A-LEVEL ECONOMICS

COURSE COMPANION

Ray Powell MA, MSc (Econ)

Lecturer in Economics, Kingston College of Further Education
Chief Examiner, A-Level Economics,
the Associated Examining Board

First published 1982

Second edition, 1984
Reprinted 1985, 1986, 1987
Third edition, 1988
Revised edition, 1991

Illustrations: Tek-Art 1982, 1984, 1991

Text © Ray Powell 1982, 1984, 1988, 1991

© BPP (Letts Educational) Ltd
Aldine House, Aldine Place
142-144 Uxbridge Road
London
W12 8AW

British Library Cataloguing in Publication data
Powell, Ray
A-level economics: course companion.—
3rd ed.—(Letts study aids).
1. Economics
I. Title
330   HB171.5

ISBN 1 85758 022 2

Printed and bound in Great Britain by
WM Print Ltd, Frederick Street, Walsall, West Midlands WS2 9NE. (0922) 643008.

Note for readers: Some of the information in this book is liable
to change, particularly that which is directly influenced
by Government policy. Such information is correct at the time of
going to press but the reader should keep in touch with current
affairs to ensure an up-to-date knowledge of the subject.

Preface

This book is written for all students taking the Advanced Level and Advanced Supplementary examinations in economics. In recent years, both the style of the examination and the knowledge and skills required of candidates have undergone significant and sometimes fundamental change. As an experienced teacher and Chief Examiner who has worked for two of the larger examining boards, I have written this book to acquaint students with the standards and skills now required by all the examining boards.

The core of the book comprises twenty-seven topic units, which I have chosen after a careful analysis of the syllabus of the examining boards and the subject areas on which questions have been set most frequently in recent years. At the end of each topic unit I have discussed a number of representative questions, many of which are selected from recent examination papers.

At all times in writing the book, I have tried to help students to make the most of the information and skills learned in a taught course but which, sadly, many students fail to reproduce amidst the pressures and stresses of an examination. Answering an examination is not merely a matter of learning and displaying a factual knowledge, important though that can be. Conventional textbooks, excellent as they are, seldom provide guidance on how to develop and make use of the wider range of skills that modern examinations seek to test. The purpose of this book is to provide exactly such an aid to students. It has **not** been designed **either** as **an examination crammer, or** to provide **a simple means of spotting questions**, nor does it contain model answers to be learned parrot-fashion. The questions at the end of each unit are there to provide guidance on the different approaches to a particular topic area, and the type of skills required to answer a question satisfactorily. In any case, spotting questions is a dangerous business: Chief Examiners change frequently, and in a discipline such as economics different issues become fashionable and topical.

The following examination boards have given permission to reproduce questions set by them in previous examinations, for which I am most grateful:

AEB : Associated Examining Board for the General Certificate of Education

JMB : Joint Matriculation Board

London : University of London University Entrance and School Examinations Board

Cambridge: University of Cambridge Local Examinations Syndicate

Oxford : Oxford Delegacy of Local Examinations

O & CSEB : Oxford and Cambridge Schools Examination Board

WJEC : Welsh Joint Education Committee

SEB : Scottish Examination Board

The answers to the questions are my own and none of the above boards can accept any responsibility whatsoever for the accuracy or method of working in the answers given.

I wish to express my special thanks to Keith West who wrote the larger parts of Units 15, 16, 25 and 26 and who contributed many ideas to other units throughout the book. I am also most grateful to Bill Stevenson who read through the manuscript and suggested many improvements, to Jeremy Lawrence for editing the typescript, to the staff at Letts Educational for their support and patience during the preparation of the book, and to my wife Christine for her encouragement and for all the hard work and long hours spent typing the manuscript in a form fit for the printer. However, any shortcomings the book may possess are entirely my own responsibility.

Ray Powell

iv

Contents

Introduction and guide to using this book

This book has been written specifically to prepare candidates for the Advanced and Advanced Supplementary Level examinations in economics set by the various GCE examining boards. It should also prove useful as a preparation for the many business studies and professional examinations in economics of a comparable standard to A Level. The book is organized in a series of Topic Units chosen both to represent the subject areas with which examination questions deal, and also to prepare candidates for answering questions on 'new' subject areas as yet not well covered in existing textbooks. Thus, while the topic units are conventionally ordered, proceeding from **micro-** to **macro-economics**, units are included on such topics as the determination of agricultural prices, market 'failures', the implications of budget surpluses and supply-side economics, and areas of controversy between Keynesian and monetarist economists.

Since the book does not attempt to cover every aspect of the Advanced Level syllabuses of the various examining boards, it should not be regarded as a substitute for the many excellent and detailed textbooks that are available, or for sources of up-to-date information such as the *British Economy Survey*, *The Economic Review* and *Treasury Economic Briefing* and *Bulletin*. It is designed for use throughout a taught economics course, and it should prove especially useful in preparing examination technique in the period immediately before an examination. Make sure that you obtain a copy of your examination syllabus. Each topic unit contains two distinct but complementary parts. The first section provides a detailed summary of the underlying concepts used by economists of different schools of thought and points of perspective in approaching the topic, together with a summary of essential, largely factual, information, and a note on how the topic links with the other units in the book. The last part contains a selection of representative questions chosen largely from the examination papers set in recent years by the principal examining boards. Each question is discussed in detail, and suggestions are made on examination technique and on how to avoid the pitfalls that may be present in the question.

The book's aim is to help examination candidates gain the knowledge, techniques and skills, not only to be sure of passing at Advanced Level, but also to realize what is required to achieve the highest possible grades. At all times the book tries to explain in a clear but precise way the new developments taking place in the subject, and to show how these are reflected in recent examination questions and in the answers expected by the examiners.

The difference between GCSE and A-Level study

The majority of students who start an A-Level course in economics are completely new to the subject; only a minority have studied GCSE economics. For this reason, no mention is made in the individual topic units of the difference between what is required at GCSE and A Level. There is in fact little difference in the range of subjects included in the 'straight' economics syllabuses at GCSE and A Level, though the A-Level syllabus tends to be rather wider. However, some examination boards offer 'combined subject' syllabuses at Advanced Level, or subjects such as social economics, which is offered as an option by the Southern Examining Group at GCSE. At Advanced Level, the Oxford and Cambridge Board allows the combination of economic principles and British economic and social history in a single examination, as an alternative to the 'straight' economic combination of economic principles and applied economics. Similarly, economics can be combined with English social and economic history, or the structure and working of British government, or world affairs since 1945, in the Economic and Public Affairs option offered by the Cambridge Local Examinations Syndicate. Again, this is an alternative to the 'straight' economics Advanced Level syllabus available through the Cambridge Board.

The principal differences between GCSE and A-Level economics lies not in the syllabus content but in the order of the skills that the examinations try to test. The GCSE examination is largely concerned with testing the **'lower order' skills** of **factual recall** and **description** together with the **understanding** and **application** of simple ideas. In contrast, at Advanced Level much more emphasis is placed on the **'higher order' skills** involved in **theoretical analysis** and evaluation. Although the practice of each examining board is slightly different, students should derive useful guidance from the introductions to the syllabuses of the Joint Matriculation Board and the

Associated Examining Board; two boards that publish in detail the aims and objectives of their economics syllabuses. By the end of the AEB course, candidates are expected to display the ability to:

(a) recall knowledge of the institutions and main features of the United Kingdom economy and its place within the world economy;

(b) demonstrate knowledge and understanding of the basic concepts and techniques of analysis used by economists;

(c) select and apply appropriate methods and techniques to the interpretation and analysis of economic problems and economic data;

(d) organize and present economic ideas and statements in support of an opinion or conclusion;

(e) evaluate the logical consistency or accuracy of economic statements on the basis of factual evidence and/or theoretical analysis;

(f) synthesize an argument by drawing on different facts or analytical approaches and demonstrate an appreciation of the economic approach.

Most helpfully, the JMB syllabus specifies **six areas of knowledge and skill** which the A-Level examination is designed to test, providing a guide which should prove very useful to all students of Advanced Level economics, irrespective of examination board:

1 Knowledge (30% of total marks)

(i) Knowledge of the terminology of economics.

(ii) Knowledge of specific facts relating to economics and economic institutions.

(iii) Knowledge of general and specific methods of enquiry and of the main sources of information about economic matters and ways of presenting economic information.

(iv) Knowledge of the main concepts, principles and generalizations employed within the field of economics and of the major economic theories held.

2 Comprehension (25%)

(i) The ability to understand and interpret economic information presented in verbal, numerical or graphical form and to translate such information from one form to another.

(ii) The ability to explain familiar phenomena in terms of the relevant principles.

(iii) The ability to apply known laws and principles to problems of a routine type.

(iv) The ability to make generalizations about economic knowledge or about given data.

3 Application (15%)

The ability to select and apply known laws and principles to problems which are unfamiliar or presented in a novel manner.

4 Analysis and synthesis (15%)

(i) The ability to recognize unstated assumptions.

(ii) The ability to distinguish between statements of fact, statements of value and of hypothetical statements.

(iii) The ability to make valid inferences from material presented.

(iv) The ability to examine the implications of a hypothesis.

(v) The ability to organize ideas into a new unity and to present them in an appropriate manner.

(vi) The ability to make valid generalizations.

5 Evaluation (15%)

(i) The ability to evaluate the reliability of material.

(ii) The ability to detect logical fallacies in arguments.

(iii) The ability to check that conclusions drawn are consistent with given information and to discriminate between alternative explanations.

(iv) The ability to appreciate the role of the main concepts and models in the analysis of economic problems.

6 Expression

The ability to organize and present economic ideas and statements in a clear, logical and appropriate form.

The Board notes also that questions frequently overlap these broad objectives, and that although no specific allocation of marks is given to the skill of **expression**, candidates will inevitably penalize themselves if they fail to express themselves clearly.

An analysis of question styles

In order to test a range of skills such as those illustrated in the extract from the JMB syllabus, most examining boards have recently introduced new examination papers and new types of question. A typical A-Level economics examination now includes (i) an **essay paper**, (ii) a **multiple choice** (or **objective test**) **paper** and (iii) a **data response** (or **stimulus**) **paper**. However, there are variations from board to board which you are advised to check, particularly concerning the type of data response material the board includes in its examination.

1 Essay questions

There is little doubt that Advanced Level economics has become a more difficult and testing examination over the many years since the day when, with fear and trepidation, the author faced the JMB examination in the subject. In those days it was common practice for the examining boards to set just two essay papers which allowed candidates a fair degree of scope in choosing the parts of the syllabus to revise, and which included a number of questions testing factual recall and description.

Since the introduction of multiple choice and data response questions, the essay paper has become rather more specialized. Questions answerable simply by factual recall may allow candidates to do well simply by 'rote-learning' pages of notes. Such questions have fallen out of favour with examiners because they fail to discriminate between 'good' and 'bad' candidates on the basis of the ability of a good candidate to practise the higher order skills we have listed. Some, but not all, examining boards have shifted the testing of factual knowledge to the multiple choice paper, leaving the essay paper free to test analytic evaluation and similar skills.

Most boards which have not as yet introduced a separate data response paper have kept two essay papers supplemented by a multiple choice paper. Where two essay papers are set, it is usual for the first paper to cover **micro-economics** and for the second paper to test the **macro-economic** topics in the syllabus, though the papers of the Oxford and Cambridge Board divide between **economic principles** and **applied economics**. Among the boards which have only one essay paper, the JMB, London and the AEB place a strong emphasis on **'applied' questions** (questions related to current economic problems and government policy). Most boards allow a candidate the 'free choice' of selecting questions (usually five) from any part of the essay paper. The London paper is the most restrictive, including only ten or twelve questions (compared with as many as sixteen set by some other boards), divided into two sections corresponding roughly to the division between micro- and macro-economics. Candidates are required to answer four questions, choosing at least two from each section.

Because of these differences in both the structure of the essay paper and the 'house style' of questions set by each board, it is vital for a candidate to study the precise regulations of the examination for which he or she is sitting, and also to analyse a selection of recent papers or specimen papers set by the board. When important changes are made in the syllabus, or when the method of examination is changed, it is usual for the examining board to publish a specimen paper or papers. Each year your teacher should get an **Examiner's Report** which discusses the previous year's examination. He should go through the report with you as it will provide a useful insight into the Chief Examiner's approach and demands. Increasingly, via the publications of the **Economics Association** and schools conferences, the chief examiners are becoming better known and more accessible. If the chief examiner gives a lecture in your area, go and listen! If your teacher does not know who the Chief Examiner is, get him or her to find out and study any textbook he may have written recently.

2 Multiple Choice Questions

Almost all the examining boards now either set a separate multiple choice paper or include multiple choice questions in a separate section of one of their other papers. Candidates are usually required to answer about fifty compulsory questions within an hour and a quarter or an hour and three-quarters. (The length of the examination depends upon the number of questions in the paper and the 'house style' of questions–the questions in the common paper set by the Cambridge Local, Oxford Local, Welsh, and Oxford and Cambridge Boards involve more calculation than is usual in the papers set by the other boards, so more time is allowed.)

The multiple choice paper tests the whole range of the syllabus and it can also test certain types of numerical and logical skills that essay questions cannot adequately do. The AEB and the London Board use their multiple choice papers to test descriptive knowledge, but this is not a noticeable feature of the JMB paper or of the common paper shared by the other boards.

The structure of the multiple choice paper also varies between boards. Two main types of question are used: **single completion** and **multiple completion**. Most **single completion** questions contain a **stem** (the question itself) and **five possible answers** (a single **correct** answer and four incorrect **distractors**), though the AEB now sets questions with only four possible answers. **Multiple completion** questions are similar, but one or more of the possible answers may be correct. (The JMB also sets two other types of multiple choice question: 'assertion/reason' and 'matching pairs'. **Assertion/reason** questions are perhaps the most difficult type of question. The candidate must first decide whether the two statements in the question are correct when considered as separate statements. If both are correct, he must then decide whether the second statement provides an explanation of the first. A **matching pairs** question requires the candidate to select items from one list to match up with items from a second list provided in the question.)

Some multiple choice papers include only single completion questions, whereas others are divided into separate sections with each section devoted to a different type of question. (The common paper shared by many of the boards is of the first type, whereas the London Board, the AEB and the JMB favour the latter approach.) Subject-areas listed at the beginning of the board's published syllabus are usually tested first, with the questions then proceeding through the remaining syllabus topics. (If the paper is divided into different types of question, it is usual for each section to cover the syllabus in this manner; the largest section of the paper contains single completion questions which thoroughly cover the syllabus, but the coverage of the other sections may be rather sketchy.) Some of the examining boards publish details of the number of questions they intend to set on each broad division of the syllabus, together with the skills the questions are designed to test.

3 Data Response Questions

Most of the examining boards have now introduced a new **data response** or **stimulus** paper, or have incorporated questions of this type into one or other of their existing papers. Data response or statistical questions have been introduced in response to a growing dissatisfaction felt by many teachers, universities and employers that economics students have lacked the ability and confidence to handle empirical data, whether in written, numerical or graphical form. However, there are considerable differences in both the stimulus material that the boards include in their questions, and in the skills which the questions are designed to test.

The Cambridge Board sets statistical questions which require a considerable amount of calculation to work out a correct answer. The JMB sets a single, hour-long compulsory question containing perhaps two or three detailed sources of data which may be in either numerical or written form. Both the JMB and the AEB appear to favour the **'incline of difficulty' approach** to the setting of data response questions: the question is structured into separate parts, each succeeding part becoming more difficult, in order to test the 'higher order' skills. Thus the first part of a JMB or AEB data response question may require the candidate to **describe** some aspect of the data, while later parts require an **explanation of the data in terms of economic theory and an evaluation.** Properly constructed questions of this type discriminate well between good and bad candidates. The London Board, which previously set very general questions not noticeably different from essay questions, changed its data response paper in 1986 to include more structured questions which resemble closely the questions set by the AEB and JMB. These boards set questions requiring interpretation and analysis of the data rather than a set of calculations yielding unique correct answers, arguing that the skill of calculation can be tested more appropriately on the objective test paper.

We have noted only some of the differences between the styles of question set by the examining boards. It is vitally important that a candidate should be familiar with the 'house style' of a board's data response questions. Some boards set a compulsory data response question or questions; with other boards there is free choice. The Oxford and Cambridge Board offers perhaps the most interesting range of choice; data response questions form an optional section within the Board's applied economics paper, a paper which also includes a **Documents and Commentaries** option. This option, which is the only one of its type offered by any of the examining boards, contains questions which resemble data response questions, the principal difference being that questions are set on government publications and other documents which are similar to 'set books'. The Oxford and Cambridge Board notifies schools and colleges some time before the examination about the publications that candidates are expected to read.

The examination

Once you have prepared for the examination as thoroughly as time allows, the most daunting task still remains to be faced: to do yourself justice when presented with unseen questions amid the stresses and strains of the examination room. In this section of the book we shall discuss some 'golden rules' that, if followed, should stand you in good stead and make your task rather easier, providing of course that that most useful ingredient, luck, is also at least a little on your side.

1 Revision technique

You can reduce the need for luck by preparing a revision programme. Since you will have to face a multiple choice paper containing compulsory questions covering the whole of the syllabus, plan a thorough programme and begin it several weeks before the examination, time-tabling periods of each day when you know you can work for up to two or three hours completely free of distraction. It is a good idea, however, to allow yourself a brief relaxation period every half hour or so to facilitate the absorption of the knowledge, ideas, and concepts intensively revised in the previous period. Although you must cover the whole syllabus, concentrate on key concepts and on essential economic theory rather than on detailed historical and descriptive fact.

There are various methods of revising, and not all may suit every candidate. Generally it is not a good idea to read through sheaves of notes or chapters from a textbook, and certainly it is not good practice to 'rote-learn' pages of notes. Nevertheless, you must learn key definitions, though it is even more important to learn how and when to use them. Remember that, as a properly prepared candidate, you will only be able to use a small fraction of your total economic knowledge in a single essay or data response paper. Provided that you have revised in a reasonably structured way in the weeks before the examination, it is certainly not a good idea to work late into the night on the day preceding the examination. Answering an examination paper is a tiring task, especially if you are to display the type of skill the paper is testing; you need to arrive in the examination room as refreshed as possible and capable of thinking clearly not just for a few minutes, but for up to three hours.

If you decide to arrange your revision programme around the use of this book, we suggest that you select one or at most two topic areas for coverage at each revision session. Quickly read the first half of a topic unit, making a mental note of key definitions or concepts. Then try to write your own answer plans to two or more questions at the end of the unit. Check your completed answer plan against the one included in the book and read through the notes on understanding the question. Go back over the topic unit to make sure you understand the most important definitions and concepts, which you should now write out in a revision list. Several hours later or on the next day, write **in your own words** the meaning of the concepts and key definitions. Check what you have written against the explanations given in the topic unit. Repeat this exercise frequently throughout your revision period until you feel confident that you **thoroughly understand** all the concepts and definitions. You might also attempt on later dates to write answer plans to the questions omitted when you first revised the topic unit.

2 Essay technique

Most examination boards require a candidate to answer four questions in a three-hour essay paper, allowing about forty-five minutes for each question. It is vital to arrange your time so as to answer all four questions, since all carry equal marks and no allowance is made for answering too few. Spend at least a couple of minutes at the beginning of the examination in carefully reading the paper, paying close attention to the wording of each question. Carefully select four and read each through again; subconsciously you will be thinking about the other questions while working on your first answer! Choose the easiest question to answer first, but remember again to divide your time equally. When a question contains more than one section it is also important to divide your time between each part, assuming, unless the question specifies otherwise, that each carries equal marks. Examiners frequently complain that the second section of a question is either ignored or treated in cursory fashion, with the answer being little more than a footnote.

Nevertheless, if you find that you have allocated your time badly you must take action to remedy the situation. It may be a good idea to answer one or both of the last two questions with an elongated though carefully written essay plan. In general, marks are awarded for relevant points made. It follows that you should make as many relevant points as possible and avoid dwelling on any single point. Of course in a properly developed essay you should have time to elaborate appropriately the points you make, but even so it is easy to spend too much time on a single argument—a variation of the 'law of diminishing returns' applies to economics essays written under examination conditions! The marking scheme may allocate perhaps two, three, or four marks for a particular relevant argument, and a brief mention of the argument can earn you at least half and possibly all the allocated marks if it is properly related to the question. Candidates frequently waste valuable time by unnecessarily elaborating one argument, while failing even to mention a range of others. It is surprising how often an answer written as a series of points by a candidate pressed for time at the end of an examination earns more marks than the answer the candidate attempted first! Examiners *always* prefer short, well-structured and concise answers to long, rambling and repetitive essays.

Whether your essay is long or short, it must always be addressed to the set question. You will earn no marks at all for writing a 'model answer' to a question not on the examination paper! Long introductory and concluding paragraphs are generally inadvisable since they seldom pick up many marks. Nevertheless, it is good practice to use the first paragraph both to define precisely the terms mentioned in the question and also to state any assumptions you are making in interpreting the meaning of the question. If you think the question is open to more than one interpretation, then tell the examiner and explain why you are favouring a particular interpretation. Many questions are capable of different interpretations and there may be no 'single correct answer'. At all times try to 'get behind the question' to the underlying assumptions and economic theories necessary for a proper development of the answer.

While diagrams and particularly graphs are often appropriate, they should complement rather than simply repeat the information you are providing in written form. Diagrams are often included which fail to earn any extra marks yet which waste valuable examination time. If you cannot correctly remember a particular graph or diagram, then leave it out. A wrongly drawn graph will serve no purpose other than to signal to the examiner in the clearest possible way that a candidate has not understood the essential theory required for answering a question! Draw your graphs large rather than small, and pay careful attention to how you label the axes and all curves.

Every essay question includes at least one key instruction, e.g. calling for a discussion, evaluation, comparison or contrast. Very few questions can be answered simply by factual description or by an uncritical historical account. Most examination questions test whether you can introduce basic economic theory in a simple but clear way in order to cast light on the specified problem. We include difficult or more advanced theories in this book where relevant to specific examination questions, though as a general rule simple theories used well are always preferable to the latest, most advanced theories obviously misunderstood by the candidate.

Questions asking for comparisons or contrasts should not be answered with two separate accounts. Strictly, a 'comparison' notes points of similarity whereas a 'contrast' notes points of difference, though in practice examiners are unlikely to be pedantic about this distinction. However, it is important to avoid confusing questions asking for a discussion of **causes** with those concerned with the **economic effects** resulting from a particular government policy or change in the economy. When discussing causes and effects it is as well to remember the central importance in economics of the **price mechanism** and of the concept of the **margin**. Most economic changes occur at the margin in response to movements in relative price or income, when an economic agent decides it is no longer worthwhile to engage in its earlier pattern of economic behaviour.

Small adjustments rather than **massive structural changes** are the rule; even the 1973 oil crisis, an event regarded as cataclysmic at the time, produced rather slow adjustments that are still taking place. Changes usually take a time to work through; a **trigger event, event A** (such as the 1973 oil crisis or a change in government policy), may directly cause **event B**, which in turn causes **event C** and so on. In general the immediate direct effects of A on B are easier to predict than the later indirect effects further down the 'causal chain'. The chain of direct and indirect effects may be either **dampened** or **explosive**; in the former case event B is smaller than event A, and C is smaller than B, and so on. In contrast, a causal chain is explosive if each succeeding event is more powerful than the previous one. Because most economic changes are eventually 'absorbed' through relative price changes and minor adjustments at the margin, economic chains may often be dampened.

Nevertheless a further complication may be caused by the existence of **feed-backs**, when for example event B feeds back to change the variable associated with the original event A. In terms of essay technique, you should at all times avoid being dogmatic when discussing economic cause and effect, and remember that in economics it is often the case that 'everything depends upon everything else'.

3 Data response technique

Many of the examination techniques relevant to essay questions are also applicable to the data response paper. It is perhaps even more important to read through the questions to make sure that you thoroughly understand both the data content and the questions. Where a choice is allowed, the rubric at the beginning of the paper will usually advise you to spend at least fifteen minutes reading through the paper; take this instruction seriously and carefully read through each question before you make your final choice.

We have already noted how stimulus questions frequently start by asking for the extraction of simple facts from the data. Avoid the temptation to elaborate your answer to this part of the question since it is unlikely that more than a couple of marks will be allocated for simple description. Conversely, you must not simply describe or **paraphrase** the data when tackling the parts of a question that require the 'higher order' skill of interpreting or evaluating. Search for the conclusions that can reasonably be **inferred** from the data, and the more tentative conclusions that really require stronger supporting evidence. Sometimes a question will explicitly ask for a statement of the **assumptions** upon which the arguments in the data are based or upon which you are making your inferences. It may also ask for a discussion of **other sources of information or data** that might allow you to draw **stronger inferences** and conclusions.

Very often the limited amount of data included in a stimulus question is consistent with more than one interpretation, not by itself either proving or refuting a particular **economic theory** or **hypothesis**. Nevertheless, the examiner is hoping that candidates will be able to handle basic economic method by stating the assumptions being made in interpreting the data and by discussing how far the data appear consistent with at least one economic theory. So even if a question does not formally ask for a statement of basic assumptions or for a discussion of the limitations of the data, a good answer will show that a candidate is thinking about these issues. You should clearly show the examiner when you are drawing conclusions based solely on the data, and when you are bringing in 'outside knowledge', either in the form of economic theory or descriptive fact, to help in its interpretation.

Numerical questions may be based upon various forms of data including tabulated schedules, charts and different types of graph. They may also involve either data extracted from **real-world sources** or **simulated data** made up specially for the question. Whereas data from real world sources may contain various inaccuracies, being an estimate of what has happened in the real world, simulated data are completely fictitious. Simulated data on such topic areas as supply and demand, the theory of the firm, the multiplier and comparative advantage may be included to test whether candidates can use basic economic theory to perform simple **calculations**. Most examining boards now allow the use of electronic calculators in the data response paper (and also now in the multiple choice paper). Nevertheless it is vital to show all your workings, and you should explain to the examiner what you are trying to do at each stage in the manipulation of the data. Stimulus questions try to test economic knowledge rather than arithmetical skills, though there will usually be a single correct answer to a question or part of a question involving a calculation. However, an arithmetic slip should not be heavily penalized, providing that you have clearly shown that you are using the correct economic method to answer the question.

When answering questions based on real-world data sources, it is useful to know the difference between **time-series** and **cross-sectional** data, and to be aware of the uses and limitations of data expressed in such forms as **index numbers** and **percentages**. **Time-series data** observe how economic variables change over time, from year to year, quarter to quarter, or month to month. For example, British national income figures for 1990, 1991, and 1992 would form a short time-series. Whereas time-series data are often highly **aggregated, cross-sectional data** divide up or disaggregate the data into its various components. (The division of annual national income data into wages, profits and rent provides a simple example. Cross-sectional and time-series data can of course be combined together, in which case they are known as **pooled data**.)

Time-series data measuring changes in economic variables such as national income, output, and expenditure usually fluctuate both **seasonally** and also with the upswings and downswings of the **business cycle**. Seasonal fluctuations cannot of course be detected unless the data are presented in **quarterly** or **monthly** form, in which case they may be presented in either **seasonally adjusted** or **unadjusted form**. Adjusted data pick up the long-term trend from year to year whereas unadjusted data show the fluctuations occurring from season to season.

If the data contain observations for only two or three years, great care must be taken in interpretation. It is very easy to confuse the **long-term trend** of the data with relatively **short-term fluctuations** associated with the business cycle. As a general rule, a time-series must extend over at least five or six years to allow a long-term trend to be detected, and even then there is a danger that structural changes taking place in the economy may have altered the trend. Where it is possible to detect a long-term trend in the data, it may also be possible to **extrapolate** the trend in order to **predict** the future. Beware, however, of basing a forecast upon data subject to violent fluctuations, and always be prepared for the possibility that a structural change or 'outside shock' occurring in the future may upset the forecast.

Many economic variables measured in money units are affected by inflation, which can seriously distort time-series data. Check whether data are unadjusted for inflation, in the current prices of each year, or whether the data have either been converted to the **constant prices** of a particular year, or been expressed in **index numbers**. Index numbers, which are usually based on 100, can sometimes be confused with data expressed in **percentages** which must, of course, add up to 100. Cross-sectional data are often expressed in percentages, sometimes in the form of a chart or pie graph. Great care must be taken in interpreting both index numbers and percentages, particularly if absolute totals are not included in the data. A 1% change is seldom exactly equivalent to a one-point movement in an index, and the percentage share of, for example, income tax in total government revenue can fall, yet the absolute total of income tax revenue may still be rising.

As a final word of warning, be especially wary of reading economic interpretations into the apparent steepness or flatness of curves when data are presented in graphical form. By altering the scales on the vertical and horizontal axes it is possible to show changes in an economic variable either by a steep or a flat curve (providing that the variable is rising or falling). So look carefully at the chosen scales whenever a question requires graphical interpretation.

4 Multiple choice technique

A multiple choice paper allows candidates to spend only a minute or two on each question. Some questions can usually be answered in a few seconds, but others which involve calculation or deep thought may require several minutes. It is important to avoid being delayed by such questions occurring early in the paper, in which case you may never reach some 'easier' questions in the later sections. Try to go through the paper three times in all. On the first occasion, quickly move on from any question proving difficult or involving a calculation, making sure to draw a heavy pencil line around all the questions you do not attempt. Similarly, place a question mark against any question you do attempt, but which gives you serious cause for doubt. If one and a quarter hours are allowed for the paper, try to complete your first run-through in about fifty minutes. On the second run, return to the questions you have placed a mark against, and be prepared to spend several minutes on each. If time allows, scan through the paper a third time, checking whether you have correctly interpreted the wording of each question. If you have second thoughts about any of your answers, take great care to erase completely your initial mark on the answer sheet. Indeed, make sure that all your marks are in the correct positions on the answer sheet since the computer which checks the sheet cannot award credit for any slips on your part.

Finally, allow at least half a minute to guess the answers to any questions still unanswered. Your aim is to maximize your marks, so do not leave any questions unattempted. There is always at least a twenty per cent chance that your guess will turn out to be correct!

Guidance for Scottish Higher students

The Scottish Examination Board offers two certificates in Economics for the post sixteen year old age group.

The Certificate of Sixth Year Studies which is based largely on an in-depth study of one selected topic and is only open to students with previous examination success in Economics, and the Higher Grade which is normally a one year post-Ordinary Grade course intended for seventeen year olds, although often taken by older or Further Education candidates, for which this book is more suited. The course covers the same range of economic theory and analysis as most A-level courses, but, because of its shorter duration, the questions set may require less depth or development in order to reach a pass standard. A and B passes are required for university entrance. There are few differences between this course and a typical A-level course in the field of Economic analysis covered by the syllabus. However, here there is not the same emphasis on factual knowledge recall nor on the memorising of traditional theory. More time is spent on the acquisition of numerate and interpretive skills and the application of key concepts and principles to real world problems (similar to JMB).

The syllabus aims to develop in candidates:

1 An understanding of the basic concepts and principles of economics;
2 The capacity to apply this understanding to the analysis of economic problems;
3 An understanding of the nature and extent of economic inter-dependence;
4 An appreciation of the economic dimension of life and of the changing economic framework of the United Kingdom;
5 Economic literacy and numeracy;
6 An appreciation of the applicability and limitations of economic theory in contemporary society.

The Examination has three papers. A multiple choice objective test consisting of thirty items of the four-response type and worth thirty per cent of the total marks. These items do not specifically test the knowledge of economic facts and figures but concentrate on the understanding and application of concepts and principles. Paper two is a one hour interpretation paper similar to the data-response type. Here skills tested are mainly those of number and interpretation. The higher skills of evaluation and synthesis are tested along with the others in a two and a half-hour essay paper which breaks down to two analysis questions and two questions of applied economics from a total of twelve. Contemporary and, where possible, Scottish examples are used, and study is normally confined to the decade prior to the examination. Comparative and development economics are largely excluded at this level, but the effects of EEC membership on the British economy are studied.

The Scottish Board has several key marking principles which stress the positive and tolerant approach to candidate's work. In general the aim is to give credit to what is correct and relevant and to ignore all else, that is, wrong statements carry no weight and marks are not deducted. The whole emphasis of the examination is on the testing of economic understanding rather than on strict factual accuracy from the candidates.

Table of Analysis of Examination Syllabuses

The table on the next two pages shows how the topic units that make up the main body of the book relate to the specific syllabuses set by the examining boards. As we have already noted, there is a common core to most of the syllabuses. The main differences lie in the style of the examination papers and in the questions they contain, rather than in the coverage of the syllabus. Syllabuses change from time to time, so some of the information provided in this guide may already be out of date. If in doubt consult either your teacher or an up-to-date syllabus provided by your examining board.

Advanced Supplementary Level

Traditionally, most students in sixth forms and on equivalent courses in colleges have studied three A-level subjects, knowing that three good pass grades are usually required by universities and polytechnics for entry to a degree course in higher education. However, following the introduction of the Advanced Supplementary (AS) examination in 1989, pass grades in two subjects at AS level are now regarded by universities and polytechnics as equivalent to a pass in one subject at A level.

The objective of the new AS examination is to give greater choice and flexibility, enabling you to study more of the subjects you enjoy up to A-level standard, and helping to keep your higher education and careers options open. Universities, other higher education institutions and employers recognize the value of more broadly based sixth-form studies. While it is theoretically possible to study six subjects at AS level instead of three subjects at A level, a more usual combination is likely to be two subjects at A level and two at AS level.

Schools and colleges are expected to offer AS level primarily on two-year courses. Some schools may decide to enter their students for AS level at the end of one year, half-way through a two-year course leading to A level.

Other schools and colleges may plan to enter their 'weaker' students for AS level rather than A level, believing that it represents an 'easy option'. However, because AS level requires the same standard of work as A level, with AS level passes being graded A to E in the same way as A levels, it must not be regarded as easier than A levels. In each subject, the AS syllabus has been designed to contain approximately half the syllabus content of A level, but will be examined to test skills of exactly the same degree of difficulty. Indeed, it may very well be the case that rather more than half the equivalent A-level syllabus is included in the new AS syllabuses, meaning that ½ + ½ does *not* equal 1, in terms of the amount of work you are expected to do! Nevertheless, while the same general calibre of work is expected at AS level as at A level, the syllabuses aim to take account of the shorter teaching and studying time available.

Not all the GCE examining boards offer economics as an AS-level subject. Oxford, the AEB, the JMB, the London Board and the Cambridge, Oxford and Southern School Examinations Council (COSSEC) have all prepared syllabuses in economics at AS level. This leaves the Welsh, Northern Ireland and Scottish boards as the only examining boards which do not offer economics as an AS-level subject.

Summary of A-level examination papers set by the examining boards

Board	AEB	London	JMB	WJEC	Oxford
Syllabus	618	9120		0011	9840
Subject Name	Economics	Economics	Economics	Economics	Economics
Number of Papers	3	3	2	3	3
Paper 1	1¼ Hours Multiple Choice 50 compulsory questions (25%)	3 Hours Essays 4 questions to be answered from a choice of 12; choosing two from each section of the paper (40%)	*Part 1* 1½ Hours Multiple Choice approximately 50 compulsory questions (30%) *Part 2* 1 Hour Data Response 1 compulsory question (20%)	2½ Hours Section A: 2 Data Response questions of which one must be answered. Section B Essays (largely Micro-Economics) 4 Questions to be answered from 7 (35%)	3 Hours Essays 5 questions from a cho of approximately 14 (40%)
Paper 2	1½ Hours Stimulus Paper 2 compulsory questions (25%)	2¼ Hours Data Response 3 questions to be answered from a choice of 6, divided into two sections: Section A (numerical data) and Section B (written passages); with at least one question to be chosen from each section (30%)	3 Hours Essays 4 questions to be answered from a choice of 12 (50%)	2½ Hours As in Paper 1 but largely macro-economics (35%)	1¾ Hours Multiple Choice ● 50 compulsory question (40%)
Paper 3	3 Hours Essays 4 questions to be answered from a choice of 10 (50%)	1¼ Hours Multiple Choice 50 compulsory questions (30%)		1¾ Hours Multiple Choice ● 50 compulsory questions (30%)	1½ Hours Comprehensive & Analysis Paper 2 compulsory question one presenting numeri data, the other a writte passage (20%)
Paper 4					

Table of topics common to the syllabuses of all the Boards

Topic Area	Comments
1 The central problem of all economic societies The problem of scarcity, choice, opportunity cost, allocation of resources; the market mechanism; free goods, economic goods, private and public goods; types of economic system.	All boards set questions asking for a comparison of market and comm economies and a discussion of their virtues and disadvantages, together those mixed economies, See Unit 9, and also Units 1 and 8.
2 Demand Theory Individual and market demand curves; consumer behaviour; utility theory, movements along and shifts of demand curves; price, income and cross elasticities of demand; substitution and income effects; complementary and competing demand; consumer surplus.	The London and Associated Examining Boards do not require a knowl of indifference curves, a topic on which most of the other Boards set spe questions. See Units 2 and 4, and also Unit 5.
3 Cost and Supply Theory Firm and industry supply curves; the behaviour of firms; the law of returns and the economic short run; increasing returns to scale and the economic long run; economies and diseconomies of scale; the derivation of marginal total and average cost curves; price elasticity of supply in the market period, short run and long run; movements along and shifts of supply curve.	There is a tendency for all the Boards to set questions best answered some knowledge of alternative theories of the firm (managerial behavioural). However, the syllabuses only specify the orthodox p maximizing theory of the firm. Most Boards expect a knowledge o structure of industry in the British economy, the size and growth of firms capital market, etc., but there has been a movement away from expecte detailed descriptive knowledge of topics such as the various types of busi enterprise in the British economy. For theory: Unit 3, 4 and 5. Fo institutional approach: Units 10 and 11.
4 Market Equilibrium and the Equilibrium Firm The concept of equilibrium in economics; the interaction of supply and demand and industry (or market) equilibrium; marginal, total and average revenue; short- and long-run equilibrium. The determination of a firm's equilibrium price and output in different market structures (perfect competition, monopolistic competition, oligopoly, and monopoly).	Questions are being increasingly set on 'market failures' and the circumstance which goods and services are provided outside the market (public goods, n goods, externalities); the revised syllabus of the AEB explicitly recognizes new topic area. Also questions increasingly require an evaluation of equilib in different market structures in terms of their desirable and undesir properties – productive and allocative efficiency, etc. For market equilibrium Units 1 and 9. For the equilibrium firm: Units 6 and 7, and for market fail Unit 8.
5 The Theory of Distribution Demand for and supply of factors of production; the determination of wages, interest, profits and rent; economic rent, quasi-rent and transfer earnings; wage determination and bargaining in the British economy; the role and effectiveness of trade unions.	See Unit 13.

Cambridge	Cambridge	Oxford & Cambridge	Oxford & Cambridge	SEB	NISEC
9070	9072	9633	9635		
Economics	Econ. & Public Affairs	Economics	Econ. & Polit. Studies	Economics	Economics
3	4 (Paper 1 compulsory and one other to be taken)	4 (Papers 1 and 2 compulsory Papers 3 & 4 are options)	4 (Paper 1 compulsory Papers 2, 3 & 4 are options)	3	3
Hours tiple Choice ● ompulsory stions %)	3 Hours Economics Essay Paper (50%)	1¾ Hours Multiple Choice ● 50 compulsory questions	3 Hours Principles of Economics Essays (As an alternative either Paper 3 or Paper 4 of subject 9633 may be taken)	1 Hour Multiple Choice 30 compulsory questions (30%)	1¾ Hours Multiple Choice ● Approximately 50 compulsory questions. (30%)
Hours istical Questions ompulsory questions %)	3 Hours Structure and working of British Government Essay Paper (50%)	1½ Hours Essays 2 questions from a choice of 6 covering 'Principles of Economics'	3 Hours Political Thought Essays	1 Hour Interpretation (Data Response) 2 compulsory questions (a) prose interpretation (b) statistical material interpretation (20%)	3 Hours Essay Paper 4 questions to be answered with 2 from a choice of 5 from each of 2 sections. Section 1: Micro-economics and Methodology. Section 2: Macro-economics. (40%)
ours ays uestions to be wered from a choice pproximately 13 %)	3 Hours World Affairs since c. 1960 Essay Paper (50%)	3 Hours Applied Economics 4 questions must be answered: 2 from each section: Section A: Choice of 9 questions on 'The British and Other Economies'. Section B: Choice of 3 'either/or' questions on 'Documents, Commentaries and Numeracy'.	3 Hours Representative Government Essays	2½ Hours Essay Paper 4 questions to be answered; 2 from Section A covering economic theory and 2 from Section B covering government policy and the external economic relations of the UK (50%)	2 Hours Data Response Paper 3 compulsory questions using different types of real world data. (30%)
	3 Hours English Social and Economic History, 1815–1973 Essay Paper (50%)	3 Hours British Economic and Social History since 1780. Essays, Documents, commentaries, and statistical questions.	3 Hours British Constitutional History since 1830		

Key: ● Common Shared Multiple Choice Paper

---

ic Area	Comments
he System of National Income Accounts definition and measurement of income expenditure and output; net and s; national and domestic; market prices and factor cost; relationship veen measures; problems of comparison over time and between countries; Balance of Payments as a part of the National Accounts.	Questions frequently ask for a discussion of the extent to which National Income figures provide a useful measure of economic welfare. Scottish candidates may be required to analyse National Income Accounts in the Interpretation paper. See Unit 18.
he Theory of Income and Output Determination circular flow of income; injections into and withdrawals from the flow; consumption function; the multiplier; theories of investment; the lerator; the equilibrium level of income; inflationary and deflationary ; the determinants of the aggregate levels of employment and prices ation theory).	The syllabus content of this topic area reflects the 'Keynesian orthodoxy' of the 1950s and 1960s. Increasingly however, the questions being set require a knowledge of the theoretical issues separating Keynesians and monetarists and their different views of 'how the economy works'. Knowledge of the 'aggregate demand/aggregate supply' model will be very useful, even though the AD/AS model may not be mentioned explicitly in the syllabus. Look mainly at Units 19, 20 and 21, but also at Units 22, 23 and 24.
ioney and Banking nature and functions of money and credit; the demand for and supply of ey; the money market; the fuctions of the Bank of England and com-cial banks; reserve ratios and the operation of monetary policy; interest s, open market operations and special deposits.	Questions are now set which require knowledge of Keynesian and monetarist views on the role of money, the demand for money, interest rate theory and the role and effectiveness of monetary policy. See Units 14, 16, 17 and 24.
ternational Economics theory of specialization and trade; the gains from trade and the principle of parative advantage; the case against trade; the theory of the Balance of Pay-ts and fixed and flexible exchange rates; the terms of trade; the UK Balance ayments; international economic institutions including the International etary Fund, World Bank, General Agreement on Tariffs and Trade and the pean Economic Community; free trade areas and customs unions.	Questions are frequently set requiring an application of the principle of comparative advantage to a discussion of the regional problem or division of labour and specialization *within* a country. Other questions require some knowledge of the operations of macro-economic policy within an open economy, the effects of the foreign trade multiplier, the Balance of Payments and the money supply, exchange rates and inflation, etc. Use Units 25, 26 and 27.
The Economic Role of the Government lic provision and distribution of goods and services; the distinction veen private and social costs; the management of national, regional and economies; policy instruments and objectives; fiscal policy; monetary ry; incomes policy; direct controls; micro-economic policies; industrial, nal and employment policies; competition policy; the nationalized stries; the determinants of government revenue and spending; the nal Debt and the Public Sector Borrowing Requirement.	In recent years, questions have increasingly reflected the Keynesian v monetarist debate on the correct role of the government in the economy, demand management v 'supply side' policies, fiscal v monetary policy, the implications of taxation, public spending and the Public Sector Borrowing Requirement, etc. Questions on 'the mixed economy' are a key feature of Scottish Higher Grade papers. For micro-economic policy use Units 5, 8 and 12. For macro-economic policy use Units 15, 16, 17, 20, 22, 23 and 24.

Summary of the AS syllabuses set by the examination boards

In contrast to A level, for which all the examining boards set syllabuses in economics based on the same common core, there are significant differences in syllabus content at AS level. The differences arise from the fact that each board has had to select approximately half the A-level syllabus, and the boards have used rather different criteria for making this choice. All the boards offering economics at AS level, with the exception of the AEB and JMB, have decided to divide their syllabus content into a compulsory section and two or more optional sections from which a choice can be made. The nature of the choice and the content of the options vary considerably from board to board, so we have summarized separately the main details of syllabus content, structure and choice for each board.

AEB

No choice available, all the syllabus must be covered. The syllabus is divided into four subject areas: (1) *the market mechanism and resource allocation*; (2) *money and exchange*; (3) *the creation and distribution of income*; and (4) *the economic role of government*. The syllabus broadly covers the range of the A-level syllabus; major exceptions are the omission of most aspects of the theory of the firm, the derivation of supply and demand curves, a detailed knowledge of financial institutions and measures of the money supply, the theory of the demand for money and rate of interest determination, international economic institutions, the national income accounts, the structure and theory of taxation, local government, growth theory, competition and region policies.

London

The syllabus is divided into four sections:
Section 1 A compulsory core covering basic principles: the economic problem, demand, supply, the price mechanism and the allocation of resources, the circular flow of income, the determinants of the level of national income, government expenditure and revenue, money and banking and international trade and exchange.

Additionally, a candidate must select one of three options covering *economic issues and policy*. The options are:
Section 2 The price mechanism, market failure and government intervention.
Section 3 Unemployment, inflation and macro-economic policies.
Section 4 The international economy.

JMB

The syllabus specifically focuses on economic policy and the role of government. There are three subject areas:

(1) *The nature of economics and economic systems*
    (a) Economies and their problems.
    (b) The role of government in a mixed economy.
    (c) The methods and techniques of economic analysis.

(2) *Macro-economic problems and policies*
    (a) Unemployment.
    (b) Inflation.
    (c) Economic growth.
    (d) International economic relations.

(3) *Micro-economic problems and policies*. Candidates must be familiar with *two* of the following:

    (a) Industrial policy.
    (b) Urban and regional policy.
    (c) Social policy.
    (d) Distribution policy.

Oxford

The syllabus is divided into 3 sections:

Section A A compulsory section covering the whole syllabus, but not in detail.
(1) Demand.

(2) Supply.
(3) Price and output determination.
(4) Factor markets.
(5) The central problem of economic societies.
(6) The theory of income determination.
(7) Money and prices.
(8) International economics.
(9) The role of government.

Section B Candidates choose from Part I *or* Part II, in which the micro-economic part of the syllabus is examined in more depth.
Part I Firms and markets
Part II Individuals and markets

Section C Candidates choose from Part I *or* Part II, in which the macro-economic part of the syllabus is examined in more depth.
Part I Money and inflation
Part II The international economy

COSSEC

Candidates must study Module I and *one* other module, II, III, or IV. For each of the optional modules a special subject is set. Centres will be notified by COSSEC if there is a change of special subject after 1990.

Module I (compulsory): resource allocation and economic systems
(1) Resources.
(2) The economic problem.
(3) Allocative mechanisms.
(4) The model of circular flow of national income.
(5) Specialization, trade and exchange.

Module II (optional): Industrial economics
(1) Production.
(2) Motivation.
(3) Market structures.
(4) Labour market.
(5) Government and industry.
   Special subject: Privatization.

Module III (optional): The macro-economic system
(1) National income.
(2) Money and prices.
(3) Policy objectives.
(4) Policy instruments.
   Special subject: De-industrialization.

Module IV (optional): International economics
(1) International trade.
(2) International capital markets.
(3) Trade and protection.
(4) Economic development.
   Special subject: The international debt problem.

Coursework

Currently, London is the only board to include coursework as part of its AS-level economics syllabus. (None of the boards include coursework at A level.) However, given the strong likelihood that compulsory coursework will be required at both A and AS level (following the major syllabus revision due to take place in the mid 1990s), students and teachers might like to study the requirements and assessment criteria, together with the assessment objectives, outlined by the London board for the 'investigative study' which has formed part of the AS-level requirements. Why not write off for your copy!

Board	AEB	London	JMB	Oxford	COSSEC
Syllabus	984	8120			8430
Subject Name	Economics	Economics	Economics	Economics	Economics
Number of Papers	2	3	2	2	2
Paper 1	2 Hours Written Paper Section A: Between 8 and 12 compulsory short-answer questions. (20%) Section B: 2 compulsory stimulus questions (40%) (60%)	2 Hours Essay Paper 3 questions must be answered, with at least 1 question from Section 1, and 1 question from either Section 2, 3 or 4. Section 1, 2, 3 and 4 correspond to the sections of the syllabus. 3 essay questions will be set in each of the 4 sections (40%)	1¼ Hours Section A: 20 compulsory multiple choice questions covering the whole syllabus (20%) Section B: One compulsory stimulus question drawn from Sections 1 and 2 of the syllabus (20%) (40%)	2 Hours Written Paper Section 1: Choice of 8 short answer questions from 16 (20%) Section II Choice of 2 Essay questions from 12. One question must be answered on micro-economics and 1 on macro-economics (40%) (60%)	1¼ Hours Section A: A mixture of about 10 short answer questions and 10 multiple choice questions based on Syllabus Module I (20%) Section B: Choice of 1 data response question from 3, one question being set on each of the Modules II, III, IV* (20%) (40%)
Paper 2	1½ Hours Essay Paper Choice of 2 essay questions from 5 (40%)	2 Hours Data Response Paper A range of compulsory data response questions will be set in Section 1 of the paper. One question from section 2, 3 or 4 must also be answered. Two questions will be set in each of these sections which correspond to the sections of the syllabus (40%)	1¾ Hours Section A: Choice of 1 from 4 essay questions drawn from Section II of the syllabus. (20%) Section B: Choice of 2 from 12 essay questions drawn from Section III of the syllabus. Three questions are set on each of 4 policy groups. *Each chosen question must be from different policy groups. (40%) (60%)	1½ Hours Comprehension and Analysis One numerical data response question must be answered from a choice of 2. One prose passage question must be answered from a choice of 2 (40%)	2¼ Hours 3 questions must be answered, one from each of three sections. The questions may involve stimulus material. Section A: 3 essay questions on Module I* Section B: 2 essay questions will be set on each of the special subjects for each Module II, III IV*. Section C: 3 essay questions will be set on the content of Modules II, III, IV* without reference to the special subject. (60%)
Paper 3 (London)		Coursework 1 investigative study from a choice of topics, based on Sections 2, 3 and 4 of the syllabus. (20%)			

* See summary of syllabuses on pp. xvi – xvii.

Examination boards

AEB	The Associated Examining Board, Stag Hill House, Guildford, Surrey GU2 5XJ	*NISEC*	Northern Ireland Schools Examinations Council Beechill House, 42 Beechill Road, Belfast BT8 4␣
Cambridge	University of Cambridge Local Examinations Syndicate, Syndicate Buildings, 1 Hills Road, Cambridge CB1 2EU	*Oxford*	Oxford Delegacy of Local Examinations, Ewert Place, Summertown, Oxford OX2 7BZ
COSSEC (AS only)	As for Cambridge, Oxford and Cambridge.	*O and C*	Oxford and Cambridge Schools Examinations Board 10 Trumpington Street, Cambridge and Elsfield Way, Oxford OX2 8EP
JMB	Joint Matriculation Board, Devas Street, Manchester M15 6EU	*SEB*	Scottish Examinations Board, Ironmills Road, Dalkeith, Midlothian EH22 1B␣
London	University of London Schools Examinations Board, Stewart House, 32 Russell Square, London WC1B 5DN	*WJEC*	Welsh Joint Education Committee, 245 Western Avenue, Cardiff CF5 2YX

1 Price Determination

1.1 Points of perspective

According to Professor Lionel Robbins's well-known and long-established definition, economics is 'the science which studies human behaviour as a relationship between ends and scarce means which have alternative uses'. Although by no means all economists agree that this is the best definition of the subject, it does emphasize the importance (except perhaps in Marxist economics) of **resource allocation** as the central problem to be studied. Economics is literally the study of economizing, with consumption as the ultimate end to which economic activity is directed.

Production converts the primary resources of the earth's surface into **economic goods**, which are then consumed to satisfy human wants or needs. Some goods, such as air, are known as **free goods** because no scarcity exists and nobody can charge a price for them. Most goods and all services, however, are economic goods. Scarce resources are used up and costs are incurred in the production of economic goods. The cost involved is an **opportunity cost**, which to economists means rather more than just a money cost. Resources which are allocated to one particular end-use cannot simultaneously be used elsewhere; the opportunity cost of using resources in a particular way is the value of the alternative uses foregone. For example, the opportunity cost of a visit to the theatre might be the sacrificed opportunity to spend the same time and money at a football match.

In all forms of society or economic system, some mechanism must exist to allocate or ration economic goods (and the resources contained in them) between competing uses. In a market economy, the **price mechanism** operating in a system of interrelated markets acts as the rationing device, determining **what** is produced, **how** it is produced and **for whom** it is produced.

Examination candidates at Advanced Level are often rather better at discussing the relative advantages and disadvantages of economic systems–market economies, mixed economies and planned economies–than they are at showing a detailed understanding of how a simple market operates. In particular, **market plans** and **market action** are almost always confused. The objective of this first topic is to explain, from basic principles, how market price is determined in a single market–leaving the 'market versus planned economy' issue for considering rather later in the book, after other important aspects of market behaviour have been introduced in the intervening units.

1.2 Underlying concepts

1 The nature of a market

A market is a meeting of buyers and sellers in which goods or services are exchanged for other goods or services. The exchange is usually indirect, by means of money; in modern economies goods are seldom bartered for each other. Instead, one good is exchanged for money which is then traded a second time for other goods, usually after a time delay. The exchange must be voluntary; a forced transaction is not a market transaction.

A market need not exist in a single geographical location, although transport costs and lack of information may create barriers which separate markets. Markets are decentralized and usually unorganized in the sense that there is no central authority, such as the government, to decide how much is going to be traded and how much each buyer and seller in the market must trade. Price is the only information which needs to be known by each trader in the market.

2 The functions of price

If the price mechanism is to work efficiently in a market economy, it must simultaneously fulfil two functions:

(i) The signalling function. Prices must convey sufficient information to all traders in the market for their economic activities and plans to be co-ordinated. Markets will function inefficiently if prices signal wrong or misleading information, leading in extreme cases to complete market failure or breakdown (see Unit 8).

(ii) The incentive function. Markets will only operate in an orderly and efficient manner if the buyers and sellers in the market respond to the incentives provided by the price mechanism. If demand rises relative to supply, the price will tend to rise. This provides the incentive for firms to shift resources into producing goods and services whose relative price has risen, and to demand more resources such as specialized labour in order to increase production. This may bid up wages and other input prices, causing households to switch their supply of labour into industries where relative wages are rising.

3 The 'goods market' and the 'factor market'

You will have noticed from the preceding section that both households and firms are simultaneously operating within two sets of markets. On the one hand, consuming households face business enterprises in the retail or goods market, where households are the source of demand. For this demand to be an **effective demand** (demand backed up by money), the households must sell their labour services in the labour market, where it is now the firms who exercise demand. Although a market economy will usually be made up of a vast number of different and often specialized markets, for many purposes we can generalize and consider just a **'goods' market** and a **'factor' market** (one where households sell the services of the labour and capital they own) – the two markets being linked together through the decisions of both households and firms.

1.3   Essential knowledge

1 Demand and supply curves

For the rest of the unit we shall ignore the factor market and restrict ourselves to exploring in greater detail the process of price determination within a single market in the goods market. Figure 1.1a illustrates the essential features of such a market.

A **demand curve** D_1 represents household or consumer behaviour in the market, while the **supply curve** S_1 maps out the supply decisions of firms. You will notice that the downward-sloping demand curve shows that consumers demand more of a good at low prices than at high prices. Be very careful of how you interpret this. It is insufficient to say that a demand curve slopes downward because more is demanded at low prices than at high prices; we need to go further than this and to 'get behind' the demand curve by developing a theory of consumer behaviour to explain demand. This is done in Unit 2. In a similar way, Unit 3 develops a theory of the behaviour of firms to 'get behind' the supply curve and explain supply. For the time being, however, we shall accept that normal demand curves slope downwards and normal supply curves slope upwards.

2 Market plans and market action

The distinction between market plans and market action is of crucial importance to a proper understanding of the way a market works, yet it is a distinction which appears unknown to a significant proportion of candidates at Advanced Level. A demand curve, such as D_1 in Figure 1.1a, shows how much of a good all the consumers in the market intend to demand at the various possible prices. **Intended demand** is also known as **planned demand** or **ex ante demand**. Similarly, the supply curve S_1 shows **intended supply (planned supply** or **ex ante supply)**. It is easy to show that, at almost

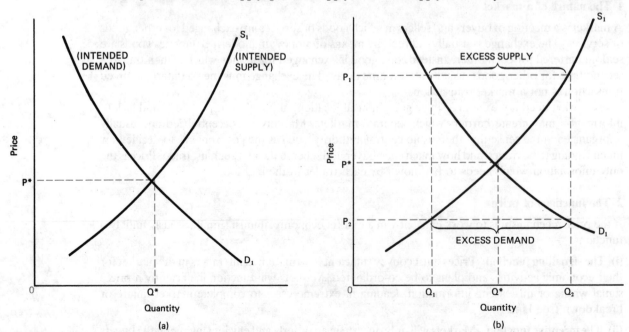

Fig 1.1 The determination of equilibrium price in a single market: (a) equilibrium requires intended demand to equal intended supply; (b) the price mechanism ensures convergence towards equilibrium

all prices, it is impossible for both the firms and the consumers to fulfil their plans simultaneously. Suppose that for some reason the price in the market is P_1, as represented in Figure 1.1b. Firms would like to supply quantity Q_2 at this price, but households are only willing to purchase Q_1: intended supply is greater than intended demand and **excess supply** results.

You should now ask yourself what will be the quantity actually traded if the price remains at P_1. The answer is quantity Q_1. The amount bought is Q_1, and the amount sold is Q_1; the two are the same, as indeed they must be. Now the amount bought is just another name for **realized demand (actual demand** or **ex post demand)**, and the amount sold is another name for **realized supply (actual supply** or **ex post supply)**. It follows that realized demand will always equal realized supply whatever the price. This represents an **identity**.

3 The equilibrium price

The concept of equilibrium is of the utmost importance in economic theory and analysis. Equilibrium is a **state of rest**, when there is no reason for anything to change unless disturbed by an outside shock. Households and firms will be in equilibrium if they can both fulfil their market plans. In Figure 1.1b, the price P_1 is not an equilibrium price because the firms are unable to fulfil their plans at this price. Realized demand, of course, equals realized supply at Q_1, but this is largely irrelevant: the crucial point is that intended supply is greater than intended demand at this price.

We now introduce a very important assumption about economic behaviour, which will recur throughout the book: if any economic agent (such as a household or firm) is unable to fulfil its market plans, a reason exists for it to change its market behaviour. At the price of P_1 in Figure 1.1b, the firms are unable to fulfil their market plans. If firms react to their unsold stocks (or excess supply) by reducing the price that they are prepared to accept, then the market will **converge** towards the equilibrium price.

Similarly, if the initial price is P_2 in Figure 1.1b it may be supposed that the households, who are unable to fulfil their market plans at this price, will bid up the price to eliminate the **excess demand** in the market.

The equilibrium price, P^*, is the only price which is **consistent** with the market plans of both households and firms, who consequently have no reason to change their plans. At the equilibrium price, intended demand = intended supply. This is often known as the **equilibrium condition** to clear the market; it must not be confused with the **identity**: realized demand $\equiv$ realized supply.

In Figure 1.1b, the market mechanism ensures a **convergence** towards the equilibrium price of P^*. Consider, however, Figure 1.1c, which includes a (theoretically possible) downward-sloping supply curve. We leave it as an exercise for the reader to work out why this is a **divergent** equilibrium. What will happen if excess supply $(Q_4 - Q_3)$ or excess demand $(Q_2 - Q_1)$ exists in the market? Would the same events happen if the supply curve is drawn steeper than the demand curve?

To summarize the main conclusions of this very important section of the unit:

 (i) if intended supply > intended demand, price will fall (disequilibrium condition);
 (ii) if intended supply < intended demand, price will rise (disequilibrium condition);
 (iii) if intended supply = intended demand, price stays the same (equilibrium condition);
 (iv) realized supply $\equiv$ realized demand, at all prices (identity).

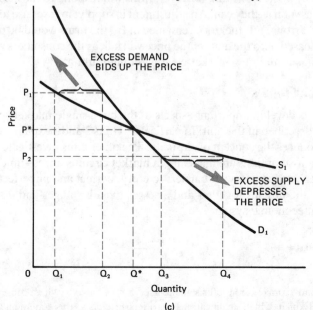

(c)

Fig 1.1 (c) Different assumptions about supply would cause a divergence away from equilibrium

4 Shifts in demand and supply

When we draw a demand curve to show how much of a product households intend to demand at the various possible prices, it is assumed that all the other variables which may also influence intended demand are held unchanged or constant. This is known as the *ceteris paribus* assumption. (In economic shorthand we write: $Q = f(P)$, ceteris paribus.) In a similar way, all the other variables which may influence supply are held constant when a supply curve is drawn. Common sense suggests that household income and fashion will influence demand, and costs of production will affect supply decisions, but you should refer to Units 2 and 3 for a more detailed explanation. In this section, we shall restrict the analysis to a brief investigation of a change in the **conditions of demand**, when one of the variables which influences demand is assumed to change. The reader should have little difficulty in extending the analysis to a change in the conditions of supply.

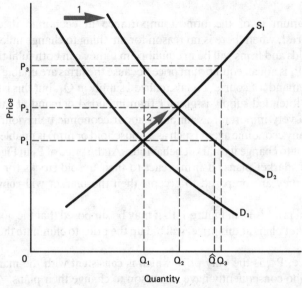

Fig 1.2 The effect of a shift in the demand curve within a single market

In Figure 1.2, the demand curve D_1 and the supply curve S_1 are drawn to show the initial condition of supply and demand. The equilibrium price which clears the market is at P_1, where quantity Q_1 is traded. A successful advertizing campaign persuades households to demand more at all prices and the demand curve shifts upwards (or rightwards) to D_2 (arrow 1). At the existing price of P_1, households now demand $\hat{Q}$. But because conditions of supply have not changed, firms still only intend to supply Q_1 at this price, which is therefore no longer an equilibrium price. Excess demand exists in the market.

It is worthwhile at this point to take a closer look at how the price mechanism eliminates excess demand. If the firms are unable to increase supply immediately, the supply curve will be temporarily vertical and the price will be bid up to P_3. (Unit 4 explains how supply is completely **inelastic** in the momentary time period.) In the short run, however, firms will respond to the incentive provided by P_3 and increase supply as soon as they can. An adjustment in supply, in response to price, takes place along the supply curve (arrow 2). If the price remained at P_3, the firms would be prepared to supply Q_3. If this amount is released onto the market the price will fall, as the consumers will only take Q_1 at this price. The price falls to the new market-clearing equilibrium at P_2.

1.4   Links with other topics

The next nine topic units develop important aspects of the basic single-market supply and demand model which has been described in this unit. In particular, Units 2 and 3 explain demand and supply curves, and Unit 4 introduces the concept of elasticity. The other units investigate how markets may function when different assumptions are made about market circumstances–time-lags in the supply of agricultural products, producer power, barriers to entry, perfect and imperfect information, etc. Finally, Unit 10 draws the threads together and assesses the advantages and disadvantages of the market economy as an economic system.

1.5   Question practice

Essay Questions

Question 1 'Changing relative prices and profits signal a need for a change to which consumers and producers respond.' (R G Lipsey) Explain which qualifications need to be made to this statement?

(Oxford: June 1987)

Understanding the Question You must firstly explain, clearly and carefully, the signalling function of prices and the way that prices and profits create incentives. The second part of your answer should be a survey of some of the circumstances in which the price mechanism, and the profit motive, may fail to perform these functions adequately in a market economy. (We cover these circumstances in Unit 8 on 'Market Failures'.) You might also argue that when prices are administered (e.g. in a Prices and Incomes policy) these functions are performed inadequately and, perhaps, not at all. Divide your answer fairly equally between the two parts of the question; a candidate may underachieve through writing too little on the second part.

Answer plan

1 Explain how, in a market economy, prices signal what is available; conveying the information which allows all the participants in the market to plan and co-ordinate their economic activities.

2 Explain how buyers and sellers respond to the incentives provided by these signals, drawing special attention to the role of profits in creating incentives for firms to enter or leave markets and to decide on how much to produce.

3 But, if prices signal wrong or misleading information, markets will function inefficiently (sometimes breaking down completely). List several examples, e.g. under-production: (i) by monopolists; (ii) of public goods; (iii) of merit goods; (iv) of positive externalities; over-production of; (i) demerit goods; (ii) negative externalities.

4 With the aid of examples from the above list, or from other examples of market failure, explain why qualifications to Lipsey's statement are necessary.

Question 2 Assuming an initial situation where beef prices and output are determined freely by demand and supply, predict the effect of each of the following:

(a) An increase in the price of chicken   (6)
(b) An increase in the price of cattle hides   (6)
(c) The introduction of government guaranteed prices for beef producers above the free market level   (7)
(d) The introduction of an *ad valorem* subsidy paid to beef producers   (6)

(WJEC: June, 1987)

Understanding the Question This is a straightforward question, for the most part, testing your understanding of causes of shifts in demand and supply. For each part of the question, draw a supply and demand diagram to show an initial market equilibrium. Then identify whether the event specified in the question shifts the supply curve or the demand curve and the direction of the shift. Draw on the new curve accordingly and describe the adjustment to the new equilibrium. The concept of elasticity (explained in Unit 4) provides an additional tool of analysis; for example the cross-elasticity of demand for beef, with respect to an increase in the price of chicken, determines both the direction and the proportionate shift of the demand curve in your answer to (a). Also, the assumption of perfectly price-elastic (i.e. horizontal) and inelastic (i.e. vertical) demand, and/or supply curves, might affect all your answers.

Answer plan

(a) (i) Explain that chicken and beef are substitutes and that an increase in the price of chicken will shift the demand curve for beef towards the right.
    (ii) Show the initial and subsequent equilibria on a supply and demand diagram.
    (iii) Briefly note how cross-elasticity of demand and the price elasticity of the supply curve may influence the outcome.

(b) (i) Here the relationship is joint supply. If the increase in the price of cattle hides causes more of the existing stock of cattle to be slaughtered, the supply curve of beef (the by-product) will shift towards the right. Illustrate.
    (ii) The long-term effects are less predictable. One possibility is that an accelerated rate of slaughter might diminish the total size of the cattle stock, causing a long-run shift in supply towards the left.

(c) (i) A guaranteed price for beef, above the free market price, causes the demand curve (representing consumer demand plus government demand) to become horizontal at the guaranteed price. Market equilibrium will be determined where this horizontal demand curve intersects the market supply curve. Illustrate.

(d) (i) Explain that an *ad valorem* subsidy is paid to farmers as a percentage of the price without the subsidy. The higher the price, the greater the absolute subsidy paid.
    (ii) Payment of the subsidy causes the supply curve to shift to the right, but not parallel to the original supply curve. The new curve will be 'flatter'.
    (iii) Show the new equilibrium at a greater output and a lower price. You might also adapt the analysis of the effects of an expenditure tax, presented in Unit 15, and explain how the extent to which the subsidy falls in price depends on price elasticity of demand.

Question 3 Explain what is meant by the statement that a market is in disequilibrium and indicate how this disequilibrium may arise. Discuss how trade unions are likely to affect the equilibrium of the labour market.

(JMB: June, 1989)

Understanding the Question Equilibrium and disequilibrium are amongst the most important of all economic concepts. In this unit we have concentrated on the market aspect of these concepts. In the next few units we shall be examining how a particular economic agent (i.e. a consumer or a firm) may be said to be in equilibrium. To answer the last part of the question, you should draw upon the analysis (presented in Unit 13) on the effects of introducing a trade union into both competitive and monopsonistic labour markets (i.e. one employer only).

Answer plan

1 Clearly explain market equilibrium in terms of the price and level of output at which the planned demand of buyers equals the planned supply of sellers. Illustrate on a supply and demand diagram.
2 Disequilibrium occurs when the market fails to clear and one or other of the set of buyers (or sellers) fails to fulfil their market plans. Explain how prices above and below the equilibrium price on your diagram represent disequilibrium, exhibiting either excess supply or excess demand.
3 Show on your diagram how a shift of supply (or demand) causes disequilibrium to arise (assuming trading was initially taking place at the equilibrium price you have already described). Briefly explain some causes of shifts in supply or demand.
4 The introduction of a trade union into a competitive labour market is likely to lead to a shift of the supply curve. There are various possibilities. Two extreme scenarios are: **(a)** the union restricts supply of labour to the left of the initial equilibrium level of employment, with the union-determined supply curve of labour depicted as a vertical line at this supply; and **(b)** the union fixes the minimum wage at which it will allow its members to supply their labour. In this situation, the supply curve of labour is horizontal at the union-determined wage. In both cases, the new equilibrium is determined where the new supply curve intersects the employers' demand curve for labour. The wage rate will be higher but employment will be lower, compared to the initial equilibrium. But, as Unit 13 explains, the new equilibrium in a monopsony labour market might represent an increase in employment as well as wages.

Multiple Choice Questions

Question 4 Which of the following statements that refer to the price mechanism is NOT true?
(a) In a private enterprise system the sovereignty of the consumer is not always complete.
(b) Lack of information may prevent the price mechanism from working perfectly as an allocative device.
(c) Exchange can only take place at equilibrium prices in a market economy.
(d) A rise in the relative price of a good tends to attract resources from markets where relative prices have fallen.

Understanding the Question These are all general statements about the nature of a market economy. All are true except for the third statement. If a private enterprise system conformed to the conditions of perfect competition, then consumer sovereignty would follow from the basic assumptions of the model, but perfect competition seldom, if ever, exists. Information problems, which prevent the price mechanism from working, have been referred to in the unit, which has also shown that trading can take place at disequilibrium prices.

Question 5 Which of the following will cause the demand curve of butter to shift to the right?
(a) A fall in the price of butter.
(b) A rise in the costs of producing butter.
(c) A subsidy granted to milk producers.
(d) A successful advertizing campaign by the dairy industry.

Understanding the Question This type of question is testing whether you can correctly identify the variables which are responsible for the positions of the supply and demand curves. It also tests whether you can distinguish between a shift in the demand curve and an adjustment in response to a price change along a curve (statement **(a)**). The correct answer is **(d)**.

Data Response Questions

Question 6

Mounting commercial stocks of unsold rubber have been weighing down prices for many months. There are few signs that free market forces will succeed in lifting prices in the short term. Natural rubber consumption is down worldwide so far this year; the destocking prompted by high interest rates shows signs of continuing, thus restricting import demand.

Earlier this month London rubber dealers, Lewis and Peat, said that prices were unlikely to rise significantly before February or March next year when the onset of winter in the Far East cuts the yield from rubber trees. The company appeared sceptical about the ability of the International Rubber Agreement to boost prices by mopping up surplus rubber for its buffer stock.

The producers, however, are relying on the International Rubber Agreement to act as a counterbalance to the present depressing free market influences. The International Rubber Agreement entered into force in October 1980, but it is only within the past few weeks that the Pact has had funds at its disposal to finance support-buying operations. It has been reported that only some £20 million has been received so far from members – enough to buy up only 50 000 tonnes of rubber. Some traders argue that considerably more than this needs to be taken off the market to bring supply and demand into balance over the next few months.

(Adapted from an article in *The Guardian*, 16 November, 1981)

(a) Why should high interest rates cause destocking of natural rubber? (2)

(b) With the aid of supply and demand diagrams explain, according to the passage:

    (i) how market forces depressed the price of natural rubber in 1981;   (3)

    (ii) why prices were expected to rise after February 1982.   (3)

(c) (i) Explain how the members of the International Rubber Agreement might use support-buying operations to boost the price of natural rubber.   (6)

    (ii) What difficulties might the International Rubber Agreement encounter through operating their support buying scheme?   (6)

(AEB: November, 1984)

Understanding the Question This question is testing your ability to use simple supply and demand analysis by showing an understanding of which of the conditions of supply or demand change in response to the events noted in the passage. It is also testing your knowledge of how a buffer-stock policy can be used to stabilize agricultural prices (see Unit 5).

Answer Plan

(a) Explain how the opportunity cost to a manufacturing firm investing in stocks of rubber includes the loss of the interest that would be earned if the funds were deposited instead in a financial institution such as a bank. The higher the interest rate, the higher the opportunity cost, so the greater the incentive to destock.

(b) With the use of diagrams, show:

  (i) How destocking of *existing* rubber stocks shifts the demand curve for rubber imports from the Far East leftwards. You might also argue that the world-wide depression in the early 1980s also shifted demand leftwards, thereby depressing the price of natural rubber.

  (ii) The onset of winter in the Far East would shift the supply curve of natural rubber leftwards.

(c) Draw on Unit 5 to explain:

  (i) The working of a buffer-stock and support-buying scheme.

  (ii) Difficulties involved in possible over-supply, financing problems and in securing the continuing cooperation of all members of the International Rubber Agreement.

1.6 Further reading

Begg, D., Fischer, S., and Dornbusch, R., *Economics*, 3rd edition (McGraw Hill, 1991).
Chapter 3: Demand, Supply and the Market.

Lipsey, R. G., *An Introduction to Positive Economics*, 7th edition (Weidenfeld & Nicolson, 1989).
Chapter 4: Basic Economic Concepts.
Chapter 5: Demand, Supply and Price.

2 Demand

2.1 Points of perspective

In this unit we 'go behind' the market demand curve in order to demonstrate how its shape and essential characteristics are derived from basic economic principles, and from a set of initial assumptions about how consumers behave. Different assumptions about consumer behaviour lead to differently shaped demand curves, so that although conventional downward-sloping demand curves are normally to be expected, it is best to avoid describing this characteristic as a 'law' of demand (which suggests a misleading inevitability about the existence of downward-sloping demand curves).

1 Market demand and individual demand

Students often confuse the **market** (or industry) demand curve, which shows how much of a commodity all the consumers in the market intend to buy at all possible prices, and the **individual** demand curve of a single consumer or household in the market. The relationship between the two is very simple: the market demand curve is obtained by adding up all the individual demand curves for every consumer in the market. Henceforth in this unit, 'demand' will mean individual demand rather than market demand. It will also mean **effective demand** – a demand backed by purchasing power or money.

2 The utility approach and the indifference curve approach

Two different methods can be used to derive demand curves from a set of initial assumptions – the **utility** approach and the **indifference curve** approach. While both approaches lead to the same conclusions, the indifference curve method is preferred at a university level because it is more rigorous and the technique can be extended to other aspects of advanced economic theory. However, at the school or college level, our experience is that students are far better advised to learn simple theories well rather than risk fouling up a more complicated, if academically respectable, theory. For this reason, only the utility approach is explained in this unit.

Nevertheless, you should check whether or not the syllabus of your particular examining board requires a knowledge of indifference curves. The books which are recommended for further reading at the end of this unit include a thorough coverage of indifference curve analysis.

2.2   Underlying concepts

1 Utility maximization

The basic or fundamental assumption of demand theory is that consumers always seek in the market place to maximize the total **utility** they obtain from the set of goods they buy. Utility cannot be seen, touched, or even properly measured. It is sometimes defined as the pleasure which a consumer obtains from using a good or service. However, it really means rather more than this. Some goods, such as medicine for example, are consumed because they **fulfil a need** rather than because they give the consumer direct pleasure. The assumption of utility maximization also implies that consumers act **rationally**, which in the sense used here means that people act in their own self-interest.

2 The existence of constraints

If consumers had unlimited income, or if all goods were free, a consumer would maximize utility by obtaining those goods which gave him utility up to the point of **satiation**. However, all but a few lucky and very wealthy consumers face a number of **constraints** which limit their freedom of action in the market place. The principal constraints are:

  (i) **Limited Income.** Consumers do not possess unlimited means with which to purchase all the goods which would give them utility. The **opportunity cost** to a consumer of choosing one good is the lost opportunity to choose the next best alternative. (Note that the assumption of rationality implies that the 'best' alternative will always be chosen!) A limited income constrains a consumer's freedom of choice, and so, together with the given set of prices the consumer faces, it imposes a **budget constraint** on his market action.
 (ii) **The consumer faces a given set of prices.** A single consumer is unable to influence the market prices of any of the goods he might wish to buy: he is a **'price-taker'** rather than a **'price-maker'**.
(iii) **Tastes and preferences are fixed.** A consumer who prefers Good A to Good B today will also prefer Good A tomorrow: the consumer is said to behave *consistently* if his preferences are stable over time.

3 Maximizing v minimizing behaviour

Demand theory is thus essentially concerned with the way in which a consumer with a limited income and fixed tastes behaves in the face of changing prices. The consumer attempts to maximize a desired objective (utility), subject to a set of constraints. The assumption of maximizing or minimizing behaviour (on the part of consumers, firms, workers and even perhaps the government) is central to orthodox micro-economic theory. You should note that a **maximizing objective** can always be rewritten in minimizing terms. Thus, we can rewrite the consumer's assumed objective 'to maximize the utility obtained from a purchased bundle of goods' as: 'to minimize the outlay, expenditure or cost of obtaining the same set of goods'. They are different sides of the same coin.

Whether we set up an assumed objective in maximizing or minimizing terms depends upon our convenience; we can do either. The reader will find further examples of 'maximizing and minimizing behaviour' in later units, for example in distribution theory and in the theory of the firm.

2.3   Essential information

1   Diminishing marginal utility

The principle of diminishing marginal utility states that although the total utility derived from a good increases with the amount consumed, it does so at a decreasing rate. It is quite possible that a person may experience increasing marginal utility when more of a good is consumed, at least for the first few units of that good. This is why we refer to diminishing marginal utility as a **'principle'** rather than as a **'law'**. The principle is illustrated in Figure 2.1. The upward (or positive) slope of the total utility curve in Figure 2.1a indicates that **total utility** rises with consumption. The last unit purchased is always the **marginal unit**, so the utility derived from it is the **marginal utility**. (Formally, the marginal utility derived from the n'th unit = the total utility of n units minus the total utility of $(n-1)$ units. If 20 units are consumed, $n = 20$.) You will notice that the principle of diminishing marginal utility is shown by the **diminishing rate of increase** of the slope of the total utility curve in Figure 2.1a. The marginal utility derived from each unit of consumption is plotted separately in Figure 2.1b. The principle of diminishing marginal utility is represented by the negative or downward slope of the curve in this diagram.

Figure 2.1 illustrates an important lack of rigour in the utility approach to demand analysis. The vertical axes are measured in degrees of utility, 'utils' or 'subjective units of pleasure', which are not really measurable because a 'unit of pleasure' will vary from person to person.

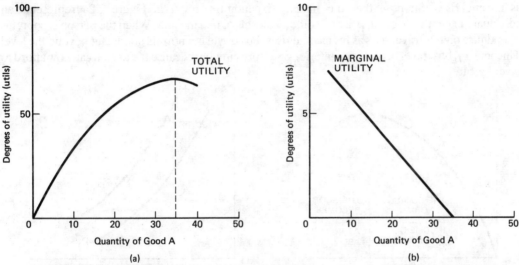

Fig 2.1 Utility curves (a) total utility rises at a diminishing rate as an individual's consumption of Good A increases (b) this can also be shown by a marginal utility curve—note that at the peak of the total utility curve marginal utility drops to zero

2   Consumer equilibrium and the derivation of the demand curve

A consumer, constrained by limited income, fixed tastes and the prices which he faces in the market place, will continue to buy units of a commodity until the marginal utility which he gains is the same as that he could have obtained by spending a similar amount of money on another commodity. The equilibrium condition with respect to a single commodity is, therefore, where Marginal Utility = Price. It is an easy matter to extend the analysis to the case where a consumer buys many commodities. Successive units will be bought of each commodity to the point where its marginal utility equals its price. The multi-commodity equilibrium condition is:

$$\frac{\text{Marginal Utility of Good A}}{\text{Price of A}} = \frac{\text{Marginal Utility of Good B}}{\text{Price of B}} = \frac{\text{Marginal Utility of any Good}}{\text{Price of any Good}}$$

Suppose that a consumer can only choose between Good A and Good B and he starts off from a position of consumer equilibrium. At existing prices he is satisfied with the combination of Goods A and B that he buys. The price of Good A now falls, and the situation can now be represented by:

$$\frac{\text{M.U. of Good A}}{\text{Price of A}} > \frac{\text{M.U. of Good B}}{\text{Price of B}}$$

The consumer is no longer in equilibrium: he would be better off substituting more of the good whose relative price has fallen for a good whose relative price is now higher. He is not now maximizing utility, and so he has a motive for changing his market behaviour.

When he consumes more of Good A, he moves 'down' the marginal utility curve for Good A, and 'back up' the marginal utility curve for Good B. As he substitutes more of Good A for less of Good B, the marginal utilities adjust until he is once again in equilibrium, when no alternative reallocation will increase his total utility. The equilibrium is achieved at a point of **equi-marginal utility**, where the marginal utility derived from each good as a ratio of its price is the same for all goods. The essential point is that more is demanded of the good whose relative price has fallen. The **substitution effect**, whereby consumers substitute more of a good whose relative price has fallen for goods whose relative price has risen, helps to explain the downward-sloping demand curve.

3 The substitution effect and the income effect

If consumer behaviour was determined only by the substitution effect of a price change, demand curves would only slope downwards. This is provided that customers are utility maximizers who experience diminishing marginal utility, and assuming also that they are uninfluenced by future uncertainty and status. However, if consumers expect even higher prices in the future, they may demand more at high prices for speculative reasons. Similarly, if a high price indicates status, 'status maximizers' may be expected to demand more of a good at higher prices.

When we introduce the **income effect** of a price change, matters become rather more complicated. If the price of one good falls, a consumer's **real income** rises. The nature of this income effect depends upon whether the good is a **'normal' good** or an **'inferior' good**. If expenditure on a good rises when a consumer's real income rises, then the good is a normal one. Conversely, if expenditure on the good falls when income rises, then that good is classed as inferior. It is important to stress that the same good can, for a particular individual, switch from being normal to inferior as his income rises. Suppose that the Income-Expenditure graph in Figure 2.2a represents an individual's expenditure on bus travel at different levels of real income. When the person is poor, his expenditure on bus travel rises as his income rises: bus travel is a normal good. But beyond the level of income Y_1, bus travel becomes an inferior good, presumably because the person can now afford to travel by car.

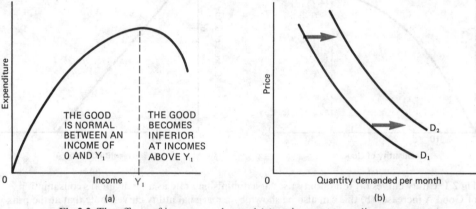

Fig 2.2 The effects of income on demand (a) an income expenditure curve for a good which is inferior at high levels of income (b) a shift in the price demand curve for a normal good following an increase in income

For normal goods, the substitution effect of a price change is reinforced by the income effect, and the two effects together explain the downward-sloping demand curve. But in the case of inferior goods, the income effect works in the opposite direction to the substitution effect. The income effect is, however, likely to be much smaller than the substitution effect, because expenditure on a single good is probably only a tiny proportion of a consumer's total spending; real income hardly alters at all if the price of a single good changes. Nevertheless, a theoretical possibility exists that the income effect of a price change will not only be in the opposite direction to the substitution effect but that it will also be stronger. This is the special case of an inferior good known as a **'Giffen' good** – less of a Giffen good is demanded as the price falls, hence the demand curve slopes upward.

4 Shifts of demand

In the previous section, the analysis explains how a change in real income, resulting from a change in the price of a good, influences the shape of the demand curve. It is important to separate this effect from the effects of a change in real income which is independent of a change in the good's own price. If a person's real disposable income rises as a result of a wage increase or a cut in income tax, then the demand curve of each of the goods that the person buys may shift. If the good is a normal one, the demand curve will shift to the right (or upwards) and more will be demanded at every price. This is illustrated in Figure 2.2b. In the case of an inferior good, however, a rise in real income causes the demand curve to shift to the left (or downwards).

A change in real disposable income is only one of the possible causes of a shift in the demand curve. In general, a change in any of the constraints facing the consumer (sometimes known as the

conditions of demand) will shift the demand curve. The good's own price is not listed as one of the conditions of demand because the demand curve is itself a 'map' showing how demand responds to price changes. However, changes in the price of a **complementary** or **substitute** good will normally shift a demand curve. Most people in Britain regard bread and butter as complementary goods. If the price of bread rises, the demand curve for butter will probably shift to the left and less butter will be demanded at all prices. Conversely, a rise in the price of a substitute for butter, such as margarine, will normally cause the demand curve for butter to shift rightwards.

The time-period under consideration will also influence demand. Strictly speaking, the horizontal axis of a demand graph should specify the time-period for which demand is being measured. If the time-period is changed, for example from monthly to yearly demand, the ability of consumers to respond to a change in price will also alter. This aspect of demand theory will be investigated in Unit 4 on elasticity.

5 Consumer surplus

The concept of consumer surplus is illustrated in Figure 2.3, which shows the market demand curve of all the consumers in the market.

In Figure 2.3, the equilibrium price of 10 pence is the price which every consumer in the market pays for the good in question. It is also the price which the marginal consumer is only just prepared to pay in order to obtain the good. If the price rose above 10 pence, the marginal consumer would either

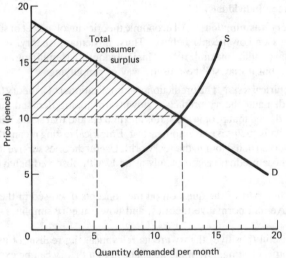

Fig 2.3 Consumer Surplus: the shaded area shows total consumer surplus when the market price is 10 pence

drop out of the market or reduce his demand. However, some consumers, who value the good more highly, would be prepared to pay 15 pence for it. They gain a consumer surplus (or **surplus utility**) equal to the difference between what they would be prepared to pay and what they actually need to pay. The total consumer surplus, the utility which consumers enjoy but do not pay for, is shown by the shaded area of the graph.

2.4 Links with other topics

Although the determination of the shape of the demand curve has been the central theme of this unit, we have largely ignored a very important aspect of the shape and slope of demand curves: the concept of **elasticity of demand**. Unit 4 on elasticity should be regarded as a very useful follow-up to this unit.

In this unit we have dealt only with the **micro-economic theory of consumer behaviour**–how consumers choose between alternative goods and services. The **macro-economic theory of consumption** (covered in Unit 19) explains how consumers divide their limited income between **aggregate consumption** on all goods and **saving**. Although economists agree that a sound macro-economic theory should be based firmly on micro-economic foundations, students are often confused by the parallel existence of micro- and macro-consumption theory. Think carefully about the context of the question, when you decide how to structure and plan your answer to a question on consumer behaviour.

2.5 Question practice

Essay Questions

Question 1 Explain, with examples, the nature and purpose of economic theory and outline the characteristics of a useful theory. Discuss how far the theory of consumer behaviour with which you are familiar possesses these characteristics.

(JMB: June, 1980)

Understanding the Question Most economic theories claim to be **positive theories**: they attempt to **explain** how the economy works, and to predict what will happen in the future if certain actions are taken now. However, some economic theories are **normative theories** about what ought to happen: a theory of optimal government policy is a 'normative' theory because it is essentially concerned with how a government should make value judgements when choosing between different policy options.

The theory of demand (or consumer behaviour) is a positive theory: the problem or puzzle to be explained is how consumers make decisions when faced with the choice of how to spend their incomes. (The theory does not say how they ought to spend their incomes.) Restricting ourselves to positive theories, the usefulness of a theory may be judged by three criteria: (i) relevance, (ii) realism of assumptions, and (iii) ability to survive empirical tests.

(i) How relevant is a theory? If a 'good' theory explains a trivial problem of no interest to anybody, then it is hardly a useful theory. This, for instance, is the basic Marxist criticism of orthodox economics. Marxists argue that orthodox economics is dominated by the study of the 'uninteresting' problem of individual behaviour in a 'timeless' economy, thereby ignoring or side-stepping the 'interesting' problems (to a Marxist) of how a capitalist economy comes into existence and changes over time, and the economic relations between **classes** (as distinct from relations between **individuals**).

(ii) How realistic are the theory's assumptions? All economic theories involve a set of simplifying assumptions about economic relationships or how people behave. Thus, in demand theory, economists assume that consumers have the single aim of utility maximization. This is obviously a simplifying assumption as sometimes people will have other aims, but it may still be a useful way of simplifying.

(iii) Can a theory survive empirical tests? The predictions (or implications) of a theory follow logically from its initial assumptions. Thus, demand theory predicts a downward-sloping demand curve, but if the initial assumptions of the theory had been that people are status maximizers and that status is indicated by high price, then the theory would be unlikely to survive an empirical test. Empirical testing means that the predictions of a theory are tested against observed behaviour in the real world. Useful theories survive the process of empirical testing, whereas theories whose predictions are plainly at odds with observed behaviour are discarded.

Answer plan

1 Base your answer to the first part of the question on the concepts discussed in the previous section: the distinction between positive and normative theories, and how a theory simplifies—yet explains—the real world.
2 The characteristics of a useful (positive) theory are its relevance, the realism of its assumptions, and its ability to stand up to empirical testing. Often the mechanism of a theory can be expressed with the use of mathematics in an economic model.
3 Assess the usefulness of demand theory in terms of these three characteristics. Do downward-sloping demand curves conform to observed behaviour?

Question 2 Explain how an individual reallocates expenditure on goods when the price of one good changes.

(O & CSEB: June, 1987)

Understanding the Question This is a straightforward question on the demand theory covered in this unit. You can answer using either the utility theory or indifference curve analysis. Either way, you must relate your explanation to the maximizing (or optimizing) objective of the consumer, and clearly explain the substitution and income effects of the price change. The distinction between the positive income effect of a normal good and the negative income effect of an inferior good should also be emphasized, together with a brief explanation of the possible Giffen good phenomenon.

Answer plan

1 State the utility maximizing objective of the individual consumer.
2 List the constraints facing the consumer, emphasizing the budget constraint posed by limited income and the set of prices the individual faces.
3 Explain diminishing marginal utility.
4 Introduce the condition of equi-marginal utility and explain that utility can only be maximized over the set of goods available to purchase if the condition or equality holds for all of them.
5 Show how a price decrease for one good disturbs the equality and creates an incentive to substitute more of the good whose relative price has fallen for the other goods whose relative prices have risen, until the equality holds again.
6 Introduce the income effect of the price change.
7 Explain how the substitution and income effects combine and affect the allocation of expenditure in the case of normal goods, conventional inferior goods and Giffen goods.

Question 3 Why do households need to exercise choice? Explain how maximizing principles influence household choice in the goods market and in the factor market.   (*AEB: June, 1988*)

Understanding the Question There are three parts to this question and it is important to divide your time fairly equally between each part. The first part centres upon the fundamental economic problem of scarcity, economizing and opportunity cost (Unit 1). Then, assuming a utility maximizing objective on the part of households (the maximizing principle) and firmly stating the constraints facing the consumer, you must explain the conditions necessary for successful exercise of choice in the goods market: MU=P and/or the condition of equi-marginal utility. You must conclude your answer by drawing upon the extension of the analysis to the factor market where households choose between supplying labour and enjoying leisure time. This is covered in Unit 13.

Answer plan

1 Introduce the fundamental economic problem of scarcity, and mankind's relatively limitless wants, in the face of limited means with which to satisfy those wants.
2 Relate the need to exercise choice to the opportunity cost of any choice.
3 Introduce the assumption of a utility maximizing objective on the part of households.
4 Explain how utility maximization is brought about in the goods market by choosing a combination of available goods so that MU=P for each good and, the condition of equi-marginal utility holds for all the goods.
5 Drawing on Unit 13, explain how utility maximization is brought about in the factor market by supplying labour up to a point at which the MU of working = MU of the substitute, leisure time.

Multiple Choice Questions

Question 4 The Law of Diminishing Marginal Utility states that the more you consume of a commodity:
1 the higher the price you will be prepared to pay;
2 the slower the rate of increase in the total utility you derive from it;
3 the less the pleasure that you get from having an additional unit of it.

Directions

(a)	(b)	(c)	(d)
1, 2, 3 are all correct	1, 2 only correct	2, 3 only correct	1 only correct

Understanding the Question The objective questions included in Unit 1 are examples of **simple completion questions** where there is a straightforward choice between four or five possible answers, of which only one is correct. The second type of question is a **multiple completion question** where, although there is only one correct response you can make, this can depend on one or more of the completion items being correct. In this particular example, completion item 1 is wrong because it has nothing whatever to do with diminishing marginal utility, but items 2 and 3 are both correct. Thus the answer to the question is **(c)**.

Question 5

Table 1: *Average weekly household income in the United Kingdom*

	1970	1975	1980	1983
Gross weekly income	£35.40	£72.87	£147.18	£187.86
Weekly disposable income	£29.54	£58.16	£121.50	£152.50

Source: *Family Expenditure Survey*

Table 2: *The Retail Price Index (1975 = 100)*

1970	1975	1980	1983
54.2	100.0	195.6	248.6

Source: *Economic Trends*

Table 3: *Selected commodities or services as a percentage of total household expenditure in the United Kingdom*

	1970	1975	1980	1983
Housing	12.6	13.1	15.0	16.8
Fuel, light and power	6.3	5.5	5.6	6.4
Food	25.7	24.8	22.7	20.8
Alcoholic drink	4.5	5.1	4.8	4.8
Tobacco	4.8	3.6	3.0	2.9
Clothing and footwear	9.2	8.7	8.1	7.0
Durable household goods	6.5	7.4	7.0	7.2
Transport and vehicles	13.7	13.8	14.6	14.7
Services	9.0	9.9	10.8	11.3

Source: *Family Expenditure Survey*

(a) Explain the terms 'gross weekly income' and 'weekly disposable income'.

(2)

(b) Discuss whether the average household in the United Kingdom became better or worse off over the period shown by the data.

(6)

(c) **(i)** Summarize the significant features of the data in Table 3. (4)

(ii) Suggest possible reasons which might explain the changes or the lack of change in the pattern of household expenditure shown by the data.. (8)

(AEB: June, 1986)

Understanding the Question

(a) Gross weekly income is the income from all sources before deductions (such as income tax and national insurance contributions): weekly disposable income is residual income available to spend after these deductions.

(b) You must calculate whether the real weekly disposable income of the average household rose or fell over the period shown by the data. Divide the nominal figure for each year by the Retail Price Index (RPI) for the year and multiply by 100. This converts the data into the constant prices of 1975, the base year for the RPI. This calculation (correctly performed), together with a conclusion, is quite sufficient to earn all 6 marks, but you might also mention that your conclusion also depends on certain assumptions, such as no significant change in factors contributing towards feelings of being 'better' or 'worse' off; leisure time; intangibles such as 'quality of life'; and services provided by the state.

(c) **(i)** It is important to give an 'overview', highlighting the key changes, rather than to adopt a 'shopping list' approach going through each of the items, but without showing any real understanding of the data. For example, try to group the items into necessities and luxuries and see if there are any changes common to the necessities which separate them from the luxuries.

(ii) A good answer might concentrate on price effects and income effects and show an awareness that proportionate expenditure did not change by very much on many of the items. Your answer to part **(b)** will tell you whether real income rose or fell over the period. If real income rose and expenditure rose, you could conclude that the good is normal. But if expenditure fell, the good would be inferior. (But be careful! The expenditure data shows proportional changes in household expenditure rather than absolute rises or falls in expenditure on particular items. Also, the changes in the pattern of expenditure may be caused by relative price changes rather than by changes in income.)

2.6 Further reading

Anderton, A. G., *Economics, A New Approach*, 2nd edition (Unwin Hyman, 1990).
Chapter 22: Demand theory.

Burningham, D., editor, *Economics*, 3rd edition (Hodder & Stoughton, 1987).
Chapter 6: Consumer behaviour.

3 Cost and Supply

3.1 Points of perspective

In much the same way that the characteristics of demand curves depend upon the typical behaviour of consumers, so the properties of supply curves depend upon the behaviour of **producers** or **firms**. The **market supply curve**, which shows how much all the firms in an industry intend to supply at various possible prices, is obtained by adding up the separate supply curves for individual firms. For the rest of this unit, we shall assume that there are a large number of firms within a well-defined industry and that each firm is a passive **'price-taker'**, unable to influence the market price by its own decisions on how much to supply. We are really constructing the theory of supply within a **perfectly competitive** industry, though a more comprehensive treatment of perfect competition is delayed until Unit 6.

3.2 Underlying concepts

1 The firm

A firm is a **productive unit** or business enterprise which sells its output at a price, within the market economy. In the **private sector** of the economy, firms may range from a one-man window-cleaning business (a **sole trader** or **individual proprietor**) to huge 'multinational' public joint-stock companies, such as ICI, with branches and plants in many countries. Most **public corporations** or nationalized industries in the **public sector** of the economy are also considered as firms because they sell their output within the market economy. It is not usual, however, to regard **public services**, such as the National Health Service, as firms or business enterprises. Although the NHS is a major customer or market for firms which supply it from within the market economy, most of its own activities take place outside the market economy.

2 Profit-maximizing behaviour

In constructing a theory of supply we are not especially interested in the organizational complexities of firms, such as the different forms of ownership and control and the existence of multi-product and multi-plant enterprises. These are aspects of the **internal** structure of firms, which is the subject matter of Unit 10. In this unit we **abstract** from the internal organization of firms and concentrate instead upon the **external** behaviour of firms when they make decisions on the production and sale of a good or goods within the market. In the context of this unit, it does not matter who makes the decisions within the firm, as long as the decisions are consistent with a desired goal or objective which is assumed to exist for all firms. In the traditional theory of the firm it is assumed that all firms, whatever their internal structure and whatever the form of market in which they exist, share the common goal of profit maximization.

3 Factors of production

Economists conventionally divide all the inputs necessary for production to take place into four categories, or **'factors of production'**. These are land, labour, capital and enterprise (or the entrepreneurial factor). For the rest of this unit we shall simplify and assume that just two inputs, labour and capital, are all that is needed for production to take place.

4 The short run and the long run

In economic theory the short run is defined as a period of time in which at least one factor of production is fixed. Thus, in the short run a firm can only increase output or supply by adding more of a variable factor, in this case labour, and combining it with the fixed input, capital. In the long run it is assumed that all factors of production are variable. The **scale** of the fixed factors can only be altered in the economic long run. From a firm's point of view, the short run is thus a time-period in which its ability to increase supply is **constrained** by the size of its fixed capital. We must distinguish between a firm's short-run or constrained supply curve, and its long-run supply curve, which is unconstrained except by factors such as the available technology and the prices it must pay to obtain the services of labour and capital.

3.3 Essential information

1 The principle of diminishing returns

If a firm attempts to increase output or supply in the economic short run by adding a variable input, such as labour, to a given amount of fixed capital, then eventually diminishing marginal returns to labour will set in: an extra worker will add less to total output than the previous worker. (Diminishing marginal **output** and diminishing marginal **product** are alternative expressions of the same principle.) You should note that the principle of diminishing marginal returns refers to the physical productivity of labour and not to either the money cost of employing labour (the wage) or to the money value of the output which labour produces. The principle of diminishing returns is sometimes known as a 'law', but it must be stressed that when the first units of labour are added to fixed capital **increasing marginal returns** are likely to be experienced. This is because the employment of an extra worker allows greater **specialization** and **division of labour** to take place, with the result that total output increases more than proportionately as workers are added to the labour force.

There are two useful ways of illustrating the principle of diminishing returns in a diagram. In Figure 3.1, a **production possibility curve** has been drawn to show how many cars or bicycles a labour force of 100 men can produce if combined with fixed amounts of capital in either the car or the bicycle

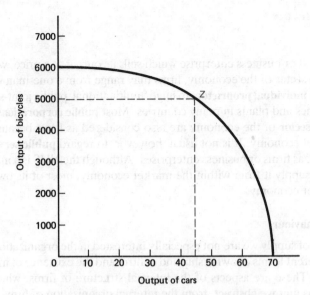

Fig 3.1 A production possibility curve

industry. If all the men are employed in the bicycle industry, the maximum output is 6000 bicycles and no cars. Similarly, seventy cars and no bicycles can be produced if all the men are switched to the car industry. The production possibility curve, drawn between these two extremes, represents all the combinations of bicycles and cars which are possible if some of the men are employed in one industry and some in the other. The point Z on the production possibility curve shows that the total possible output is 5000 bicycles and forty-five cars if fifty men are employed in each industry.

Now ask yourself what will happen if workers move out of the car industry into the bicycle industry (or vice versa). Whereas the first fifty workers in the bicycle industry produce a total of 5000 bicycles, the addition of a second fifty workers only increases output by an extra 1000 bicycles. The slope of the production possibility curve, which is concave to origin, is evidence of diminishing marginal returns in both industries.

Figure 3.2a again illustrates the principle of diminishing returns to labour, but in this example within a single industry. You will notice that the diagram distinguishes between diminishing **marginal** returns to labour and diminishing **average** returns–a source of confusion to many students. The concept of marginal returns refers to the addition to output attributable to the last worker added to the labour force. (Formally, the marginal returns of the n'th worker = total returns of n workers minus total returns of (n-1) workers.) The average return per worker is simply the total output divided by the number of workers employed (total returns/n).

The mathematical relationship between any marginal variable and the average to which it is related is:

(a) if the marginal > the average, the average will rise;
(b) if the marginal < the average, the average will fall;
(c) if the marginal = the average, the average will neither rise nor fall.

This is a universal mathematical relationship with a host of economic applications. It is essential for students to understand what it means and to avoid the very common error of misrepresenting the relationship. It does *not* state that an average will rise when a marginal is rising, or that an average will fall when the marginal is falling. Figure 3.2a clearly shows that the marginal returns curve begins to fall as soon as the point of diminishing marginal returns is reached. Nevertheless, the average returns curve continues to rise as long as the marginal output of an extra worker is greater than the existing average output–thereby, 'pulling up' the average curve. The point of diminishing average returns is reached only when the output of an extra worker falls below the existing average.

2 Short-run cost curves

The total cost of producing a particular output is made up of the cost of employing both the variable and the fixed factors of production. This can be expressed as the identity:

$$TC \equiv TVC + TFC$$

Likewise, average total cost can be written as:

$$ATC \equiv AVC + AFC$$

In Figure 3.2b, the average variable cost (AVC) curve is illustrated alongside (in Figure 3.2a) the average returns curve from which it is derived. Variable costs are the wage costs of employing the variable factor, labour. If all workers are paid the same wage, total wage costs will rise

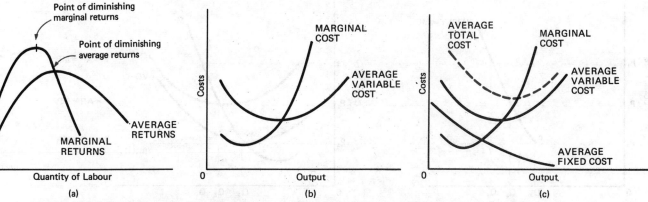

Fig. 3.2 The derivation of the firm's short-run cost curves (a) diminishing marginal returns and diminishing average returns to labour set in (b) these can be translated into money costs as the marginal cost curve and the average variable cost curve (c) the average total cost curve is obtained by including average fixed costs in the diagram

proportionately with the number of workers employed. However, while increasing average returns are being experienced, workers on average are becoming more efficient. It follows that average variable costs per unit of output will fall as output rises, but once diminishing average returns set in, average variable costs will rise with output.

In a very similar way, the marginal cost (MC) curve is derived from the nature of marginal returns to the variable inputs. If an extra worker adds more to total output than the previous worker, yet the wage cost of employing him remains the same, then the MC of producing an extra unit of output must fall. When diminishing marginal returns set in, however, the MC curve will rise.

While the nature of average and marginal returns to the variable factors of production determines the shapes of the AVC and MC curves, a separate, but very simple, explanation is needed for the average fixed cost (AFC) curve. Because total fixed costs do not vary with output in the economic short run, AFC per unit of output will fall as the fixed costs or 'overheads' are spread over larger and larger outputs. A falling AFC curve is drawn in Figure 3.2c, which also includes the average total cost curve obtained by adding up the AVC and AFC curves. The short-run ATC curve is typically U-shaped, showing that average total costs first fall and later rise as output is increased. You should note that the MC curve cuts both the AVC and the ATC curves at their lowest points. Check back to the preceding section to make quite sure that you know why this must be so. However, the point where the MC curve cuts the AFC curve is of no significance because the MC curve is derived only from variable costs and not from fixed costs.

3 The firm's short-run supply curve

We are now in a position to show how the short-run supply curve of a firm in a perfectly competitive industry is derived from its marginal cost curve. (The characteristics of perfect competition as a **market form** are examined in Unit 6.) A perfectly competitive firm, being a price-taker, will sell its output at the same market-determined price or **average revenue**, whatever the output it decides to supply to the market. This means that **total revenue** will always rise by the amount of price or average revenue when the firm decides to release an extra unit of output on the market. Now, **marginal revenue** is defined as the addition to total revenue resulting from the sale of an extra unit of output. It follows that **marginal revenue equals average revenue** for a perfectly competitive firm and is represented by a horizontal price-line such as P_1 in Figure 3.3.

It can easily be shown that any profit-maximizing firm, whatever the market form or structure, will produce the output where MR = MC. (We are now using MR as the economic shorthand for marginal revenue and not marginal returns!)

(a) If MR > MC, the firm is sacrificing the profit it could make from an extra unit of output. Therefore, it should increase output.

(b) If MR < MC, the firm is making a loss on at least the final unit of output produced. Therefore, it should decrease output.

(c) If MR = MC, there is no incentive to increase or decrease output. This is the **equilibrium condition** for a profit-maximizing firm.

Returning to Figure 3.3, let us suppose that the market-determined price is P_1. Using the equilibrium condition, the firm will choose to supply Q_1 onto the market, but if the price falls to P_2, supply will be reduced to Q_2. This is the **break-even price**, since the firm will start to make a loss if the price falls below the ATC curve. Nevertheless, if the price falls below P_2 it may still be consistent with profit-maximizing behaviour for the firm to continue to supply an output, in the short run at least,

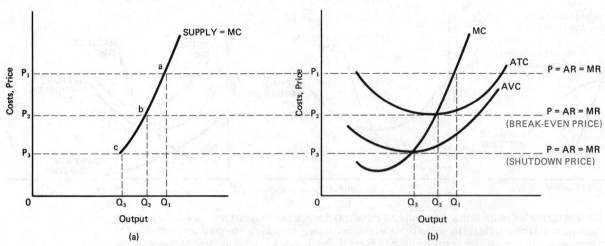

Fig 3.3 (a) The derivation of the firm's short-run supply curve from its MC curve (b) only the part of the MC curve above AVC is the firm's supply curve

even though it is making a loss. As long as the price covers AVC, the size of the loss will be less than the fixed costs the firm will incur if it produced zero output. The **shut-down price** is P_3, at which the firm just covers its variable costs.

Our conclusion is that the firm's MC curve, above AVC, is its short-run supply curve. The curve maps out how much the firm is prepared to supply to the market at each price. We have shown that the MC curve slopes upwards because of diminishing marginal returns to the variable factors of production. It is extremely useful to remember that the slope of the supply curve is derived from the principle of diminishing marginal returns and the assumption of profit-maximizing behaviour by firms. You should note the parallel between this analysis and the derivation, in Unit 2, of the demand curve from the principle of diminishing marginal utility and the assumption of utility-maximizing behaviour by households.

4 Shifts in supply

In the preceding analysis, the productivity of labour reflected in the principle of diminishing returns, and the wage or money costs of hiring labour determined the position of the firm's MC curve or short-run supply curve. If either productivity or wage costs change, the position of the supply curve will shift. Generalizing, a change in any of the **conditions of supply** will shift the supply curve. If labour becomes more productive, if wage costs fall, or if taxes on the firm are cut, then the supply curve will shift rightwards (or downwards), showing that the firm is prepared to supply more at existing prices.

5 Long-run costs and supply

In the long run, a firm can change the **scale** of the fixed factors of production and move to a new size of productive unit (or new short-run situation). The long-run average cost curve, which is illustrated in Figure 3.4, is a mathematical line drawn as a tangent to a 'family' or set of short-run cost curves, each representing a feasible size of productive unit. A firm can thus move in the long run from one short-run supply curve to another, which is associated with a different scale of fixed capacity. (It is useful to remember that firms can also enter or leave the industry in the long run. This means that the **industry** short-run supply curve, obtained by adding the individual supply curves of each firm, can shift its position in the long run when firms enter or leave the industry.)

The shape of the long-run ATC curve depends upon whether economies or diseconomies of scale are experienced. Long-run costs may be falling, rising, or constant. If an increase in all the inputs or factors of production results in falling long-run average total costs, **economies of scale** exist. Eventually **diseconomies of scale** may set in when the long-run ATC curve begins to rise. The textbook example of a U-shaped long-run ATC curve is drawn in Figure 3.4a. There is no reason, however, why the curve must be U-shaped. An industry, such as the automobile industry, with **economies of large-scale production** is represented in Figure 3.4b, while Figure 3.4c illustrates the **economies of small-scale production** which might be more typical of agriculture. (Further explanation of industries with economies of large- and small-scale production and a description of the main economies and diseconomies of scale are included in Unit 10.) Statistical studies have suggested an absence of significant economies and diseconomies of scale in many industries, in which case the correct long-run ATC curve would be the horizontal line in Figure 3.4d.

If the firm's long-run marginal cost curve is also its **long-run supply curve**, this would imply a

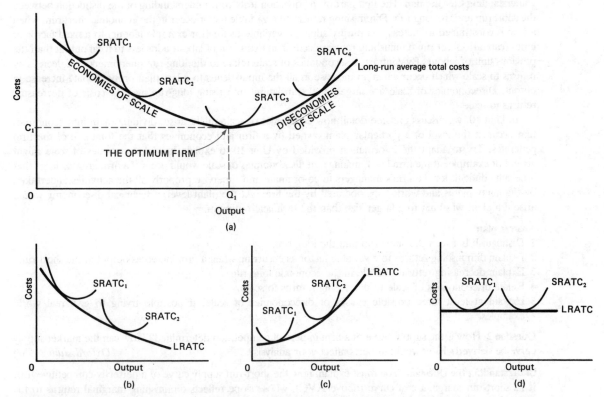

Fig 3.4 Long-run average total cost curves (a) economies of scale followed by diseconomies of scale
(b) an industry with economies of large scale production (c) an industry with diseconomies
of large scale production (d) an industry without economies or diseconomies of scale

horizontal (or perfectly elastic) long-run supply curve in industries with constant long-run average costs. Firms of many different sizes could co-exist without significant differences in costs.

6 Returns to scale

Many textbooks confuse economies of scale with the closely related concept of **increasing returns to scale**. Economies of scale refer to long-run **money costs** of production, whereas long-run returns to scale relate only to the **physical output** of the factors of production or inputs. If physical output increases more than proportionately as the scale of all the inputs is changed, increasing returns to scale occur. (**Decreasing returns to scale** and **constant returns to scale** are other possibilities.) Increasing returns to scale contribute to economies of scale (in the form of **technical economies**), but some economies of scale are not explained by increasing returns to scale–for example, **'bulk-buying' economies**, when a firm uses its market power to buy inputs at low prices.

While it is useful to understand the difference between economies of scale and increasing returns to scale, it is much more important for the student at Advanced Level to be absolutely clear about the difference between short-run returns, explained earlier in the unit, and the long-run returns to scale described in this section. It is the impact of diminishing marginal returns on the costs and profits of a firm in the economic short run that encourages the firm to change the scale of its operations in the long run.

3.4 Links with other topics

In this unit it has been assumed that a firm exists within a perfectly competitive industry. Further aspects of the supply and output decisions of firms in conditions of perfect competition and monopoly are developed in Unit 6, while Unit 7 extends the analysis to imperfect competition. Elasticity of supply is explained in Unit 4, which is followed in Unit 5 by a survey of the special problems of agricultural supply.

3.5 Question practice

Essay Questions

Question 1 Explain the distinction between diminishing returns to a variable factor and diseconomies of scale.

(60)

With reference to examples, explain how diseconomies of scale might result.

(40)

(London: June, 1989)

Understanding the Question The first part of the question tests your understanding of the distinction between the short run and the long run. Diminishing returns to a variable factor occur in the economic short run, when a firm is constrained to increase output by adding a variable factor (for example labour) to a fixed factor or input (capital). Short-run diminishing returns occur if an extra unit of labour adds less to total output than the previous unit of labour. By contrast, diseconomies of scale relate to the long-run phenomenon of decreasing returns to scale which occur when an increase in all the inputs leads to a less than proportionate increase in output. Diseconomies of scale are largely the 'translation' into rising long-run average costs of decreasing returns to scale.

In Unit 10, we discuss in some detail how economies of scale might arise; dividing them into economies that occur at the level of a particular plant owned by a firm and economies that the total size of the firm generates. Try to adapt the information provided by Unit 10 to explain how diseconomies of scale might arise. For example, at the firm level, managerial diseconomies of scale would occur if a firm grew so large that it became difficult for the firm's managers to co-ordinate and supervise properly all the activities undertaken by the many plants and workshops operated by the firm. At the plant level, a technical diseconomy would arise if a plant was built to a larger size than the technical optimum.

Answer plan
1 Distinguish between the short run and the long run.
2 Explain diminishing returns to a variable factor as occurring when a firm increases output in the short run.
3 Explain decreasing returns to scale in the economic long run.
4 Relate diseconomies of scale to decreasing returns to scale.
5 Explain at least three possible causes of diseconomies of scale, if possible trying to give real world examples.

Question 2 How is the supply curve of a firm in perfect competition determined? How can the market supply curve be derived? How would imports affect your analysis?   *Oxford: June, 1987)*

Understanding the Question You must explain how the short-run supply curve of a perfectly-competitive firm is its short-run marginal cost curve (above AVC), whose slope reflects diminishing marginal returns to the variable factors of production. The market supply curve is simply the summation of the supply curves of each of the firms that comprise the market.

You could then explain that a firm's long-run supply curve is its long-run marginal cost curve, with the long-run market supply curve again being the summation of the long-run supply curves of each of the firms. Assuming constant input prices, the shape of the long-run supply curve will depend on whether the firms experience increasing, constant, or decreasing returns to scale. For example, constant returns to scale result in constant long-run marginal costs and a horizontal long-run supply curve. The supply of imports is also often represented by a horizontal supply curve. For example, refer to Figure 5.3 in Unit 5 for an illustration of the impact of imports upon the market supply curve.

Answer plan
1 Derive a firm's short-run supply curve from its short-run MC curve.
2 Explain how the market short-run supply curve is the sum of each firm's short-run supply curve.
3 Repeat for the long run.
4 Explain that the supply curve of imports shows the quantities that all overseas firms are prepared to supply at different prices onto the domestic market, supplementing domestic supply.
5 Explain the circumstances in which a horizontal (infinitely elastic) supply curve of imports can be assumed.

Multiple Choice Questions

Question 3 A firm's total fixed costs are £1200. If at a certain output its average total costs per unit are £10 and the average variable cost per unit is £7, then that level of output is:
(a) 200 units   (b) 300 units   (c) 400 units   (d) 500 units

Understanding the Question The correct answer (c) is obtained in two stages:
(i) calculate average fixed costs per unit by using the identity:
    average total costs ≡ average fixed costs + average variable costs;
(ii) the level of output = total fixed costs ÷ average fixed costs.

Question 4 Diminishing returns occur in the short run when there is a reduction in:
(a) the average product of the fixed factor
(b) the total product of the variable factor
(c) the marginal product of the fixed factor
(d) the marginal product of the variable factor

Understanding the Question This is a straightforward question on the short-run 'laws' of returns. Although average and total returns will eventually diminish as more and more of a variable factor is added to fixed capacity, the principle of diminishing returns usually refers to the **marginal** returns of a variable input – alternative (d).

Data Response Questions

Question 5 A profitable airline is considering the introduction of a new trans-Atlantic flight and is faced with the following costs per flight:

	£
Fuel charges	10 000
Depreciation	700
Insurance	300
Landing charges	500
Interest	500
Labour	5000
Other fixed costs	5000

(a) From the above table distinguish between fixed and variable costs. Give reasons for your choice. (4)

(b) **(i)** Given a maximum seating capacity of 300 persons per aircraft, what is the *minimum* price per seat that the airline must charge on this flight to avoid making a loss? (5)

  (ii) If the above costs were representative of all flights, what price must the airline charge to remain in business in the long run? (5)

(c) Discuss the factors that are likely to determine the *actual* price charged. (6)

(London: January, 1987)

Understanding the Question Numerical or statistical data response questions are of two types: those based on a real-world data source and those containing fictional data. Most of the examination boards only set questions containing real-world data, arguing that the other type is not really a true data response question and that the skills being tested can be tested just as adequately on the multiple choice paper. Before spending time studying any simulated data questions in this book, check past papers of your own examining board to see what the board's policy is. The London board is the major exception to the rule, usually setting one question of this type in each examination.

This is a deceptively difficult question. Usually with questions of this type, it is possible to calculate a correct answer. However, the answers to questions **(b)(i)** and **(ii)** depend upon demand at each price and no data is provided on the matter on demand. To avoid a loss, total revenue per flight must at least equal total costs per flight. Total costs per flight are £22 000 so, providing all 300 seats are sold, the airline must charge £73.34 per passenger. However, it would have to charge a higher price to avoid a loss if less than 300 passengers wished to fly at a price of £73.34. If, at all prices, only one passenger wished to fly, the airline would have to charge £22 000 to avoid a loss! The answer to part **(b)(ii)** depends upon similar assumptions about demand. We might also add that an amount for 'normal profits' (see Unit 6) would have to be added to the costs shown in the table for an economist to conclude that it is worthwhile for a firm to stay in business in the long run.

Amongst the factors that you might discuss in your answer to part **(c)** are: the airline's assumed objectives; the extent to which it is a 'price taker' or 'price maker'; the existence of cartel-style agreements with other airlines; product diffentiation and price discrimination; the influence of government regulation or price administration; and the economics of offering cheap stand-by flights to fill seats when immediately before departure the marginal cost of accepting an extra passenger is very low.

3.6 Further reading

Lipsey, R. G., *An Introduction to Positive Economics*, 7th edition (Weidenfeld & Nicolson, 1989).
Chapter 10: The Firm, Production and Cost
Chapter 11: Costs and Output
Begg, D., Fischer, S. and Dornbusch, R., *Economics*, 3rd edition (McGraw-Hill, 1991)
Chapter 8: Developing the Theory of Supply; Costs and Production

4 Elasticity

4.1 Points of perspective

Consider the demand curves which are drawn in Figure 4.1 and which show the demand for a product such as electronic calculators in two separated markets, the London area market and a market for the rest of the United Kingdom. Demand curve D_2 is quite clearly flatter than D_1. Students are often tempted to use the flatness or steepness of a demand or supply curve to describe its elasticity–the responsiveness of demand or supply to a change in price. However, a careful inspection of Figure 4.1 reveals that the slope of the curves is misleading and that flatness or steepness is not a proper indicator of elasticity. In each market a twenty per cent reduction in price from £20 to £16 results in a doubling of the quantity which households intend to buy: despite their different slopes, the demand curves display identical elasticities whenever the price changes. In this example we could calculate the **average elasticity** when the price changes from £20 to £16. Strictly, however, elasticity is a measure of the response of demand to a price change at a **specific point** on a curve, and the concept should not be used to describe quite large changes in price.

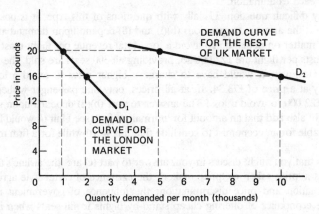

Fig 4.1 Demand curves with the same elasticities but different slopes

Whenever one variable responds to another variable, an elasticity can be estimated. Elasticity is an especially useful **descriptive statistic** of the relationship between any two variables because it is independent of the units, such as quantity and price units, in which the variables are measured. A knowledge of supply and demand elasticities is particularly useful to decision-makers both in firms and in government. If we are told, for example, that the demand elasticity of Scotch whisky is 2, then this single statistic contains the information that a one per cent price-rise causes a two per cent fall in quantity demanded. (Strictly, the elasticity is −2 as the price-rise causes a fall in quantity demanded, but the minus sign is frequently omitted.) The size of the elasticity will indicate the extent to which sales may drop when a tax is imposed upon Scotch whisky: the more elastic the demand (and supply) curves, the greater will be the fall in sales. Since the government's tax-revenue equals the amount of the tax multiplied by the after-tax quantity of sales, the government will experience the least loss in tax-revenue when it imposes a tax on goods with low demand and supply elasticities.

4.2 Underlying concepts

1 The estimation of elasticity

Suppose that a businessman wishes to estimate how his customers will respond when the price of his product is increased. If he possesses perfect market information, as in perfect competition, there will be no problem: he simply reads off, from a chart or graph displayed on his office wall, the quantities that would be demanded at all possible prices. Unfortunately, many students at Advanced Level seem to think that all business decisions are made in this way! Businessmen, however, seldom if ever possess perfect information and this means that they cannot be sure how their customers will react to price changes. One method of estimating the elasticity of demand for a good is to collect data on the quantities actually bought at different prices in previous years–but the elasticity statistic which is obtained from such an exercise must be treated with caution. It will have been calculated on **ex post** rather than **ex ante** data: the amount **actually bought** may not have been the same as the quantity that households had planned or intended to buy. Also, conditions of demand and the general price-level may have changed over the years. To overcome these problems, a businessman could hire a market research team to go into the street with questionnaires, to ask people how much they would buy at various prices.

4.3 Essential information

1 Elasticity formulae

When an examination question requires you to discuss the measurement and interpretation of elasticity statistics, you must bear in mind the data-collecting problems described in the preceding section: measurement of elasticity involves more than just a textbook formula. Nevertheless, once the information on the planned demand of households or the supply intentions of firms has been collected, a simple formula is used to estimate the elasticity:

(i) Price elasticity of demand $= \dfrac{\text{Proportionate change in quantity demanded}}{\text{Proportionate change in price}}$

(ii) Price elasticity of supply $= \dfrac{\text{Proportionate change in quantity supplied}}{\text{Proportionate change in price}}$

(iii) Income elasticity of demand $= \dfrac{\text{Proportionate change in quantity demanded}}{\text{Proportionate change in income}}$

(iv) Cross-elasticity of demand for Good A with respect to Good B $= \dfrac{\text{Proportionate change in quantity of A demanded}}{\text{Proportionate change in price of B}}$

For example, if the price rises by a third and consumers respond by reducing the quantity demanded by two-thirds, the price elasticity of demand–formula (i) above–is 2 (strictly −2).

2 Price elasticity of demand

If a price change results in a more than proportionate change in demand, demand is said to be **elastic**. The elasticity statistic, calculated from the formula, will be greater than 1. Similarly, if the change in demand is less than proportionate, demand is **inelastic**, and the elasticity statistic will be less than 1. It is usually misleading, however, to refer to the whole of a demand curve as elastic or inelastic since the elasticity will generally vary from point to point along the curve.

Before we show how the elasticity varies along the curve, it is useful to introduce an alternative way of describing demand elasticity in terms of price changes:

(i) If total **consumer expenditure increases** in response to a **price fall**, demand is relatively elastic.
(ii) If total **consumer expenditure decreases** in response to a **price fall**, demand is relatively inelastic.
(iii) If total **consumer expenditure remains constant** in response to a **price fall** elasticity of demand = unity.

Figure 4.2 illustrates some possible changes in consumer expenditure which might follow a reduction in price. When the price falls from P_1 to P_2 in Figure 4.2a, total consumer expenditure **increases** by the shaded area k, but **decreases** by the area h. The area k, which represents the proportionate increase in the quantity demanded, is clearly larger than area h, which represents the proportionate change in price. Demand is thus elastic at all points on the demand curve between a and b on curve D_1. However, if the price falls from P_3 to P_4 on the same demand curve, the shaded area k′ is smaller than the area h′. Total consumer expenditure falls, and demand is inelastic at all points between c and d on the demand curve.

We are now in a position to explain the misleading generalization that a 'flat' demand curve is elastic and a 'steep' curve is inelastic. Moving along all linear (straight-line) demand curves that slope down from left to right, elasticity of demand falls from point to point along the curve. The 'flat' demand curve illustrated in Figure 4.2b is really only the upper part of a curve which, if extended far enough rightwards or downwards, would eventually become inelastic in its lower reaches. Similarly, the 'steep' inelastic demand curve in Figure 4.2c is the lower part of a curve which would become elastic in its upper reaches if these could be included in the diagram.

Intuition suggests that if elasticity varies from point to point along a downward-sloping **linear** curve, then we require a **non-linear** curve to show a constant elasticity at all points. The rectangular hyperbola illustrated in Figure 4.2d is the special case of a non-linear demand curve which shows a unit elasticity at all points on the curve.

3 Infinite elasticity and zero elasticity

Infinitely elastic (or perfectly elastic) demand or supply can be represented by a horizontal curve,

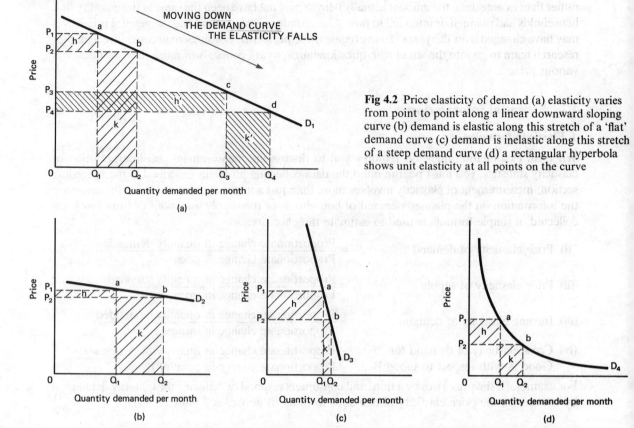

Fig 4.2 Price elasticity of demand (a) elasticity varies from point to point along a linear downward sloping curve (b) demand is elastic along this stretch of a 'flat' demand curve (c) demand is inelastic along this stretch of a steep demand curve (d) a rectangular hyperbola shows unit elasticity at all points on the curve

such as those drawn in Figure 4.3a. The diagram illustrates a trap awaiting the unwary student. In the case of the perfectly elastic demand curve, consumers demand an infinite amount at a price of P_2 or below; if the price rises above P_2, demand falls to zero as consumers switch to the perfect substitutes which are assumed to be available. In the case of the perfectly elastic supply curve, however, firms are prepared to supply an infinite amount at a price of P_1 or above. If the price falls below P_1, the firms refuse to supply any output onto the market!

Figure 4.3b illustrates a completely inelastic supply curve: whatever the price, the same amount is supplied onto the market. Similarly, completely inelastic demand would be shown by a vertical demand curve.

4 The determinants of demand elasticity

Substitutability When a perfect substitute for a product exists, consumers can respond to a price-rise by switching their expenditure to the substitute product. Commodities–for example, British

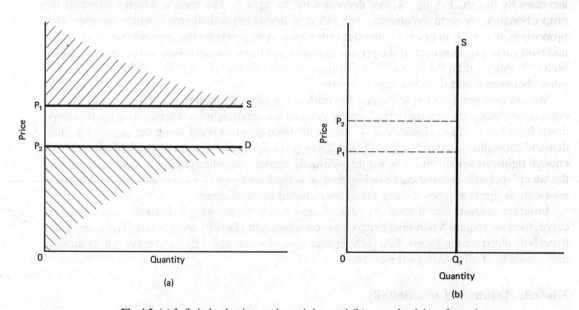

Fig 4.3 (a) Infinitely elastic supply and demand (b) zero elasticity of supply

motor-cars – which have close substitutes available tend to be in more elastic demand than those that do not.

Percentage of income Items on which many people spend a large proportion of their income, such as summer holidays, tend to be in more elastic demand than goods such as matches, on which only a fraction of income is spent.

Necessities v luxuries Necessities tend to be in inelastic demand, luxuries in elastic demand. Salt is often cited as a commodity with a very inelastic demand: it is a necessity, with no close substitutes, and expenditure on it is only a small part of most households' total spending.

The width of the definition The wider the definition of a commodity, the lower the elasticity. Thus, the demand for a particular brand of a commodity will be more elastic than the demand for the commodity as a whole. In a similar way, the elasticity of demand for bread will be greater than that for food as a whole.

Time The longer the time-period involved, the greater the elasticity of demand is likely to be. This is because it takes time to adjust to a change in price. If the price of gas rises, people may be unable to switch immediately to alternative household heating systems because they are 'locked in' to their existing investments in gas-fired appliances. However, the opposite may be true in certain circumstances: some consumers might react to a sudden increase in the price of cigarettes by giving up smoking altogether, and then gradually drift back to their old habits.

5 Price elasticity of supply

Supply curves normally slope upwards from left to right, and the mathematical properties of upward-sloping (or positive) curves are different from those of downward-sloping (or negative) curves. The key points to note are:

(i) **Any** straight-line (linear) supply curve drawn from the origin (point O) will display unit elasticity of supply **at all points** along the curve. This is illustrated in Figure 4.4a, where a doubling of the price causes an exact doubling of the quantity supplied.

(ii) The 'flat' supply curve drawn in Figure 4.4b is **elastic** at all points along the curve, since any price-change would result in a more than proportionate change in supply. But the elasticity **falls towards unity,** moving from point to point up the curve to the right.

(iii) Similarly, the 'steep' curve in Figure 4.4c is **inelastic** at all points, since any price-change results in a less than proportionate change in supply. But in this case the elasticity **rises towards unity,** moving from point to point up the curve.

(iv) However, as in the case of demand curves, the 'flatness' or 'steepness' of a supply curve is a misleading guide to its elasticity. The key point is not the flatness or steepness of the curve, but **whether the supply curve intersects the price axis or the quantity axis.**

The rule is:

(a) If a linear supply curve intersects the price axis, the curve is elastic at all points.

(b) If a linear supply curve intersects the quantity axis, the curve is inelastic at all points.

(c) If a linear supply curve intersects the origin, the elasticity is unity at all points along the curve.

In the case of non-linear supply curves, it is possible to use the rule to check the elasticity at a particular point on the supply curve by drawing a **tangent** to the point, and by noting the axis which

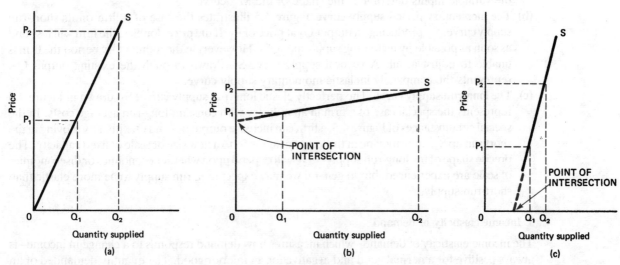

Fig 4.4 Price elasticity of supply (a) unit elasticity of supply (b) elastic supply (c) inelastic supply

the tangent intersects. We leave it as an exercise for the reader to do this, and also to draw a 'steep' supply curve intersecting the price axis. You will find that the curve is elastic at all points, showing that a 'steep' curve can be elastic!

6 The determinants of supply elasticity

Suppose that the demand for a good such as a car-component suddenly doubles at all prices. The factors which may determine whether supply is able to respond include:

(i) **The number of firms in the industry** Generally, the greater the number of firms in an industry, the more elastic is the industry supply.

(ii) **The length of the production period** If production converts inputs into outputs in the space of a few hours, supply will be more elastic than when several months are involved, as in agriculture.

(iii) **The existence of spare capacity** If spare capacity exists and if variable inputs such as labour and raw materials are available, it should be possible to increase production quickly in the short run.

(iv) **The ease of accumulating stocks** If it is easy to store unsold stocks at low cost, firms will be able to meet a sudden increase in demand by running down stocks. Likewise, they can respond to a sudden fall in demand and price by taking supply off the market and by diverting production into stock-accumulation.

(v) **The ease of factor substitution** Many firms produce a range of different products and are able to switch machines and labour from one type of production to another. If factors of production can be switched in this way, then the supply of one particular product will tend to be elastic.

(vi) **Time** The longer the time-period under consideration, the greater the ability of firms to adjust to a price-change. It is useful to distinguish three separate time-periods, the short run, the momentary period, and the long run:

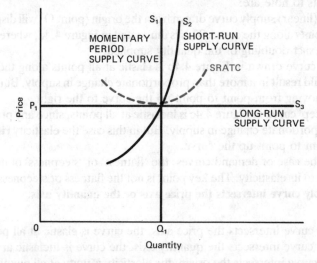

Fig 4.5 The elasticity of the supply curve varies with the time period

(a) **The short-run supply curve** The short-run supply curve of an individual firm is its short-run marginal cost curve. In Unit 3 it is explained how the impact of diminishing marginal returns to the variable inputs determines the shape of the MC curve.

(b) **The momentary period supply curve** Figure 4.5 illustrates the case of a firm on its short-run supply curve, S_2, producing an output Q_1 at price of P_1. If the price doubles, the firm will respond as soon as possible by increasing supply along S_2. However, in the momentary period the firm is unable to adjust at all. A vertical supply curve S_1, drawn through the existing output Q_1, represents the completely inelastic momentary supply curve.

(c) **The long-run supply curve** The perfectly elastic long-run supply curve, S_3, drawn in Figure 4.5 represents the special case of a firm in an industry with constant long-run average costs. In the special circumstances of Figure 4.5, a firm can increase output beyond Q_1 either by moving in the short run up S_2, or by moving in the long run along S_3 to a new size or scale of fixed capacity. The precise shape of the long-run supply curve will depend upon whether economies or diseconomies of scale are experienced, but in general we may expect long-run supply to be more elastic than short-run supply.

7 Income elasticity of demand

The income elasticity of demand–which measures how demand responds to a change in income–is always **positive** for a **normal** good and **negative** for an inferior good. The quantity demanded of an inferior good **falls** as income **rises**. Normal goods are sometimes further subdivided into **luxuries** or

superior goods, for which the income elasticity of demand is greater than unity, and **essential** or **basic** goods with an elasticity of less than one. Although the quantity demanded of normal goods always rises as income rises, it rises more than proportionately with income for superior goods (such as dish-washers). Conversely, demand for a basic good such as soap rises at a slower rate than income.

8 Cross-elasticity of demand

This is a statistic which describes the complementary or substitute relationship between two commodities. A cross-elasticity of demand of -0.1 for bread with respect to the price of butter indicates that a ten per cent rise in the price of butter is associated with a one per cent fall in the demand for bread. In contrast, a cross-elasticity of $+0.8$ for margarine with respect to the price of butter shows that a ten per cent rise in the price of butter will result in an eight per cent increase in the demand for margarine. Whereas the mathematical sign of a cross-elasticity statistic depends on the nature of the relationship between the two commodities, the absolute size of the statistic indicates the strength of the relationship. Cross-elasticities are negative for complementary goods, and positive for substitutes. A cross-elasticity statistic very close to zero is likely when there is no complementary or close substitute relationship between two goods.

4.4 Links with other topics

There are three important applications of the elasticity concept in public finance, exchange-rate policy, and agriculture. The possible effects of the elasticity of supply and demand on government tax revenue are explained in Unit 15. Elasticity of demand for exports and imports has an important effect upon exchange-rate policy, which is the subject of Unit 27. Meanwhile, Unit 5 develops the theme of how the inelastic supply and demand for agricultural products results in very unstable prices and incomes for primary producers.

4.5 Question practice

Essay Questions

Question 1 Define 'price elasticity of demand' and outline the factors which determine its value. Show the relevance of price elasticity in analyzing the effects of a rise in the price of petrol on the demand for different forms of transport. *(JMB: June, 1980)*

Understanding the Question You must start off by correctly defining price elasticity of demand as a measure of the responsiveness of demand to changes in **price only**. Briefly describe problems of measurement, but avoid the temptation to write too much on the mathematics of demand curves! Develop the answer by drawing on the coverage in the unit of the various factors, such as the existence of substitutes, which determine the value of the elasticity. The last part of the question is particularly important because it is impossible to rely on textbook definitions and formulae in answering a question of this type: your ability to think for yourself is being tested. Because of the lack of substitute fuels, demand for petrol for all forms of motor transport tends to be inelastic, though under some circumstances cycling, walking, and trains powered by electricity will provide alternatives. Demand for a particular form of motor transport, such as that provided by private cars, will be rather more price-elastic, as motorcycles and buses are substitutes. In each case, the effects of a petrol price-rise will vary with the percentage cost increase that this has on each form of transport.

A general rise in the price of petrol and oil-based products, resulting from a rise in the price of imported oil, would probably cause real incomes to fall. Some of the effects on the demand for different forms of transport might be the result of the income effect, as for example when people who feel poorer give up cars and switch to bus travel. It is of course completely impossible to analyze *all* the effects and 'feedbacks' in an examination answer. The examiner will be hoping that you can make intelligent use of the concept of price elasticity of demand in developing *some* of the possible lines of argument–perhaps noting at the same time that income and cross-elasticity of demand will also be involved.

Answer plan This question is in two fairly equal parts. The first requires recall of knowledge and explanation of a key economic concept. A fair attempt at the second part would be needed to secure a pass grade.

1 Define price elasticity of demand, stating the formula.
2 Explain, with diagrams, the main determinants.
3 Analyze the effects of a petrol price-rise. Credit is unlikely to be given for a detailed consideration of the *causes* of the price rise. The types of transport to consider would seem to be car, bus, train, aeroplane, cycling and walking. Choose perhaps two or three forms and look at the immediate direct effects, bringing in elasticity.
4 Finally, consider the more difficult indirect effects, for example the income effects and feedbacks.

Question 2

(a) Discuss briefly what is measured by the concept of 'the price elasticity of demand'.
(b) Explain how the value of the relevant price elasticity will play a critical role in determining the degree of success of the following policies:

(i) An increase of 0.5 pence per unit in the price of electricity intended to reduce consumption by 10 per cent.

(ii) An increase in admission charges by Football League clubs intended to increase gate receipts.

(iii) The introduction of subsidies paid to producers of certain foods intended to reduce the cost of living.

(WJEC: June, 1980)

Understanding the Question We have included this question as an example of some of the policy-making applications of the elasticity concept. In the first of the examples specified in the question, the success of the increase in the price of electricity is measured by the fall in the quantity demanded. If the price-rise represents a 20 per cent increase, for example, then the elasticity would have to be 0.5 in order to achieve the required fall in demand. If the true elasticity is 1.0, the policy would 'overshoot', causing a 20 per cent drop in demand.

In the second example, success is measured by the change in revenue (which equals **consumer expenditure**) rather than by the change in the quantity traded. This is a simple application of the rule which states that demand must be inelastic if a **rise** in consumer expenditure is to result from a **rise** in price.

The effects of a subsidy on the price of food is illustrated in Figure 4.6. Because demand for **all foods** is inelastic, a general food subsidy would result in a substantial fall in food prices. This is shown in Figure 4.6a. According to the question, however, only certain foods are to be subsidized. If consumers are able to switch from unsubsidized substitute foods, demand is likely to be elastic. Figure 4.6b shows how the main effect will be on sales and on producers' revenue rather than on the price of food and the cost of living.

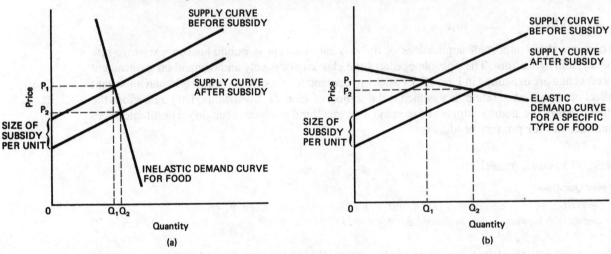

Fig 4.6 Food subsidies and the price of food (a) a substantial fall in the price of food when demand is inelastic (b) the main effect of the subsidy is on producer's revenue when demand is elastic

Answer plan

1 Describe how the elasticity is a descriptive statistic measuring the responsiveness of demand to a change in price.

2 A precise knowledge of the elasticity is required by the electricity board in order to reduce demand by an exact amount.

3 A general knowledge of the elasticity or inelasticity of demand is sufficient for the Football League clubs.

4 Whether a subsidy will reduce food prices and the cost of living will depend upon the range and type of foods being subsidized.

Question 3

(a) Examine the significance of income elasticity of demand to:
   (i) car telephone producers and (ii) potato farmers.   (50)

(b) Discuss the significance of cross-elasticity of demand to the Post Office when considering higher postal rates.   (50)

(London: June, 1990)

Understanding the Question

(a) After defining clearly the concept of income elasticity of demand, you must explain how the elasticity will vary for normal goods and inferior goods. You might further subdivide normal goods into those with a positive income elasticity of demand greater and less than unity (sometimes respectively called superior goods, or luxuries) and basic goods. You might then argue that a car telephone is a superior good, but that potatoes are basic goods (or possibly inferior goods). In each case you must explain what is likely to happen to the demand for the good if real incomes rise or fall. You could conclude that the income elasticity of demand may not be significant from the producers' point of view, either because the income elasticities may not be significantly different from zero (i.e. income changes may not have a significant effect on demand), or because real income change is slow, or because income effects are overwhelmed by other influences upon demand such as relative price changes or the effect of advertising campaigns.

(b) Carefully define cross-elasticity of demand and explain how it varies for goods in joint demand and for substitutes. An increase in postal rates will reduce demand for the postal services provided by the Post Office and also reduce demand for any complementary services that the Post Office might provide, e.g. insurance of mail. The significance of this will depend upon the absolute rise in real postal rates and the size of cross-elasticity of demand. However, the cross-elasticity of demand for substitute services provided by rival firms is likely to be of much more interest to Post Office decision-makers when deciding whether or not (or by how much) to raise postal rates. A high cross-elasticity will imply a significant loss of business to rival means of communication (telephone, fax and dispatch delivery services), unless, of course, these rivals introduce similar price rises.

Multiple Choice Questions

Question 4 If there is a free market in potatoes and if demand is completely inelastic, the most likely effect of an outstandingly good crop will be:

(a) to increase the total income of potato farmers   (c) to increase the quality demanded

(b) to increase the price of potatoes   (d) to reduce the total income of potato farmers

Understanding the Question The correct answer (d) is obtained from simple supply and demand analysis. The demand curve is vertical, showing that the same quantity is demanded at all prices–so alternative (c) is clearly wrong. The new equilibrium will be where a 'lower' supply curve intersects the vertical demand curve. The new equilibrium price is lower than the old price, and farmers' income falls.

Questions 5 and 6 are based on the table below.

Demand Schedule for carrots	
Price in pence	Quantity demanded per week (tons)
3	600
4	480
5	400
6	300
7	280
8	245

Question 5 If the price increases from 5p to 6p the demand is

    (a) inelastic   (c) elastic

    (b) of unit elasticity   (d) perfectly elastic

Question 6 Between which prices is the elasticity of demand unitary?

    (a) 4p and 5p   (c) 6p and 7p

    (b) 5p and 6p   (d) 7p and 8p

Understanding the Questions You may encounter a problem if you use the elasticity formula to answer these questions. The elasticity statistic calculated for a price **rise** from 5p to 6p will differ from the statistic calculated for a price **fall** from 6p to 5p. This is because the formula calculates the **average elasticity** between two points on the demand curve and the answer obtained depends upon whether the upper or lower point is used as the base for the calculation. It is better, and much quicker, to use the simple rule described in the unit, to obtain the answers. Firstly calculate the total consumer expenditure at each price. The answer to question 5 is (c) because a **rise** in price is associated with a **fall** in consumer expenditure. Total consumer expenditure remains the same at 1960 pence between a price of 7p and 8p, so the answer to question 6 is (d).

Question 7 Which of the following statements concerning supply is (are) correct?

(1) The momentary period is that period in which supply is completely inelastic.

(2) In the short run, part of a firm's marginal cost curve is also its supply curve.

(3) Supply is usually more elastic in the short run than in the long run.

(a)	(b)	(c)	(d)
1, 2, 3 correct	1, 2 only correct	2, 3 only correct	1 only correct

Understanding the Question This is a straightforward question which is testing your understanding of the supply curve and elasticity of supply. The correct answer is (b). Sometimes the **momentary period** may be called the **market period**: it is the period in which firms cannot bring extra supplies onto the market, or remove supply from the market.

Data Response Questions
Question 8

High tax weapon in smoking battle

Higher taxation on cigarettes is likely to reduce smoking, Mrs Joy Townsend a research scientist at Northwick Park Hospital, Harrow, told the association.

Mrs Townsend argued that the effect of public education about smoking and health had changed the pattern of smoking. The difference between men's and women's smoking habits had narrowed. Most importantly, by 1964, 49 per cent of unskilled workers, the lowest social class, smoked cigarettes, while only 17 per cent of the professional class still did so.

In 1981, the then Chancellor, Sir Geoffrey Howe, imposed one of the largest post-war increases in tobacco tax, putting the price up by 20 per cent. Since then the tax has been increased in line with inflation.

An important aspect of taxation was that it impinged differently on different income groups. Tobacco tax rises did not fall more heavily on the poor, because low income earners reduced their smoking in response to tax increases. The downward drift in real cigarette prices over twenty years had effectively increased smoking levels of the lower socio-economic groups and had been an important factor in the divergent habits of the social classes.

In the past four years, cigarette prices had risen by 26 per cent in real terms and consumption had fallen by 20 per cent. Government revenue had increased by 10 per cent providing an extra £435 million.

Tax was therefore working as an ally of preventative medicine and health education costing less than £200 per life per year compared with some £800 per life per year for bypass surgery or £5000 for heart transplant programmes.

Source: adapted from *The Guardian*, 4 September 1986

(a) Explain what is meant by the phrase 'The downward drift in real cigarette prices' (4th paragraph).   (2)
(b) (i) Use the figures in the article to calculate the price elasticity of demand during the 'past four years' (5th paragraph).   (1)
    (ii) Why might this figure not provide a correct measure of the responsiveness of the demand for cigarettes to a change in price?   (2)
    (iii) According to the article, how does the price elasticity of demand for cigarettes for people in the higher socio-economic groups differ from the price elasticity of demand for those people in the lower socio-economic group?   (2)
(c) Explain and illustrate, using a demand and supply diagram, the likely effect of the change in cigarette prices in 1981 upon the market for cigarettes and government tax revenues.   (5)
(d) Outline the **economic** arguments in favour of high levels of taxation on tobacco.   (8)

(AEB: June, 1988)

Understanding the Question Increasingly, the examining boards set data response questions that range across the syllabus, testing your skill at drawing upon relevant theory to answer a particular part of the question, before moving on to quite different theory appropriate for answering other aspects of the question. Thus parts (b) and (c) of this question specifically test the concept of elasticity, whereas parts (a) and (d) are testing other areas of your economic knowledge–though you might argue in your answer to (d) that a high level of taxation upon tobacco can be justified as an efficient revenue raiser for the government because demand is price inelastic. But while this argument is relevant, a developed answer to part (d) should also discuss the economic case for taxing tobacco as a demerit good (*see* Unit 8 on Market Failures). You can answer part (a) by arguing that cigarette prices have probably risen by less than the rate of inflation for all goods and services. The main point to make in your answer to part (b)(ii) is that over the years the *ceteris paribus* assumption has not held, i.e. the demand curve for cigarettes has shifted, with changes in the determinants of demand other than price (e.g. income, health scares) causing the change in demand for cigarettes. Part (b)(iii) of the question asks 'how' not 'why'. The article implies that the price elasticity of demand of people in the higher socio-economic groups is lower (i.e. more inelastic) than that of people in the lower-income groups. (However, the better-off and more educated groups might be more responsive to health scares, though less influenced by price changes.)

4.6 Further reading

Begg, D., Fischer, S., and Dornbusch, R., *Economics*, 3rd edition (McGraw Hill, 1991).
Chapter 4: The effect of price and income on demand quantities.

Burningham, D., editor, *Economics*, 3rd edition (Hodder and Stoughton, 1987).
Chapter 6: Consumer behaviour.

Lipsey, R. G., *An Introduction to Positive Economics*, 7th edition (Weidenfeld & Nicolson, 1989).
Chapter 6: Elasticity and Consumer's Surplus.

Maunder, P., Myers, D., Wall, N., Le Roy Miller, R., *Economics Explained*, 2nd edition (Collins, 1991).
Chapter 7: Demand and supply elasticity.

5 Agricultural Prices

5.1 Points of perspective

Agriculture is an industry in which there are thousands of producers, few of whom can influence the market price by individual decisions to supply or not to supply. At the same time many agricultural products, for example soft wheat, are relatively uniform or **homogeneous** commodities for which the world price is a ruling market price. In other words, it would seem that agriculture approximates to the economist's abstraction of **perfect competition** as a market form. Yet, if we look more closely, we also see that agriculture is the industry in which governments of a variety of political persuasions have consistently intervened in order to support farm prices and agricultural incomes. In this unit we examine the causes of fluctuating prices and incomes, and compare some of the ways in which governments can intervene to create greater stability.

5.2 Underlying concepts

Throughout history, agriculture has experienced two closely related problems. Firstly, there has been a **long-run downward trend in agricultural prices** relative to the prices of manufactures and services, and secondly, **agricultural prices and incomes have been unstable from year to year**. The long-run trend is largely explained by **shifts** in agricultural supply and demand curves through time, while the short-run instability results from the **inelastic nature** of agricultural supply and demand, and the effects of good and bad harvests on the position of the short-run supply curve from one year to another.

5.3 Essential knowledge

1 The long-run downward trend in the relative price of agricultural products

In Figure 5.1, the equilibrium price and output of food in an earlier historical period is shown at point E_1. Over time, both the supply and the demand for foodstuffs have increased, but the supply curve has shifted further to the right. Thus the new long-run equilibrium at E_2 represents a larger output at a lower price. The shift in the demand curve for food is explained mainly by an increase in the population and higher incomes. However, food is a necessity with a low income elasticity demand: when real income doubles, food consumption also increases, but by a smaller proportionate amount. Meanwhile, improvements in agricultural technology, such as the introduction of machinery and fertilizers, have rapidly increased farm yields, thereby causing the much greater long-run shift in supply.

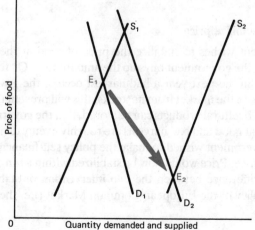

Fig 5.1 The long-run fall in agricultural prices

2 Price instability

The year-to-year instability in farm prices is caused by **low short-run elasticities of supply and demand** combined with **random fluctuations** in the harvest. Because of the length of the production period between planting and harvesting a crop, it is often appropriate to depict the short-run supply curve as a vertical or completely inelastic line. We are assuming that once the crop is harvested, it will be sold for whatever it will bring. The supply curve S_1, drawn in Figure 5.2a, represents supply in a 'normal' year. However, weather conditions and other factors outside the farmers' control will shift the position of the supply curve from year to year. The size of the resulting price fluctuations will depend upon the price elasticity of demand. Demand for foodstuffs in general is inelastic because food is a necessity, so significant fluctuations in price occur as the vertical supply curve shifts up or down the relatively inelastic demand curve.

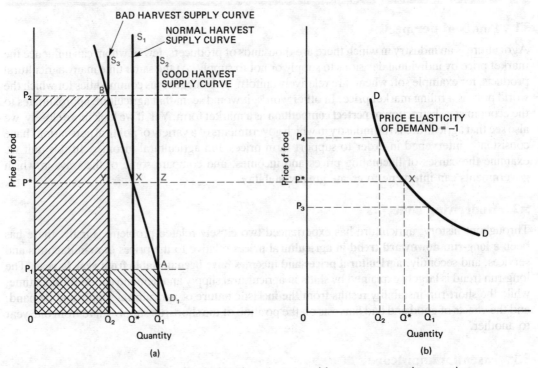

Fig 5.2 Short-run price instability of agricultural products (a) without government intervention, both prices and farm incomes fluctuate (b) target prices to stabilize farm incomes

3 Fluctuations in agricultural incomes

From a farmer's point of view, fluctuations in his income are more serious than fluctuations in price. If demand is elastic, a **fall** in price causes a **rise** in farm income, but when demand is inelastic the opposite is true: income **falls** when price falls. Following a bad harvest, the supply curve in Figure 5.2a shifts to S_3 and agricultural incomes are represented by the rectangle OP_2BQ_2. In the event of a good harvest, the diagram shows that farm incomes decline to the area OP_1AQ_1. Paradoxically, therefore, a farmer may benefit more from a bad harvest than from a good one, when demand is inelastic.

4 Government policy to stabilize price

Suppose that a government wishes to stabilize the price of food at the 'normal' year price, P^*. Following a good harvest, the government buys up the amount $Q_1 - Q^*$ to prevent the market price falling below P^* to P_1. If in the next year a bad harvest occurs, the government will supplement supply by releasing food onto the market from its stocks; this will prevent the price from rising above P^* to P_2. Providing that agricultural products can be stored, that the government is prepared to meet the cost of storage, and that good and bad harvests are roughly evenly divided, then the price can be stabilized at P^*. If the government wished to make the policy self-financing, it could buy at a lower price and sell at a higher price. Price would now be stabilized within a range, and the costs of storage could be met from the difference between the two **intervention** or **stabilization** prices, as in the Common Agricultural Policy of the European Common Market (i.e. the European Community).

5 Government policy to stabilize agricultural incomes

The policy described in the previous section is an example of a **buffer stock policy**. Although such a policy may successfully stabilize price, it does not necessarily stabilize agricultural incomes. In the event of a good harvest, farmers' income will be the rectangle OP^*ZQ_1 if the price is stabilized at P^*. Incomes will decline to the area OP^*YQ_2 following a bad harvest. Farm incomes thus vary directly with the size of production, the exact opposite of the situation in which prices are left free to fluctuate in conditions of inelastic demand.

How then can a government use a buffer stock policy to stabilize incomes rather than prices? The answer is provided by Figure 5.2b. The curve DD, with a unit elasticity, is drawn through X, the point which determines farm incomes in a normal year. DD shows the complete range of prices at which the government must operate its buffer stock policy if it is to stabilize incomes. Following a good harvest in which output Q_1 comes onto the market, the government must buy at the price P_3: farm incomes will then be exactly the same as in the normal year. Symmetrically, the government must release part of its buffer stocks onto the market at the price of P_4 in order to stabilize incomes when output falls to Q_2 in a bad year.

6 Agricultural support policies in the United Kingdom

A fundamental change in British agricultural policy took place when the United Kingdom joined the **European Community**. British farmers are relatively high-cost producers when compared with their counterparts in areas such as the American Mid-West, although they are efficient within the constraints imposed by farm size and the British climate. In most agricultural sectors, British farmers are relatively low-cost producers when compared with European farmers.

In Figure 5.3, the high British costs of production are represented by the long-run domestic supply curve S_1. On the same diagram, the world price of food is shown by a perfectly elastic supply curve drawn at a lower level of costs P_1; this perfectly elastic supply curve represents an infinite supply of imports at the ruling world price. The diagram implies (perhaps unrealistically) that, without some system of protection or support, British farmers would produce no food: the supply curve S_1 cuts the price axis at a price higher than P_1.

Before the United Kingdom joined the EC, **deficiency payments** or **producer subsidies** were the main form of agricultural support. Essentially, the policy was a **'cheap food' policy**, financed out of general taxation: the price of food in Britain was determined by the world price and subsidies were paid to British farmers to keep them in business. This is illustrated in Figure 5.3a. British farmers were guaranteed a price of P_2 at which they supplied Q_2. Nevertheless, domestic production was sold to the consumer at the world price P_1, the difference in the two prices being the deficiency payment to the farmers provided by the government. Under this system, the total demand Q_1 was determined at A. Quantity Q_2 was domestically produced and the remainder was imported.

In contrast, the **Common Agricultural Policy** (CAP) of the EC has dealt with the problem of cheap imports by imposing an external **tariff** or **levy** which brings the price of imports up to the level of cost, plus normal profits, of European farmers. Suppose that the tariff is fixed at P_2 in Figure 5.3b. The total amount demanded will be reduced to Q_3 as compared to Q_1 in the deficiency payment scheme. Quantity Q_2 will still be domestically produced and the rest imported.

The external tariff on food imports is only one part of the CAP. As earlier indicated, the Community also operates a buffer stock policy with upper and lower stabilization prices. The problem has been that for many products the lower of these two intervention prices has been set too high, at a level such as P_3 in Figure 5.3b. An excess supply of XY is encouraged and the price can only be sustained if the Community continuously intervenes to purchase the over-production. This is represented by the shift in the demand curve to D_2. The effects of bad harvests in causing temporary leftward shifts in the short-run supply curve have been insufficient to reverse the accumulation of the butter 'mountains' and wine 'lakes' which have resulted from the policy.

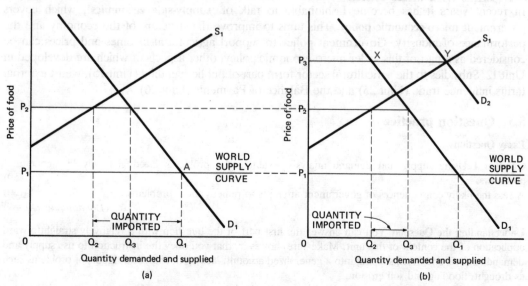

Fig 5.3 Farm price support systems (a) A deficiency payment system (b) A buffer stock system plus an external tariff

7 Dynamic causes of price instability

Because of the length of the production period, there may be a **supply lag** between the decision to produce and the actual supply coming onto the market. We can assume that this year's price has no effect on this year's supply but instead determines next year's supply. Year-long supply lags can be typical of crops such as wheat, though the original **'cobweb' model**–described below–was based on the market for hogs in the USA.

Figure 5.4 illustrates how the **adjustment mechanism** from one year to the next may be **unstable**, being associated with ever-increasing fluctuations in price and output. Suppose that equilibrium is at E where long-run supply and demand intersect. An outbreak of pig disease now disturbs the system and reduces the number of hogs coming onto the market to Q_2. Within the current year, an inelastic short-run supply curve can be depicted by a vertical line drawn through Q_2. A new price P_2, determined at point A on this vertical line, encourages farmers to supply Q_3 onto the market in the next year. Again, a vertical line can be drawn through Q_3 to represent the inelastic short-run supply curve next year. When the supply Q_3 comes onto the market, the price drops to P_3. Price and output then continue to oscillate around the equilibrium in a series of increasing fluctuations.

Although in the above example the cobweb model is associated with increasing instability, this is not inevitable. Try drawing a cobweb diagram in which the long-run supply curve is steeper than the long-run demand curve. Following a disturbance, price and output will again fluctuate, but the adjustment mechanism will now be stable, converging towards the long-run equilibrium at E.

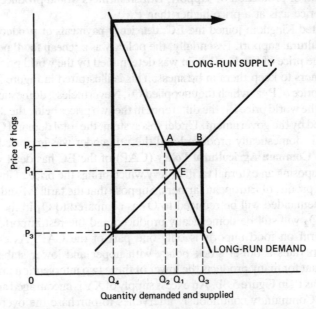

Fig 5.4 Dynamic causes of price instability: the cobweb theory

5.4 Links with other topics

In recent years it has become fashionable to talk of **'supply-side economics'**, which covers government **micro-economic policy**. This aims to improve the structure of the economy and the performance of industry. Government policy to support agricultural incomes and prices can be considered as a part of this wider micro-economic policy, other aspects of which are developed in Unit 12. Subsidies to the agricultural sector form part of public spending (Unit 15), whilst external tariffs influence trade (Unit 25) and the Balance of Payments (Unit 26).

5.5 Question practice

Essay Questions

Question 1 Using supply and demand analysis, examine the problems faced generally by agricultural producers.   (50)
Assess the likely consequences of government attempts to remedy these problems.   (50)

(London: June, 1989)

Understanding the Question You can answer the first part of the question with a relatively straightforward application of the content of this unit. Make sure, however, that you obey the instruction to use supply and demand analysis and avoid slipping into a generalized account, lacking in analytical rigour, of problems such as drought, flooding and soil erosion.

Be careful with the second part of the question: it asks for an assessment of consequences, rather than a detailed description of methods of remedying problems such as over- and under-production, fluctuating prices and farmers' incomes, etc. Nevertheless, you must briefly state a method of remedying a problem before you can launch into an assessment of the consequences of implementing the method. An obvious point to make is that the problem may be successfully dealt with! You will however, be expected to go further in your assessment, discussing possible failure to achieve the desired objective and any distortions or unintended consequences that might result.

Answer plan

1 List three or four problems faced by farmers that can usefully be evaluated in terms of supply and demand analysis. Examples could include: fluctuating prices; fluctuating farmers' incomes; persistent over-production; vulnerability to the market power of food processing firms.
2 Examine each in terms of supply and demand analysis, making sure to include diagrams.
3 Briefly state how the government can attempt to remedy each of the problems you have described (e.g. by support buying; subsidies; import controls; encouragement of farmers' co-operatives, etc). Give real world examples where possible.
4 Assess the likelihood of success of each remedy, and indicate any unintended consequences. Where possible draw on evidence from the real world, but avoid turning your answer into an historical account of UK or EEC agricultural policy.

Question 2 Explain why the prices of agricultural products tend to fluctuate more than those of manufactured products.
(*AEB: November, 1986*)

Understanding the Question This question provides a good test of your ability to apply the theoretical analysis explained in this unit. You will be expected to include the key analysis on how inelastic short-run supply and demand and random fluctuations in supply cause year-to-year fluctuations in agricultural prices and output. You could then go on to explain the long-run downward trend in agricultural prices and, if you have the time, the cobweb theory.

Answer plan

1 Agriculture is dominated by a large number of small producers who are 'price-takers'. In contrast, industrial firms are more likely to be monopolists or 'price-makers', with the market power to stabilize prices if they wish.
2 The agricultural production period is usually longer and individual farmers may be unable to accumulate stocks. Explain how an inelastic short-run supply curve results. Conversely, as manufacturers produce more durable goods, their supply curve tends to be more elastic.
3 Analyze year-to-year price instability in conditions of inelastic supply and demand.
4 Explain the long-run downward trend in agricultural prices relative to the price of manufactured goods. Manufactured goods are more income-elastic and producers may have the ability to create demand.
5 Supply lags in agriculture, illustrated by the cobweb theory, may also cause fluctuating prices.

Multiple Choice Questions

Question 3 When the demand for agricultural products is *elastic*
(a) a price fall results in a fall in a farmer's receipts
(b) a price fall makes no difference to a farmer's receipts
(c) a price rise makes no difference to a farmer's receipts
(d) a price rise results in a fall in a farmer's receipts.

Understanding the Question Figure 5.2a in the unit illustrates the effect on a farmer's income when the price changes in conditions of **inelastic** demand. This question tests your ability to extend the analysis to conditions of elastic demand. The correct answer is **(d)**. Alternatives **(b)** and **(c)** would only be correct if elasticity was unity at all points on the demand curve, and **(a)** would be correct if demand was inelastic.

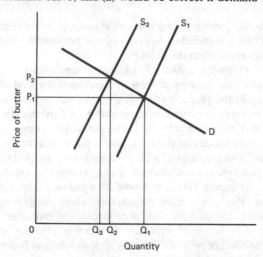

Question 4
In the above diagram, the demand curve for butter is constant but the supply curve has been shifted to S_2. The European Commission uses its butter mountain stockpile to stabilize the price at P_1. Thus the change in the

butter mountain will be:
(a) $Q_1 - Q_3$
(b) OQ_2
(c) $Q_2 - Q_3$
(d) $Q_1 - Q_2$

Understanding the Question This is a straightforward case of excess demand at the fixed price of P_1. The quantity supplied of Q_3 is less than the quantity demanded Q_1, thus the difference $Q_1 - Q_3$ is the reduction in the butter stockpile. This quantity is put on the market by the European Commission to satisfy the excess demand. Thus **(a)** is the correct alternative.

OQ_2 shows market quantity without price controls.
$Q_2 - Q_3$ is the difference between quantity supplied at different prices on the new supply curve.
$Q_1 - Q_2$ shows the reduction in quantity demanded when price rises to P_2.

Data Response Questions

Question 5 Study the graphs below and then answer questions **(a)** to **(d)**.

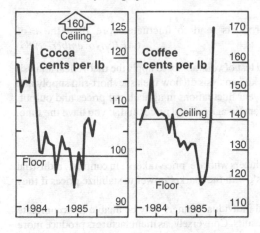 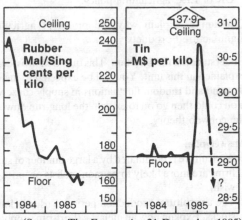

(Source: *The Economist,* 21 December 1985)

Trading in the markets for the commodities referred to above is (or has been) affected by the operation of commodity agreements. These agreements attempt to achieve some degree of price stability.
(a) (i) Suggest *two* causes of the price changes for coffee.   (2)
    (ii) Suggest *two* different causes of the price changes for rubber.   (2)
(b) (i) What do you understand by the terms 'ceiling' and 'floor' as used in the above graphs?   (2)
    (ii) Using a diagram or diagrams, analyse how the authorities attempt to stabilise the price of *one* of the four commodities shown above.   (6)
(c) Why is it difficult to make commodity agreements totally successful?   (4)
(d) What would be the effect of price *instability* in commodity markets on (i) the consuming countries and (ii) the producing countries?   (4)

(*London: June, 1988*)

Understanding the Question
(a) Price changes for any commodity can be caused either by a shift of the demand curve along the supply curve or by a shift of the supply curve along the demand curve. Identify the price increase or decrease which you wish to explain and then suggest two plausible causes of shifts of one or other of the curves (in the appropriate direction).
(b) You can answer this part of the question by drawing on the coverage of 'support-buying' or 'buffer-stock' policies in the unit. Make sure you include a diagram, similar perhaps to Figure 5.2(a), but adapted to one of the four commodities specified in the question.
(c) Reasons for the complete or partial failure of commodity agreements include: **(i)** a tendency for continuous overproduction because the support-buying price is fixed at a level high enough to attract new producers into the market; **(ii)** the producers' inability to continue to finance support-buying; **(iii)** the agreement is undercut by non-member countries or producers; and **(iv)** members may cheat on a cartel-type agreement, selling part of their output below the support-buying price.
(d) Just as the price instability in commodity markets may lead to fluctuations in producers' incomes, so it can affect the real incomes and purchasing power of consumers and the profit margins of any firms in consuming countries that purchase the commodities. Falling commodity prices shift the terms of trade (the ratio of export prices to import prices) in favour of consuming countries and against producing countries, but rising commodity prices have the opposite effect. Highly volatile commodity prices therefore lead to rapid shifts in the terms of trade of producers and consumers and also to instability in the balance of payments of both sets of countries. Consuming countries might attempt to protect themselves from the adverse effect of price instability by such measures as building up stocks and seeking alternative sources of supply.

5.6 Further reading

Maunder, P., *et al, Economics Explained*, 2nd edition (Collins, 1991).
Chapter 8: Governments and markets.
Lipsey, R. G., *An Introduction to Positive Economics*, 7th edition (Weidenfeld & Nicolson, 1989)
Chapter 7: Applications of Price Theory.

6 Perfect Competition and Monopoly

6.1 Points of perspective

1 Market structure and the theory of the firm

Perfect competition and monopoly are examples of **market structures** or **market forms**. They are opposite or polar extremes which separate a spectrum of market structures known as **imperfect competition**. Figure 6.1 illustrates the main types of market structure, including monopolistic competition and oligopoly which we shall examine in Unit 7 on imperfect competition. Monopoly itself can be considered to be the most extreme form of imperfect competition, since there is no competition at all within an industry if a single firm produces the whole of an industry output. Nevertheless, monopoly is usually a relative rather than an absolute concept. This is because a firm will almost always experience some competition from substitute products produced by firms in other industries, even when it has an absolute monopoly in the production of a particular good or service.

Although the analysis in this unit is restricted to perfect competition and pure monopoly, you must avoid the temptation to consider either of these two market structures as typical or representative of the real world. Pure monopoly is exceedingly rare; the **public monopolies** or nationalized industries, such as the electricity industry, provide perhaps the best examples. Perfect competition is actually non-existent—it is a **theoretical abstraction** or model, defined by the conditions which are listed in Figure 6.1. Some economists argue that the emphasis given to perfect competition encourages students to adopt a false perspective in the belief that a perfect market is an attainable 'ideal'. This view will be explored in rather greater depth in Unit 9. As you proceed through this unit, remember how perfect competition is essentially an unrealistic market structure, but note how it provides a 'bench-mark' by which we may judge the desirable or undesirable properties of the imperfectly competitive market structures of the world we live in.

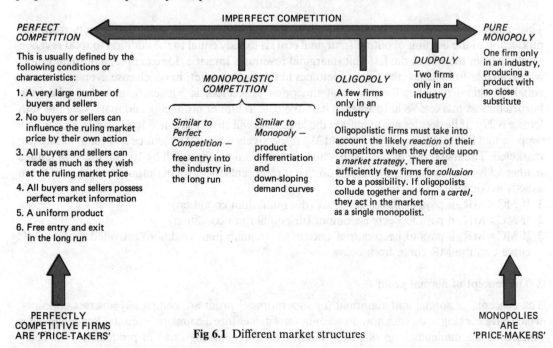

Fig 6.1 Different market structures

2 The traditional theory of the firm

For many years the theory of the firm was principally concerned with the nature of perfectly competitive markets. The development of this theory owes much to the great nineteenth century British economist, Alfred Marshall. During Marshall's lifetime the British economy was still dominated by a large number of small firms, for many of which a single owner/decision-maker, or **entrepreneur**, could be identified. Thus, perfect competition may have been a reasonable approximation to what the economy was like in the late nineteenth century.

3 Alternative theories of the firm

During the first half of the twentieth century, many economists became dissatisfied with perfect competition as *the* theory of the firm. Their dissatisfaction was a response to the growth in the size of firms and the increasing domination of markets by a small number of large business enterprises. Theoretical models of monopoly and imperfect competition were developed by Edward Chamberlin and Joan Robinson in an attempt to give a greater realism to the theory of the firm. More recently, some economists have attacked the **profit-maximizing** assumption that is fundamental to the traditional theories of monopoly, imperfect competition and perfect competition. The 'new' theories of the firm are called **managerial theories** and **organizational** (or **behavioural**) **theories**: both claim to be more **realistic** and hence better at explaining actual behaviour than the traditional profit-maximizing theories of the firm. Managerial theories, popularized by J. K. Galbraith in his book *The New Industrial State* (1967), take as their starting point the split between shareholders as owners and managers as decision-makers in large modern business corporations. It is argued that managers aim to maximize **managerial objectives**, such as sales, growth, and managerial career prospects, rather than shareholders' profits. In contrast, organizationalists such as Professor Herbert Simon, a winner of the Nobel Prize for Economics, see the firm as an organization or **coalition** of different groups, such as managers, production workers, research scientists, etc. The firm is a **'satisficer'** rather than a **maximizer**, attempting to satisfy the aspirations of the groups which make up the coalition.

6.2   Underlying concepts

1 Profit-maximizing behaviour

This assumption is fundamental to the traditional theory of the firm. Profit can be represented by a simple identity:

$$\text{Total Profits} \equiv \text{Total Revenue} - \text{Total Cost}.$$

The firm aims to produce the level of output at which $\text{TR} - \text{TC}$ is maximized. This is one way of stating the **equilibrium condition** of the firm, for if profits are being maximized, there is no reason or incentive for the firm to change its level of output.

Nevertheless, it is usually more convenient for analytical purposes to state the equilibrium condition in alternative form:

$$\text{MC} = \text{MR}$$

This means that profits are maximized when the addition to total costs that results from the production of the last unit of output (marginal cost) is exactly equal to the addition to total revenue resulting from the sale of the last unit (marginal revenue). Imagine, for example, a horticulturalist who is unable to influence the price of lettuces in the local market, in which case average revenue equals marginal revenue. Suppose that the price of lettuces is 30p each, and that when the horticulturalist markets 98 lettuces each day, the cost to him of producing and marketing the 98th lettuce is 29p. If he decides not to market the lettuce he will clearly sacrifice 1p of profits. Let us now suppose that his total costs rise by 30p and 31p respectively when a 99th lettuce and 100th lettuce are marketed. The marketing of the 100th lettuce causes total profits to fall by 1p, but the 99th lettuce neither adds to nor subtracts from total profits: it represents the level of output at which profits are exactly maximized. To sum up:

1 If $\text{MC} < \text{MR}$, it pays to increase output (disequilibrium condition)
2 If $\text{MC} > \text{MR}$, it pays to decrease output (disequilibrium condition)
3 If $\text{MC} = \text{MR}$, it pays to keep output unchanged (equilibrium condition) provided that the MC curve cuts the MR curve from below.

2 The concept of normal profit

The concepts of normal and abnormal (or supernormal) profit are completely abstract concepts, which have nothing to do with how an accountant will measure a company's profits. **Normal profit** is defined as the minimim level of profit required to keep existing firms in production, yet being insufficient to attract new firms into the industry. As such, normal profit is regarded as a necessary cost of production, which is included in the average cost curve. **Abnormal profit** is defined as any extra profit over and above normal profit. We shall now examine what happens to abnormal profits in conditions of perfect competition and monopoly.

6.3   Essential information

1 Short-run equilibrium in conditions of perfect competition

Perfect competition can be defined in terms of the **conditions of perfect competition**, which are listed in Figure 6.1. While you must learn the conditions of perfect competition, it is seldom relevant to an examination question merely to repeat the list. Instead, you must learn to use the conditions to analyze the essential properties of a perfectly competitive firm and industry in equilibrium, compared with those of a monopoly in equilibrium. For example, the assumptions that a perfectly competitive firm can sell as much as it wishes at the ruling market price, and that it cannot influence the ruling market price by its own actions, allow us to say that the firm is a **'price-taker'**. The perfectly competitive firm faces an **infinitely elastic demand curve**, determined by the ruling market price in the industry as a whole. This horizontal demand curve or price line is also the perfectly competitive firm's **average revenue** and **marginal revenue curve**.

To show the equilibrium output of a perfectly competitive firm in the short run, we superimpose this horizontal average and marginal revenue curve upon the average and marginal cost curves which were derived in Unit 3. Using the equilibrium condition $MC = MR$, the resulting equilibrium output is illustrated at Q_1 in Figure 6.2a. Total abnormal profits at this output are represented by the shaded area obtained by subtracting the total cost area (OC_1xQ_1) from the total revenue area (OP_1yQ_1).

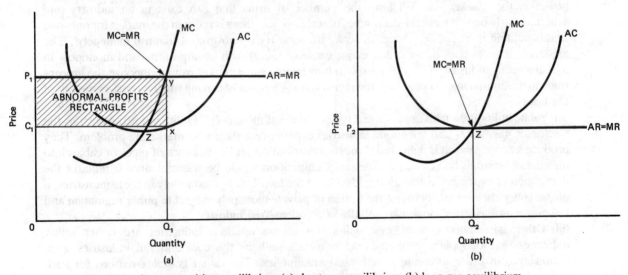

Fig 6.2 Perfect competition equilibrium (a) short-run equilibrium (b) long-run equilibrium

2 Long-run equilibrium in conditions of perfect competition

In order to distinguish between short-run and long-run equilibrium in perfect competition, we assume complete freedom of entry and exit by firms in and out of the industry in the economic long run. The market price signals to firms whether abnormal profits, normal profits or losses can be made. The existence of abnormal profits will provide the **incentive** for new firms to enter the industry, and, in a similar way, existing losses will create the incentive for firms to leave. As illustrated in Figure 6.3, the entry of new firms causes the industry supply curve to shift rightwards and the ruling market price falls. Symmetrically, the departure of firms causes the industry supply curve to shift leftwards and the price line rises. Long-run equilibrium will occur when there is no incentive for firms to enter or leave the industry: this is represented by the output Q_2 at the price of P_2 in Figures 6.3 and 6.2b. The total revenue area now equals the total cost area, illustrating the fact that abnormal profits have been competed away. It must be stressed at all times that it is **impersonal market forces** and individual self-interest, operating in conditions of freedom of entry and exit, which bring about this long-run equilibrium outcome.

3 The causes of monopoly

An effective monopoly must be able to exclude competitors from the market through **barriers to entry**. However, the closer the substitutes that competitors can produce, and the more elastic the demand curve facing the firm, the weaker the monopoly position. A monopoly is strongest when it

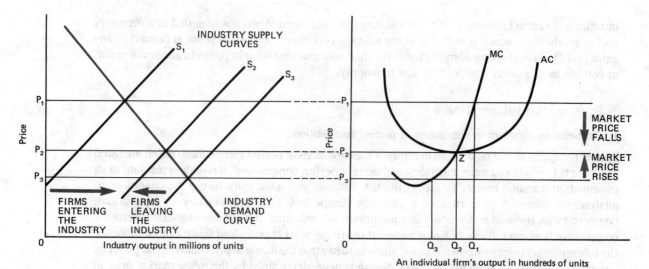

Fig 6.3 Perfect competition long run equilibrium: the entry and exit of firms produces a long-run equilibrium for an individual firm output Q_2 and price P_2

produces an essential good for which there are no substitutes. Monopoly is likely to exist under the following circumstances:

(i) Economies of scale Many industries, for example the aircraft-building industry, are **'decreasing cost' industries** with scope for perhaps unlimited economies of scale. In most circumstances, however, the **market size** will limit the number of firms that can exist in an industry and simultaneously benefit from full economies of scale. Where there is room in the market for only one firm benefiting from full economies of scale, the industry is known as a **'natural monopoly'**. The existence of economies of scale is a major cause of the growth of large firms and monopoly in manufacturing industry. It may also explain how a large supermarket can monopolize the grocery trade in the limited market of a small town or suburb as a result of driving small grocery stores out of the business.

(ii) Public utility industries are a special type of 'natural monopoly'. Utility industries such as the electricity, gas, water and telephone industries experience a particular marketing problem. They produce a service which is delivered through a distribution grid or network of pipes or cables into millions of separate homes and businesses. Competition would be wasteful since it requires the duplication of expensive distribution grids. Given the likelihood of monopoly in these industries, a **public policy choice** exists between the option of **private monopoly subject to public regulation** and the **public ownership of monopoly**, usually as a **nationalized industry**.

(iii) Other government-created monopolies Not all nationalized industries are either utility industries or monopolies. Nevertheless, industries such as the coal and rail industries were nationalized in order to create state-owned monopolies. The rather complex reasons for such nationalizations are explored in Unit 14 on nationalized industries. In other instances, the government may deliberately create a private monopoly, for example by granting a **franchise** to a TV company which operates without competition within a particular geographical area. As another example, the **patent law** creates an exclusive right for an inventor to exploit his invention for a number of years.

(iv) Control of raw materials and market outlets Firms may try to establish exclusive control over the source of raw materials for their products in order to deny access to competitors. In a rather similar way, British breweries have been known to buy up public houses in order to establish exclusive market outlets for the beer they produce.

(v) Advertizing as a barrier to entry It is sometimes argued that small firms are prevented from entering an industry because they cannot afford the minimim level of advertizing which is necessary to persuade retailers to stock the goods they produce. Their products are 'crowded out' of the market by the mass advertizing, brand-imaging, and other marketing strategies of much larger established firms.

4 Monopoly equilibrium

Despite the likelihood of economies of scale in conditions of monopoly, for the time being we shall assume that we are investigating an industry with **no economies or diseconomies of scale**. It follows from this assumption that the lowest long-run average costs which a firm can achieve will be the same in conditions of perfect competition and monopoly. Nevertheless, the **revenue curves** will be different in the two market forms. Since the monopoly is the industry, the monopolist's demand curve and the industry demand curve are identical. There are two ways of looking at this. If we regard the monopolist as a **'price-maker'**, then when he sets the price he must be a **'quantity-taker'**. If the price is set at P_1 in Figure 6.4a the maximum quantity the consumers will buy at this price is Q_1. Alternatively, if the monopolist acts as a **'quantity-setter'**, the demand curve determines the maximum price the monopolist can charge in order successfully to sell the chosen quantity. This is an example of a **'trade-off'**, an important economic concept which is closely related to **opportunity cost**. A problem of choice exists because the monopolist does not possess the freedom to set both price and quantity: if he acts as a price-maker, the demand curve determines the maximum output he can sell and vice versa.

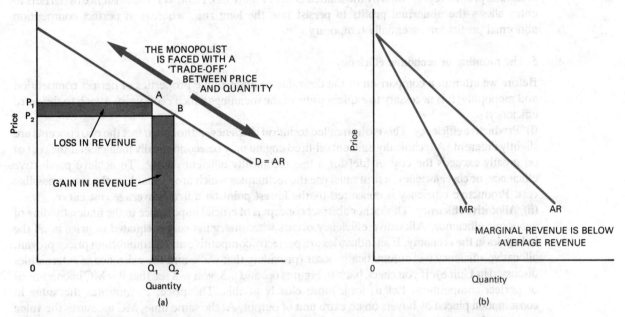

Fig 6.4 The relationship between average revenue and marginal revenue in monopoly. (a) MR equals the gain in revenue minus the loss in revenue (b) the MR curve is always below the AR curve

Since the demand curve shows the price the monopolist charges for each level of output, it is also the monopolist's average revenue curve. The demand curve is not the marginal revenue curve, which must be below the average revenue curve. We can use Figure 6.4 to explore the relationship between the AR and MR curves in conditions of monopoly. If the monopolist decides to produce output Q_1 in Figure 6.4a, the area OQ_1AP_1 will represent total revenue. When output is increased by one unit to Q_2, total revenue changes to the area OQ_2BP_2. Two shaded areas are drawn on the diagram. The area marked as the **'gain in revenue'** represents the extra unit sold multiplied by the new price–or the average revenue per unit at the new level of output. The other shaded area shows the **'loss in revenue'** which results from the fact that all the units of output comprising the previous level of output Q_1, must now be sold at the price of P_2 rather than P_1. The marginal revenue associated with Q_2 is obtained by subtracting the loss in revenue from the gain in revenue (or average revenue). The

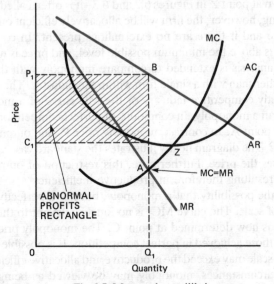

Fig 6.5 Monopoly equilibrium

resulting MR curve which is drawn in Figure 6.4b is twice as steep as the AR curve. This will always be the case providing that the monopolist's demand or AR curve is linear (a straight line), though this mathematical property will not apply if the AR curve is non-linear.

The equilibrium output in conditions of monopoly is illustrated in Figure 6.5. Equilibrium is determined at point A, where MC = MR. It is worth repeating that the equilibrium condition MC = MR applies to **any firm**, whatever the market structure, as long as the firm is a profit-maximizer. You must avoid the temptation to read off the equilibrium price at point A: point B on the AR curve locates the monopolist's equilibrium price.

As in the case of short-run equilibrium under perfect competition, the monopolist makes abnormal profits, represented by the shaded area of Figure 6.5. However, the existence of barriers to entry allows the **abnormal profits to persist into the long run**, whereas in perfect competition abnormal profits are essentially temporary.

5 The meaning of economic efficiency

Before we attempt a comparison of the desirable or undesirable properties of perfect competition and monopoly, it is necessary to explain *some* of the meanings which economists attach to the word efficiency:

(i) Productive efficiency This is often called **technical efficiency**, although in fact the two concepts are slightly different. A technically efficient oil-fired engine may be economically inefficient if the cost of oil greatly exceeds the cost of fuel for a less technically efficient engine. To achieve productive efficiency, or **cost efficiency**, a firm must use the techniques which are available **at the lowest possible cost**. Productive efficiency is measured by the **lowest point on a firm's average cost curve**.

(ii) Allocative efficiency This rather abstract concept is of crucial importance to the understanding of economic efficiency. Allocative efficiency occurs when **marginal cost is equated to price in all the industries in the economy.** If all industries are perfectly competitive and if equilibrium prices prevail, allocative efficiency will automatically occur (providing that we ignore the existence of **externalities** discussed in Unit 8). If you check back to Figures 6.2 and 6.3, you will see that P = MC in conditions of perfect competition. Let us look more closely at this. The price, P, indicates the **value in consumption** placed by buyers on an extra unit of output. At the same time, MC measures the **value in production** of the resources needed to produce the extra unit of output. Suppose that P > MC, as is the case in monopoly: households will pay for an extra unit an amount greater than the cost of producing it. At this price the good will be **underconsumed**. If in contrast P < MC, the value (P) placed on the last unit of the good by consumers will be less than the cost (MC) of the resources used to produce the extra unit. At this price the good will be **overconsumed**.

Whenever P > MC or P < MC, **allocative inefficiency** will occur. For any given employment of resources, total consumer utility or **welfare** can be increased if resources are shifted out of industries where P < MC and into those where P > MC, until a state of allocative efficiency (P = MC) exists in all industries.

6 Evaluating perfect competition and monopoly

If you refer back to Figures 6.2b and 6.3, you will see that a perfectly competitive firm achieves both productive and allocative efficiency in long-run equilibrium. (The productively efficient output is the lowest-cost output, shown at point Z in Figures 6.2 and 6.3 – it is often called the **optimum output** of the firm.) Strictly speaking, however, the firm will be allocatively efficient only if all other industries are perfectly competitive and if there are no externalities present. In contrast, in conditions of monopoly, average cost is above the minimum possible level, and price is not equated to marginal cost. In Figure 6.6, the analysis is extended to compare monopoly with the whole of a perfectly competitive industry, rather than with a single firm within the industry. The curve S_1 represents the supply curve of a perfectly competitive industry or the MC curve of a monopoly if all the firms aggregate together to form a monopoly. In conditions of perfect competition, industry price P_1 and output Q_1 are located at point A. In contrast, monopoly price P_2 and output Q_2 are determined at point B where MR = MC. The diagram neatly illustrates the standard case against monopoly that it **restricts output** and **raises the price**. Furthermore, this restriction of output is at a point above minimum average cost, resulting therefore in productive inefficiency.

Consider, however, the possibility that a monopoly, but not a perfectly competitive firm, can **benefit from economies of scale**. The curve MC_1 is no longer relevant to the analysis of monopoly price and output, which is now determined at point C. The monopoly price P_3 is now lower and output Q_3 is higher than those achieved in perfect competition. It is possible that the benefits which result from economies of scale may exceed the productive and allocative efficiency losses which occur in monopoly. In these circumstances, monopoly may be viewed as being preferable to perfect competition.

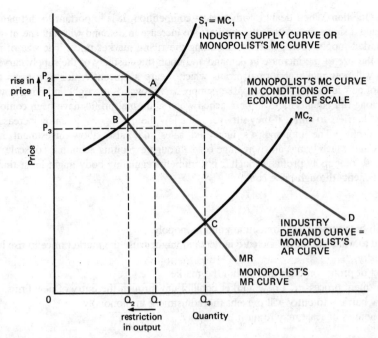

Fig 6.6 The effects of economies of scale on price and output in monopoly

6.4 Links with other topics

Various other aspects of the behaviour or conduct of monopolies, such as price discrimination towards different groups of customers, are examined in Unit 7 on imperfect competition. Because the market price conveys misleading information in conditions of monopoly, the existence of monopoly provides a very important form of market failure, the subject of Unit 8. Some descriptive aspects of the growth of monopoly are introduced in the context of the size and growth of firms (Unit 10), while Unit 12 examines government policy towards monopoly and some possible justifications for the existence of monopoly, additional to the economies of scale argument introduced in this unit.

6.5 Question practice

Essay Questions

Question 1 What is an economic model? Describe briefly the model of perfect competition and discuss whether it is realistic and useful.
                                                                                    (AEB: June, 1988)

Understanding the Question Model building is a technique used by economists first to understand the working of the economy and, secondly to predict what might happen. Models are small-scale replica of real world phenomena. An economic model, however, is better thought of as a simplification of the real world in which the essential features of an economic problem are explained using diagrams, words, or even algebra. The basic model we have described in earlier units is the 'supply and demand model' of a single market within the wider model of a market economy. Within the 'supply and demand model', we construct 'sub-models': of consumer behaviour to explain demand curves; and firms' behaviour to explain the nature of supply.

This is where the model of perfect competition fits in. Briefly describe the assumptions of the model, i.e. the conditions of perfect competition, together with the profit maximization assumption common to all 'traditional' theories of the firm. The model predicts that, in the long run, the 'invisible hand' of market forces 'competes' away abnormal profits and brings about an outcome that is efficient (subject to possible qualification) both productively and allocatively.

You can then argue that the model is unrealistic; but that many economists regard it as useful both as a benchmark against which the competitiveness and efficiency of real-world firms and markets can be measured and as an 'ideal' towards which to try to shift the economy.

Answer plan

1 Explain the meaning of an economic model as a simplification of the real world.
2 Give examples of economic models other than the model of perfect competition.
3 Explain the assumptions of perfect competition.
4 Describe the predictions of the model.
5 Argue that the assumptions of the model are unrealistic.
6 Explain how many economists nevertheless regard the model as useful.

Question 2 Compare and contrast the possible long run effects of an increase in demand for the products of:
(a) a perfectly competitive industry;
(b) a monopoly.
                                                                                  (Oxford: June, 1989)

Understanding the Question When dealing with perfect competition, it is important to distinguish between the whole market and a single firm within the market. An increase in demand will shift the market-demand curve along the market-supply curve, thereby increasing the ruling market price. The size of increase will depend both upon the size of the increase in demand and upon the elasticity of the supply curve. Each firm within the market will now make abnormal profits which create an incentive for new firms to enter the market. The entry of new firms will shift the market-supply curve towards the right and bring down the price. Eventually, a new long-run equilibrium will be reached when abnormal profits have been competed away.

With monopoly, barriers to entry, if they survive, will allow the monopolist to enjoy increased abnormal profit (monopoly profit). The monopolist's increased sales may also allow investment in expanded production capacity and which brings down average costs through exploiting economies of scale. This in turn might further increase monopoly profits, though a government regulating body might insist that consumers share some of the benefits through price cuts.

Answer plan

1 Briefly distinguish between perfect competition and monopoly.
2 Explain how, and to what extent, the increase in demand might cause the market price to rise in a perfectly competitive industry.
3 Explain the effect of profits on each firm within the market.
4 Discuss the adjustment process to a new market equilibrium through the entry of new firms.
5 Show clearly how barriers to entry will prevent this adjustment in monopoly.
6 Discuss how economies of scale may result in monopoly.

Question 3

(a) Explain what is meant by monopoly profits. (15)
(b) What reasons are there for believing that a monopoly agreement between a number of firms may be more harmful than a single-firm monopoly, from society's point of view? (5)
(c) Why does the state grant monopoly rights in the form of patents to particular firms? (5)

(*WJEC: June, 1989*)

Understanding the Question:

(a) Monopoly profits are supernormal or abnormal profits; they persist into the long run because of barriers to market entry. Since this part of the question carries most of the marks, you must elaborate (using diagrams) to explain monopoly equilibrium and give examples of barriers to entry.
(b) Make sure you carefully explain 'society's point of view', for example: in terms of productive and allocative efficiency; or 'producer sovereignty' versus 'consumer sovereignty'. A single-firm monopoly may be technically integrated, benefiting from economies of scale. (In Unit 12 we call such a firm a **'fully-unified' monopoly**.) By contrast, a multi-firm monopoly agreement is likely to be a **cartel agreement**, where firms keep their separate identity but exploit an artificially created monopoly position by raising prices and restricting output. Because of the lack of technical integration of productive capacity, the monopoly position created by the cartel agreement is unlikely to result in economies of scale.
(c) To give firms an incentive to innovate by guaranteeing monopoly profits during the period of the patent.

Multiple Choice Questions

Questions 4, 5 and 6

(a) Both the assertion and the reason are true statements, and the reason is a correct explanation of the assertion.
(b) Both the assertion and the reason are true statements, but the reason is not a correct explanation of the assertion.
(c) The assertion is true but the reason is a false statement.
(d) The assertion is false but the reason is a true statement.

Assertion		Reason
Question 4 A profit-maximizing monopolist will charge the lowest possible price for his product	because	the monopolist may benefit from economies of scale.
Question 5 In long-run equilibrium firms in perfect competition make only normal profits	because	firms in perfect competition always act in the public interest.
Question 6 The demand curve facing a perfectly competitive firm is infinitely elastic	because	perfect substitutes exist for the firm's output.

Understanding the Questions These are examples of the 'assertion/reason' type of question set by the Joint Matriculation examining board. Alternative (d) is the correct answer to question 4. The second statement is true, but the first statement is false because the lowest possible price would require the sacrifice by the monopolist of his abnormal profits; this course of action would be inconsistent with profit maximization. In question 5, the first statement is true and the second statement is false. The desirable properties of perfect competition result from impersonal market forces, not from an assumption that entrepreneurs are any less motivated by self-interest! Question 6 provides an example of both statements being true with the second statement being the reason for the truth of the first statement. If a perfectly competitive firm charged a price above its demand curve, all the customers would switch to the identical goods produced by other firms in the industry.

Data Response Questions

Question 7 'The classical theory of the firm relied heavily on the notion that firms are small, owner-managed organizations operating in highly competitive markets whose demand functions are given and where only normal profits can be earned. If the firm did not therefore maximize profits it would fail to survive under those conditions. Setting aside the question as to whether this ever was a valid description . . . it is certainly far removed from the actual characteristics of firms in many branches of economic activity today. It is only when the main features of the organization of modern corporations are taken into account that the questions of the goals of the firm and its decision processes can be effectively discussed.'

(J. F. Pickering, *Industrial Structure and Market Conduct,* Martin Robertson & Co. Ltd., 1974)

(a) Explain, within the context of classical theory, how profit maximization is crucial for a firm's survival.
(b) What 'main features of modern corporations' would you consider the author had in mind when he questioned the adequacy of the traditional theory of the firm? Giving your reasons, state whether you would agree that such theory is now obsolete.   (*London: January, 1980*)

Understanding the Question You should be able to infer from the passage that the author is using the classical theory of the firm as a label for perfect competition, though, as the next unit explains, the profits of firms in monopolistic competition are also competed away in the long run. You must show how long-run equilibrium in perfect competition comes about and how high-cost firms are competed out of existence. An understanding of the meaning of normal profit is important. In answering the second part of the question, one approach is to argue that alternative theories, such as the managerial and behavioural theories of the firm, are more realistic because they model the split between owners and managers, which is a 'main feature of modern corporations'. Alternatively, you could argue that the most significant feature is the fact that large corporations exist in monopolistic markets and that barriers to entry prevent the competing away of abnormal profits. To earn a very high grade, you must attempt to answer the final point in the question. Perfect competition is regarded by some economists and politicians as an 'ideal' towards which the system should be shifted. Milton Friedman has defended perfect competition by arguing that it does not matter if the assumptions of a theory are unrealistic. The managers of large corporations need not be consciously profit-maximizing, but in a competitive world only the firms which operate close to the profit-maximizing path will survive.

Answer plan

1 Explain what the author means by the classical theory of the firm.
2 Show how surviving firms make only normal profits in perfect-competition long-run equilibrium. It is **not** necessary to write a list of the conditions of perfect competition.
3 Discuss what is meant by a modern corporation.
4 The main features of modern corporations may be monopoly power, survival of inefficient firms, and different market behaviour and goals. Develop some of these points.
5 State whether you regard the traditional theory to be obsolete. Offer some reason for your viewpoint.

Question 8 The firm represented in the diagram below is nationalized and follows a marginal cost pricing policy.

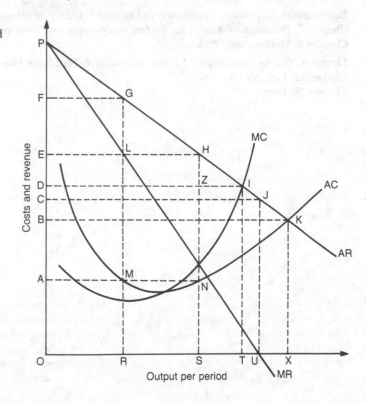

(a) With specific reference to the diagram on page 45, comment on the relationship between price elasticity of demand and marginal revenue.   (3)

(b) What price would a nationalized industry charge and what output would it produce if pursuing a marginal cost pricing policy?   (1)

(c) State the change in price that would occur if the firm were to adopt an average cost pricing policy.   (2)

(d) (i) What is meant by 'consumer surplus'?   (2)

(ii) Assume: 1 the firm is now privatized and, instead of following a policy of marginal cost pricing, it follows a policy of profit maximization;

2 cost conditions are unchanged and the firm charges the same price to all consumers.   (3)

What is the change in consumer surplus?   (3)

(e) Subsequently, if this firm were to pursue a policy of price discrimination, explain with the aid of a diagram how profits could be increased.   (4)

(f) Examine the circumstances in which a nationalized firm following a marginal cost pricing policy would incur a loss. Use a diagram to illustrate your answer.   (5)

Understanding the Question

(a) Demand is elastic when marginal revenue is positive; unit elastic when marginal revenue is zero; and inelastic when marginal revenue is negative.

(b) Marginal cost pricing means setting price equal to marginal cost. This can only occur at point I on the graph, with price equal to OD.

(c) Average cost pricing means setting price equal to average cost (point K on the graph). Price therefore falls from OD to OB.

(d) (i) Consumer surplus is surplus utility enjoyed over and above utility actually paid for.

(ii) When the price is OD, consumer surplus is shown by the triangular area DPI. Since the profit maximizing price (determined via the marginalist rule MR = MC) is OE, then following privatization, consumer surplus falls to the area bounded by EPH. The loss of consumer surplus is shown as the area DEHI.

(e) Price discrimination is explained in Unit 7, and illustrated in Figure 7.4 which shows the special case of price discrimination in which a monopolist or oligopolist divides the total market into two submarkets. However, the other extreme limiting case occurs when the monopolist charges each customer in the market a price equal to the maximum he is prepared to pay. In effect, a range of prices is charged, lying along the demand curve, and all the consumer surplus previously enjoyed by households is transferred to the monopolist as extra profit.

(f) The marginal cost curve included in the diagram in the question is a short-run marginal cost curve. If the firm sets price equal to long-run marginal cost, losses may be incurred. This will happen if the firm experiences economies of scale, with the long-run marginal cost curve being below the long-run average cost curve. In this situation a price equal to long-run marginal cost must be less than average cost, resulting in a loss.

6.6   Further reading

Burningham, D., editor, *Economics*, 3rd edition (Hodder & Stoughton, 1987).
Chapter 7: Determination of price: perfect competition and monopoly
Chapter 9: Markets and efficiency

Lipsey, R. G., *An Introduction to Positive Economics,* 7th edition (Weidenfeld & Nicolson, 1989).
Chapter 12: Perfect Competition
Chapter 13: Monopoly

7 Imperfect Competition

7.1 Points of perspective

Imperfect competition is the label attached to the wide variety of market structures between the extremes of perfect competition and pure monopoly. A great many theoretical models of imperfect competition have been devised, each model pertaining to a precisely defined market structure and a set of assumptions about how the member firms behave. In this unit we shall examine just three of the possible market structures:

1 **monopolistic competition,** in which it is assumed that firms act independently of each other.
2 **competitive oligopoly,** an example of a market structure in which **interdependent** firms must take account of the reactions of one another when forming a **market strategy.**
3 **collusive oligopoly**, which occurs when firms attempt to overcome the **uncertainty** associated with guessing how competitors will react by colluding together and forming a cartel.

7.2 Underlying concepts

As in the theories of perfect competition and monopoly, the **profit-maximizing assumption** is fundamental to the models of imperfect competition considered in this unit. If you refer back to the introduction to Unit 6, you will see how **managerial** and **behavioural theories** of the firm attack the assumption of profit-maximizing behaviour as being an **unrealistic** objective for large modern business corporations.

Even if imperfectly competitive and monopolistic firms aim to maximize profits, they may simply not possess the accurate information about their market situation needed to equate marginal cost and marginal revenue. For this reason, imperfectly competitive firms are often modelled as **price-searchers**, seeking by trial and error the price which will maximize profits. In some circumstances, firms may produce a wide variety of differentiated products and services, for which the marginal cost of producing each particular good or service is different. In these conditions, imperfectly competitive firms commonly resort to **'rule of thumb' pricing**, without ever consciously setting MC equal to MR. Businessmen may ask their accountants to estimate the cost of one unit of output when producing at near to full-capacity. This estimate is called a **standard cost** and is used for price setting. On the basis of this standard cost, firms may adopt **'cost-plus'** or **'mark-up' pricing**, by adding a profit margin to the standard cost. The choice of the profit margin may itself be based on rule of thumb, or historical experience, or what a firm thinks it can charge without falling foul of a government monopoly investigation.

Nevertheless, many economists argue that the gap between the MC = MR rule and actual business pricing-behaviour can be bridged. When cost-plus pricing gets businessmen too far out of line with what they would achieve with profit-maximizing pricing, they will modify their pricing. Firms which stray too far from the profit-maximizing path will experience low profits and falling share-prices. While such firms are unlikely to be competed out of business in a highly imperfect market, they may become vulnerable to **'discipline by the capital market'**. This means that firms which perform badly are vulnerable to **take-over** by managers who believe that they can manage the firms' assets more successfully.

7.3 Essential knowledge

1 The theory of monopolistic competition

The theory of monopolistic competition was introduced by Edward Chamberlin in 1933 as an early attempt to model the characteristics of imperfect competition. As the name implies, monopolistic competition resembles both perfect competition and monopoly in some respects. Each firm's product is assumed to be a little different from those of its competitors; if it raises its price slightly, it will not lose all its customers. Thus a firm faces a **downward-sloping demand curve,** rather than the horizontal or infinitely elastic demand curve of perfect competition. Nevertheless, the **absence of barriers to entry** allows market forces, through the entry of new firms, to shift the demand curve and to **compete away abnormal profits** in the long run.

The short-run equilibrium in monopolistic competition is little different from the monopoly equilibrium illustrated in Figure 6.5, except that the demand or average revenue curve is likely to be rather more elastic. Figure 7.1 shows the long-run equilibrium, achieved after the entry of new firms has eliminated abnormal profits. As in the case of monopoly, monopolistic competition involves both **productive inefficiency** (the lowest-cost output is not produced) and **allocative inefficiency** (P > MC). However, the consumer is presented with a **considerable choice between differentiated goods**. There may be circumstances in which consumers prefer a wider choice at the expense of an improvement in productive efficiency.

Nevertheless, it is also possible that firms are using advertizing and brand-imaging to present the consumer with a false choice between essentially similar goods, in which case advertizing is an unnecessary cost and a waste of resources. Advertizing may manipulate consumer 'wants' by persuading people to buy products through the association of the product with other desirable properties such as social success. Many economists distinguish between **informative advertizing**, which helps the consumer to make a more rational choice between products, and **persuasive advertizing**, which distorts the choice.

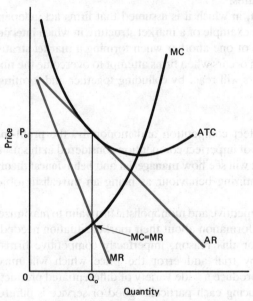

Fig 7.1 Long-run equilibrium of a firm in monopolistic competition

2 Competitive oligopoly

Monopolistic competition shares with perfect competition and monopoly the characteristic that member-firms choose their market strategy in a way which is completely **independent** of the likely **reactions** of other firms. However, this may not be very realistic, particularly when there are only a few large firms competing within an industry. An **oligopoly** is sometimes defined in terms of an industrial **concentration ratio**: for example, a four-firm concentration ratio of 70% means that the four largest firms account for 70% of sales. Alternatively, an oligopoly can be defined in relation to the behaviour or market strategy of the member-firms. Oligopolists are **mutually interdependent** since each firm is concerned about the reactions of its competitors. There are a great many separate theories of oligopoly, each modelling a different set of assumptions about how the rivals react. Many of these theories are examples of **games theories**, in which each oligopolist is regarded as a player in a game, choosing a best strategy subject to retaliations.

3 Reasons for the existence of oligopoly

In many industries there are economies of large-scale production, but diseconomies of scale begin to set in while output is still well below the total market size. The result is a **natural oligopoly** in which a few firms can produce the total industry output and simultaneously benefit from full economies of scale. In other circumstances, **countervailing power** may explain the existence of an oligopoly: large duopolists such as Unilever and Proctor & Gamble may each possess sufficient **market power** in the detergent industry to prevent the other emerging as a sole monopolist. **Government monopoly legislation** may also deter the creation of an outright monopoly.

4 Price stability and the kinked demand curve

Although oligopolistic markets are characterized by competitive behaviour, the competition often takes the form of **non-price competition** such as:

(i) advertizing competition, packaging, brand-imaging and product differentiation;

(ii) marketing competition, including the attempt to obtain **'exclusive outlets'** through which to sell the product;

(iii) quality competition, including the provision of after-sales servicing.

Figure 7.2 illustrates the theory of the kinked demand curve, a theory originally proposed in 1939 by Paul Sweezy as an explanation of supposed price rigidity and the absence of price wars in conditions of oligopoly. Suppose that an oligopolist, for whatever reason, produces an output Q_0 at a price P_0, determined at point X on the diagram. He perceives that **demand will be relatively elastic in response to an increase in price**, because he **expects** his rivals to **react** to the price rise by keeping their prices stable, thereby gaining customers at his expense. Conversely, he **expects** his rivals to react to a decrease in price by cutting their prices by an equivalent amount; he therefore expects demand to be relatively inelastic in response to a price fall, since he cannot hope to lure many customers away from his rivals. In other words, the oligopolist's initial position is at the junction of two demand curves of different relative elasticity, each reflecting a different assumption about how the rivals are expected to react to a change in price. If the oligopolist's expectations are correct, sales revenue will be lost whether the price is raised or cut. The best policy may be to leave the price unchanged.

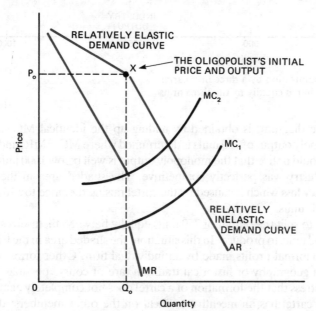

Fig 7.2
The 'kinked'
oligopoly theory

A second explanation of price rigidity is also suggested by Figure 7.2. In mathematical terms, a **discontinuity** exists along a vertical line above output Q_0, between the marginal revenue curves associated with the relatively elastic and inelastic demand (or average revenue) curves. Costs can rise or fall within a certain range without causing a profit-maximizing oligopolist to change either price or output. At output Q_0 and price P_0, MC = MR as long as the MC curve is between an upper limit of MC_2 and a lower limit of MC_1.

Although the kinked demand curve theory provides a neat and perhaps plausible explanation of price rigidity, it has been subject to many attacks. It is an **incomplete theory** because it does not explain how and why an oligopolist chooses to be at point X in the first place. **Empirical evidence** casts great doubt on whether oligopolists respond to price changes in the manner assumed. Oligopolistic markets often display evidence of **price leadership**, which provides an alternative explanation of orderly price behaviour. Firms come to the conclusion that price-cutting is self-defeating and decide that it may be advantageous to follow the firm which takes the first step in raising the price. If all firms follow, the price rise will be sustained to the benefit of all the firms.

5 Collusive oligopoly

The theory of the kinked demand curve illustrates an important characteristic of competitive oligopoly: the existence of **uncertainty**. An oligopolist can never be sure how his rivals will respond, yet he must take their **expected reactions** into account when determining his own market strategy. An incentive may exist for oligopolists to **collude** together in order to **reduce uncertainty**. Also, by acting collectively the firms may achieve an outcome which is better for all of them than if they had remained a competitive oligopoly. This can be shown by the principle of **joint profit maximization,** which is illustrated in Figure 7.3. We shall assume that there are three firms with similar cost curves in an industry. The cost curves of one of the firms are drawn in the left-hand panel of Figure 7.3. Suppose that the firms now decide to get together and act as a single monopolist, yet at the same time maintaining their separate indentities. The monopoly MC curve, which is illustrated in the

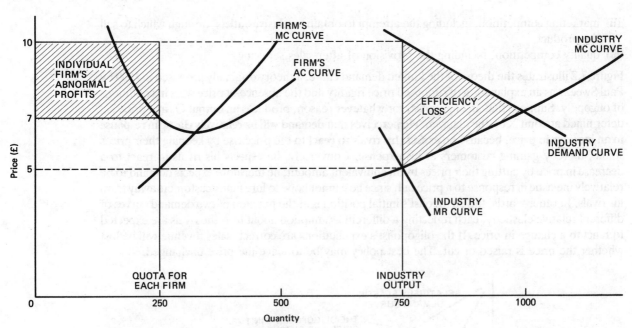

Fig 7.3 Joint profit maximization by a three firm cartel
in which the market is shared equally by the three firms

right-hand part of the diagram, is obtained by adding up the identical MC curves of the three separate firms. Monopoly output of 750 units is determined where MC = MR, and each firm charges a price of £10. You should notice that the monopoly output is well below 1000 units, which would be the output if the industry was perfectly competitive. The shaded area in the right-hand panel represents the **efficiency loss** which is caused by the cartel raising the price to £10 and restricting the industry output to 750 units.

If the firms decide to split the output of 750 units equally between themselves, each firm will be allocated a **quota** of 250 units to produce. In this situation, the shaded area in the left-hand part of the diagram shows the abnormal profits made by an individual firm. Other forms of market-sharing, based for example on geography or historical tradition, are of course possible.

It is important to stress that the formation of a cartel does not completely eliminate uncertainty. Each member of the cartel has an **incentive to cheat** on the other members: this is because the marginal cost of producing the 250th unit is only £5, yet the marginal revenue received, which equals the price, is £10. A firm can increase its total profit at the expense of the other members of the cartel by **secretly** selling an output over and above its quota at a price which is less than £10 but greater than the marginal cost incurred. This is an example of a **divergency** between **collective and individual interest**. The firms' collective interest is to maintain the cartel so as to keep sales down and the price up. Nevertheless, an individual firm can benefit if, while the other members maintain the cartel, it secretly undercuts the agreement by selling more than its allotted market share.

6 The possibility of price discrimination

Monopolies, and other firms in highly imperfect markets, regularly charge a number of different prices to different groups of customers. Sometimes more than one product is involved, as in the case of first- and second-class rail travel; in other instances the prices may reflect the different transport and handling costs which are incurred in delivering the good or service to the customer. You must not confuse these examples of differentiated prices with the concept of monopoly or oligopoly **price discrimination**. Price discrimination occurs when a firm is able to charge different prices for an **identical** product. The costs of production must be the same, irrespective of the type of customer to whom the product is sold. Price discrimination will benefit a firm if it increases the firm's total profits. The necessary conditions for successful price discrimination are:

  (i) It must be possible to identify different groups of customers or markets for the product.
 (ii) There must be a different elasticity of demand in each market.
(iii) Total profits will be increased by selling at a higher price in the market where demand is **less** elastic. (Demand will **never** be inelastic, since this would imply that marginal revenue is negative.) The markets must be **separated** to prevent **seepage**, which occurs when customers buy at the lower price in one market in order to resell in the other market at a price which undercuts the monopolist.

Figure 7.4 illustrates the simplest case of price discrimination, when a firm's MC curve is assumed to be constant. Profits are maximized by equating MR to the constant MC curve in each market. Output Q_1 is sold at a price of P_1 in the industrial market, while household customers buy Q_2 at price P_2. Marginal revenue is the same in each market at these outputs. If this was not the case, the firm would be able to increase profits by reallocating its output between the markets.

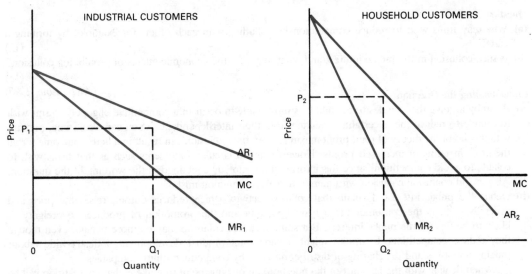

Fig 7.4 Price discrimination

Although price discrimination can benefit the producer in terms of higher profits, there may be circumstances in which it is also in the interest of consumers. The classic case concerns the demand for the services of a doctor in an isolated small town. If all the townspeople are charged the same price for health care, the town's doctor is unable to make a sufficient income to cover his opportunity cost: it is in his interest to move to a larger city, thus leaving the townspeople without any medical care. If, however, the doctor is permitted to charge a higher price to the few rich citizens who can afford to pay, he may be able to earn sufficient income to make it worth his while to treat the poorer people at a lower price. Everybody ends up by getting some benefit from the introduction of price discrimination–though, as the next unit explains, **collective provision** of a **merit good** such as health care **outside the market** may be judged more desirable than **private provision through the market**.

7.4 Links with other topics

This unit has followed on from Unit 6 in extending the coverage of market structures to include the main forms of imperfect competition. Certain aspects of the behaviour or conduct of large firms which have been examined in some depth in this unit are equally applicable to the case of pure monopoly. Likewise, the descriptive aspects of the growth of firms covered in Unit 10, and the policy-making implications of industrial concentration (Unit 12), relate to the highly imperfect market structures introduced in this unit as well as to conditions of pure monopoly.

7.5 Question practice

Essay Questions

Question 1 Examine the main differences in the determination of price and output in conditions of monopoly and oligopoly.

(London: January, 1988)

Understanding the Question Having defined the two market structures, briefly mention similarities before proceeding to a more in-depth analysis of differences. Conventional theories of monopoly and oligopoly both assume the profit-maximizing objective and the importance of the MR = MC rule but, whereas there is a definitive theory of monopoly price and output determination, oligopoly lacks such a theory. Avoid the temptation to elevate the kinked demand curve theory of oligopoly to such a status, though, having emphasized its rather tarnished reputation, you can use it as a basis for comparison. Draw attention to the interdependence of oligopoly compared to the independence of a monopolist, and discuss the uncertainty that results in oligopoly. Price and output might, of course be determined by collusive activity in oligopoly and you could well argue that in the form of a cartel, collusive oligopoly in effect becomes a form of monopoly.

Answer plan

1 Define the two market structures.
2 Note the usual assumption of a profit maximizing objective and the marginalist rule (MR = MC) for price and output determination in both monopoly and oligopoly.

3 Explain why there is no definitive theory of price and output determination in oligopoly.

4 Explain how the need to anticipate other firms' reactions and the resulting uncertainty will affect price and output determination in oligopoly, but not in monopoly. Illustrate if you wish, with the aid of the kinked demand curve theory, but do not overdo.

5 Argue that collusive oligopoly can resemble monopoly.

Question 2

(a) Why may firms wish to reduce competition by colluding with each other: for example, by forming a cartel?   (12)

(b) Is such collusion in the public interest and what might be the economic effects of prohibiting collusion?
(13)

(AEB: June, 1990)

Understanding the Question

(a) Begin by arguing that the desire to collude is most likely to occur in a competitive oligopoly. Firms wish to collude to reduce the uncertainty resulting from their interdependence. You can also argue, perhaps with the aid of the theory of joint profit maximization, that collusion can result in a better outcome for all the firms in terms of increased profits. However, avoid circular statements such as that firms wish to collude to avoid competition, since this information is already contained in the wording of the question. Also, avoid confusing collusion with merger activity, a common mistake.

(b) Define the public interest. Explain that collusive activity which reduces output, raises the price and generally exploits the consumer through manipulation and the promotion of producer sovereignty, is likely to be against the public interest. But some forms of collusion may be more benign, even though they reduce competition. Examples might include joint product development, industry-wide labour training initiatives and the sharing of distribution grids by competitive utility companies.

When dealing with the last part of the question, an obvious point to make is that competition will be promoted! Output may rise and price fall. Covert collusive activity could also replace overt cartel agreements.

Multiple Choice Questions

Question 3

(a)	(b)	(c)	(d)
1, 2 and 3 are all correct	1 and 2 only correct	2 and 3 only correct	1 only correct

The market conditions necessary for a producer successfully to undertake price discrimination include:
(1) different demand conditions in different market sectors
(2) different marginal cost conditions in different market sectors
(3) demand must be price-inelastic in at least one market sector.

Understanding the Question Item 1 is correct. Indeed the essence of price discrimination is the charging of higher prices to customers who are prepared to pay more. The remaining statements are incorrect yet students regularly fail to see why. If different marginal costs are incurred, then we are really dealing with two slightly differentiated products. The **service** provided in delivering coal to a consumer in London is **not the same service** as that provided indelivering coal to a consumer who lives near the coal-mine. Firms can obviously charge different prices for different products or services, but this is **irrelevant** to the question. Price discrimination refers to the charging of different prices for the same good or service, produced at identical cost.

We assume that a discriminating monopolist is a profit-maximizer. Therefore it is illogical for the firm to produce an output for which demand is inelastic, since MR will be negative. **Profit-maximizing firms must always produce in the elastic section of their demand curve where MR is positive!** Alternative **(d)** is therefore the correct answer.

Question 4

Output (units)	Total Revenue (pence)	Total Cost (pence)
1	15	5
2	27	12
3	36	21
4	42	32
5	45	45

The firm described in this table is operating under conditions of:
(a) Imperfect competition and decreasing marginal cost.
(b) Imperfect competition and increasing marginal cost.
(c) Perfect competition and increasing marginal cost.
(d) Perfect competition and decreasing marginal cost.

Understanding the Question You must carefully distinguish between average and marginal cost and revenue. In this example, the extra cost of producing one more unit of output is increasing (by 7, 9, 11 and 13 pence); thus alternatives **(a)** and **(d)** must be wrong. The changes in total revenue indicate the nature of the market. In order to sell more units of output, the firm has to accept a price which falls from 15 to 13½ to 12 to 10½ to 9 pence; this implies a downward-sloping demand curve. Hence the firm is in some form of imperfect competition. Alternative **(b)** is clearly the correct answer.

Data Response Questions

Question 5 A monopolist has separated its customers into two markets, A and B. The prices and quantities in these two markets are as follows:

Market A		Market B	
Price (£)	Quantity	Price (£)	Quantity
10	10	5	10
9	20	4.50	20
8	30	4	30
7	40	3.50	40
6	50	3	50
5	60	2.50	60
4	70	2	70
3	80	1.50	80
2	90	1	90
1	100	0.50	100

(a) What conditions are necessary for the monopolist to be able to separate the two markets in this case? (2)

(b) (i) *On graph paper* plot the monopolist's demand and marginal revenue curves in markets A and B. (4)
   (ii) Assuming that the marginal cost of production is constant at £1.90, what quantity will the monopolist sell in each market if it is a profit maximizer? (2)
   (iii) What price will the monopolist charge in each market? (2)

(c) Comment on the relationship between the price elasticity of demand and marginal revenue in market B. (4)

(d) Assume that the monopolist now cuts its price in market A by £0.50. What is the price elasticity of demand at the new price charged? (3)

(e) Assume that the monopolist now faces an increase in the rates payable on its premises. How will the profit maximizing monopolist adjust the prices charged in each market? (3)

(London: June, 1989)

Understanding the Question

(a) The necessary conditions for market separation are: (i) the ability to indentify the customers who are prepared to pay different prices; and (ii) the prevention of market seepage.

(b) Set out your diagrams in a format similar to Figure 7.4. The data provided in the tables represents the demand or average revenue curves in both submarkets. The easiest way to plot the marginal revenue curves is to extend the demand curves you have drawn to both axes and then draw the MR curves from the vertical intercept to bisect the horizontal axis between origin and the horizontal intercept. Draw a horizontal MC curve through a price of £1.90 and locate the profit maximizing output in each market where MR is £1.90. Read up to the demand curve to locate the profit maximizing price in each market.

(c) Demand must be elastic at the profit-maximizing level of output because MR is positive.

(d) You should find that the monopolist is now producing exactly half way down the demand curve and that MR is zero at this level of output. Price elasticity of demand will be unity.

(e) Business rates are a fixed cost, so the MC curve remains unchanged at £1.90. Profit maximizing output and price remain unchanged but total profits will be reduced because total costs have risen.

7.6 Further reading

Burningham, D., editor, *Economics*, 3rd edition (Hodder and Stoughton, 1987).
Chapter 8: Oligopoly.

Lipsey, R. G., *An Introduction to Positive Economics*, 7th edition (Weidenfeld & Nicolson, 1989)
Chapter 14: Imperfect Competition.

8 Market Failures

8.1 Points of perspective

1 Failure associated with market structure

Monopolistic and **imperfectly competitive** market structures provide the best-known examples of **market failure**. The 'wrong' quantity is produced and sold at the 'wrong' price. In comparison with perfect competition, too little is produced at too high a price, and the market outcome is neither **allocatively efficient** nor **productively efficient**. Nevertheless, the market can still function in conditions of imperfect competition, producing at least **some** of the good or service.

2 Failure associated with the market mechanism

Even when most of the conditions of perfect competition are met, **informational problems** may prevent the market mechanism from working properly. A certain **minimum level of organization** of a market is required to allow information about market prices to be transmitted to all the participants. A lack of sufficient information about prices in other parts of the market may cause a market to degenerate into **bilateral bargaining**, where a buyer and seller enter into an exchange in a state of ignorance about prices in other parts of the market.

In other instances, the adjustment process towards equilibrium may be **too slow** or **unstable**, and equilibrium may never be reached. As a result, trading may always take place at disequilibrium prices.

3 Market failure and the 'new' micro-economics

In this unit, attention is concentrated upon some examples of market failure which have been largely ignored, at least until fairly recent times, in the more traditional textbooks designed for Advanced Level students. In particular we shall investigate **public goods** (and **'bads'**), **merit goods** and **externalities**. Traditionally, micro-economics has been concerned with the manner in which markets function smoothly, relegating the coverage of market breakdown to something of a footnote, if indeed the subject was mentioned at all. In contrast, a modern micro-economic approach is to acknowledge that markets may function inadequately, perhaps more often than they function smoothly, and that in certain situations the market may completely fail to provide any quantity at all of a desired good or service. In response to this change of emphasis, questions on market failure are regularly appearing in the Advanced Level papers of all the examining boards.

8.2 Underlying concepts

1 Market failure v market inadequacy

A market fails completely when there is no incentive for firms to produce a good or service, even though utility would be gained from its consumption. We shall show why markets fail to provide **pure public goods** such as national defence, which by its nature has to be consumed **collectively** rather than individually. Markets also fail to regulate the production and consumption of **externalities**, with the result that too much of an external **'bad'** such as pollution and too little of an external **good** such as a beautiful landscape may be produced.

In other circumstances, markets will provide some of the good or service, but an inadequate quantity: monopoly and imperfect competition have already been mentioned in this respect. The market mechanism may provide too little of a **merit good**, such as education or health care, and too much of a 'good' such as narcotic drug or alcoholic drink – goods which are sometimes classed as **demerit goods**.

2 The problem of self-interest

Merit goods, demerit goods, and externalities all illustrate the existence of **divergencies**, and possible conflicts, between **private and social costs and benefits**. A central proposition of economic theory is that an economic agent in a market situation only considers the private costs and benefits to the agent itself of its market actions, *i.e.* it always seeks to maximize its self interest. However, if in maximizing its private benefit or interest, it imposes costs on other economic agents or the wider community, **private benefit maximization** will not coincide with **social benefit maximization**. In an unregulated market, the 'wrong' quantity of the good will be produced and consumed–the 'correct' quantity being that which maximizes the social benefit rather than merely the private benefit of individuals.

8.3   Essential knowledge

1 Pure public goods and quasi-public goods

A **pure** public good such as national defence is defined by the properties of **non-exclusion** and **non-diminishability**. A person can benefit from national defence without having to pay for it. Furthermore, if an extra person benefits from defence, this in no way diminishes the benefits available to others. Most public goods, for example roads, street lighting and broadcasting, are **quasi-public** goods or **non-pure** public goods. Markets could, in principle provide the goods, but for various reasons they do not. Instead, the goods or services are usually **collectively** provided by the state, often at zero price, and financed out of general taxation.

The essential properties of a public good can be explained with the use of the well-known example of a lighthouse. This is illustrated in Figure 8.1.

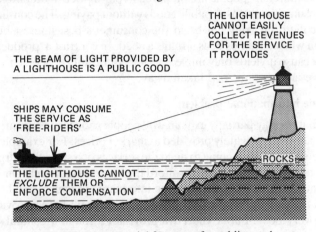

Fig 8.1 The essential features of a public good

The lighthouse provides a service (a beam of light) for which there is a need; if the service is not provided more ships will be wrecked and transport costs will rise. Lighthouses could be provided through the market if entrepreneurs were able successfully to charge a price to passing ships. Now, most goods are called **private goods** because an entrepreneur who provides them can **enforce private property rights** and exclude people who do not wish to pay for consuming the goods. In the case of quasi-public goods, it is theoretically possible to exercise private property rights and to exclude **free-riders**–people who consume without paying. A motor toll-road provides an example. However, in many cases the difficulty and cost of collecting revenue may prove prohibitive. A lighthouse company might try moral persuasion in order to collect revenue from passing ships, relying on the fact that it is in the interest of all ship-owners for the service to be provided; an incentive nevertheless exists for any individual ship-owner to become a free-rider, providing that the other ship-owners still pay up. In these circumstances, most ship-owners may be expected to become free-riders, thereby destroying the incentive for the private provision of the lighthouse.

While **non-excludability** explains how private provisioning of a public good through a market may break down, the property of **non-diminishability** (or **non-rivalry**) suggests why the good should be provided at zero price or 'free'. Whenever an extra person consumes a public good such as defence or a lighthouse beam, no additional resources are used up. Thus the consumption can be met without transferring resources out of other industries. The marginal cost of meeting the extra consumption is zero. Consumer welfare will be maximized if the greatest possible consumption is achieved–and this will only happen if the price is zero.

2 Public goods and government goods

A public good is sometimes defined as any good or service provided by the public sector. This is not a very satisfactory definition. A good such as coal produced by a nationalized industry should be regarded as a private good provided through the market. Other goods and services such as education and health care are merit goods rather than public goods, though they share with public goods the characteristic of being collectively provided at zero price, and being financed out of taxation. It is useful to note that **public collective provision** is **not inevitable** in the case of public goods: in some instances, **private collective provision** is possible. A co-operative of ship-owners could provide lighthouses, though it might be necessary to make membership legally compulsory. **Modified market provision** is another alternative. For example, the difficulty of charging a price to consumers of commercial TV and radio programmes is circumvented by charging advertizers for access to the public good!

3 Merit and demerit goods

A **merit good** such as health care or education is a good or service from which the **social benefits** of consumption to the community as a whole exceed the **private benefits** to the consumer. In the case of a **demerit good** such as tobacco or alcohol, the **social costs** of consumption exceed the **private costs.** If merit and demerit goods provided through markets at prices unadjusted by any subsidy or tax, people will choose to consume **too little** of a merit good and **too much** of a demerit good. It is worth stressing that an incentive certainly exists for merit and demerit goods to be provided through the market, but merit goods will be underconsumed and demerit goods will be overconsumed.

The government can try to encourage the consumption of merit goods and to discourage and sometimes outlaw the consumption of harmful products or demerit goods. Demerit goods must not be confused with nuisance goods or economic 'bads'. Most products and services are economic **goods** that yield utility in consumption–people are prepared to pay a price in order to obtain them, unless of course they can consume the goods as public goods without paying. The consumption of a demerit good, such as a narcotic drug, may not be in the consumer's best interest but it certainly gives pleasure to the person who consumes it, as it fulfils a need. In contrast a 'product' such as garbage is an economic **'bad'** because it yields only unpleasantness or disutility: people are prepared to pay a price in order to have an economic bad taken away.

4 Merit goods and the informational problem

Uncertainty of information may partially explain why people choose to consume too little of a merit good such as health care if it is privately provided at market prices. For example, a person does not know in advance when, if ever, he is going to need the services of a specialist surgeon: sudden illness may lead to a situation in which he is unable to afford the surgeon's services. One market-orientated solution is for a private insurance market to come into being, in which case health care would be collectively provided through the market. However, this may still fail to provide a service for the chronically ill or the very poor. **Public collective provision** through a compulsory state insurance scheme is therefore another solution. It is interesting to note that both private and public collective schemes are a response to the fact that the demand or need for medical care is much more predictable for a large group of people than for an individual–an application of the 'Law' of large numbers.

5 Externalities

An externality is a special type of **public good** or **'bad'**, its crucial characteristic being that it is generated and received **outside the market**. This can be demonstrated by considering the well-known example of pollution as an **external cost**. Figure 8.2 illustrates the generation of pollution by a brickworks. The nearby laundry is an **unwilling free-rider** receiving the pollution as a nuisance good or economic 'bad'.

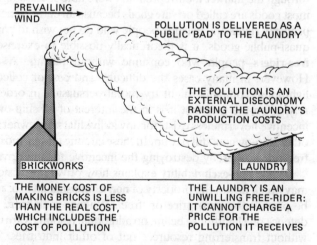

PREVAILING WIND

POLLUTION IS DELIVERED AS A PUBLIC 'BAD' TO THE LAUNDRY

THE POLLUTION IS AN EXTERNAL DISECONOMY RAISING THE LAUNDRY'S PRODUCTION COSTS

BRICKWORKS

LAUNDRY

THE MONEY COST OF MAKING BRICKS IS LESS THAN THE REAL COST, WHICH INCLUDES THE COST OF POLLUTION

THE LAUNDRY IS AN UNWILLING FREE-RIDER: IT CANNOT CHARGE A PRICE FOR THE POLLUTION IT RECEIVES

Fig 8.2 Case study of an externality: Pollution

External costs such as pollution, which increase the production costs of the firms that receive them, are examples of **external diseconomies**. Symmetrically, a firm may generate **external benefits** which are **external economies** if they lower the production costs of other firms. The laundry is unable to charge a price through the market to the brickworks for the pollution it unwillingly consumes. In a similar way, a power-station discharging warm water into a lake cannot charge a price to fishermen for the external benefit they receive in the form of larger catches of fish. The market thus **fails to provide an incentive** for the brickworks to generate **less** pollution and for the power-station to discharge **more** warm water. Without such an incentive, **too much** of an external cost and **too little** of an external benefit are likely to be generated. Thus governments may become involved in adjusting markets via taxes and subsidies in order to discourage economic bads and to encourage external benefits.

The different types of externality

	External costs	*External benefits*
Generated in production and received in production.	Pollution discharged by a brickworks and received by a nearby laundry. (External diseconomies)	Warm water discharged by a power-station and received in the form of bigger fish catches by nearby commercial fishermen. (External economies)
Generated in production and received in consumption.	Pollution discharged by a brickworks and received by nearby households.	Warm water discharged by a power-station and received in the form of bigger fish catches by private anglers.
Generated in consumption and received in production	Congestion caused by private motorists increasing production costs for firms. (This is another type of external production diseconomy.)	Commercial bee-keepers benefiting from the private gardens of nearby households. (This is another type of external production economy.)
Generated in consumption and received in consumption.	Congestion caused by private motorists causing a utility loss to other private motorists, pedestrians and households.	Passers-by enjoying the view of nearby private gardens.

Externalities are essentially **'spin-offs'** which are generated by one economic agent in the pursuit of its private self-interest and received outside the market by other agents. **Divergencies** are likely to arise between the **private cost and benefit** of the generator of the externality and the **social cost and benefit** to all who receive them. An external cost such as pollution can be regarded as part of the production cost of bricks which is evaded by the brickworks by being 'dumped' on others. The **real cost** of bricks is greater than the **money cost** at market prices because the real cost includes the cost of pollution; bricks are therefore **underpriced** at market prices, price being less than the true marginal cost. Too many bricks are produced, causing a **misallocation of resources** (allocative inefficiency).

In this example, pollution is an externality which is both **generated** and **received in production**, thereby increasing the production cost of the firms receiving the pollution. Externalities may also be generated and received in consumption. This, and the other possibilities, are summarized in the table at the top of the page.

6 Public policy and market failure

Public goods are usually provided 'free' by the state since otherwise they would not be provided at all. This is an example of public provision **replacing** the market. In the case of merit and demerit goods, the government can either **replace** or **modify** the market. A demerit good such as heroin may be judged so harmful that its consumption and sale are made illegal. A complete ban on a good is the ultimate **quantity control** which a government can use to regulate sale or consumption. Nevertheless a market may still exist in the form of an illegal **black market**. Black markets emerge when free markets are severely regulated or suppressed. In other circumstances, a government may decide that less severe quantity controls are more appropriate, such as the creation of no-smoking areas and restrictions on the sale of tobacco and alcohol. The symmetrical equivalent to a complete ban on heroin is to make the consumption of a merit good such as education or vaccination compulsory.

At the same time, price controls provide another form of regulation which can be used to modify the market. **Minimum price legislation** can discourage the consumption of demerit goods, whereas **maximum price legislation** increases the demand for merit goods–though problems of excess supply and demand are likely to result. For this reason governments may prefer to influence demand by **taxing** demerit goods and by **subsidizing** merit goods. If a 100% subsidy is given to the private producers of a merit good, it becomes effectively 'free', in the sense that it is available at zero price. An example occurs when free places in private schools are financed by the state. Alternatively, the state can provide the merit good itself at zero or token price, similarly financed out of general taxation.

The problem of externalities can be tackled in a rather similar way with a combination of quantity controls or regulations, and taxes and subsidies to influence price. Discharge of pollution may be made illegal or restricted to certain times of the day or year. Maximum emission limits can be imposed. Since the central problem is the failure of the market to provide incentives to generate fewer external costs and more external benefits, taxes and subsidies can be used to provide the desired incentives. The government could, in principle, calculate the money cost of pollution and impose this as a **pollution tax** upon the polluter. The imposition of such a tax **internalizes** the externality! More controversially, subsidies can be paid to encourage external benefits, for example those which result from the planting of trees.

8.4 Links with other topics

In this unit we have investigated in some depth the circumstances in which the **signalling** and **incentive** functions of prices (described in Unit 1) may break down, resulting in the failure of markets to function smoothly. In some situations markets may fail to function at all. The relative merits of the market economy and the planning mechanism (the subject of Unit 9) link directly to the question whether individual markets function smoothly or badly. Units 8 and 9 are thus very closely related. If a case exists for the public provision of public goods and some merit goods, then this will influence the level and pattern of both government spending and government revenue. These examples of market failure are reintroduced in Unit 15 on taxation and public spending.

8.5 Question practice

Essay Questions

Question 1 In what senses could the market system 'fail'? To what extent could your arguments be used to justify the production and distribution of goods and services by the public sector?   (*Oxford: June 1989*)

Understanding the Question A good answer might discuss how, if the signalling and incentive functions of prices break down, the various desirable attributes of the market economy may not be attained. Goods and services might not be produced or they might be over-produced or under-produced. You might also distinguish between the inefficient and the inequitable functioning of market forces. Illustrate your answer with the standard examples covered in the unit (public goods, merit and demerit goods and externalities) but make sure you discuss thoroughly any chosen example in terms of the sense in which the market system has failed. It is also worth discussing monopoly as an example of market failure, together with more 'macro' examples such as the failure of a market economy to achieve full employment or an equitable distribution of income. In the latter context, 'North/South' inequalities between rich and poor countries, and the possibility that standards of living achieved by market economies cannot ultimately be sustained (because the earth will run out of resources), might represent the ultimate 'global' market failures.

Reintroduce public goods and merit goods in your answer to the second part of the question. The provision of pure public goods by the public sector is most easy to justify since merit goods can be privately provided, aided by public subsidy. Public provision by nationalized monopoly industries might be linked to monopoly as a market failure, nationalization being a method of controlling monopoly abuse.

Answer plan

1 Briefly explain the signalling and incentive functions of price and note how, in principle, competitive market forces might achieve efficient production and allocation of resources.
2 List examples of market failure.
3 Choose at least three examples, and explain how the market system malfunctions in each example.
4 Explain the case for public sector provision of public goods and merit goods.
5 Assess whether public sector provision is the most efficient provision.
6 Discuss whether the case for nationalized industries can be made in terms of market failure.

Question 2

(a) Explain why the emission of pollution by a firm into the atmosphere or into a river may be economically inefficient.   (13)
(b) Evaluate two ways of reducing any economic inefficiency caused by pollution.   (12)
    (*AEB: June, 1990*)

Understanding the Question With this question there is a danger of writing too much about 'environmental science' and not enough economics. You must explain why pollution is a negative externality and how the emission of negative externalities results in allocative inefficiency. Describe how a pollution tax and regulation might reduce the inefficiency and then evaluate their effectiveness. 'Evaluate' is the key word in the second part of the question, and an answer restricted to description would not gain many marks. Also avoid the temptation to write about more than two methods of reducing inefficiency. (Other methods might include: education programmes; fines; subsidy and compensation; and even the promotion of more economic growth to create both the 'educated' population and the extra resources with which to improve the environment.)

Answer plan

1 Firmly state that pollution is an example of a negative externality.
2 Explain how negative externalities result in a misallocation of resources.
3 Briefly mention other inefficiencies that might result, e.g. an inefficient workforce due to pollution harming health.
4 State two methods of reducing the inefficiency, e.g. taxation and regulation.
5 Describe how each method might operate.
6 Evaluate the effectiveness of each method.

Question 3

What is cost-benefit analysis? (25)
With reference to examples, discuss its application to public sector investment. (75)

(London: January, 1989)

Understanding the Question

Cost benefit analysis (CBA) is a technique for evaluating all the costs and benefits of any economic action or decision, *i.e.* the **social costs** and **benefits** to the whole community and not just the **private costs** and **benefits** accruing to the economic agent undertaking the action. CBA is most often used by governments to help decide whether to invest in a major public project such as a motorway, a Channel tunnel or a third London Airport, or a major investment by a nationalized industry. However, there is no reason in principle why a private sector investment, or indeed any action by a private economic agent or by the government, cannot be examined by CBA.

CBA is really just an extension of the **Discounted Cash Flow** technique of investment appraisal explained in Unit 21. Using DCF, a firm attempts to calculate all the **private** costs and benefits occurring **in the future** as a result of an investment undertaken now. The central problem is guessing and putting money values to an unknown and uncertain future. CBA is even more difficult because many of the social costs and benefits resulting in the future from an action undertaken now take the form of **externalities** that are difficult to quantify. How does one put a monetary value to the saving of a human life resulting from fewer accidents on a proposed motorway? What is the social cost of the destruction of a beautiful view? It is extremely difficult to decide on all the likely costs and benefits, 'to draw the line' on which to include or exclude, to put monetary values to the chosen costs and benefits, and to make a suitable comparison between costs and benefits accruing immediately with those that will only be received in the distant future.

Critics of CBA argue that it is 'psuedo-scientific' – value judgements and arbitrary decisions disguised as objectivity. CBA is also criticized as being a costly waste of time and money, a method whereby politicians distance themselves from, and induce delay in, unpopular decisions, deflecting the wrath of local communities away from themselves and onto the 'impartial experts' undertaking the CBA. Nevertheless the supporters of CBA argue that for all its defects it remains the best method of appraising public investment decisions because all the likely costs and benefits are exposed to public discussion.

Answer plan

1 Explain that CBA is a technique of appraisal, similar to DCF in discounting a future stream of costs and benefits, but including all the costs and benefits, social rather than merely private.
2 Explain that CBA is applicable, in principle, to public sector investment because, in pursuit of the aim of social welfare maximization, **all** the costs and benefits generated by the project should be assessed, **not just** the private costs and benefits.
3 Give examples of public sector investment projects that might generate significant externalities that affect social welfare, e.g. a motorway, airport or nuclear power station.

Questions 4, 5 and 6

(a) Both assertion and reason are true statements and the reason is a correct explanation of the assertion.
(b) Both assertion and reason are true statements but the reason is not a correct explanation of the assertion.
(c) The assertion is true but the reason is a false statement.
(d) The assertion is false but the reason is a true statement.

Assertion		*Reason*
Question 4 Services, such as defence, which are collectively provided and produced are called 'public goods'.	because	the provision of public goods for one person means that others in society benefit and are not impeded in their consumption.
Question 5 All the people who benefit from public goods are termed 'free-riders'.	because	free-riders receive a service without paying for it.
Question 6 Aircraft noise and other forms of pollution are called 'economic bads'.	because	they are all examples of externalities.

Understanding the Questions

Question 4 Alternative **(a)** is correct because public goods have the characteristics of non-excludability and non-rivalry as stated in the reason. Conversely, other people can be excluded from consuming a private good.
Question 5 Free-riders are correctly explained in the reason part of the question, but the assertion is false. Public goods can usually be provided to consumers who are not free-riders, but the temptation to become a free-rider or the costs of excluding free-riders are likely to cause the market to break down. It is also the case that consumers pay for the good through taxation when public goods are provided by the government. Therefore the consumers are not free-riders.
Question 6 Both the assertion and the reason are true statements, but the reason does not explain the assertion. Economic bads are so named because they are harmful and diminish economic welfare, rather than because they are externalities.

Question 7
Which of the following is an example of an external economy?
(a) A firm which obtains bulk supplies of raw materials at a discount.
(b) A firm uses its market power to obtain bulk supplies of raw materials at a discount.
(c) An increase in production costs caused by traffic congestion.
(d) An increase in a farmer's crop yield which results from a new drainage scheme installed by a neighbouring farmer.

Understanding the Question
Alternative **(a)** is an example of an **internal** economy of scale, since the economy results from the bargaining power which results from the firm's size and market power. Alternative **(b)** is also wrong because the overseas subsidiary is a part of the firm. Traffic congestion causes an external diseconomy, leaving **(d)** as the correct answer.

Data Response Questions

Question 8 The following passage is adapted from a 'Social Cost-Benefit Study of Two Suburban Surface Rail Passenger Services', by C. D. Foster.

> Several studies have been done to estimate the social worth of retaining railway passenger services that are financially unprofitable. What distinguishes this study is that it is one of the first which seeks to justify the retention of rail passenger services because of road congestion in urban areas. The essential case, if proven, must be that the traffic the railways divert from the roads reduces congestion by an amount sufficient to justify the rail subsidies required. Underlying this is the proposition that users of city roads pay less through taxation for using them than covers the real costs of their use.
>
> Road users in cities pay substantially less than the costs they occasion. The greater the congestion, the truer this is. The extra cost or, as economists would call it, the marginal social cost, of an extra vehicle coming onto a road is quantifiable. Wherever there is congestion, the marginal social cost will be greater than the actual cost to the individual road user (often called the marginal road user) since the costs to him of using the road are his vehicle costs and his time. He does not have to take into account the costs he imposes on other road users–and on pedestrians.
>
> On the other hand, if rail transport in cities is required to cover costs, it will then be over-priced relative to users of urban roads, since rail users will be required to cover all the real costs they give rise to, while road users will not. The effect of this difference in pricing policy is an inefficient distribution of traffic between road and rail. Less traffic travels by rail, especially in the peak, than is efficient.
>
> One way of getting prices right would be to raise the price of urban road use until both public and private road transport covered its real costs. But if we accept that it is politically imprudent or undesirable to raise the cost of using roads to a level where marginal social costs are covered, one can attempt to get the correct relationship between road and rail by the opposite course of action; that is by keeping rail fares lower than they would be if the railways charged what the market would bear rather than raising road prices. This is the essence of the case for rail subsidies.

(a) What is meant by the term 'marginal social cost' (paragraph 2)?   (3)
(b) Why is the marginal social cost of an extra road user on a congested road greater than the cost to the marginal road user (paragraph 2)?   (3)
(c) Why was the existing system of prices for road and rail transport considered to be inefficient?   (6)
(d) Describe and discuss the relative merits of the two policy options outlined in the passage that would improve the allocation of traffic between road and rail.   (8)

(AEB: June, 1984)

Understanding the Question The author of the passage argues that negative externalities are generated by road transport but not by rail transport. Whereas, taken in isolation, users of rail transport pay the 'correct' price, road users pay too low a price because part of the true cost of road transport is dumped on others as a negative externality. The relative prices of the two forms of transport are therefore wrong, leading to a misallocation of resources. Too many people travel by road and too few by rail. The public policy problem is to achieve the correct relative prices of the two forms of transport. The 'best' solution might be to tax road users so that P = MSC for both road and rail. But because the 'best' solution may be politically inopportune, the 'second best' strategy would be to introduce a compensating distortion, via subsidy, into rail pricing, so that P < MSC for both forms of transport. But although this might achieve the 'correct' relative prices for road and rail, it would promote a wider misallocation of resources, since both road and rail would now be too cheap compared to other goods and services.

8.6 Further reading

Hardwick, P., Khan, B., Langmead, J., *An Introduction to Modern Economics*, 3rd edition (Longman, 1990).
Chapter 12: Public goods and externalities.

Begg, D., Fischer, S. and Dornbusch, R., *Economics*, 3rd edition (McGraw Hill, 1991).
Chapter 15: Introduction to Welfare Economics.

9 Market Economies and Planned Economies

9.1 Points of perspective

In the first eight units we have examined how the price mechanism is assumed to work, both in the 'ideal' circumstances of a perfect market, and in the more realistic conditions of monopoly, market imperfection and market failure. We are now in a position to draw together themes and strands of reasoning from earlier units, in order to make a comparison of **market economies** and **planned economies** as **economic systems**.

1 Ownership and economic systems

One way to define an economic system is in terms of **ownership** of the means of **production**, **distribution** and **exchange**. This approach is favoured by **Marxist economists**, who analyse the conflict between the **employed class** and the **class which owns the means of production**. Marxists are particularly interested in the dynamic change over time of society (and economic systems), in response to the apparent conflict between **economic classes**. Most Marxian economic analysis has centred on **capitalism** as an economic system. Capitalism is usually defined as a system in which the means of production are owned by private individuals who employ labour in order to produce output for private profit. Marxists believe that the supposed conflicts and contradictions of capitalism will eventually culminate in a final crisis out of which will develop **socialism**. In socialism the community as a whole, usually through the state, owns the means of production, distribution and exchange. Of course, it is not nearly as simple as this, and to many economists capitalism and socialism may have a number of different meanings.

2 Allocative mechanisms and economic systems

Market economies and **planned economies (command** or **collective economies)** are defined in terms of the **allocative mechanism** which is assumed to exist in the economic system. In a pure market economy all resources, goods and services other than free goods would be allocated through the market, whereas in a centrally planned economy a central authority would make all the allocative decisions. Both these extreme situations are obviously unrealistic. Where a very large proportion of economic activity takes place through the market, as for example in the Swiss economy, it is usual to refer to it as a market economy. Where, however, the bulk of economic activity is determined by a central planning authority, as in the Soviet Union (at least, until recent times), it is customary to refer to it as a planned or command economy even though some activities such as market-gardening may be outside the system.

3 Other possibilities

It is often wrongly stated that private ownership (or **'free enterprise'**) is a **necessary condition** for the existence of a market economy. While it is certainly usual for capitalism to exist within a largely market economy, it is by no means inevitable. Nationalized industries in Britain have provided an example of socially owned enterprises operating in the market sector of an economy. Indeed, most of the economies of the advanced industrial nations outside the USSR are referred to as **mixed economies** and many of the former Eastern bloc countries have begun the process of transforming from command economies to Western-style mixed economies. The mixed economy is a very broad label that covers a variety of possible systems. A mixed economy is sometimes defined in terms of ownership, as an economy containing large **private** and **public sectors**. It is equally possible to define a mixed economy in terms of allocative mechanisms; in this case, the co-existence of **market** and **non-market** sectors defines a mixed economy, each sector usually providing different categories of goods and services. However, some services such as health and education may be provided by both sectors.

Until recently there was a wide measure of agreement in the United Kingdom on the virtues of a mixed economy, the main discussion and controversy being on where to draw the line, within fairly narrow limits, between private and public ownership and between market and non-market provision. This consensus has now been attacked by the advocates of a **social market economy**, which is much closer in concept to a pure market economy. In a social market economy, as much as possible would be privately provided through the market, the state restricting its economic role to that of 'nightwatchman': maintaining orderly conditions in which markets can operate, providing some public goods, and using taxation and transfers to provide a minimum state 'safety net' to protect the victims of a largely unregulated market economy. Advocates of a social market economy are usually **monetarist** in their approach to macro-economics.

9.2 Underlying concepts

1 The problem of scarcity revisited

The problem of what, how and for whom to produce in a situation where scarce resources have alternative uses was briefly mentioned in the introduction to Unit 1. Since a major part of the evaluation of market and planned economies must be in terms of how well they perform these allocative tasks, we shall restate the scarcity problem with the use of a **production possibility** diagram.

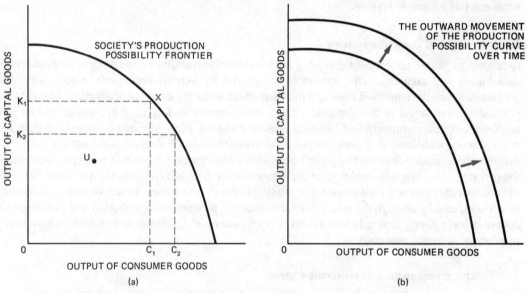

Fig 9.1 (a) The economic problem and society's production possibility curve
(b) economic growth causes the frontier to move outwards over time

The **production possibility frontier** drawn in Figure 9.1a shows what can be produced with the existing quantity of labour, capital, and land at a country's disposal, for a given level of technology or 'technical progress'. Although resources and capacity are limited, a choice of which type of good to produce exists. If we assume just two classes of goods, **capital** and **consumer** goods, the production possibility frontier represents the **technological choice** available to society between the two groups of goods. A point such as X on the frontier is associated with the output K_1 of capital goods and C_1 of consumer goods. The production possibility diagram also illustrates the following points of interest:

(i) If society is on its production possibility frontier, at a point such as X, more of one good can only be produced at the expense of some of the output of the other good. For instance, if the output of consumer goods is increased to C_2, the output of capital goods must fall by $K_1 - K_2$. The **opportunity cost** of the extra output of consumer goods is $K_1 - K_2$, the alternative output of capital goods which is given up.

(ii) If you refer back to Unit 3, you will see that the shape of the production possibility curve reflects the nature of **returns** to the resources as they are switched between the capital and consumer goods industries. Figure 9.1 shows **diminishing returns** in both industries: as more and more resources are transferred into the consumer goods industries, output rises by a smaller extra quantity for each unit of resource transferred.

(iii) All points on the production possibility frontier represent **full employment** of society's resources. A point such as U inside the frontier is associated with unemployment. Here it is no longer true that the opportunity cost of increasing the output of consumer goods is the sacrifice of some production of capital goods—production of both capital and consumer goods can be stepped up by utilizing unemployed resources.

(iv) An increase in the resources available to the society, or technical progress which improves the efficiency with which resources are used, can shift the production possibility curve outwards. This is illustrated in Figure 9.1b. Of course, the choice as to which original quantities of capital and consumer goods to produce may influence the outward movement of the frontier. **Capital goods** are goods which are used to produce other goods and services, whilst **consumer goods** represent the final goods and services purchased by households. The output of capital goods has two purposes. Firstly it replaces the capital that is worn out in producing the current **flow** of capital and consumer goods (**depreciation investment** which maintains the society's capital **stock**). Secondly it may also add to the capital stock (**net investment**), thereby enabling a larger output to be produced in the future. In conditions of full employment it may be possible to increase the standard of living by producing more consumer goods at the expense of capital goods. However, in the long run the standard of living can best be increased by producing more capital goods now, thereby creating the growth in the economy's productive capacity which shifts the production possibility frontier outwards.

2 General equilibrium in a perfectly competitive market economy

In Unit 1 we considered how the equilibrium price is determined within a single market, and in Unit 6 we investigated the equilibrium of a single firm within a perfectly competitive industry or market. For a **general equilibrium** to occur within a whole system of perfectly competitive inter-related markets, equilibrium prices and quantities must be simultaneously determined in each market. Such a general equilibrium would be both **productively** and **allocatively** efficient since it would be impossible either:

(i) to produce more of one particular good or service without diverting resources away from another, or

(ii) to make one consumer better off without making some other consumer or consumers worse off.

It is important to stress that these **'optimal properties'** of a perfectly competitive general equilibrium hold for a **given distribution of income**. Theré will be a different optimal general equilibrium for each and every alternative distribution of income! In these circumstances a strong normative case may exist for redistributing income in the interests of social fairness, for example, when 1% of the community is very rich and 99% are very poor.

9.3   Essential knowledge

1 The advantages of a market economy

Subject to some very strong assumptions about the absence of externalities and economies of scale, a perfectly competitive market economy in general equilibrium would possess the following advantages:

(i) **Economic efficiency** (productive and allocative) would be achieved.

(ii) **Consumer sovereignty.** The goods and services produced would be determined by price signals which reflect consumer wants.

(iii) **Decentralized decision-making.** The optimal production and allocation of resources would be achieved without the need for an expensive bureaucracy. In a market economy the price system acts as a **social control mechanism**. This is often referred to as the **'invisible hand'** principle, describing the proposition that economic order rather than chaos results from the pursuit of individual self-interest in a market economy.

2 The disadvantages of a market economy

(i) **Economic inefficiency.** Productive and allocative efficiency will only be achieved if every market in the system is perfectly competitive and if trading takes place always at equilibrium prices in every market. Unless these almost impossible conditions are met, we cannot be sure that a perfectly competitive market system would be economically efficient.

Of course, the market economies of the real world are in no sense perfectly competitive. In a perfectly competitive system, price (and wage) flexibility would bring about **full employment** of all available resources in equilibrium. A criticism of the market economies in the actual world is the **persistence of unemployment** and the tendency for **business cycles** in the pattern of economic behaviour. Both these phenomena are indicators of inefficient utilization of resources.

(ii) **Producer sovereignty**. The existence of **increasing returns to scale** and **economies of scale** helps to explain why actual market economies are only distant approximations to the perfectly competitive 'ideal'. If markets are dominated by monopoly and imperfect competition, firms may decide what to produce, perhaps manipulating consumer wants through advertizing. In any case, price now functions as a misleading signal, contributing to resource misallocation.

3 The case for replacing the market

Supporters of the principle of a market economy argue that, however imperfectly the price mechanism works, it still results in sufficient efficiency and consumer sovereignty to justify the system. Nevertheless, many advocates of a **mixed economy** claim that in a number of specific instances the government planning mechanism should either **modify** or **replace** the market:

(i) **The problem of income distribution.** The best that can be claimed for a perfectly competitive market system is that it may be economically efficient **for a given initial income distribution**. It is completely **'value neutral'** on the desirability or otherwise of the initial pattern of incomes. It is a function of government to use tax and public spending policies to achieve a 'satisfactory' distribution of income.

(ii) **Goods which the market fails to provide.** We examined in Unit 8 the nature of **public goods**, **merit goods** and **externalities**. In each case the market either completely fails to provide the goods in question, or provides the 'wrong' quantities. Governments usually plan the public collective provision of public goods such as national defence, and of merit goods such as education. Governments may also modify the market through regulation, taxation and subsidies, in order to encourage the consumption of market-provided merit goods, or to reduce the **divergency** between **private** and **social cost and benefit** in the case of externalities. You should refer back to Unit 8 for a detailed explanation of these examples of market failure.

4 Command economies

A command economy, in which markets would be largely replaced by a command or planning mechanism, would of course be very different from the type of mixed economy we have just described. In theory at least, it is possible for a **centrally planned** command economy to achieve exactly the same distribution of resources as would occur in general equilibrium in a perfectly competitive market economy. As a result, there is no **theoretical** reason why a market economy must be more economically efficient than a command economy. Consider, however, the implications of the complete abolition of prices as sources of information. It has been calculated that in an economy such as the USA the central authority would have to issue over 200 billion orders in respect of a **single** commodity, allocating precise amounts of the good to each consumer. The costs of a completely centralized control system governing all production and consumption decisions would be immense! Such a command economy is as abstract and unreal an economic concept as the model of a perfectly competitive market economy.

The command economies of the real world, such as the Soviet economy before the onset of *perestroika*, have tended to be **command economies with some household choice**. The command system concentrated on the **production decision** of what to produce, rather than on the final allocation of goods and services to consumers. A **central plan** allocated resources to particular industries and productive units which were required to meet the output targets of the master plan. In some circumstances, factory managers were free to set final prices, though it was more usual for the central planners to decide the prices of important commodities such as bread and meat. Prices which were chosen by a central authority with the object of encouraging individual consumers to behave in a certain way are known as **shadow prices**.

Sometimes, shadow prices are deliberately set so as to ration final goods and services which are scarce in relation to an overwhelming unfulfilled consumer demand. In this respect, shadow prices imitate at least one of the functions of market prices. However, in a market economy the price would provide an incentive for producers to enter the industry. This incentive is lacking in a command economy, unless the planners respond to the signals of scarcity by diverting more resources into the particular industry.

9.4 Links with other topics

We have nearly completed our necessarily brief coverage of micro-economic theory. In Units 10 and 11 the emphasis is switched away from economic theory as we look at the way firms have grown in the British economy and how they raise finance. We then see in Unit 12 how government **micro-economic policy** attempts to make the British economy more competitive. In these units, the theory which we have developed in Units 1 to 9 will be used to **evaluate** the **aims** and **effectiveness** of government policies.

9.5 Question practice

Essay Questions

Question 1   How are resources allocated in a free market and in a planned economy? Examine the relative merits, in terms of economic efficiency, of each method of resource allocation.

(London: June, 1987)

Understanding the Question
The wording of the question allows a candidate some considerable scope in interpreting the concepts involved. For example, a free economy may mean a perfectly competitive market economy, but it can also include highly imperfect market economies in which economic agents are free to own private property, buy and sell labour services, etc., within the constraints of the imperfect market system. It would be as well to define what you mean by 'free' at the beginning of the essay. Good answers should suggest that the concept may mean different things to different economists. Similarly, a planned economy can refer to a completely centrally planned economy, a command economy with some household choice, or an economy in which planning is locally delegated.

You must stick to the economic aspects of resource allocation in both systems, avoiding the temptation to discuss political systems and wider concepts of personal freedom except in so far as they impinge upon resource allocation. The best approach is to show how the market and the planning systems both attempt to solve the central problem of scarcity, but that the methods differ in each system. Whereas a free market system is more efficient in avoiding administrative costs and shortages, a planned system could, in principle, be more efficient in considering the long-run rather than just the short-run and social welfare rather than just individual welfare. Consider also whether 'real world' market and planned economies exhibit the various efficiencies and inefficiencies you discuss.

Answer plan

1 Briefly describe some of the meanings of free and planned economies.
2 Describe how free economies are characterized by private property and individual decentralized decision-making. This contrasts with the socialized ownership and centralized decision-making of planned economies. Compare the incentive motive in the two systems.
3 Firmly state that all economies are similar in having to deal with the problem of scarcity.
4 Contrast how the market mechanism and the decisions of a central authority deal with the problem.
5 A perfectly competitive market economy in a state of general equilibrium would display characteristics of consumer sovereignty and economic efficiency. In principle, economic efficiency but not consumer sovereignty could be achieved in a planned economy.
6 However, in real-world versions of both systems, inefficiencies are likely. Free economies will contain the problem of monopoly and producer power. In a planned economy, the decisions of the central authority may not accord with consumer preferences, and shortages will result.

Question 2   Outline, briefly, the main characteristics by which economic systems may be classified. Discuss what influences, if any, the nature of the economic system can exert on the level, rate of increase and distribution of national income.

(JMB: June, 1988)

Understanding the Question   Start your answer by introducing the standard classification of economies into market, mixed and command economies. You might also mention social market economies and market socialism within this classification; do not confuse the two. Develop your answer by discussing both allocative mechanisms (the price mechanism and the planning mechanism) and ownership of the means of production (capitalism versus socialism). The question instructs you to be brief, but you might mention an alternative approach to classification; based on the historical stages through which an economy moves in the process of economic development. For example, the American economic historian, W. W. Rostow, has identified five stages of development: the traditional society; the traditional society preparing for 'take-off'; 'take-off' into self-sustained growth; the drive to maturity; and the age of high mass-consumption. Alternatively, you could simply make a division into pre-industrial, industrial and post-industrial economic systems.

You must devote most of your answer to the second part of the question. The level, rate of increase and distribution of income are not independent and you should firmly state this fact, and briefly explain why. For example, right-wing economists argue that a highly unequal distribution of incomes might, through the promotion of saving amongst the better-off and the creation of incentives, accelerate the rate of growth of income, with the poor eventually benefiting from an increased level of income through a 'trickle down' effect. According to this view, a pure market economy promotes the fastest rate of growth, though many would argue that the accompanying inequalities do not operate in the benign manner described above. One possible way of answering the question would be to draw on the events taking place in Eastern Europe in the early 1990s as former command economies transform into versions of market and mixed economies.

Answer plan

1 Briefly explain the characteristics of command, market and mixed economies in terms of how resources are allocated and ownership of the means of production.
2 Perhaps mention other classifications, e.g. in terms of stage of economic development reached.
3 Carefully explain the meanings of level, rate of increase and distribution of national income and illustrate how they can interact.

4 Discuss different views as to whether decentralized decision making (the pursuit of self-interest and incentives created by the profit motive in a market economy) or the planning mechanism in a command economy, can achieve the fastest rate of growth and the highest level of income.

5 Illustrate your answer from the experience of real-world economies. The recent and current experience of Eastern European economies might back up some of your arguments.

6 You might conclude that some version of a mixed economy produces an acceptable level and rate of growth of income combined with a relatively equitable distribution of income, representing a compromise between efficiency and equity attractive to the electorate at the ballot box in a political democracy.

Question 3

(a) How are resources allocated in a mixed economy?   (15)

(b) In the light of the economic changes that have occurred within the United Kingdom economy in recent years, discuss whether it is still correct to describe the United Kingdom economy as a mixed economy.

(10)

(AEB: June, 1990)

Understanding the Question Having defined a mixed economy in terms of both allocative mechanisms (price and planning mechanisms) and ownership (private and public ownership), you must explain how resources are allocated in some detail. Explain how in the market sector resource allocation may stem ultimately from consumers' ability and willingness to pay, with both households and firms responding to the signals and incentives provided by market prices. Then outline the allocation of resources via the command mechanism and the public sector in the provision of public goods and merit goods. The question asks 'how' rather than 'why', so don't let your answer drift into a detailed explanation of market failure. An important element of resource allocation in a mixed economy involves the use of taxation and transfers or subsidies. Resources or spending power is allocated away from taxpayers towards the beneficiaries of the transfers. The latter might include nationalized industries and also private sector producers such as farmers and firms receiving regional aid. By contrast, if nationalized industries were instructed to act commercially and be self-financing, then their role in resource allocation would be little different from that of private sector firms in a market economy.

The second part of the question invites you to discuss the extent to which policies of privatization, deregulation and the promotion of market forces have changed the nature of the mix in the United Kingdom economy and whether we can conclude that it is still a mixed economy.

Answer plan

1 Define a mixed economy.
2 Explain how the price mechanism functions in the market sector to allocate resources.
3 Explain how the planning mechanism decides on the levels of public goods and merit goods to produce.
4 Explain the role of taxation and transfers to modify the market.
5 Discuss the extent to which nationalization in a mixed economy may affect resource allocation.
6 Note the policies of privatization, deregulation and marketization introduced in the United Kingdom since 1979. Explain how the role of the state has been reduced.
7 Assess whether the UK economy is still a mixed economy.

Multiple Choice Questions

Question 4 The statement 'There is no such thing as a free lunch' relates to the application of

(a) the concept of a merit good
(b) the working of the price mechanism
(c) the concept of opportunity cost
(d) the law of diminishing marginal utility

Understanding the Question This is a straightforward question on the concept of opportunity cost and the problem of choosing between the alternative uses of scarce resources. Free meals, for example for pensioners or school-children, can be examples of merit goods. Nevertheless, the provision of the free meals uses up scarce resources, and they have to be paid for by somebody. The correct answer is therefore **(c)**.

Question 5 Under the command economy system, the economic problem of deciding what goods shall be produced is decided mainly by

(a) advertizing
(b) profit levels
(c) government direction
(d) relative prices

Understanding the Question The decision will be based on the planning authority's perception of the wants of consumers, which may be judged subsidiary to other needs of the community or of the planners themselves. Many command economies have concentrated on capital goods rather than on providing consumer goods. **(a)**, **(b)** and **(d)** are all features of a market economy, whereas **(c)** is characteristic of centralized decision-making.

Data Response Questions

Question 6 'The protagonists of the free market system explicitly state its advantages as freedom and efficiency. . . . They regard men and women as primarily motivated by individual economic self-interest. The laws of supply and demand are held to operate because individuals are so made that they seek to sell to the highest bidder and buy from the cheapest (supplier). It follows that a person's income or wealth reflects his economic worth. Thus, man is seen as economic man. . . .'.

(Source: R. Holman, *Poverty: explanations of social deprivation*, Martin Robertson, 1978)

(a) In what sense does the behaviour of economic man lead to efficiency in the free market system?

(b) Discuss the assertion that an individual's productivity is a sound basis for determining the distribution of income.

(London: June, 1980)

Understanding the Question Although this data response question resembles an essay question, you are expected to make use of the concepts included in the quoted passage. Answers which fail to refer to the 'data' will usually be penalized, perhaps heavily. You should be able to answer the first part of the question by drawing on the coverage of economic efficiency in Unit 6 and the application of the concept to a perfectly competitive market system explained in this unit. You can show that, subject to the strong assumption about perfect information, mobility of factors of production, no economies of scale and an absence of externalities, a state of allocative and productive efficiency can be brought about in perfect competition general equilibrium. However, perfect competition in all markets is a necessary condition for the achievement of economic efficiency, so the behaviour of economic man may not lead to efficiency in the markets of the real world. Indeed, it may lead to such inefficiencies as unemployment.

The **'determination'** of the distribution of income can have two quite distinct meanings, one **positive** and the other **normative**. In the perfectly competitive free market system which is implied in the passage, incomes are **determined** by the price system within the assumed mechanism of the market economy. Unit 15 explains how the wage in a particular industry is determined by the productivity of the marginal individual worker to be employed. This is simply a matter of logical deduction from the basic assumptions of perfect competition.

It is vital to distinguish between a government's **normative** view on how the distribution of income should be determined and the way in which a **positive economic theory**, such as the theory of perfect competition, determines wages and profits as a part of the mechanism of the theory. Governments make value judgements on the desirable distribution of income. A distribution of income based on individual productivity might be economically desirable, in providing incentives, and socially desirable if people believe they should be rewarded for individual effort.

However, governments might also decide that individual productivity is only one of a number of criteria to take into account when determining the distribution of income. It is highly unlikely in any case, in a market economy free from government interference, that individuals would be rewarded on the basis of labour productivity alone. Initial inheritances of capital and land would be significant. The existence of monopoly would reward the strong, who possess market power, at the expense of the weak. In these circumstances governments may decide to alter the distribution of income on some criterion of 'social fairness'. The old and sick, who have no factor services to sell, will deserve some sort of income. Public opinion surveys indicate strong support for the idea of determining wages using the criterion of the **social value** of a job in some system of **job evaluation**. On this basis nurses would be rewarded more highly than casino croupiers. In practice, however, it would be almost impossible to determine incomes in this way without the complete destruction of market incentives. Within mixed economies, governments have preferred to use **taxes and transfers** to **modify** the **market-determined** distribution of income, rather than to **completely replace** the market.

Answer plan

1 Briefly explain the meaning of economic efficiency.

2 Explain the meaning of the passage: 'men and women do not **consciously** attempt to achieve an economically efficient system. Within a perfectly competitive system, economic efficiency or the "good of all" would result from the self-interest of individuals' (Adam Smith's *Invisible Hand*).

3 Nevertheless, the free markets of the real world may fail to achieve a state of economic efficiency, and they produce inefficiencies of their own, such as unemployment.

4 Interpret the second part of the question in a normative sense. There may be a case for basing the distribution of income on individual productivity, but other criteria such as protecting the weak should also be taken into account.

9.6 Further reading

Burningham, D., editor, *Economics*, 3rd edition (Hodder and Stoughton, 1987).
Chapter 2: Economics Systems.

Maunder, P., *et al*, *Economics Explained*, 2nd edition (Collins, 1991).
Chapter 2: Economic systems: the capitalist economy
Chapter 3: Economic systems: the command economy
Chapter 4: Economic systems: the mixed economy.

10 The Size and Growth of Firms

10.1 Points of perspective

This unit describes important aspects of the structure of British industry, emphasizing in particular the manner in which the size of firms has changed, Together with Unit 11 on the finance of industry, the unit provides a link between the micro-economic theory of Units 1 to 9, and the evaluation of British micro-economic policy in Unit 12. In this unit we shall be concerned with business enterprises in the private sector of the economy; nationalized industries are the subject of Unit 12.

10.2 Underlying concepts

In micro-economic theory, understanding is facilitated by considering the behaviour of a **single firm** operating a **single manufacturing plant** to produce a **specific product** within a **well-defined industry**. Reality, however, is much more complicated. Though single-plant/single-product firms certainly exist, particularly in the **small business sector** of the economy, large firms tend to be much more diverse. J. K. Galbraith has divided the economy into two parts: the thousands of small and traditional businesses on the one hand, and the few hundred technically dynamic, massively capitalized and highly organized corporations on the other. Large businesses in this **corporate sector** of the economy commonly operate in a variety of different industries, producing many different products from a number of separated plants. The largest business corporations are **multinational companies**, such as BP or ICI, controlling subsidiary enterprises and plants throughout the world. Some companies, such as Shell, are also **transnationals**, with ownership and control located in more than one country.

1 Industrial structure in the United Kingdom

Published statistics of the output of different British industries are usually based on the **Standard Industrial Classification**. This was first published in 1948, with revisions in 1958 and 1968. The latest revision, introduced in 1980, follows as closely as possible the classification of economic activities used by the EC. It comprises 10 major **industrial divisions**, including manufacturing, which are then further divided and subdivided into 60 **classes**, 222 **groups** and 334 **activity headings**. In the new structure, the energy-producing industries have been grouped, together with water supply, in a self-contained division. Other features are that, apart from agriculture, forestry and fishing, the various raw material producing industries are included within the same divisions as the corresponding processing industries, e.g. the slaughtering of animals is now included with food manufacturing, and the production of man-made fibres is a separate class adjacent to the chemical industry rather than a part of the textile industry. The SIC does not, therefore, always correspond to the normal description of 'industries' in economics text books. In service industries, the SIC draws a distinction between principals and agents e.g. in the distributive trades, dealers, buying or selling on behalf of others, are classified separately from wholesalers who actually take ownership of the goods in which they deal.

In comparison with similar industrial countries, the United Kingdom has a relatively small agricultural sector, reflecting the reliance on food imports. In 1989, agriculture accounted for less than 2% of Gross Domestic Product. Mining and quarrying industries had risen to about 10% of GDP, with the massive growth in the output of North Sea oil and gas more than offsetting a decline in the output of coal. However, the outputs of oil and gas probably peaked in the mid-1980s. The manufacturing sector is not particularly large in comparison with the relative share of manufacturing in countries such as Japan and West Germany. The share of manufacturing in GDP has fallen from 37% in 1955 to about 22% by 1989. In part, this reflects the importance of financial service industries, largely located in the City of London, to the British economy. It may also reflect the fact that many services, including utility industries such as the gas and electricity industries are in the **sheltered economy**, rather than in the **competitive economy**. By the nature of the service they provide, they are sheltered from import competition. The service sector has not experienced the **de-industrialization** or

structural decline, in response to import penetration and loss of export markets, that occurred in the manufacturing sector in the late 1970s and early 1980s. Some economists, notably R. Bacon and W. Eltis, have argued that the growth of employment in public sector services financed 'outside the market' was an important cause of the decline of manufacturing, through the 'crowding out' effects of taxation, However, in more recent years, the de-industrialization process may have ended, at least in terms of the absolute rather than the relative decline of manufacturing. By the end of 1987, the output produced by a much reduced or 'slimmed down' manufacturing sector had climbed back to the level previously achieved before the big decline in 1979, though it began to fall again in the 1990/91 recession.

2 Firms

A **firm** or **enterprise** is a unit of control and ownership. A common method of classifying firms is in terms of the legal status of the enterprise. On this basis the main types of business enterprise in the United Kingdom are **sole proprietors** or **traders, partnerships,** and **private** and **public joint stock companies**, though other types of enterprise such as co-operatives and building societies may be important in certain specialized areas of the economy. The concepts of **small businesses** and **large businesses** are less easy to define, since they do not refer to a precise legal status. Most small businesses are sole proprietors, partnerships and private companies, whereas the overwhelming majority of large businesses are public companies. In the early 1980s there were about 800 000 private companies and 8 000 public companies in the UK, though not all were actively trading. Some private companies such as the Littlewoods retailing group are sufficiently big to be regarded as large businesses, and a significant number of public companies are relatively quite small. When in 1971 the Bolton Committee reported on the role of small firms in the national economy, it found that there were 820 000 small firms responsible for 14% of GNP and 18% of the net output of the private sector. The inclusion of agriculture and the professions would have increased the 1971 total to 1 250 000 enterprises employing 29% of the working population. More recently it has been estimated that there are upwards of 2 million sole-traders or unincorporated businesses alone, without taking account of small companies. The government had recommended to the Bolton Committee that a 'small firm might be defined broadly as one with not more than 200 employees', but the Committee decided that this definition was unsuitable for most industries. It used other criteria such as turnover in distribution, and the number of vehicles in road haulage, to classify small businesses. Generally, the Bolton Committee decided to include three further criteria in addition to the employment criterion recommended by the government in its definition of the small firm. These were:
  (i) that it has a relatively small share of its market;
 (ii) that it is managed by its owners or part-owners in a personalized way;
(iii) that it is independent.

3 Plants

A **plant** or **establishment** is an individual productive unit within an enterprise, such as a factory, shop or farm. Many manufacturing processes require the separation of production into specific technical operations conducted in different buildings and workshops. The manufacture of most automobiles, for example, involves a large number of **vertically related** processes from the casting of engines and the pressing of car bodies to the final assembly of the completed vehicle. Many of these processes may be **internally integrated** within the various plants owned by an enterprise. Sometimes a firm may own several plants, which are vertically integrated, operating in different geographical locations. In other circumstances the separated tasks may be performed in different workshops within a single plant or large factory. In the case of a multi-product firm (a diversified firm operating in different industries), it is of course usual for different plants to produce the different products, except when products are **jointly supplied** from a common raw material and manufacturing process.

10.3   Essential information

1 The growing size of British firms
(i) The aggregate concentration ratio This ratio measures the share of the 100 largest firms in manufacturing output. For most of the twentieth century, the aggregate concentration ratio increased, thus indicating the growing importance of large firms. The 100 largest firms accounted for 16% of manufacturing output in 1909; 22% in 1940; and 38% in 1985. Nevertheless, in a world context, British firms are not very large and, where British companies compete in world markets,

they may be substantially smaller than their main competitors. Since 1979, the aggregate concentration ratio has decreased (falling to 38% by 1985), reflecting the decline and bankruptcy of many large manufacturing firms in the recession of the early 1980s. The onset of further recession in the early 1990s appears likely to continue to reduce the importance of both manufacturing industries and large manufacturing firms within the economy.

Evidence on concentration outside manufacturing industry is less satisfactory, though retailing in general, and grocery retailing in particular, have become increasingly concentrated in a few large firms. In 1972 the 100 largest manufacturing firms supplied two-thirds of the output of the food and motor vehicle industries, and half the output of the chemical industry. The importance of the 100 largest firms was least in timber and furniture, and in leather clothing and footwear, accounting for less than 10% of output.

The evidence also indicates that the growth in aggregate concentration has been much more rapid in Britain than in other countries, despite the relative smallness of even the largest British firms.

(ii) **The market concentration ratio** A common measure of concentration within a particular industry is the **five firm concentration ratio**. This ratio shows that, since 1968, the five largest firms have accounted for over 90% of domestic output in a quarter of manufacturing industries. Again, for many products, market concentration ratios are higher in the UK than in the USA, France and W. Germany. However, the concentration ratio can be a misleading indicator of monopoly power when there is substantial international trade and import penetration. Some economists believe that manufacturing industries in the United Kingdom are subject to much more competition than the concentration ratio suggests.

The fact that little of the growth in manufacturing concentration in the United Kingdom is explained by increasing plant size is of some significance. Between 1930 and 1968 the share of the 100 largest plants in manufacturing output remained the same at 10.8%. The explanation for increasing concentration must lie in **the increase in the average number of plants owned by the largest firms**. This suggests that an important cause of the increased size of firm is due to **take-overs** and **mergers** between existing firms, rather than a result of internal growth and the technical expansion of plants.

2 Economies of scale

External economies There are two sets of circumstances in which external economies occur:
(i) **External economies of scale** These occur when an individual firm within an industry, irrespective of its size or scale, benefits from a change in the scale of the industry as a whole. For example, the expansion of a firm which supplies components, in response to the growth of the whole industry, may allow an individual firm to buy components at a lower average cost. Such economies, which are **external to individual firms**, are **internal to the industry**.
(ii) **External benefits** External economies of the first type are **received through the market**. This enables an individual firm to buy its inputs at a lower price than would otherwise be the case. In contrast, an external benefit is an **externality received outside** the market, for example when a farmer benefits from the drainage installed by his neighbour. You should refer back to Unit 8 for a more detailed explanation of externalities, including external costs as examples of **external diseconomies**.

Internal economies of scale It is useful to distinguish between **plant-level economies of scale**, **firm-level economies of scale**, and **learning or experience effects**, all of which can result in a larger size of firm having a greater opportunity to achieve lower unit production costs. An internal economy of scale occurs whenever an increase in the scale of the inputs, including factors of production which in the short run are fixed, results in a fall in the average cost of producing a unit of output. Internal economies of scale can only occur if the size of either the plant or firm is increased. In contrast, **learning effects** occur after a new technology has been adopted. A learning effect occurs when managers and workers learn from experience how to operate particular technologies more effectively. Although learning effects will usually be associated with a change in the scale of operations, this is not inevitable. Nevertheless the existence of learning effects suggests that the full benefit of economies of scale will not be experienced until some time after the change in scale has taken place.
(i) **Plant-level economies of scale** The main sources of economies of scale at the plant level are increased possibilities for the division of labour, better integration of technical processes within a particular plant, and better utilization of indivisible items of plant. Most of these advantages are **technical economies of scale**, though there may be some scope for **managerial economies** of scale at the plant level as a result of managerial division of labour. **Volume economies** are a further type of technical economy: as the volume of a plant such as a blast furnace increases, the input of energy required to produce a unit of output may diminish.
(ii) **Firm-level economies of scale** Presumably, firms will try to benefit as much as possible from the

available plant-level economies of scale. They will also try to take advantage of economies associated with the growth of the firms which are independent of plant size, for example:

(a) **risk-bearing economies:** spreading risks over a number of products.

(b) **capital-raising economies:** large firms can often borrow from banks at a lower interest rate than small firms. The next unit explains how large firms have **access to the capital market**.

(c) **bulk buying and bulk marketing economies:** Large firms may be able to use their **market power** to buy supplies at lower prices and to market their products on better terms negotiated with retailers.

(d) **economies in overheads:** The costs of management and research and development can be distributed over a larger output.

(iii) The importance of economies of scale Empirical evidence suggests that there are considerable economies of scale at the plant level in bulk chemicals and in assembly operations where mass production methods can be applied, *e.g.* motor vehicles and refrigerators. However, in some cases scale economies may be as easy to obtain in a number of closely associated plants, not necessarily owned by the same firm, as in a single plant. In many industries the penalty of operating below **Minimum Efficient Plant Size** is small. The fact that the increase in concentration in the UK since 1945 has been through an increase in the number of plants owned or controlled by firms, rather than through an increase in plant size, suggests that firms have believed that more scope exists for economies at the firm level than at the plant level. Nevertheless, recent studies have concluded that firms which have grown through merger have performed less well after the merger. This may indicate that **diseconomies of scale**, resulting at the firm level from merger and acquisition, have exceeded the hoped-for scale economies. One such diseconomy is **X-inefficiency**, which has been identified in American research into mergers. X-inefficiency occurs when because of social attitudes or institutional factors, a firm is unable to make proper use of its capital, or the technology at its disposal, or its labour force. A company will be X-inefficient if it is unable to implement new ideas and methods, for example if a group of shop-floor workers or managers successfully resists change. The existence of X-inefficiency means that a firm incurs a level of costs greater than the lowest possible cost of producing any output.

3 Vertical, horizontal and conglomerate integration

There are various ways in which the activities of a firm can be integrated. At the plant level there is an obvious technical **internal integration** of processes, which are often carried out in separate workshops. This is an example of **vertical** integration. Vertical integration of processes is also a motive for a firm to grow by **internal growth,** *i.e.* to invest in new plant in order to extend its operations into producing its own raw materials, components, or market outlets.

Integration can also take place by **acquisition**. A firm may take over or merge with an existing independent firm in order to integrate the existing capacity of the other firm into its operations.

(i) Vertical integration A firm can expand through vertical integration forwards or backwards. **Backwards integration** occurs when a firm buys into its **sources of supply**, for example when a car-assembly firm buys a manufacturer of gearboxes. **Forwards integration** involves the buying up of **market outlets**. This type of integration would take place if a car-assembly firm acquires a chain of retail showrooms.

(ii) Horizontal integration results when a firm takes over a similar firm at the **same stage of production** in the **same industry**. The merger between British Motor Holdings and Leyland Motors which created British Leyland (later to become the Rover Group, now owned by British Aerospace) in the late 1960s was largely horizontal.

(iii) Conglomerate integration This is also known as **lateral** or **diversifying integration.** The defining characteristic of a lateral merger is the acquisition of a firm producing a different product in a separate industry. Large firms which have grown through lateral integration into highly diversified companies are known as **conglomerates**, for example Trafalgar House, whose interests range from construction to publishing.

(iv) Statistics on mergers Many take-overs or mergers will contain elements of vertical, horizontal and conglomerate integration. The Office of Fair Trading has compiled a classification of mergers in the United Kingdom:

	\multicolumn{10}{c}{Percentages}

Type	1970 No.	1970 Value	1974 No.	1974 Value	1980 No.	1980 Value	1984 No.	1984 Value	1987 No.	1987 Value
Horizontal	84	70	68	65	65	68	63	79	67	80
Vertical	1	0	5	2	4	1	4	1	3	1
Diversified	15	30	27	33	31	31	33	20	30	19
	100	100	100	100	100	100	100	100	100	100

The data indicates that most mergers are horizontal but a significant minority are conglomerate, perhaps because the opportunity for further horizontal amalgamation has diminished. Vertical motives for merger have been of no significance.

(v) Motives, advantages and disadvantages.

(a) The underlying motive for a merger of any type is a company's belief that it can profitably use the assets of the firm which is being acquired. We have already indicated that this belief may be misguided, since the results of many mergers have been disappointing.

(b) Economies of scale. This is an important motive in vertical and horizontal mergers. However, a proper **productive integration** of the **plant** of the merged companies must take place if the benefits are to be realized. Otherwise, diseconomies of scale may result and the merged firm may perform less well than the previously separate companies.

(c) Financial motives. Economies of scale at a plant level are not an important motive behind conglomerate mergers. Financial motives, including the hope of financial economies of scale, are often significant in lateral mergers.

(d) Monopoly power motives. Horizontal and vertical mergers may be planned in order to create a monopoly position in the market. The merged company may intend to use its market power to restrict output and raise price so as to increase its profits.

(e) Other motives. Vertical mergers sometimes try to achieve **security of supply** or **access to the market**. The **spreading of risks** and the **wish to diversify** into growing markets are frequently cited as motives behind conglomerate mergers. Many mergers in the 1960s and 1970s had an **asset-stripping** motive. Asset-stripping mergers can be horizontal, vertical or conglomerate. The asset-stripper takes over a company in order to close it down, usually sacking the labour force and selling off the company's assets which are redundant to his plans. The asset-stripper believes that he can profitably convert the **hidden assets** of his 'victim' to an alternative use. In many examples of asset-stripping, the land owned by the take-over victim was the most important hidden asset. Asset-stripping earned a bad reputation because it was often associated with closing down productive firms and converting the premises to property speculation. However, some economists view asset-stripping as merely a part of the process of rationalization which any economy must experience if it is to adapt to changing technology and demand. In the late 1980s, the asset-stripping motive for mergers resurfaced in the form of 'junk-bond' financed take-over bids. ('Junk bonds' are explained in Unit 11.)

10.4   Links with other topics

You should refer back to Unit 3 for a theoretical coverage of economies of scale, and to Unit 8 for examples of externalities which illustrate external economies and diseconomies. In the next unit, Unit 11, we examine the way firms finance growth in the British economy, and then in Unit 12 we introduce further aspects of economies of scale and merger activity, in the treatment of competition policy.

10.5   Question practice

Essay Questions

Question 1 Explain what the economist means by a 'firm' and why organizations as diverse as ICI and a corner shop can be said to possess the same essential characteristics from the economic viewpoint. Consider the possible reasons why approximately 90 per cent of firms in the UK are 'small'.   (*JMB: June, 1987*)

Understanding the Question A firm is a business enterprise producing (or dealing in) an output of goods or services for sale in the market. As we have seen, a profit-maximizing objective is usually assumed, though other objectives such as attaining a target market share (or even simply survival), can be fitted into the economist's view of the firm and its activities. Nationalized industries can be classified as firms, providing that they are predominantly concerned with market activity, but public sector services such as the National Health Service and state education are not normally regarded as firms by economists. Nevertheless, the logical thrust of 'reforms' of these services, introduced by the Conservative Government in the early 1990s, is to make hospitals, doctors' surgeries, schools and universities function much more as if they are firms driven largely by commercial profit and loss criteria.

You must explain how such profit and loss criteria affect businesses as diverse as ICI and a small corner shop. Start the last part of your answer by stressing that, although there are many more small than large firms, large firms account for a much greater proportion of total output nevertheless. It would take scores of thousands of corner shops to produce an output equal to ICI, especially when the value of the overseas output of this UK based multi-national is taken into account. Reasons for the existence of and survival of small firms include:

(i) entrepreneurial choice–the owners of small firms may prefer the intimate surroundings and personal contacts of the business environment.

(ii) limited market size–this applies particularly to the provision of services such as hairdressing in local geographical areas.

(iii) the demand for a personal or specialized service–again hairdressing provides a good example.

(iv) the existence of diseconomies of scale–in these circumstances, cost advantages will create a competitive advantage for small firms.

(v) the absence of economies of scale–many industries display an absence of noticeable economies or diseconomies of scale, and there is likely to be a wide distribution of different-sized firms competing side by side in such an industry. In other industries there may be 'niches' in the market, or in the supply of specialist services to bigger firms, which can best be filled by small businesses.

(vi) 'sunrise' industries–a 'sunrise' industry is a completely new industry based on a new technology or a new product, such as digital watches. To start with, demand is small (accounting for the fact that firms are small). However, the small firms may grow into large businesses or be taken over by large firms in other industries, as the market expands over time.

(vii) 'sunset' or 'geriatric' firms–small firms sometimes survive for a while in a terminal stage of decline before their eventual demise, having shrunk from a much larger previous size. Such firms may be members of a declining industry or they may simply be badly managed firms or enterprises which have run out of entrepreneurial drive.

Answer plan

1 Define a firm as a business enterprise, producing or dealing in goods or services for sale.
2 Show how ICI and a small corner shop fit into the economist's definition of a firm.
3 Offer a definition of a 'small' firm, and suggest how small firms compare to large firms in terms of contribution to national output.
4 Carefully explain (with examples) a number of reasons why small firms are significant.

Question 2 Distinguish briefly between internal and external economies of scale. How might economies of scale affect market structure? *(AEB: November, 1989)*

Understanding the Question Internal economies of scale are those economies resulting in lower long-run average production costs, that result from the growth of a firm's scale of operations and fixed capacity. They come from the firm's own decision-making processes. By contrast, external economies of scale occur when individual firms within the industry benefit from lower average production costs as a result of the growth of the scale of the whole industry. If all member firms merged to form a monopoly, these external scale economies would become internal. If there is only room in the market for one firm benefiting from full internal economies of scale, a 'natural' monopoly is promoted. Likewise, a 'natural' oligopoly would be expected in a market with room for several firms benefiting from full scale economies. External economies of scale may affect geographical aspects of market structure; for example, the emergence of specialist subcontracting firms within the industry in a particular region may encourage other firms within the industry to locate close to the firms offering the specialist production services.

Answer plan

1 Carefully distinguish between internal and external economies of scale.
2 Illustrate internal economies of scale with a LRATC curve.
3 Briefly suggest causes of internal economies of scale (at plant and firm level).
4 Explain, with examples, how internal scale economies may promote monopoly and oligopoly.
5 Explain, with examples, how external scale economies may affect the geographical structure of markets.

Multiple Choice Questions

Question 3

Industry   *Number employed (thousands)*

Industry	Year 1	Year 2	Year 3
Shipbuilding and marine engineering	243	211	205
Textiles	836	776	767
Vehicles	891	886	862

The conclusion that these industries are declining is valid if
(a) the industries have become more capital intensive
(b) output varies directly with the number employed
(c) the size of the working population has remained the same
(d) diseconomies of scale have been experienced.

Understanding the Question The correct answer to the question is **(b)**. Alternative **(a)** is completely incorrect since a growth in capital intensity could accompany a growth in output and a decline in the labour force. Alternatives **(c)** and **(d)** are simply irrelevant to the meaning of the question.

Question 4 Which of the following statements offers the best explanation of the existence of economies of scale?
(a) Demand for some products is greater than for others.
(b) Labour becomes more efficient when added to fixed capital.
(c) Large firms can obtain the benefits of monopoly.
(d) Some factors of production are not easily divisible.

Understanding the Question Demand must of course be sufficient to allow a firm to benefit from economies of scale, but demand does not explain such economies. Alternative **(b)** refers to the short-run laws of returns which should be carefully distinguished from long-run returns to scale and economies of scale. The benefits of monopoly are not directly related to economies of scale, though the market power which a large firm may possess can reduce the cost of inputs. The best answer is **(d)**, which is based on the concept of **indivisibilities**.

Data Response Questions

Question 5 Read the passage below and then answer the questions which follow.

An important part of the case for big business rests on the claim that across a wide range of industries modern technology requires plants of a very large absolute size and this means that they can supply a relatively large fraction of the domestic market. Anything less would mean that unit production costs are higher than they need be and are therefore certainly above those of foreign competitors.

But an efficient allocation of a given set of resources is one which yields both a maximum and 'correct' (in the sense of best meeting consumers' demands) output. The central result from monopoly theory is that resource allocation will be distorted by the ability of monopolists to restrict output below a level that would best accord with consumer demand (that is price would be greater than marginal cost). Hence from a given bundle of resources economic welfare is likely to be lower in the presence of monopoly. To the extent, therefore, that large size is correlated with monopoly (itself a subject of some dispute) allocative inefficiency will result.

However, this may still strike an uncommitted bystander as not getting to the heart of the matter. Increasingly high on the list of problems associated with very large firms is their alleged effect on the environment. What is the point of these firms ensuring, for example, that they are both technically and economically efficient in a *private* sense if, in their achievement, they are simultaneously generating very high social costs which do not enter their accounts but which nevertheless impose enormous burdens on the community?

Michael Utton, *The Political Economy of Big Business*, Blackwell

(a) Explain in your own words the economic argument lying behind the first paragraph.   (5)
(b) Why, under monopoly, is price normally greater than marginal cost?   (6)
(c) Why might the correlation of large size with monopoly be 'a subject of some dispute', (paragraph 2)?   (7)
(d) Discuss the implications for the community of large firms 'generating very high social costs which do not enter their accounts' (paragraph 3).   (7)

(Oxford: June, 1988)

Understanding the Question
(a) You should base this part of your answer on plant-level economies of scale; the concept of minimum efficient plant size; and the long-run average total cost curve.
(b) Although the profit-maximizing level of output may be located where MR = MC, price will be higher than MC since AR > MR, due to the nature of the demand curve facing the monopolist. The assumption of the profit-maximizing objective on the part of the monopolist leads to this result.
(c) Although big firms may produce a large proportion of domestically-produced output, they often produce internationally-traded goods and are vulnerable to competition from imports. At the other extreme, a small corner shop may effectively be a monopoly in an isolated village without a bus service to the nearest town.
(d) The firms are generating negative externalities leading to a misallocation of resources. This implies the need for public policy (such as taxation and regulation) to try to correct the market failure by closing the divergency between private and social costs (*see* Unit 8).

10.6 Further reading

Artis, M. J., editor, *The UK Economy*, 12 edition (Weidenfeld & Nicolson, 1989).
Chapter 4: Industry.

Morris, D., editor, *The Economic System in the UK*, 3rd edition (Oxford University Press, 1986).
Chapter 3: The Behaviour of Firms.

A Review of Monopolies and Mergers Policy, A Consultative Document (HMSO Command 7198, 1978).

11 The Capital Market and the Stock Exchange

11.1 Points of perspective

In Unit 10 we explained how firms grow through a process of either **internal** or **external** growth, or through a combination of both. We now examine how a firm might finance the process of growth, involving as it does the investment in new plant and productive capacity in the case of internal growth, and the acquisition of other firms by take-over or merger when external growth takes place.

11.2 Underlying concepts

1 Saving and Investment

Although saving and investment have a similar meaning in everyday language, the economist uses each word in a distinct way. **Saving** is defined as **income which is not spent on consumption**, including funds that simply lie idle. In contrast, **investment** involves the **productive use of savings** in the purchase of capital goods, stocks, and raw materials. As a generalization, **households** make **savings decisions** and **firms** make **investment decisions**. Nevertheless, 60 to 75% of the investment carried out by British firms is financed by **internally generated funds**, when a firm provides its own savings out of revenue from the sale of its output.

Alternatively, firms may be able to obtain savings directly from households, for example by advertizing the sale of **shares**. It is more usual, however, for firms to gain access to the savings of households via **financial intermediaries** such as banks, insurance companies and pension funds, known generally as the **financial institutions**.

2 Alternative sources of finance

It is useful to distinguish between **internal** and **external** sources of finance, taking care not to confuse these terms with the concepts of internal and external growth which were mentioned earlier:

(i) Internal finance. We have already defined internal finance as the savings which a firm generates internally out of revenue. These funds are sometimes known as **ploughed-back profits**. It is worth repeating that self-finance provides by far the most important source of funds for British industry.

(ii) External finance. Some 25 to 40% of the financial requirements of firms in the private sector of the economy are raised through borrowing, the sale of shares, and government grants or subsidy. The main forms of external finance are:

(a) Trade credit. This refers to the practice of delaying the payment of bills for as long as possible while trying to persuade customers to settle their debts as quickly as possible in order to improve cash flow. Trade credit is equivalent to an interest-free loan.

(b) Borrowing from banks. Bank loans account for approximately 10 to 20% of the funds which are available to firms from all sources in the United Kingdom. British banks have often been criticized for failing to provide long-term risk capital to British industry. But traditionally British banks have lent to finance investment in **working or circulating capital**, such as the building-up of stocks, in preference to **fixed investment** in new plant. We shall examine this criticism later in the unit, paying particular attention to the financial needs of small firms.

(c) Provision of finance by the government. This takes two main forms: firstly, the provision of loans to the private sector, and secondly, government grants and subsidies, for example in the form of regional aid and support policies to agriculture.

(d) Raising funds on the capital market. Students commonly confuse the **capital market** and the **Stock Exchange**, and exaggerate the importance of both markets as sources of finance for British industry. The capital market is not a single institution. It comprises all the institutions, including banks, insurance companies and pension funds, which are concerned with either the supply of or demand for long-term funds, or securities which are claims on existing capital. It is thus the market for **long-term loanable funds,** as distinct from the **money market** which is the market for short-term funds.

11.3   Essential knowledge

1 The role of the Stock Exchange

'When the capital development of a country becomes a by-product of the activities of a casino, the job is likely to be ill done.'–J. M. Keynes, in the *General Theory*.

The Stock Exchange is often criticized as being a place of mere speculation, a casino where dealers are interested only in making immediate capital gains through buying securities at one price and selling at another. This criticism stems from the fact that the Stock Exchange is the **secondary** or 'second-hand' part of the capital market. The Stock Exchange is viewed as a casino by its critics because it has little direct role in the raising of long-term funds or risk capital for industry. Figure 11.1 illustrates why this is so. The actual raising of new capital takes place when public companies or the government decide to issue and sell new **marketable securities**. Companies may sell long-dated securities which guarantee a fixed rate of interest (**debentures or corporate bonds**) or they may sell a stake in the ownership of the company (**shares,** including **equity**). New issues of shares can be sold when a company goes public for the first time, or when an existing public company decides to raise extra capital by a new equity issue, usually a **rights issue**. A rights issue gives existing shareholders the right to buy at a favourable price. In the 1980s, a pernicious fashion started in the USA: the finance of 'hostile' take-over bids through the medium of 'junk-bonds'. A 'junk-bond' is a corporate bond which carries a big element of risk since the company that issues it has few assets to secure the loan. Consequently, 'junk-bonds' earn a high rate of interest to compensate for the risk. The funds raised from the 'junk-bond' sale are used to finance the take-over of the 'victim' company, whose assets are then liquidated to pay the interest on the bonds!

New issues are not sold on the Stock Exchange, though occasionally the new issues of small companies are **placed** through Stock Exchange firms. Instead, new issues are sold on the **primary part** of the capital market, usually through newspaper advertisements arranged by merchant banks, or through direct contact with existing shareholders when a rights issue is made. It is important to stress that the amount of new capital raised through new issues in any one year is only a small fraction of the total trading taking place in existing securities on the Stock Exchange. It follows that most share sales are second-hand deals in which one member of the general public or a financial institution sells an existing security to another person or institution. The person who buys the security prefers to hold an interest or dividend-earning financial asset instead of money, whereas the seller is switching out of securities in order to store his wealth in the more liquid form of money. Thus the majority of security sales reflect individual decisions, called **portfolio balance decisions**, to adjust the form in which personal wealth is held, rather than a decision to supply risk capital to industry.

Nevertheless, it is often argued that the Stock Exchange has important **indirect roles** in the provision of capital and the promotion of efficiency in British industry:

(i) When a private company decides to 'go public', its principal objective is to raise capital by securing access to the capital market. A Stock Exchange quotation, whereby the company's shares are *listed* and the market price *quoted* on the Stock Exchange, is certainly useful, and perhaps essential, if the general public are to be persuaded to buy the shares. New issues of shares would find fewer buyers if it was impossible to resell the securities on the Stock Exchange.

(ii) The Stock Exchange Council examines the financial structure and control of all quoted companies. There may be greater public confidence in companies if only the shares of 'reputable' companies are quoted.

(iii) The Stock Exchange has an important role in the restructuring of British industry in the face of changing technology and demand. Companies which fail to adapt will perform badly, and low profitability will cause share prices to fall. The quotation of a public company's shares on the Stock Exchange provides both an indicator of performance and a means through which the company can be taken over by new owners who believe they can use the company's assets more profitably. The threat of a future take-over can also provide an incentive for the existing managers to improve their performance.

Fig 11.1 The stock exchange and the capital market

2 The Government and the capital market

Only a small proportion of the securities traded on the capital market and the Stock Exchange represent either new or old capital raised by British industrial companies. A large proportion of securities are **overseas securities**. Others are **British Government Securities**, usually called **gilt-edged securities** or simply **gilts**. Gilts are similar to debentures although the government sells far more gilts than the private sector sells debentures. Thus gilts secure a fixed-term loan to the government, after which the gilts mature and the face value is paid back. In addition, the government guarantees to pay a fixed interest each year during the life of the security. What is not guaranteed is the day-to-day market price at which the security can be resold second-hand on the Stock Exchange, or indeed the price which the government can persuade the general public to pay when it sells the gilt as a new issue.

The total quantity of new gilts which the government sells each year is strongly dependent on the size of the budget **deficit** or **surplus** and the **Public Sector Borrowing Requirement** (PSBR) or **Public Sector Debt Repayment** (PSDR). Generally speaking, the higher the level of public spending in relation to tax revenue, the larger the PSBR and the government's need to borrow on the capital market. A large issue of gilts tends to depress their price, thereby converting the guaranteed interest rate or yield into a higher effective or true interest rate. In this way, public spending may 'crowd out' the private sector in the capital market, since the sale of gilts eventually raises interest rates and the cost of borrowing by companies. By contrast, a budget surplus and PSDR allow the government to repay a debt. There is less need to sell new gilts so pressure on interest rates may be relieved.

3 The role of the financial institutions

It is widely believed that a large proportion of the shares in British companies are owned by small shareholders who are ordinary members of the general public. As the following table shows, this is no longer the case.

These figures indicate that individuals now directly own well under half of all shares whereas financial institutions, including insurance companies, pension funds, and unit and investment trusts, own the greater proportion. However, one result of the privatization of previously nationalized industries such as British Telecom and British Gas in the 1980s was to increase, at least temporarily, the number of individuals owning shares. This was part of a policy of 'popular capitalism' i.e. extending share ownership by reserving a proportion of newly issued shares for employees and small shareholders, rather than for the financial institutions. Banks own relatively little equity, though they control a substantial amount through the management and advice given to pension funds and to ordinary shareholding customers of the banks. In fact, the degree of concentration of control over shares in the hands of the financial institutions is greater than the statistics of ownership suggest. The growing power of the financial institutions is an important cause of imperfection in the capital market. Nevertheless, it can be said in defence of the institutions that they represent the growth of the **indirect** ownership of industry by ordinary workers via their contributions to pension and insurance schemes. Yet while it is undoubtedly true that workers receive the benefit of ownership from the pensions and insurance endowments which are financed through company profits, it is much more debatable whether the growing indirect ownership of shares via the financial institutions gives workers any real control over industry.

The ownership of company shares (percentages)

	1963	1975	1981	1983
Persons and charities	56.0	39.8	30.4	27.0
Insurance companies	10.1	16.0	20.5	22.0
Pension funds	6.5	16.8	26.7	29.0
Investment trusts	11.2	10.6	6.8	6.0
Unit trusts	1.4	4.0	3.6	4.0
Banks	1.4	0.7	0.3	—
Industrial and commercial companies	5.1	2.9	5.1	5.0
Public sector	1.4	3.6	3.0	3.0
Overseas holders	6.9	5.6	3.6	4.0
	100.	100	100	100

(Source: *Stock Exchange Surveys*)

4 The financing of small businesses

Access to the capital market tends to be restricted to public companies, especially those with a Stock Exchange quotation. Since most small businesses are sole traders, partnerships or private companies, they must rely on bank borrowing, rather than on the sale of securities on the capital market, as their principal source of external finance. Many owners of small businesses complain that banks treat them much less favourably than large companies when providing loans to finance investment. This view was supported in the report of the **Wilson Committee** on **The Financing of Small Firms**, published in 1979. Nevertheless, there are several reasons why investments by small firms are riskier than those undertaken by large companies:

(i) Large firms are likely to engage in a wider range of investments. If one investment fails, the likelihood that at least some of the other projects will succeed reduces the risk of bankruptcy. In any case, large firms usually have greater cash reserves to draw upon in just such a crisis.

(ii) Large public companies are less highly **geared**. A high gearing means that a large proportion of a company's assets are financed by borrowing rather than by shareholders' funds (accumulated profits and shares). Firms must usually pay a fixed rate of interest on their bank loans and debentures, even when no profits are being made. A high **gearing ratio** increases a firm's vulnerability to bankruptcy when business is bad. In contrast, a low-geared public company may survive a recession by suspending the payment of dividends to shareholders. Small businesses are usually highly geared, since they possess little or no equity capital. Banks may simply regard them as less attractive risks in comparison with lower-geared larger companies.

Yet **bank overdrafts** have always been the principal source of external funds for small businesses, be they unincorporated sales traders or private companies. Outside the banks, the **Industrial and Commercial Finance Corporation** (ICFC) is an important provider of start-up finance. Between 1945, when it was set up, and 1983, the ICFC invested £900 million in small and medium-sized firms, supporting more than 7000 companies.

In the 1980's the Conservative Government actively encouraged the growth of small businesses as a means of reducing unemployment and as an escape from recession. An **Enterprise Allowance Scheme** has encouraged the unemployed to start up their own businesses. Applicants to the scheme receive a weekly cash payment to offset loss of unemployment pay while establishing their businesses, also offsetting, it is hoped, the difficulties caused by a lack of start-up capital and the reluctance of banks to lend to the unemployed. The Government also created **Enterprise Zones**, which are inner-city areas exempt from rates and various bureaucratic controls. These may also have attracted new businesses though there is some debate as to whether they have simply caused firms to shift their location, thereby causing areas of 'blight' to emerge in areas insufficiently lucky to have been designated as Enterprise Zones.

The Wilson Committee suggested a number of ways in which the financial position of small businesses could be assisted. The recommendation of a **state-backed guarantee scheme for bank loans** was adopted in 1981. Under the scheme the state rather than a bank takes most of the risk if a business fails and cannot pay back a bank loan. The scheme has encouraged banks to grant **term loans** to finance long-term growth, thus replacing the more traditional shorter-term overdraft. The Wilson Committee further proposed the creation of **'over-the-counter' markets** throughout the UK in which the shares of small public, but unlisted, companies could be traded. Such 'share-shops' might encourage a revival of personal share ownership and the local financing of businesses. While 'over-the-counter' markets have yet to emerge in any numbers, the Stock Exchange itself created in 1980 an **unlisted securities market** (USM) as a means for small companies to go public and to tap the capital market, without the expense of a full Stock Exchange listing. Compared to a full Stock Exchange launch, a company can go public on the USM by selling only a very small proportion of its equity. Few of the many companies launched since 1980 on the USM have actually used it to raise new capital; most have simply been floated to enable the company's owners to obtain a market valuation of their capital. Indeed within its short life the USM has established a reputation for volatility, largely because the few shares made available in the 'high-flying' companies launched on the USM have created conditions for speculation and rapid fluctuations in share price. Before the Stock Exchange crash of 1987, the USM provided a useful route, or half-way stage, for an eventual full Stock Exchange listing and quotation for successful and fast-growing companies (e.g. Amstrad). Indeed, because of the success of the USM, the Stock Exchange launched a new Third Market in 1987; to provide a market in the shares of very small, growing, public companies. However, both markets have become moribund, and the Third Market is likely to be merged with the USM, whose own future is in some doubt.

Finally, the Wilson Committee advised the Government to establish a **Small Firms Investment Company** (SFIC) and an **English Development Agency**, intended to be the beginning of a full-scale **Small Business Agency**. These bodies would function as intermediaries through which small businesses might raise equity capital in the manner of the successful **Scottish and Welsh Development Agencies**. Although this idea has not yet been taken up, the 1981 Budget announced a **Business Start-up Scheme** to provide tax allowances for investment by individuals in new businesses. Because of its complexity and limited nature, the Business Start-up Scheme had little impact. In 1983 it was replaced by a **Business Expansion Scheme**, a rather simpler and more attractive package of tax advantages. Under the scheme, a number of managed funds have been set up to attract savings from private individuals for investment in growing new firms.

11.4 Links with other topics

In this unit we have considered the financing of businesses in the private sector of the economy. We go on to examine government financial assistance to industry and the financing of investment by nationalized industries in Unit 12. The financing of public investment in roads, schools and other forms of **social capital** is discussed in Unit 15 on public finance.

11.5 Question practice

Essay Question

Question 1 How many firms finance growth? Discuss whether shortages in the supply of funds have caused the low rate of investment in manufacturing industry in the United Kingdom.   (*AEB: November, 1988*)

Understanding the Question The first part of the question requires a brief coverage of each of the alternative sources of finance explained in the unit. Draw special attention to the distinction between internal and external sources of finance, indicating that successful businesses of all sizes rely extensively upon self-finance or ploughed-back profits. Mention the distinction between public and private companies and the fact that only public companies have easy access to the capital market as a source of externally-provided finance. The role of bank borrowing also deserves some explanation.

It is well known that UK firms invest a smaller percentage of their turnover in new capacity and research and development than their competitors in Europe and Japan. (If you have the information, then briefly quote the evidence.) Many businessmen and economists blame the banks, and other financial institutions, together with the 'short-termism' of the City of London. In the latter context, it is argued that the nature of the UK capital market makes UK public quoted companies much more vulnerable to unwelcome 'hostile' take-over bids than German and Japanese companies. United Kingdom public companies may be tempted to divert profits away from investment and 'R and D' in order to increase dividends paid to shareholders. This may boost share prices, at least in the short run, thus making public companies more expensive and less attractive to purchase. By contrast, there are proportionately many more private companies and fewer public companies in Germany and Japan and a much smaller proportion of the equity of public quoted companies is available for purchase.

To earn a high mark you must discuss the demand for investment funds as well as their supply. Low business confidence or poor expectations of future profitability are relevant here and you must also discuss the possibility that high interest rates reduce the demand for investment funds. Finally, you might introduce 'vicious circle' arguments to provide a link between 'supply-side' and 'demand-side' explanations. For example, low investment may lead to lack of competitiveness, reducing profitability and business confidence, leading to further cuts in investment and so on.

Answer plan

1 List the sources of finance, emphasizing the distinction between internal and external sources.
2 Briefly explain each source you have listed.
3 Quote evidence on the UK's low comparative investment rate.
4 Explain how shortages in the supply of funds may be responsible, e.g. poor profitability reduces sources of internal finance; inadequacies of financial institutions and the capital market.
5 Introduce alternative explanation, e.g. 'demand-side' explanations; the effects of City 'short-termism'; the high cost of funds.
6 Link 'supply-side' and 'demand-side' explanations, e.g. in terms of 'vicious' circle arguments.
7 Reach an overall conclusion as to whether shortages in the supply of funds have caused a low rate of investment.

Question 2 Distinguish briefly between the money market and the capital market. Evaluate the role of the capital market in the United Kingdom economy.   (*AEB: November, 1989*)

Understanding the Question There is not necessarily a clear-cut distinction between the money market and the capital market but the money market is usually regarded as the set of financial markets dealing in highly liquid or short-dated financial assets and securities whereas the capital market is the set of financial markets dealing in the long-dated and undated counterparts. If the government, a company or a financial institution wishes to borrow for a few days or weeks in order to relieve a temporary liquidity problem, it may raise funds in the money market. By contrast, as the name implies, the capital market is the appropriate market in which to raise funds (by share issue or long-term borrowing) to finance long-term investment in fixed capital. In this unit we have covered the 'traditional' capital market (comprising the new issues market and the secondary market) in which UK-based firms and the government raise long-term finance. You might also draw attention to the much more rapid growth in recent years of the 'international' capital market (or Eurobond market) which encompasses all the world's major financial centres such as London, New York and Tokyo. This is a truly global capital market in which securities—predominantly fixed interest bonds—are sold worldwide. Typically, a large multi-national company or the government of a developing country may raise funds on the Eurobond market because the size of the issue is too large for the capital market of a single country.

We explain the money market in Unit 17. The main money market with which A-level candidates are familiar is the Discount Market upon which commercial bills and Treasury bills are traded. However, there are other money markets, such as the inter-bank market where banks lend funds to each other as a part of the process of managing their asset portfolios.

Answer plan

1 Explain the money market as a source of short-term finance, and the capital market as a source of long-term finance.
2 Mention the main institutions of the London Discount Market (one of the money markets), and the principal financial assets traded (*see* Unit 17).
3 Briefly distinguish between the 'traditional' capital market and the Eurobond or 'international' capital market.
4 Distinguish between the 'primary' (new issues) market and the secondary market within the capital market. Also, distinguish between the main financial assets traded (shares, corporate bonds, gilts).
5 Draw on the section in the unit on the role of the Stock Exchange (which forms the main secondary market).
6 Critically evaluate this role (and the role of the new issues market) drawing again on the material in this unit.

Data Response Questions

Question 3 'The Stock Exchange's new **unlisted securities** market was started yesterday with two new issues to join the ten companies already in the new class of stocks. Both new stocks **outperformed the market**. Jobbers and brokers maintained that the new market had not made any difference and that the success was due to the quality of the new companies. The new market is designed to give a home to smaller companies which want their shares traded regularly and easily. Previously, such companies had used the facilities under rule 163(2) originally intended for companies which wished to issue shares on a one-off basis such as football clubs. Companies had been using the 163(2) rule when they were too small for a **full Stock Exchange quotation**.'

(*Times Newspapers Ltd*)

(a) Explain what is meant by the three phrases which are in bold type in the passage.
(b) What factors would lead a small company to use the new market facilities?

(*London: January, 1983*)

Understanding the Question This is a question testing the knowledge and understanding of recent changes in the United Kingdom capital market, changes that are fully explained in the unit. Although a company might use the USM as a means of raising capital, it has largely been used as a means by which the owners of a company can **capitalize** (achieve a market value for) the assets they own.

11.6 Further reading

Artis, M. J., editor, *The UK Economy*, 12th edition (Weidenfeld & Nicolson, 1989).
Chapter 2: The Monetary Credit and Fiscal Systems.

Griffiths, A., and Wall, S., *Applied Economics*, 4th edition (Longman, 1991).
Chapter 2: Company accounts as a source of financial information.

12 Industrial Policy

12.1 Points of perspective

In this unit we examine the meaning of industrial policy and assess the effectiveness of the industrial policy implemented by the UK government in recent years. We shall examine three main elements of industrial policy: **competition policy**; **private versus public ownership of industry** and **regional policy**, before concluding the unit with a discussion of the policy mix appropriate for tackling the important industrial problem of **deindustrialization**, or the decline of manufacturing industry.

12.2 Underlying concepts

1 The meaning of industrial policy

Industrial policy is part of the government's **micro-economic policy** which aims to improve the economic performance of individual economic agents, firms and industries on the **'supply-side'** of the economy. Since the 1930s, when industrial policy first began as a response to the Great Depression, all British governments have had some sort of industrial policy. However, significant changes have occurred in the nature of the policy and also, the importance attached by different governments to industrial policy in comparison to other aspects of economic policy. The most far-reaching changes occurred in the 1980s after the decline of **Keynesianism** as the prevailing orthodoxy influencing British governments and the ascendancy of **monetarism**, **supply-side economics** and other elements of the **neo-classical revival**.

2 Industrial policy before 1979

For much of the period from 1945 until 1979, successive British governments pursued an **interventionist** industrial policy, reflecting the Keynesian view that economic problems result from a failure of market forces and industrial problems can be cured (or at least reduced) by appropriate government intervention. During the Keynesian era, industrial policy (and Keynesian economic policy in general) extended the roles of government and state planning in the economy.

3 Industrial policy under the Conservatives after 1979

By way of contrast, the industrial policy pursued by Conservative Government in the 1980s and early 1990s has been **anti-interventionist** and based on the belief that the correct role of government is as an **enabling agency**, to encourage rather than reduce the role of market forces and to create the conditions in which market forces can work effectively and efficiently. But although recent Conservative governments have disbanded an interventionist industrial policy in favour of a more free-market approach, in some respects the importance attached to industrial policy in the government's overall economic strategy has actually increased. During the Keynesian era, industrial policy and micro-economic policy were generally subordinate and subserviant to macro-economic policy. **Keynesian macro-economic policy** was aimed overwhelmingly at the **'demand-side'** of the economy, attempting to influence and control output and employment by **managing the level of aggregate demand** in the economy. But monetarists and other 'free-marketeers' believe that Keynesian demand management policies led to inflation rather than to full employment and economic growth. They also believe that the Keynesian concern with demand management diverted attention away from the 'supply-side' of the economy, where the real problems that must be tackled stand in the way of increased output and employment. It is perhaps not surprising, therefore, that after the monetarist or neo-classical 'counter-revolution' of the 1970s, the 1980s and after, macro-economic policy has generally been subordinated to a 'supply-side' micro-economic policy in which a **free-market orientated industrial policy** has been elevated to a key position.

12.3 Essential information

1 Competition policy

For over 40 years since its inception in 1948, competition policy has formed an important part of the UK government's wider industrial policy. **Competition policy** is part of industrial policy that covers **monopolies**, **mergers** and **restrictive trading practices** and we shall now look at each of these in turn.

2 Statutory monopoly

Monopoly policy in the UK is seldom concerned with **pure monopoly** – rather it attempts to regulate **highly concentrated industries** dominated by a few large firms. **'Oligopoly policy'** might be a better descriptive label. For policy purposes, the UK government defines a **statutory monopoly** as existing if: either one firm has at least 25 per cent of the market for the supply or acquisition of particular goods and services (a **scale monopoly**); or a number of firms, which together have a 25 per cent share and so conduct their affairs to restrict competition (a **complex monopoly**).

3 The theoretical background to monopoly policy

In Unit 6 we have seen how economic efficiency and output are likely to be maximized and consumer sovereignty and welfare promoted, when industries and markets are perfectly competitive. This provides the theoretical basis of the government's policy towards monopoly, mergers and restrictive trading practices. Compared to a perfectly competitive market, monopolies may be expected to reduce output and raise prices and they may have less incentive to innovate. Monopolies may also exploit their producer sovereignty by manipulating consumer wants, restricting choice and discriminating 'unfairly' between different customers.

Nevertheless, as we have also seen, the argument that monopolies restrict output and raise prices assumes that monopolies and perfectly competitive firms have similar cost curves. When **economies of scale** are possible, this is unlikely to be the case. Indeed a **'natural' monopoly** exists when limited market size makes it impossible for more than one firm to benefit from full economies of scale. It has been argued that splitting up of a 'natural' monopoly (such as the gas industry) into a large number of competitive firms would lead to unnecessary duplication of distribution networks. Thus, there is a strong case for these industries to continue to be organized as monopolies. The public policy choise is not so much a choice between competition and monopoly; rather it is a choice between **state monopolies run as nationalized industries** and **private monopoly subject to severe and effective public regulation**. Monopolies are also sometimes justified on the grounds that they promote rather than reduce innovation (since the expectation of monopoly profits allowed by barriers to entry, creates an incentive to develop new products and technologies). They are also justified on the grounds that large domestically-based firms might be able to compete in world markets.

4 Cartels and fully-unified monopolies

Whether innovation is likely to be increased or diminished by monopoly will depend to some extent upon the reason for the creation of the monopoly. It is useful to divide monopolies into:
(a) Cartels. A cartel is usually regarded as the worst form of monopoly, as regards to public interest, since it is likely to exhibit most of the disadvantages of monopoly with few (if any) of the benefits. A **cartel** is a **price ring** which is formed when independent firms make a restrictive agreement to charge the same price, and possibly to restrict output. A cartel acts as a monopoly in the marketing of goods, but the benefits of economies of scale are unlikely to occur because the physical or technical integration of the productive capacity of the cartel's members does not take place. Consumer choice is restricted, and cartels tend to keep inefficient firms in business while the more efficient members make monopoly profits. In these circumstances, it is probable that the incentive to innovate by developing new products and methods of production will be lacking. Cartels are thus **dynamically inefficient**.
(b) Full-unified monopoly. A **fully-unified** or **fully-integrated monopoly** may result by accident rather than design. A dynamic firm grows and benefits from economies of scale, becoming a monopoly as the reward for successful competition! The monopoly position is the result of the firm's success in innovation and reducing costs – all of which indicate that the firm is **dynamically efficient**. A fully-unified monopoly is thus likely to be the 'spin-off' of essentially 'benign' motives for growth. Once the monopoly has been established, the firm may continue to behave well, retaining its innovative habits and using its monopoly profit to finance new developments, though government regulation may be necessary to ensure continued 'good behaviour'.

5 The cost-benefit approach of monopoly policy

Because it is recognized that monopoly can be good or bad depending upon circumstances, UK monopoly policy has always taken the pragmatic view that each case of a monopoly or trading practice that restricts competition must be judged on its merits. If the likely costs resulting from the reduction of competition exceed the benefits, the monopoly should be prevented but, if the likely benefits exceed the costs, monopoly should be permitted, provided that it does not abuse its position and exploit the consuming public.

6 The Monopolies and Mergers Commission and the Office of Fair Trading

UK monopoly policy is implemented by the **Office of Fair Trading (OFT)** and the **Monopolies and Mergers Commission (MMC)**, which are responsible to a government ministry, the **Department of Trade and Industry (DTI)**. The OFT uses **market structure, conduct and performance indicators** to systematically scan or screen the UK economy for evidence of monopoly abuse. **Concentration ratios** provide evidence of monopolistic market structures, while market conduct indicators allow the OFT to monitor anti-competitive business behaviour. **Conduct indicators** include:

  (i) consumer and trade complaints;
 (ii) evidence of parallel pricing, price discrimination and price leadership;
(iii) evidence of merger activity;
(iv) the ratio of advertising expenditure to sales.

The four main **performance indicators** used to measure business efficiency are:

  (i) price movements;
 (ii) changes in profit margins;
(iii) the ratio of capital employed to turnover;
(iv) the return on capital employed.

  When the OFT discovers evidence of statutory monopoly which, it believes is likely to be against the public interest, it refers the firms to the MMC for further investigation. In most cases, the OFT asks the MMC to decide the relatively narrow issue of whether a particular trading practice is in the public interest, and not to address the wider issue of whether the firm should be split up. The MMC interprets the public interest largely in terms of the effect upon competitiveness of the trading practices it is asked to investigate. The Commission does not possess any powers to implement or enforce its recommendations. Instead, it reports to the DTI, which may either implement some or all of the recommendations, shelve the report and do nothing, or take action completely contrary to the MMC's recommendations. For example, in 1989 the MMC recommended in its report into monopoly in the brewing industry, that the major breweries should be forced to sell off all public houses they owned in excess of 2000. However, the Government eventually rejected this recommendation. Usually, however, the government complies with the spirit of the MMC's report. The government has quite wide powers to take action (including the ability to make an order requiring that firms split up or sell off assets). But in practice, these order-making powers are seldom, if ever, used. Currently, it is usual for the Government to ask the OFT to talk with the firms to persuade them to alter their business behaviour voluntarily. Firms may be asked to abandon any undesirable practices and to give undertakings about their future conduct.

7 Alternative strategic approaches to monopoly policy

Ever since the establishment of the Monopolies Commission in 1948, UK monopoly policy has been based on a pragmatic **regulatory and investigatory approach**, **watching out** for monopoly abuse and **investigating** firms or industries where abuse or inefficiency is suspected. Relatively few firms and takeover bids are actually investigated—the rationale being that the possibility of an MMC investigation creates sufficient incentive for most large firms to behave themselves and resist the temptation to exploit their monopoly power. However, although the '**watchdog' investigatory/ regulatory role** of the MMC has been central to UK monopoly policy, there are a number of alternative strategic approaches that might be used. These include:

  (i) The compulsory breaking-up of all monopolies;
 (ii) The use of price controls to restrict monopoly abuse;
(iii) Taxing monopoly profits;
(iv) The public ownership of monopoly;
 (v) Privatizing monopolies;
(vi) Removal of barriers to entry.

8 The growing influence of the 'theory of contestable markets'

It is generally agreed that **privatization** alone cannot eliminate the problem of monopoly abuse, since it merely changes the nature of the problem back from **public** or **state monopoly** to **private monopoly** and the commercial exploitation of a monopoly position. The fact that the privatization of the telecommunication and gas monopolies has been accompanied by the setting up of regulatory bodies such as **OFTEL** and **OFGAS**, which provide a source of regulation additional to that available from the MMC and the OFT, is a recognition of this problem.

One method of exposing monopolies – including the newly-privatized utility industries – to increased competition, is to **remove artificial barriers to entry**. The government can remove the protected legal monopoly status enjoyed for example, by the Post Office for letter deliveries and by bus companies, airline and commerical TV and radio companies. Access to British Telecom's distribution network of landlines can be given to a competitor such as Mercury Communications and private power companies can be allowed to rent the services of the national electricity distribution grid. Import competition can also be encouraged. This can be quite effective in reducing the market power of public and private monopolies producing internationally traded goods and services but it would be less effective in reducing the monopoly power of utility industries, whose products are not generally traded internationally, and consequently are not vulnerable to import competition.

Support for the belief, that the most effective (and simplest) way of dealing with the problem of monopoly is to remove any artificial barriers to entry, has been provided by an important 'new' theory known as the **theory of contestable markets**. Before the advent of this theory (and of the wider neo-classical revival of which the theory of 'contestable' markets is a part), monopoly policy and other aspects of industrial policy involved an ever-increasing extension of regulation by government into the activities of private sector firms. Increased intervention was justified by the belief that regulatory powers must be strong enough to countervail the growing power of large business organizations and make monopolies behave in a more competitive fashion. But, one unforeseen result of the spread of government regulation of industry has been that powerful established firms, that the system of regulation was intended to control, have often been able to use the regulatory system to their own advantage. The beneficiaries of regulation have become the regulated firms themselves, rather than consumers or outside firms attempting to gain entry to the market. This has been because large established firms, already within the market, possess: political lobbying power to influence government and the regulators; and a monopoly of much technical information relevant to their industry.

Before the advent of the theory of 'contestable' markets, monopoly was normally defined by the number of firms in the market and by the share of the leading firms, measured by a concentration ratio. The basic dilemma, facing the policy makers, centred on how to reconcile the potential gains in productive efficiency, (that a monopolist's large scale of operation could allow) with the fact that lack of competitive pressure can lead to monopoly abuse and consumer exploitation. But in the theory of 'contestable' markets, monopoly is defined, not by the number of firms in the market nor by concentration ratios, but by the potential ease or difficulty with which new firms may enter the market. Monopoly is not regarded as a problem, even if there is only one established firm in the market; providing that an absence of barriers to entry and exit creates **the potential** for new firms to enter and contest the market. **Actual competition** in a market is not essential; **the threat of entry** by new firms is quite sufficient, according to the 'contestable' market theory, to ensure efficient and non-exploitive behaviour by existing firms within the market.

The theory of 'contestable' markets has had a major impact upon recent UK monopoly policy, under the Conservative Government, because it implies that a conventional regulatory policy is superfluous providing there is adequate potential for competition. Instead of interfering with firms' pricing and output policies, the government should restrict the role of its monopoly policy to discovering which industries and markets are potentially contestable and then developing conditions, by policies of deregulation, to remove barriers to entry and exit, ensuring that contestability is possible.

Appropriate **deregulation policies** suggested by the theory of 'contestable' markets include:
  (i)   the removal of licensing regimes for public transport and TV and radio transmissions;
 (ii)   removal of controls over ownership, such as exclusive public ownership;
(iii)   removal of pricing controls which act as a barrier to entry, such as those practised in the aviation industry.

9 Merger policy

Recent UK merger policy has also reflected the influence of the theory of 'contestable' markets, since a merger is only referred by the government for investigation by the MMC if the OFT has advised that, on the face of it, the merger might have significant anti-competitive effects. The OFT cannot itself make merger references to the MMC but the Office has important screening and advisory roles. The OFT keeps itself informed of all merger situations that might be eligible for a reference to the MMC, by picking up information from the firms themselves and from the financial press. Currently a merger is eligible for reference to the Government if the merger creates a combined company with at least 25 per cent of the market, or if the assets of the company being acquired are valued at £30m or more. It is generally assumed by the Government that mergers are beneficial; unless it can clearly be shown that the effects are likely to be adverse. In fact, very few eligible mergers are investigated; even fewer are declared against the public interest and prohibited. Critics argue that the policy is applied inconsistently and is much too weak. They believe that the stance of merger policy should be significantly changed to a presumption that mergers have adverse rather than beneficial effects, and that factors such as the 'national interest' should be considered as well as anti-competitive effects, (to prevent UK-owned firms falling into foreign hands).

10 EC merger policy

In 1990, a new EC merger policy came into operation to control the growing number of mergers within the European Community. The European Commission has long had powers to control mergers but, before 1990, it did not apply them systematically. Under the new system, the UK and other EC countries, will continue to use national policy to deal with smaller mergers, but the European Commission will adjudicate on larger mergers with a 'Community dimension'. As in UK merger policy, nearly all the EC's criteria for judging a merger are competition related. However, although the new EC policy is intended to provide a 'one-stop' regulatory system by clarifying the borderline between EC and national jurisdiction, many commentators fear that the opposite will be the case. They fear that the new system will be an unclear, time-consuming, bureaucratic 'paradise for lawyers', which will cause companies contemplating a merger to register their plans with both national and EC authorities to minimize the chance of falling foul of either.

11 Restrictive trading practice policy

Restrictive trading practices undertaken by firms in imperfect product markets can be divided into two broad kinds: those undertaken **independently** by a single firm; and **collective** restrictive practices which involve either a written or an implied agreement among two or more firms.

(i) **Independently undertaken restrictive practices**. In the UK there is no separate legislation dealing with independently undertaken restrictive practices. These might include: the decision taken by a firm to charge discriminatory prices; the refusal to supply a particular resale outlet; and 'full-line forcing' (whereby a supplier forces a distributor who wishes to sell one of his products to stock the full range of his products). Instead, such practices are covered by the monopoly policy we have already described—they are considered as evidence of anti-competitive market conduct or behaviour when the OFT decides on monopoly references. As we have seen, the MMC frequently recommends in its reports that firms drop any trading practices which offend the public interest.

(ii) **Collective restrictive practices**. In contrast to independently undertaken restrictive practices, collective restrictive agreements and practices can be referred by the OFT to a court of law, the **Restrictive Practices Court** (RPC). The current legal position is that a firm must register any restrictive agreement (such as a cartel agreement) with the OFT. The OFT then automatically notifies the RPC. The restrictive agreement is presumed to be illegal unless the firm can persuade the court that the practice is in the public interest.

12 The need to modernize restrictive practice legislation

Some economists argue that the introduction of restrictive practice legislation, in the 1950s, was a major cause of takeover activity in the next three decades. Firms successfully circumvented the outlawing of collusive practices, such as cartel agreements, by **internalizing** the restrictive practice through merger! However, it is now generally agreed that the current legislative framework is less effective than it ought to be and is in need of revision. The main weaknesses in the current system are:

(i) Once a collective agreement is registered, it can continue to operate lawfully until the RPC rules whether or not the agreement is in the 'public interest'. But, in practice, it can take several years for an agreement to come to court, unless the OFT pushes for an early decision.

(ii) Companies are able to avoid prosecution by skilfully drafting an agreement to take advantage of the loopholes provided by the eight 'gateways' that allow a 'public interest' defence of an agreement.

(iii) The present laws are ineffective because of concessions granted to many industrial sectors and in particular, to the professions. These are currently 43 separate exemptions, ranging from agreements concerning the marketing of eggs to long-established restrictive practices within the professions.

(iv) Although agreements that are not registered are automatically declared illegal if uncovered by the OFT, all too often they remain uncovered. This is because the OFT's powers of investigation are limited. At present OFT officials can act only when they have firm evidence that a cartel exists (evidence which is usually provided by a disgruntled ex-member of the cartel).

(v) The maximum fines that the RPC can impose upon guilty firms are much too small to act as an effective deterrent to misbehaviour. The maximum fines bear no relation to the scale of cartel agreements.

To take account of the weaknesses outlined above, the Government published plans, in 1989, to reform the law relating to restrictive practice, but has not found parliamentary time as yet in which to introduce the necessary legislation.

13 Public ownership and industrial policy

The history of nationalization in the UK extends back to the middle of the 19th century when the Post Office was established as a civil service department. The first public corporation was the Port of London Authority, created in 1908. Other early public corporations were the Central Electricity Board, London Passenger Transport Board and the BBC; set up by Acts of Parliament in the 1920s. Most of the early public corporations represent what has been called **'gas and water' socialism**; the regulation, through public ownership, of an essential utility or service regarded as too important to be left to the vaguaries of private ownership and market forces. However, the main periods of nationalization and extension of public ownership in the UK have occurred during the periods since the Second World War when Labour governments have been in office.

In 1929 the British Labour Party adopted the commitment to 'common ownership of the means of production, distribution and exchange'. Although nationalization has at times been regarded by some Labour Party supporters rather as an end in itself, socialist theoreticians have argued that increased public ownership is necessary to give the government proper control of the key industries (or 'commanding heights' of the economy), deemed vital for the socialist planning of the economy. Socialists have also believed that nationalization leads to improved industrial relations, and to a more equitable distribution of income and wealth amongst the population. In the former case, greater industrial democracy can be promoted as class conflict between capitalists and workers giving way to co-operation between workers and managers to serve the public interest. At the same time, the abolition of private ownership and monopoly profit can allow the payment of higher real wages to the employees of nationalized industries and the charging of lower prices to consumers; both of which should improve distributional equality within society. Nevertheless, it was not originally envisaged by Labour Party politicians that nationalized industries would be subsidized and run at a loss, whether to save the industries from bankruptcy or to provide a subsidized service to the public. Indeed, the Labour Party believed that the key industries, once nationalized, would immediately begin to function more efficiently than under private ownership, thus allowing employers, consumers and taxpayers and the 'wider' public interest all to benefit.

14 Other reasons for nationalization

Industries have therefore been nationalized in the UK for two main reasons: as an **instrument of socialist planning** and control of the economy and as a method of **regulating the problem of monopoly** – in particular the problem of **'natural' monopoly** in the utility industries. There are however, other possible reasons for nationalization, some of which have been used by supporters of public ownership as part of an ad-hoc justification for keeping industries in the public sector and resisting privatization. These include:

 (i) To regulate the production of demerit goods, such as alcohol or gambling;
 (ii) To regulate the production of merit goods and ensure public health;
(iii) Defence and national security;
 (iv) To use monopoly profit as a source of state revenue;
 (v) National prestige;
 (vi) The rescue of uncompetitive manufacturing industries ('lame ducks' or 'hospital cases').

15 Nationalized industry pricing and investment policies

In terms of pricing policy, the nationalization statutes which established the major public corporations in the 1940s, were vague; simply requiring that the industries should pay their way 'taking one year with another'. Thus, from the beginning, a potential conflict was created between the commercial objective of being profitable and the public interest duty to provide social, and often uneconomic services, e.g. to citizens living in remote areas.

By the 1960s, much more thought was being given to the 'correct' pricing and investment policies nationalized industries should adopt. It was suggested that the pricing policies of nationalized industries should be based on the principle of **marginal cost pricing**, while investment decisions should follow the best practice adopted in the private sector: namely to use the **discounted cash flow techniques** (explained in Unit 21) to decide whether particular investment projects are worthwhile.

16 Marginal cost pricing

We have seen that many of the industries taken into public ownership in the UK have been monopolies and that nationalization can prevent consumer exploitation by the monopoly deliberately restricting output and raising prices. Left to itself, and functioning as private profit maximizer, a nationalized industry would choose a level of output and set a price at which $P > MC$. But as we have explained in Unit 5, this is **allocatively inefficient**: too little of the good or service would be produced and consumed because the price is too high. To produce the **allocatively efficient** level of output, a nationalized industry should therefore adopt marginal cost pricing, so that $P = MC$. By setting a price equal to marginal cost, the conditions of perfect competition are approximated, while still achieving the productive efficiency or low average costs that economies of scale and the monopoly position of the industry allow.

However, there are a number of difficulties in both the theory and the application of marginal cost pricing. These include:

(i) Marginal cost pricing can be guaranteed to improve allocative efficiency only if all other prices in the economy equal marginal costs. Since many prices charged in the private sector do not equal the relevant marginal costs, it is therefore by no means certain that by instructing a nationalized industry to charge marginal cost prices, allocative efficiency will improve.

(ii) In any case, to ensure allocative efficiency throughout the economy, each industry – including the nationalized industries – would have to **set price equal to marginal social cost ($P = MSC$)** rather than just the marginal private production cost incurred by the industry itself. Thus, if the pricing decision of a nationalized industry were to reflect the wider public interest, which is measured by social costs and benefits, the value of all the external costs and benefits generated in the course of production would have to be calculated and included in the price charged by the industry. **External costs (or negative externalities)** would include the costs of pollution and environmental destruction; while any environmental improvement 'spun off' from production would be an example of an **external benefit (or positive externality)**.

(iii) The question of whether price should be set equal to short-run or long-run marginal cost is significant, since the decision affects a nationalized industry's profitability. Most of the nationalized industries benefit from economies of large scale production and falling 'long-run average total costs' (LRATC). In this situation, **long-run marginal costs (LRMC)** must be below LRATC. If $P = LRMC$, the industry inevitably makes a loss and requires a subsidy to finance the resulting deficit. But the use of taxation to finance the deficit of a nationalized industry causes fresh allocative distortions and is likely to reduce industry morale. By contrast, if an industry is instructed to set $P = SRMC$, profits are made normally, though these are smaller than they would be if the industry were allowed to act 'commercially', as a private profit-maximizer, producing the output at which $MR = MC$.

(iv) Because of **'lumpiness'** or **indivisibilities**, it may be difficult or impossible (in practice) to calculate the marginal cost of providing an extra unit of a good to a single consumer.

17 Nationalized industry pricing in practice

Partly because of the difficulties we have just listed, the theory of marginal cost pricing has had only a very limited impact upon the actual pricing decisions of nationalized industries in the UK. In practice, the instruction that nationalized industries should set prices equal to marginal cost has been subordinated by successive UK governments who have used nationalized industry pricing as an instrument to achieve other objectives of government policy. In the 1970s, Conservative and Labour governments both used the prices charged by nationalized industry as a **counter-inflation policy instrument**. Prices were kept artificially low and the industries made large losses. More recently, this policy has been reversed. In the 1980s, the Conservative Government instructed the industries to **act 'commercially'**, just as if they were private profit maximizers. Since the profits (or trading surpluses) of nationalized industries go to the Exchequer; this represents a form of **'implicit' taxation**, with government revenue from the profits of nationalized industries allowing the level of formal or 'official' taxation to be kept down. Many commentators also believe that the current policy of instructing nationalized industries to set profit-maximizing prices ignoring any wider 'public interest' issues, represents the 'fattening up' of the few remaining industries for eventual privatization.

18 Privatization

Following the major nationalizations of the 1940s, the next 30 years saw little movement on that front. Many of the Acts of Nationalization, passed by Labour governments, merely reorganized assets already in the public sector. But, equally, there was relatively little **denationalization** or **privatization** when Conservative governments were in office. The 1950s to the 1970s were the decades of the mixed economy; when the major political parties agreed that the mix of public and private enterprise worked and was 'right for Britain'. But with the election of a radical free-market orientated administration, under Mrs Margaret Thatcher in 1979, this consenus broke down. The Conservative Government of the 1980s and early 1990s set about the task of **breaking up the mixed economy** and replacing it with a **social-market economy**.

This has involved an industrial policy based on the inter-related processes of **privatization**, **marketization** and **deregulation** which are illustrated in Table 12.1.

Table 12.1 Privatization and related industrial policies

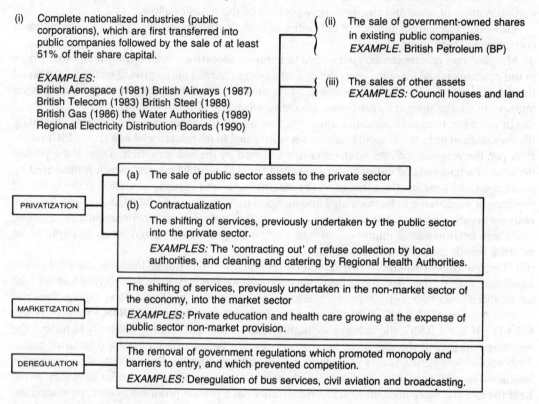

(i) Complete nationalized industries (public corporations), which are first transferred into public companies followed by the sale of at least 51% of their share capital.

EXAMPLES:
British Aerospace (1981) British Airways (1987)
British Telecom (1983) British Steel (1988)
British Gas (1986) the Water Authorities (1989)
Regional Electricity Distribution Boards (1990)

(ii) The sale of government-owned shares in existing public companies.
EXAMPLE. British Petroleum (BP)

(iii) The sales of other assets
EXAMPLES: Council houses and land

PRIVATIZATION

(a) The sale of public sector assets to the private sector

(b) Contractualization
The shifting of services, previously undertaken by the public sector into the private sector.
EXAMPLES: The 'contracting out' of refuse collection by local authorities, and cleaning and catering by Regional Health Authorities.

MARKETIZATION

The shifting of services, previously undertaken in the non-market sector of the economy, into the market sector
EXAMPLES: Private education and health care growing at the expense of public sector non-market provision.

DEREGULATION

The removal of government regulations which promoted monopoly and barriers to entry, and which prevented competition.
EXAMPLES: Deregulation of bus services, civil aviation and broadcasting.

19 The case for privatization

The general case for privatization can only be understood properly when seen as part of the 'revolution' (or 'counter-revolution') in economic thinking known as the **neo-classical revival**.

We have already noted that socialists often seem to regard nationalization as an end in itself, apparently believing that by 'taking an industry into public ownership', efficiency and equity are automatically improved and the public interest served. In much the same way, many **economic 'liberals'** (at the opposite end of the political and economic spectrum) seem to believe that private ownership and capitalism are always superior to public ownership, whatever the circumstances; and that the privatization of state-run industries must inevitably improve economic performance.

Rather more specific arguments that have been used to justify the privatization programme include:

(i) Revenue raising Privatization (the sale of state-owned assets) provides the government with a short-term source of revenue which in some years has reached £3-4 billion or more. Clearly an asset cannot be sold twice; eventually privatization must slow down when there are no more assets left to sell.

(ii) Reducing public spending and the PSBR Since 1979, the Conservative Government has aimed to reduce both public spending and the Public Sector Borrowing Requirement (PSBR). By classifying the monies received from asset sales as 'negative expenditure' rather than as 'revenue', the government has been able to reduce the level of public spending as well as the PSBR from an accounting point of view. Clearly there are other more concrete reasons why privatization may cause public spending to fall besides those related to 'creative accounting'. If the state can successfully sell loss-making industries, such as the Rover Group, public spending on subsidies falls. The PSBR can also fall if private ownership returns the industries to profitability since corporation tax revenue will be boosted.

(iii) The promotion of competition and efficiency Most nationalized industries were monopolies. For reasons already explained, Conservative governments believe that nationalized industries are inefficient. Before the beginning of the privatization programme in the early 1980s, Conservative politicians frequently argued that a major reason for privatization was to 'promote competition' through the break-up of the state monopolies. However, as we have seen, many of the nationalized industries were 'natural' monopolies, difficult to break up into competitive smaller companies without a significant loss of economies of scale and productive efficiency. There has also been a practical conflict between the aims of promoting competition and raising revenue. To maximize revenue from the sale of a nationalized industry, such as British Telecom or British Gas, the government chose to sell the industry whole, without breaking up the monopoly. Therefore, privatization has tended to switch industries merely from public to private monopoly; with little evidence that either competition or efficiency has been promoted, despite the introduction of some market discipline via the capital market.

(iv) 'Popular capitalism' Undoubtedly an important reason for the privatization programme in the UK has been the motive of extending share ownership to individuals and employees (who previously did not own shares) so as to widen the stake of the electorate in supporting a private enterprise economy. Privatization has proved generally popular with voters so the Conservative Government has seen no point at all in changing a winning programme.

20 The case against privatization

(i) Monopoly abuse. As we have already seen earlier in this chapter (in the context of competition policy), opponents of privatization argue that far from promoting competition and efficiency, privatization increases monopoly abuse by transferring socially-owned and accountable public monopolies into weakly-regulated, less accountable private monopolies. Evidence of consumer dissatisfaction with the service provided since privatization by British Telecom and British Gas has been used to support this argument.

(ii) 'Selling the family silver'. Opponents of privatization argue that if a private-sector business were to sell its capital assets, simply in order to raise revenue to pay for current expenditure, it would rightly incur the wrath of its shareholders. The same should be true of the government and the sale of state-owned assets: taxpayers ought not to sanction the sale of capital assets, owned on their behalf by the UK government, to raise revenue to finance current spending on items such as wages. In reply, supporters of the privatization programme argue that, far from 'selling the family silver', privatization merely 'returns the family's assets to the family', i.e. from the custody of the state to direct ownership by private individuals.

(iii) The 'free lunch' syndrome. Opponents of privatization also claim that state-owned assets have been sold too cheaply, encouraging the belief amongst first-time share buyers that there is such a thing as a 'free lunch'. This is because the offer-price of shares in newly-privatized industries has normally been pitched at a level which has guaranteed a risk-free capital gain (or 'one-way bet') at the taxpayer's expense for people buying the government's sell-offs; thereby encouraging the very opposite of an 'enterprise' economy of risk-taking venture capitalism.

21 Regional policy and the regional problem

Much of the industrial policy, implemented by United Kingdom governments since the Great Depression in the 1930s, has been specifically regional in character; aiming to improve the overall performance of the UK economy by reducing regional inequalities and by making better use of all the nation's resources wherever they happen to be located.

For much of the 20th century, it has been possible to divide the UK into a **'successful half'** (broadly the southern part of Britain including London and the South East, the Midlands and East Anglia) and an **'unsuccessful half'** (in the north and west of the UK). The 'successful' south-eastern half of Britain is part of the **'Golden Triangle'** – a 'core' area of post-war growth in Western Europe, stretching between the English Midlands, North Germany and the Paris Basin in France. By contrast, most of the rest of Britain is part of a **European 'periphery' region**: outside the core of the 'Golden Triangle'. The European periphery is sometimes further subdivided into an **'outer' and an 'inner' periphery**. In Britain, the 'outer periphery' includes the older area of 18th and 19th century industrialization, together with the geographically remote, lowly populated and generally non-industrialized 'highlands and islands' which make up the northern and western fringe of the UK. The 'outer periphery' experienced a much slower rate of growth of output than the rest of the UK during the 1950s and 1960s. By contrast, the 'inner periphery', stretching in a broad belt across central Britain and including parts of the south-west, the Midlands, Lancashire and Yorkshire, achieved neither the prosperity of the 'core' nor the stagnation typical of the outer region. Instead, its experience lay between these extremes.

22 The convergency approach to regional problems

In large part, the modern British regional problem is a **problem of mismatching capital and labour**. The northern 'unsuccessful' half of Britain has combined a **surplus of labour** with a **capital shortage**; whereas the southern 'successful' part of Britain has been a region of plentiful capital but relative labour shortage.

In this situation, conventional market theory would predict that wage levels should rise in the south in response to the relative shortage of labour. At the same time capital should flow northwards and labour southwards; being attracted respectively by the wage differentials emerging between the two halves. Thus, by encouraging capital and labour mobility in this way, the market mechanism should ultimately lead to a process of regional convergence in which differences between regions are equalized, thereby causing the regional problem to disappear.

23 The free-market approach to regional policy

The 'free-market' approach to regional policy, which broadly argues the case against an interventionist regional policy, is based on the 'convergency theory' described above. Economists of the 'free-market' (or neo-classical) school believe that the market mechanism alone can solve the regional problem and that the **proper function of regional policy is simply to create the free-market environment in which the price mechanism can operate efficiently**. Indeed, according to this view, an interventionist or 'active' regional policy, far from reducing regional differences, actually makes the inequalities worse because it interferes with the efficient working of the market. Free-market economists argue that, over many decades, the policies and legislation of successive British governments created inflexible markets which prevented the price mechanism from functioning properly. They blame planning controls for preventing firms from choosing low-cost locations; and national collective bargaining for preventing the emergence of the regional wage differentials, regarded as necessary for the convergency process to work.

24 The 'interventionist' approach to regional policy

Economists who argue in favour of an **'active' or interventionist regional policy**, reject both the 'convergency theory' and the belief that market forces alone can cure the regional problem. The case for a much more interventionalist regional and industrial policy is based upon two important arguments:

(i) **Regional divergency** Many Keynesian economists believe that market forces actually widen differences between regions rather than reducing, and eventually eliminating, regional disparities in income, employment and standards of living. Although, in principle, low wages should attract firms to regions of high unemployment, by creating depressed regional markets, they can have the opposite effect. Market forces might only be successful, in pulling individual firms to depressed regions, if the regions possess sufficient **external economies**, attractive to modern industries. Such external economies are provided, in part, by government investment in infrastructure and social capital; but also by other firms supplying components, specialist services or market outlets, already located in the region. However the regional problem may exist, in part, precisely because the depressed regions lack a system of established external economies, sufficient to attract inward investment by new firms. Indeed, far from possessing sufficient external economies attractive to modern industry, the disadvantaged regions may contain significant **external diseconomies** which act as deterrents to incoming firms. Diseconomies result from: remoteness from the European 'core'; derelict buildings; polluted land; unsuitable transport facilities; and a labour force trained in the wrong skills and unused to modern working practices. These may all counter the pull of low wages and a plentiful supply of labour, serving to intensify rather than reduce the regional problem.

(ii) **The social cost argument** When making an economic decision in an unregulated market economy, a firm need consider only the private costs incurred by the enterprise itself, together with the private benefits received. Thus, when choosing a suitable location for production, a firm can ignore any externalities received by the wider community, which may result from its private choice. But while the firm can ignore externalities, it is the government's duty to take account of external costs and benefits, generated by the private locational decisions of firms, and to formulate public policy that maximizes the welfare of the whole community, rather than just the private interests of individual firms. In the absence of externalities, there is no public policy problem; the social (or public) interest coincides with the private interests of firms. In these circumstances, and in the absence of other arguments to justify intervention, the government should refrain from interfering with market forces. But supporters of an active regional policy argue that a case for government intervention exists precisely because the location of industry generates externalities received as social costs by the wider community. These include the costs of under-utilized social capital (for example, schools and housing) in the areas of high unemployment from which workers migrate, and the costs to the community of financing unemployment benefits for the workers who remain. Further social costs, of congestion and over-utilization of social capital, may be generated in areas such as the South East where industry chooses to locate. By encouraging firms to locate in depressed regions, away from the South East, the savings in social and external costs may exceed any increase in private costs to individual firms, especially if industry is relatively 'footloose' and private costs are much the same throughout the country. In these circumstances, regional policy results in a net welfare gain to the whole community; the actual financial costs to government and taxpayers which are paid to firms as compensation for increased private costs are less than the savings in total social costs.

25 Capital mobility versus labour mobility

We have already explained how the market disequilibrium of a labour surplus in one half of Britain and a relative shortage of labour in the other half can be cured either by a greater capital mobility, or by greater labour mobility. Essentially, the former type of policy **takes work to the workers**; whereas the latter attempts to **take workers to the work** (assuming that job opportunities exist in the southern 'successful' half of Britain). In principle, regional policy can be based on either approach, or indeed upon both approaches; but under successive British governments, **policies to improve capital mobility** have been dominant. Governments have generally accepted that a successful improvement in labour mobility, sufficient to reduce regional unemployment, would worsen other aspects of the regional problem. In particular, the social costs of congestion would be increased in the south, with further social costs resulting from a declining population in the north. For this reason, government employment policies have placed most emphasis on improving the **occupational** rather than the **geographical mobility** of labour. Job Centres for labour recruitment and job advertising; training schemes for the young; and retraining schemes for older workers have been established, and in recent years employment legislation has been used to reduce restrictive labour practices which prevented workers from changing occupations.

26 UK regional policy before 1984

For the most of the period since the Second World War, British regional policy was based on the active or interventionist approach already described. British regional policy has always involved **'market modification'** rather than **'market replacement'**, i.e. the use of policy instruments to create signals and incentives to encourage firms, voluntarily, to locate in the depressed regions; rather than the enforced location of investment through the command or planning mechanism. In essence, a 'carrot and stick' approach to the regional problem was adopted. Incentive 'carrots' were offered to attract firms to the depressed regions, while at various times planning restrictions were enforced as a 'stick' (or deterrent) to prevent location in the 'successful' southern half of Britain. The country was divided into **Assisted Areas**, in which the 'carrots' were offered to incoming firms, and the rest of Britain, where planning restrictions were enforced and regional assistance was unavailable. Currently the assisted areas are called **Development Areas** and **Intermediate Areas**. The main form of regional assistance available in the assisted areas has always been financial; namely **investment grants**, **Regional Development Grants (RDGs)**, and **investment tax allowances**, together with **government investment in social capital or infrastructure**.

27 The 'catalytic cracker syndrome'

Pre-1984 regional policy was expensive to the taxpayer in terms of the cost of each new job created. An explanation for this lies in the **'catalytic cracker syndrome'**. This refers to the spending of millions of pounds of regional aid on expensive and capital-intensive equipment, such as catalytic crackers in the oil-refining industry, with very few resulting jobs. The 'catalytic cracker syndrome' was encouraged because, prior to 1984, regional aid was channelled largely into the finance of investment by manufacturing firms in new plant and fixed capacity.

28 The 'branch factory syndrome'

The structure of regional financial assistance available before 1984 also encouraged the **'branch factory syndrome'**. Much of the investment in new manufacturing industry in the regions, which took place before 1984, established branch factories owned by large companies with headquarters and main plants outside the assisted areas. Partly because financial assistance was directed at encouraging and rewarding investment, and partly because service industries were largely excluded from receiving aid, pre-1984 regional policy did little to encourage the growth of small businesses indigenous to the regions. Successful growth of such small and often labour-intensive businesses, in service industries as well as in manufacturing, might well have created better balanced regional economies than in fact resulted from the 'branch factory syndrome'. A greater proportion of service industries could have made the regional economies less vulnerable to the changes in demand that affect heavy capital goods industries, especially severely in times of recession. It is also possible that the growth of businesses, indigenous to the regions, might have produced a situation in which many more owners of businesses actually live within the assisted areas, with profits and higher managerial income circulating within the regional economies. Instead, regional aid largely financed the growth of branch factories owned by British and overseas multinational companies. Typically, such factories were peripheral to the main activities of the parent company, often manufacturing a narrow range of components with which to supply other factories in the multinational's wider sphere of operations. Perhaps more importantly, these branch factories tended to generate only relatively low 'production line' incomes to employees living within the assisted areas. Profits generated by the factories, together with higher managerial incomes, usually leaked out of the regional economy; being transferred to the parent company, or to shareholders and the upper echelons of management living outside the regions. Leakages of income out of a region also contributes to a low regional multiplier. The **regional multiplier** measures the relationship between an injection of government spending into the regional economy and the resulting change in regional income. The smaller the regional multiplier, the less effective the regional financial assistance.

Perhaps the most serious effect of the 'branch factory syndrome' occurred in the severe recessions that affected the whole of British industry in the early 1980s and 1990s. Manufacturing, in general, faced serious difficulties; but it was usually the outlying branch factories, located in the regions, which were the most vulnerable to closure.

29 Recent changes in UK regional policy

In 1984 and 1988 significant changes were made in British regional policy. In part, these were a response to the 'catalytic cracker' and 'branch factory' syndromes we have just described but, at a more deeper level, they represented the return to free-market principles by the Conservative Government and a rejection of Keynesian and interventionist approaches to economic policy. Before 1984, all manufacturing firms investing in assisted areas (at the time comprising a three-tier structure of Special Development Areas, Development Areas and Intermediate Areas), were automatically entitled to RDGs. Financial aid was not generally available to service industries. The main changes introduced in 1984 by the Conservative government were:

(i) The map of assisted areas was redrawn and reduced to a two-tier structure of Development Areas and Intermediate Areas. Approximately 35 per cent of the UK population now lives within the assisted areas.

(ii) The new changes were intended to reduce the cost of regional policy to the government and to the taxpayer. Besides demoting some areas from assisted area status, the rate at which Regional Development Grants were offered to firms investing in new plant and buildings in Development Areas was reduced from 22 per cent to 15 per cent.

(iii) An element of selectivity (or discretion) was introduced into regional policy. Before 1984, RDGs were automatically available to manufacturing firms expanding in Development Areas and Intermediate Areas. After 1984, RDGs were available automatically at the reduced rate of 15 per cent in Development Areas, but only on new and not on replacement investment. In Development Areas, any further assistance over and above the 15 per cent RDG was made selective; while Intermediate Areas qualified for selective assistance only. Following the example of other countries in the EC, regional policy was made selective by introducing a cost-per-job limit for the RDG of £10,000, designed to reward investment by labour-intensive firms and to avoid the 'catalytic cracker syndrome'. However the cost-per-job limit was not applied to small firms employing less than 200 employees, in the hope that capital-intensive small firms would be encouraged to grow to a viable size.

(iv) In one significant area, regional policy was extended. For the first time, service industries, such as advertising and data processing (but not tourism), became eligible for regional financial assistance. A new grant was created which has proved to be especially attractive to labour-intensive service industries. As an alternative to the RDG, which is available only to finance capital investment, labour intensive firms were offered a grant of £3,000 for each new job created;

provided that the total turns out to be worth more than 15 per cent of the capital cost of the project.

In 1988, automatic entitlement to RDGs was finally abolished, completing the change to a discretionary regional policy designed to encourage the growth of indigenous small businesses rather than branch factories. The assisted areas and overall cost of regional aid was left unchanged (though at about £400m compared to £700m a few years earlier).

30 The EC regional fund

In some areas of economic policy, such as agricultural policy, the UK has had to adopt common EC policies replacing, in effect, independent national policy. This is not the case with the regional policy of the European Community, which essentially supplements rather than replaces each country's regional policy. Before 1975, regional assistance from the EC was available from a number of funds such as the **EC Social Fund** which financed the training of young workers. In 1975 a **European Regional Development Fund** (ERDF) was established to create a more unified Community regional policy. Financial assistance from the ERDF is channelled through the British government and is intended to be additional to the government's own regional aid. However, there have been criticisms that the British government has used the receipt of EC funds as an excuse for reducing its own financial assistance to the regions. Development Areas are classified as **European Peripheral Regions**, which qualify for a higher level of community assistance than other parts of Britain; designated **Central Regions**. In general, the EC frowns upon continuous subsidies to the regions, preferring instead investment in regional infrastructure. The EC also prefers aid to be selectively available to finance specific projects, rather than automatically available to all firms investing in assisted areas. The changes in British regional policy, introduced in 1984 and 1988, were, in part, a response to the need to bring British policy in line with EC regional policy.

31 The effectiveness of regional policy

Studies undertaken into the effectiveness of regional policy have shown that at best, it has prevented regional disparities from widening; while in years of recession (such as the period 1978-82), regional differences grew worse. However, in 1990, the Confederation of British Industry published an inter-regional comparison showing, for the first time in recent memory, more industrial capacity was employed in northern England than in the south. In part, this probably reflects the effect of high interest rates and bigger mortgages reducing consumer spending much more in the south of England than in the north. But it might also provide support for the 'anti-interventionist' changes in regional policy which we have described. It is claimed that a 'new dynamic' was at work in the second half of the 1980s; with the survivors of the recession of 1979-82 doing well and new businesses working to better management standards. Not only has a restructured manufacturing sector performed well in the north in recent years; it is also argued that the regional economy has been boosted by the growth of successful indigenous businesses providing financial and professional services that no longer have to be 'imported' from London and the south-east. It remains to be seen however, whether the regeneration of the northern economy, that took place in the late 1980s, will survive the return to recession in 1990/91 and the **deindustrialization process** that so affected the UK economy in the early 1980s.

32 Deindustrialization

In the 1970s and the early 1980s, the UK regional problem became submerged in the wider problem of deindustrialization. As a result, UK governments switched the emphasis of policy away from regional problems to a more general industrial policy; aimed at halting and reversing the deindustrialization process wherever it was occurring.

Deindustrialization refers to the structural decline of industrial output in the face of international competition. Some commentators use the term to refer only to the absolute decline of manufactured output which occurred in the severe recession of the early 1980s; but if the term is used in a relative, rather than an absolute sense, deindustrialization has been occurring for a much longer period (and is still continuing), despite the slow recovery in manufacturing output in the UK after 1981. Indeed, with the onset of recession in the early 1990s, many commentators believe that deindustrialization will re-emerge as the most significant economic problem affecting the UK economy in future years. Nor should the term be restricted to manufacturing industry; extractive industries such as coalmining and fisheries and possibly also construction and utility industries, have been subject to the deindustrialization process. Although defined in terms of industrial output, deindustrialization has been accompanied by an often rapid fall in industrial employment. This has continued despite the recovery in the UK economy, as firms have sought to reduce their loss of competitiveness by 'shaking out' the workforce in order to increase labour productivity.

33 Government policy towards deindustrialization before the 1979 election

Labour governments recognized the problem of deindustrialization and introduced a set of interventionist policies, aimed at reversing the structural decline of manufacturing. The Labour government believed that deindustrialization was caused, primarily, by failure of capitalism and the market economy; arguing that private sector firms (especially multinational companies) were becoming unaccountable to the national interest and that markets–including the capital and financial markets–were taking too short-term a view of economic prospects. As a result, industry, in general, was underinvesting in new capacity, and the financial institutions were failing in their function of providing risk or venture capital to industry on a long-term basis. On this diagnosis, the Labour government introduced an interventionist policy to reverse the deindustrialization process; based on such measures as nationalization and the creation of a **state holding agency**, the **National Enterprise Board** to take an ownership stake in the private sector in return for providing finance.

34 Deindustrialization and the Conservative Government

The policies adopted by the Conservatives, in the 1980s and early 1990s to deal with de-industrialization, have been different in almost all respects from those of the Labour government in the 1970s. Recent Conservative policy has been based on the assumption that any problems, caused by deindustrialization, along with the regional problem, result from decades of too much (rather than too little) government intervention. State intervention has prevented the market mechanism from working properly, particularly in the labour market. Firms have been faced with high wage costs which, together with the crippling burden of taxation necessary to finance state intervention, have reduced international competitiveness. According to the 'radical right' philosophy, adopted by the Conservative Government, the correct way to deal with the deindustrialization problem is to 'roll back' state intervention, creating conditions in which private enterprise and entrepreneurial initiative, can regenerate the British economy by operating in competitive and efficient markets.

The free-market 'supply-side' orientated policies, adopted by the Conservative Government to deal with the deindustrialization problem, have included: (i) the encouragement of small business; (ii) tax cuts; (iii) abolishing labour restrictive practices and reducing the power of trade unions; (v) establishing Enterprise Zones and Urban Development Corporations.

35 Enterprise Zones and Urban Development Corporations

Since the Second World War, population and employment have both declined in large conurbations (built-up areas) throughout the United Kingdom. Population decline has affected large cities (such as London and Birmingham) in the 'successful' south as well as industrial cities in the north. This decline, particularly acute in manufacturing, has reduced employment opportunities for the skilled and semi-skilled manual workers who make up a large part of the working population in industrial cities. Service industries have generally been unable to grow sufficiently to make up for the decline of manufacturing in the large cities. Inner-city decline has also contributed to the growth of a high level of public expenditure provided by the local authorities. But increased spending by local authorities, in areas of urban deprivation, has required higher local taxation to finance the spending. By the 1980s, Britain's inner-cities were becoming locked into a vicious spiral of decline. Falling employment led to a consequent narrowing of the local tax base; accompanied by growing demands for local public spending from a population increasingly dependent upon welfare benefits. This in turn led to an even faster rate of decline in local employment as firms went out of business or moved out of the inner-cities to escape the taxation required to pay for the high levels of local public expenditure.

Before 1979, governments either ignored the growing **'micro-regional' problem** of the inner-cities, concentrating instead on the more conventional problems of **'macro-regions'**; or they chose to deal with the problem by increasing the level of central government funding for local authorities in the city centres affected. After 1979, the Conservatives adopted a completely different approach; reducing the level of intervention by local and central government alike, and attempting to create an environment attractive to private enterprise.

Enterprise Zones were established, conceived of as areas of reduced 'red tape' and bureaucracy. Firms locating in Enterprise Zones (usually sited on previously derelict urban land in inner-cities), benefit from a 10-year 'rates holiday' during which they pay no local taxation and are exempt from the need to obtain planning permission or to make redundancy payments to laid-off workers. By 1986, 28 Enterprise Zones had been established but a number of studies have cast doubt on their effectiveness in reducing the inner-city problem. It is doubtful whether Enterprise Zones have attracted many completely new businesses; indeed, areas of blight have tended to grow up around Enterprise Zones, as businesses have moved into the zones from the surrounding area to benefit from the 'rates holiday'. The Enterprise Zones have tended to attract service industries (such as retail super-stores and warehouses) rather than manufacturing; creating employment for low-paid unskilled workers. Their critics argue that Enterprise Zones have failed to make sufficient impact upon the unemployment and social problems of inner-cities; and that they are not an appropriate base for the regeneration of areas of urban deprivation.

To supplement the Enterprise Zones, the Conservative Government also set up privately sponsored **Urban Development Corporations** (UDCs). UDCs, such as the **London Docklands Development Corporation** are, like Enterprise Zones, largely outside the political control of the municipalities in which they are located. Critics argue that far from decentralizing power away from the state, the UDCs erode the power of local democracy in the UK; and represent a further step towards the centralization of effective power or decision making in Westminster and Whitehall.

12.4 Links with other units

Other aspects of United Kingdom industrial structure, and the role of government in industry, are covered in Units 10 and 11, while Units 6, 7 and 8 explain the causes of market imperfection and failure towards which industrial policy is often addressed. The issue of whether industrial policy should be 'interventionist' or anti-interventionist' is further developed in Unit 23 on supply-side economics and Unit 24 on Keynesianism and monetarism.

12.5 Question practice

Essay Questions

Question 1 'Restrictive practices by firms obviously run counter to the public interest and should be severely punished by the government.' Discuss, illustrating with examples.   (*SUJB: June, 1987*)

Understanding the Question The current UK legislative position (which is fully explained in the Unit) is that it is possible to justify certain trading restrictive practices on public interest grounds. However, the government has announced its intention to abolish the 'public interest' defence and to introduce a general prohibition on agreements and practices deemed anti-competitive and levy heavy fines on firms that disobey OFT rulings. Nevertheless, the government has yet to find parliamentary time to introduce the proposed changes.

Answer plan

1 Define a trading restrictive practice, distinguishing between non-collective restrictive practices (such as a refusal to supply goods) and collective practices (such as a cartel agreement). If possible, give real-world examples.
2 Perhaps drawing on the eight 'gateways', allowed by current UK legislation, suggest why a public interest defence may be allowed. Give examples.
3 Explain the anti-competitive effects of many restrictive practices. Give examples.
4 Argue a conclusion as to whether a public interest defence can be justified.
5 Discuss the issue of severity of punishment if restrictive practices are made illegal.

Question 2 Why do economies have a public sector? Discuss how and why the size and composition of the public sector in Britain have changed in recent years.   (*JMB: June, 1989*)

Understanding the Question You can answer the first part of the question by explaining market failure in the case of public goods and merit goods; and how the public sector of an economy may provide these goods and services more effectively and efficiently than a private sector. Explain also how socialist governments are likely to extend a country's public sector by nationalizing industries in pursuit of such goals as effective socialist planning of the economy, monopoly control and egalitarianism. This could then provide a lead into the second part of the question since the changes in the size and composition of the UK public sector in the 1980s reflect the determination of the Conservative Government to eradicate socialism from the British economy.

Answer plan

1 Briefly define the public sector, distinguishing it from the private sector.
2 Relate the public sector to market failure and the provision of public goods and merit goods.
3 Explain how in the political process in Western democracies, the electorate has voted for a mix of private and public ownership.
4 Socialist governments have extended the role of the public sector in pursuit of socialist objectives.

5 The changes occurring in the UK economy in the 1980s result from the rejection by the Conservative Government of all aspects of socialism.
6 With examples, describe the principal changes: privatization, marketization, deregulation.

Question 3
(a) In what ways has the regional policy of the UK Government changed since 1979?   (13)
(b) Consider the view that present policies are unlikely to have much impact in reducing regional unemployment disparities.   (12)

(*WJEC: June, 1988*)

Understanding the Question The question requires you to explain how the interventionist and Keynesian-inspired regional policy implemented before 1979 gave way during the 1980s to an anti-interventionist policy. The Keynesians believed that regional problems and disparities resulted from the operation of unregulated market forces and that Government intervention to modify and, if necessary, replace the market through the planning mechanism could improve upon this 'market failure'. But the changes introduced in the 1980s follow the rejection of this view by 'classical' inspired Conservative governments. For them, the regional problem resulted from too much (rather than too little) government intervention. You can agree or disagree with the second part of the question, though the evidence does seem to indicate that regional disparities have remained as wide as ever. As each part of the question carries approximately half the marks, make sure you develop both your answers.

Answer plan
1 Briefly explain the meaning of regional policy.
2 Explain how the overall strategy of UK regional policy changed from being Keynesian and interventionist to 'classical' and anti-interventionist.
3 Give examples of particular changes, e.g. the cuts in total regional spending; the abolition of automatic entitlement to regional assistance, etc.
4 Explain that the second part of the question relates to Keynesian criticism of the anti-interventionist approach.
5 Introduce evidence of the effectiveness of regional policy in recent years, e.g. have regional disparities narrowed?
6 Reach an argued conclusion as to whether you agree or disagree.

Multiple Choice Questions

Question 4 For the purposes of British monopoly policy, a statutory monopoly is defined as an industry in which
(a) there is only one firm
(b) one firm produces 33% of the industry output
(c) one firm produces 25% of the industry output
(d) the dominant firm has assets valued at £30 million or more.

Understanding the Question This question tests factual recall and your knowledge of the qualifying condition for industries or firms to be referred to the MMC. Alternative (a) defines a pure monopoly rather than a statutory monopoly. Alternative (b) is the definition of a statutory monopoly which was applicable before 1973, whereas (d) introduces the distraction of the size of an acquired company if a merger is to be eligible for investigation. This leaves (c) as the correct answer.

Question 5 Which of the following would be unlikely to reduce regional unemployment?
(a) Information about employment vacancies in Job Centres.
(b) An increase in unemployment benefits as a ratio of average pay.
(c) A reduction in Corporation Tax paid by firms in assisted areas.
(d) The introduction of government-sponsored retraining schemes.

Understanding the Question Policies (a) and (d) are examples of standard government policies to improve labour mobility and reduce frictional unemployment. Policy (c) is also likely to reduce regional unemployment by making it more attractive for firms to locate in the problem regions, though unemployment elsewhere might rise. This leaves alternative (b) as the correct answer; the incentive to find a new job would be reduced, causing a lengthening in the 'search period' for a new job, and an increase in frictional unemployment.

Question 6 The public sector of the economy comprises the economic activities of:
(a) nationalized industries and public authorities   (c) public corporations
(b) public utilities   (d) public companies.

Understanding the Question Public utilities and public corporations are, of course, included in the public sector, but neither provides a definition of what constitutes the public sector of the economy. Alternative (a) is a much more comprehensive definition of the public sector, since it includes the activities of central and local government in the provision of non-marketed services and the ownership of municipal enterprises. Alternative (d) is a complete red herring; public companies are predominantly in the private sector.

Data Response Questions

Question 7

What has emerged is that until the mid 1960s concentrations of declining industries, including coal, textiles and shipbuilding, were chiefly to blame for job losses in depressed areas. But since then the causes of decline have been very different.

The main problem, it now seems, is that regions such as Scotland and the North are being dragged down by their big cities. In other parts of these regions employment trends are not nearly as bad. Throughout Britain a massive shift of jobs from cities to smaller towns and rural areas is occurring on a scale which swamps most other trends in industrial location.

Source: S. Fothergill and G. Gudgin, *The Guardian* 1982

(a) Explain how the changed pattern of industrial location may have been the result of:
    (i) more capital intensive production methods;   (4)
    (ii) market forces affecting industrial location.   (8)
(b) What are the implications of the described change for government investment in social capital?   (4)
(c) Discuss the use of Enterprise Zones as a response to the observed trend.   (4)

(*SUJB: June, 1987*)

Understanding the Question The question relates to the replacement of the 'traditional' regional problem of the 'two halves of Britain' by the more micro-problem of depressed inner-cities. New manufacturing industries and service industries which are located in rural and semi-rural areas away from the traditional manufacturing cities, are generally much more 'footloose', lacking the requirement of a specific location in a port or on a mineral outcrop. Capital intensivity may (or may not) have much to do with the newer locational influences. The more automated newer manufacturing industries are capital intensive since little labour is required in the production process, but many newer industries are quite labour-intensive, especially in the service sector. The predominance of road transport, both for receiving raw materials and components and for delivering finished products to customers; and the importance of electricity (or gas) as energy sources, have probably been more significant in contributing to the newer pattern of industrial location than any change in capital intensivity *per se*. The availability of 'greenfield' sites uncluttered by existing urban dereliction and congestion and the desire of a business's owners and also its employees to live and work in an attractive environment have been other locational influences.

The shift in the locational pattern tends to leave the inner-cities with ageing populations and a large fraction of the declining population dependent on welfare benefits. By contrast, activity rates are much higher in the newer employment areas which attract an inward migration of younger workers and their families. Central or local government will need to invest in hospitals and schools–and possibly in public sector housing–in the expanding areas, while the provision of facilities for retraining redundant workers and for meeting the needs of the elderly poor, together with the investment in a modernized infra-structure to attract new private sector investment, will be required in the inner-city areas. Enterprise Zones, however, represent an attempt to get the private sector to invest directly in the infrastructure, thus reducing the need for investment in social capital by central or local government.

Question 8 Study the graph which shows the summer and winter demands on the Central Electricity Generating Board system in the United Kingdom.

(a) What pricing and investment problems are implied for the United Kingdom electricity industry from an examination of the data opposite?

(b) In 1981 electricity consumers were offered a 'new' Domestic Economy 7 Tariff which involved a night unit charge of 1.82p and a standing charge of £7.25 per three months. The ordinary domestic tariff remained unchanged at 4.48p per unit throughout the 24 hour period, plus a standing charge of £5.50 per three months.
Comment on the introduction of the new tariff.

(*London: June, 1985*)

Demands on CEGB system

Source: *The Guardian*, 13 March 1980

Understanding the Question Utility industries (such as electricity and gas) and transport industries (such as British Rail) face the problem that they are expected to provide a continuous service to meet demand, but there are considerable fluctuations in the level of demand at different times of day, and also seasonally.

If the electricity industry invests in power station capacity to meet the maximum peak demand (of 45 000 megawatts) in the early evening period of a typical winter's day, a large part of the capacity will lie idle during the daily offpeak, and also during the summer months. The costs of providing the capacity to meet winter peak-time demand include the costs of under-utilization at other times. Suppose also that demand increases, both at peak and off-peak times. The marginal cost incurred by the electricity industry in meeting extra winter peak demand will be very high, since it will be a **long-run marginal cost** of investing in new capacity which will be underutilized at other times. By contrast, the marginal cost of meeting an increase in off-peak demand, both daily and seasonally, might be low: simply the **short-run marginal cost** of operating existing capacity that would otherwise lie idle.

Pricing can be used to try to smooth out the shape of the daily and seasonal demand curves. High prices can be charged in the peak (reflecting the high peak-time marginal costs we have just described) and low-prices in the off-peak. The Economy 7 prices quoted in the question are examples. If successful, the marginal cost pricing structure will encourage consumers to switch consumption from peak to off-peak hours, leading to better utilization of a smaller overall production capacity. New customers may also be attracted to off-peak consumption in preference to substitute fuels, such as gas. However, the success of the policy depends on customer's price elasticity of demand for electricity at different times of day and at different seasons. Economy 7 type pricing structures may encourage households to switch to night storage electric central heating and to load their washing machines and dishwashers at night. Industrial customers might also operate their energy intensive processes at night to benefit from the lower prices charged. However, differential pricing would have little effect on the demand for electricity to power electric trains or domestic TV sets and lighting, and in some circumstances it could lead to customers abandoning electricity for alternative fuels.

12.6   Further Reading

Artis, K. J., editor, *The UK Economy*, 12th edition (Weidenfeld & Nicolson, 1989).
Chapter 4: Industry.

Morris, D., (editor), *The Economic System in the UK*, 3rd edition (Oxford University Press, 1985).
Chapter 26: Competition Policy, Chapter 25: Nationalized Industries.

Griffiths, A. and Wall, S., *Applied Economics*, 4th edition (Longman, 1991).
Chapter 8: The Nationalized Industries and Privatization.
Chapter 19: Regional and Urban Policy.

13   The Labour Market and the Determination of Wages

13.1   Points of perspective

In earlier units we examined the behaviour of firms and how prices are determined when firms sell their output in the **goods market** or **product market**. We generally assumed that the **prices of the inputs** necessary for production, or the **prices of factor services**, were given. We now reverse the assumption, and examine how the prices of **factors of production** are determined in the **factor market**, assuming that conditions and prices in the product market are generally given. We shall concentrate on the labour market and the determination of wages, applying our analysis where necessary to the other factors of production and their prices.

We shall follow the convention of dividing the factors of production into **land** and **labour**, which earn **rent** and **wages** respectively, and **capital**, which is further subdivided into **loan capital**, earning **interest**, and **entrepreneurship**, or **enterprise**, earning **profit**. This is strictly a theoretical division which conforms neither to official statistics nor to the everyday use of such words as rent and interest. For example, a businessman will think of rent as the payment he makes for the use of a building. However, from a theoretical point of view, part of the payment is the rent of land, but the rest is an interest payment on capital.

The distribution of income between the factors of production is called the **functional distribution of income**. This should not be confused with the **size distribution of income**, which measures, for example, the proportion of total income received by the top ten per cent of income earners, compared with the bottom fifty per cent. Table 13.1 illustrates both distributions of income.

Table 13.1

The Functional Distribution of Income Distribution of total income by percentage				*The Size Distribution of Income* Distribution of pre-tax income by percentage			
	1976	1981	1986	Income received by	1976	1981	1986
Income from employment	70.6	68.3	68.8	Top 20% of population	44.4	46.4	50.7
Gross trading profits and				Next 21–40% of population	26.2	26.9	26.9
surplus of private and				Next 41–60% of population	18.8	18.0	16.4
public enterprises, minus				Next 61–80% of population	9.4	8.1	5.7
stock appreciation	12.1	14.8	16.5				
Other income, including							
cost and income from				Bottom 20% of population	0.8	0.6	0.3
self-employment	17.3	16.9	14.7				

Although the official statistics do not exactly match the theoretical distinctions between the factors of production, they tend to show that the share of wages rose slightly at the expense of profits in the 1970s, but that the reverse was true in the 1980s. Indeed in recent years there has been a sharp recovery in the profitability of industry. The size distribution also shows a growing inequality in the distribution of income, with the gap increasing between rich and poor.

13.2 Underlying concepts

Distribution theory introduces no new methods of analysis and only a few new theoretical concepts. It is merely the **price theory** of the earlier units, but viewed from the 'other side'. As we shall see, it can be subjected to the same criticisms as other aspects of conventional price theory. In earlier units we examined the interaction of **households** and **firms** in the goods market, where households are the source of demand for goods and services supplied by firms. We now view households as the source of supply of factor services, which are demanded by firms in the pursuit of profit.

You should note:

(i) Wages and other factor prices are assumed to be determined by **supply** and **demand**.

(ii) The assumption of maximizing behaviour. The assumptions of **profit-maximizing behaviour** on the part of firms and **utility maximization** by households are as crucial to distribution theory as they are to the rest of price theory. Firms will only demand the services of factors of production if profits can be increased by their employment. Similarly, households will only supply more labour, or hire out the capital or land they may own, if it maximizes their **net advantage**. The concept of **net advantage** covers all the rewards, **monetary** and **non-monetary**, which a household gains from the sale of its factor services. For example, if a person enjoys his work, the net advantage obtained from employment will include the pleasure gained from the work itself, as well as the **utility of the wage**–or more strictly, the utilities obtained from the goods and services bought with the money wage.

(iii) The demand for factor services is a derived demand. The essential difference between consumer demand in the goods market, and a firm's demand for factor services, is that the latter is a **derived demand**: the services of labour or land are demanded only because they are necessary in the production of goods and services to sell for profit.

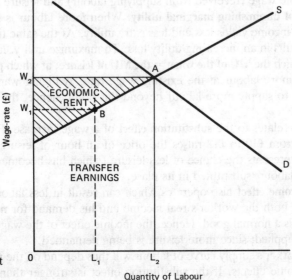

Fig. 13.1 Economic rent and transfer earnings

(iv) Entrepreneurial profit, and indeed the **entrepreneurial function**, is regarded as different from those of the other factors of production. The entrepreneurial function of **risk-taking** and the bearing of **uncertainty** is undertaken by the owners of a business, who bear the financial risks. However, the existence of such a separate entrepreneurial function in modern companies can be questioned. Very often all the important decisions are made by **management**, who are a part of the labour force. In so far as entrepreneurial profit exists, it is essentially a **residual**, the difference between the total revenue obtained from the sale of output in the product market, and the other factor rewards which constitute the firm's costs of production.

(v) Transfer earnings and economic rent. So far we have used the term **rent** in its everyday meaning as the price which must be paid to hire the services of land. To the economist, however, rent or **economic rent** has a rather different meaning. It is a more general meaning which applies to all the factors of production, yet it is more specific since it refers to only a part of the earnings of each factor. Figure 13.1 illustrates the demand and supply for a particular type of labour. L_1 represents a worker who is just prepared to supply labour if the wage is W_1, but who would withdraw from this particular labour market if the wage fell below W_1. We now assume that the firm pays the same wage to all the workers it employs. This is the equilibrium wage W_2, determined where the demand and supply curves intersect at A. Worker L_1 receives the wage of W_2 even though he would be prepared to work for the lower wage of W_1. The part of his wage above the supply curve at point B is **economic rent**, while the part below is **transfer earnings**. Transfer earnings represent the factor's **opportunity cost**, while economic rent is the difference between what the factor is actually paid and its opportunity cost. If the wage falls below W_1, worker L_1 will transfer out of this particular labour market, or at least decide to supply less labour. Taking all the workers together, their economic rent is shown by the shaded area above the supply curve, while their transfer earnings are shown by the area below. Worker L_2 is the marginal worker, who is only just prepared to supply labour at the wage of W_2. All his wage is transfer earnings.

The concept of economic rent is sometimes applied to entrepreneurial profit, as well as to the earnings of the other factors of production. In this case, **normal profit** is regarded as a transfer earning, since the entrepreneur will leave the industry if normal profit is not earned. **Abnormal profit** which is earned over and above normal profit becomes the 'economic rent of enterprise'.

13.3   Essential information

1 The supply of labour

The aggregate supply of labour in the economy is ultimately constrained by the size of the total population. Nevertheless, for a given total population size, the aggregate supply can increase or decrease if, for example, married women decide to enter or leave the working population, which is determined by demographic factors and migration. However, for the purpose of this unit we are more interested in examining the supply of labour within a single labour market than with investigating the factors which cause the aggregate supply of labour to change.

The market supply curve of labour is the sum of the supply curves of each worker in the labour market. A worker's supply curve of labour can either **slope upwards**, showing that more labour is supplied as the wage rises; or it can **bend backwards**, a case where wage rises cause less labour to be supplied. In both cases, the supply curve reflects the **choice between work and leisure**. The decision to supply an extra hour of labour means that an hour of leisure time is sacrificed. This choice affects both the wage (received from supplying labour) and leisure yield utility which both respond to the **law of diminishing marginal utility**. When more labour is supplied at a particular wage rate, the extra income yields less and less extra utility. At the same time, each extra hour of leisure sacrificed results in an increasing utility loss. To maximize utility, labour must be supplied up to the point at which **the MU of the wage = the MU of leisure**; at which point the worker has no incentive to supply more labour at the existing wage rate. A higher wage would be needed to encourage a worker to supply more labour beyond this point; hence, the upward-sloping supply curve of labour.

This explanation relates to the **substitution effect** of a wage increase. For example, an hourly wage rate increase from £10 to £12 raises the price of an hour of leisure from £10 to £12. The substitution effect represents the choice of less leisure (which has become more expensive), with the supply of more labour, substituted in its place.

However, an **income effect** also operates which can result in less labour being supplied. The wage increase raises both the worker's real income and his demand for **normal goods**. For most people, leisure time is a normal good. Hence, the income effect of the wage increase suggests that less labour will be supplied; since more leisure is being demanded.

The slope of a worker's supply curve of labour will thus depend on the relative strengths of the substitution and income effects. If the substitution effect is stronger than the income effect, an

upward-sloping supply curve results: but, if the income effect is the more powerful, the supply curve is **backward-bending** or **regressive**.

An alternative approach to the backward-bending supply curve is to assume that workers aim to achieve a target real income, measured in terms of bought goods and services. A wage increase allows the target to be reached with a lower input of labour, allowing the worker to enjoy more leisure time rather than extra material goods. This is a plausible behavioural assumption when the work itself is unpleasant, (e.g. coal mining).

A backward-bending supply curve has an important implication for tax policy. If the supply curve is upward-sloping, an increase in income tax results in less labour being supplied, because the tax is equivalent to a cut in wages. If, however, the supply curve is backward-bending, the rise in income tax causes people to work longer hours in order to maintain their target incomes.

2 The demand curve for labour

We have already indicated that the demand curve for a factor of production is a **derived demand**. We assume that a firm will only voluntarily employ an extra worker if this increases total profit. To find out whether profits will indeed increase, a firm must know (a) how much the worker adds to total output, and (b) the money value of the extra output when it is sold in the product market. The amount which is added to a firm's revenue by employing one more worker is called the **marginal revenue product** (MRP) of labour. The two elements which comprise the MRP of labour are represented by the identity:

$$\underset{\text{(MRP)}}{\text{Marginal Revenue Product}} \equiv \underset{\text{(MPP)}}{\text{Marginal Physical Product}} \times \underset{\text{(MR)}}{\text{Marginal Revenue}}$$

In Unit 3 we explained the 'Law' or principle of diminishing marginal returns, which states that a variable factor such as labour will **eventually** add less and less to total output as labour itself is added to other factors which are held fixed. In the context of distribution theory it is usual, if rather confusing, to refer to the **marginal physical product** (MPP) of labour. This is exactly the same as the marginal returns of labour. The falling MPP curve which is drawn in Figure 13.2a is explained by the principle of diminishing returns!

To find the money value of the MPP of labour, we multiply the MPP by the addition to total revenue resulting from the sale of the physical output in the goods market. In other words, we must multiply MPP by **marginal revenue**. In Figure 13.2 it is assumed that conditions of perfect competition exist in the goods market. In a perfectly competitive market, MR is identical to the good's price. Thus the MRP curve is derived by multiplying MPP by a constant price at each level of output. In these conditions, the slope and elasticity of the MRP curve are determined by MPP alone, though a change in the good's price will shift the position of the MRP curve. If the goods market is a monopoly or imperfectly competitive, MR will decrease with output. This causes the MRP curve to be steeper than when the goods market is perfectly competitive.

3 The equilibrium wage

In a competitive labour market, the MRP curve of labour is the employer's demand curve for labour. An employer demands labour up to the point where MRP = the marginal cost of employing an extra worker. If the employer goes beyond this point and hires a worker who adds more to total costs than to total revenue, profits must fall. Conversely, if the firm decides to limit the size of the work-force at a point where the MRP of the last worker is greater than the MC of employing him, the firm is

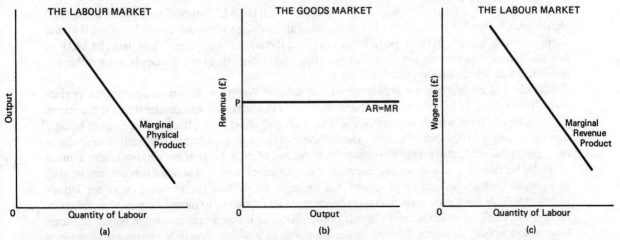

Fig 13.2 How the demand curve for labour (the MRP curve) is derived, assuming a perfectly competitive goods market

sacrificing potential profits. It follows that a **profit-maximizing firm** must demand labour up to the point where MRP = MC. However, the nature of the resulting equilibrium wage depends upon the assumptions made about the competitive state of the labour market. We shall explore some of the possibilities:

(i) A perfectly competitive labour market This is illustrated in Figure 13.3a. In these conditions, there are a large number of firms and a large number of workers, all acting independently in the market. An individual firm is a **price-taker**, in a position to employ as much labour as it wishes at the **ruling market wage**. The ruling wage is determined at the intersection of the supply and demand curves for labour in the labour market as a whole, but for an individual firm in the market the ruling wage is its supply curve. In Figure 13.3a, this is shown by the perfectly elastic supply curve SS. We assume that a firm can employ any quantity of labour it wishes at this wage. In these market conditions, employment is L_1. Each worker receives the equilibrium wage W_1, which is equal to the MRP of labour.

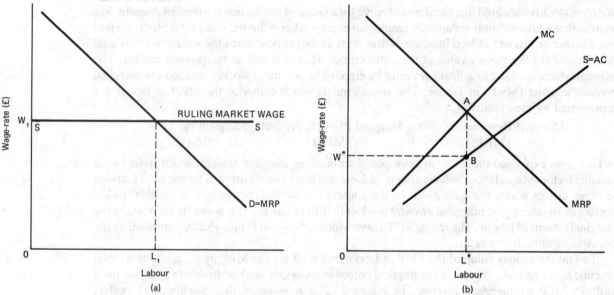

Fig 13.3 The equilibrium wage in different labour markets (a) a perfectly competitive labour market (b) a monopoly buyer of labour

(ii) A monopsony buyer of labour Figure 13.3b illustrates a particular case when the equilibrium wage is not equal to the MRP of labour–though the size of the labour force is still determined where MRP = MC of labour. A single employer is a **monopsony** buyer in the labour market. Assuming an upward-sloping supply curve of labour, the intersection of the supply and MRP curves no longer determines either the equilibrium wage or the size of employment. The supply curve S, or **average cost curve of labour**, shows the wage which must be paid to **all** workers at each size of employed labour force in order to persuade them to supply labour. However, the supply curve S is **not** the **marginal cost curve of labour!** The employer will have to pay a higher wage to attract an extra worker, and the higher wage must be paid to all the other employed workers. Thus the MC of an extra worker incudes the total amount by which the wage bill rises. The MC curve of labour is **above** the AC or supply curve!

If the firm wishes to maximize profits, employment will be at L^*, immediately below point A on the diagram where MRP = MC. However, the equilibrium wage W^* is determined at point B on the supply curve of labour. In this type of labour market, the equilibrium wage is **less** than the MRP of labour. It is useful to note the similarity between this analysis and that for a **monopoly seller within the goods market**, which we explained in Unit 6.

(iii) Trade unions and the monopoly supply of labour We have so far assumed that perfect competition exists in the labour market and that workers always act **independently**. If the workers join together to form a trade union, they will now act **collectively**–an effective trade union being a monopoly supplier of labour. We shall examine some of the possible effects a trade union might have on wages in the context of one of the questions at the end of the unit. In some circumstances a union may only be able to raise wages at the expense of employment, whereas at other times it may be able to increase both wages and employment, for example by shifting the demand curve for labour rightwards. This can happen when a union encourages an employer to introduce new technology or methods of working which increase labour productivity, or if a general increase in wages resulting from union activity increases demand in the economy as a whole. Lastly, a union can sometimes exercise sufficient power, through the threat of strikes and the disruption of the continuous flow upon which modern industry is often dependent, to persuade a firm to sacrifice profit-maximization for the sake of securing at least some profit from uninterrupted production. In this situation, both the wage and the level of employment are determined at a point 'off' the employer's demand curve for labour. The union forces the firm to employ more workers than it would wish to at the wage-rate achieved by the union; hence the firm incurs extra avoidable costs and cannot be maximizing profits.

4 Explanations of different wage levels

Many economists argue that the real reason for the existence of different wage levels lies outside the explanation provided by distribution theory. For example, **social** and **political** factors must surely be highly relevant to any explanation of why female workers are paid less than men in many occupations which require similar skills. Nevertheless, the following reasons are suggested by conventional distribution theory to explain differences in wages:

(i) The separation of labour markets The economy comprises many separated labour markets rather than one large market. In each market, demand and supply conditions are different, resulting in different equilibrium wages. If perfect competition existed throughout the economy, differences in wages would create **incentives** for labour to move between markets and for entrepreneurs to substitute capital for labour. In this way, market forces would reduce wage variations between different industries and occupations. The continuing persistence of wage differences is explained by the forces which prevent labour mobility and factor substitution:

(a) It takes time for a worker to acquire the skills required in another occupation. Costs are also involved in acquiring the skill.

(b) Not all workers will possess the necessary aptitude or ability for a particular type of work.

(c) There are man-made barriers which prevent a worker from moving between labour markets, for example a union closed shop, or restrictions on entry to medical school.

(d) Technical considerations can make it impractical for a firm to employ more capital in place of labour.

(ii) Differences in the elasticities of supply and demand The elasticities of both the supply of and demand for labour are likely to differ between separated labour markets. If the demand for labour is relatively elastic, a rightward shift of the supply curve will have a greater effect on employment than on the wage level. In a similar way, the effect of a shift in demand will depend on the elasticity of the supply curve. A shift in either curve will have the greatest effect on the wage in a particular market when both the supply and demand curves are relatively inelastic. The **time period** in question is an important influence on both elasticities, with elasticities being higher in the long run than in the short run. It follows that a sudden change in the conditions of either supply or demand in a particular labour market will cause a larger change in the equilibrium wage in the short run than in the long run. In the long run, market forces serve to reduce wage differentials through the impact of labour mobility and factor substitution.

The supply of unskilled labour is generally more elastic than the supply of a particular type of skilled labour, since the training period of unskilled labour is usually very short. The existence of unemployed labour will also influence the elasticity of supply.

In general, the demand for labour will be relatively inelastic if:

(a) wages costs are only a small part of total production costs–this is sometimes known as the 'importance of being unimportant';

(b) the demand for the good produced by the firm is inelastic;

(c) it is difficult to substitute other factors of production for labour, or other types of labour for the particular type in question.

(iii) The relative importance of monetary and non-monetary rewards This varies between different occupations. A worker who enjoys his job may be prepared to accept a lower wage than a worker of similar skill and ability employed in an unpleasant occupation. Similarly, the existence of perks and fringe benefits in kind contribute to differences in money wages.

5 Criticisms of distribution theory

(i) The most important propositions of conventional distribution theory are that:

(a) in competitive markets, the equilibrium wage will equal the value of the marginal product of labour in each market, and

(b) the condition that the wage equals the marginal product of labour in each market is a necessary condition to achieve **allocative and productive efficiency** throughout the economy;

(c) the actual combination of labour and other factors of production employed will depend upon their relative prices. In competitive markets, where the price of each factor equals its marginal cost, a firm will employ factors until the

$$\frac{\text{MRP of labour}}{\text{wage}} = \frac{\text{MRP of land}}{\text{rent}} = \frac{\text{MRP of capital}}{\text{rate of interest}}$$

The most fundamental criticism of distribution theory is that it does not really explain anything at all. The theory is **circular**. The demand or MRP of a factor depends upon the value of what is produced; this in turn depends upon the effective demand of consumers exercised in the goods market; finally, the consumers' effective demand depends upon the distribution of income. Hence, the distribution of income is dependent upon the distribution of income! To give the theory some sense, an initial distribution of income must be assumed, and this initial distribution cannot of course be explained by the theory.

(ii) Even within its own terms, the theory can only explain the distribution of income within a small part of the total economy, assuming that conditions in the rest of the economy are held constant. In these conditions, a fall in the wage may cause an employer to demand more labour. However, if the wage level falls throughout the economy, the resulting decrease in aggregate demand can cause the demand curve for labour in each labour market to shift inwards. Unemployment may follow from the wage cut. This is the **Keynesian critique** of the micro-economic theory of distribution.

(iii) The theory assumes that the marginal productivity of labour can be separated from the marginal productivity of capital. However, in many technical processes capital and labour are **complementary** rather than substitutes. Output can only be raised by increasing both capital and labour in some fixed ratio. In these circumstances the marginal productivity of labour is impossible to isolate and identify.

(iv) The MRP theory of wage determination can only be used to explain the wages of workers employed in the market economy. It is impossible to place a market value on the labour productivity of the growing proportion of the British labour force employed in the **public services** provided by central and local government. The determination of public sector pay provides one example of the importance of **differentials, comparability** and **relativity** in wage-bargaining. It is by no means always clear, however, whether public sector pay is determined by comparability with the 'rate for the job' for similar employment in the private sector, or vice versa.

(v) Distribution theory is sometimes criticized for **unrealistically** ignoring the role of **collective bargaining** and other methods of pay determination in the British economy. In one sense the lack of realism is not very important. The theory states that a firm can only maximize profits if it employs labour up to the point where the MRP of labour equals the MC of labour. If this equality does not hold, the firm cannot be maximizing profits! In a perfectly competitive world it would be the forces of competition rather than the deliberate decisions of firms that would bring about the situation where MRP = MC. Firms which strayed away from profit-maximization would either be competed out of existence, or they would have to mend their ways. However, in a world in which firms may not be profit-maximizers, and in which markets are imperfectly competitive, there is no reason why the predictions of distribution theory should come true.

Nevertheless, distribution theory does tend to encourage the attitude that perfectly competitive markets are normal, that workers are paid what they **deserve** in terms of the value of what they produce, and that real-world bargaining patterns and institutions such as trade unions are distortions in otherwise perfect markets. While the markets for capital and land may be closer to the conditions of perfect competition, labour markets would probably be highly imperfect even without the existence of trade unions. Indeed, the principal argument used to justify trade unions is that, in their absence, market power would lie in the hands of employers. It is doubtful if labour markets ever existed in which all employers and all workers act as passive price-takers. More typically, market power would lie in the hands of the employers in a labour market in which a small number of employers bargained individually with a large number of workers unrepresented by a trade union. By bargaining collectively through a trade union, workers are seeking to create a market power to equal or exceed that possessed by the employer.

6 Methods of wage determination in the UK

In distribution theory it is generally assumed that wages are determined by individual negotiation between workers and employers and that market forces eventually bring about a ruling market wage. When trade unions are introduced into this analysis, it is assumed that firms decide how much labour to employ at a wage level determined by the union acting as a monopoly supplier of labour. The actual process of wage and salary determination in the UK is both more complicated and more varied.

(i) Collective bargaining In 1986 there were over 10 million trade union members in the UK, though this represents a significant fall in union membership as compared to a decade earlier. Between 1979 and 1986, union membership fell by over 20%. Less than half of the labour force are now trade union members. The pay of most trade union members is determined by collective bargaining. The union represents its members' interests collectively by bargaining with employers to improve pay and other conditions of work. For further discussion of the nature of collective bargaining and its effectiveness, you should refer to the question practice at the end of this unit.

(ii) Individual negotiation generally takes place in non-unionized parts of the economy. Highly paid managers, executives and consultants who offer specialist professional services will normally negotiate on an individual basis. At the other extreme, unorganized low-paid workers such as fruit-pickers and other casual workers also negotiate individually. In these circumstances the employer usually has much more bargaining power than the individual worker. Consequently the wage may effectively be determined by the employer on a 'take it or leave it' basis.

(iii) State determination There are various ways in which the state intervenes to influence both market forces and the collective bargaining process:

(a) Protecting low-paid workers In low-paid industries such as catering, trade unions are difficult to organize and they tend to be ineffective. **Wages councils** have been established to determine minimum rates of pay. Wages councils represent a form of **minimum wage legislation**. In some countries, a minimum wage has been established by law, to cover all industries.

(b) Statutory incomes policies At various times since the Second World War, British governments have imposed a statutory incomes policy on the process of wage determination. An incomes policy usually lays down an **upper limit** to wage settlements. During a statutory incomes policy, 'free' collective bargaining is either **constrained** or perhaps even **suspended**. Trade unions have often been suspicious of incomes policies which they believe may undermine the bargaining function of a union. The government's main purpose in introducing an incomes policy has usually been to attack the **cost-push** causes of inflation which result in part from the nature of wage bargaining in the UK. Incomes policies have also been justified as a method of ensuring a **fairer distribution of income** than that resulting from the collective bargaining process.

(c) The state as an employer In most industries where the state or a public authority is the employer, unions are recognized and wages are determined by collective bargaining. However, there are exceptions, such as the armed forces and the police, where normal trade union activity is not allowed. Pay in the armed forces is effectively determined by the state.

(d) Arbitration and conciliation In the process of free collective bargaining, a trade union will often demand a pay rise which is greater than the increase the employer is initially prepared to pay. Bargaining is a process in which each side modifies its offer or claim until agreement is reached. The vast majority of agreements are reached without a breakdown in the bargaining process and without dispute. Occasionally, however, agreements cannot be reached and a dispute either occurs or is threatened. Many collective agreements contain negotiating procedures to be followed when the next round of bargaining takes place. The procedural arrangements commonly specify the stage in the breakdown of bargaining at which outside **arbitrators** or **conciliators** should be brought in to help both sides reach agreement. In 1975 the Employment Protection Act established the **Advisory Conciliation and Arbitration Service** (ACAS). If both sides in a dispute agree, ACAS may be called in to try to settle a dispute.

13.4 Links with other topics

The process of wage determination, in particular labour markets, is an important part of inflation theories (see Unit 22). The shape of the supply curve of labour is crucial to the 'supply-side' theory explained in Unit 23; whilst in Unit 24, the different views of Keynesians and monetarists are discussed concerning the labour market and the wage determining process.

13.5 Question practice

Question 1 Examine the role of trade unions in the determination of money wages and real wages.

(London: January, 1986)

Understanding the Question In the main body of the unit we restricted our analysis of trade unions in the context of distribution theory to the rather general statements that (i) unions can increase both wages and employment for their members if union activity results in the MRP curve shifting rightwards, and (ii) if the main result of union activity is to shift the supply curve of labour leftwards by restricting entry to the labour market, wage rises will normally be at the expense of employment. Figure 13.4a also illustrates a situation in which wages rise at the expense of employment. We assume rather unrealistically that the union can fix any wage-rate it chooses, and that employment is then determined by the amount of labour which employers will hire at this wage. If the wage is fixed at W_2, above the competitive wage determined by supply and demand at W_1, the line W_2AS becomes the supply curve of labour. Employers are faced with a perfectly elastic supply of labour at the union-determined wage, up to a supply of L_3. Beyond this point they will have to offer a higher wage in order to attract more labour. However, they will only willingly employ a labour force of L_2, thereby restricting employment below the competitive level of L_1. At the union-determined wage-rate, there is an excess supply of labour of $L_3–L_2$. This will create a pressure to undermine the union if unemployed workers are prepared to supply labour at a wage below W_2. Whether W_2 continues as the wage rate will depend upon the union's power to resist wage-cutting.

Figure 13.4b illustrates a market structure in which the introduction of a union can increase both the wage-rate and employment, without the need to shift the MRP curve rightwards! This is when a **monopsony buyer of labour** bargains with a trade union which is a **monopoly seller of labour**. We explained earlier, in the context of Figure 13.3b, how in the absence of a trade union the competitive supply of labour would result in an equilibrium wage rate at W^*, and an employment level at L^*. Suppose now that a trade union fixes the wage-rate at W_1. At this wage-rate the supply curve of labour is the line W_1XS, and the marginal cost curve of labour is W_1XZ MC. You should note that the MC of employing another worker is the same as the union-determined wage, as long as the labour force is below L_1. If a labour force above L_1 is to be employed, the wage must rise in order to persuade additional workers to supply their labour. Because all workers must be paid the higher wage, the MC of employing an extra worker is now above the supply curve. Between the horizontal section of the MC curve for levels of employment below L_1, and the 'competitive' section of the curve Z MC, is a vertical line or discontinuity, XZ. The equilibrium level of employment at the wage of W_1 is L_1. This is determined where the MRP curve intersects the vertical section of the MC curve between X and Z. The union can increase both the wage-rate and the level of employment as compared with the situation without a union. Providing of course that the union possesses the required power, both the wage-rate and the level of employment can be increased up to an employment level of L_2 determined at point Y. Wages can be increased beyond Y up to a level fixed at A, but only at the expense of some of the extra employment which the union created.

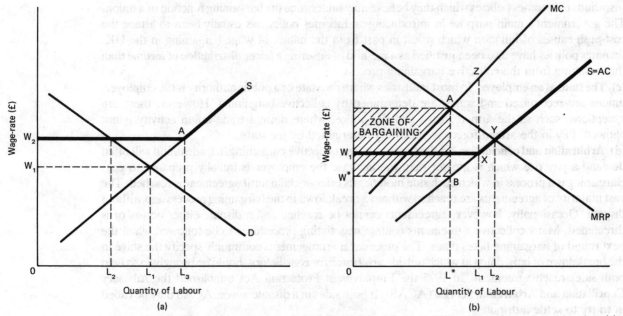

Fig 13.4 The effect of the introduction of a trade union into different labour markets (a) competitive demand for labour (b) monopoly demand for labour

Answer plan

1 Distinguish between an increase in the **money wage** and the **real wage**. If an increase in the money wage causes or is associated with an equal increase in prices, there is no increase in the real wage. In order to increase the real wage of its members, a union must secure a rise in the wage-rate which is greater than the rate of inflation.

2 In these circumstances, employment and the real wage may rise if the MRP curve shifts rightwards. Whether such a shift in the demand curve for labour is the result of the union's existence, or would have taken place anyway, is open to debate.

3 If the union raises the real wage by restricting entry to the labour market, thereby shifting the supply curve of labour leftwards, employment is likely to fall. However, the unemployed may not be members of the union!

4 Introduce and explain other market situations such as those we have explained in these notes.

Question 2

'Britain's top-paid City executive earns more than £2.5 million a year . . . up to 250 times higher than that of an average school teacher . . . Economics textbooks are packed with rationales for big pay differentials'
Financial Times, 9 October 1987. M. Prowse, 'Why the City Pays Too Much'.

Outline an economic theory of pay differentials and explain whether or not you feel it gives a satisfactory explanation of the example quoted.
(JMB: June, 1988)

Understanding the Question The actual quotation used in the question need not form a key part of your answer; though it would be useful to relate your explanation to the pay differentials between a top businessman and a school teacher employed in the public sector. You might also make the point that the top-paid City executive is probably a part-owner (perhaps through taking advantage of share-option schemes) of the business that employs his managerial or financial skills, so not all his remuneration is a salary or payment for labour. Socialists might explain the differentials in terms of exploitation of workers by capitalists, whilst a more 'neo-classical' explanation would be in terms of supply and demand and the rewards of successful entrepreneurship. Whatever your personal views, avoid the temptation to adopt too polemic a stance and mention the existence of alternative explanations. You should draw on the explanations we have provided in the unit, such as: the separation of labour markets and market imperfections; differences in productivity and elasticities of demand and supply; and the differing relative importance of monetary and non-monetary rewards.

Answer plan

1 Introduce a theory to explain pay differentials (e.g. the neo-classical distribution theory covered in this unit or Marxian theory).
2 Carefully show how your chosen theory explains pay differentials.
3 Point out and explain any inadequacies in the theory.
4 Indicate if other theories complement your chosen theory; or offer more adequate explanations.
5 Reach an overall conclusion as to the adequacy of your explanation.

Multiple Choice Questions

Question 3 An employer with a labour force of 10 men, each paid at the rate of £20 per day, raises the wage-rate by £1 per day to attract one more worker. If other costs remain constant, the marginal cost of employing the additional worker is
(a) £1.00   (b) £11.00   (c) £21.00   (d) £31.00

Understanding the Question Figures 13.3b and 13.4b are especially useful in understanding this question. If the wage-rate is increased to attract one more worker, the marginal cost of labour will include the increase in the wage paid to all the other workers as well as the wage paid to the new worker. MC = £10 + £21. **(d)** is therefore the correct answer.

Question 4 A pop-singer earns £10 000 a week. He would be prepared to remain in his present occupation even if his wage fell as low as £50 a week. £9950 therefore represents his
(a) transfer earnings   (c) economic rent   (b) opportunity cost   (d) quasi rent

Understanding the Question This is a straightforward question on the division of wages, and other factor incomes, between economic rent and transfer earnings. In this case, the singer's transfer earnings are £50 and the economic rent, which is the difference between what he actually earns and the minimum he would be prepared to accept, is £9950. Thus **(c)** is the correct answer. The concept of **quasi rent** in alternative **(d)** is closely related to economic rent. The short-run supply curve of a factor of production is likely to be less elastic than the long-run curve. This means that a factor which will eventually be transferred to an alternative use in the long run, in response to a fall in its factor price, may not be transferred in the short run. That part of its earnings which is economic rent in the short run, but transfer earnings in the long run, forms a **quasi rent**.

Data Response Questions

Question 5 Using the data in the table below and making use of your knowledge of economics, answer the following questions.
Earnings, unemployment rates and employment growth in selected regions of the United Kingdom, 1976 and 1985.

	South East	East Anglia	East Midlands	Yorkshire/ Humberside	North	Scotland
Men						
Gross weekly earnings in £						
April 1976	77.0	66.4	67.3	68.9	71.4	71.6
April 1985	213.8	182.7	175.5	180.7	179.3	189.7
Growth rates						
(% per annum)	12.0	11.9	11.2	11.3	10.8	11.4
Unemployment rate (%)						
1976	5.5	6.1	5.8	6.8	8.8	8.5
1985	11.7	11.9	14.9	17.7	23.0	19.1
Employment						
Growth rates						
(% per annum)	0.1	0.5	−0.5	−0.6	−1.5	−0.3
Women						
Gross weekly earnings in £						
April 1976	50.5	43.4	42.9	43.3	45.0	44.6
April 1985	140.9	118.6	114.3	117.3	119.7	119.1
Growth rates						
(% per annum)	12.2	11.8	11.5	11.7	11.5	11.5
Unemployment rate (%)						
1976	2.3	2.8	2.9	3.4	5.2	4.8
1985	7.5	8.9	9.7	11.2	13.0	11.2
Employment						
Growth rates						
(% per annum)	1.0	1.4	1.0	0.3	0.2	1.0

Source: *Employment Gazette*

(a) (i) Compare and contrast the earnings of men and women in the various regions.   (3)
    (ii) How have men's and women's relative earnings changed over the period 1976–1985?   (3)

(b) How has the incidence of unemployment amongst women compared with men changed over this
period?   (4)

(c) **(i)** Would economic theory suggest that areas with lower wages should have lower unemployment?
                                                                                           (4)

  (ii) Do the data support your answer in **(c)(i)**?   (3)

(d) **(i)** Why might unemployment influence the rate of wage increases?   (5)

  (ii) Do the data seem to fit the theory?   (3)

(Oxford: June, 1988)

Understanding the Question

(a) **(i)** When answering this question, you must avoid the temptation simply to translate numerical data
into words. The question is testing your skill to extract key similarities and differences but take
note of the mark allocation. Only 3 marks are available for this part of the question, so restrict
your answer, at most, to two similarities and two differences. Be careful also to avoid overlap
with part **(ii)** of the question. The gross income of both men and women grew in all regions during
the decade, being highest in the South East throughout the period and lowest in the East
Midlands. Regional differentials were reasonably stable over the decade. Male earnings in East
Anglia rose from the second bottom to the third top position but the rank order of female
earnings in East Anglia did not improve.

  (ii) There was little change in men's and women's relative wages (as distinct from their absolute
wages). Men remained just over 50 per cent better off in all regions throughout the decade.

(b) The incidence of unemployment approximately doubled for men over the decade, but tripled for
women in many regions. (However, male unemployment rates were significantly higher in all regions
throughout the period and female employment grew in all regions while male employment fell in the
majority of the selected regions.)

(c) **(i)** Low relative wages should attract firms to a region (and lead to outward migration from the
region), thus causing regional unemployment to fall. But as regional unemployment falls, we
would expect an equalization of wage rates between regions to occur. However, a region may be
so unattractive to employers (because of a poor resource base or isolation from buoyant markets)
that low wages and high unemployment persist together. Sources of labour market friction may
also have this effect.

  (ii) The evidence could support a number of arguments. Unemployment is lowest in the South East
where earnings are highest, but both unemployment and male earnings were relatively high in
Scotland and the Yorkshire/Humberside region in 1985.

(d) **(i)** The existence of unemployment means there is an excess supply or labour, the effect of which is
to depress regional wage rates. This assumes that employed workers are in competition for jobs
with the unemployed. Labour market frictions may reduce this competition, so that the rate of
regional wage increases can be little affected by regional unemployment.

  (ii) The data displays a significantly greater variation in regional unemployment rates than in the
regional growth rates of earnings. It gives tentative support to the argument that unemployment
has a relatively small effect on the rate of wage increase. However, it is worth noting that the
data relates to absolute rather than real wage levels. When inflation is taken into account, the
rate of increase of real wages may have been much higher in some regions than in others.

13.6 Further reading

Williamson, H., *The Trade Unions,* 7th edition (Heinemann, 1983).

Burningham, D., editor, *Economics*, 3rd edition (Hodder & Stoughton, 1987).

Chapter 11: Factor Markets and the Distribution of Income.

Lipsey, R.G., *An Introduction to Positive Economics*, 7th edition (Weidenfeld & Nicolson, 1989).

Part Five: The Theory of Distribution.

14 Money

14.1 Points of perspective

1 Money as a medium of exchange and unit of account

In a developed market economy, nearly all the exchanges involved in production and distribution require the use of money as a **medium of exchange**. In a very simple economy, exchange could be based on **barter**, but barter is inefficient and impractical in a more complex economic system. Successful barter requires a **'double coincidence of wants'**: if someone wishes to buy a typewriter, he must find another person who not only has a typewriter to sell, but who also wants the goods which the purchaser is selling. Time and energy will be wasted in searching the market to establish the double coincidence of wants. The existence of such **transactions and search costs** is likely to discourage specialization and large-scale production in an economy.

Besides functioning as a medium of exchange, money usually acts as a **unit of account**, allowing the prices of all goods to be compared. In modern economics the unit of account is almost always the medium of exchange, but there are exceptions—the prices of antiques or racehorses offered for sale at an auction are sometimes expressed in guineas, even though the guinea has long ceased to be a monetary unit.

2 Money as a store of value

Monetarists and **Keynesians** hold rather different views on the nature and functions of money. Monetarists have inherited what is sometimes known as the **classical tradition**, which separates the role in the economy of **'real'** and **'monetary'** forces. They believe that the **relative prices** of goods, which are determined in the real economy by the forces of supply and demand, are independent of money even though they are commonly expressed in monetary units of account. Money merely determines the **general price level**. For example, if the amount of money in the economy doubles, all prices double, but relative prices and equilibrium outputs in the economy remain the same.

Keynesians argue that this view of the role of money ignores the essential function of money as a **store of value**. For example, a person who sells his labour and receives money in exchange may decide to store the income he received in the form of idle money instead of using it to demand goods and services. This can result in a lack of demand for the output which is currently being produced, resulting in the breakdown of the **monetary linkage** between the **markets of the real economy**. Thus, the function of money as a store of value is an important part of the Keynesian argument that unemployment can be caused by a lack of **effective aggregate demand** in an economy.

3 The historical development of money

(i) Commodity money In order to function as money, an asset must be an acceptable medium of exchange and a possible store of value. Early forms of money which replaced barter were **commodities**, such as beads, shells, cattle and slaves, usually with an **intrinsic value** of their own. Gradually the **precious metals**, gold and silver, replaced other forms of commodity money because they possessed to a greater degree the other desirable characteristics necessary for a commodity to function as money: relative **scarcity, portability, durability, divisibility,** and **uniformity**.

(ii) Representative money Nevertheless gold and silver are vulnerable to theft and difficult to store, and it became the custom for precious metals to be deposited with goldsmiths for safekeeping. The goldsmiths developed into banks, and the gold receipts which they issued became bank-notes or paper money. The notes were acceptable as a means of payment since they could be exchanged for gold on demand. Although relatively worthless in itself, the money **represented** ownership of commodities with an intrinsic value.

(iii) Token money Banks discovered that they could increase their profits by issuing notes to a value greatly in excess of the gold deposits which they held. Imprudent banks would over-expand the note issue, and depositors suffered in the crashes which periodically occurred when banks could not meet demands by the public to convert notes into gold. As a direct result of these bank crashes, the 1844 Bank Charter Act largely removed from English and Welsh banks the right to issue their own notes, though some banks continued to issue notes on a limited scale until the last 'country' bank merged in 1921. This change in the law encouraged a new development in banking, the creation of **deposit money**. Instead of issuing its own notes when a customer requested a loan, a bank would make a

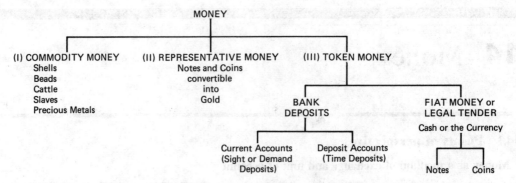

Fig 14.1 Historical and present-day forms of money

ledger or book-keeping entry crediting the customer's account with a loan or bank deposit. Such a bank deposit is obviously a store of value. However, a bank deposit is also a medium of exchange if it is customarily accepted that payment can be made by shifting ownership of the deposit, for example through the medium of a cheque.

Bank deposits are of course **token money**. They are **customary money** rather than **legal tender**, and generally accepted as money because of people's confidence in the banks and the monetary system. Bank deposits make up by far the largest part of modern money, between about two-thirds and 85 per cent of the money supply, depending on how money is defined. In contrast, **cash** (notes and coins, or the **currency**) is just the 'small change' of the system. Nowadays the state has a monopoly of the issue of cash, in England and Wales at least, and cash has gradually developed to become purely token money, just like a bank deposit. Unlike a bank deposit, however, cash is usually legal tender – 'fiat money' made legal by government decree – which must be accepted as a medium of exchange.

14.2 Underlying concepts

1 Money, near money, and money substitutes

It is generally agreed that bank **current accounts (sight deposits** or **demand deposits)** function as money. They are both a store of value and a medium of exchange since cheques can be drawn on the deposit and are accepted in payment of a debt. Nowadays many people use credit cards as a medium of exchange. However, a credit card is not a store of value, and its use merely delays the settling of a debt through a cash transaction or the shifting of a bank deposit. A credit card is a **money substitute** rather than a form of money in its own right.

Whereas a money substitute is a medium of exchange but not a store of value, the reverse is true of **near money**. Financial assets such as building society deposits were until recently regarded as near monies. A building society deposit is a substitute for a bank current account or a cash holding as a convenient form of storage for wealth or value, but it does not serve directly as medium of exchange unless cheques can be drawn on the deposit.

2 The problem of defining the money supply

Thirty years ago, neither economists nor politicians gave much attention to the precise definition of the money supply, since it was generally accepted that 'money did not matter' in the macro-economic management of the economy. As we shall see in later units, this is no longer the case. According to the monetarists, money does matter, and the **control of the money supply** is an important part of monetarist economic management in general, and monetary policy in particular. Even if it is accepted that monetarist theory is correct (we shall later see that Keynesians dispute this) **practical monetarism** may be impossible if the money supply is a 'will-o'-the wisp' which cannot by its nature be controlled. Suppose that the **monetary authorities** (the Bank of England and the Treasury) decide either to restrict the rate of growth of the money supply or to reduce the absolute size of the money stock. The more successful they appear to be in controlling whatever they define as the money supply, the more likely it is that **near monies**, outside the existing definition and system of control, will take on the function of money as a medium of exchange. The phenomenon is related to **Goodhart's Law**, which states that as soon as a measure of the money supply (e.g. M4) is adopted as a target for monetary control, any apparently stable, former relationship between it and the price level will break down, rendering the measure useless as a control variable. In this sense, 'money is as money does'! Keynesians sometimes argue that the money supply is impossible to control, since it **passively** adapts to whatever level is required to finance the transactions which are desired at the existing price level. We shall examine the implications of this argument in the context of monetary policy in Unit 17 and inflation in Unit 22.

Whether or not this view on the impossibility of controlling the money supply is completely accepted, it does help to explain why policy-makers have commonly used more than one definition of the money supply. The 'narrow definition' favoured in Britain has been **M1**, comprising cash and bank sight deposits. However, wealthy individuals and companies will normally hold interest-earning **deposit accounts** or **time deposits** alongside their current accounts or sight deposits. Should time deposits be defined as money? Unlike a sight deposit, the ownership of a time deposit cannot be shifted by cheque; hence a time deposit is not a medium of exchange. But to compete with the building societies, the banks have allowed deposit accounts to become increasingly more liquid. A customer may keep a very low balance in a current account, upon which cheques can be drawn; when a large payment is due to be made, part of the deposit account is simply shifted into the current account. Bank customers therefore treat their deposit accounts as money, a practice encouraged by the banks in order to attract funds away from building societies and National Savings Certificates. For this reason, time deposits are included in the wider measure of money **M3**. But because building society deposits have become as liquid as bank deposits, M1 and M3 have now given way to **M2** and **M4** (which include building society deposits) as the main measures of 'narrow' and 'broad' money respectively.

Because of the tendency for near monies to become money, in the 1970s the authorities widened from M1 to **Sterling M3 (£M3)** the definition of money used as the principal target or indicator in British monetary policy. The narrow definition M1 concentrates on the medium of exchange function of money, whereas wider definitions, such as M3, include financial assets that are both temporary stores of value and are sufficiently liquid to be converted into a

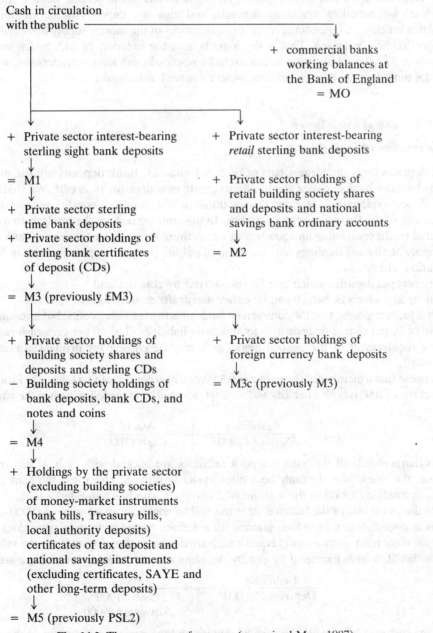

Fig. 14.2 The measures of money, (as revised May, 1987)

medium of exchange quickly and without capital loss. £M3, as distinct from M3, included only sterling bank deposits. Foreign currencies deposited in the UK banking system were excluded from £M3 for the simple reason that since they are unlikely to be spent in the UK, it would be misleading to include them in a measure of the money supply used primarily as an indicator of, and to control, domestic monetary conditions. But perhaps in reaction to the difficulty in 'hitting' announced £M3 targets, in 1983 the authorities introduced a new measure of the money stock, MO. **MO** is the narrowest possible measure of money, being mainly notes and coins – cash or '**high-powered money**', or the '**monetary base**'.

In the 1987 Budget, the Chancellor of the Exchequer announced the dropping of £M3 as a formal target of monetary policy, as distinct from its role, along with the other measures of money, as a general indicator of monetary conditions. Shortly afterwards in May 1987, the Bank of England published a reclassification of the official measures of money, which we have summarized in Figure 14.2. £M3 was renamed, becoming simply **M3**, while 'old' M3 was redesignated **M3c**. Perhaps the most significant measures of money are now **M2** and **M4**. We have already noted how illogical it is to include time deposits in a measure of money such as M3, but to exclude building society deposits which are essentially similar. In recognition of this, a distinction is now made between **retail** and **wholesale** deposits. **Retail deposits** are liquid – or relatively liquid – deposits held by the general public **which are likely to be spent**. They may be held in banks, or in other financial institutions such as building societies. In contrast, **wholesale deposits** are normally owned by banks and financial institutions, and held in other banks and financial institutions. Wholesale deposits, which reflect the asset portfolio management decisions of banks and other financial institutions, have relatively little effect on the retail spending decisions of the general public. There is a case, therefore, for excluding wholesale deposits, and also any deposits which are unlikely to be translated quickly into spending power, from measures of the money supply designed primarily to monitor 'retail' conditions. This is the logic behind the creation of M2, which includes retail deposits in all financial institutions, but excludes wholesale and long-term deposits, while **M4** also includes time deposits held in building societies as well as in banks.

14.3   Essential knowledge

1 The creation of bank deposits

Bank deposits form the largest part of both M1 and M3. Bank deposits are the main form of money because banks possess the ability to create new deposits or **credit**. We shall delay until Unit 17 an explanation of how this is done in the complex conditions and institutional framework of the British monetary system. In this unit we restrict the analysis to a very simple model of credit creation in an economy in which there is just one **commercial bank** which has a monopoly of all bank dealings with the general public. For our purposes a bank is defined as an institution which:

(i) accepts **deposits** which can be transferred by cheque; and

(ii) makes **advances** (which can be either **overdrafts** or **term loans**).

We shall further assume that the commercial bank aims to maximize profits, but is required to hold a reserve of 10 per cent cash against its total deposit liabilities. The 10 per cent **cash ratio** may be a **reserve requirement** of the **central bank**, or it may be chosen for **prudential reasons** by the bank itself.

Suppose that a member of the public now makes a new deposit of £1000 in cash. From the bank's point of view £1000 is both a **liability** and an **asset**, and will be recorded as such in the bank's balance sheet:

Liabilities	Assets
Deposit £1000	Cash £1000

As things stand, all the bank's deposit liabilities are backed with cash. If this remained the position, the 'bank' would simply be a safe-deposit institution. However, the bank can increase profits by crediting £9000 to the account of a customer who has requested a loan.

On the assets side of the balance sheet this will be shown as an **advance** of £9000 – whether the loan is an overdraft or a term loan granted for a definite period or term of years does not matter. Since the bank must honour any cheques which are drawn on the account up to the value of £9000, **deposit liabilities** have increased by exactly the same amount as **interest-earning assets**:

Liabilities	Assets
Deposits £10 000	Cash £1000
	Advances £9000

Both the customer who made the original deposit and the customer in receipt of the advance can draw cheques to a combined value of £10 000 on their deposits. The initial £1000 has expanded deposits, and hence the money supply, to £10 000. As we are assuming a monopoly bank, there is no danger of customers drawing cheques payable to customers of other banks. Nevertheless, there could be a **cash drain** from the bank, if customers decide always to keep some proportion of their money assets in the form of cash. A cash drain would limit the bank's ability to create deposits to a figure somewhat below that illustrated in our example.

Deposits will be expanded whether the bank expands advances or purchases interest-earning assets such as securities or bonds from the general public. Suppose the bank creates £6000 of advances and purchases £3000 of bonds. The bank pays for the bonds with a cheque for £3000 drawn on itself, thereby increasing total deposit liabilities to £10 000 when the payment is credited to the account of the person who sold the bonds. The spectrum of assets owned by the bank is different from the previous position, but the deposit liabilities, which represent the creation of money, are the same as in our last example:

Liabilities	Assets	
Deposits £10 000	Cash	£1000
	Bonds	£3000
	Advances	£6000

Of course, the assumption of a monopoly commercial bank is completely unrealistic, but it does illustrate the central principle of credit creation–that the banking system as a whole can create an expansion in bank deposits (and thus the money supply) which is a **multiple** of the **liquid reserves** held by the banks. Because, in our example, cash is the only liquid asset or reserve held to **fractionally back** the bank's deposit liabilities, the ability of the banks to expand deposits is dependent on the cash ratio. The **money multiplier** measures the maximum expansion of deposits (or **'low-powered'** **money**) which is possible for a given increase in cash (or **'high-powered' money**) deposited in the banking system. Assuming that there is no cash drain, for our model we can write:

$$\text{money multiplier} = \frac{1}{\text{cash ratio}}$$

In Unit 17 we shall see that British banks have usually kept some form of **liquid assets ratio** or **reserve ratio**, rather than the simple cash ratio of our model. It is useful, therefore, to write the money multiplier more generally as:

$$\text{money multiplier} = \frac{1}{\text{liquid assets ratio}}$$

When we assume a **multi-bank system**, similar to that in the UK, the general conclusions of our model still hold. If the increase of £1000 in cash deposits is spread over all the banks, deposits can expand to £10 000 providing that every bank is prepared to create deposits to the full extent the cash ratio allows. However, if only one bank is willing to expand deposits to the full, it will soon face demands for cash which it cannot meet. Customers will draw cheques on their deposits which will be paid into the accounts of the customers of the banks that have refused to expand credit. When the cheques are cleared, the bank must pay cash to the other banks, equal to the shift in deposits. To avoid this possibility, the bank will restrict the extent to which it is prepared to expand deposits. However, if all banks expand credit to the full, payments to customers of other banks will largely cancel out. The banking system as a whole can expand deposits to £10 000, though some banks may gain business at the expense of others.

2 The demand for money

So far we have assumed implicitly that banks will create new bank deposits, and hence increase the supply of money, to the fullest extent possible. In our model, the ability of the banks to create new deposits is constrained, firstly by the size of the **cash base** of the banking system, and secondly by the **prudential requirement** to maintain a cash ratio–in Unit 17 we shall extend the analysis to the situation where the monetary authorities decide the reserve ratio and then attempt to influence the reserve assets in the implementation of monetary policy.

However, we have begged the question of whether bank customers actually **demand** and take up all the new deposits or credit which the banks are prepared to create. The **actual money stock** in the economy will be determined by both the demand and the supply of money.

The nature of the demand for money is one of the most important areas of debate between Keynesian and monetarist economists, a debate which is significant both in terms of economic theory and practical policy-making. Unfortunately, in a book of this type we can do no more than scratch the surface of the issues involved. Keynesians and monetarists share common ground in believing that part of the demand for money results from **transactions** and **precautionary motives**:

(i) The transactions demand for money A certain amount of money is required as a medium of

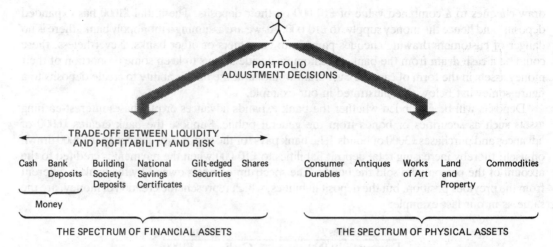

Fig 14.3 An example of some of the financial and physical assets in which an individual may decide to store his personal wealth

exchange so that people can undertake day-to-day purchases of goods and services. The transactions demand for money depends upon:

(a) **real income**–people with high incomes are likely to require larger transaction balances to finance their purchases for the simple reason that they usually plan to spend more than poorer people.

(b) **the price level**–a rise in the price level is likely to increase the transactions demand for money, since more money is needed to finance the same real expenditure.

(c) **institutional factors such as the length of time between pay days**–if a worker is paid a salary of £800 once every four weeks instead of £200 weekly, he is likely to keep a larger balance, on average, in his bank deposit or in cash in order to finance the expenditure planned over the month. Financial innovation, such as the development and availability of near monies and money substitutes, may also affect the transactions demand for money.

(ii) The precautionary demand for money A certain amount of money may be held to meet unforeseen emergencies, though it is more usual nowadays to hold such assets in building society deposits and other near monies. For most purposes the precautionary demand for money can be merged into the transactions demand, since it is also likely to be determined by real income, the price level and institutional factors.

(iii) The speculative demand for money If money balances were required only for transactions and precautionary purposes, the **demand for money function** would be **inelastic** with respect to the rate of interest, resembling the curve labelled L_{t+p} in Figure 14.4(a). However, Keynes argued the existence of a third **speculative** motive for holding money balances in which changes, and expected changes, in the rate of interest become the crucial influences over people's demand to hold money. The speculative demand for money is shown as the curve L_s in Figure 14.4(b).

The speculative demand is sometimes called the demand to hold **passive** or **idle** money balances as a **store of value or wealth**–in contrast to the essentially **active** nature of transactions and precautionary balances which are held essentially as a medium of exchange. Figure 14.3 illustrates how money is just one of the assets in which an individual may decide to store his **portfolio** of wealth. However for our purposes we can simplify and assume that an individual can store in wealth in just two assets: **money and bonds**. Money possesses the advantage of instant spending power, or complete **liquidity**, but it earns little if any interest or income. In contrast, bonds earn fixed rates of interest but suffer from being relatively illiquid.

Now, the higher the rate of interest the more attractive it becomes to store wealth in bonds rather than money. **Thus the demand for idle money balances is inversely related to the rate of interest**. However, **speculation** about **future interest rates** explains the particular **non-linear** slope of the L_s function shown in Figure 14.4(b). Although bonds have the advantage of earning an income, we saw in Unit 11 how the **price of bonds varies inversely with the rate of interest**. If the rate of interest rises, then bond prices must fall, and owners of bonds must suffer **capital losses**. Clearly, it is in the interest of bond owners to guess correctly **future changes** in interest rates. If they expect, or **speculate**, that interest rates will rise, they should sell bonds and hold their wealth in money since changes in the rate of interest do not involve any change in the value of money. Bond holders will **prefer liquidity**, to evade capital losses that would result from holding bonds. But if interest rates are expected to fall, people should move out of money and purchase bonds so as to benefit from future capital gains.

Finally there will be a value of the rate of interest which people regard as 'normal'; if the actual rate is below the 'normal' rate people will expect the actual rate to rise, and if it were above they

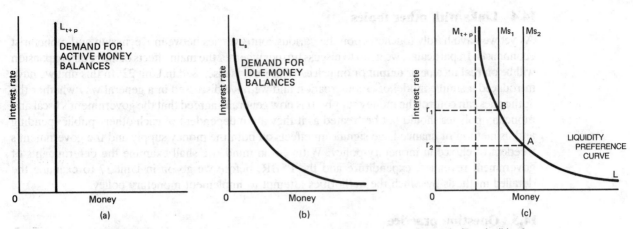

Fig 14.4 The demand for money (a) the transactions and precautionary demand (L_{t+p}) (b) the speculative and asset demand (L_s) (c) the demand for money curve (liquidity preference curve) and the determination of the rate of interest

would expect it to fall. This part of Keynes' theory of the speculative demand for money explains the upper (vertical) and the lower (horizontal) sections of the L_s curve. Keynes argues that at some low rate of interest everyone will expect the rate to rise, thus making them unwilling to hold bonds. For any further fall in the interest rate below this level, demand for money will be perfectly elastic. The resulting horizontal section of the L_s function Keynes called the **liquidity trap**. In a similar way, there will be some high rate of interest at which everyone will expect the rate of interest to fall, making them unwilling to hold money as a passive wealth asset. For any further rise in the interest rate above this level there will be no further movement out of money and into bonds; hence the L_s function will be completely interest-inelastic or vertical.

3 The determination of the rate of interest
In Figure 14.4(c) we bring together the demand for, and the supply of, money to illustrate the Keynesian theory of the determination of the rate of interest. The rate of interest can be regarded simply as the **price of money**, and as in any market, an equilibrium price will be determined where demand equals supply. We obtain the demand for money function, (which is often called the **Liquidity Preference** function), by adding up the transactions, precautionary, and speculative demands for money. The supply of money is shown as a vertical, and completely interest-inelastic, line labelled Ms_1. This is derived from the simplifying, and rather unrealistic, assumption that the money supply is a **policy instrument** completely controlled by the **monetary authorities**. If the authorities fix the money supply at Ms_1, the rate of interest is determined at r_1; if they then increase the money supply to Ms_2, the rate of interest falls to r_2. However, in Unit 17 we shall suggest that the reverse relationship is perhaps more relevant to the conduct of monetary policy – changes in the rate of interest being used to achieve change in the money supply!

4 Some implications for monetary policy
In later units we shall explain how Keynesians have often argued that **fiscal policy** is both more powerful and predictable than **monetary policy** as a method of influencing the level of output in the economy. The theory developed in the preceding sections can be used to illustrate why Keynesians doubt the effectiveness of monetary policy. In Keynesian theory, the main **transmission mechanism** through which monetary policy affects output and the 'real economy' is via the effect of the interest rate upon businessmen's investment decisions. But even supposing that investment is highly responsive to changes in the rate of interest – and Keynes' theory of the **marginal efficiency of capital** which is explained in Unit 21 suggests that it is not – monetary policy may have little effect if the Liquidity Preference curve is flat or interest-elastic. In these circumstances a large change in the money supply is likely to cause little or no change in the rate of interest, and hence investment. Conversely, if the demand for money curve is nearly vertical or interest-inelastic, the effect on the rate of interest may be quite powerful.

It is therefore not surprising that Keynesians and monetarists often disagree on the interest-elasticity of the demand for money, which, as we have seen, depends upon the existence of a speculative motive for holding money. Monetarists usually adopt the old 'classical' view that denies the existence of the speculative demand. Their argument is that the demand for money is interest-inelastic, people holding money balances largely to finance spending or transactions. Any increase in the money stock can cause significant changes in interest rates, but according to monetarists, the main effect will not be on investment and output but on prices as people spend their suddenly-increased money holdings.

14.4 Links with other topics

As yet we have hardly touched upon the various controversies between Keynesian and monetarist economists. In particular, we need to discuss further whether the main effects of monetary expansion will be on **real income or output** or on **prices**. This issue is discussed in Unit 22. In this unit we have introduced a simple model of credit creation and we have discussed in a general way whether the authorities can control the money supply. It is now generally agreed that the government's fiscal and monetary policies should not be treated as if they are independent of each other–public spending and its method of finance have significant effects on both the money supply and the government's freedom of choice in monetary policy. With this in mind, we shall examine the determinants of government revenues, expenditure and the PSBR, before we go on in Unit 17 to examine the detailed methods by which the authorities attempt to implement monetary policy.

14.5 Question practice

Essay Questions

Question 1

(a) Explain how the banking system creates bank deposits. (15)

(b) How might total bank deposits be affected by:

  (i) The government's budget moving from deficit into surplus? (5)

  (ii) A large-scale sale of shares to the general public resulting from the privatization of the electricity industry? (5)

(*AEB: June, 1990*)

Understanding the Question This question displays a clear 'incline of difficulty'; part (a) is relatively straightforward, typical of many past examination questions, part (b) is more difficult, requiring the candidate to think carefully about events topical (or about to be topical) at the time of the examination.

You can answer part (a) either with any of the standard models of deposit creation ('monopoly' bank or multi-bank systems) or with illustation from actual British experience. State the assumptions of your chosen model and indicate the constraints operating on the deposit-creating process.

Begin your answer to part (b) (i) by noting that a budget deficit, through its financing by borrowing from the banking system, can lead to the growth of bank deposits. It follows that a budget surplus, by removing this need to borrow, should have a contractionary effect on bank deposits. An alternative approach is to trace the linkages stemming from taxpayers drawing cheques on their bank deposits which are paid to the government. If these deposits are taken out of circulation (i.e. not spent by the government), bank deposits will contract. However, there may be a more neutral effect if the government 'spends' the surplus on debt redemption, since deposits will recirculate back to the banking system.

In much the same way, the sale of shares to the general public in a major privatization will be paid for with cheques drawn on the general public's bank deposits. Again, if these deposits are taken out of circulation, bank deposits fall. But, if the government simply spends the proceeds of the privatization, the effect is likely to be neutral again because the deposits return to the banking system.

Answer plan

1 Briefly explain what a bank deposit is; state that the banking system can create as well as accept deposits.

2 Introduce a model of deposit creation, clearly indicating its simplifying assumptions.

3 Develop the model of deposit creation. Indicate the constraints limiting the process and explain the deposit multiplier.

4 Explain that the government's budget moving from deficit into surplus leads to a negative PSBR and the possibility of debt repayment (a PSDR).

5 Explain how the effect on bank deposits may be contractionary or neutral, depending on what happens to the surplus.

6 Show that a rather similar process happens with privatization revenues, depending on whether they are spent by the government.

Multiple Choice Questions

Question 2 The following table gives details of items comprising the money stock of the UK in 1979:

Notes and coins in circulation	£9701 m
Private sector sterling current accounts	£20 345 m
Private sector sterling deposit accounts	£27 376 m
Public sector sterling deposit accounts	£1255 m
UK residents' deposits in other currencies	£5306 m

In 1979 the money stock defined as Sterling M3 amounted to:

(a) £30 046 m (b) £57 422 m (c) £58 677 m (d) £63 983 m

Understanding the Question Alternative (a) is M1, the sum of notes and coins in circulation and private sector sterling current accounts, the most liquid measure of money apart from actual cash. Alternative (b) is equivalent to M1 plus private sector sterling deposit accounts. However this does not equal Sterling M3 because it excludes public sector sterling deposits. Thus (c), which includes public sector deposits, is the correct answer. Alternative (**d**) is the wider measure of M3 (as it was defined before 1987), which includes foreign currency deposits as well as holdings of sterling.

Questions 3 and 4

(a)	(b)	(c)	(d)
1, 2, 3 all correct	1, 2 only correct	2, 3 only correct	1 only correct

Question 3 There will be positive real interest rates if:
1 The Bank of England increases its lending rate.
2 Nominal interest rates rise above the rate of inflation.
3 The capital values of fixed interest securities are index-linked.

Understanding the Question The real rate of interest may be positive if the Bank of England raises its lending rate, but we cannot be certain without knowing the lending rate and the rate of inflation. The correct answer is (**c**). Alternative 2 is a necessary condition for real interest rates to be positive, while the linking of the capital value of a security to an index of the inflation rate, such as the Retail Price Index, ensures that the fixed interest rate is a real yield on the security–providing of course, that the index accurately measures the inflation rate.

Question 4 In Keynesian theory, which of the following are determinants of the demand for money?
1 The rate of interest.
2 The level of real income.
3 Expectations about the future level of security prices.

Understanding the Question The answer is (**a**) since, according to Keynesians, all three of the specified variables influence the demand to hold money balances. The demand for money depends upon expectations of future interest rates and security prices (the speculative demand for money) and upon the present interest rate (asset demand and liquidity preference). The level of real income is accepted by Keynesians as well as by monetarists as a determinant of the demand for money (transactions demand).

Question 5 Study the table below, then answer the questions which follow.

Table of percentage changes

	M0	*£M3*	*Money GDP*	*Prices*
1980-81	5.2	17.5	14.9	18.6
1981-82	4.3	16.3	9.4	10.1
1982-83	6.0	12.2	9.4	7.1
1983-84	6.1	12.1	7.6	4.4
1984-85	2.4	10.0	6.5	4.6

(Derived from statistics in *Economic Trends* and the *Bank of England Quarterly Bulletin*)

(a) Explain what is meant by M0 and £M3. (5)
(b) What, if anything, do the data imply about the relationships between the monetary aggregates in the table and prices over this period? (5)
(c) What can be inferred from the table regarding the direction of the changes in **real GDP** or output over the period? (5)
(d) Government policy in the early 1980's was based on an assumed close relationship between movements in £M3 and **money GDP**. What do the data suggest? What can be inferred about the income velocity of circulation of £M3 comparing 1980-81 with 1984-85? (5)
(e) What theory suggests that there will be a relationship between M0 and £M3? What do the data suggest about this relationship in practice? (5)

(*WJEC, June 1988*)

Understanding the question This question covers the monetary aggregates, or measures of the money supply which we have explained in this unit, together with the monetarist theory of inflation (the quantity theory of money) and aspects of monetary policy, which are explained respectively in Units 22 and 17. Note that the measure of money, £M3, is now known simply as M3. The question is testing a number of skills: factual recall in (**a**); ability to detect correlation (perhaps involving lagged correlation) or lack of correlation between the variables in the data in (**b**) and (**d**); the ability to convert nominal data into real data (using the information given on the rate of inflation in (**c**)); and, finally in (**e**), the bank-deposit multiplier relationship between the monetary base (M0) and 'broad' money (M3), which includes mostly bank deposits.

14.6 Further reading

Burningham, D., editor, *Economics*, 3rd edition (Hodder & Stoughton 1987).
Chapter 15: Money and banking. Chapter 16: The control of the monetary system.

Lipsey, R. G., *An Introduction to Positive Economics*, 7th edition (Weidenfeld & Nicolson, 1989).
Chapter 30: Money and the Price Level.
Chapter 31: Monetary Equilibrium.

15 Taxation and Public Spending

15.1 Points of perspective

This is the first of two units devoted to important aspects of **public finance**. This unit, which covers the **structure** of **taxation** and **public expenditure** in the United Kingdom, emphasizes the more **micro-economic elements** of public finance, leaving until Unit 16 a consideration of what happens in the economy as a whole when government expenditure is different from revenue and a **budget deficit** or **surplus** occurs. The **macro-economic** and **monetary** implications of public finance are further developed in later units.

It is worth stressing at the outset that taxation and public spending are 'opposite sides of the **fiscal** coin'. Thus an argument for (or against) public spending is usually also an argument for (or against) taxation.

A large part of the **public sector** exists in the **non-market economy**, which means that the output of goods and services produced is not sold at a **market price**. There are of course important exceptions, particularly the activities of **nationalized industries**, which exist largely in the **market economy**. In some cases the distinction is rather unclear, when for example an art gallery is largely financed out of taxation even though a **token price** is charged for admission. We shall, however, follow the convention of excluding from our definition of public spending the direct spending by nationalized industries, since the expenditure is largely financed from the revenue raised by selling the industries' output in the market place. In this unit we restrict our analysis to the direct spending by **central** and **local government** and the taxation which largely finances this spending.

15.2 Underlying concepts

1 Types of taxation

A **tax**, which is a **compulsory levy** charged by a government or **public authority** to **pay for its expenditure**, can be classified in a number of ways:

(i) According to who levies the tax Most taxes are levied by **central** government in the UK, but the **community charge** (or **poll tax**) and the **uniform business rate** are examples of local government taxation. Due to its unpopularity, the poll tax will be replaced with a property tax.

(ii) According to what is taxed The major categories here are **taxes on income, expenditure and capital**, though other categories include **pay-roll** and **poll taxes**. **Personal income tax** is the most important tax on income in the UK, though employees' **National Insurance contributions** (NIC) and **corporation tax** (a tax on company income or profits) are other examples. The **Inland Revenue** is the department of the civil service mainly responsible for collecting taxes on income and capital, whereas the **Board of Customs and Excise** collects expenditure taxes. Expenditure taxes are usefully divided into *ad valorem* or **percentage taxes** such as **value-added tax** (VAT), and **specific taxes** (or **unit taxes**) which include the excise duties on tobacco, alcohol and petrol. A specific tax on, for example, wine is levied on the quantity of wine rather than on its price. Thus a bottle of expensive vintage claret bears the same tax as a bottle of cheap table-wine. Similarly, a **user tax** such as a **television licence** or **motor vehicle tax** is levied irrespective of either the price or the current market value of the TV set or car.

The poll tax has temporarily replaced the local rates as the main form of local taxation in the UK. Prior to its introduction in 1989 in Scotland and 1990 in England and Wales a poll tax, which is a tax 'on being a human being', was last levied in the United Kingdom in the 14th century, when it triggered a peasants' revolt that caused its hasty withdrawal! Viewed as a 'community charge', the poll tax can be classified as an expenditure tax levied to pay for local government services provided. Taxes on wealth and capital have never been significant in the United Kingdom. The main current capital tax is **inheritance tax**, a tax on gifts from the dead to the living, which replaced **capital transfer tax** (CTT). CTT was a short-lived tax levied during the 1970s and early 1980s which had extended the taxation of wealth to cover gifts made during life as well as the inheritance of estates. Finally, amongst a number of miscellaneous taxes, are employers' National Insurance contributions, a form of **pay-roll tax** in which the amount of tax paid varies with the number of workers employed.

(iii) Direct and Indirect Taxation These concepts are often used interchangeably with taxes on income and expenditure, though it is not strictly true that a tax on spending *must* be an indirect tax. Income tax is a direct tax because the income receiver, who **benefits** from the income, is **directly liable** in law to pay the tax (even though it is frequently collected through the PAYE scheme from the employer). In contrast, **most** taxes on spending are indirect taxes since the **seller** of the good, and not the purchaser who benefits from its consumption, is liable in law to pay the tax. Nevertheless, as we shall see later, the seller usually tries to **pass on the incidence** of the tax to the purchaser by raising the price of the good by the amount of the tax! There are, however, examples of **direct taxes on expenditure**, such as the **stamp duty** paid by the purchaser rather than by the seller of a house.

(iv) Progressive, Regressive and Proportionate Taxation In a progressive tax system a **progressively larger proportion** of income is paid in tax as income rises, while in a **regressive** system a **progressively smaller proportion** is paid. A tax is **proportionate** if exactly the same proportion of income is paid in tax at all levels of income.

You should note that in these definitions the word **progressive** is completely **'value neutral'**, implying nothing about how the revenue raised by the government is spent. Nevertheless, progressive taxation is likely to be used by the government to achieve the social aim of a 'fairer' distribution of income. However, progressive taxation cannot by itself redistribute income – a policy of **transfers** in the government's public spending programme is required for this. Progressive taxation used on its own will merely reduce **post-tax income differentials** compared with **pre-tax differentials**.

Progressive, regressive and proportionate taxes can also be defined in terms of the **marginal** and **average tax rates**. The **marginal tax rate** measures the proportion of the last pound paid in tax as income rises, whereas the **average tax rate** at any level of income is simply the total tax paid as a proportion of total income. In the case of a progressive income tax, the marginal rate of tax is higher than the average rate, except when no tax at all is paid on the first band of a person's income. If income tax is regressive, the marginal rate of tax is less than the average rate, while the two are equal in the case of a proportionate tax.

2 Types of public spending

We have already noted why we are excluding the direct spending by nationalized industries from our definition of public spending. Amongst the various divisions that can usefully be made between types of public spending are those between **central** and **local government spending**, and between **capital** and **current spending**. Capital spending involves **public** or **social investment** in a project (or **public work**) such as a new hospital, school or motorway. Current spending includes items such as the wage costs of staffing and the maintenance costs of running existing capital assets.

Perhaps the most important distinction to be made between types of public spending is between **real** and **transfer expenditure**:

(i) Real expenditure Real expenditure occurs when the government directly provides goods and services which add to national output. All capital spending is real expenditure, as is the current expenditure on the wages and salaries of civil servants, local government officers, teachers, police, the armed forces and workers in the National Health Service. In contributing directly to output, real expenditure **uses up scarce resources**; indeed it is sometimes known as the **'direct command of resources'** by the government.

(ii) Transfer expenditure Conversely, transfer expenditure merely redistributes income between different members of the community. Tax revenues are used to provide **income** via pensions, welfare benefits, grants and subsidies both to households in the personal sector and to firms within the corporate sector. The various forms of regional and industrial aid and assistance, including the transfers to nationalized industries, are an important part of total transfers. Transfers do not contribute directly to production although their administration uses up scarce resources, and indeed transfers to low-income groups usually encourage consumption since poorer people have high **marginal propensities to consume**. Massive transfers from central to local government also take place **within** the public sector. A large part of the spending of local authorities is financed in this way. **Interest payments** on past government borrowing (which we cover in more detail in the context of the PSBR and the **National Debt** in Unit 16) are a form of transfer from taxpayers to those people who have lent to the government. Strictly, however, the term **transfer payment** (which must not be confused with the **transfer earnings** of Unit 13) is restricted to payments which are not made in return for some productive service.

Statistics which show public spending as a percentage of either GDP or GNP are sometimes used to indicate the relative importance of real expenditure by the government. However, great care must be taken in using such statistics; the figures can be very misleading unless both transfers and the spending by nationalized industries have first been excluded.

15.3   Essential information

1 The principles of taxation

Adam Smith's four **principles** or **canons** of taxation are commonly used as the starting-point for analyzing and evaluating the operation of a tax system. Adam Smith suggested that taxation should be **equitable, economical, convenient** and **certain**, and to these we may also add the canons of **efficiency** and **flexibility**:

(i) Equity   A tax should be based on the taxpayer's **ability to pay**. This principle is sometimes used to justify **progressive taxation**, since the rich have a greater ability to pay than the poor. A tax system should be **fair**, but there are likely to be different and possibly conflicting interpretations of what is fair or equitable.

(ii) Economy   Collection of a tax should be easily and cheaply administered so that the yield is maximized relative to the cost of collection.

(iii) Convenience   The method of payment should be convenient to the taxpayer.

(iv) Certainty   The taxpayer should know what, when, where and how to pay, in such a manner that **tax evasion** is difficult. (**Tax evasion** is the **illegal** failure to pay a lawful tax, whereas **tax avoidance** involves the arrangement of personal or business affairs **within the law** to minimize tax liability.)

(v) Efficiency   A tax should achieve its intended aim without side-effects. If for example the raising of the top rate of income tax, in order to raise revenue, results in increased disincentives to work, then the tax is inefficient. Since it is usually impossible to avoid all the undesirable side-effects of a tax, the tax system should attempt to minimize them.

(vi) Flexibility   If the tax system is used as a means of economic management then, in order to meet new circumstances, certain taxes may need to be easily altered.

2 The aims of taxation

The **aims** of taxation should not be confused with the **principles** or **canons** of taxation, although an aim may well be to arrange the tax system as much as possible in accordance with the principles of taxation. It is useful to distinguish between a number of aims or objectives of taxation and to note how the importance attached to some of the objectives has varied according to the changing fashions in economic thought:

(i) Revenue raising   One of the oldest and most obvious aims of taxation is to raise revenue so as to pay for government expenditure. Before the **Keynesian 'revolution'** of the 1930s most economists believed that revenue-raising was by far the most important objective of taxation. Indeed many went further and argued that the levels of both public spending and taxation should be as low as possible, with the government restricting its activities to the provision of goods and services that could not be provided adequately and privately through the market. According to this **pre-Keynesian** or **neo-classical** view, recently revived in modern **monetarism**, a government should engage in the **financial orthodoxy** or **'sound finance'** of **balancing its budget**.

(ii) The correction of market 'failures'   In the traditional view we have just described, the primary purpose of government intervention in the economy is to correct or to reduce the various **market failures** which we first introduced in Unit 8. A government may be justified in using taxation to:

(a) Tax monopoly profits, both to deter monopoly and to remove the 'windfall gain' accruing to a monopolist as a result of barriers to entry and inelastic supply.

(b) Finance the collective provision of public goods and merit goods. The market might **fail to provide public goods** such as roads and defence, while education, health care and other **merit goods** might be **underconsumed** at market prices.

(c) Discourage the consumption of demerit goods. Demerit goods such as tobacco might be **overconsumed** at market prices. Note that a conflict may arise between the revenue-raising aim of taxation and this aim of reducing the consumption of demerit goods.

(d) Alter the distribution of income. The government may decide that the distribution of income resulting from unregulated market forces is undesirable. Taxation and transfers can be used to modify the distribution of income resulting from market forces.

(iii) Keynesian economic management   While **Keynesians** certainly accept that taxation should be used to achieve such objectives as the provision of public goods, and the switching of expenditure away from demerit goods, they go much further by arguing that taxation should also be used to correct what they regard as arguably the **greatest market failure of all**: the tendency for unregulated market forces to produce **unemployment** and **unacceptable fluctuations** in economic activity. In subsequent units we shall explain how Keynesians have advocated the use of taxation, public spending and the **budget deficit** as **policy instruments** in a **discretionary fiscal policy** aimed at controlling the level of **effective aggregate demand** in the economy to achieve the objectives of full employment and stable economic growth, without an excessive inflationary cost. We shall also show how monetarists reject the use of the **demand management techniques** involved in a discretionary fiscal policy, supporting instead the older view that the government should balance its budget and restrict the role of public finance to the correction of more conventional market failures at the micro-economic level.

3 The meaning of fiscal policy

Fiscal policy has various meanings. It is sometimes used as a rather general term referring to any aspect of a government's policy towards the level and structure of taxation and public spending. During the Keynesian era, fiscal policy took on the narrower and more specific meaning we introduced in the previous paragraph involving the use of taxation and public expenditure in the **macro-economic management of demand**. Such a **discretionary fiscal policy** can be contrasted with the **fiscal stance** currently advocated by monetarists based on an automatic **fiscal rule** to balance the budget or to reduce public spending as a percentage of gross domestic product (GDP). Increasingly, attention is also devoted by both Keynesians and monetarists to the **micro-economic** objectives and effects of fiscal policy on the **supply-side** of the economy, examining such areas as the role and effectiveness of government grants, subsidies and tax allowances in **regional and industrial policy**, and the general question whether public spending financed by taxation or borrowing displaces or 'crowds out' private spending.

4 Taxation and the level and pattern of expenditure

Indirect taxes such as VAT will affect **consumer preferences** and **spending patterns** by causing **relative price changes**. The total level of expenditure can be reduced by levying higher taxes, assuming there is no dis-saving and that the tax revenue is not spent by the government. Some taxes are also considered as **automatic stabilizers** which reduce the amplitude of fluctuations in the business cycle. For instance, when there is full employment, inflationary pressures may be caused by money incomes rising faster than production. A progressive income tax can then drain off some potential consumption into taxation. Conversely in a recession, transfers such as unemployment pay will tend to boost consumption while the government's tax revenue will fall at a faster rate than national income.

5 The incidence of taxation

The **formal incidence** of a tax refers to which particular tax-payer is directly liable to pay the tax to the government. In the case of indirect taxes upon expenditure such as VAT, the question arises whether the seller of the good who bears the formal incidence can **shift the incidence** or **burden** of the tax onto the purchaser by raising the price by the full amount of the tax. A firm's ability to shift the incidence of a tax depends upon price elasticity of demand. Figure 15.1a illustrates the situation where demand is relatively elastic and only a small proportion of the tax can be successfully shifted.

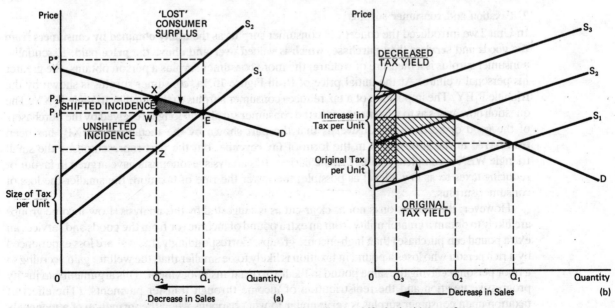

Fig 15.1 Elasticity and taxation (a) the ability of a supplier to shift the incidence of an expenditure tax depends upon elasticity of demand (b) an example of a tax increase producing a fall in the government's tax revenue when demand and supply are both relatively elastic

The imposition of a tax raises a supplier's costs; thus at each price the firm is prepared to supply less. If the tax is a specific or unit tax charged at the same rate irrespective of the good's price, the supply curve will shift **upwards**, from S_1 to S_2, the **vertical distance** between the two curves showing the tax per unit. If all the tax is to be successfully shifted, the price must rise to P*. **This will only happen if demand is completely inelastic**. In any other circumstance, **some** consumers will reduce their purchases as the price rises. However, many consumers will still want the good and so the price is bid up from P_1 to P_2. The size of the government's tax revenue is determined by the amount bought and sold at the new equilibrium (Q_2) multiplied by the tax per unit. This is shown by the rectangle $TZXP_2$. You should now note that the part of the tax rectangle **above** the initial equilibrium price, P_1, represents the successfully shifted incidence of the tax, whereas the part of the tax rectangle **below** P_1 cannot be shifted and must be borne by the supplier. When demand is relatively elastic, only the smaller proportion of the tax can successfully be shifted.

We leave as an exercise for the reader the tasks of drawing appropriate diagrams to show what happens when demand is inelastic and to show the converse effects resulting from the imposition of a **unit subsidy** paid to the supplier.

6 The tax yield

If the principal aim of a tax is to raise revenue, the government will wish to maximize the tax's **yield**. In the case of taxes upon expenditure the government needs to consider the price **elasticities of both demand and supply** of the goods upon which taxes are levied. When a tax is first introduced, it will produce a positive yield providing that at least some of the good is bought and sold after the imposition of the tax. However, the quantity bought and sold will usually fall after the imposition of a tax, so the government may not receive the revenue it was expecting. If the size of the tax is increased, the absolute size of the government's revenue may rise, fall, or indeed stay the same, depending on the elasticities of supply and demand. Figure 15.1b illustrates the effects of an increase in taxation when demand and supply are both relatively elastic. In this case the tax yield falls. Although the government receives a larger tax revenue from each unit bought and sold at the new equilibrium, the loss in revenue resulting from the fall in sales more than offsets the revenue gain. When demand and supply are relatively inelastic, however, government revenue will increase.

Some important public policy implications result from this analysis. If the government wishes to **maximize revenue** it should tax as many goods and services as possible. Not only will this **widen the tax base**, but it will also reduce the elasticity of demand for the bundle of goods and services being taxed, taken as a whole. If only one good is taxed, demand is likely to be relatively elastic since untaxed goods are likely to contain some fairly close substitutes! Conversely, if the government aims to use taxation to **switch expenditure**, for example away from a **demerit good** such as tobacco, it should tax specific types of goods rather than wide categories. On this basis it could introduce different rates of taxation, for example taxing high tar and low tar cigarettes at different rates in order to switch expenditure away from the more harmful good. In a similar way, it can use **tariffs** or **import duties** to switch expenditure towards home-produced goods. In this way there may be a significant 'trade-off' between the **revenue-raising** and the **expenditure-switching** aims of taxation.

7 Taxation and consumer surplus

In Unit 2 we introduced the concept of consumer surplus as the **utility obtained by consumers from the goods and services they purchase, which is valued over and above the price paid**. Essentially, consumer surplus is a measure of **welfare**; the more consumer surplus a person obtains, the greater his personal welfare. At the initial price of P_1 in Figure 15.1a, consumer surplus is shown by the triangle P_1EY. The imposition of a tax reduces consumer surplus to the smaller triangle P_2XY. The question now arises as to what happens to the consumer surplus no longer received by the purchasers of the good or service. The answer is that the part shown by the rectangle P_1WXP_2 has been **transferred to the government** in the form of **tax revenue**, but the part represented by the small triangle WEX is **completely 'lost'**. On the basis of this analysis, economists have argued in favour of reducing taxes to as low a level as possible; the lower the rate of taxation, the smaller the loss of consumer surplus.

However, the conclusion is not as clear-cut as is suggested by this analysis. Low-income groups are likely to obtain a greater utility from an extra pound of income (or from the goods and services an extra pound can purchase) than high-income groups. Correspondingly, the welfare loss experienced by a rich person who loses a pound in taxation is likely to be smaller than the welfare gain accruing to a poor person receiving the same pound in the form of a transfer payment. This argument can justify progressive taxation and the redistribution of income through transfer payments. (The effect of taxation upon consumer surplus is very similar to what happens when the **formation of a monopoly** raises the price of a good. Part of the consumer surplus is transferred to the monopolist as a **monopoly profit**, but part is 'lost' to everyone.)

8 Other aspects of taxes on income and expenditure

(i) Taxation and Incentives It is often argued that a progressive income tax damages the economy through its effects on personal incentives. After all, the most obvious way legally to avoid an income tax is to work fewer hours, or even to stop working altogether. It is argued that expenditure taxes are preferable to income tax because they have no effect on the **choice between work and leisure**. Instead expenditure taxes affect the choice between **saving** and **spending**, and they also switch expenditure into the consumption of untaxed goods and services.

Nevertheless, economic theory **does not prove** that an increase in income tax **inevitably** must have a disincentive effect upon personal effort. If the supply curve of labour is upward-sloping, a disincentive effect will result, since a tax increase is equivalent to a wage cut and less labour is supplied as wages fall. But in circumstances where workers aspire to a 'target' disposable income, when the supply curve of labour is perverse or backward-bending, a tax rise will mean that people have to work longer to achieve their desired target income. The tax is an incentive to effort!

(ii) Fiscal drag and fiscal boost **Fiscal drag** occurs in a progressive income tax structure when the government fails to raise **tax thresholds** or personal tax allowances at the same rate as inflation. Suppose that prices and all **money incomes** double. In the absence of taxation **real incomes** will remain the same. However, **real disposable incomes** will fall if inflation drags low-paid workers, who previously paid no tax, across the tax threshold to pay tax for the first time. In a similar way, higher-paid workers may be dragged deeper into the tax net, possibly into higher tax bands where they will pay tax at steeper marginal rates. In these circumstances the government's total revenue from income tax will rise faster than the rate of inflation, even though the tax structure has not been changed.

Conversely, in times of inflation **fiscal boost** is likely to reduce the **real value** of specific expenditure taxes (but not of *ad valorem* taxes such as VAT). Unless the government adjusts the rate of specific taxes to keep pace with inflation, their **nominal value** will stay more or less the same, but their real value will be eroded.

The simultaneous occurrence of fiscal drag and fiscal boost (such as occurred in the period of rapid inflation in the UK in the 1970s) shifts the structure of taxation away from taxes on expenditure and towards taxes on income. This can be avoided either by replacing progressive income tax with a proportionate tax, and specific expenditure duties with *ad valorem* taxation, or by **indexing** personal tax allowances, income tax bands, and the rates at which specific duties are levied.

(iii) The poverty trap and the unemployment trap The vulnerability of the tax structure in the UK to the process of fiscal drag is closely related to the emergence of a phenomenon known as the **poverty trap**. The poverty trap occurs because the **tax threshold at which income tax is paid** overlaps with the **ceiling at which means-tested welfare benefits cease to be paid**. If a low-paid worker is caught within this zone of overlap, he not only pays tax and National Insurance contributions on an extra pound earned, but he also loses part or all of his right to claim benefits. The resulting 'marginal tax rate' may be very high indeed, sometimes over 100 per cent.

The existence of the poverty trap supports the argument that the major disincentives to personal effort resulting from the structure of taxation and welfare benefits in the UK are experienced by low-paid rather than by highly paid workers. Not only is the 'effective marginal tax rate' paid by the lower income groups frequently higher than the top rate of 40 per cent paid by the well-off; poorly paid workers are likely to experience less job satisfaction and to have less scope for perks and fringe benefits. Indeed the low-paid may be tempted to escape from the poverty trap either by **avoiding** tax through not working at all and living off benefits, thus becoming trapped in unemployment, or by **evading** tax through working in the untaxed **'hidden economy'** or **black economy**.

The poverty trap is undoubtedly made worse when fiscal drag draws low-paid workers into the tax net. Amongst the policies which could eliminate or reduce the effects of the poverty trap are the **raising of tax thresholds** and the replacement of **means-tested benefits** either by untaxed benefits granted as of right (such as **child benefit**) or by benefits subject to tax **'clawback'**. In the latter case, the government grants a benefit as of right and without a means test, but 'claws back' a fraction of the benefits through the income tax system from recipients who are above the tax threshold. Alternatively, the introduction of a **negative income tax** (NIT) has been suggested to merge the existing income tax and benefits structures. In a NIT scheme there would be a **single tax threshold**, above which people would pay (**positive**) income tax, and **below which** they would receive payments from the Inland Revenue (negative income tax) in lieu of welfare benefits. Amongst possible disadvantages of a NIT scheme are its tendency to reinforce the means-testing principle (though some may consider this an advantage), and the argument that civil servants in the Inland Revenue Department are not the most appropriate 'experts' to assess welfare needs. Avoid confusing the poverty trap with the unemployment trap. **Low-waged** people in work are caught in the poverty trap whereas the unemployment trap affects some of the **unwaged** or unemployed people. As we have noted, the low-waged may escape the poverty trap by choosing voluntary unemployment instead, thus entering the unemployment trap. Also avoid confusing the poverty trap with real poverty. Low-income families in the poverty trap are **relatively** poor but the real poor are not in work.

9 How progressive is the British tax system?

The poverty trap and occasional fiscal drag, particularly in the 1970s, have tended to reduce the advantages to the low-paid accruing from the progressive structure of British taxation. In any case the British income tax structure is probably much less progressive than is commonly supposed. Employees' National Insurance contributions are generally a regressive tax falling most heavily as a proportion of income on low-paid and middle-income groups, while the degree of progression in the upper reaches of the income tax structure is greatly reduced by the possibilities in the upper reaches of the income tax structure is greatly reduced by the possibilities of legal tax avoidance open to the better-off. On the expenditure side, some excise duties such as tobacco duty are probably regressive whereas others, including petrol duty, are progressive. Value-added tax is probably slightly progressive since some necessities are currently excluded from the tax, but this may be countered by the fact that the low-paid spend a larger fraction of their income than the well-off, their savings being correspondingly lower. Moreover, the introduction of VAT in 1972 was a **regressive change** to the tax structure since VAT replaced **purchase tax**, which had been a distinctly progressive tax levied on a narrower base composed largely of luxuries. Finally, the poll tax is an extremely regressive tax; a duke paying the same as a dustman.

10 The control of public expenditure

Textbooks sometimes portray the level and pattern of public spending as a tractable policy instrument capable of being 'fine-tuned' or easily adjusted in the macro-economic implementation of fiscal policy and the management of the economy. In practice, however, the control of public expenditure presents a number of formidable difficulties:

(i) Much expenditure is on necessary services such as education, the police and health care which are difficult to cut.

(ii) Control of public expenditure is made more difficult in a democracy by the popularity of state spending and the unpopularity of cuts.

(iii) As we have already explained, many types of expenditure change autonomously for reasons outside the government's direct control, and sometimes these changes occur automatically in the upswings and downswings of the business cycle.

(iv) Central government may have little direct control over local government. It can attempt to impose limits (and to place **external financing limits** upon nationalized industries), but in practice these limits may often be exceeded.

11 The relative importance of the different types of taxation in the UK

The table which follows shows the approximate importance of the major categories of taxation in total tax revenue, including National Insurance contributions in the United Kingdom in 1989/90.

Table 15.1

Income	%	Capital	%	Expenditure	%	Miscellaneous	%
Income Tax	24.6	Capital Gains Tax	1.1	Value Added Tax	15.5	Rates/Poll Tax	10.8
Corporation Tax	11.7	Inheritance Tax	0.6	Excise and Customs		North Sea	
				Duties	11.9	Oil Revenues	0.7
National Insurance				Vehicle Excise		Others	3.5
Contributions	17.8			Duties	1.5		
Total	54.1		1.7		29.2		15.0

Less than 20% of local authority expenditure was financed by the domestic rate and poll tax. Central government transfers accounted for nearly 50% of local government revenue, with the remainder divided between the business rate and income from other sources, such as the sale of assets and services.

12 Cash limits

Each year the British government publishes a **White Paper** outlining its planned expenditure and use of resources over a medium-term period of about five years. The White Paper is usually published a month or two before the government's **Budget** before the beginning of a new financial year. In recent years, the White Paper and Budget have been supplemented by a mid-year **autumn financial statement** – almost a 'mini-budget' – in which the **Chancellor of the Exchequer** (the government's **Finance Minister**) has on occasion softened the way for unpopular tax changes to be introduced in the next year. Traditionally, the Chancellor has undertaken two main tasks on Budget Day. He introduces the government's **Finance Bill** (later to become a **Finance Act**) in which tax proposals are put into effect, and secondly he publishes a **Financial Statement** or 'red book' containing the Treasury's review of the economy over the past year. Since the Chancellor's freedom of manoeuvre on the **revenue side** in the Finance Bill is ultimately constrained by the plans announced on the **spending side** in the White Paper, a careful reading of the expenditure White Paper can often indicate likely tax changes in the Budget.

Before 1976 the annual survey on public spending contained in the White Paper was conducted in **constant prices**, or in **'volume'** terms. This approach meant that expenditure estimates were based on **physical inputs** such as people, buildings and equipment needed. This emphasis on the use of **real resources** reflected the Keynesian approach to demand management in the economy.

However, the pricing of the inputs included in the White Paper was based on out-of-date figures, causing a serious problem in the 1970s when in a period of increasing inflation government expenditure rose rapidly and actual spending exceeded the budgetary projection. If the prices paid by a department rose, more cash was made available to enable the volume of the programme to be maintained. This caused budget deficits and increased the PSBR, as explained in Unit 16. To prevent this happening, the government introduced **cash limits** for the first time in 1976. These were grafted onto the volume system of planning, requiring volume plans to be revised each year at the expected prices of the year subject to the cash limit. In 1981 the Government decided to plan all public expenditure from the outset in cash rather than volume terms. By 1981 cash limits were covering about 60% of total public expenditure. If inflation is faster than the government anticipates or allows for, and the volume of spending cannot be maintained within the cash limit, then the volume must now be reduced and factor inputs dispensed with. As a result **'finance now determines spending'** rather than spending determining finance.

Until recently, government expenditure (on transfers such as pensions, unemployment pay and welfare benefits) lay outside the system of cash limits. This part of public expenditure is largely 'demand-led'. Thus, an ageing population tends to increase expenditure on pensions whilst spending on unemployment pay and welfare benefits fluctuate with the business cycle, providing further examples of automatic stabilizers. Demand-led growth of expenditure on welfare budgets reduces the ability of the government to control public spending. In an attempt to improve its overall control of welfare expenditure, the Conservative Government extended cash limits by establishing a 'capped' Social Fund in 1988.

15.4 Links with other topics

This unit is closely linked with Unit 16 because the levels of taxation and public spending largely determine government's budgeting position and the PSBR. This in turn influences the **money supply** and **monetary policy** as explained in Unit 17. We then go on in Units 19, 20, 22, 23 and 24 to develop the roles of taxation and public spending as **fiscal policy** instruments in the Keynesian theory of aggregate demand management, comparing the **discretionary** fiscal policy of the Keynesians with the older **balanced budget tradition** revived by the monetarists.

15.5 Question practice

Essay Questions

Question 1 Assess the case for the introduction of an annual community charge or poll tax upon adult residents, as a means of financing local government expenditure. (*AEB: June, 1988*)

Understanding the Question Although the poll tax was introduced in 1989 (Scotland) and 1990 (England and Wales), this issue of comparing different forms of local government finance is likely to continue to remain topical, at least in the early 1990s. With this particular question, you can assess the advantages and disadvantages of a poll tax, both in comparison with the local residential rating system which the poll tax replaced and in comparison with alternatives such as a local income tax, sales tax or property tax.

In 1981, the Conservative Government published a Green Paper inviting discussion on the options of: a poll tax; a local sales tax; a local income tax, and reformed domestic rates. It also rejected other possibilities such as: local duties on petrol; alcohol and tobacco; a local vehicle excise duty; and a local payroll tax. Very much in line with such canons of taxation as economy, efficiency and equity, the Green Paper assessed each potential tax against seven criteria:

(i) Is it practical?

(ii) Is it fair?

(iii) Does it make councillors, who take decisions on local expenditure, properly accountable to the local taxpayers?

(iv) Are the administrative costs acceptable?

(v) Are the implications for the rest of the tax system acceptable?

(vi) Does it encourage proper financial control?

(vii) Is is suitable for all tiers of local government?

You can base your assessment against this type of criteria. The poll tax (at least in an 'uncapped' version) can score quite well in terms of accountability but much less well when measured against the criteria of economy and equity. The poll tax is about three times more expensive to collect than the local rate it replaced; although the local rate could be severely regressive in particular instances (e.g. an elderly, single person and a large family including several income-earners live in identical accommodation), on average the poll tax is much more regressive. The local rate promoted inefficiencies (for example, deterring home improvement), but so does the poll tax. The poll tax encourages inefficient use of housing; retired people continuing to live in large houses after their families have grown up and moved away. It may also promote widespread evasion and deregistration from electoral roles. For these and other reasons, the 1981 Green Paper came out strongly against a poll tax but, as we have seen, this did not prevent the government which had commissioned the Green Paper from introducing such a tax! The new tax has proved to be short-lived.

Answer plan

1 Carefully explain the meaning of a poll tax.

2 Specify the alternatives, such as: a continuation of the local rating system; a property tax; a local income tax; and a local sales tax. Mention also, that other alternatives might include: an extension of central government funding of local authorities; or an abolition of local government, with its activities being taken over by central government or by non-governmental bodies like Urban Development Corporations.

3 State the criteria against which you are going to assess a poll tax: e.g. efficiency; economy; equity; accountability, etc.

4 Carefully assess the poll tax against each of these criteria in turn. By all means mention alternative taxes for the purposes of comparison but avoid drifting into an assessment of those alternatives, thereby neglecting the poll tax itself. Also mention the political context but don't drift into political abuse.

5 Reach an argued conclusion.

Question 2 Examine the arguments for and against a shift from direct to indirect taxation.

(London: January, 1987)

Understanding the question Although the concepts are not identical, you can base your answer on a shift from income tax to expenditure taxes (such as VAT) and specific customs and excise duties on items like tobacco, alcohol and petrol. During the 1970s, the combined processes of fiscal drag and fiscal boost (which we have explained in the Unit), contributed to a shift of the UK tax system in the opposite direction, namely towards direct taxation. By contrast, during the 1980s, many of the tax reforms and adjustments made by the Conservative Government were introduced with the intention of significantly restructuring the balance back towards indirect taxation. The underlying reason for this is the growing influence, during the 1980s, of 'supply-side' economics; and the role, within 'supply-side' economics, of a micro-economic fiscal policy aimed at creating incentives for individual economic agents acting as workers, entrepeneurs and consumers in particular, desirable ways. For a full coverage, refer to Unit 23 on 'supply-side' economics.

A prominent exponent of 'supply-side' economics is Professor Arthur Laffer who, with the aid of the **'Laffer curve'** (illustrated in Unit 23), argued that because of their disincentive effects, high average and marginal rates of income tax eventually become counter-productive as revenue raisers. He further argued that by cutting income tax rates, the government can actually increase total tax revenue because people will work harder. The government's tax revenue from the resulting larger economic 'cake' will grow, despite reduced income tax rates.

Answer plan

1 Define direct and indirect taxation, relating the concepts to income and expenditure taxes.

2 Explain that a case for a shift towards indirect taxation may be made to correct an unplanned drift in the opposite direction, resulting from fiscal drag and fiscal boost.

3 Make the point firmly that income tax may have a disincentive effect on effort whereas indirect taxes don't; affecting instead the choice between spending and saving. (Mention that this argument depends in large part upon the assumption of a conventional 'upward-sloping' supply curve of labour but avoid drifting into a developed discussion of 'backward-bending' versus 'upward-sloping' supply curves.)

4 Develop the incentive argument in terms of 'supply-side' economics and the 'Laffer curve'.

5 Explain that the main case against a shift towards indirect taxation is that it will tend to make the tax system much more regressive, countering the principle of 'equity'.

Multiple Choice Questions

Question 3 For which of the following taxes would the amount paid in tax become a larger proportion of taxpayers' income in a period of inflation, if tax rates and allowances, and the quantities of goods bought and their relative prices, remained unchanged, but incomes kept pace with inflation?

(a) Value-added tax   (b) Specific tax on alcohol   (c) Motor vehicle tax   (d) Progressive income tax

Understanding the Question This question is based on the concepts of **fiscal drag** and **fiscal boost**. Fiscal boost refers to the tendency for the real value of **specific taxes** on spending to fall during a period of inflation unless tax rates are adjusted to keep pace with rising prices. The specific tax on alcohol and the specific motor vehicle tax will therefore tend to fall as a proportion of income as taxpayers' income rises. In contrast, an **ad valorem** tax on expenditure, such as VAT, will keep pace with inflation, but it will not rise as a proportion of income unless conditions specified in the question are relaxed. However, in a period of inflation a larger proportion of taxpayers' income will be drawn across the tax threshold and into the tax net, and some people on low incomes who previously paid no tax will begin to pay tax for the first time. This is known as fiscal drag. The answer is therefore **(d)**.

Question 4 A transfer payment is recognised by the fact that
(a) No goods or services are produced in exchange
(b) The distribution of income is made more equal
(c) National Income is reduced
(d) People receive incomes from the state

Understanding the Question The correct answer is **(a)** since a transfer payment involves the redistribution of income from taxpayers to people who do not produce any productive service in return for the income received. Taxation is a transfer payment to the government, whereas pensions, unemployment and other benefits are transfers from the government. A large proportion of transfers do indeed reduce income inequality, but it is perfectly possible for transfer payments to be made to the better-off sections of the community. As a further example, significant transfers are made from wages to profits in the form of various government subsidies and grants to industry. Transfer payments have no **direct** effect on National Income, though indirectly they may either increase or reduce income and output, depending on their effect on demand, production and incentives. Lastly, transfers are only one form of income from the state; people who work for or sell goods to the government and holders of the National Debt also receive incomes from the state.

Data Response Questions

Question 5 The following passage is adapted from an article by Michael Meacher, MP, in *The Guardian*, 4 August 1982.

> Three years after the present Government reduced the highest rate of income tax to 60 per cent, there are still 120 000 families today who are subject to a marginal tax rate of more than 80 per cent. However, they are not the rich, but the poor.
> They are families with children where the working head earns between £47 and £87 a week, that is as little as only a quarter to a half of the current national average wage. Yet liability to income tax at 30 per cent and national insurance contributions at 8¾ per cent, plus the loss of 50p of family income supplement for each extra £1 earned, cripple such families with poverty surtax.
> Their position is even worse if rent and rate rebates are added in. As a result, the Department of Health and Social Security estimates from the evidence of its Family Expenditure Survey, that there are more than 250 000 poor families subject to a marginal rate in excess of 50 per cent (not reached at the top end of the income scale till the £19 000–£23 500 bracket). Within these 250 000 there are even 50 000 poor families subject to a marginal rate in excess of 100 per cent i.e. each extra pound they earn makes them actually worse off than before. These extraordinary consequences flow from a tax structure which has become distorted out of all recognition as a result of decades of incremental adjustment at successive annual budgets.

(a) What does the author mean by the marginal rate of taxation?

(b) Explain how the tax structure may have caused the consequences outlined in the passage.

(c) Discuss the likely economic effects of the situation described in the passage.

(d) Explain how the government could reduce or eliminate the problem outlined in the passage.

(AEB: June, 1985)

Understanding the Question Although it is not mentioned explicitly, the problem being discussed by Michael Meacher, the Labour Party's 'shadow' social security spokesman in 1982, is the 'poverty trap'.
(a) By the marginal rate of taxation, he appears to mean not just the proportion of the last pound earned paid in tax, but also the proportion paid in National Insurance contributions and the proportion 'lost' in benefits no longer claimable.

(b) The consequences outlined in the passage are caused by whatever caused the poverty trap. You could mention how the separate planning and administration of the tax system (by the Treasury and Inland Revenue) and the social security system (by the DSS) have caused the zone of overlap between the tax threshold and the benefits ceiling. Also explain the role of fiscal drag in reducing the tax threshold in real terms.

(c) Effects include the creation of disincentives for low-paid workers to work overtime, together with the 'incentive' to work illegally in the 'black' economy. Closely related, but not identical, to the poverty trap is the unemployment trap. This describes the situation in which unskilled workers with large families may be better off out of work, living off state benefits than in work in a low-paid job paying tax and NIC and losing means-tested benefits.

(d) When answering the last part of the question, do not confuse the 'poverty trap' with 'poverty'. The people caught in the poverty trap are **relatively poor**, but the real poor are the unwaged, too poor to be in the trap. The abolition of all welfare benefits would, of course abolish the trap at a stroke, but it would hardly reduce poverty! Instead, discuss a negative income tax, raising or indexing tax thresholds and the replacement of means-tested benefits with universal benefits, untaxed or subject to tax 'clawback'.

15.6   Further reading

Griffiths, A., and Wall, S., *Applied Economics*, 4th edition (Longman, 1991).
Chapter 13: Public Expenditure.
Chapter 14: Taxation.

Morris, D., editor, *The Economic System in the UK*, 3rd edition (Oxford University Press, 1985).
Chapter 19: Public Finance.

16   Budget Deficits and Surpluses

16.1   Points of perspective

In this unit, we examine the overall financial position both of central government and of the wider public sector. We also consider the implications of the **borrowing requirement**, that results when the government runs a **budget deficit**, and of the **debt repayment** that becomes possible in the event of a **budget surplus**.

1 Keynesian deficit financing

Until quite recently (1987/88), UK governments almost always ran budget deficits. Budget deficits were largely the result of the dominance of **Keynesian views** on the role of economic management and fiscal policy. Broadly speaking, the Keynesian view has been that when households save too much and firms invest too little, unemployment will be caused by a lack of effective **aggregate money demand** (AMD) in the economy. In these circumstances, the government should borrow the excess savings of households in order to inject demand back into the economy through public spending. For much of the post-war era, until the late 1970s, such deliberate **deficit financing** occupied a central place in the discretionary fiscal policy used by Keynesians to 'fine-tune' the level of aggregate expenditure in the economy.

2 Monetarists and the government's budgetary position

Since the 1970s, the use of discretionary fiscal policy and the budget deficit as a policy instrument to manage demand, has been successfully attacked by the **monetarists**. We shall explain, later in this Unit (and in Units 17 and 22) how monetarists regard the level of public spending, and its method of finance through the **public sector borrowing requirement** (PSBR), as an underlying cause of inflation (via an excessive rate of growth of the money supply). To finance the budget deficit and PSBR, the authorities borrow from: private individuals, (i.e. the general public); from overseas; or from the banking system. If the funds are borrowed from the general public, monetarists argue that competition for funds takes place which raises interest rates and **'crowds out'** private sector consumption and investment. Overseas borrowing eventually leads to a drain of national resources in interest payments while borrowing from the banking system expands the money supply. It is therefore not surprising that, since monetarists believe that each method of financing a budget deficit and PSBR gives rise to undesirable consequences, they argue against the principle of deficit financing and large-scale public-sector borrowing.

Monetarist theory first began to influence UK governments in the mid-1970s, becoming a dominant influence upon the Conservative administrations of Mrs Margaret Thatcher, (especially in the early 1980s). In the late 1980s and early 1990s, 'pure' monetarism has arguably been of less significance, certainly as an influence upon practical policy, than other aspects of the 'neo-classical revival', such as 'supply-side' theory. Nevertheless, although Mrs Thatcher's first administration (elected in 1979) was firmly committed to monetarism, the government's aim was to **reduce** rather than to **eliminate** the budget deficit and the PSBR. The government was not committed to balancing the budget, let alone to securing a large budget surplus and negative PSBR or **public sector debt repayment** (PSDR).

In the outcome, Mrs Thatcher's administrations were much more successful than they dared hope (until 1991 at least) with respect to the **fiscal policy elements** of their central macro-economic strategy: the MTFS. (This contrasts with the **monetary policy elements** of the MTFS, which have seldom been 'on target'!) The budget deficit and the PSBR fell rapidly from the early 1980s onwards (both in absolute terms and as proportions of GDP) until, in 1987/8, the budget moved into a significant surplus and the positive PSBR gave way to a PSDR. This gave the Government the opportunity to reduce the National Debt by 'retiring' (or redeeming) existing debt without having the need to undertake any net new borrowing which, in the era of budget deficits, would have expanded the National Debt.

However, the Conservative Government's 'success' in achieving a large budget surplus and PSDR was more the result of autonomous changes taking place 'naturally' in the economy than of deliberate government planning. After the deep recession of 1979/81, the economy entered a period of continuous growth for the rest of the 1980s. During a period of rising incomes (and falling unemployment after 1986), government revenues from progressive taxation rose faster than income, while **demand-led** public spending on unemployment pay and welfare benefits fall. Thus, the budget deficit tends automatically to fall in the upswing and boom of a business cycle, and to rise when the economy enters a recession. This is the **'automatic stabilizer'** or **'built-in stabilizer'** effect of progressive taxation and government expenditure that we mentioned in Unit 15. In the years of continuous growth in the late 1980s, the stabilizing effect was sufficiently powerful to move the budget into surplus. But the Government has not been able to sustain a continuing surplus and PSDR. With the economy entering recession in 1990, the budget moved into deficit in 1991. The Government now recognizes the 'counter-cyclical' nature of the budgeting position and aims for a balanced budget 'over the course of the business cycle' rather than in any particular year, thereby accepting the effect of automatic stabilizers on its finances.

16.2 Underlying concepts

1 Components of the public sector

The United Kingdom public sector is made up of three parts: **central government**; **local government**; and **public corporations** or **nationalized industries**. Central and local government, considered together, are known as **'general government'**. When defining and measuring the budget deficit or surplus, and its related borrowing requirement (or debt repayment position), it is important to make clear whether the whole of the public sector is being discussed or just central government alone. The PSBR is the difference each year between the income and expenditure of the whole of the public sector; a difference which (when expenditure exceeds income) has to be met from borrowing. In the case of a public sector surplus, income exceeds expenditure and the PSBR is negative. As we have already mentioned, a negative PSBR is also known as a PSDR; though this implies that the public sector surplus is actually used for the early 'retirement' (or redemption) of debt or past public sector borrowing. (This need not be the case because, as a part of monetary policy, the government could use its excess revenues to purchase private sector financial assets (such as commercial bills) rather than to redeem its own debt. But, since the public sector budget surplus that emerged in 1987 has been used by the government for debt repayment rather than for other purposes, we shall continue to describe a negative PSBR as a PSDR.)

In the event of a public sector deficit, the PSBR is made up of the CGBR, the LABR and the PCBR, which are respectively the **borrowing requirements of central government, local government,** and **public corporations**. The CGBR and LABR taken together are known as the **GGBR (general government borrowing requirement)**.

Expressed as identities, the relationship is:

PSBR ≡ CGBR + LABR + PCBR

and GGBR ≡ CGBR + LABR

Likewise, in the event of a public sector surplus:

$$PSDR \equiv CGDR + LADR + PCDR$$
and $GGDR \equiv CGDR + LADR$

As already indicated, the public sector finances were in deficit for most of the period from 1945 until 1987 (with the PSBR averaging over £10bn, during the earlier years of Mrs Thatcher's administration, from 1979 to 1984). The PSBR was greatly reduced in 1985 and 1986, falling to £2.25bn in 1986, before the budget moved into surplus in 1987, creating a PSDR. The surplus rose to £14.5bn in 1988, or 3 per cent of GDP, but fell to £7bn in 1989/90. In its 1990 budget, the government predicted a further fall in the surplus/PSDR to £3bn in 1991/2, with a balanced budget returning in later years. However, for the 'counter-cyclical' reasons already explained, the public sector's budgetary position deteriorated at a much faster rate than the government predicted, leading to a quite rapid return to budget deficits and a positive PSBR.

2 The budgetary position and the National Debt

The budget deficit (or surplus) and the related borrowing requirement (or debt repayment) are all examples of **financial flows** (not to be confused with **stocks**). The budget deficit or surplus is the difference, measured per month, quarter, or year, between the much larger flows of income (mostly from taxation) and expenditure. The PSBR is the **flow of new borrowing** that must be undertaken to finance a public sector deficit. In each year for which the public sector is in deficit, the **flow** of net new borrowing undertaken, (the PSBR), adds to the **stock** of public sector debt. Conversely, the **flow** of debt repayment (or negative borrowing), allowed by a public sector surplus, causes the **stock** of accumulated public sector debt to fall.

Just as it is important to distinguish between the budgetary positions of central government and the whole of the public sector, so care must be taken to avoid confusing the **public sector debt** with the **National Debt**. The National Debt is a confusing term since it usually refers to central government alone rather than to the wider public sector. The National Debt is the **stock of all historically accumulated borrowing** which central government has not yet paid back. The total outstanding public sector debt is larger than the National Debt, which only records central government debt. (You should refer to Question 2 at the end of this unit for further discussion of the economic significance of the National Debt.)

3 Privatization and the PSBR/PSDR

Although taxation is the main source of government revenue, government income from taxation is boosted by revenue from other sources such as: (i) sale of assets; (ii) sale of services (such as the publications of Her Majesty's Stationery Office); (iii) profits (trading surpluses) of nationalized industries; (iv) royalties, (v) dividends paid on government owned shareholdings; (vi) rents; (vii) interest payments paid to the government. (**Borrowing** by the government is not classified as a source of revenue; as we have seen, when expenditure exceeds revenue, borrowing finances the resulting deficit!) As a result of the privatization programme, income from the sale of assets has been a significant source of government revenue (in most of the years since the early 1980s), contributing several billion pounds each year to the public purse. However, in its financial accounts, the Conservative Government has classified the privatization proceeds as 'negative expenditure' rather than 'revenue'. Thus in 1989/90, privatization revenues of £4bn, resulting mainly from the sale of the water authorities, succeeded in bringing general government expenditure down from £202bn to £198bn! Privatization revenues have also contributed significantly to the budget surplus and PSDR. If we exclude government income from privatization, the PSDR of £7 billion for 1989/90 reduces to £3 billion.

We should note that privatization can only continue to earn a substantial income for the government as long as there are significant public sector assets available for sale which the general public also wishes to buy. The longer the privatization programme continues, the fewer are the remaining assets that the government can sell, with the list including, for example, motorways, prisons and police stations. Thus, in the 1990s, dwindling revenues from the sale of assets are likely to be a further contributory factor (along with the economy being in recession) to a disappearing budget surplus and PSDR; and the re-emergence of the budget deficit and a positive borrowing requirement. (We might also note that some commentators claim that the 'real' value to the taxpayer, of asset sales in the privatization programme, is much smaller than the nominal value recorded in the government's accounts. To make an industry attractive to buy, the government has often 'written-off' large amounts of debt owed by the industry to the government.)

16.3   Essential information

1 Financing the budget deficit and PSBR

Budget deficit and PSBR financing can be looked at in two ways:

(i) By the type of liability used to raise funds The largest part of the PSBR is financed by the sale of long-term government securities (gilts), though if the government is unable to sell new issues of gilts at acceptable prices and interest rates, Treasury bills are sold.

(ii) By the economic sector which provides the funds Before the advent of a budget surplus and a negative PSBR, the non-bank private sector accounted for approximately three-quarters of the funds provided to finance the deficit. Part of this was provided by households (the **personal sector**), largely through National Savings. However, **financial institutions or intermediaries** such as Pension Funds and Insurance Companies accounted for the bulk of the funds provided by the non-bank private sector, though indirectly the funds they provide represent the **contractual savings** of households. The institutions are the principal purchasers of long-dated gilt-edged securities. The **banking sector** provided the bulk of the remaining funds, purchasing Treasury bills or the **residual government debt**, therefore financing the part of the PSBR which the government could not finance through the non-bank sector. The **overseas sector** was a very small contributor. Its importance varies with the exchange rate and with changes in official reserves.

2 Effects of the PSBR

(i) The traditional Keynesian view of the PSBR Until the 1970s the Keynesians paid very little attention to the effects of the PSBR on the economy. Instead, the Keynesian emphasis was placed on the **direct fiscal effects** of the budget deficit and increased government expenditure on aggregate demand, and then on the levels of output and employment in the economy. We shall explain in Units 19 and 20 how and why the Keynesians believed that an increased budget deficit could increase or '**crowd in**' output and employment via the national income multiplier. Keynesians either ignored or played down the importance of the **indirect monetary effects** which result from the method of financing the deficit. The PSBR itself was viewed as a marginal influence on the 'real' economy. Keynesians believed that the principal monetary effect of a rising PSBR occurs through increased interest rates which result from the increased need of the government to sell securities. But, as we explain in Unit 21, the Keynesians also believe that interest rate changes have a rather weak effect on private sector investment and the level of economic activity.

(ii) Monetarism and the indirect monetary effects of the PSBR In complete contrast to the Keynesians, monetarists place great emphasis on the indirect monetary effects of the PSBR and dispute the strength of the direct fiscal stimulus to output and employment of a budget deficit. According to the monetarists, the monetary effects of an increase in the PSBR include:

(a) The '**crowding out**' of private sector investment as a result of increased interest rates caused by the growth in the PSBR. The crowding-out theory helps to explain why monetarists believe that fiscal policy is ineffective in stimulating output and employment; in the extreme case of crowding out, an extra £ of public expenditure simply displaces a £ of private sector spending.

(b) An expansion of the money supply In some years in the 1970s, movements in the PSBR appeared to be highly correlated with movements in the money supply. This led monetarists to claim that an increase in the PSBR must cause a direct and predictable increase in the money supply. However, in other years the correlation was not nearly so strong, and there is now a more general agreement that the effects of an increase in the PSBR on the money supply depend on how the government borrows.

A budget deficit and positive PSBR can be financed in four ways:

$$\text{PSBR} \equiv \begin{array}{c} \text{New} \\ \text{currency} \\ \text{issue} \end{array} + \begin{array}{c} \text{Borrowing} \\ \text{from the} \\ \text{banks} \end{array} + \begin{array}{c} \text{Borrowing from} \\ \text{the non-bank} \\ \text{private sector} \end{array} + \begin{array}{c} \text{Borrowing} \\ \text{overseas} \end{array}$$

Of these, the financing of the public sector deficit by the issue of currency and by borrowing from the banking system **directly** increase the money supply, but borrowing from the non-bank private sector and from overseas do not.

(1) The issue of new currency The government can finance the PSBR by borrowing directly from the Bank of England. It sells its own securities to the Bank in return for an increase in the note issue which enters into circulation when spent by the government. Eventually, the increased note issue finds its way into the asset structure of the commercial banks, enabling a multiple expansion of the money stock to take place via the deposit creation process.

(2) Borrowing from the banks The same effect will take place if the government finances its increased spending by borrowing directly from the banks through the sale of **Treasury bills**. Money is directly created because the banks purchase the bills by drawing cheques on themselves, thereby creating bank deposits. Less directly, money may also be created through the money multiplier process because Treasury bills are highly liquid assets which, as we shall explain in Unit 17, form part of the banks' reseve assets.

(3) Borrowing from the non-bank private sector If the government sells gilts and National Savings Certificates to the general public (the non-bank private sector) the effect on the money supply is generally neutral. The increase in bank deposits resulting from the injection of government spending into the economy is countered by a fall in bank deposits as a result of the purchase of government securities by the general public.

(4) Overseas borrowing If the balance of payments on current account is in deficit, the government can simultaneously finance part of the **internal deficit** (the budget deficit) and any **external deficit** (a balance of payments deficit) by selling government securities to the residents of other countries. The effect on the money supply is neutral since the government is essentially borrowing sterling which has flowed into foreign ownership in payment for goods and services imported by British residents. The same result occurs if British residents pay for imports in foreign currencies. In this case, the general public sell sterling to the Bank of England in exchange for foreign currencies. This brings into the public sector sterling which can then be used to finance the borrowing requirement, and the country's foreign exchange reserves fall by an amount exactly equal to this method of financing. Whether the government borrows directly overseas, or whether it runs down foreign currency reserves, there is no effect on the domestic money supply.

(iii) The 'New Cambridge School' and the PSBR In the late 1960s a crisis occurred in Keynesian economics, which continued to develop in the 1970s. A consequence of the failure of traditional Keynesian demand management policies to secure continuing full employment, economic growth and price stability, was the emergence of a breakaway 'New School' of Keynesian economists, the **Cambridge Economic Policy Group** (CEPG). Traditionally, Cambridge has been the academic centre of Keynesianism. The older-generation Keynesians at Cambridge University are sometimes known as the 'Old School' Keynesians. There are a number of well-publicized differences which separate the 'Old' and 'New' School Keynesians. Paradoxically, the New School shares with the monetarists a belief in the virtues of **medium-term economic policy** and a distrust of short-term demand management via the traditional Old School instrument of discretionary fiscal policy. However, unlike the monetarists, the New School retains the essentially Keynesian belief in the need for extended government intervention in the economy, particularly through **incomes policy** and **import controls**.

An important element of the New School model of 'how the economy works' is the **net acquisiton of financial assets** (NAFA) of each of the three broad sectors in the economy, the **private sector, the public sector, and the overseas sector**. Any net accumulation of **financial assets** by one sector must be exactly balanced by an increase in the **financial liabilities** of one or both of the other sectors. In a two-sector economy comprising just the private and public sectors, the private sector surplus (or net saving) must exactly equal the public sector deficit. The principle holds true with the inclusion of a third sector, the overseas sector, and can be expressed as an **identity in which the net acquisition of financial assets by each sector must sum to zero**:

$$\text{Private sector NAFA} + \text{Public sector NAFA} + \text{Overseas sector NAFA} \equiv 0$$

Thus a public sector deficit (or PSBR) must mean that the other two sectors are net accumulators of financial assets or claims against the public sector. It also follows that, unless there is an increase in the net saving or surplus of the private sector (households and firms), an increase in the public sector deficit must lead to the overseas sector accumulating financial claims against the UK, *i.e.* the **financial surplus** of the overseas sector is the **UK's balance of payments deficit**. According to the NAFA identity, the main effect of an increase in the PSBR will be to increase the balance of payments deficit, providing that the net saving of the private sector is relatively stable. This was the reasoning suggested by the CEPG to explain the simultaneous increases in the PSBR and the balance of payments deficit which occurred in the early 1970s. However, it should be noted that empirical evidence from more recent years does not support the CEPG's rather mechanical theory that the main effect of PSBR is on the balance of payments, because personal savings have varied substantially.

3 The PSBR/PSDR and economic policy

The growing importance of the PSBR (or PSDR) as economic policy variables has essentially been a part of the emergence in the 1970s and 1980s of monetarist economic policies. The PSBR first became prominent in official policy when the Labour government signed a 'Letter of Intent' to the International Monetary Fund in 1976. The IMF insisted on the adoption by the UK government of a monetarist economic policy as the condition for the granting of an IMF loan to tide the country over the 1976 sterling crisis. Consequently, the signing of the Letter of Intent, in which for the first time the British government announced a PSBR target, marked the transition from **Keynesian short-term demand management** to **monetarist medium-term policy** in the UK. In the monetarist strategy, targets for several years ahead were announced for variables such as the PSBR and the money supply. Monetarists then implemented policies aimed at achieving the targets, at the same time hoping that the announcement of the targets would alter peoples' economic behaviour by influencing **expectations**. The monetarists argued that people would begin to behave in ways which would make the attainment of the announced targets easier, for example by reducing wage claims, once they believed that the government was both firmly committed to its targets and prepared to take whatever action was necessary to achieve the targets.

However, an important problem which strikes at the heart of this monetarist philosophy results from the fact that the key variables for which targets were announced, the PSBR, the money supply, are by their nature highly unpredictable. The 'announcement effect' on expectations may 'backfire' if the government is singularly unsuccessful in achieving its openly declared targets! In general, British governments have been rather more successful in achieving the PSBR target than the money supply target, though the need to finance increasing unemployment caused the PSBR target adopted by the Conservative Government in the early 1980s go 'off course'. Originally, in its **Medium Term Financial Strategy**, (MTFS), the Government announced a target of reducing the PSBR from 5 per cent of GDP in 1979 to 1½ per cent in 1983/4. When it became clear that this would not be met, in its 1982 budget the Government revised the target for 1983/4 to 2¾ per cent. According to the Conservative Government, the MTFS 'plots the path for bringing inflation down through a steady reduction in the rate of growth of the money supply, **secured by the necessary fiscal policies**'. The level of public spending and the PSBR target (the government's **fiscal** stance) are essentially determined by and supplementary to the **monetary stance**: the target rate of growth of the money aggregates such as M4. In recent years, formal money supply and PSBR targets have been abandoned, being regarded now as policy **indicators** rather than **targets**.

In summary, the PSBR and PSDR have been variously interpreted as **policy instruments**, **intermediate objectives**, and **economic indicators** in the pursuit of monetarist economic policies. We have described their role as **intermediate policy objectives** in the preceding paragraphs. Alternatively, the PSBR can be regarded as a policy instrument in its own right, in attaining the money supply objective. In this light the PSBR is the intermediary between fiscal and monetary policy. Finally, some monetarists argue that since the PSBR (and the money supply) are notoriously difficult to forecast and control with any degree of accuracy, they are best used as general economic indicators rather than as either policy instruments or objectives in their own right.

Indeed in recent years, the 'other PSBR' – the **private sector borrowing requirement** – has attracted a growing attention. This is because monetary growth in the 1980s, and early 1990s, seems to be much more closely related to the mushrooming growth of private sector borrowing from the banking and financial system, rather than to public sector borrowing, which became negative during the period of budget surplus from 1987/8 until 1990/1.

16.4 Links with other topics

Because of the central importance of the PSBR and PSDR in the economy, many of these links have inevitably been demonstrated in the earlier sections of the unit. The PSBR is intertwined with fiscal policy (discussed in Units 15 and 21) and monetary policy (Unit 17); it is also central to many of the issues between Keynesians and the monetarists (Unit 24). The size of the PSBR and its method of financing have direct implications for inflation and unemployment (Unit 22), and interest rates and investment (Unit 21).

16.5 Question practice

Essay Questions

Question 1 'Since 1987 the United Kingdom Government has moved from a position of having a budget deficit to a budget surplus.'
(a) Explain what is meant by this statement. (5)

(b) What may be the effects upon an economy of a budget surplus sustained over several years?   (20)

(*AEB: November, 1990*)

Understanding the Question Although the quotation refers to recent UK experience, the actual question is more general and hypothetical. However, it is quite acceptable to answer it in terms of the effects of the UK budget surplus upon the British economy in the late 1980s and early 1990s. The UK budget surplus happened by accident rather than design since the Conservative Government initially planned a reduced deficit, and PSBR, moving towards a balanced budget rather than an actual surplus. However, buoyant tax revenues resulting from continuous growth in the mid to late 1980s (from a starting point in the depths of recession in 1981), together with the Government's success in keeping public spending under control, moved the budget into surplus from about 1987 onwards. But by 1991, a much slower growth rate was dampening tax revenues and increasing demand-led public spending on unemployment pay, thus moving the budget back into deficit.

There are various ways of approaching the main part of the question. Obvious points to make are that the effects will depend on the size of the surplus relative to the economy and whether, in the absence of the surplus, excess or deficient aggregate demand exists in the economy. Introduce the 'traditional' Keynesian argument that a surplus might be used as a deliberate instrument of fiscal policy to remove excess demand in an otherwise 'overheated' economy. By removing such excess demand, the surplus reduces inflationary pressures and it also reduces the balance of payments deficit caused by excess demand sucking imports into the economy. You might also argue that the surplus has an automatic stabilizing effect upon the economy, thereby inducing milder fluctuations in the business cycle. But if a surplus occurs in an already deflated economy, it may prevent any recovery of demand and condemn the economy to a lengthy depression.

From a more monetarist perspective, you can argue that the surplus could be part of a strategy to reduce the levels of both public spending and borrowing in the economy so as to counter any 'crowding-out' taking place in the economy. You can link the surplus explicitly to monetary policy, arguing that if a budget deficit leads to government borrowing from the banking system which expands the money supply, then a budget surplus can reduce government borrowing and have the opposite effect. Whether the budget surplus reduces the money supply depends to an extent upon what the government does with its surplus tax revenues. If used for debt redemption (via a PSDR), the revenues recirculate back to the general public in return for redeemed gilts and National Savings securities; thereby causing the surplus to have a more neutral effect on the money supply. But, if sustained over several years, debt redemption will reduce both the absolute and real size of the National debt; decrease government's debt-servicing costs and, perhaps, contribute to a fall in interest rates.

Answer plan

1 Carefully distinguish between a budget deficit and a budget surplus, making clear whether you are referring to the central government's budget or to the budgetary position of the whole of the public sector.
2 Explain how a government's budget may move from deficit into surplus either as a result of deliberate policy, e.g. through public spending cuts, or via the automatic stabilizing effects occurring in the upswing of a business cycle.
3 Discuss the effects of the surplus in reducing aggregate demand.
4 Discuss the effects of the surplus in countering 'crowding-out'.
5 Discuss the effects upon the money supply, interest rates and the National Debt.

Question 2 Explain what is meant by the National Debt and describe its main components. Examine critically the view that the National Debt is always a burden upon the economy.   (*AEB: June, 1987*)

Understanding the Question The first part of the question is straightforward and requires simple recall of facts and ideas. The National Debt is the total **stock** of outstanding borrowing which the **central government** has not yet paid back. It can be considered in terms of **marketability**, **liquidity** and **source** *i.e.* from whom the government has borrowed. Most of the National Debt is **marketable**, comprising Treasury bills and gilts. Gilts are examples of long-term securities or stock which promise to pay the purchaser a specified rate of interest for a certain length of time, and then repay the original nomimal sum. Gilts and Treasury bills can be resold before they mature, on the capital market and money market respectively. However, National Savings Certificates, premium bonds and certain other paper assets are **not marketable** and can only be redeemed, or cashed in, by the original buyer or his agent selling them back to the government.

The **liquidity** of the National Debt is also significant, varying from three months for Treasury bills to twenty years or more in the case of gilts. In the past, 'undated' stock, such as Consols and the famous 1939 War Loans, were issued with no redemption date, thus leaving repayment at the option of the government. The government may decide to issue more long-dated stock and fewer 'shorts'. This is known as **funding**. We shall explain in the next unit how funding has been used as a technique of monetary control, because fewer shorts, such as Treasury bills, mean fewer liquid assets in the banking system and less potential for the multiple creation of bank deposits.

The National Debt can also be categorized by **source**. The main holders are **internal**, public and private financial institutions and individuals. The Bank of England, commercial banks, insurance companies, pension funds, building societies, public companies and trust funds all hold government debt. The **external** debt is that part of the National Debt which has been sold overseas. External holdings may be either in sterling or in other currencies.

The second part of the question seeks a careful consideration of the economic importance of the National Debt. It needs to be related to other factors, such as Gross Domestic Product (GDP), growth, national resources, inflation and the PSBR (and CGBR).

In the UK, National Debt is a declining percentage of GDP and national income. This could be explained by economic growth, if the economy grows in real terms faster than the National Debt. However, the main explanation lies in inflation. If the rate of inflation is greater than the rate at which the CGBR adds to the National Debt, the money value of the debt as a proportion of money GDP will usually fall. Similarly, if the rate of inflation is greater than the nominal interest rate the government pays to debt-holders, the government gains and debt-holders lose. In these circumstances the real burden of the debt on tax-payers is falling. However, debt-holders may begin to realize that they have been suffering from 'money illusion' in lending to the government at negative real rates of interest. When this happens, the government may experience considerable difficulty in persuading the general public to buy new debt, at least at current interest rates.

The larger the National Debt, the greater the money cost of debt **servicing**. The cost of servicing depends on the average liquidity of the debt, its total size, and the rate of interest offered when the debt was first issued. This servicing has to be met out of current income and borrowing. The greater the cost of servicing, then the greater the level of taxation and the PSBR. Current income which could be used for other purposes finances debt interest incurred by earlier generations. Effectively, this is a transfer from tax-payers to holders of the debt, rather than a burden on the community as a whole. The National Debt is also classified as, and divided into, the **Deadweight Debt** and the **Reproductive Debt**. Suppose that the government sells gilts and uses the revenue to build a hospital or some other **capital project**. The hospital will deliver a stream of consumer services during the life of the gilts. This type of borrowing is not a burden on future generations. In contrast, if borrowing finances **current spending**, for example on wars, it can be regarded as a burden on future generations whose taxes will pay the interest on **deadweight spending** indulged in by the government today. A large part of the National Debt is deadweight debt incurred to pay for past wars. Since the deadweight debt does not cover any real asset, interest payments on the debt are a burden on the country's citizens.

If the holders of the debt are external, however, then interest payments are a drain on national resources. In Britain's case the external burden is small, but a less developed country, without either large domestic savings or a developed banking sector, could be heavily reliant on outside lenders. Much of current income might be needed to pay interest on foreign borrowing, resources would flow out of the economy, and development could be impeded.

Answer plan
1 Define the National Debt.
2 Distinguish between the main forms of debt on the basis of marketability, liquidity, and source.
3 The importance of the National Debt depends in part upon whether it is regarded as a burden. Discuss the circumstances in which it may and may not be burden. Take care to distinguish between the absolute size and the relative size of the debt, its money value and its real value.

Multiple Choice Questions

Question 3 The idea that interest payments on the National Debt constitute a future claim on the country's resources is true if
(a) the debt is partly or wholly incurred abroad.
(b) there is unemployment in the economy.
(c) the debt is long-term rather than short-term.
(d) interest rates are rising.

Understanding the Question The correct answer is (a) because part of government income which could be used in domestic production or consumption is spent on debt servicing and represents a drain from the domestic flow of income. Interest payments to people living within the country are a claim on the government, but they are merely a transfer as far as the country's resources are concerned. Although rising interest rates may affect future borrowing, the interest rate on the existing debt was fixed when the stocks were issued. (c) is incorrect because the maturity/liquidity profile of the debt affects the frequency of redemption, not the obligation. Alternative (b) is simply irrelevant, although the need to finance unemployment pay may be a cause of an increasing National Debt.

Data Response Questions

Question 4 The following passage is adapted from *Controlling the Money Supply* by David Cobham (Open University Press, 1985)

There are two separate ideas involved in 'control' of the public sector borrowing requirement (PSBR): one is accuracy, that is whether the government can hit its PSBR target; the other is reduction, that is whether the government can reduce the PSBR below some allegedly 'excessive' level.

As regards accuracy there are three major problems for the government. First, the size of the PSBR depends partly on the levels of economic activity and employment in the economy. Second, the size of the PSBR will be affected by inflation, which the government may not be able to forecast accurately. A third problem affecting whether the government can hit its PSBR target results from the fact that the coordination of the whole range of public expenditure is a vast bureaucratic undertaking, and it may be impossible precisely to control the total, especially in the short run, without unacceptable disruption in particular areas of expenditure.

These three problems also impinge on the question of controlling the PSBR in the sense of reduction rather than accuracy. But here there is an obvious political problem as well, resulting from political infighting between government ministries and departments as well as between political factions in the Cabinet. Public expenditure cuts as a method of reducing the PSBR will necessarily offend, and therefore face obstruction from, some vested interests within as well as outside the administrative system.

Controlling the PSBR is thus far from straightforward and large errors have occurred in both directions at different times in the past. PSBR control is therefore an inefficient and inflexible instrument for controlling monetary growth.

(a) What is the public sector borrowing requirement (PSBR)?
(b) Explain and discuss the difficulties, noted in the passage, which face a government when attempting to control and to reduce the PSBR.
(c) Explain briefly why governments might wish to control the PSBR.   (*AEB: November, 1987*)

Understanding the Question Part **(a)** of the question required a fairly precise definition of the PSBR as the flow of borrowing required by the whole of the public sector to finance the difference between its expenditure and income. Part **(b)** relates closely to many of the issues we have discussed in the main body of the unit, including the fact that measures to reduce the PSBR affect the real economy, which in turn may affect the PSBR, via effects upon unemployment and tax revenues. When answering part **(c)** you might mention that a traditional Keynesian government would probably not have indulged in PSBR control *per se*, but nevertheless deficit financing as a part of demand management has PSBR implications. However, the main body of your answer to this question must state that a monetarist government, or a government under the influence of monetarism, may wish to control the PSBR with the immediate objective of controlling monetary growth, in pursuit of ultimate objectives of controlling inflation and creating stable financial conditions in the economy.

Answer plan
1 Define the PSBR. Do not over-elaborate.
2 Identify each of three difficulties noted in the passage related to PSBR control.
3 Briefly explain each.
4 Then relate each of these difficulties to PSBR reduction.
5 Discuss the political problems involved in reducing the PSBR.
6 Explain why a monetarist government might wish to control the PSBR.
7 If you have time, explain why a non-monetarist government might wish to control the PSBR, but avoid the temptation to discuss whether a government **should** attempt to control it.

16.6 Further reading

Artis, M. J., *The UK Economy*, 12th edition (Weidenfeld & Nicolson, 1989).
Chapter 2: Monetary Credit and Fiscal Systems.

Morris, D., editor, *The Economic System in the UK*, 3rd edition (Oxford University Press, 1985).
Chapter 12: Demand Management Policy: Theory and Measurement.

17 Monetary Policy

17.1 Points of perspective

Monetary policy refers to any deliberate attempt by the **monetary authorities** (the **Bank of England** and the **Treasury**) to achieve their economic **objectives** using monetary **instruments**, such as changes in interest rates, the money supply and controls over bank lending. The traditonal approach to monetary policy adopted by many textbooks is rather artificial; implying that over the years British monetary policy has been largely concerned with controlling the supply of money with a view to controlling the level of aggregate demand in the economy. Textbooks often describe monetary policy in a simple mechanical way, emphasizing how the authorities attempt to control the banking system's ability to create new deposits or credit by influencing the size of a **reserve or liquid assets ratio**. In fact, the objectives and methods of implementation of monetary policy have changed very significantly in recent years, as has its importance relative to other policies such as **fiscal** and **incomes policies**. We shall spend some time, therefore, describing the background to monetary policy in the UK before we deal with the more precise detail of how the policy is currently implemented.

17.2 Underlying concepts

1 Instruments and objectives

At the risk of gross oversimplification, it is useful to conceive of economic policy as a problem of assigning particular **policy instruments** to particular **objectives**. Post-War British governments have faced the same broad range of objectives, namely:

 (i) to create and maintain **full employment**;
 (ii) to achieve **economic growth** and improved living standards;
 (iii) to achieve a fair or **acceptable distribution of income**, both between regions and different income groups in society;
 (iv) to **control or limit inflation**, or to achieve some measure of price stability;
 (v) to attain a **satisfactory balance of payments**, usually defined as the avoidance of an external deficit which might create an exchange rate crisis.

The order in which we have listed these objectives is by no means accidental. There is general agreement that objectives (i) to (iii) are the **ultimate objectives** of economic policy–though there is considerable disagreement both on the nature of full employment and social fairness, and on how to attain them. In contrast, objectives (iv) and (v) are **intermediate objectives**, or possibly **constraints** in the sense that an unsatisfactory performance in terms of controlling inflation or the balance of payments can prevent the attainment of one or other of the ultimate policy objectives.

2 Keynesian monetary policy

For most of the post-war period, until about 1970, British monetary policy under both Conservative and Labour governments could be described as **Keynesian**. Keynesian monetary policy displayed the following characteristics:

(i) Monetary policy was regarded as independent of fiscal policy, which was the principal Keynesian policy instrument used to **manage demand** in the pursuit of full employment and stable growth. In general, Keynesians have believed that fiscal policy is more effective than monetary policy in influencing the level of **aggregate money demand** in the economy, while monetarists adopt the reverse view.

(ii) Nevertheless, the Keynesians did use monetary policy on occasions as a **supplementary policy** to 'back up' or reinforce fiscal policy in the task of demand management.

(iii) More usually, however, monetary policy was assigned other objectives, particularly **National Debt management**. Being the largest borrower in the economy, the government stands to benefit from low interest rates. For much of the Keynesian period, the overriding aim of monetary policy was to procure **orderly financial markets** in which the government could sell new securities (gilts and Treasury bills) at favourable prices, thereby easing the problems of financing the National Debt and the PSBR. Since Keynesians have believed, until recently at least, that the money supply is both impossible and unnecessary to control, they gave little attention to this aspect of monetary policy. (As we explain in Unit 22, Keynesians do not locate the cause of inflation in an excess supply of money.) Instead, Keynesian monetary policy usually allowed the money supply to adapt passively to whatever level was consistent with the government's interest rate target. However, some attempt was made to influence consumer demand (and thus indirectly the supply of money) in the course of demand management via the **structure of interest rates** and **controls on bank lending**.

(iv) Occasionally, the interest rate target of Keynesian monetary policy was switched away from the 'normal' objective of **low and stable interest rates** and **National Debt management** to a 'crisis' objective of **high interest rates** to **protect the exchange rate**. During most of the period we are discussing, the British Balance of Payments was in persistent deficit. **Capital outflows** occurred, which meant that the authorities had to sell **reserves** and buy pounds in order to maintain the **fixed exchange rate**. In the resulting sterling crisis, monetary policy and high interest rates were usually used to support the exchange rate and stem the capital outflow. This aspect of monetary policy became much less significant in the 1970s when the authorities allowed the pound to *float*. Nevertheless, in the 1980s monetary policy was used to support and maintain an 'unofficial' exchange rate target before the exchange rate was fixed upon EMS entry in 1990.

3 Monetary policy under the monetarists

The 1970s were a decade of transition in which monetary policy changed in a rather haphazard way from the Keynesian policy we have just described to a policy displaying the following monetarist characteristics:

(i) An important monetarist objective is the **control of inflation**. As we shall explain in Unit 22, monetarists believe that inflation is caused by an excess supply of money. The **immediate objective** of economic policy must therefore be to **control the rate of growth of the money supply** in order to reduce the rate of inflation. By 1980, under a broadly monetarist Conservative

Government, attempted control of the rate of growth of the money supply had replaced the other aims of monetary policy.

(ii) We have already noted that monetarists believe that monetary policy can have a greater expansionary or contractionary effect on aggregate money demand and the level of money national income than fiscal policy. Sometimes textbooks imply that monetarists wish, therefore, to use monetary policy in place of fiscal policy in order to manage the level of demand in the economy. In Unit 24 we shall explain why this view of monetarism is essentially misconceived. Under monetarism, monetary policy is a **medium-term policy** for influencing and stabilizing the general economic environment, rather than a tool of **short-term** or **discretionary** demand management. The framework of monetary policy in the 1980s was the **Medium Term Financial Strategy** adopted by the Conservative Government in its 1980 budget. The MTFS incorporated the monetarist view that the **firm announcement** of a money supply target for several years ahead would itself bring down the rate of inflation, through its effect on **expectations**.

Nevertheless, for the reasons we suggested in Unit 14, the government has found that a **money supply target** is almost impossible to achieve, and according to the monetarists' own philosophy, a failure to achieve an announced target may influence expectations adversely! Consequently, since 1979 the Conservative Government has moved away from the announcement of a **single** money supply target, such as M3. In some years in the early 1980s, the Conservative Government responded to M3's 'misbehaviour' by 'moving the goalposts', i.e. by raising and widening the M3 target band for the next year, while still claiming that the MTFS was necessary for the control of inflation. Finally, the Government abandoned the formal announcement of targets for measures of money such as M3. Currently, M4, M0 and other monetary aggregates are used as mere indicators of the 'tightness' or 'looseness' of monetary conditions. These are monitored along with other monetary indicators – the value of **money GDP** (also known as **nominal GDP**) and the exchange rate – to assess whether the MTFS is 'on course'.

(iii) Monetarists place great emphasis on the **interdependence** of fiscal and monetary policy, arguing that the ability to control the money supply depends upon the fiscal policy adopted by the government. In general, monetarists believe that increased levels of government spending financed by increased borrowing from the banks are mainly responsible for excessive monetary growth, and hence ultimately for inflation. Accordingly, lower levels of public spending and a smaller PSBR are regarded as a necessary condition for controlling the money supply and reducing the rate of inflation. (If however, the PSBR is financed through the non-bank sector, there is no reason why the money supply should expand.)

4 The money supply and the rate of interest

We explained in Unit 14 how the rate of interest is the price of money. Simple supply and demand analysis indicates that if the supply of any commodity is restricted relative to demand at the existing price, then price will rise. This suggests that monetary policy cannot hope to achieve simultaneously the twin objectives of restraining the growth of the money supply and low interest rates. In the next sections we shall describe the very important changes in the implementation of monetary policy which occured in the 1970s and 1980s. During the 1970s, in the transition from Keynesianism to monetarism, it was often unclear whether the objective of monetary policy was the control of the money supply or the traditional Keynesian target of interest rate stability. However, by the end of the decade the Conservative Government, under strong monetarist influence, was committed to the money supply target and the acceptance that interest rates would have to be both higher and more volatile than they had been in the past.

17.3   Essential knowledge

1 The banking system in the UK

In Unit 14 we defined a bank as an institution which accepts deposits that can be transferred by cheque and which makes loans and advances. Until the **1979 Banking Act** there were no legal restrictions to prevent any institution calling itself a 'bank'. Officially, however, the **UK banking sector** comprised all the **listed banks** which recognized the **uniform reserve ratio**, together with the **Banking Department** of the **Bank of England** (the *central bank*) and the **discount market institutions**. In order to regularize the situation, the 1979 Banking Act introduced restrictions on authorized banks by establishing a two-tier system of **'recognized banks'** and **'licensed deposit-taking institutions'**. It is now an offence to take deposits unless authorized to do so by the Bank of England. The authorized listed banks are divided into three main groups, the **British banks, overseas banks** and **consortium banks**. In recent years there has been a rapid growth in the operations in the UK of overseas and consortium banks, and also the more specialized British banks. In response to this growth, the controls which formerly applied only to the clearing banks have been extended to all listed banks. A consortium bank is a bank which is owned by a group of other banks, including at least one overseas bank, but no one bank owns more than 50 per cent of the share capital.

For our purposes we shall concentrate attention on the clearing banks, the institutions in the Discount Market, and the Bank of England:

(i) The clearing banks All the banks which we have mentioned, with the exception of the Bank of England, are **commercial banks** in the sense that the ultimate objective of their owners is to make a profit. The clearing banks, and in particular the **London clearing banks**, are by far the most important of the commercial banks, both in terms of the volume of their deposits and in the fact that the **current accounts** or **sight deposits**, which they accept and create, function as a most important part of the supply of money. The clearing banks are also known as **primary banks** and **retail banks**, since most of their deposit business is with the firms and members of the general public.

(ii) The banks and the Discount Market In Unit 14 we used a simple model of the banking system to explain the principle of credit or deposit creation. We assumed in this simple model that banks possess just three assets: cash, bonds and advances. Before we explain the role of the Discount Market and its important relationships with the clearing banks on the one hand, and the Bank of England on the other, we shall firstly introduce a rather more detailed version of the assets side of the balance-sheet of a clearing bank:

Table 17.1: The asset structure of a UK clearing bank

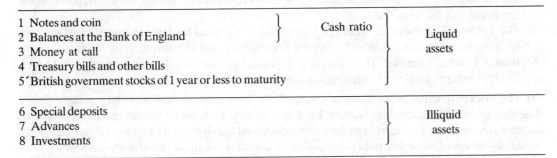

1 Notes and coin		
2 Balances at the Bank of England	Cash ratio	Liquid assets
3 Money at call		
4 Treasury bills and other bills		
5 British government stocks of 1 year or less to maturity		
6 Special deposits		
7 Advances		Illiquid assets
8 Investments		

In arranging the structure of its assets, a bank faces a 'trade-off' between **liquidity** and **profitability**. Since the illiquid assets in the balance sheet are the most profitable of a bank's assets, it will expand deposits by as much as possible through the purchase of bonds or securities (investments) or through the creation of advances. However, in the event of a loss of deposits to other banks or a cash drain to the general public, the bank must be able to convert some at least of its interest-earning assets into cash. (It is important to note that **balances at the Bank of England** are equivalent to cash.) Banks come to possess highly liquid interest-earning assets, **money at call, Treasury bills** and **commercial bills** as a direct result of their special relationship with **discount houses** and brokers of the **London Discount Market** or **money market**. The money market is a market in short-term money or funds, as distinct from the long-term market, the **capital market**. Firms in the private sector may decide to raise funds in the money market by the sale of **commercial bills** (or **bills of exchange**) for the purpose, for example, of financing trade or a temporary cash-flow problem. In a similar way the government can obtain temporary funds through the sale of Treasury bills, which the Bank of England sells on behalf of the government. A commercial bill becomes a marketable security when it is endorsed or accepted, usually by a merchant bank in its function as an **accepting house**. Specialized financial institutions known as **discount houses** then purchase the accepted bills of exchange and Treasury bills. Instead of receiving a formal rate of interest, the discount house earns a **discount rate**, which is the difference between the **discount price** paid for the bill on the day of issue and the face value received when the bill matures three months or ninety-one days later.

In practice, many bills are resold by the discount houses to the banks before they mature, thereby accounting for item 4 in Table 17.1. Item 5, **government stocks with one year or less to maturity**, is essentially similar. From a bank's point of view, short-dated government securities, including Treasury bills, are highly liquid. If the banks are ever in a situation in which they need to restore their cash ratio, the banks can either encash their securities as they mature or sell them to the general public at only a small capital loss.

Money at call, which is item 3 on the balance sheet, also results from the relationship between the banks and the discount houses. Each week the discount houses may purchase new issues of bills to the value of many millions of pounds. Money at call, which comprises overnight and very short loans or advances that the clearing banks can quickly recall from the discount houses, is a very cheap source of finance which enables the discount houses to conduct their discounting business at a profit.

(iii) The Bank of England Although the 'narrow function' of the money market is as a source of short-term money for the private sector and the government, its wider function, with which we are much more interested, is to act as a 'buffer' between the Bank of England and the clearing banks: a buffer through which the Bank of England implements monetary policy. And just as we make a distinction between the narrow and wider functions of the money market, so it is useful to separate the wider function of the Bank of England, the **implementation of monetary policy**, from the narrower functions which we shall first consider:

(a) The 'narrow' functions of the Bank of England.
The Bank of England is the country's **central bank**. It is organized in two departments, the **Issue Department** responsible for note issue, and the **Banking Department** which conducts the banking business which we shall now describe. The Bank of England is:

(1) **The government's bank**, keeping the government's principal bank accounts, receiving tax and other revenue, and paying for goods and services bought by the government. The Bank **manages the National Debt** on behalf of the government, selling new issues and redeeming maturing Treasury bills and gilts. The Bank also manages and holds Britain's gold and foreign currency reserves, implementing the government's exchange rate policy and any exchange control regulations which are in force.

(2) **The bankers' bank** The commercial banks hold deposits at the Bank of England (item 2 in Table 17.1), which enable the settlement of debts between the banks.

(3) **General banking supervisor** The Bank of England decides who can operate as a bank and the ways in which banks must operate in order to protect depositors. Recent banking legislation has expanded this function.

(4) **The 'lender of last resort'** Traditionally, the Bank of England has been prepared to supply cash to the banking system in order to maintain confidence and to prevent bank failures.

(5) **Banker to other countries** The Bank acts as banker to other countries that wish to hold their foreign currency reserves in sterling on deposit in London.

(b) The 'wider' function of the Bank of England: the implementation of monetary policy.
Together with the Treasury, the Bank of England controls the banking system and implements the country's monetary policy. Earlier in the unit we discussed the changes which have taken place in the broad objectives of monetary policy; we shall now examine the more detailed changes which have occurred in the Bank of England's **techniques of monetary control**.

2 The techniques of monetary control

In this section we explain the various **policy instruments**, or **techniques of control**, which the monetary authorities can use to try to 'hit' one or other of targets of monetary policy. We shall examine: **(i) open market operations; (ii) funding; (iii) imposing required reserve ratios upon the banks; (iv) direct controls upon bank lending;** and **(v) control via interest rates**. It is important to realize that not all these instruments or techniques of control will necessarily be used; some which found favour during the Keynesian era have been rejected as unsuitable under monetarism.

(i) Open market operations Traditionally, a main technique of control used in the United Kingdom's monetary policy has been through **open market operations** (OMO) – a policy of the Bank of England buying or selling gilts on the capital market (and also bills on the Discount Market). In principle, a sale of gilts to the general public should lead, via the money multiplier, to a multiple contraction of credit and bank assets (shown on the right-hand side of a bank's balance sheet) and to an equal fall in total deposits (shown on the left-hand side). **Contractionary OMO** reduce total bank deposits by proceeding through the following stages:

(a) The public buy gilts by drawing cheques on their deposits in the clearing banks.

(b) The cheques are paid into the Bank of England, causing a shift of deposits away from the clearing banks and into the Bank. The balance sheets of the clearing banks will now show an equal fall in customers' deposits on the liabilities side, and balances at the Bank of England on the assets side.

(c) The cash ratio thus falls, followed (in principle) by a multiple contraction of deposits and credit when the banks reduce their rate of deposit creation in order to restore their cash ratios.

In practice, however, banks can restore the cash ratio by recalling 'money at call'. This passes the cash squeeze initiated by the Bank of England onto the discount houses, who find themselves in the classic exposed position of 'borrowing short and lending long'. At this stage, the discount houses go to the Bank of England (in the Bank's role as **lender of last resort**), and obtain cash with which to repay the clearing banks. If this were the end of the story, it would appear that the cash squeeze initially started by the Bank of England, would be rendered ineffective by the Bank's subsequent willingness (in order to maintain confidence and liquidity), to re-supply the cash back to the banking system, via the discount houses. But although the clearing banks restore their cash ratios with cash supplied in this way by the Bank of England, they do so by running down their holdings of other liquid assets. And, if the banks were initially operating close to their desired ratio of liquid assets to total deposits, they must now reduce lending and total deposits to restore their liquid assets ratio. Thus in practice, a clearing bank's **liquid assets ratio** (or **reserve assets ratio**) tends to be a more important fulcrum of control in the operation of monetary policy than its cash ratio.

The Bank of England can, of course, use open market operations to **expand** rather than to **contract** total bank lending and deposits. In this case the central bank buys securities from the general public, paying for the gilts with cheques drawn on itself.

(ii) Funding The term 'funding' can be applied both to the **stock** of National Debt and to the **flow** of the PSBR; but the effects on the money supply are rather different. Funding the **National Debt** has a **contractionary** effect on bank deposits whereas the effect is **neutral** when **funding the PSBR** (strictly **'fully-funding'** the PSBR). The government funds the National Debt by selling long-dated debt (mostly gilts) to replace maturing short-dated debt (Treasury bills). The general public thus buy illiquid securities from the government, paying for them with bank deposits which are taken out of circulation. The effect is broadly similar to contractionary open-market operations, supplemented by a further possible contraction resulting from a reduction in the supply of bills to the banking system, as funding alters the composition of the National Debt in favour of long-dated securities.

In the event of a budget deficit, the government **fully-funds the PSBR** by selling just sufficient new long-dated debt to cover its borrowing requirement. Once again, the public buy illiquid securities and pay for them with bank deposits; in this case the bank deposits circulate back to the banking system when spent by the government in its public spending programme. The overall effect on the money supply is thus neutral. However, **'over-funding' the PSBR** would occur if the government sold more long-dated debt than needed to fully-fund its borrowing requirement. The effect on the money supply would again be contractionary – indeed 'over-funding' the PSBR is really just another name for contractionary open-market operations.

(iii) Imposing required reserve ratios upon the banks Open-market operations and funding the National Debt are examples of techniques of monetary control which seek to influence the credit- and deposit-creating abilities of the commercial banks by acting on the supply of cash and liquid assets available to them. In principle, both OMO and funding can engineer a multiple contraction of total bank lending and deposits because, as a part of normal banking practice, the commercial banks choose to keep prudent cash and liquid asset ratios. But instead of leaving the clearing banks free to decide their own **prudent ratios**, the monetary authorities have sometimes imposed **required reserve asset ratios** upon the banks. When left to themselves, the banks might, for example, choose to operate on a liquid assets ratio of 20 per cent. But, if the central bank imposes a required ratio of 30 per cent, the commercial banks must undertake a multiple contraction of bank deposits until liquid assets equal the required ratio, unless the banks are able to purchase extra liquid assets from the general public by offering bank deposits in exchange. In order to bring about a further reduction in lending and bank deposits, the central bank could simply **raise the required reserve assets ratio**. Conversely, the authorities could reduce the ratio if they wished to encourage an expansion in lending and deposits.

For many decades, until 1981, the United Kingdom monetary authorities did indeed impose required cash and liquid assets upon the British clearing banks, though since that date, for reasons we shall shortly explain, required ratios have been largely abandoned. However, the UK authorities have never engaged in a policy of raising or lowering the required ratios from year to year in order to contract or expand total bank lending. Instead, the authorities operated **special deposits policy**, which had an effect similar to the raising or lowering of a required reserve ratio.

As a part of normal banking practice, the UK clearing banks keep working (or operational) balances at the Bank of England (item 2 in Table 17.1) which form part of their cash ratios. In the 1960s and 1970s the Bank of England frequently called for special deposits, equal for example, to 2 per cent of the clearing banks' deposit liabilities. Immediately upon the call for special deposits, part of the banks' operational balances at the Bank of England became frozen or completely illiquid, ceasing, therefore, to be a part of the cash ratio. The effect was equivalent to raising a required cash ratio by 2 per cent. Similarly, the release of special deposits was equivalent to reducing the required cash ratio. There have been no calls for special deposits in the UK since about 1980.

Required reserve ratios were abandoned by the Bank of England in 1981 and there is little sense in calling for special deposits in the absence of required ratios imposed on the banking system. Indeed, even when required ratios were imposed, calls for special deposits were probably more effective as a 'tax' upon the banking system than as a serious constraint upon the banks' lending and deposit-creating ability. Although the Bank of England usually paid money-market rates of interest on all special deposits, a call for special deposits 'taxed' the banking system because it prevented the banks from using more profitably the funds that became tied up at the Bank of England.

(iv) Direct controls on bank lending As seen above, the imposition of required reserve asset ratios, and calls for special deposits, are forms of control imposed on the commercial banks which limit the banks' freedom to act commercially, in their self-interest. However, the monetary authorities can, if they wish, impose a form of control that interferes much more severely and directly in the banks' freedom to make their own commercial decisions. Such controls are known as **direct controls**, of which are two types: **quantitative** and **qualitative**.

(a) Quantitative controls These involve imposing maximum limits upon the amount that banks can lend, or upon the rate at which banks can expand total deposits.

(b) Qualitative controls These are **'directional' controls** which instruct or 'persuade' banks to lend only to certain types of customers, e.g. business customers requiring credit to finance investment or exports might be given a high priority, with consumer credit relegated to a much lower position. Selective higher purchase controls represent another form of directional control.

Direct controls on bank lending were widely used as a technique of monetary control in the United Kingdom in the 1960s and 1970s. However, for reasons which we shall explain shortly, direct controls on lending, together with required ratios, have been abandoned in the 1980s and 1990s, though a future Labour administration might reintroduce them.

(v) Control via interest rates All the techniques of monetary control which we have so far described operate on the ability of the clearing banks to supply credit and to create bank deposits – though by causing security prices to rise or fall, open market operations and funding affect interest rates also. The final technique of control we shall consider attempts to influence the **supply of credit and bank deposits** through an **indirect route**, by acting on the general public's **demand for bank loans**. Whereas the **direct controls** on bank lending which we described in the previous section **ration the quantity or supply of credit** available, by raising or lowering interest rates, the monetary authorities can seek to **ration demand via price**.

As well as using open market operations to raise or lower interest rates, the Bank of England has another instrument at its disposal: the **discount rate** or **lending rate** at which it undertakes the **lender of last resort function** of supplying cash to the banking system through the discount market. Changes in the Bank of England's lending rate affect interest rates in two ways. In the first place, it usually has an immediate effect on the bill discount rate at which the discount houses conduct business with the clearing banks and, therefore, on other short-term interest rates. The bill discount rate is normally a fraction of a per cent below the Bank of England's lending rate; if it were higher, then the clearing banks might find that there were no bills on offer since the discount houses could obtain a better price by selling their bills to the Bank of England instead! It follows, therefore, that the Bank of England can force the bill – discount rate down by reducing its own lending rate. Secondly, changes in the Bank of England's lending rate tend to act as a psychological signal to financial institutions and markets that the Bank of England wants interest rates to move in a particular direction.

3 The abandonment of required ratios and direct controls

We have already mentioned how, under monetarism, monetary policy has been used primarily to control the growth of the money supply. Yet, in achieving (or failing to achieve) this control, the monetarists have rejected and largely abandoned the use of required reserve ratios, calls for special deposits and direct controls on bank lending. How do we explain this paradox? The answer is really quite simple. Most monetarists belong to the 'classical' or 'free-market' school of economic thought, which regards markets as inherently stable and efficient; and government interventionism as destabilizing, distortive and inefficient. Monetarists apply this view of the world to monetary policy as well as to other aspects of economic theory and policy making. Thus, although monetarists wish to achieve control over monetary growth, they reject as unsuitable the more interventionist techniques of monetary control which constrain artificially the commercial freedom of the private enterprise banks to act in their own best interest in the market economy.

4 Disintermediation

Disintermediation is an example of a distortion or inefficiency caused by direct controls on bank lending. In the 1960s, UK monetary policy (which was then basically Keynesian) relied heavily upon the more interventionist forms of control which we have described: required reserve ratios; calls for special deposits; and quite stringent qualitative and quantitative controls on bank lending. These controls discouraged competition amongst the clearing banks. But the controls encouraged other financial institutions to become banks by developing banking business in competition with the high street clearing banks. At that time, the finance houses and the other financial institutions which developed into 'fringe' banks or 'secondary' banks were not subject to the interventionist controls imposed on the 'primary' banks by the Bank of England as a part of monetary policy. This competitive advantage allowed the 'fringe' banks to 'cream' banking business away from the clearers who were subject to restrictive controls. This process is called **disintermediation** – when only part of the banking system is controlled, banking business **disintermediates** away from the banks subject to the restrictions, towards those that are not. When quantitative and qualitative controls on bank lending were removed in the UK in the 1970s, much banking business **'reintermediated'** back to the primary banks. The clearing banks' 'financial economies of scale' enabled them to charge lower interest rates than the secondary banks, and their branch networks allowed easy access.

Disintermediation has also had an international dimension, which has been especially significant for the UK since 1979 when the British Government abolished foreign exchange controls. In the conditions of free movement of funds between countries which have existed since 1979, banking business would simply disintermediate overseas if the Bank of England imposed controls on UK banking operations that limited their commercial freedom and raised their costs. This is perhaps the main reason why the Bank of England has largely abandoned required reserve ratios. The monetary authorities now believe that all banks operating within the UK must be free to choose their own liquidity ratios if they are to compete on an equal footing in what has become a truly international and global market for banking services. Thus, while the Bank of England has tightened up and extended its supervisory role over all banks and financial institutions, domestic and overseas-owned, operating within the UK, at the same time it has largely abandoned direct intervention in commercial banking activities undertaken by the banks.

5 Monetary base control

The abolition in 1981 of a required liquid assets ratios imposed upon the banks and the suspension in 1982 of an officially announced **Minimum Lending Rate** (MLR), were thought at the time to herald a move to switch monetary policy towards a system of **monetary base control**. In the 1970s many 'academic' monetarists such as Professor Milton Friedman, then of the University of Chicago, had argued that once 'monetarist' governments were elected in countries, such as the UK and the USA, they should pursue control of the money supply by adopting a strict policy of monetary base control. The basic principle of monetary base control is quite simple. The state (or the monetary authorities) can, in principle, exercise monopoly control over the supply of **cash** or **'high-powered' money** which forms the **monetary base**. By reducing the supply of cash to the banking system (using techniques such as open market operations and funding), the authorities can engineer a multiple contraction in the part of the money supply which they do not themselves issue, namely **bank deposits**. Required reserve ratios need not be imposed on the banks. The banks can be left to choose their own liquidity ratios as a part of normal prudent banking practice. But, for monetary base control to have **predictable** effect upon the total money supply, the **money multiplier must be fairly stable**, i.e. it is assumed that the commercial banks will not react to a cash squeeze simply by altering their ratios, leaving total bank deposits unchanged.

To be effective, a system of monetary base control would require the abandonment by the central bank of its lender of last resort function. Normally, when the Bank of England squeezes cash through contractionary open market operations or funding, it immediately gives the cash back to the banking system via the discount market, in its role as lender of last resort. In a strict system of monetary base control, this practice would cease. Once cash was squeezed, it would not be re-supplied by the authorities and the banks would have no option but to reduce total deposits in order to restore their ratios.

6 Recent monetary policy

In the early 1980s, the Conservative Government claimed to be firmly committed to monetarist theory and policy, including a strict adherence to a 'tight' monetary policy aimed at controlling the growth of the money supply in order to combat inflation. However, during the 1980s, the Conservative Government's monetary policy proved to be much more pragmatic or discretionary than originally intended. The band within which the monetary target, Sterling M3, was set in MTFS was first widened, and eventually in 1983 its targeting was dropped. Indeed, monetarist 'purists' have on occasion claimed that the Government's monetary policy has not really been 'monetarist' at all, but a form of 'quasi-Keynesianism'. Other commentators argue that the success in reducing inflation (which nevertheless remained high in the 1980s relative to inflation in the economies of the UK's main competitors) had much less to do with monetary policy than with external events such as the falling prices of oil and of other commodities. Indeed, in terms of domestic policy alone, the success of the 'battle against inflation' may have owed more to a 'good old-fashioned deflation of demand', which raised unemployment to over three million, than to any success in 'hitting' monetary targets. The Sterling M3 target was seldom achieved successfully.

In so far as the Government attempted in the 1980s and early 1990s, to operate monetary policy so as to control the rate of growth of the money supply, we can identify the following main strands of policy:

(i) The move to a system of monetary base control has not been pursued We have already noted that the changes in the system of monetary control introduced in 1981 were thought at the time to indicate the possibility that a fully fledged monetary base control system would eventually be introduced. This has not happened, perhaps because there are two potential problems involved in a strict system of monetary base control. These are:

(a) To have a predictable effect upon the total money supply – which is made up largely of bank deposits – control of cash or the monetary base relies on a **stable money multiplier**. If the money multiplier varies, changes in the monetary base may simply be 'absorbed' in a change in the money multiplier, without a predictable effect upon the total stock of money.

(b) Strict monetary base control might produce politically unacceptable fluctuations in interest rates which also conflict with other objectives, such as National Debt management. The effective abandonment of the lender of last resort function might also lead to bank crashes with unacceptable effects on financial confidence.

We can use Figure 17.1 to illustrate how the limited system of monetary base control introduced in 1981 contrasts with both the largely Keynesian monetary policy of the previous years and a notional system of strict monetary base control.

(i) We have already noted that monetary policy cannot simultaneously reduce both the money supply and interest rates and that a successful reduction of the former will almost inevitably be at the cost of higher rates of interest. During the Keynesian era, monetary policy was aimed principally at an interest rate target, usually chosen to reduce the cost of managing the National Debt. Such an interest rate target is shown as $\bar{r}$ in Figure 17.1(a). Suppose the demand by the general public to hold

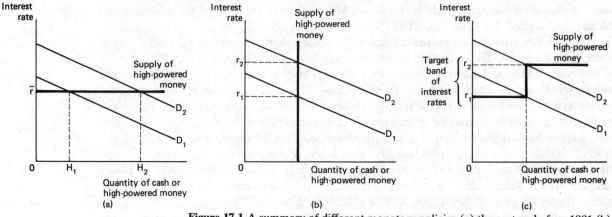

Figure 17.1 A summary of different monetary policies (a) the system before 1981 (b) a monetary base control system (c) the modified base control system introduced in 1981

cash shifts from D_1 to D_2; then the authorities were always willing to supply cash to the banks to enable the interest rate to be attained. This is illustrated by the perfectly elastic supply curve of cash, or high-powered money, with respect to the rate of interest shown in Figure 17.1(a).

(ii) In contrast, in a monetary base control system illustrated in Figure 17.1(b), the authorities choose a target stock of cash or high-powered money that is completely inelastic with respect to the interest rate. In Figure 17.1(b) the supply of high-powered money is shown by a vertical line; if the general public's demand for cash increases from D_1 to D_2, successful control of the monetary base must mean that the rate of interest is allowed to rise from r_1 to r_2.

(iii) Figure 17.1 (c) summarizes the main features of the limited system of base control introduced perhaps experimentally, in 1981. Under this system, the authorities have attempted to control the monetary base, but only within a narrow and undisclosed range of interest rate flexibility. Thus the supply of cash or high-powered money is completely inelastic within the range, shown by r_1 and r_2 in Figure 17.1(c). But the supply of cash becomes perfectly elastic if interest rates move outside the target range as the authorities increase or reduce the cash supply so as to keep the rate of interest within the target band.

(ii) PSBR control When first elected in 1979, the Conservative Government believed that excess monetary growth was caused largely by the growth of public spending and its method of finance via the PSBR. The Government therefore put into motion a policy of cutting public expenditure and the PSBR to achieve control over the rate of growth of the money supply. In the early 1980s, the Government also **over-funded the PSBR**; it sold more new gilts than were needed to finance or fund the PSBR. (Over-funding the PSBR is essentially the same as the **contractionary open-market operations** explained in Unit 16.) For various technical reasons, over-funding was dropped in 1985. Since then, the authorities have followed a **'Full Fund' rule** instead; designed to have a **neutral** rather than a **contractionary** effect on the money supply.

When there is a budget deficit and a **positive PSBR**, the government puts more money into the economy than it receives from taxation. The 'Full Fund' rule requires that it must take the same amount out again by funding. However, with a budget surplus and a **negative PSBR** (as existed from 1987 to 1991), 'full funding' means repaying just sufficient government debt to offset and neutralize the money taken out of the economy by the surplus. In these circumstances, the negative PSBR can be called a **Public Sector Debt Repayment (PSDR)**.

(iii) Interest rate manipulation In Unit 14 we stated that if the money supply is regarded as a **policy instrument**, completely controlled by the monetary authorities, the rate of interest is determined when the demand by the general public to hold money balances equals the supply of money. By expanding or reducing the money supply, the authorities can, in principle, alter market interest rates.

It is now realized that this is perhaps completely the wrong way of looking at things. Instead of regarding the **money supply as exogenous**, with the **rate of interest endogenously determined** within the supply and demand framework, it may be more correct to treat the **rate of interest as exogenous**, and the **money supply as endogenous**, i.e. a complete reversal of roles. According to this view, the rate of interest can be used as the policy instrument to achieve a money supply objective, rather than vice versa. Referring back to Figure 14.4(c) in Unit 14, let us suppose that the rate of interest is r_2. According to the revised view we have just explained, the general public wishes to hold money balances equal to Ms_2 at this rate of interest. We now assume that the money supply or stock of money **passively adapts** or **accommodates** itself to exactly equal the size of money balances the public wish to hold at the current interest rate. The money supply is therefore endogenously determined at Ms_2. If the authorities wish to reduce the money supply to Ms_1, they raise interest rates to r_1, thereby achieving their money supply target by acting on the demand for money, effectively rationing the demand for money via price or the cost of borrowing.

There is no doubt that during the 1980s and early 1990s, the Government's monetary policy has often been implemented in the manner we have just described, acting **indirectly** on the demand for money, rather than **directly** on its supply. In part this no doubt reflects Goodhart's Law and the difficulties involved in directly controlling the money supply.

17.4 Links with other topics

In this unit we have developed the simple theory of deposit and credit creation explained in Unit 14. On several occasions we have referred to the links between monetary policy and fiscal policy and the PSBR (Unit 16). In the next units we largely ignore the roles of money and monetary policy in the economy, as we construct and explain an essentially Keynesian national income/expenditure model of the economy. However, the debate and controversy about the importance and roles of the money and monetary policy are reintroduced in Unit 22 on inflation and Unit 24 on the Keynesian/monetarist conflict.

17.5 Question practice

Essay Questions

Question 1 Outline briefly the main differences between Keynesian and monetarist approaches to monetary policy. In 1986 the money supply (Sterling M3) grew by about 18 per cent, whereas price inflation was about 3 per cent. What are the implications of this for government policy to control inflation? (*JMB: June, 1987*)

Understanding the Question You can answer the first part of the question by drawing on the sections in the unit on Keynesian monetary policy and monetary policy under the monetarists. It might be useful to make a clear distinction between Keynesian monetary policy, as it was implemented in the UK economy nearly 30 years ago, and how you believe a Keynesian-inspired government would approach monetary policy in the 1990s. Thirty years ago, before the impact of monetarism, the monetary causes of inflation were either not realized or ignored; and in any case the control of inflation occupied a relatively low position in the order of

Keynesian priorities. These days, no government could afford to implement a monetary policy that took no account of the possible inflationary consequences of the policy. Thus Keynesians, as well as monetarists, would use monetary policy primarily to reduce inflationary pressures in the economy. Keynesians might, however, accuse monetarists of advocating a 'one-club golfer' approach. They argue that, however good his skills, a golfer could not hope to win a major tournament if he relied on just a single golf club. Why use one club when other golf clubs are available for specialist strokes? In much the same way, why use monetary policy (and interest rates in particular) as the single instrument for managing the economy, when (according to Keynesians) a range of other effective policies and instruments of government intervention are available, such as tax increases.

Likewise, a Keynesian might argue that the implication of the money supply growing far faster than the price level, is to throw doubt on the central tenet of monetarism; the quantity theory of money. A monetarist could reply in a number of ways. First, he would point out that, in monetarist theory, the relationship beteen the money supply and the price level is a lagged relationship: growth in the money supply in 1986 might be expected to cause inflation about two to three years later (i.e. 1988/99). Indeed, the monetary expansion of the mid-1980s was diverted, to a large extent, into the purchase of property; fuelling house-price inflation which is not measured in the Retail Price Index. Increased property prices made house-owners much wealthier, which then fuelled severe inflationary pressures in the late 1980s and early 1990s as house-owners began to spend part of their increased wealth. The conventional monetary policy instrument, of increasing interest rates to reduce consumer spending, has proved ineffective and slow to operate in dampening inflationary pressures induced by the property boom of the mid to late 1980s.

Goodhart's Law is also relevant to the question (i.e. as soon as a measure of money is used as a policy target, it begins to 'misbehave' and lose its value as an instrument of control). Thus, you might suggest reasons why, in 1986, Sterling M3 was a misleading indicator of monetary conditions in the economy.

Answer plan
1 Explain the main differences between 'traditional' Keynesian and monetarist approaches to monetary policy.
2 Discuss whether these differences are significant at the present time.
3 Discuss whether the data quoted in the question refutes, or is consistent with, the quantity theory of money.
4 Argue that if the relationship between the money supply and the price level in the quantity theory has broken down, it implies that strict control of the money supply will be ineffective in controlling inflation. Other policy measures would be needed. Even if the relationship still exists, simplistic monetarist policies might not be successful.

Question 2 Why has monetary policy in the United Kingdom, in the 1980s, moved towards the control of interest rates whereas monetary theory tends to concentrate on control of the money supply?
(Oxford: June, 1989)

Understanding the Question 'Monetarist' theory centres on the quantity theory of money which predicts that an increase in the stock of money will cause a lagged increase in the price level. Hence, to control inflation, the rate of growth of the stock of money (or 'money supply') must first be controlled. But as we have seen, there are great difficulties in controlling the supply of money directly. In principle, a monetary policy, based on a system of monetary base control, could be used but there is no guarantee that it would be successful; the UK authorities have resisted introducing such a system on the grounds that the costs involved may exceed the benefits. Therefore, the 'practical' (or pragmatic) monetarism implemented in the UK in recent years has centred almost exclusively on trying to control the supply of money by acting on the general public's demand for money, via interest rate manipulation. 'Purist' monetarists, employed usually in academic institutions rather than at the Treasury or Bank of England, have argued that such policies do not constitute proper monetarism but, perhaps, a form of 'closet' Keynesianism.

Answer plan
1 Explain how 'monetarist' theory focusses on the role of the money supply in the inflationary process, via the quantity theory of money.
2 Discuss practical difficulties of directly controlling the money supply. Goodhart's Law is relevant here, together with the difficulties of implementing a system of monetary base control.
3 Discuss whether the money supply should be regarded as exogenous or endogenous.
4 Explain how the rate of interest may be used to act on the demand for money to influence the money supply indirectly.

Multiple Choice Questions
Question 3 The revision of the system of monetary control in 1980 and 1981 included all but one of the following measures. The exception was
(a) Increasing the number of banks under government control
(b) Suspension of Minimum Lending Rate
(c) Introducing a ½ per cent ratio for cash balances at the Bank of England
(d) Replacing Sterling M3 as a monetary target

Understanding the Question Under the 1979 Banking Act the government officially differentiated between institutions allowed to call themselves **'banks'** and others known as **'licensed deposit-takers'**. This extended the number of banks to 96. MLR was suspended in 1981, giving freer rein to market forces in the setting of interest rates. At the same time, the required reserve asset ratio was abolished and replaced by the new requirement that all 96 banks should keep ½ per cent of their assets as a ratio of eligible liabilities in balances at the Bank of England. Thus (a), (b) and (c) were all implemented, leaving (d) as the answer to the question. Sterling M3 remained as the government's stated monetary target, despite its volatility and inaccuracy as a measure of the money supply, though it was eventually dropped as a monetary target in 1987.

17.6 Further reading

Artis, M. J., editor *The UK Economy*, 12th edition (Weidenfeld & Nicolson, 1989).
Chapter 2: Money and Finance: Public Expenditure and Taxation.

Brown, R., *A Guide to Monetary Policy*, (Banking Information Service, 1982).

Morris, D., editor, *The Economic System in the UK*, 3rd edition (Oxford University Press, 1985).
Chapter 10: Monetary Policy

18 National Income Accounting

18.1 Points of perspective

The macro-economics which we know today originates in the publication in 1936 of *The General Theory of Employment, Interest and Money* by J. M. Keynes. In the pre-war years Keynes's predecessors, the **neo-classical school of economists**, who then dominated economic thought in western economies, concentrated their attention on how individual markets function and on how relative prices are determined in those markets. Before Keynes, economics usually meant micro-economics! When attention was turned to the determination of the general level of employment in the economy, it was believed that the economy automatically tended towards a **full-employment equilibrium**, provided only that market forces in the individual markets which made up the economy were allowed to work.

However, in the United Kingdom of the 1920s and '30s it occurred to some economists, and in particular to Keynes, that the economy had settled into an **underemployment equilibrium**, in which mass unemployment could persist from year to year. Keynes formed the opinion that the existing body of economic thought failed to provide an adequate explanation of the persistence of mass unemployment. The growth of modern macro-economic theory was a direct result of the need felt by Keynes and his followers to construct what they thought was a better and more general theory capable both of explaining the inter-war depression and of suggesting how full employment could once again be achieved. In the next three units we shall introduce and explain the essential elements of Keynes's theories of income, output, and expenditure, which provide the theoretical framework for understanding the modern macro-economics with which the name of Keynes is so closely associated.

Keynes was just as interested in practical policy as in abstract theory, and indeed the logic of his theory suggested that governments could achieve and maintain full employment by intervening in the economy and **managing the level of demand**. Such policies would require accurate information on what was being produced and on the composition and level of income and expenditure. During Keynes's lifetime there was a distinct lack of such information. The growth, in the post-war era, of a **system of National Income Accounts** developed directly out of the need to have comprehensive and up-to-date statistics on national income, output and expenditure if government was to intervene successfully in the economy. The principal function of the National Income Accounts has always been to provide the basic data for economic policy-making, particularly at the macro-economic level, and for economic forecasting.

18.2   Underlying concepts

1 Accounting identities

Many of the problems experienced by students in the understanding of macro-economic theory stem from an initial failure to recognize and understand the meaning of an **accounting identity**. The most basic of all the identities used in the system of national income accounts is:

National Income ≡ National Product ≡ National Expenditure

or in economics shorthand (in which it is convenient to use the letter Y for income):

(i) $NY \equiv NP \equiv NE$

We shall keep to the mathematical convention of using the ≡ sign to indicate an identity, in which the **left-hand side** of the ≡ sign **always equals the right-hand side**. By definition, the two sides of an identity expression **must** be equal! It is also useful to note that all the identities used in the system of national accounts are **ex post identities**, measuring what has **actually** happened in the economy, rather than what people wish or intend to happen.

2 The circular flow of income

The identity $NY \equiv NP \equiv NE$ tells us that **actual incomes received** in the economy are equal to both **actual expenditure** and the **actual output** produced in the economy. The identity holds because all three are measures of the same thing, the **flow of new wealth** or **income** produced in an economy in a specific time period, usually a year. This can most easily be explained by assuming a highly simplified economy in which all income is spent on consumption and where there is no government sector or foreign trade.

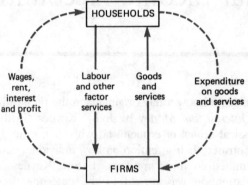

Fig 18.1 The circular flow of income

Figure 18.1 illustrates the **circular flow of income** in such a **two-sector closed economy** comprising households (the **personal sector**) and firms (**the corporate sector**), and two flows, the **'real' flow** of goods and services shown by the continuous line, and the **money flow** of income and expenditure represented by the broken line.

In such an economy it is obvious that if all income is spent on consumption, total expenditure must equal total output, since the value of total output is itself equal to the wages, rent and other factor rewards which go to make up income.

It is less obvious that the identity still holds when we relax the simplifying assumptions, for example by assuming that households now **save** part of their income in idle money balances. In this situation, consumption expenditure will indeed be less than national output, part of which will accumulate as **unsold stocks**. However, as a further part of the system of accounting identities, investment is defined not only as **planned** or **intended investment** on new machinery or raw materials but also as **actual** or **ex post** investment, which includes unsold stocks or **unintended inventory accumulation!** In these circumstances, national expenditure (actual consumption + actual investment) will still equal national output or product!

3 Capital, wealth and income

In Figure 18.2, national income is represented as the continuous **flow** of new wealth produced from the **national capital stock**. It is essential to distinguish **capital** and **wealth**, which are **stock concepts**, from income, which is a flow, measured for a particular period of time. The **national wealth** comprises all those assets which have value, whereas the **national capital stock** is that part of the national wealth which is capable of productive use. It follows that all capital is wealth, but not all wealth is necessarily capital. The national capital stock, which includes **social capital** such as roads and schools as well as **private capital** in the form of machines, raw material stocks and factories, is a measure of the physical wealth assets which are capable of producing more wealth. (The value of labour skills possessed by the population is sometimes defined as **human capital**. While such human

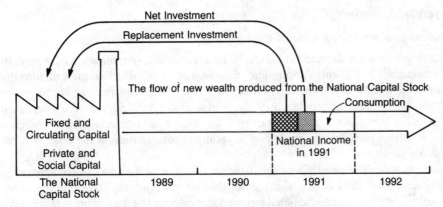

Fig. 18.2 National income as an economic factor

capital is undoubtedly a national resource, it is not included in the definition of the national capital stock.)

We can use Figure 18.2 to illustrate some very important economic relations:

(i) The size of national income or output which can be produced in a particular year is ultimately limited by the size of the national capital stock.

(ii) Part of the national capital stock will be worn out in producing this year's national income. Assuming conditions of full employment in which the capital stock is being used to capacity, part of this year's national income must make good the national capital stock if the economy is to be capable of producing the same size of national income next year. Investment which makes good the national capital stock is known as **replacement investment** or **depreciation investment**. Gross national product and **gross national income** measure the size of output or income produced before allowing for depreciation, whereas **net national product** and **income** measure the goods and services available after replacing the national capital stock. As an accounting identity:

$$\text{(ii)} \qquad NNP \equiv GNP - I_{\text{REPLACEMENT}}$$

A similar distinction can be made between **gross** and **net national income**. However, in the presentation of official national income statistics it is conventional to treat national income as already being net of depreciation or capital consumption. Hence, in the official statistics, identity (ii) can be rewritten as:

$$\text{(iia)} \qquad NY \equiv GNP - I_{\text{REPLACEMENT}}$$

Official statistics also measure **money national income**, which should not be confused with **real national income**, the flow of real goods and services produced. Money national income is simply real national income valued at current prices.

(iii) If **economic growth** is to occur, real national income or output must increase over time. Of course, if there is already spare capacity, including unemployed labour, in the economy, some growth in output can take place without the need to increase the size of the national capital stock. But once full capacity is reached, economic growth requires that extra investment, known as **net investment** be undertaken, over and above the depreciation investment which merely replaces the existing national capital stock. Total investment in the economy may be expressed as:

$$\text{(iii)} \qquad I_{\text{GROSS}} \equiv I_{\text{REPLACEMENT}} + I_{\text{NET}}$$

(iv) Finally, we can use Figure 18.2 to illustrate the **'trade-off'** between current and future consumption and standards of living. The higher the rate of net investment, the smaller is the current output available for consumption purposes. However, the diagram implies that the higher the rate of net investment out of current national income or output, the higher the growth rate and hence the greater the future ability to produce goods and services for consumption. Thus higher living standards in the future require the sacrifice of consumption now! According to this rather simple analysis, it would seem that all a society has to do is to decide how much of current income should be consumed, and how much should be saved and made available for investment. Unfortunately, even if people could agree on this decision, the problem of procuring economic growth is not as simple as this. For example, a reduction in current consumption might make existing investments unprofitable. It may well be that a high rate of private sector investment is linked to the level of business confidence associated with a buoyant consumer market. We shall examine some of these problems in the subsequent units.

18.3 Essential knowledge

1 The three ways of measuring national income

The circular flow of income depicted in Figure 18.1 is a very great simplification of reality. We have already introduced some complications into the circular flow, which represent **injections** and **withdrawals** from the flow of income: households save part of their incomes, and firms retain profits in order to finance investment, and they may also hold stocks of unsold goods. We reserve until Unit 19 an analysis of how saving and investment, together with other important injections and withdrawals resulting from foreign trade and government intervention in the economy, affect the level of income or output.

Nevertheless, it remains true that even with the introduction of the government and foreign trade sectors into our model, the identity which states that income, output, and expenditure totals are equal, still holds. Any one of these **national income aggregates** can be used to measure the economy's flow of output.

(i) The income method We have already explained why, conceptually, national income must equal national output, since all payments for goods and services produced are also incomes. Income in this sense is a payment for productive services rendered, whether by labour or the services of land and capital. **Transfer payments**, such as pensions, welfare benefits and unemployment pay, must be excluded from the estimate of national income, since they are simply transferred from one group of people to another without the recipients adding to production. If such transfers were wrongly included in national income, the error of **double-counting** would occur.

Nevertheless, the national income statistics include arbitrary judgements on what is and is not 'productive work'. Thus an **imputed rent** is estimated for the values of the services received by owner-occupiers from the houses they live in, equal to the rent which would be paid if they were tenants of the same properties. But the housekeeping allowance paid by a husband to his wife is excluded, implying that housework is unproductive! It follows that if a man marries his house-keeper, or if he decides to paint his own house where previously he employed a decorator, the estimates of national income will fall!

The gap between the GDP total obtained by the income and expenditure methods is often used to approximate the size of the so-called '**black economy**' – this refers to unrecorded income where a good or service is provided and the cash payment is not declared officially. Various estimates of the black economy have been made. The Inland Revenue has estimated that activity in the black economy accounts for up to 7.5 per cent of national income, while independent authorities have guessed that the figure might be as high as 15 per cent. Supply-side economists argue that punitive tax rates caused the growth of the black economy, and that tax cuts ought to result in its decline.

An estimate of British national income in 1988, based on the measurement of factor incomes, is shown in Table 18.1, taken from the 1989 National Income and Expenditure 'Blue Book'.

Table 18.1 illustrates the important distinction between **national** and **domestic** income (and product). **Total domestic income**, which is shown in row 8, is obtained from the addition of the various factor incomes in rows 1–7. Total domestic income is converted into **Gross Domestic Product** in row 10 by subtracting **stock appreciation**, which results from inflation and is not a reward to a factor of production. A **statistical discrepancy** (which used to be known as a residual error) is then added to make the income-based estimate of GDP equal to the expenditure-based estimate. The decision as to where in the national accounts to include a residual error is essentially arbitrary. Although, conceptually, national income must equal national product and expenditure, the national income statistics are only **estimates** of what has happened in the economy. Mistakes in data collection inevitably occur, so a 'mistakes item' must be inserted in this table to ensure its equality with the expenditure table. Thus **Gross Domestic Product** (GDP) **at factor cost** in row 12 is a measure of the incomes received by factors of production through employment in the UK economy. GDP is not the same as **Gross National Product** (GNP) because part of the domestically generated incomes may flow overseas to foreign owners of companies operating in the UK. Similarly, citizens living in the UK may receive incomes in the form of dividends and other profits remitted on assets they own abroad. GDP (in row 12) is converted into GNP (in row 14) by adding the **Net Property Income from Abroad** which results from such dividends flows. You will notice that the estimate for net property income from abroad in 1988 is positive. If this figure is correct (National Income estimates are continuously revised in the months and years following first publication) it shows that dividends and profits flowing into Britain exceed those remitted from the UK.

Finally, the estimate for National Income (or Net National Product) in row 15 is obtained by deducting capital consumption or depreciation from Gross National Product.

(ii) The output method of calculating national income involves adding up the money values of all

Table 18.1

Factor Incomes 1988	£m
1 Income from employment	249 775
2 Income from self-employment	42 617
3 Gross trading profits of companies	70 242
4 Gross trading surplus of public corporations	7286
5 Gross trading surplus of general government enterprises	−70
6 Rent	27 464
7 Imputed charge for consumption of non-traded capital	3408
8 Total domestic income	400 722
9 *less* Stock appreciation	−6116
10 Gross Domestic Product (GDP) – income based	394 606
11 Statistical discrepancy (income adjustment)	181
12 Gross Domestic Product (GDP) – average estimate at factor cost	394 787
13 Net property income from abroad	5619
14 Gross National Product (GNP) at factor cost	400 406
15 *less* Capital consumption	−54 769
16 National Income ≡ Net National Product at factor cost	345 637

goods and services produced in the economy. As with the income method there is a danger of double-counting. Only the **money values of final goods and services** sold to consumers must be totalled, or alternatively the **'value added'** by each industry, including the producers of raw materials and capital (or intermediate) goods. A distinction must also be made between Gross National Product (and Gross Domestic Product) at **market prices**, and GNP (and GDP) at **factor cost**. Market prices, or the prices consumers pay for final goods and services, are inflated by the effect of **indirect taxes**, but deflated by government **subsidies** paid to firms. National income aggregates at market prices must be converted to factor cost by **subtracting indirect taxes** and **adding subsidies**. The distinction between GNP at market prices and at factor cost, and other important national income aggregates, are summarized in Figure 18.3.

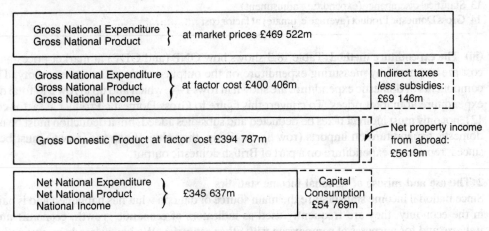

Fig. 18.3 The national income aggregates in 1988

One of the most significant problems in the estimation of national product results from the fact that a large part of national output is not sold at a market price. In the case of public services, such as education, health care, police and administration, the **value of inputs**, including wages, is used as the measure for the value of output. In the case of production which takes place in the **'non-monetized' economy**, such as 'do-it-yourself' home improvement and housekeeping, either an **imputed value** must be estimated or, as we have seen, a decision is taken not to include such estimates in the measurement of national income. In developed industrial countries this may not be a serious problem; but quite obviously it would be rather absurd to omit an estimate of the non-monetized flow of output in a developing economy with a proportionately large subsistence agricultural sector.

Table 18.2 illustrates the calculation of GDP at factor cost by totalling the value added by groups of industries and services. You will notice that stock appreciation has already been deducted from the figures. As before, GDP could be converted into GNP by adding the net property income from abroad.

Table 18.2

Gross domestic product by industry, 1988	£m
1 Agriculture, forestry and fishing	5625
2 Energy and water supply	21 845
3 Manufacturing	93 433
4 Construction	25 745
5 Distribution, hotels and catering, repairs	55 131
6 Transport and communication	28 657
7 Banking, finance, insurance, business services and leasing	76 922
8 Ownership and dwellings	21 407
9 Public administration, national defence and compulsory social security	27 023
10 Education and health services	35 237
11 Other services	25 785
12 Total	416 810
13 Adjustment for financial services	−22 204
14 Gross Domestic Product (GDP) at factor cost (income based)	394 606

Table 18.3

Expenditure 1988	£m
1 Consumers' expenditure	293 569
2 General government final consumption	91 847
3 Gross domestic fixed capital formation	88 751
4 Value of physical increase in stocks and work in progress	4371
5 Total domestic expenditure at market prices	478 538
6 Exports of goods and services	108 533
7 Total final expenditure	587 071
8 *less* Imports of goods and services	−125 194
9 Gross Domestic Product at market prices (expenditure based)	461 877
10 *less* Taxes on expenditure	−75 029
11 Subsidies	5883
12 Gross Domestic Product at factor cost (expenditure based)	392 731
13 Statistical discrepancy (expenditure adjustment)	2056
14 Gross Domestic Product (average estimate) at factor cost	394 787

(iii) The expenditure method Table 18.3 shows how GNP (and GDP) at market prices and factor cost are estimated by measuring expenditure on the outputs produced in the economy. The main components of domestic expenditure are shown in rows 1–4, which add up in row 5 to total domestic expenditure at market prices. To convert this figure to Gross Domestic Product at factor cost (row 12), not only must indirect taxes be deducted and subsidies added, but a deduction must be made for domestic expenditure on imports (row 8). Similarly, the value of exports (row 6) must be added, since it represents expenditure on a part of British domestic output.

2 The use and misuse of national income statistics
Since national income statistics are the main source of data on what has happened and is happening in the economy, they are frequently used as **indicators of economic growth, economic and social welfare**, and for **purposes of comparison with other countries**. We have already mentioned some of the various problems in the construction and use of national income statistics, particularly the distinction between **money** and **real** national income, and the problem of imputing or excluding the value of activity in the non-monetized sector of the economy. We shall now summarize the most important problems which arise in the use of national income statistics.

(i) Comparisons over time
(a) Money national income is a misleading indicator of economic growth. For the growth rate to be calculated, money national income for each year, expressed in **current prices** of that year, must be **deflated** to show real income in the **constant prices** of a single year. An index number, such as the Retail Price Index, used to deflate GNP to constant prices is known as a **GNP deflator**.

(b) Population usually grows over time, so real GNP per head of population (per capita) is a better indicator of living standards than the aggregate real GNP figure.

(c) The quality of goods and services available is likely to change over time, presenting a particularly difficult problem in the use of GNP statistics.

(d) More generally, the GNP figures cannot measure changes in intangibles, which affect the quality of life and the general level of welfare in society. **Externalities**, including both external benefits and costs, usually escape measurement in national income statistics, as do such intangibles as the value people place on leisure time and living close to work. When externalities are measured, what is in effect a welfare loss may appear as a welfare gain! For example, if motorists spend more time each day sitting in congested traffic, they will regard this as a welfare loss. However, as far as the national income statistics are concerned it will appear as extra consumption expenditure on the outputs of the vehicle and petroleum industries.

(ii) Comparisons between countries

(a) We have already mentioned how comparisons of GNP per head between countries are misleading if the relative importance of the non-monetized economy is greatly different.

(b) Further problems occur in the comparison of real income per head if different commodities are consumed. For example, expenditure on fuel, energy and building materials is likely to be greater in a country with a cold climate than in a warmer climate.

(c) A reliable comparison of real GNP per capita requires the accurate deflation of money GNP figures to constant prices in each country. There are considerable differences in statistical method and sophistication between countries, in the construction of both national income accounts and price indices. In addition, artificially managed exchange rates may distort comparison of internal price levels within countries, and even if exchange rates reflect the prices of goods which are traded internationally, they will not reflect the prices of goods and services which do not enter into international trade.

18.4 Links with other topics

Throughout this unit we have stressed that the system of national income accounts measures what has **actually happened** in the economy. We now go on in the next three units to introduce an essentially Keynesian national income/expenditure model of an economy, in which we are interested in whether **planned** or **intended** expenditure in the economy is consistent with the national output which is actually being produced. In particular, we shall examine what is likely to happen in the economy if planned expenditure either exceeds or falls short of actual output.

18.5 Question practice

Essay Questions

Question 1 Consider the uses and limitations of the statistics for 'national income' in gauging changes in a country's standard of living over time.   *(WJEC: June, 1990)*

Understanding the Question We have explained in the Unit some of the main limitations of national income statistics for measuring changes in welfare and living standards over time. However, the question does refer to the uses of national income statistics; so do not restrict your answer to a discussion of limitations alone. The point to make is that, despite their limitations, national income statistics provide one of the best measures available for assessing changing living standards. Perhaps make a brief note that other measures could be used to give a fuller picture, e.g. mortality and health statistics and indicators of food intake or consumer goods per household. It would also be useful to begin your answer by offering a definition of 'standard of living', e.g. total welfare (or utility) per person, derived from goods and services consumed (whether purchased or received 'outside the market' as free goods, services provided by the state, or as positive externalities and other 'intangibles').

Answer plan

1 Explain the components of the 'standard of living'.
2 Describe how national income statistics can be used to measure changes in living standards over time.
3 List and explain each of the limitations on their use.
4 Suggest briefly how these limitations might be overcome (for example, with the use of supplementary measures or indicators).

Multiple Choice Questions

Question 2 From the following information, calculate the Gross National Income of a country:

	£m		£m
Wages	10 000	Unemployment pay and other social benefits	1000
Salaries	6000	Profits	1000
Government Pensions	2000	Rent and Interest	1000

£m
The Gross National Income is: **(a)** 18 000   **(b)** 20 000   **(c)** 22 000   **(d)** 23 000

Understanding the Question The question is testing your understanding of the fact that transfer incomes (pensions, unemployment pay and social benefits) are not included in national income, since they do not result from production. Double-counting would occur if they were included. The correct answer is therefore **(a)**.

Question 3 The following information shows the changes experienced by an economy:

	Size of population	National Income	Price Index
Year 1	100m	200 bn	100
Year 2	110m	240 bn	120

Which of the following would be true?
(a) Real national income has risen   (b) Real national income has fallen
(c) Real national income per head has remained constant   (d) Real national income per head has fallen

Understanding the Question Since money national income and prices have both risen by 20 per cent, real national income has remained constant. However, population has risen by 10 per cent, so real national income per head has fallen. The answer is therefore **(d)**.

Data Response Question

Question 4 Answer the questions below with reference to the table:

Growth and Use of Resources in the UK at 1980 Market Prices
(Note: All figures are in £ million apart from the index numbers.)

	1979	1980	1981	1982	1983	1984
Consumers' expenditure	137.6	137.0	136.6	137.6	143.1	145.5
General government current expenditure on goods, wages, salaries and other services	48.3	48.9	48.8	49.3	50.2	50.7
Gross domestic fixed capital formation	43.9	41.6	37.7	40.1	41.9	45.4
Increase in stocks and work in progress	2.5	−2.9	−2.6	−1.0	0.7	0.1
Exports	63.1	63.1	62.0	62.8	64.1	68.5
Total final expenditure	295.3	287.7	282.6	288.7	300.1	310.1
Less imports	−59.9	−57.7	−55.8	−58.5	−62.0	−67.8
Gross Domestic Product	235.4	230.0	226.8	230.3	238.1	242.3
Index numbers (1980 = 100)	102	100	99	100	104	105

(Source: *Social Trends*, H.M.S.O., 1986.)

(a) Explain the meaning of the phrase 'use of resources at 1980 market prices'. (4)
(b) With specific reference to the data, what can be inferred about:
  (i) changes in living standards; (5)
  (ii) changes in the state of the economy? (5)
(c) Explain what further information you would require in order to make a more accurate assessment of changes in living standards and the state of the economy over the period shown. (6)
(*London, June 1988*)

Understanding the Question The table shows some of the main components of national expenditure on resources; measured at 1980 prices so as to get rid of the effects of inflation from the data. Consumers' expenditure and imports indicate the 'bought' component of living standards, whilst government spending might reflect, in part, the contribution of state-provided public goods and merit goods. However, the data does not indicate the less tangible elements of living standards, such as those arising from externalities and reductions in the length of the working week. Therefore, further information on these would be useful, together with details of employment and distribution amongst different income groups. The data also indicates the trough and upswing of the business cycle and the state of the balance of payments.

18.6 Further reading

Stanlake, G. F., *Macro-economics, an Introduction*, 4th edition (Longmans, 1989).
Chapter 2: The Meaning and Measurement of National Income.

Maunder, P., et al., *Economics Explained*, 2nd edition (Collins, 1991)
Chapter 13: Measuring Economic Activity: National Income.

19 Equilibrium National Income

19.1 Points of perspective

In Unit 18 we briefly mentioned the fundamental difference between the **neo-classical** (or **pre-Keynesian**) view of 'how the economy works', and the view of Keynes himself. According to the older view, the operation of the price mechanism in each of the individual markets which make up the economic system automatically tends towards a situation in which there is full employment of all resources, including labour, in the economy – in other words towards a **full employment equilibrium**. We shall see in Unit 24 how modern **monetarists** adopt essentially the same view of the **stabilizing** nature of market forces (and the **destabilizing** effects of government intervention).

In contrast, the Keynesians believe that the price system contains no self-regulating mechanism that automatically produces full employment, and that government intervention can be a stabilizing force in the economy. Left to itself, a market economy may tend towards an equilibrium in which there is either **mass unemployment** resulting from **deficient demand**, or **demand-pull inflation** in conditions of **'over-full' employment** and **excess demand**. In this unit we develop and explain an elementary **national income and expenditure** model of the economy and illustrate these Keynesian propositions.

19.2 Underlying concepts

1 The interrelationships between markets

A market economy is of course an interrelated system of markets. At the macro-economic level we usually consider such markets in highly aggregated form, dividing the economy into three great markets: the **goods market** (or product market) in which **output** is produced, the **labour market** (which is a part of the wider factor market) and the **money markets.** In this unit we concentrate attention on the interrelationships between the goods market and the labour market – the markets of the 'real' economy. At the outset we must stress, as a word of warning, that more advanced analysis than that considered in this unit investigates the simultaneous interrelationships between all three sets of markets in which the role of the money markets is particularly important. In this unit we largely ignore the role of money in the economy, though in Unit 21 on investment we shall consider the effects of money and the rate of interest on the level of output in the goods market.

2 Equilibrium national income

In Unit 1 we introduced the concept of equilibrium in the context of a single market within an economy. We defined equilibrium as a **state of rest**, or a condition in which the **plans** of all the economic agents in the **economic model** are **fulfilled** and **consistent with each other**. We shall continue to use this concept of equilibrium in examining the conditions necessary to achieve an **equilibrium level of national income or output** within the goods market of an economy. Nevertheless, equilibrium is a state towards which the economy is heading; the equilibrium will not necessarily be reached. It is more realistic to think of the economy as being in a state of **disequilibrium**, tending, in the absence of outside disturbances or 'shocks', towards the equilibrium level of national income. Essentially, national income and output will be in equilibrium when the **planned** or **intended aggregate money demand (AMD)** of all the economic agents in the economy in the current period equals the output (or income) produced in the previous period.

19.3 Essential information

1 A two-sector model of the economy

For the time being we shall construct a two-sector model of the goods market in the economy by pretending that there is no foreign trade and no government sector. We are assuming a **closed** economy in which **households** (or the personal sector) exercise **consumption demand** for final goods and services, and **firms** (or the **corporate sector**) demand **investment goods**. In this highly simplified economy, AMD (or **planned expenditure**) is represented by the identity:

$$\text{(i) } AMD \equiv C + I$$

This identity is essentially different from all the identities introduced in Unit 18. It is an **ex ante** identity defining **planned** or **intended** demand in the economy in terms of the consumption and investment intentions of households and firms. In contrast, the national expenditure identity in the economy is an **ex post** identity, measuring what has actually been spent on consumption and investment:

$$\text{(ii) } E \equiv C + I$$

We must now introduce theories to explain how and why households and firms make consumption and investment decisions. For the sake of simplicity we shall delay the discussion of theories of investment until Unit 21, for the time being assuming that the level of investment in the economy is given outside our model, at a level $\bar{I}$. We must, however, introduce a theory to explain how consumption decisions are made by households. Such a **behavioural theory**, which explains how consumption plans are formed, is called a **consumption function**.

2 The consumption function

(i) The pre-Keynesian consumption function In Unit 2 we constructed a micro-economic theory of demand for one particular good or service, where households or consumers choose between a large number of available goods and services. We saw that an important variable influencing the demand for a specific good or service is its price relative to the prices of all other goods and services. The micro-economic theory of demand can be expressed as the functional relationship:

$$Q_d = f(P), \text{ ceteris paribus}$$

When in contrast we construct a macro-economic consumption function we take the relative prices of goods as given, and concentrate attention instead on how household decisions are made to divide expenditure between **consumption** on all goods and services, and **saving**. The choice between consumption and saving is expressed by the identity:

$$\text{(iii) } Y \equiv C + S$$

Ex ante, the identity states that, at each level of income, planned consumption and saving must add up to equal the level of income. By rewriting the identity, we can define **planned savings** as being simply that part of income which households do not intend to spend on consumption:

$$\text{(iv) } S \equiv Y - C$$

In the pre-Keynesian era, the predominant view was that the **rate of interest** was the main variable influencing the division of income between C and S. The pre-Keynesian savings and consumption functions can be written as:

$$\text{(v) } S = f(r)$$
$$\text{and (vi) } C = f(r)$$

The lower the rate of interest, the greater the consumption and the lower the saving at each level of income. Saving is a **positive function** and consumption a **negative function** of the rate of interest.

(ii) The Keynesian consumption function Keynes accepted that the rate of interest was a variable which influenced consumption decisions, but he believed that the **level of income** was a much more important influence. In general terms, we can write the Keynesian consumption function as:

$$\text{(vii) } C = f(Y)$$

and, from identity (iii), the Keynesian saving function is:

$$\text{(viii) } S = f(Y)$$

The essential features of the Keynesian consumption and savings functions are expressed in Keynes's own words in the *General Theory*:

'The fundamental psychological law, upon which we are entitled to depend with great confidence . . . , is that men are disposed, as a rule and on average, to increase their consumption as their income increases, but not by as much as the increase in their income.'

Figure 19.1, which illustrates the Keynesian consumption function, also introduces the importance of the '45° line' in national income and expenditure models of the economy. Providing that the axes of the diagram are measuring in the same scale, a line drawn at 45° to origin locates all points at which output or income on the horizontal axis equals expenditure measured on the vertical axis.

Figure 19.1 also shows that planned consumption (C) is made of two elements:

(a) autonomous consumption This is the part of consumption which does not vary with the level of income. In Figure 19.1, autonomous consumption is equal to the vertical distance (a) at all levels of income.

(b) income-induced consumption Because the consumption function in Figure 19.1 is drawn as a straight line (a **linear** consumption function) it can be expressed as the equation:

$$\text{(ix)} \quad C = a + cY$$

At any level of income, cY measures **income-induced** consumption, since an increase in income of $\triangle Y$ *induces* an increase in planned consumption equal to $c \triangle Y$. The greater the value of (c), the **steeper** will be the **slope** of the consumption function and the larger the increase in consumption resulting from an increase in income. In fact (c) is the measure of the **marginal propensity to consume**, a concept to which we shall shortly return.

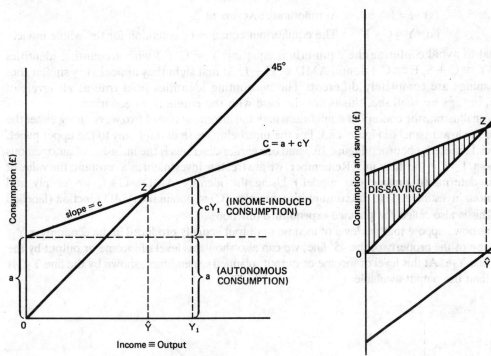

Fig 19.1 The Keynesian consumption function

Fig 19.2 Deriving the savings function

In Figure 19.1, the consumption function crosses the 45° line at point Z, indicating that at the level of income $\hat{Y}$ households plan to consume all their income. At any level of income below $\hat{Y}$, planned consumption is greater than income, from which it follows that planned saving must be negative! Similarly, at any level of income above $\hat{Y}$ households plan to consume less than their income, and planned saving is therefore positive. This relationship between consumption and saving is clearly shown in Figure 19.2, both in the separately plotted savings function (S) and in the shading between the consumption function (C) and the 45° line.

3 The propensities to consume and save

In order properly to understand the Keynesian consumption and saving functions, it is necessary to introduce and define the propensities to consume and save:

(i) The average propensity to consume (APC) is the proportion of income which households plan to consume. (Formally, $\text{APC} \equiv \dfrac{C}{Y}$.) If income is £10 and households plan to consume £8, the APC is 0.8. When the APC is 0.8, the **average propensity to save** (APS) must be 0.2, since the APC and APS always add up to unity. in Figure 19.1, the APC falls as income rises, though total consumption of course rises. APC is greater than unity at all levels of income below $\hat{Y}$, equals unity at $\hat{Y}$, and falls below unity at levels of income above $\hat{Y}$. Conversely, the APS rises from negative to positive values as income rises, equalling zero at $\hat{Y}$.

(ii) The marginal propensity to consume (MPC) is the proportion of the **last** unit of income which households intend to consume. Formally, $\text{MPC} \equiv \dfrac{\triangle C}{\triangle Y}$ and $\text{MPS} \equiv \dfrac{\triangle S}{\triangle Y}$

Again, the MPC and the **marginal propensity to save** (MPS) must total unity. As we have already indicated, the **slope** (c) of the consumption function in Figure 19.1 is the marginal propensity to consume. In this diagram, the MPC is assumed to be constant at all levels of income. Since however, the MPC is likely to decrease as income rises (though remaining between unity and zero), it would be more realistic to draw a consumption function whose slope diminishes at higher levels of income.

(iii) The relationship between the average and marginal propensity to consume Returning to our previous example in which household income is £10, planned consumption £8, and the APC 0.8, we shall now assume that if income increases by £1 to £11, planned consumption will rise by just 60 pence. The MPC is 0.6 and MPC < APC. The APC must now fall as income increases, in this case from 0.8 when income is £10 to 0.78 when income is £11. Since APC falls as income rises, it follows that the MPC must be less than the APC.

4 Equilibrium national income revisited

We can now represent our simple two-sector model of the economy in just three equations:

(ix) $C = a + cY$: The consumption function

(x) $I = I$: Autonomous investment

(xi) $Y = C + I$: The equilibrium equation or condition for the whole model

It is vital to avoid confusing the equilibrium equation $Y = C + I$ with accounting identities such as $Y \equiv C + S$, $E \equiv C + I$, and $AMD \equiv C + I$. At first sight they appear very similar, but the meanings are completely different! The accounting identities hold true at **all** levels of income, but, as we shall see, this is not the case with the equilibrium equation.

We can illustrate the concept of equilibrium national income in one of two ways, using either the upper or the lower panel of Figure 19.3. For the time being we shall refer only to the upper panel. The crucial difference between Figure 19.3 and our earlier diagrams is the inclusion of autonomous investment, $I = \bar{I}$, in the diagram. (Remember, we are treating investment as a constant, the value of which is determined outside our model.) Using the identity $AMD \equiv C + I$, we simply add autonomous investment (I) to the consumption function (C) to obtain the AMD function (labelled C+I). This is also called the **planned expenditure** function.

Let us now suppose that the level of income or output actually produced in the economy is Y_1. Making use of the property of the 45° line, we can also show this level of income or output by the vertical line Y_1e. At this level of income or output, planned expenditure, shown by the line Y_1f, is greater than the output available.

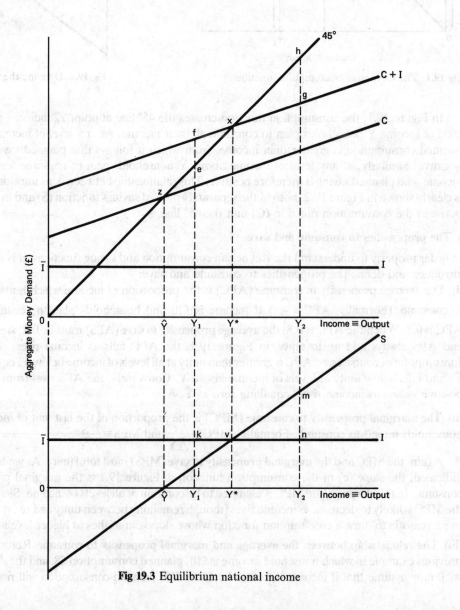

Fig 19.3 Equilibrium national income

Thus, at income Y_1, $Y<C+I$. This is a **disequilibrium condition**, since the planned expenditure of the households and firms is greater than the output produced.

In a similar way we can show that a level of income such as Y_2 is also a disequilibrium level of income, since at income Y_2, $Y>C+I$, which again is a disequilibrium condition. At Y_2, actual output Y_2h exceeds planned expenditure Y_2g by the amount gh.

At Y_1, firms can only meet the planned expenditure in the immediate period by **destocking**, whereas at Y_2 they will experience **unintended stock accumulation**. Because, in each situation, planned expenditure differs from the output firms have actually produced we now assume that firms react by changing the output they plan to produce in the next period. More precisely, we assume that firms react to destocking by increasing output to meet demand, and they react to unintended stock accumulation by reducing output. (For the time being we are also assuming that spare capacity exists so that firms can increase output, and that prices remain constant.)

If, when $Y<C+I$, firms increase output

and, when $Y>C+I$, firms decrease output,

it follows that only when $Y=C+I$ will output remain unchanged.

In Figure 19.3, national income is in equilibrium at Y^*, the only level of income where $Y=C+I$. Only at this level of income are the plans of the households and firms fulfilled and consistent with each other. At any other level of income or output, unintended destocking or stock accumulation creates an incentive for firms to change the level of output.

Figure 19.3 is an example of a **'Keynesian cross'** diagram in which equilibrium is determined at point x where the AMD or aggregate expenditure function crosses the 45° line. In the most simple and unrealistic version of the Keynesian theory we assume that output quickly responds to any change in demand. This means that the 45° line is the **aggregate supply** function in the model. Thus the equilibrium condition can also be stated as:

aggregate expenditure = aggregate supply

Be sure to avoid confusing point x on the AMD function with point z on the consumption function. The equilibrium level of income is determined at x, whereas z merely determines the single level of income at which APC $=1$!

5 Saving and investment

The lower panel of Figure 19.3 illustrates an alternative way of stating the equilibrium condition of national income. You will notice that the equilibrium level of income Y^* is located where the savings function (S) crosses the investment function (I). Thus the equilibrium condition can be written as:

Planned Saving = Planned Investment

or (xii) $S=I$

It is important to stress that this statement of the equilibrium condition is merely an alternative to $Y=C+I$, adding nothing new to the model. This is shown when we derive equation (xii) by **substituting** the ex ante accounting identity (iii) into the equilibrium condition (xi):

substituting   (iii) $Y\equiv C+S$
into   (xi) $Y=C+I$
we get $C+S=C+I$
or   (xii) $S=I$

Nevertheless this method of expressing the equilibrium condition possesses the advantage of showing that income is in equilibrium when **injections** of demand into the circular flow of income equal **leakages** or **withdrawals** of demand. In a simple two-sector model of the economy, saving is the only leakage and investment is the only injection. More generally we can write the equilibrium condition as:

Planned Leakages = Planned Injections

It is vital to avoid confusing the equilibrium condition $S=I$ with the **ex post identity** which states that **actual saving** will always equal **actual investment** whatever the level of income. Consider once again the level of income Y_2, but this time in the lower panel of Figure 19.3. Planned saving exceeds planned investment by the amount nm. You should notice that nm equals gh in the upper panel, which we earlier defined as **unintended stock accumulation** at this level of income. Actual investment at any level of income is defined by the identity:

(xiii) I ACTUAL $\equiv$ I PLANNED + I UNPLANNED

and unplanned investment occurs precisely when firms 'invest' in unsold stocks of finished goods. We can now explain why actual investment equals actual saving at the level of income Y_2, even though planned saving is greater than planned investment. In the first place, households are able to fulfil their savings plans, so actual saving equals planned saving. However, this creates the situation in which firms accumulate unsold stocks (resulting in unplanned investment) exactly equal to the excess of saving over planned investment! It follows from the way we have defined actual investment that actual savings and investment are equal. We shall leave it as an exercise for the reader to work out why the identity still holds at the income level Y_1 where destocking occurs and unplanned investment is negative.

6 The equilibrium equation in a four-sector economy

We shall complete the unit by extending our model in a very simple way to include a **government sector** and an **overseas** or **foreign trade sector**. Government spending (G) and overseas demand for the country's exports (X) represent additional injections of demand into the circular flow of income, whereas taxation (T) and import demand (M) are leakages. The AMD identity now becomes:

$$(xiv) \quad AMD \equiv C+I+G-T+X-M$$

In order to keep the model as simple as possible, we shall treat the values of G, T, X and M as being **autonomously** determined outside the model, just as we have already treated I in this way. This is a highly artificial assumption since we might expect some at least of these components of planned expenditure to be related to the level of income. However, we shall delay relaxing this assumption until we examine the **multiplier theory** in Unit 20. We are also rather artificially assuming that households plan consumption decisions out of **pre-tax income** and that the level of taxation, T, is not determined by the level of income. In Unit 20 we see how the model changes when we assume that consumption decisions are made out of **post-tax disposable income**.

Since we are making the assumption that all the components of planned expenditure, with the exception of consumption, are autonomously determined outside the model, the AMD function drawn in Figure 19.4a has the **slope** of the consumption function (the MPC), and its position is determined by adding the values of I, G and X to, and subtracting the values of T and M from, the consumption function. The equilibrium condition for the model now becomes:

or alternatively:

$$(xv) \quad Y = C+I+G-T+X-M$$
$$(xvi) \quad S+T+M = I+G+X$$
$$\text{(leakages)} \qquad \text{(injections)}$$

As in the two-sector model of the economy, the equilibrium level of national income is depicted in Figure 19.4a and b at Y^*, where the AMD function crosses the 45° line.

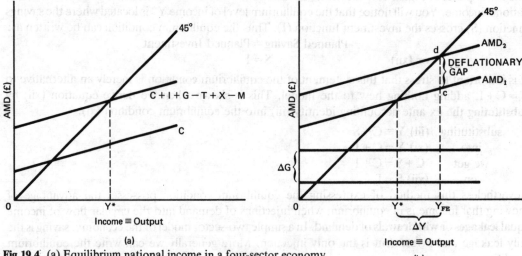

Fig 19.4 (a) Equilibrium national income in a four-sector economy
(b) Equilibrium national income and full employment equilibrium

7 Equilibrium national income and full employment equilibrium

Suppose that the equilibrium level of income Y^* is insufficient to employ fully the available labour force in the economy. We can represent the size of national income or output which will employ all the labour force at Y_{FE} in Figure 19.4b. The existing level of planned expenditure represented by AMD_1 brings about an equilibrium level of national income at Y^* rather than at Y_{FE}. In Keynesian terms, unemployment is caused by **deficient demand** in the economy. If any of the components of planned expenditure such as C, I, G or X autonomously increase, the **deflationary gap** between AMD_1 and AMD_2 might be closed, bringing about an equilibrium level of income at the full employment level.

Keynes, writing in the depression economy of the inter-war years, believed that the deficient demand was either caused in the first place, or certainly reinforced, by a **collapse** of private sector consumption and investment demand. (The tendency of households to save too much is called the **'paradox of thrift'**. According to the Keynesian view, saving, which is an individual virtue, becomes a vice in the economy as a whole if unemployment is caused by too little consumption. We shall examine Keynes's theory of deficient investment demand, the **marginal efficiency of capital** theory, in Unit 21.)

If Keynes was correct, it would be unwise to rely on an autonomous recovery in consumption and investment to close the deflationary gap and bring about full employment. Instead the government could deliberately use the **policy instruments** at its disposal, government spending (G) and taxation (T), to inject demand into the economy through a **budget deficit**. Essentially, the government **borrows** the excess savings of the private sector, which are injected back into the circular flow of income in public spending. This is the theoretical basis of **Keynesian demand management** or **discretionary fiscal policy**, used by the Keynesians to control the level of aggregate demand in the economy to a level consistent with achieving equilibrium national income at full employment.

19.4 Links with other topics

In Units 20, 21 and 22, we expand on important aspects of the Keynesian income/expenditure model of the economy. Then, in Unit 23, we introduce the **aggregate demand/aggregate supply (AD/AS) macro-model** which, in recent years, has begun to replace the income/expenditure model as the theoretical framework within which macroeconomic issues are investigated.

19.5 Question practice

Essay Questions

Question 1 Distinguish the equilibrium level of National Income from the full employment level of National Income. Why may they differ? *(London: January, 1981)*

Understanding the Question To answer the question you must firstly show an understanding of the meaning of the equilibrium level of national income. You can use any of the methods of writing the equilibrium condition, but it is probably best in this particular question to use $Y = C + I + G - T$. It is not necessary to introduce exports and imports, though the introduction of the government sector allows you to show how government policy can bring about equilibrium at the full employment level, assuming that the initial equilibrium was not at the full employment level. You should draw a 'Keynesian cross' diagram similar to those in the unit, to illustrate the deflationary or inflationary gap which will exist if equilibrium is below or above the full employment level.

To earn a high grade you must answer the second part of the question at some length, suggesting reasons why there can be too little or too much demand in the economy. In particular, you can explain how Keynes's theories of the consumption function and marginal efficiency of capital (Unit 21) suggest that households may save too much and firms invest too little in a depressed economy, which settles into an underemployed equilibrium.

Not all economists agree that the equilibrium and the full employment levels of national income differ. We have noted in the introduction to both this unit and Unit 18 how the pre-Keynesians believed that the economy is automatically self-adjusting to a full employment equilibrium. After the publication of Keynes's *General Theory* in 1936, the debate continued. Properly to understand the debate between 'Keynes and the Classics', our analysis would have to be extended to the interrelationships between the goods and labour markets and the money market. For example, Keynes's opponents argued that in conditions of excess supply of labour prices would fall along with money wages. There would be a reduction in the transactions demand for money (Unit 14), causing the equilibrium rate of interest in turn to fall. If businessmen's investment decisions are responsive to the rate of interest, aggregate demand in the economy may now increase to close the deflationary gap. Thus market forces cure unemployment, and according to this view of 'how the economy works' Keynes's unemployment equilibrium is a special case in which wages and prices are inflexible downwards.

Answer plan

1 Explain the meaning of the equilibrium level of National Income, clearly stating the equilibrium conditions, and showing how the level of income or output will change towards the equilibrium if the condition is not met.
2 Draw a 'Keynesian cross' diagram to show equilibrium national income above or below the full employment level of income. Draw a planned expenditure function consistent with equilibrium at the full employment level, and indicate the inflationary or deflationary gap.
3 Explain the possible causes of excess or deficient demand in the economy.
4 Possibly discuss the fact that not all economists believe that the two concepts are different.

Question 2

(a) What are the main injections and withdrawals in the circular flow of income model? (10)
(b) An open economy experiencing a **deflationary gap** receives an increase in investment of £100m. Analyse the likely consequences for the economy's national income. (10)

(Cambridge AS: June, 1989)

Equilibrium national income

Understanding the Question Part **(a)** of the question is straightforward, testing your ability to set out a Keynesian income/expenditure model, illustrated with a circular flow diagram or a 'Keynesian cross' diagram. Show clearly the main injections of demand into the flow of income: investment; government spending; and export spending—and the main withdrawals or leakages: saving; taxation; and imports. Only a brief explanation is needed.

For part **(b)** you must explain the cause of a deflationary gap, in terms of deficient aggregate demand and withdrawals of demand from the flow of income depressing the equilibrium level of income below full employment. The injection of investment will trigger the multiplier process (explained in Unit 20), with the level of national income growing by £100m × the multiplier. The size of the multiplier will, itself, depend upon the nature of the leakages from the circular flow of income–the larger the marginal propensities to save, tax and import; the smaller is the multiplier. In an open economy, any stimulation of demand will tend to draw imports into the economy (via the marginal propensity to import), reducing the size of the multiplier. Finally, it is worth mentioning that the investment will shift the economy's production possibility frontier outwards and it may also promote greater future growth of output by contributing to competitiveness.

Answer plan

1 Briefly explain the Keynesian model, illustrated on a circular flow diagram, with all the injections and withdrawals of demand clearly indicated.
2 Explain the injections and withdrawals and how equilibrium income occurs when planned injections equal planned withdrawals.
3 Illustrate a deflationary gap on a 'Keynesian cross' diagram and distinguish between equilibrium income and full employment income.
4 Explain how the increase in investment causes a multiplier effect, with the size of the multiplier dependent on the nature of withdrawals.
5 Discuss whether the deflationary gap will be fully closed and whether increased imports and inflation may also be promoted by the demand stimulation.
6 Note other consequences, e.g. on competitiveness and the position of the production possibility frontier.

Multiple Choice Questions
Questions 3, 4 and 5

Assertion		Reason
3 The marginal propensity to consume usually increases with income.	because	People usually consume more as their incomes rise.
4 An increased budget surplus (given constant government expenditure) will have a deflationary effect.	because	Given constant government expenditure, an increased budget surplus will reduce aggregate demand.
5 Other things being equal, an increase in the propensity to import will reduce the level of income.	because	Imports represent a leakage from the circular flow of income.

(a) Both the assertion and the reason are true statements and the reason is a correct explanation of the assertion.
(b) Both the assertion and the reason are true statements but the reason is not a correct explanation of the assertion.
(c) The assertion is true but the reason is a false statement.
(d) The assertion is false but the reason is a true statement.

Understanding the Questions The answer to question 3 is **(d)**. This question tests your understanding of the relationship between total and marginal consumption. According to Keynes's theory of aggregate consumption, total planned consumption increases with income, but less than proportionately. Therefore the marginal propensity to consume decreases as income rises.

The correct answer to both question 4 and question 5 is **(a)**. An increased budget surplus represents a leakage of demand from the circular flow of income, causing the AMD curve to shift downwards. A similiar effect occurs in the case of question 5, but with one notable difference. The **slope** of the AMD curve reflects the marginal propensities to consume, import (and tax) in the economy–although in the diagrams in the unit we dealt only with the marginal propensity to consume. Therefore an increase in the marginal propensity to import will reduce the slope of the AMD curve, shifting the curve downwards at all positive levels of income.

Data Response Questions

Question 6 The following data refers to a hypothetical closed economy where money prices and wages are constant and the Central Bank allows the money supply to expand or contract as necessary to maintain the interest rate at a certain level.

    (i) Household consumption spending is defined by the equation:
$$C = 1000 + 0.8\,Y_D$$
Where C = consumption and Y_D = household disposable income in £ billion.
(Household disposable income = national income minus tax revenue.)

(ii) Tax revenue is raised by way of a proportional income tax with a rate of 25%.
(iii) Private investment spending = £600 billion.
(iv) Government spending on goods and services = £2,400 billion.

(a) At what level of disposable income will household savings be zero?
How does the average propensity to save vary as disposable income increases? (5)
(b) What is the equilibrium level of income? (5)
(c) Suppose the government wishes to increase the level of income by £100 billion by additional government spending on goods and services.
How much additional spending should the government undertake? (5)
(d) How does the budgetary position of the government alter, comparing the new equilibrium level of income with the initial position? (5)
(e) What action must the Central Bank take when income is increased by £100 billion if it wants to maintain interest rates at their original level? (5)

(WJEC: June, 1990)

Understanding the Question

(a) If the consumption function is $C = 1000 + 0.8 Y_D$, then the savings function must be
$S = -1000 + 0.2 Y_D$. Set S at zero and solve for the size of Y_D.

(b) Algebraically, the equilibrium equation for the model specified in the question (a closed economy with a government sector) is:

$$Y = a + c(Y - tY) + \bar{I} + \bar{G}$$

or; $Y = £1000\ bn + 0.8(Y - 0.25Y) + £600\ bn + £2,400\ bn$

Solve this equation for the value of Y.

(c) The multiplier in this model (see Unit 20) is: $\dfrac{1}{s + ct}$

or $\dfrac{1}{0.2 + 0.2} = 2.5$

Divide the desired change of income (£100 bn) by the multiplier to solve for the size of the increase in government spending needed to bring about the desired change.

(d) The budgetary position of the government is $(G - T)$ or $(\bar{G} - tY)$.
Plug the relevant numbers into $(\bar{G} - tY)$ for the situations before and after the increase in government spending and national income, and compare the two budgetary positions. If the budget was initially in deficit, has the demand stimulation increased or reduced the size of the government's deficit?

(e) At a higher level of income, the transactions and precautionary demands for money will increase; causing the liquidity preference curve to shift to the right. In order to prevent the rate of interest from rising, the authorities must allow the money supply to increase to accommodate the general public's desire to hold larger money balances.

19.6 Further reading

Stanlake, G. F., *Macro-economics: an Introduction*, 4th edition (Longman, 1989).
Chapter 4: Output, Demand and Equilibrium.   Chapter 5: Consumption.
Chapter 7: The Determination of Equilibrium.   Chapter 8: Output and Employment.

Lipsey, R. G., *An Introduction to Positive Economics*, 7th edition (Weidenfeld & Nicolson, 1989).
Chapter 26: Macro-economic Concepts and Variables.
Chapter 27: National Income in a Two-sector Model.
Chapter 29: National Income in More Elaborate Models.

20 The Multiplier

20.1 Points of perspective

In this unit we develop an important aspect of the Keynesian national income/expenditure model of the economy which we introduced in Units 18 and 19. In Unit 19 we explained that when aggregate money demand (AMD) is greater (or less) than the income or output produced in the previous period, national income will rise (or fall) until an equilibrium is reached when AMD equals the available output. We now introduce the **multiplier theory** and investigate in more detail the process by which income or output changes when an autonomous change occurs in any of the components of planned expenditure.

The concept of the multiplier was first developed in 1931 by R. F. Kahn, who at the time was a colleague and former pupil of Keynes at Cambridge. The early theory was essentially an **employment multiplier**, which modelled how a change in public investment, for example in road-building, might cause a subsequent multiple expansion of employment. Keynes first made use of Kahn's employment multiplier in 1933 when he discussed the effects of an increase in government spending of £500, a sum assumed to be just sufficient to employ one man for one year in the construction of public works. Keynes wrote: 'If the new expenditure is additional and not merely in substitution for other expenditure, the increase of employment does not stop there. The additional wages and other incomes paid out are spent on additional purchases, which in turn lead to further employment . . . the newly employed who supply the increased purchases of those employed on the new capital works will, in their turn, spend more, thus adding to the employment of others; and so on.'

By the time of the publication in 1936 of Keynes's famous *General Theory,* the multiplier had become a vital part of Keynes's explanation of how an economy can settle into an **underemployment equilibrium**. In the *General Theory*, Keynes focused attention on the **investment multiplier**, explaining how a collapse in investment and business confidence can cause a multiple contraction of output. From this, it was only a short step to suggest how the **government spending multiplier** might be used to reverse the process. Analytically, in terms of the Keynesian expenditure/income model of the goods market in the economy, an increase in public spending which is unaccompanied by an increase in taxation has an identical expansionary effect to an autonomous increase in investment. Indeed, nowadays the concept of the **National Income multiplier** is used as a generic term to include the multiplier effects which result from a change in **any** of the components of demand. Thus the **autonomous consumption multiplier**, the **investment multiplier**, the **government spending multiplier**, and various forms of **tax** and **foreign trade multipliers** are all examples of specific National Income multipliers. At a local level, the **regional multiplier**, which we briefly mentioned in Unit 12, is sometimes identified. A regional multiplier indicates by how much regional income or output will increase when additional demand is injected into the regional economy. However, the **money multiplier** discussed in Units 14 and 17 should not be classified amongst the Keynesian or National Income multipliers, though its existence serves to illustrate that multiplier effects occur whenever a change in one variable cause **multiple and successive** stages of change in another variable. Indeed, if fiscal and monetary policy are interdependent, an increase in government spending can result in simultaneous fiscal and monetary multiplier effects.

20.2 Underlying concepts

1 The dynamic multiplier

It is often forgotten that the multiplier process is essentially a dynamic process which takes place over a considerable period of time. In order to illustrate this, we shall continue to adopt for the time being the assumptions of Unit 19: namely that the values of all the components of aggregate expenditure, with the exception of consumption, are determined autonomously. Only the consumption decisions of households are related to level of income through the marginal propensity to consume (MPC). We shall assume that the MPC is 0.8 at all levels of income, which of course means that the marginal propensity to save (MPS) must be 0.2. Saving is the only income-related **leakage** of demand in the economy. Whenever income increases by £10, consumption spending increases by £8, and £2 is saved. Finally, we shall assume that prices remain constant in the economy and that a margin of spare capacity and unemployed labour exists which the government wishes to reduce.

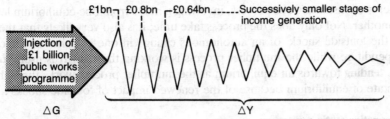

Fig 20.1 The multiplier process when the marginal propensity to consume is 0.8

Suppose that the government now increases public spending by £1 billion, but keeps taxation at its existing level. The government could, for example, decide to increase **transfer incomes** such as pensions, welfare benefits and unemployment pay, or even aid to industry. Alternatively, the government might invest in **public works** or **social capital**, for example in road construction. Figure 20.1 illustrates that the increase in public spending represents an initial increase in incomes for the factors of production who are now employed in the construction scheme. At the second stage, demand for goods and services produced largely by the private sector will increase when the households employed in the public works spend 0.8 of their increase in income on consumption, in total £800 million. Further stages of income generation then occur, with each succeeding stage being smaller than the previous one. In our particular model, each successive stage is exactly 0.8 of the previous stage because the MPC is 0.8 at all levels of income and saving is the only income-induced leakage. Assuming that nothing else changes in the time it takes for the process to work through, the eventual increase in income resulting from the initial injection is the sum of all the stages of income generation.

The value of the government spending multiplier $= \dfrac{\text{change in income}}{\text{change in government spending}}$

$$\text{or } k = \frac{\Delta Y}{\Delta G}$$

where k is the symbol for the government spending multiplier. Providing that saving is the only leakage of demand, the value of k depends upon the marginal propensity to consume. In fact, the formula for the multiplier in this model is

$$k = \frac{1}{1-c} \text{ where c is the MPC}$$

$$\text{or } k = \frac{1}{s} \text{ where s is the MPS}$$

The larger the MPC (and the smaller the MPS), the larger is the value of the multiplier. In our model, the value of the multiplier is 5 (i.e. $\frac{1}{1-0.8}$), indicating that the initial increase in public spending will subsequently increase income by £5 billion in total.

We have stressed the dynamic nature of the multiplier process in order to emphasize that the economy is likely to be in a permanent state of **disequilbrium**. It is wrong and artificial to imply that

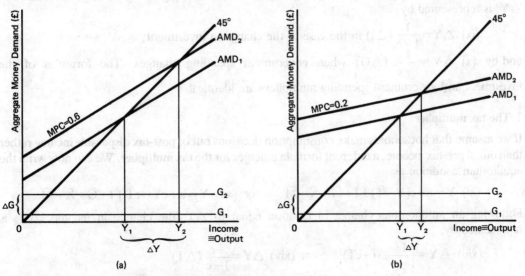

Fig 20.2 How the size of the multiplier is determined by the marginal propensity to consume (a) MPC = 0.6 (b) MPC = 0.2

the multiplier is an instantaneous process, involving a move from one equilibrium level of national income to another. Not only does the process take time; it is also very likely that the economy will experience the 'outside shock' of an autonomous change in one or other of the components of planned expenditure while the multiplier process is working through. It is useful to think of the economy as **tending** towards an equilibrium as the multiplier process works through, yet unlikely to reach a state of equilibrium because of the renewed impact of 'outside shocks'.

2 The comparative static multiplier

Figure 20.2 illustrates the multiplier concept in terms of the change in the level of AMD necessary to change the equilibrium level of national income from one **static equilibrium** to another. Since saving is the only income-induced leakage of demand from the economy, the slope of the AMD function depends on the value of the MPC. An initial equilibrium level of income, Y_1, is determined by the level of planned expenditure AMD_1. When the MPC is 0.6, as in Figure 20.2a, an injection of government spending shown by $\triangle G$ increases the equilibrium level of income to Y_2. The change in income from one equilibrium level to another, $\triangle Y$, is two and a half times the change in government spending. However, a comparison of the equilibria indicates nothing about the length of the time path from one equilibrium to the other. The slope of the AMD function is less, and the MPC is smaller in Figure 20.2b. Thus the multiplier is also smaller, equal to 1.25 when the MPC is 0.2.

20.3   Essential information

1 The simple multiplier

Our purpose is to show that there is **no unique formulation** for the multiplier; as we change the assumptions of our model, treating taxation and import demand as income-related, we shall arrive at different formulas for the relevant multiplier. Firstly, however, we shall restate the elementary multiplier in a model of the economy in which all the components of aggregate demand except consumption are **autonomously** determined outside the model.

Equation (i) is a behavioural equation showing the consumption function, and equations (ii) to (vi) depict the other components of aggregate demand, which are autonomous:

> (i) $C = a + cY$, where c is the MPC.
> (ii) $I = \bar{I}$: investment
> (iii) $G = \bar{G}$: government spending
> (iv) $T = \bar{T}$: taxation
> (v) $X = \bar{X}$: exports
> (vi) $M = \bar{M}$: imports

The equilibrium condition for the model is:

> (vii) $Y = C + I + G - T + X - M$ or (viii) $Y = a + cY + \bar{I} + \bar{G} - \bar{T} + \bar{X} - \bar{M}$

Since saving is the only income-induced leakage of demand, the simple multiplier in this model is $\dfrac{1}{1-c}$ or $\dfrac{1}{s}$, where s is the marginal propensity to save. If for example private investment changes by $\triangle I$, or government spending changes by $\triangle G$, then the resulting change in the level of income, $\triangle Y$, is represented by

> (ix) $\triangle Y = \dfrac{1}{1-c} (\triangle I)$ in the case of the change in investment;

and by (x) $\triangle Y = \dfrac{1}{1-c} (\triangle G)$ when government spending changes. The formulas of the investment and government spending multipliers are identical.

2 The tax multiplier

If we assume that households make consumption decisions out of **post-tax disposable income** rather than out of pre-tax income, a different formula emerges for the **tax multiplier**. We can now write the equilibrium condition as:

> (xi) $Y = a + c(Y - \bar{T}) + \bar{I} + \bar{G} + \bar{X} - \bar{M}$ or (xii) $Y = a + cY - c\bar{T} + \bar{I} + \bar{G} + \bar{X} - \bar{M}$

Following an autonomous change in taxation equal to $\triangle T$, the change in income, $\triangle Y$, is represented by:

> (xiii) $\triangle Y = \dfrac{1}{1-c} \triangle(-cT)$ or (xiv) $\triangle Y = \dfrac{-c}{1-c} (\triangle T)$

> where $\dfrac{-c}{1-c}$ is the tax multiplier.

This expression tells us two important things about the tax multiplier. In the first place, it is **negative**, which means than an autonomous **increase** in taxation results in a **fall** in the equilibrium level of income, the size of the fall being a multiple of the absolute change in taxation. Secondly, since the value of c (the MPC) is less than unity, the value of the tax multiplier in this model is **always** less than the value of the government spending multiplier $\frac{1}{1-c}$. For example, if the MPC is 0.8 the government spending multiplier $\frac{1}{1-c}$ will be 5, and the tax multiplier $\frac{-c}{1-c}$ will be 4. As an exercise, you might calculate the size of the two multipliers for other values of the MPC. Whatever the chosen value of the MPC, you will find that the absolute size of the government spending multiplier (forgetting the plus and minus signs) is always equal to the tax multiplier plus one! Thus a given increase in tax revenue has a smaller multiplier effect than a similar change in government spending. The explanation for this lies in the fact that disposable income falls by an amount equal to the size of the tax increase, but since part of disposable income is saved, spending does not fall by the full amount of the increase in taxation. In the initial stage of the multiplier effect, the change in spending is $-c\triangle T$ rather than $-\triangle T$. Summing all the successive stages of the multiplier process, the total change in spending and income equals $\frac{-c}{1-c}$ ($\triangle T$) rather than $\frac{-1}{1-c}$ ($\triangle T$).

3 The balanced budget multiplier

Now let us suppose that the government decides to increase public spending and taxation by equal amounts, so that $\triangle G = \triangle T$. The combined multiplier effects of $\triangle G$ and $\triangle T$ are shown by:

(xv) $\triangle Y = \frac{1}{1-c} (\triangle G) + \frac{-c}{1-c} (\triangle T)$

Since $\triangle G = \triangle T$, we can rewrite this as:

(xvi) $\triangle Y = (\frac{1}{1-c} + \frac{-c}{1-c}) \triangle G$

or (xvii) $\triangle Y = (\frac{1-c}{1-c}) \triangle G$

The expression $\frac{1-c}{1-c}$ is the **balanced budget multiplier**, which must be 1. This means that an increase in public spending financed by an equal increase in taxation has an expansionary effect on the level of income exactly equal to the size of the injection of public spending. (If you find the algebra difficult, you can note from the previous section that when, for example, the MPC is 0.8, the government spending multiplier is 5, and the tax multiplier is -4. The balanced budget multiplier is simply the addition of the two multipliers; in this case $5 + (-4) = 1$!).

4 Taxation and import leakages

Up to this point in the analysis we have treated taxation and import demand in a highly artificial way. We have assumed that they are unrelated to the level of income, being determined instead **exogenously** outside our model. This is unrealistic, since a part at least of both taxation and import demand are likely to be dependent on the level of income. For the sake of simplicity, we shall now assume that **all** of taxation and import demand are **income-induced**, being determined **endogenously** within our model in the following ways:

(xviii) $T = tY$, where t is the marginal rate of taxation
and (xix) $M = mY$, where m is the marginal propensity to import.

We can write the equilibrium condition for the new version of our model as:

(xx) $Y = a + cY + \bar{I} + \bar{G} - tY + \bar{X} - mY$

In this particular model the multiplier is:

$$k = \frac{1}{1-c+t+m}$$

or $k = \frac{1}{s+t+m}$

The three income-induced leakages of demand in the model all affect the value of the multiplier. The greater the propensity to import, and the higher the rate of taxation, the smaller will be the multiplier effect resulting from a change in any of the autonomous components of demand. There is no such thing as a *unique* formulation of the multiplier, relevant to all the possible models we could specify. In general terms, however, the government spending or investment multiplier will be:

$$k = \frac{1}{\text{marginal change in income-induced leakages}}$$

5 The multiplier and economic policy

(i) Keynesian demand management In earlier units we briefly explained how Keynesians have advocated the use of **discretionary fiscal policy** to control or influence the level of aggregate demand in the economy. The greater the size of the government spending multiplier, the smaller the increase in public spending which is needed to bring about a desired increase in money national income. Similarly, the larger the tax multiplier, the smaller the tax cut which would be necessary. If the multipliers are large, and if most of the increase in money national income is in real output rather than in the price level, **fiscal policy** will be an effective way of controlling the economy.

But, as we have explained, the marginal propensity to import and high marginal tax rates reduce the size of the multiplier. The British economy is relatively small, compared for example with the USA, and open to trade. In recent years the propensity to import has noticeably increased. It is very doubtful whether the government spending multiplier is much higher than 1, and indeed, as we shall shortly explain, it may be less than 1.

(ii) Monetarism and 'crowding out' We have also indicated that the multiplier effect resulting from an increase in government spending will be greatest when taxation remains unchanged. According to this logic a government should deliberately increase the size of the budget deficit if it wishes to maximize the expansionary effects of an increase in public spending. However, our analysis has ignored the **monetary effects** of the widening budget deficit. It is precisely upon these **monetary effects of fiscal policy** that monetarists concentrate attention, arguing:

(a) That increased borrowing to finance the budget deficit causes interest rates to rise. Higher interest rates reduce private investment, thereby countering the expansionary effects of the increase in public spending. The net size of the multiplier may even be zero if the increase in public spending 'crowds out' and displaces an equal amount of private spending. Indeed 'extreme' monetarists have gone further, arguing that fiscal multipliers can be negative in the long run if 'productive' private investment is crowded out by 'unproductive' public spending. It is worth noting that the 'crowding out' view of 'modern' monetarists is by no means new–it is essentially a revival of the old 'Treasury view' against which Keynes personally argued in the early 1930s.

(b) In so far as a multiplier results from an increase in public spending financed by a budget deficit, the main effect may be on prices rather than on real income or output. Monetarists argue that expansionary fiscal policy will increase the rate of inflation if the budget deficit and PSBR are financed by methods which increase the money supply. Keynesians agree that fiscal stimulation can lead to inflation rather than an expansion of real output if the economy is at or near full capacity and full employment. The area of dispute between Keynesians and monetarists is whether the government spending multiplier will expand real output or prices when there is a considerable margin of spare capacity in the economy.

(iii) Fiscal policy multipliers We have already noted that the taxation multiplier is likely to be smaller than the government spending multiplier. However, there may also be variations in the nature of the multiplier depending on whether an increase in public spending is channelled into **public works** or **transfer incomes** and on whether changes in taxation involve **direct** or **indirect** taxation. In times of mass unemployment and gravely deficient demand, public works may be an effective fiscal policy instrument since:

(a) they can be directed to regions of especially high local unemployment;

(b) by providing lasting **social capital**, they can improve a region's economic infrastructure and create an environment attractive to private investment;

(c) the government is seen to be 'doing something about unemployment'–public works are likely to employ large numbers of manual workers;

(d) public works are not 'import intensive'; a large fraction of the initial injection of income is spent on the outputs of domestic industry, thereby increasing the size of the multiplier.

However, public works are not a very suitable policy instrument for the discretionary management of demand at or near the full employment level. Public works are slow to start, difficult to stop, and altogether difficult to 'fine-tune'. **Discretionary tax changes** may be more appropriate for controlling demand, except perhaps in conditions of very high unemployment. The multiplier effect of a tax change occurs through its impact on private sector consumption and investment. However, the size of the effect will be reduced if the propensity to import is high. As an alternative to both public works and tax cuts, a government can expand demand by increasing public spending in the form of **transfer incomes** paid to lower income groups, or even by redistributing the existing level of public spending through greater transfers. The **transfer income multiplier** tends to be larger than other fiscal multipliers because the poor have higher propensities to consume and lower propensities to import than the better-off. Nevertheless, it is not usually practicable to raise and lower the level of welfare benefits and unemployment pay as a part of discretionary demand management. Instead, transfer incomes such as supplementary benefit, which form a state 'safety net' for the poor, act as an **automatic stabilizer** dampening or reducing the multiplier effects which result when 'outside shocks' hit the economy. As incomes fall, the increase in the total volume of transfer incomes paid to the unemployed and the poor reduces the total contraction in income and demand. Similarly, the **'means tested'** nature of many transfer incomes and the **progressive** nature of income tax create an automatic stabilizer which reduces the multiple expansion that follows an injection of demand into the economy. As the economy approaches full employment, fewer people qualify for transfer incomes and the proportion of income paid in taxation increases. The volume of public spending falls while that of taxation rises.

20.4 Links with other topics

The multiplier theory is very closely related to the concept of equilibrium national income examined in Unit 19. In particular, you should refer to the discussion of **deflationary gaps** (in Unit 19) and **inflationary gaps** (Unit 22), which illustrate how the size of the multiplier determines the level of government spending needed to achieve equilibrium national income at the full employment level, without inflation. In Unit 21 we now go on to contrast the **accelerator principle** with the multiplier, showing how the two concepts can be brought together in **dynamic Keynesian models of economic growth** and of the **business cycle**. In Unit 24 we reintroduce the contrast between the Keynesian and monetarist views on the size and effectiveness of the government spending multiplier.

20.5 Question practice

Essay Questions
Question 1
(a) Briefly explain the meaning of the multiplier. (20)
(b) Examine the likely multiplier effects in the South East of England resulting from the building of the Channel Tunnel. (80)

(London: June, 1990)

Understanding the Question The first part of the question accounts for only a fifth of the marks, so be brief and avoid the temptation to write all you know about the multiplier. The second part of the question relates to regional income/output (and thence employment) resulting from an injection of spending into regional income. We have explained how the size of the multiplier will be smaller in an open economy, the greater the size of the marginal propensity to import. When we examine the effect of an increase of spending, within a particular region of an economy, the **'regional multiplier'** is likely to be even smaller since much of the initial stage of income generation will be spent, outside the region, on 'imports' from the rest of the country as well as from abroad. But, if the region is large and successful with a broad-based economy, such leakages into 'imports' from other regions may be relatively small. Conversely, however, if there is full employment and a lack of spare capacity within the South-Eastern economy, increased demand will have to be met from outside the region and local inflation may be triggered, particularly with regard to house prices and wage levels.

Answer plan
1 Explain carefully that the Keynesian or national income multiplier measures the relationship between a change in aggregate demand and the resulting change in the equilibrium level of national income.
2 Briefly distinguish between some of the various multipliers, e.g. the investment multiplier and the government spending multiplier.
3 Explain the formula for the multiplier, in either a closed or an open economy, indicating how the marginal propensities to save and import and the marginal tax rate determine the size of the multiplier. Illustrate with a numerical example.
4 Explain how the second part of the question relates to the 'regional multiplier'.
5 Discuss how 'regional imports' will reduce the size of the 'regional multiplier', drawing attention to aspects of the South-Eastern economy that would either promote or reduce regional imports, or contribute to regional inflation.
6 Explain how the construction of the Tunnel may give the South East a competitive advantage over other UK regions and integrate the region into the prosperous wider European market.
7 Perhaps discuss multiplier affects at a more micro-level within the region, e.g. in terms of the local economies around Folkestone and Dover near to the construction site.
8 Explain how the multiplier effects will extend over many years since the construction will take time to complete.

Multiple Choice Questions

Questions 2 and 3 Questions 2 and 3 refer to the following data.

Income (Y)	Consumption (C)	Saving (S)
0	150	−150
100	220	−120
200	290	− 90
300	360	− 60
400	430	− 30
500	500	0
600	570	30
700	640	60
800	710	90
900	780	120
1000	850	150

Question 2 Which of the following formulas represents the consumption schedule in the table above?

    (a)   150+0.3Y   (d) −150+0.3Y

    (b)   150+0.7Y

    (c)   150+0.8Y

Question 3 In this example, the investment multiplier is:

    (a) 0.7

    (b) 3.33

    (c) 1.43

    (d) 0.3

Understanding the Questions Question 2 puts into numerical form the Keynesian consumption function of Units 21 and 22: $C = a + cY$. Autonomous consumption, which is unrelated to the level of income, is measured by a, whereas income-induced consumption is represented by cY. The marginal propensity to consume is c. According to the consumption schedule in the question, autonomous consumption is 150. (Thus alternative **(d)** must be wrong.) The schedule also indicates that the proportion of the additional income at each stage which is spent on consumption is 0.7. Thus the correct expression for the consumption function is $150 + 0.7Y$ (alternative **(b)**). The value of the MPC (0.7) can then be used to calculate the size of the investment multiplier.

By applying the multiplier formula $k = \dfrac{1}{1-c}$, we get: $\dfrac{1}{1-0.7}$ or $\dfrac{1}{0.3}$, which equals 3.33: alternative **(b)** in Question 3.

Data Response Questions

Question 4 Study the data below, then answer the questions which follow.

The following is data for a hypothetical closed economy which initially is in short run macro-economic equilibrium.

    (i) The consumption function is given by the equation

$$C = 100 + 0.8\,Y_D$$

    where C denotes consumption in £ billion and Y_D denotes disposable after-tax income in £ billion.

    (ii) All government revenue is raised by a 25% proportional income tax. Hence

$$Y_D = 0.75\,Y$$

    where Y denotes national income in £ billion.

    (iii) Private investment spending = £1400 billion.

    (iv) Government expenditure on goods and services = £2500 billion.

    (v) National income (Y) = £10 000 billion.

(a) What are the initial values of consumption, savings and government tax revenue?   (5)

(b) What is the relationship between the average propensity to consume and the marginal propensity to consume in this economy? How does the average propensity to consume vary as disposable income increases?   (5)

(c) Suppose that private investment spending subsequently decreases to £1000 billion. What, other things being equal, is the change in national income that is predicted by the Keynesian income-expenditure model?   (5)

(d) If government expenditure and the tax rate remain unchanged, what is the government budget deficit or surplus at the equilibrium level of national income **following** the decrease in private investment?

    (5)

(e) Suppose the government wishes to achieve a return to the original national income of £10 000 billion via increasing after-tax disposable incomes by means of non-taxable cash benefits paid to households. If the consumption function is unchanged, by how much must government expenditure on cash benefits increase?   (5)

                                             (WJEC: June, 1988)

Understanding the Questions We have not explained in the main body of the unit precisely how the multiplier formula is derived from the equilibrium condition for national income, except to say that

$$k = \frac{1}{\text{marginal change in income-induced leakages}}$$

We shall now take the opportunity provided by this question to show in detail how the multiplier formula is derived in any particular national income model.

Representing the marginal propensity to consume out of disposable income as c, the marginal rate of income tax as t, and autonomous consumption as a, the equilibrium equation for this model is:

(i) $Y = c(Y - tY) + a + \bar{I} + \bar{G}$

or (ii) $Y = cY - ctY + a + \bar{I} + \bar{G}$

If we collect all the Y terms on the left-hand side of the equation, we get:

(iii) $Y - cY + ctY = a + \bar{I} + \bar{G}$

or (iv) $Y(1 - c + ct) = a + \bar{I} + \bar{G}$

Dividing both sides of the equation by the expression, we get:

(v) $Y = \frac{1}{1 - c + ct}(a + \bar{I} + \bar{G})$

The expression $\frac{1}{1 - c + ct}$ is the multiplier in this particular model.

Since c is the marginal propensity to consume, the multiplier can also be expressed as: $\frac{1}{s + ct}$, where s is the marginal propensity to save. This is the multiplier formula for an economy on which decisions to consume and save are made out of **post-tax disposable income**. If we extend the model by introducing the overseas sector; with the import equation being $M = mY$, the multiplier would become $\frac{1}{s + ct + m}$. If, in contrast, consumption and savings decisions were made out of **pre-tax** income, the multiplier would be $\frac{1}{s + t + m}$. (We introduced this multiplier earlier in the unit.) Since the MPC (c) is less than one, the value of ct must be less than the value of t. Hence the multiplier is larger when consumption decisions are made out of post-tax income because the leakages of demand are smaller.

(a) $C = £100 \text{ bn} + 0.8 (£7500 \text{ bn})$
$S = £10\,000 \text{ bn} - C$
$T = 0.25 (£10\,000 \text{ bn})$

(b) The marginal propensity to consume is constant at $0.8Y_D$ at all levels of income. APC > MPC at all levels of income. The average propensity to consume falls as income rises, being greater than unity at low levels of income and falling through unity at the level of income at which $C = Y_D$. As income rises, the APC falls towards $0.8Y_D$, but always remains above $0.8Y_D$.

(c) This part of the question tests the multiplier:

$$\Delta Y = \frac{1}{s + ct}(\Delta \bar{I})$$

(d) The government's budgetary position is $(\bar{G} - tY)$. Calculate whether the budget is in surplus or deficit at the initial equilibrium level of national income, and at the subsequently lower level of income following the fall in investment.

(e) Since the formula for the government spending multiplier is the same as for the investment multiplier, an increase of government spending or cash benefits of the same size as the decrease in investment will have the desired effect.

Question 5 Recorded below are some figures for a hypothetical economy

	Weeks				
	1	2	3	4	n
1 Output (=income)	100	90	82	75.6....	.50
2 Investment	10	10	10	10	10
3 Consumption goods produced (=consumption goods demanded in previous week)	90	80	72	65.6....	.40
4 Planned (ex-ante) savings (=20% of row 1)	20	18	16.4	15.1....	.10
5 Consumption goods demanded (=80% of row 1)	80	72	65.6	65.5....	.40
6 Excess supply (=row 3 minus row 5)	10	8	6.4	5.1....	0
7 Planned savings minus planned investment (=row 4 minus row 2)	10	8	6.4	5.1....	0

(Source: W. Beckerman, *An Introduction to National Income Analysis*, Weidenfeld & Nicolson, 1968.)

(a) Specify and briefly explain the process which is at work over time in the case of the above economy.

(b) The last column on the right shows the values of the variables for a National Income equilibrium.

(i) What assumptions are necessary for this equilibrium to be reached?

(ii) When will the equilibrium be reached? *(London: June, 1981)*

Understanding the Question

(a) The data in the question illustrate how the **national income multiplier** or **investment multiplier** (the process to be specified) is a dynamic process through successively smaller stages of income and expenditure expansion, or in this case contraction.

Explain how in the first week planned saving exceeds planned investment, causing a leakage of demand or expenditure from the economy. In week 2, income equals the value of output sold in week 1. The marginal propensities to consume and save out of income are indicated as 0.8 and 0.2 respectively at all levels of income. Therefore, in week 2 planned saving continues to exceed planned investment, but by less than in week 1. The multiple contraction of income, output and expenditure continues until, in week n, planned saving equals planned investment (and planned consumption and investment equal the output available).

(b) (i) The model assumes that saving is the only leakage of demand in the economy. This particular equilibrium would not be reached if the marginal change in income-induced leakages was greater than the marginal propensity to save, or indeed if the MPS varied with the level of income. It is also assumed that investment is the only autonomous component of demand, and that the level of autonomous investment remains unchanged as the multiplier process works through between weeks 1 and n.

(ii) You are not expected to state the answer to the question in terms of a precise number of weeks. In fact, in the dynamic multiplier process there are an infinite number of successive stages of income and expenditure generation (or contraction), each stage being smaller than the previous stage. The size of each successive stage tends towards zero as n becomes larger and larger. In the question, week n is therefore the time period when any further contractions of income are so small that we can ignore them, when income and expenditure have converged approximately to the equilibrium value of 50 at which planned saving equals planned investment.

20.6   Further reading

Begg, D., *et al. Economics*, 3rd edition (McGraw Hill, 1991).
Chapter 21: The Determination of National Income.

Stanlake, G. F., *Macro-economics, an Introduction*, 4th edition (Longman, 1989).
Chapter 7: The Determination of Equilibrium.
Chapter 8: Output and Employment.

21   Investment

21.1   Points of perspective

In developing the simple Keynesian model of Units 19 and 20, we assumed that the level of **planned** or **intended investment demand** in the economy is **autonomous** or independent of the level of income or output currently being produced. Since this is obviously a gross oversimplification, we shall devote most of this unit to an explanation and brief comparison of a number of **theories of investment**. Economists generally agree that investment decisions are made by businessmen for a variety of different reasons. Consequently there is no 'correct' investment theory; instead, each theory may explain a different and relevant aspect of how investment decisions are made. However, our general conclusion will be that a large part of investment is indeed autonomous of the level of income, being determined by factors such as the cost of borrowing (the **rate of interest**), **expectations** about future profitability, the **relative prices** of capital and labour, and the nature of **technical progress**. Nevertheless, a certain part of investment may indeed be related to the level of income, and more particularly to the **rate of change of income**, via the **acceleration principle**.

21.2   Underlying concepts

1 The different types of investment

We have explained in Unit 11 how economists distinguish between saving and investment. Investment involves the demand for, and expenditure on, **capital goods** capable of producing more income and wealth in the future. **Domestic investment** includes the purchase of new capital equipment and buildings – the **fixed capital formation** of Unit 18 – and also the accumulation in the form of **stockbuilding** of increased stocks of raw materials, work-in-progress and finished goods. Whilst the purchase of **financial claims** such as shares or debentures are not in themselves regarded as a part of domestic investment, the acquisition of paper claims on other countries is an important part of **overseas investment**, additional to the direct purchase of physical assets overseas. To the extent that they are not offset by counter-claims held by foreigners, increased holdings of foreign currencies and foreign customers' trade debts to British exporters represent a net increase in the nation's total assets.

A large part of the investment which adds to the nation's capital stock is **public** or **social investment** in such assets as roads, hospitals and schools. **House-building** can also be an important part of investment. If expenditure on new dwellings is included in investment, why not include the purchase of other **consumer durables** such as televisions and cars? Logically, there is no reason why they should be excluded, since they can be regarded as capital assets yielding a service to their owners. The exclusion of consumer durables is therefore an important omission from the official estimates of investment.

2 Investment and simple Keynesian model

In the context of our simple Keynesian income/expenditure model of the economy, 'I' represents the **ex ante net investment demand** of the **private sector**. It is worth noting that:

(i) Total or **gross investment** is much larger than **net investment** since it includes **capital consumption** or **depreciation**. Indeed over half of the gross investment in the UK economy is **replacement investment** which makes good capital consumption. Net investment adds to the nation's capital stock, thereby enabling economic growth to occur by creating the potential to produce a bigger output in future years.

(ii) The investment function I shows the **planned** or **intended** investment decisions at each level of income of all the private sector business enterprises in the economy. However, ex ante or planned investment will not always equal **ex post** or **realized** investment. Unit 19 explained how **unintended stock accumulation** (or **unplanned investment**) occurs when the actual output produced in the economy is greater than intended expenditure or AMD. Ex ante investment only equals ex post investment at the equilibrium level of national income or output!

(iii) The investment function is usually taken to include only the intended net investment of the private sector. A significant part of total investment, both gross and net, is **public investment** undertaken by the government and other public authorities such as nationalized industries. However, since 1979, spending cuts, together with the privatization of many of the formerly nationalized industries have led to a decline in public investment as a proportion of the total. An increase in public investment, for example in public works such as road construction, is usually represented by a change in government spending, G, in the Keynesian model, though investment by nationalized industries can be included along with private investment in the investment function I. However, the statistics indicate that total fixed investment in the economy is strongly influenced by government policy and factors which influence the housing market. The kind of investment decision upon which we shall now concentrate attention – that of a private sector firm considering whether to purchase extra plant or machinery – is not nearly so typical as it is often considered to be.

21.3　Essential knowledge

1 The micro-economic theory of investment

(i) Distribution theory revisited Just as the **aggregate consumption function** of Unit 19 is built up from the micro-economic theory of how individual **utility-maximizing** households choose to divide their income between consumption and saving, so the **investment function** is similarly obtained by aggregating all the individual investment decisions of **profit-maximizing** business enterprises. We start from where we left off in Unit 13 (on **distribution theory**) by stating that, in perfectly competitive markets, a profit-maximizing businessman or decision-maker will employ each factor of production, including capital, up to the point where the **value of its marginal product** equals the **marginal cost** of employing the last unit of the factor. According to this theory the demand for capital, and hence the level of investment, depends on the **marginal productivity** of capital and the rate of interest. Other things being equal, the lower the rate of interest, the greater both the demand for capital and the level of investment. The declining marginal productivity of capital means that extra capital is not worth employing unless the rate of interest falls.

If technology allows a firm to substitute one factor of production for another, then **changes in the relative prices** of factors of production will influence how a firm produces its desired level of output.

For example, a rise in the price of labour relative to the rate of interest will create an incentive for firms to employ more capital-intensive methods of production, thereby increasing the demand for capital and the level of investment.

It is likely, however, that the ability of a firm to switch between the employment of capital and labour is limited, at least in the short run. We may be justified in assuming the existence of a technologically determined **capital output ratio** which indicates the amount of capital needed to increase output by one unit. If, for example, the capital output ratio is 3, then when a firm's existing capital is fully utilized, an investment of £3 is required in order to increase output by £1 in each future year (assuming constant prices).

(ii) Discounting the future Nevertheless, a businessman's demand for capital goods is rather different from his demand for labour. It is insufficient to state that a profit-maximizing firm will invest up to the point where the **current** marginal product of capital equals the rate of interest. We must modify the businessman's **decision rule** to take account of the fact that most of the returns on a new investment are **future returns**, which are produced over the **useful economic life** of the investment. In general terms, we can state that a profit-maximizing businessman will invest in a new capital asset if:

$$\left. \begin{array}{l} \text{the rate of return per cent per period} \\ \text{he } \textbf{expects} \text{ over the life of the capital} \\ \text{assets} \end{array} \right\} > \left\{ \begin{array}{l} \text{the rate of interest per cent} \\ \text{per period that must be paid} \\ \text{for borrowed funds to finance} \\ \text{the investment} \end{array} \right.$$

Although our businessman may know the current cost of the investment and the rate of interest, he cannot know with complete certainty either the length of the asset's useful economic life or the details of the net returns or **income stream** which will be produced in each year of that life. Instead, he must **forecast** them, knowing that an asset's useful economic life may be much shorter than its **technical life**. The development of new technology or changes in input prices may render a machine **productively inefficient** long before it actually wears out. Likewise, an estimate of a machine's future net return or income stream is fraught with uncertainty: not only must the **physical product** or output of the machine be calculated for **each** year of its expected life, so also must the prices at which the output is sold, and the amounts and prices of other inputs such as raw materials and labour.

Assuming that estimates have been made of all these variables, and that the net returns have been calculated for each year of the asset's expected life, we can restate the firm's investment decision rule as:

$$\left. \begin{array}{l} \text{invest in all projects for which the } \textbf{discounted present} \\ \textbf{value} \text{ of the stream of prospective returns} \end{array} \right\} > \left\{ \begin{array}{l} \text{the known cost of} \\ \text{the capital asset} \end{array} \right.$$

This is the basis of the **discounted cash flow** (DCF) technique of investment appraisal. If a firm is to maximize the profits resulting from an investment, the year in which the profits or net returns are received is crucial, since £1000 received this year is worth more than the same amount received next year (again assuming constant prices). Income received this year can be reinvested (or lent at the current rate of interest) so as to be worth more by next year. Any money received next year must be equal to that received this year plus the rate of interest if the incomes received in each of the two years are to be of equal value. It follows that **income received earlier in the life of an investment is worth more than similar income received later**.

The DCF method of investment appraisal 'picks up' information about both the **shape** of a project's expected income stream (or cash flow), and the rate of interest. Estimate of profits in each of the years of the expected life of an investment project are expressed in terms of their value in the year of the investment–known as the **present value** (PV). The businessman or decision-maker chooses an appropriate **rate of discount** which reflects the rate of interest that would be paid to borrow the funds which finance the cost of the project. If the PV of the expected future income stream is greater than the cost of the investment, the firm can expect to 'do better' by investing in its own capital project rather than by lending out the equivalent funds to earn the going rate of interest. Quite clearly, the higher the rate of interest, the higher the appropriate **test discount rate**. An investment project judged as just worthwhile when tested against an 8 per cent discount rate would fail a 10 per cent test.

Regardless of the complexities introduced by the DCF principle and the problems of anticipating the future, the general conclusion reached is the same as that suggested by simple marginal productivity theory: that a firm's demand for investment funds is **inversely related** to the rate of interest. At higher rates of interest, fewer projects are worthwhile to a profit-maximizing firm. However, as we shall shortly see, the introduction of the **role of uncertainty about the future** into the determination of investment decisions takes on a special significance in the Keynesian macro-economic theory of investment.

2 The loanable funds theory

The pre-Keynesian theory of the determination of the **aggregate level of investment** in the economy is based in part on the marginal productivity theory of individual investment decisions which we

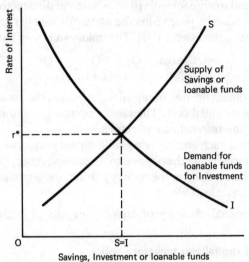

Fig 21.1 The 'Classical' loanable funds theory

described earlier in this unit. This is represented by the investment function I in Figure 21.1, which is drawn as a downward-sloping curve showing that the demand for investment funds (or loanable funds as they were known in this theory) is greater at lower rates of interest. We introduced the other part of the loanable funds theory in Unit 19 in describing the 'classical' theory of savings as a function of the rate of interest. The curve, S in Figure 21.1, shows that the supply of loanable funds or savings is greater at higher rates of interest. Thus in the loanable funds theory, the aggregate levels of both investment and saving are determined by the rate of interest. As in any market, the market price (the rate of interest) tends to rise or fall to bring about an equilibrium which clears the market. In Figure 21.1, planned investment equals planned saving at the equilibrium interest rate, r*. You should note also that the loanable funds theory is a theory of the determination of the rate of interest in the **goods market** of the economy. This contrasts with the Keynesian theory of the rate of interest, which we explained in Unit 14. In the Keynesian theory, the rate of interest is treated as a purely monetary phenomenon, whose value is determined in the **money market**.

3 The Keynesian marginal efficiency of capital theory

The 'classical' loanable funds theory has largely been discredited and replaced by Keynes's own theory of investment, the **marginal efficiency of capital** (MEC) theory (also known as the marginal efficiency of investment theory). We saw in Unit 19 how Keynes rejected the 'classical' view that the **aggregate** level of savings is largely determined by the rate of interest. (Note, however, that the rate of interest may still be important in **directing** savings between competing financial intermediaries such as banks and building societies, even though in the Keynesian theory it is the level of income that determines aggregate saving.) The rejection of the 'classical' savings function is insufficient in itself to destroy the loanable funds theory, since it merely leads to the conclusion that the savings function is vertical or **'interest-inelastic'**. Of much more significance in our present context is the Keynesian view that the rate of interest is determined in the money market (see Unit 14), being taken as given or **exogenous** by businessmen contemplating investment decisions.

It is worth noting, however, that there is one part of the loanable funds theory that Keynes did not completely reject: the **investment function** which is **inversely related to the rate of interest**. But while the pre-Keynesian investment function was stated in terms of the **current** marginal productivity of capital, Keynes incorporated into the theory the view we have already explained, that businessmen base investment decisions on their **expectations** of the future income stream resulting from each investment. Since the marginal efficiency of capital, which is the Keynesian investment function, is very closely related to the discounted cash flow technique of investment appraisal, we shall compare the two:

(a) A second look at DCF Suppose that a businessman is contemplating investing in a machine costing £1000, with an expected life of three years and no scrap value or disposal costs at the end of this life. Using the DCF method of investment appraisal, he can write the present value of the stream of prospective returns over the three years as:

$$\text{(i)} \quad PV = \frac{Q_1}{1+r} + \frac{Q_2}{(1+r)^2} + \frac{Q_3}{(1+r)^3}$$

where $Q_1 \ldots Q_3$ are the returns expected in each year and r is the *known* rate of interest or discount.

As we previously explained, the investment is worthwhile if the PV exceeds the initial cost of the investment.

(b) MEC Alternatively we can rewrite formula **(i)** so as to calculate directly the rate of return which the businessman expects to obtain by purchasing the asset. We simply replace the *unknown* PV of formula **(i)** by the **known** cost of the asset, £1000. The **unknown** is now the rate of return which we shall call i:

$$\text{(ii)} \quad \frac{\text{asset's cost}}{(£1000)} = \frac{Q_1}{1+i} + \frac{Q_2}{(1+i)^2} + \frac{Q_3}{(1+i)^3}$$

Solving formula **(ii)** for i, we obtain the rate of return which makes the present value of the expected income stream exactly equal its initial cost. The rate of return, i, is the **marginal efficiency of the capital asset**, also known as the **internal rate of return**.

If the MEC is calculated for each and every possible capital project available to all the business enterprises in the economy, we can rank the projects in descending order. With the rate of interest, r, assumed to be exogenously determined in the money market, the aggregate level of investment in the economy is now itself determined where:

the marginal efficiency of capital = the rate of interest

or   i = r

4 The marginal efficiency of capital and monetary policy

The greater the **interest elasticity** of the investment function (or the MEC curve), then the greater also the effectiveness of monetary policy in influencing the level of aggregate demand. By reducing interest rates, an increase in the money supply can induce businessmen to engage in investment projects they would not consider worthwhile at higher interest rates. Conversely, a decrease in the money supply will reduce investment.

The interest elasticity of the investment function is also important when considering whether the economic system contains the 'self-righting' property automatically to achieve an equilibrium level of national income at the full employment level. According to the 'classical' or pre-Keynesian view, falling interest rates in a depressed economy will create the incentive for businessmen to increase investment, thereby also increasing the level of aggregate demand in the economy. This effect will be greatest if investment is highly interest elastic.

5 The importance of expectations and uncertainty

Keynes doubted the interest elasticity of investment and he also believed that there was a lower limit (called the Liquidity Trap) below which the interest rate would not fall even in a depressed economy. However, even if the rate of interest is able to fall to a very low level and investment in its turn is responsive to the rate of interest, the MEC theory provided Keynes with a further very powerful explanation of why investment could collapse in a depressed economy. The **position** of the MEC curve depends on the state of **businessmen's expectations** about the future—or their **'animal spirits'**, in Keynes's colourful language. In a severe depression, business confidence is likely to be very low, causing a collapse of investment. The investment function or MEC curve shifts inwards, resulting in a situation in which little investment takes place even at very low interest rates. Indeed, given Keynes's belief that the consumption function is essentially stable, he needed a theory of an unstable investment function in order to explain how, in conditions of unregulated market forces, a collapse of investment could deepen a depression.

6 The acceleration principle

Thus, in the Keynesian view, expectations and the state of business confidence are more important determinants of investment than the rate of interest, and the level of investment is determined largely autonomously of the current level of income. Nevertheless, a part at least of net investment may be related to the **rate of change** of income or output, via the **acceleration principle**.

We have already mentioned in an earlier section how two motives exist for firms to invest in more capital equipment: firstly, when wages rise relative to the cost of capital, and secondly, when technology changes in such a way as to require larger quantities of capital than before—resulting in a larger **capital output ratio**. Assuming now that both the relative prices of capital and labour and the capital output ratio are fixed, a third motive for investment exists when firms believe that aggregate demand is increasing or will soon do so. In order to produce the extra output which they will now be able to sell, firms will need to invest in additional fixed capital, providing of course that an increase in sales is consistent with profit maximization. This is the basis of the **accelerator theory of investment**, in which it is assumed that firms try to keep to an optimal relationship between the amount of capital they possess and the volume of output. We can illustrate the acceleration principle by means of a numerical example:

Table 21.1: The acceleration principle

		Yearly Sales	Existing Capital	Desired Capital	Replacement Capital	Net Investment	Gross Investment
1st Period Steady Sales	year 1	£2000	£8000	£8000	£800	0	£800
	year 2	2000	8000	8000	800	0	800
2nd Period Rising Sales	year 3	2200	8000	8800	800	800	1600
	year 4	2400	8800	9600	800	800	1600
	year 5	2800	9600	11200	800	1600	2400
3rd Period Levelling off	year 6	3000	11200	12000	800	800	1600
	year 7	3000	12000	12000	800	0	800
4th Period Falling Sales	year 8	2800	12000	11200	0	0	0
5th Period Levelling Off	year 9	2700	11200	10800	400	0	800
	year 10	2700	10800	10800	800	0	800

We shall suppose that a firm initially sells an output of £2000 and that, because demand is unchanged, the output is stable from year to year. We shall further assume:

(a) a fixed capital output ratio of 4:1, which means that £4 of capital is required to produce £1 of output per year;

(b) the firm's capital has a life of ten years, after which it needs replacing;

(c) initially the firm possesses £8000 of capital which is exactly enough to produce its yearly output; and

(d) the initial capital has been built up evenly over the years, so that 10 per cent of it needs replacing each year.

In the first Period of Table 21.1 the demand for the firm's output remains stable. The firm has no need for additional capital so **net investment** is zero. **Gross investment** is solely replacement investment or depreciation of £800.

In Period 2, however, demand for the firm's output starts to grow. In year 3 when sales increase by £200, the firm needs additional capital of £800. A 10 per cent increase in demand or sales has had an **accelerated** effect upon investment: gross investment has increased by 100 per cent! In year 4 when sales increase by the same **absolute amount** of £200, investment remains constant, but in year 5 there is once again an accelerated effect on investment when the rate of growth of sales again increases.

In the third Period **the rate of growth** of sales **slows down** in year 6 and levels off completely in year 7. Note that investment declines in year 6 even though sales are still growing. Investment can decline without an actual decline in sales; all that is required is for the growth rate of sales or demand to slow down! In year 7 there is no need for any additional capital so net investment again is zero and gross investment equals replacement investment.

In the fourth Period, when the level of sales absolutely declines, the firm will actually need less capital. Consequently part of the capital which is wearing out need not be replaced and gross investment falls to zero in year 8.

Finally, in Period 5, we see a symmetrical effect to that observed in Period 3: in year 9 when sales continue to fall but the **rate of decline** in sales **slows down**, gross investment begins to recover. The firm must replace part at least of the capital which is wearing out if it is to meet demand, while in year 10 when capital is once again just sufficient to meet demand, replacement investment is back at its initial level of £800.

Thus the acceleration principle provides a second explanation (the first being the role of expectations and the state of business confidence) for the observed great instability of investment. In our numerical example, net investment depends upon the **change in consumption** (and indirectly, via the propensity to consume, upon the **change in income**), but investment fluctuates by a much greater percentage than consumption. The five Periods of our example broadly represent phases in the upswing and downswing of the **business cycle**. Consumption rises in the upswing of the cycle, but it must grow steadily if investment is to remain constant. However, it may be impossible to sustain a rapid growth of sales, and once the rate of growth declines, investment will begin to fall. In this way, the growth of consumption demand in the upswing of the business cycle creates the conditions for a subsequent collapse in investment and the beginning of the downswing.

7 Criticisms of the accelerator theory

(i) It is too mechanical It assumes that all firms react to increases in demand in the same way. Some firms may wait to see if the higher level of demand is maintained, whilst others may order more machinery and plant than is immediately required.

(ii) If firms already possess excess capacity left over from a previous boom in demand, they can simply utilize their spare capacity to increase output without the need to invest in any additional fixed capital.

(iii) An increase in demand may occur at a time when the capital goods industries are themselves at full capacity and unable to meet a higher level of investment demand. In these circumstances, a rise in the relative price of capital goods may encourage firms to enconomize on capital and to employ more labour, and it may also lead to technical innovation which reduces the capital output ratio.

21.4 Links with other topics

Our emphasis in this unit has been on explaining investment as one of the components of aggregate demand in the simple Keynesian model of the economy (Units 19 and 20). Essentially we have concentrated on investment as **expenditure** on new goods. However, there is another side to investment in its later effects on the **supply** of output, and as the **engine of economic growth**.

In Unit 10 on the size and growth of firms and Unit 11 on the Capital Market we examined how firms **finance** investment, while much of the basic theory of investment stems from the principle of diminishing marginal productivity, which is discussed in Unit 13.

21.5 Question practice

Essay Questions

Question 1
(a) Describe what is meant by the marginal efficiency of capital schedule.   (6)
(b) Consider the consequences of shifts in the marginal efficiency of capital schedule.   (12)
(c) Why did Keynes assert that such shifts are likely to occur in practice between different periods of
    time?   (7)
                                                                                              (*WJEC: June, 1988*)

Understanding the Question
(a) The MEC schedule is the aggregate demand curve for investment funds indentified by Keynes in his 'General Theory'. It represents the ranking, in descending order, of expected future productivity (measured by each investment's internal rate of return) of each potential investment project that could be undertaken in the economy.
(b) A shift to the right of the MEC curve, leading to a higher aggregate level of planned investment in the economy, will cause an upward shift of the investment curve ($I = \bar{I}$) on the 'Keynesian cross' diagram. A multiplier effect will result. The equilibrium level of national income will increase by $\Delta I \times$ the investment multiplier. In a depressed economy, this might close a deflationary gap and move the economy towards full employment. In a fully employed economy, there might be inflationary consequences in the short run (though we must remember that an increase in investment should be beneficial in the long run, by promoting improved competitiveness and an outward shift of the economy's production possibility frontier). By contrast a shift to the left of the MEC curve will have the opposite effect, perhaps creating a deflationary gap and under-full employment at the equilibrium level of income.
(c) According to Keynes, the state of business confidence and expectations is the significant determinant of the position of the MEC schedule. In the depressed UK economy of the 1920s and 1930s, Keynes viewed businessmen as jittery creatures subject to 'highs' and 'lows', as their 'animal spirits' swung from moods of optimism to pessimism.

Question 2 Discuss the economic relationships between consumption, income and investment.
                                                                                              (*AEB: June, 1990*)

Understanding the Question This question provides an opportunity to revise some of the most important relationships in the simple Keynesian model of Units 19 and 20, and also to indicate briefly how the introduction of the acceleration principle can extend the model:
(i) A revision of earlier concepts
   (a) We saw in our discussion of the Keynesian consumption function in Unit 19 that we may write the consumption function as

$$C = a + cY$$

   An increase in autonomous consumption (a) will have a **multiplier effect** on the equilibrium level of income.

(b) However, a part of consumption is directly related to the level of income via the **marginal propensity to consume** (c). Thus an autonomous increase in consumption results in an increase in income (via the multiplier), which in turn causes an increase in income-related consumption (via the MPC).

(c) An autonomous increase in investment will also have a multiplier effect upon income, which again induces a change in consumption.

(ii) Multiplier/accelerator interrelationships In the simple Keynesian model of the economy in Units 19 and 20 we **compared static equilibria**, noting the **multiplier effects** in the move from one equilibrium level of income to another. We ignored the possibility of subsequent **accelerator effects** resulting from the changes in income induced by the multiplier. When the acceleration principle is incorporated, the Keynesian model is converted from a simple comparison of equilibrium levels of income into a **dynamic model** of the economy showing how income, expenditure, and output continuously change through time. If k represents the multiplier, and v the capital output ratio (or accelerator), we can portray the dynamic movement of the economy through time as:

$$\triangle I \rightarrow k \rightarrow \triangle Y \rightarrow v \rightarrow \triangle I \rightarrow k \rightarrow \triangle Y \ ..... \ etc$$

multiplier accelerator multiplier
  effect   effect   effect

Depending on the values of the multiplier, k, and the accelerator, v, such dynamic Keynesian models of the economy can be used to model **economic growth**, and the cyclical fluctuations around the growth path–the **business cycle**.

Answer plan

1 Briefly explain the multiplier and show how income changes in response to an autonomous change in either C or I.

2 Show how the level of C will then change via the MPC.

3 Introduce the accelerator effect on I resulting from the changes in Y and C.

4 Suggest that a continuing interaction between the multiplier and the accelerator can take place.

Question 3 Define technical progress and outline the forms it can take. Analyze the possible economic effects of rapid technological change upon the British economy.   *(JMB: June, 1980)*

Understanding the Question There is no unique definition of technical progress. It can refer to the invention or development of new types of consumer goods, or to improvements in capital goods and methods of production, and also improvements in the quality of labour. In general it refers to the ability to increase outputs from inputs, or to maintain output with fewer inputs, thereby usually increasing the **productivity** of both labour and capital. Amongst the factors which influence the rate of technical progress are **(i)** the development of pure science, **(ii)** the ability of firms to apply the **inventions** of pure science as **innovations** in the process of production, **(iii)** the need in competitive markets to keep up with the 'best practices' of rival firms, including foreign competitors, and **(iv)** changes in the relative prices of labour and capital which may cause existing techniques of production to become uneconomic. A rising relative real cost of labour has meant that technical progress often involves the substitution of capital inputs for labour, for example in automation.

The economic effects can be considered in terms of different time periods and the bestowal of benefits and disadvantages. In the short run, rapid technical progress may lead to **technological** and **structural unemployment** (explained in Unit 22), but in the long run living standards may rise and extra employment may be created, particularly in the service sector. Of great importance is the question whether British firms can benefit from the rapid technical progress, or whether the main beneficiaries will be our overseas competitors. In the former case technical progress could promote an export-led boom created by an increased international competitiveness, whereas in the latter case British manufacturing would become less competitive, reinforcing structural unemployment and economic decline.

Answer plan

1 Define technical progress, giving different interpretations of its meaning. Distinguish between **invention** in pure science and **innovation** in the application of scientific developments to production.

2 Explain how technical progress usually means employing more capital-intensive methods of production.

3 Discuss possible effects upon employment and international competitiveness; perhaps introduce the **'virtuous circle'** argument that technical progress increases competitiveness, thereby increasing profitability and financing further technical innovation.

Multiple Choice Questions

Question 4 The cash flows shown in the table below are generated from four investment projects (A, B, C or D) available to a firm. Assuming that any funds generated can be reinvested at the current rate of interest, which is the most profitable project for the firm?

	Cash Flow (£)			
	Project A	Project B	Project C	Project D
year 1	0	20	5	80
year 2	0	20	20	15
year 3	5	20	50	5
year 4	15	20	20	0
year 5	80	20	5	0

Understanding the Question This question is based on the discounted cash flow technique of investment appraisal. All the projects earn a similar total income of £100, but each has a different shape of income stream. Project D is the most attractive to the firm since all its income is received early in the five-year period. Thus the £80 received in year 1 can be reinvested over years 2 to 5.

Question 5

year	No. of units demanded	No. of machines purchased
1	900	30
2	1800	30
3	2700	30
4	2790	33
5	2970	36
6	2970	?

The table shows how the level of investment undertaken by a small textile firm beginning production in year 1 is determined by the level of demand. Machines need replacing after three years. How many machines will be purchased in year 6?   **(a)** None   **(b)** 30   **(c)** 33   **(d)** 36

Understanding the Question This question is testing your knowledge of the acceleration principle and the relation between net and replacement investment. Since 30 machines are needed to produce 900 units of output in year 1, the capital output ratio is 1:30. In years 2 and 3 demand increases by 900 units each year, so a constant net investment of 30 machines is required. In these years, gross investment equals net investment since no replacement investment is needed. In year 4, when the rate of increase in demand is less than in years 1 to 3, less net investment is needed, but the machines purchased in year 1 have now worn out and must be replaced. Thus in years 4 and 5 gross investment equals replacement investment of 30 machines plus some net investment. However, in year 6 there is no need for any net investment since the level of demand is unchanged. Gross investment equals the investment in 30 machines to replace those bought in year 3 (Alternative **(b)**).

21.6   Further reading

Griffiths, A., and Wall, S., *Applied Economics*, 3rd edition (Longman, 1989)
Chapter 12: Investment

Stanlake, G. F., *Macro-economics, an Introduction*, 4th edition (Longman, 1989).

22   Unemployment and Inflation

22.1   Points of perspective

In this unit we introduce important theories which attempt to explain the twin economic evils of unemployment and inflation, and we also examine some suggested policy solutions. Firstly, however, we shall take a general look at the very different approaches adopted by some of the major schools of economic thought to these two problems.

The **neo-classical economists** who preceded Keynes (and whom Keynes rather confusingly labelled as 'classical') regarded the level of employment as being determined by the **'real forces'** of supply and demand in one large competitive labour market, whilst the **quantity of money** determined the price level. They accepted that there would always be a certain amount of **frictional** and **structural** unemployment–these are terms we shall define later–but believed that, provided that real and money wages were flexible, in a competitive economy **market forces** would always tend to bring about a long-run equilibrium at a minimum level of unemployment. (We shall later explain how, in recent years, **monetarists** have labelled this the **natural rate of unemployment**.)

    The neo-classical theory of aggregate employment originates in the micro-economic theory of the **diminishing marginal productivity** of labour. We saw in Unit 13 how in **competitive labour markets** a firm's equilibrium employment of labour is determined where the marginal product of labour equals the real wage. In conditions of diminishing marginal returns, firms will only employ additional workers **voluntarily** if there is a fall in the real wage. If markets are sufficiently competitive, the **excess supply** of labour will cause the real wage to fall until unemployment is eliminated. The pre-Keynesians explained persistent mass unemployment in terms of uncompetitive forces such as trade unions which prevent wages from falling. In this sense they viewed such unemployment as essentially **voluntary**. The work-force as a whole is to blame for the unemployment of some of its members, not because they are **work-shy**, but because of the refusal of those workers in employment to accept lower real wages.

For the neo-classicals, the determination of the **price-level** was completely separate from the determination of the level of employment. While the 'real forces' of supply and demand determine **levels of output and employment** and the equilibrium values of **relative** prices, **monetary forces** determine the price **level** (via the **quantity theory of money** which we shall shortly explain). Thus if the quantity of money doubles, relative prices and levels of output and employment remain the same, but all prices double.

2 The Keynesian view

Keynesians reject the older view that 'real' and 'monetary' forces are separate. Money provides a vital linkage between the markets of the real economy, and when this linkage breaks down, unemployment can result. Keynesians place great emphasis on the **store of value** function of money, arguing that **demand-deficient unemployment** can result when money incomes are stored in idle holdings of money rather than spent (Unit 14). In contrast the pre-Keynesians had never seriously entertained the possibility of such a **lack of aggregate effective demand**, accepting instead **Say's Law** that 'supply creates its own demand'. Keynes actually reversed Say's Law: instead of 'supply creating its own demand', Keynesian theory is based on the idea that 'demand creates its own supply'.

Keynes also claimed that the neo-classical theory of employment is guilty of the **fallacy of composition**. What is true for a single firm or market is not necessarily true for the economy taken as a whole. If the **money wage** paid by **one** firm falls, it will indeed be prepared to employ more workers, but if all money wages fall by the same proportion it does not follow that, collectively, **all** employers will employ more labour. Consider two possibilities. In the first place, prices of goods may fall as much as money wages. If all money wages and prices fall by the same proportion, the **real wage** will remain the same. Secondly, if prices fall by less than the money wage, the real wage will indeed fall, but a general fall in real incomes may reduce aggregate demand. If unemployment is already being caused by too little demand, a wage-cut policy may cut demand still further. Keynes argued that, far from curing mass unemployment, a wage-cut policy could make matters worse!

Keynes also rejected the **quantity theory of money**, the cornerstone of the pre-Keynesian (and the monetarist) theory of inflation. We shall explain shortly why the Keynesians reject this theory, and how Keynes adapted his theory of mass unemployment caused by **deflation** and **deficient demand** to the conditions of **inflation** and **excess demand** in the fully employed economy of World War II.

3 The Monetarist view

In many ways monetarism, or the **'New Classical Macro-economics'** as some versions of monetarism are now known, is simply a revival of the old pre-Keynesian economics. Keynes had written the *General Theory* in order to construct what he thought was a better and more general explanation than that provided by neo-classical theory of the outstanding problem on the agenda in his day: deflation or mass unemployment. Keynesian economics 'ruled' as long as its policy prescriptions ensured relative full employment, growth and price stability, although monetarist critics of Keynesianism now argue that full employment was **coincidental with**, and not **caused by**, Keynesian economic management. When, from the late 1960s onward, there was a simultaneous failure to achieve these objectives in the British economy, Keynesianism became vulnerable to attack from, amongst others, a revival of the 'old economics'. Monetarism essentially accepts the old **'Classical Dichotomy'** that the **real and monetary economy are separate**; the real forces of supply and demand determine 'real things'–output, employment and relative prices–whilst money, a **veil** behind which the real economy operates, determines 'money things'–the overall price level. Thus, growing unemployment is explained by monetarists largely in terms of workers **voluntarily** pricing themselves out of jobs, whilst, via a revival of the old quantity theory of money, irresponsible governments creating too much money are blamed for inflation.

22.2 Underlying concepts

1 Types of unemployment

The most important distinction to be made between types of unemployment is between the concepts of **voluntary** and **involuntary** unemployment. According to both the pre-Keynesians and latter-day monetarists, persistent mass unemployment is **voluntary**, explained by workers **choosing** higher real wages and fewer jobs. In contrast, Keynesians explain a part at least of mass unemployment in terms of **demand deficiency** outside the control of workers. In this sense, such unemployment is **involuntary**. Before taking the discussion further, we shall firstly introduce a more detailed classification of specific types of unemployment:

(i) Real-wage or 'classical' unemployment As we have already noted, the pre-Keynesians believed that unemployment can be caused by real wages being too high. In a competitive labour market, market forces would tend automatically to eliminate this type of unemployment. However, in uncompetitive labour markets, trade unions may resist wage cuts and price the unemployed out of jobs.

(ii) Frictional unemployment (transitional unemployment) results from the time-lag involved in the move from one job to another – note the assumption that an **unfilled vacancy** exists elsewhere. Frictional unemployment is directly related to the **geographical and occupational immobility of labour**. Factors such as the lack of information or the required skill, and the cost of moving, can prevent a worker from filling a job vacancy. Consequently the number of unfilled vacancies can be used as a measure of frictional unemployment.

(iii) Casual unemployment, which is a special case of frictional unemployment, occurs when labour is employed on a short-term basis in trades such as tourism, catering, building and agriculture. When casual unemployment results from regular fluctuations in demand or weather conditions, it can be called **seasonal unemployment.**

(iv) Structural unemployment arises when a firm or industry suffers a **structural decline**, having become uncompetitive in the face of either changing costs and technology or changing demand. The growth of international competition is a particularly important cause of structural unemployment. For many years in the 1950s and 1960s, structural unemployment in Britain was regionally concentrated in areas of declining staple industries. Such **regional unemployment** was more than offset by the growth of employment in other industries and services which took the place of the declining industries. However, in more recent years structural unemployment has afflicted all parts of the UK, spreading right across the manufacturing base. We shall argue that the return of mass unemployment in the 1970s and 1980s is explained in large part by the re-emergence of structural unemployment in the **deindustrialization** process.

(v) Technological unemployment is a special case of structural unemployment resulting from the successful growth of new industries using labour-saving technology such as **automation**. In contrast to **mechanization**, automation involves machines rather than men operating other machines. Whereas the growth of mechanized industry usually involves an absolute increase in the demand for labour, automation of production can lead to the shedding of labour even when industry output is growing.

(vi) Demand-deficient unemployment (Keynesian or **cyclical unemployment)** is the type of unemployment identified by Keynes as the cause of persistent mass unemployment between the wars. Economists generally agree that some unemployment may be caused by lack of demand in the downswing of the business cycle, but Keynes went further. He argued that the economy could settle into an underemployment equilibrium caused by a continuing lack of effective aggregate demand (see Units 19 and 20).

(vii) Residual unemployment covers any other cause of unemployment. It includes the **work-shy** (not to be confused with **voluntary** unemployment in the sense used earlier) and the **unemployable**. It is now recognized that **long-term unemployment** in itself may cause a worker to become unemployable, as a result of both the erosion of job skills and work habits, and of the employer's perception that a worker with more recent job experience is a 'better bet'. We should also mention **hidden unemployment**, which strictly is not unemployment at all but a measure of **overmanning**. Hidden unemployment occurs when firms could produce the same output with fewer workers. It can be caused by trade union pressure and restrictive practices, the high costs of making workers redundant, or by the desire of firms to hang on to skilled workers in a recession in the belief that the workers will be needed when demand picks up.

2 Inflation, deflation and reflation

Inflation is usually defined as a **persistent or continuing tendency for the price level to rise**. Although **deflation** is strictly the opposite – a **persistent tendency for the price level to fall** – the term is usually used in a rather looser way to refer to a reduction in the level of activity or output. In this sense, a **deflationary policy** reduces the level of aggregate demand in the economy. Some economists find the terms **disinflation** and **disinflationary policy** preferable. Likewise, **reflation** refers to an increase in economic activity and output, and a **reflationary policy** stimulates aggregate demand. In a sense inflation is reflation 'gone wrong', increasing the price level rather than real output.

3 Types of inflation

(a) Suppressed inflation Although inflation involves the **tendency** for the price level to rise, it is not inevitable that prices will actually rise. Strong governments may successfully introduce tough price controls which prevent the price level from rising without at the same time abolishing the underlying inflationary process. The suppression of rising prices diverts the inflationary process into quantity shortages, queues, waiting-lists and black markets.

(b) Creeping inflation The inflation rate experienced by most industrialized countries in the 1950s and early 1960s was fairly stable from year to year, averaging less than 5%. However, throughout the period it gradually crept upwards, developing into a **strato-inflation** in many countries in the late 1960s and early 1970s.

(c) Strato-inflation Whereas creeping inflations were typical of industrial countries in the post-war period, strato-inflation was the experience of developing countries, particularly in Latin America. In a strato-inflation the inflation rate ranges from about 10% to several hundred per cent, and it may be particularly difficult to **anticipate**.

(d) Hyper-inflation The transition from a creeping inflation to a strato-inflation in the early 1970s raised fears of an acceleration into a hyper-inflation. The famous German inflation of 1923 was a hyper-inflation, and similar but less publicized hyper-inflation occurred in other countries in central and eastern Europe at the end of both World Wars. However, hyper-inflations are usually short-lived and they should not be regarded as typical. A hyper-inflation usually occurs in a severe political crisis when a government turns to the printing press to create money to pay its debts. Inflation can accelerate to a rate as high as several thousand per cent a year. During the hyper-inflation, money ceases to be a medium of exchange and a store of value, and normal economic activity may completely break down.

(e) Stagflation (or Slumpflation) In the 1970s and early 1980s the incidence of both relatively high rates of inflation and increasing unemployment in the developed world led economists to coin the word 'stagflation'. It combines **stagnation** in the economy (low or negative increases in output) with **price inflation**. As we shall see, its existence made conventional Keynesian demand management policies seem inappropriate and politically damaging as a means of controlling either unemployment or inflation. In the early 1990s, there is once again a fear of a renewed stagflation affecting the UK economy.

22.3   Essential information

1 The adverse effects of inflation

The seriousness of the adverse effects of inflation greatly depends on whether the inflation is **anticipated** or **unanticipated**. It was relatively easy to anticipate more or less fully the creeping inflation of the 1950s and 1960s. Indeed in these years it was sometimes argued that a mild amount of inflation was harmless or even perhaps beneficial. This was because creeping inflation accompanied an expanding economy and became associated by businessmen with growing markets and healthy profits. This view may well explain why the control of inflation was regarded as a relatively minor policy objective.

In contrast, it is very difficult for people fully to anticipate a strato-inflation as the actual inflation rate varies substantially from year to year. The adverse effects will be much more severe and may completely destabilize the economy. Generally speaking, the main adverse effects of inflation are:

(i) It can be unfair. Weaker social groups in society such as old people on fixed pensions lose, while others in stronger bargaining positions gain. This is an example of how inflation affects the distribution of income and wealth. Nevertheless the **indexing** of pensions has reduced this particular disadvantage of inflation. In the absence of indexation, inflation also raises the average rate of taxation through the process of **fiscal drag** (see Unit 15).

(ii) A second important distributional effect occurs between borrowers and lenders. Inflation tends to redistribute wealth from lenders or creditors to borrowers or debtors. In an inflation the rate of interest may well be below the rate of inflation. This means that lenders are really paying a negative real interest rate to borrowers for the doubtful privilege of lending to them! The biggest borrower of all is usually the government. Inflation can be thought of as a hidden tax that re-distributes wealth to the government and reduces the real value of the national debt. This suggests that governments may not always be as keen as they pretend to control inflation completely!

(iii) Inflation distorts many types of economic behaviour and imposes costs upon economic agents. It can distort consumer behaviour by causing people to bring forward their purchases if they expect the rate of inflation to accelerate . This would probably affect sales of consumer durables such as washing-machines and it might also lead to the hoarding of goods such as groceries. If this were the case the **savings ratio** might be expected to fall as people borrowed or used up savings in order to finance consumption. However, an interesting feature of the inflation in the 1970s was the sharp rise in the savings ratio. This suggests that greater uncertainty may have caused people to save more. A large part of savings is intended to finance old age and retirement. If the inflation rate suddenly accelerates, existing planned savings become inadequate to finance retirement and people increase their savings to top up or supplement their existing stock of accumulated savings, in an attempt to restore the real value of accumulated savings. However, in response to a much lower and more stable inflation rate, the savings ratio fell dramatically in 1983, causing a rapid growth in consumer expenditure that fuelled, for a time at least, the growth of output and economic recovery.

(iv) Similar uncertainties affect the behaviour of firms and impose costs upon them. Long-term planning becomes very difficult. Firms may be tempted to divert investment funds out of productive investment into commodity hoarding and speculation. Profit margins may be severely squeezed in a cost inflation and firms can attempt to avoid this by making capital gains on property, land and even fine art and antiques rather than by using their funds in normal production.

(v) In a severe strato-inflation money becomes less useful as a medium of exchange and a store of value. More money may be needed to finance the buying of goods at higher prices, but this is countered by the disadvantages of holding money which is falling in value. In a hyper-inflation the use of money may completely break down and be replaced by less efficient **barter**. This imposes extra costs on most transactions.

2 Theories of inflation

(i) The Quantity Theory of Money Old theories seldom die; they reappear in a new form to influence a later generation of economists and politicians. This is certainly true of the **quantity theory of money**, which is the oldest theory of inflation. From the 18th century to the 1930s, it was *the* theory of inflation. The quantity theory went out of fashion in the Keynesian era, but modern monetarism has restored the quantity theory to a central place in the current controversy on the causes of inflation.

Early or **'naive'** versions of the quantity theory are usually distinguished from the revival of the quantity theory in a more sophisticated form by Milton Friedman in the 1950s. However, all versions of the quantity theory, old and new, form a **special case of demand inflation** in which rising prices are caused by **excess demand**. The distinguishing characteristic of the quantity theory is the location of the source of excess demand in **monetary** rather than **real forces**—in an **excess supply of money** created or condoned by the government.

At its simplest, the quantity theory is often stated as **'too much money chasing too few goods'**. Indeed to some this is a definition of inflation, though as a definition it rather begs the question of the cause of a rising price level. The theory can also be written as a simple equation:

$$MV = PT$$

This says that the **Money supply** times the number of times money changes hands **(the Velocity of circulation)** equals the **Price level** times the **total number of Transactions**. This is the famous Fisher **equation of exchange**, devised by the American economist Irving Fisher. In the Fisher equation, T includes second-hand purchases of goods and services. Strictly these should be omitted from a measure of national income or output, so it is usually better to rewrite the **equation of exchange** as:

$$MV = Py$$

in which y is a measure of transactions involving currently produced output or **real national income**. Py is thus money national income. In this form the equation of exchange is known as the **Cambridge equation**.

The equation of exchange illustrates the very important difference between an **identity** and a **behavioural equation**. As the equation stands, it is merely an identity or truism implying very little more than that the amount bought always equals the amount sold. To convert the equation into the quantity theory two strong assumptions have to be made and the theory stands or falls with these assumptions:

(a) The price level is determined by the money supply and not vice versa, or:

$$P = f(Ms)$$

where Ms is the money supply, to be distinguished from the demand for money (Md). Keynesians in particular have attacked this assumption. They argue that the money supply passively adapts or accommodates itself to finance the level of transactions taking place at the current price level. To generalize, monetarists believe that the money supply actively determines the price level whereas Keynesians have argued that the **price level determines the money supply**. Keynesians agree with what they consider to be the trivial point that an expansion of the money supply is needed if inflation is to occur, but they argue that if the money supply is restricted so that current level of transactions cannot be financed, then a drop in output and employment will occur. **Near monies** may take on the function of money, thus rendering control of the money supply ineffective. This (extreme?) Keynesian view can be summarized as:

$$Ms = f(P)$$

(b) Rewriting the Cambridge equation as:

$$Ms = \frac{1}{V}Py$$

and accepting the first assumption, it is easy to see that an increase in the money supply Ms will feed through to an increase in the price level P **provided that V and y are relatively constant**. Keynesians have attacked the quantity theory by attacking this assumption. They have argued that even if the assumption that the money supply influences the price level is correct, then the influence could be very small if an increase in the supply of money was 'absorbed' in a lower velocity of circulation, V, rather than in an increase in the price level. However, in response to evidence that V has slowed down in recent years, monetarists now argue that the velocity of circulation need only be **predictable**, and **not necessarily constant**.

This dispute extends into an argument about the **transmission mechanism** through which an increase in the money supply is supposed to increase the price level. Modern versions of the quantity theory are usually stated in terms of the **demand** for money:

$$Md = \frac{1}{V}Py$$

Monetarists believe that the demand for money is a **stable** function of the level of money income, money being required solely for transactions purposes (the **transactions demand for money**). When the government increases the money supply, people find themselves possessing larger money balances than they wish to hold. They simply spend their excess money holdings, thereby providing the mechanism by which prices are pulled up. Keynesians attack this **cash balance mechanism**, arguing that since people hold money for **speculative reasons**–the **speculative demand for money**–it does not automatically follow that an increase in the money supply is spent. If the demand for money is **unstable**, the effects of an increase in the money supply are **unpredictable**.

Even if it is agreed that the velocity of circulation is constant and that the demand for money is a stable function of money income, Keynesians have a third line of attack. An expansion of the money supply may increase **real output**, y, rather than the price level P, particularly if there is substantial spare capacity in the economy. Thus the Keynesians stress the reflationary **potential** of monetary policy, though because it is **unpredictable** it should be used as a supplement or 'back-up' to **fiscal policy**. Milton Friedman has admitted that monetary expansion can increase real output, but he argues that the effect is short-lived and that the main long-term effect is on the price level.

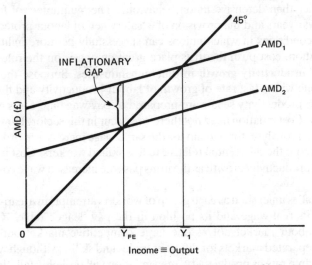

Fig 22.1 The Keynesian 'Demand-Pull' theory of inflation

(ii) The Keynesian 'demand-pull' theory of inflation In an influential pamphlet published at the beginning of the Second World War, Keynes adapted his theory of **deficient demand** in a depressed economy to explain how inflation could be caused by **excess demand** in a fully employed economy. The theory is illustrated in Figure 22.1 in which the maximum level of **real output** the economy is capable of producing with existing capacity is Y_{FE}. However, the level of aggregate money demand exercised by the various sectors in the economy, shown by AMD_1, is greater than the output that can be produced. Excess demand pulls up prices, resulting in an equilibrium level of **money national**

income at Y_1. A sustained reduction in aggregate demand to AMD_2 is necessary to close the **inflationary gap** so as to achieve full employment without inflation.

Although the monetarist and the Keynesian theories are both demand theories of inflation, the Keynesian theory locates the engine of inflation firmly in the 'real' economy. Taken together, the combined **claims** on output of households, firms, the government and the overseas sector are greater than the output that can be produced. Thus inflation is explained by the real forces which determine how people behave. In the British economy of the post-war years in which governments were committed to pursue the objective of full employment, people could behave both as **workers** and as **voters** in an inflationary way. As workers, they could bargain for money wage increases in excess of any productivity increase without the fear of unemployment, while in the political arena they could add to the pressure of demand by voting for increased public spending and budget deficits. We have already noted how in a trivial sense Keynesians admit that inflation is a monetary phenomenon, since the money stock must expand to accommodate and sustain a rising price level. But Keynesians dispute that inflation is caused by a simple prior increase in the money supply; they believe that the real causes lie much deeper.

(iii) Cost theories of inflation During the post-war years creeping inflation continued even in years when there was little or no evidence of excess demand in the economy. This prompted many Keynesians to switch their allegiance away from the demand theory of inflation to **cost-push** or **structuralist** theories which explain inflation in terms of the structural and institutional conditions which prevail on the **supply side** of the economy. Such 'Keynesians' are sometimes called **post-Keynesians** or **neo-Keynesians**.

Cost-push theorists argue that growing monopoly power in both labour and goods markets has caused inflation. Strong trade unions are able to bargain for money wage rises in excess of any productivity increase. Monopoly firms are prepared to pay these wage increases partly because of the costs of disrupting modern continuous-flow production processes, and partly because they believe they can pass the increased costs on to the consuming public in higher prices. It is often assumed in the cost-push theory that prices are formed by a simple **'cost-plus' pricing rule**. This means that monopoly firms add a standard profit margin to their costs when setting their prices.

The cost-push theory has become a very popular theory with newspapers and the general public. It suggests the simple conclusion that trade union 'pushfulness' and perhaps 'big business' are responsible for inflation. However, the question is often begged as to why unions became more militant in the 1960s and 1970s. Marxist versions of the cost-push theory locate the reason for increased labour militancy in a defensive struggle by workers to restore their real wages which are being squeezed by capitalists attempting to maintain the rate of profit. Some Marxists regard inflation as the outcome of a distributional struggle within the 'crisis of capitalism'. Other cost-push theorists argue that changed conditions in the labour market in the era of full employment led to aggressive rather than defensive union behaviour. The 'guarantee' of full employment by the state in the post-war years and the provision of a 'safety net' of labour protection legislation are said to have created conditions in which unions can successfully be more militant.

In explaining inflation, cost-push theorists place great emphasis on the roles of **pay relativities** and **different rates of productivity growth** in different industries. Suppose there are two sectors within an economy; one with a fast rate of growth of labour productivity and the other with a zero rate. Firms in the high productivity sector are prepared to pay wage increases equal to the rate of growth of productivity. Cost inflation need not therefore occur in this sector. However, workers with similar skills in the zero growth sector bargain for the same wage increases in order to maintain their comparability or to restore the differential relative to less skilled workers. Cost inflation thus occurs in the sector with zero productivity growth as the firms pass the increased wage costs on to consumers in higher prices.

A **wage-price 'spiral'** is unleashed as each group of workers attempts in a leap-frogging process to maintain or improve its real wage and its position in the pay 'league table'. Cost-push theorists essentially view the labour market not as one large competitive market but as a collection of non-competitive and separated markets for different trades and skills. Although workers realize that if **all** wages rise at the same rate as productivity, then inflation will probably fall, they also realize that what is in the interest of workers **collectively** need not be in the interest of a single group acting in isolation. A group that accepts a wage increase lower than the current rate if inflation will probably suffer if other workers do not behave in a similar fashion. Thus a group acts to preserve its relative position in the pay 'pecking order', even if its members know that by fuelling inflation a large **money wage increase** may be only a small **real wage increase** or even a decrease.

3 The rise of the Phillips curve

In the late 1950s and the early 1960s a great deal of energy was spent by economists in debating whether inflation is caused by **excess demand** or by **cost-push** forces. After 1958 the debate was conducted with the aid of a recently discovered statistical relationship, the **Phillips curve**, which is illustrated in Figure 22.2.

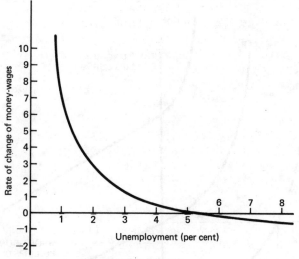

Fig 22.2 The Phillips curve

The Phillips curve purported to show a **stable** but **non-linear** relationship between the rate of change of wages (the rate of **wage inflation**) and the percentage of the labour force unemployed. Taking the rate of growth of productivity into account, Phillips estimated that in the UK an unemployment level of about 2.5% was compatible with price stability (or zero inflation), and that an unemployment level of 5.5% would lead to stable money wages. Economists grasped on the supposed **stability** of the Phillips relationship over a period of nearly one hundred years to argue that it provided statistical support for the existence of a 'trade-off' between inflation and employment. Using the Phillips curve, economists believed that they could advise governments on the **opportunity cost** in terms of **inflation** of achieving any **employment** target. In offering this advice, the **non-linearity** of the curve was significant. At low levels of unemployment a further reduction in unemployment would incur a much greater cost in terms of increased inflation than a similar reduction at a higher level of unemployment. Indeed, the Phillips curve appeared to justify the Keynesian view than an **unemployment rate of about 1½% should be regarded as full employment**; any lower level of unemployment, or 'over-full employment' would be associated with an excessive cost in terms of inflation.

Nevertheless, the Phillips curve was never, in itself, a theory of inflation. In its early years the Phillips curve was most often used by Keynesians of the demand-pull school, including Phillips himself, to illustrate how the rate of inflation varied with the amount of excess demand in the economy. In the demand-pull interpretation, the level of unemployment was used as a measure of excess demand which served to pull up money wages in the labour market. However, the Phillips curve was also accommodated in the cost-push theory, the level of unemployment being interpreted as a measure of trade union 'pushfulness'. The Phillips curve could illustrate and provide statistical support for both theories of inflation, but it could not decide between the two.

4 The fall of the Phillips curve

Around 1970 a growing level of unemployment accompanied by a much higher rate of inflation appeared to signal the breakdown of the Phillips relationship. According to the monetarists, this greatly damaged the credibility of both the cost-push theory of inflation and the demand-pull theory, at least in its Keynesian version. It is worth noting, however, that many Keynesians now claim that the Phillips curve was never a 'true' part of Keynesianism, merely excess baggage added on, the rejection of which does not destroy essential Keynesian theory. Nevertheless, neither the demand-pull nor the cost-push theorists had predicted the emergence of the **stagflation** or **slumpflation** of the 1970s. Yet a leading monetarist, Milton Friedman, had predicted the breakdown of the Phillips relationship a number of years before it actually happened. It is not surprising, therefore, that the simultaneous appearance of increased unemployment and accelerating inflation greatly boosted monetarism.

There are at least two competing theories of what has happened to the Phillips relationship. In the version favoured by some cost-push theorists, the inverse relationship between inflation and unemployment still exists, but the trade-off is now at much higher rates of inflation and levels of unemployment. The continuing growth of non-competitive forces in the structure and institutions of the economy are blamed for a rightward shift of the Phillips relationship. The cost-push school favours the use of an **incomes policy** as the only method which can once again achieve both a lower inflation rate and a lower level of unemployment.

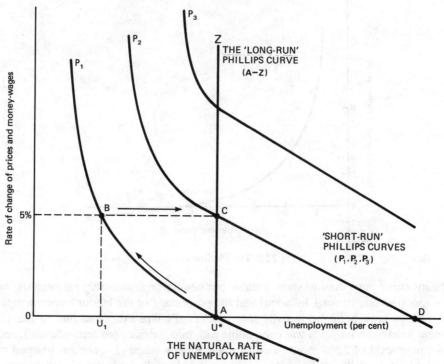

Fig 22.3 The expectations-augmented Phillips curve

In contrast, monetarists argue that even at the height of the Keynesian era there was never a **stable** relationship allowing a **long-term** trade-off between inflation and employment. The statistical relationship identified by Phillips is at best **short-run** and **unstable**. According to monetarists, the 'true' long-term relationship between unemployment and the rate of inflation lies along a vertical line, on which no trade-offs are possible, running through the **natural rate of unemployment** also known as the **'non-accelerating inflation rate of unemployment'** (NAIRU). This is shown in Figure 22.3.

To understand this conclusion we need to introduce two theories, one old and one relatively new, to help explain the monetarist view of 'how the economy works'. The old theory, the **monetarist theory of aggregate employment**, is essentially the pre-Keynesian employment theory discussed earlier in the unit, whilst the new theory introduces the **role of expectations** into the inflationary process. According to the monetarist theory of employment, the **'natural'** levels of employment and unemployment (U* in Figure 22.3) are determined at the equilibrium **real wage** at which workers **voluntarily** supply exactly the amount of labour that firms voluntarily employ. Since monetarists do not recognize **demand-deficient unemployment** it follows that, at the natural rate, unemployment is composed largely of frictional and structural unemployment.

We now introduce the **role of expectations** into the inflationary process. In order to keep the analysis as simple as possible, we shall assume that the rate of productivity increase is zero. Thus, the vertical axis in Figure 22.3 measures the rate of increase both of **money wages** and of **prices**. Suppose that the economy is initially at point A. Unemployment is at the natural rate U*, and the rates of increase of prices and money wages are zero and **stable**. In these circumstances, workers may **expect** the future inflation rate also to be zero. If the government is dissatisfied with the level of unemployment at U* and expands demand, it may believe that it can successfully trade-off along the Phillips curve P_1 to a point such as B. The cost of achieving U_1 appears to be an inflation rate of 5%. But will the new situation be stable? Not so, say the monetarists. Workers are only willing to supply **more** labour beyond the natural level of **employment** if the **real wage** rises, but a rising real wage causes employers to demand **less** labour! Initially, more workers may enter the labour market in the false belief or illusion that a 5% increase in the **money wage** is also a **real wage** increase. We call this **money illusion**. Similarly, if firms falsely believe that revenues are rising faster than labour costs, they will employ more labour. In other words, an increase in employment beyond the natural rate can only be sustained if workers and employers suffer **permanent money illusion** in equal but opposite directions!

Gradually both workers and employers will realize that they have confused money quantities with real quantities and that they have suffered from money illusion. Without permanent money illusion, employment can only stay above the natural level if inflation accelerates to keep employees' **expectations** about the rate of inflation consistently below the **actual** rate. As workers continuously adjust their **expectations of future inflation** to the **actual rate** and bargain for ever higher money wages, the **short-run** Phillips curve shifts outward from P_1 to P_2 and so on. Thus a level of unemployment below the natural rate can only be sustained if the government finances and accommodates the accelerating inflation by expanding the money supply. But even in these circumstances the inflation will eventually accelerate into a hyper-inflation and into a breakdown of economic activity, causing unemployment to rise **above** the natural rate. According to this logic, any attempt to reduce unemployment below the natural rate involves the short-run cost of accelerating inflation, whilst eventually having the perverse effect of increasing unemployment above the natural rate to an unnecessarily high level.

The theory just described is sometimes known as the theory of the **'expectations-augmented Phillips curve'**. Supporters of this theory, which was originally conceived by Milton Friedman, tend to take the view that the economy must suffer rather a long period of unemployment **above** the natural rate to rid the economy of the effect of expectations built up while unemployment was **below** the natural rate.

Suppose, once again, that the government has expanded demand and the money supply, moving the economy to point B in Figure 22.3. Unemployment is U_1. It now realizes its 'mistake', and refuses to allow the money supply to grow by more than 5% a year. According to the Friedmanite school, the economy now moves to point C as workers and employers gradually realize that the real wage has not changed. Inflation has **stabilized** at 5%. But if the government wishes to get back to point A, it must get there via point D, which is at a much greater level of unemployment. This journey is necessary in order **gradually** to reduce expectations of inflation. Just as inflation **accelerates** whenever unemployment is below the natural rate, so it decelerates when unemployment is above the natural rate. In each case this is explained by economic agents gradually adapting their expectations of inflation to the actual rate. Above the natural rate of unemployment, actual inflation is always below expected inflation.

Accordingly, expectations are continuously revised downwards and the economy can only return to zero inflation **and** unemployment at the natural rate when the expected inflation rate has fallen to zero.

5 Rational expectations

The message of the 'expectations-augmented Phillips curve' is gloomy. The economy must experience a **lengthy** period of deflation and unemployment above the natural rate as the penalty to be paid for an 'irresponsible' reduction in unemployment below the natural rate. However, in recent years many monetarists have tacked on to the Friedmanite concept of the natural rate of unemployment, an alternative theory of how expectations are formed.

According to this theory, it is unrealistic to assume that a rational economic agent acting in its self-interest will form expectations of future inflation only on the basis of past or experienced inflation. If economic agents on average **correctly forecast** the results of events taking place in the economy now, it is in their self-interest **quickly** to modify their economic behaviour so that it is in line with their expectations. Thus if workers **believe** that the government means business in reducing the money supply and the rate of inflation, they will immediately build a lower expected rate of inflation into their wage-bargaining behaviour. In this way, inflation can be reduced relatively painlessly without a lengthy period of unemployment above the natural level.

In recent years an important division has developed between **monetarists of the Friedmanite school** and those of the **rational expectations** or **'Neo-Classical' school**. According to the Friedmanites, governments can reduce unemployment below the natural rate as long as workers and employers suffer from money illusion. However, according to the rational expectations school, workers and employers instantly realize their mistakes and 'see through' any attempt by an 'irresponsible' government to reflate the economy; thus demand management policies can never succeed in reducing unemployment below the natural rate even in the short run. Monetarists of both schools usually agree that although the government cannot in the long run reduce unemployment below the natural rate, it can reduce the natural rate itself by policies designed to make the labour market more competitive, hence policies to reduce the trade union power and to abolish the closed shop, together with other 'supply-side' policies.

6 Summary: the three stages in the development of the monetarist theory of inflation:

(i) 'Mark I' of the monetarist theory of inflation was the revival by Milton Friedman in the 1950s of the quantity theory of money. This explained inflation as a purely monetary phenomenon, caused by the government creating or condoning excess monetary growth.

(ii) 'Mark II': the incorporation of the **theory of adaptive expectations** into the inflationary process. The weakness of the 'Mark I' theory is that it fails to explain why a government might be prepared to expand the money supply on a continuing basis to finance an inflation. Milton Friedman's theory of the 'expectations-augmented Phillips curve' provides an explanation and also, we should note, explains inflation in terms of the 'real' economy rather than purely as a monetary phenomenon.

(iii) 'Mark III': the 'New-Classical' school. Whereas the 'Mark II' explanation of inflation is based on a theory of **adaptive expectations**, the New-Classical School has replaced this with the **theory of rational expectations**. In the adaptive expectations theory, workers and employers **slowly** change or adapt their expectations of future inflation to the **current** rate of inflation. By contrast, in the 'New-Classical' explanation of inflation, it is rational for economic agents to **instantly** adapt their expectations of the future to all the up-to-date information that is available.

22.4 Links with other topics

The monetarist theories of inflation, the quantity theory of money, the rational expectations hypothesis, and the concept of the natural rate of unemployment, have had a great influence on British government policy in the 1980s, and in particular on the monetary policy discussed in Unit 17. In contrast, the authority of the Keynesian demand-pull theory of inflation has greatly diminished, at least in monetarist circles. This theory originates out of the Keynesian income/expenditure model of the economy described in Unit 19. Yet the other inflation theory favoured by Keynesians—the cost-push theory with all its implications for the effectiveness of incomes policy (Unit 24)—waits in the wings, ready to re-emerge if and when monetarist theories suffer a decline.

In this unit we have omitted any discussion of the **international nature** of inflation and, in particular, of the role of the **exchange rate** in the inflationary process. This defect will be remedied in Units 24 and 27. Nevertheless, we should not conclude this unit without mentioning the monetarist argument that cost-push theories suffer the defect of explaining inflation solely in terms of institutional conditions in **domestic** markets. According to the monetarists, such theories inadequately explain why similar increases in the rate of inflation have occurred in a larger number of countries with widely different domestic conditions and institutions.

22.5 Questions practice

(a) Distinguish between voluntary and involuntary unemployment.   (20)
(b) Analyse the effects of supply-side policies on both of these types of unemployment.   (80)

(London: June, 1990)

Understanding the Question In the 1920s and 1930s, Keynes believed that much unemployment was involuntary, caused by deficient aggregate demand outside the control of workers and the unemployed. In the debate today, there is perhaps less emphasis on the role of aggregate demand. Instead, 'supply-siders' and other free-market orientated economists argue that much modern unemployment is voluntary frictional, caused by the disincentive effects of the tax and benefits systems. They advocate the use of appropriate 'supply-side' policies (described in Unit 23) to reduce voluntary unemployment.

Answer plan
1 Distinguish between voluntary and involuntary unemployment in terms of the Keynes versus the 'classics' debate of the 1930s. Relate voluntary and involuntary unemployment to Say's Law.
2 Explain that modern 'supply-side' economists explain much current and recent unemployment in terms of search theories, a high replacement ratio, and the growth of 'voluntary frictional' unemployment.
3 Describe the supply-side policies such as tax and benefits cuts which free-market economists recommend.
4 Discuss neo-Keynesian views on the appropriateness of such free-market supply-side policies. State also that neo-Keynesians might recommend the use of interventionist supply-side policies to deal with involuntary structural unemployment resulting from the failure of the market, deindustrialization, etc.
5 Reach an argued conclusion on the effects of supply-side policies of various types on voluntary and involuntary unemployment.

Question 2 (a) What do you understand by the term 'economic recession'?   (5)
(b) What are the arguments for and against the idea that a country can 'spend its way   (20)
out of a recession'?
(SEB: 1981)

Understanding the Question The allocation of five marks to part **(a)** indicates that while not much development is required in the answer, something more than a one line definition of the term is required. Candidates should attempt to show their understanding of the term recession as illustrated by the various quantifiable indicators e.g. increases in the rate of unemployment, reductions in gross domestic product, a slow down in the rate and volume of investment, falling numbers of housing starts, downward trends in the retail price index, etc.

Part **(b)** calls for a discussion of the arguments for and against the Keynesian theory of employment. The first essential would be a clear presentation of the basic Keynesian macro-model and the Multiplier concept. You should follow this with a comparison of the Keynesian view of the **'crowding in'** effects of public spending and the monetarist **'crowding out'** viewpoint. According to the Keynesians, public spending stimulates the private sector, many firms in the private sector depending on government orders for their output. Essentially the Keynesians believe in high values for the government spending multiplier, whereas monetarists believe its value is very low or even negative in terms of the increase in real output rather than prices that follow on from an increase in government spending.

Answer plan

1 Define a recession.
2 Develop arguments in support of the quotation e.g. strong multiplier effects, the reflation of demand, 'crowding in' etc.
3 Develop the opposite demand-pull inflation and 'crowding-out' arguments.

Question 3 'The Phillips curve is no longer relevant to economic policy'. Discuss.

(London: January, 1988)

Understanding the Question You could usefully beg the question by noting that some economists, both Keynesian and monetarist, argue that the Phillips curve has **never** been a relevant and useful guide to economic policy. However, all answers must show how the Phillips curve was used to justify a demand management trade-off between employment and inflation. You must then go on to discuss the apparent breakdown of the relationship and one or more explanations of the breakdown.

Answer plan

1 With the aid of a diagram, explain the Phillips curve. Be careful with your labelling of the axes: the vertical axis must show the **rate of change** of wages or prices, not the wage or price **level**.
2 Discuss the policy trade-off implied by the curve, and its interpretation in both the demand-pull and the cost-push theories of inflation.
3 Describe the breakdown in the relationship, offering at least one explanation.
4 Reach a conclusion on the relevance of the Phillips cure, both now and in the past.

Question 4

(a) Explain what is meant by a change in the 'value of money' and consider how such changes are measured in practice. (10)
(b) Consider whether the stability of the value of money over time ought to be a central objective of government macro-economic policy. (15)

(WJEC: June, 1990)

Understanding the Question

(a) This is really a disguised question on how a **price index**, such as the **Retail Price Index** (RPI) can be used, in the UK, to measure inflation and the changing value of money. (By definition, the value of money falls whenever the price level rises and increases if the price level falls. You might also briefly describe how the exchange rate determines the **external** value of money, e.g. the purchasing power of the pound in terms of other currencies and the goods and services produced in other countries.)

The RPI measures monthly changes in the prices of a sample of goods and services, supposedly representative of the expenditure of a typical British family. The price of each good or service, in the sample, is represented by the **index number** 100 for a chosen **base year and month**. If the price in the shops of a particular good in the sample then rises by 2 per cent, its index number will increase to 102. Each item in the sample is also given a **weight** to reflect the importance of expenditure upon the item relative to the whole sample. For example, a weight of 10 (out of a total weighting for the sample of 1000) means that expenditure upon the item accounts for 1 per cent of total expenditure. The RPI for a particular month is calculated by multiplying each item's index number by its weight; summing the total for all the items in the sample and then dividing by the total weighting of 1000. Whether or not the resulting RPI is an accurate measure of changes in the price level and the value of money, is a matter of some dispute. Its accuracy depends upon the **representativeness of the sample** and the **accuracy of the weights** and it is also influenced by the **logistical problem** of minor civil servants accurately recording the price changes in the shops each month throughout the UK. Various items are included in the sample, which influence the cost of living, but have no direct link with the actual prices of goods and services. Currently, these include the poll tax and the mortgage interest rate. By contrast, the actual price of housing is not included in the sample. Thus, if house prices are rising rapidly but interest rates are falling (as in 1987/88), the RPI records a slowing down in the rate of inflation; whereas rising mortgage rates accompanied by a slump in house prices cause the RPI to rise (as in 1989/90). The rate of inflation measured by the RPI is sometimes called the **'headline' rate of inflation**; whereas inflation measured, excluding the effects of the poll tax and the mortgage interest rate, is known as the **'underlying' rate of inflation**.

Part **(b)** of the question asks you to assess whether control of inflation should be a prime objective of economic policy or whether it should be relegated to a subordinate position, ranked below such objectives as full employment and economic growth. Argue whichever position you wish but show an awareness of Keynesian and monetarist differences on this issue. Thus, monetarists believe there is no real choice in the long run: for them control of inflation is a necessary prerequisite for creating the conditions in which the other objectives can be attained.

Answer plan

1 Explain how the **internal** value of money (within the country) depends upon the price level and inflation.
2 Briefly mention how a rising exchange rate increases the **external** value of the country's currency whereas a falling exchange rate reduces it.
3 Explain how the British RPI measures changes in the rate of inflation and the value of money.
4 Note that the RPI might provide an inaccurate measure of changes in the value of money.
5 Suggest reasons why control of inflation and the value of money ougth to be an important objective.
6 Showing an awareness of Keynesian and monetarist perspectives, discuss whether it should always be a prime objective, or whether other objectives such as full employment should take precedence.

Multiple Choice Questions

Questions 5, 6 and 7

(a) if both statements are true and the second is a correct explanation of the first
(b) if both statements are true but the second is NOT a correct explanation of the first
(c) if the first statement is true but the second is false
(d) if the first statement is false but the second is true

	Assertion	*Reason*
Question 5	Inflation eases the burden of the existing National Debt to the government	Inflation increases the real value of a debtor's obligations
Question 6	Increased government spending increases inflation under all conditions	Increased government spending is an injection of demand into the economy
Question 7	During a sustained inflation, the money supply usually increases	Economists agree that inflation is caused by a prior increase in the money supply

Understanding the Questions The answer to question 5 is (c); the real value of the National Debt falls in a period of inflation since the maturity value of only a small part of the debt is index-linked. Thus the second statement is patently false. In question 6, the second statement is true and the first is false. Economists agree that increased government spending can increase inflation, but none would assert that it will do so under all conditions. The answer is therefore (d). (c) is again the answer to question 7. The first statement is uncontroversial, but the second statement of course separates the monetarists from the Keynesians.

Question 8

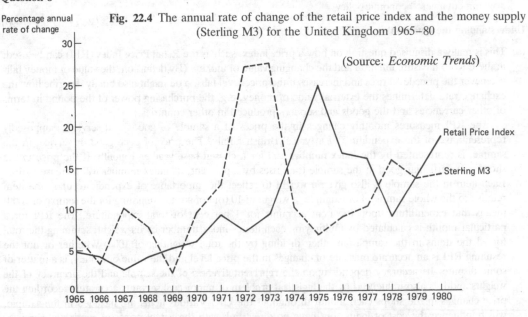

Percentage annual rate of change

Fig. 22.4 The annual rate of change of the retail price index and the money supply (Sterling M3) for the United Kingdom 1965–80

(Source: *Economic Trends*)

(a) Specify the items included in Sterling M3. (3)
(b) Describe the relationship between the retail price index and Sterling M3 in the United Kingdom between 1965 and 1980. (5)
(c) Discuss the significance of the data in the context of recent controversy about the causes of inflation. (12)

(*AEB: November, 1983*)

Understanding the Question While the first part of the question tests factual recall, the second part requires a clear understanding to be shown of the relationship between the RPI and £M3 rather than just a description of the data. You should discuss whether any correlation exists, whether it is **direct** or **inverse**, and whether a **time-lag** is involved. Do changes in the money supply appear to induce changes in the price index, or could the relationship be the other way round? Indeed could both variables simply be responding to other changes in the economy?

When answering part (c) you must identify the main controversy between monetarists and cost-push theorists (Post-Keynesians or structuralists), before going on to discuss whether the data appears to support either school. A further useful line of approach is to argue that other measures of the money supply, such as M1, might have moved completely differently during the period and it is dangerous to draw any very firm conclusions without a lot more information being available.

22.6 Further reading

Morris, D., editor, *The Economic System in the UK*, 3rd edition (Oxford University Press, 1985). Chapter 7: Inflation and Unemployment.

Maunder, P., et al., *Economics Explained*, 2nd edition (Collins, 1991) Chapter 11: Economic Indicators: Unemployment and Inflation

23 Supply-Side Economics

23.1 Points of perspective

Though first coined in 1976, by Professor Herbert Stein of the University of Virginia, the term **'supply-side economics'** came into prominence in 1980, to describe the economic policies which Ronald Reagan promised in his successful campaign for the American presidency. Supply-side economics became a dominant part of **'Reaganomics'**, the nickname given to the American Federal Government's economic programme in the early 1980s. The term was then applied to describe much of the underlying ideology, and dominant thrust of the policies, adopted by other 'free-market' orientated governments, including the Conservative administrations of Mrs Margaret Thatcher in the UK (for which the nickname **'Thatcherism'** paralleled and perhaps outlasted, the 'Reaganomics' of the USA). In terms of basic economic philosophy, supply-side economics is closely linked to the emergence of the **'radical right'** or **'New Right'** out of a more narrow **monetarism** which we shall describe in Unit 24.

There are many diverse, and often competing 'schools', of economic and political theory within the 'radical right' revival, including the **'rational expectations'** or **'New Classical' school**. Although the various schools of the 'radical right' disagree over points of both emphasis and detail, they share an extreme distrust (and often dislike), of government intervention in the economy; and a matching belief in the virtues of market forces. Thus, the ascendancy of supply-side economics and of other 'free-market' orientated ideas, in the late 1970s and during the 1980s; and the growing confidence of its academic theoreticians, have been closely related to the decline of **Keynesianism** in the face of the apparent inability, in the 1970s, of Keynesian policies to deal with **stagflation** and the **breakdown of the Phillips 'trade-off' between full employment and the control of inflation.**

23.2 Underlying concepts

1 The 'strict' meaning of 'supply-side economics'
In its original meaning, as developed by the 'radical right', supply-side economics describes a **particular way at looking at the effects of the government's fiscal policy upon the economy**. During the Keynesian era, most economists had regarded fiscal policy, and especially the government's use of taxation, as affecting the economy almost solely at the **macro-level** through its effect on aggregate demand. For Keynesians, the size of the government's budget deficit, or surplus, was the key to fiscal policy; regardless of whether a deficit resulted from higher levels of public spending or from tax cuts. The impact of public spending increases or tax changes upon the economy at the **micro-level** was largely ignored.

By contrast, supply-side economics is concerned with the **micro-economic effects of taxation and public spending**. In many respects, supply-side economics is simply a revival of the old 'classical' public finance theory that disappeared from view during the Keynesian era. Central to supply-side economics is the idea of a tax cut (not to stimulate aggregate demand Keynesian-style) but to **create incentives by altering relative prices**, particularly those of labour and leisure, in favour of work, saving and investment. **Professor Arthur Laffer**, a prominent American 'supply-sider' (and adviser to President Reagan in the 1980s), has described supply-side economics as

> providing a framework of analysis which relies on personal and private
> incentives. When incentives change, people's behaviour changes in response.
> People are attracted towards positive incentives and repelled by the negative.
> The role of government in such a framework is carried out by the ability of
> government to alter incentives and thereby, affect society's behaviour.

2 A broader interpretation of 'supply-side economics'

As we have just explained, in its original meaning supply-side economics relates exclusively to fiscal policy and tax cuts, and their effects upon incentives. However, it is useful to conceive of supply-side economics in broader terms than fiscal policy alone. In this looser interpretation, we can define supply-side economic policy as the set of government policies which aim to change the underlying structure of the economy and improve the economic performance of markets and industries and also, of individual workers and firms within markets. Supply-side policies are **micro-economic** rather than **macro-economic**, since they aim to improve general economic performance by acting on the motivation and efficiency of individual economic agents within the economy. Supply-siders, together with other 'radical-right' economists, believe that while the economy is always close to its **'natural' levels of output and employment**, these 'natural' levels can be unnecessarily low because of distortions (often blamed on 'twenty-five years of Keynesian policies') which reduce both an individual's willingness to supply labour and a firm's willingness to employ labour and supply goods. Supply-siders therefore recommend the use of micro-economic policies which they believe will remove these distortions, improve incentives and generally make markets more competitive. In the Keynesian era, micro-economic policy (along with macro-policy) usually extended (rather than reduced) government interventionism in markets, in fields such as **regional policy**, **competition policy** (or **anti-monopoly policy**), **labour market policy** and other aspects of **industrial policy**. By contrast supply-side micro-economic policy centres on a 'rolling back' of the functions of the state and a reduction of the level of government intervention in the economy. Along with tax cuts (to create incentives to work, save and invest) and welfare benefit cuts (to reduce the incentive to choose unemployment), supply-side economic policy, in its wider interpretation, includes policies of **privatization**, **marketization** and **deregulation** (described in detail in Unit 12). Supply-siders – and other schools within the 'free market revival' (be they self-styled monetarists or New Classical economists) wish to create an **'enterprise economy'**, through the promotion of **entrepreneurship** and **'popular capitalism'**; to replace the **'dependency culture'** and **statism** they see as the legacy of several decades of Keynesianism and a misguided consensus around the supposed virtues of a mixed economy. Indeed, for supply-siders, and other members of the 'radical right', the **mixed economy** is better described as a **'mixed-up' economy**!

23.3   Essential information

1 Supply-side economics and the supply curve of labour

Supply-side theory depends crucially upon the assumption that the supply curve of labour is **'upward-sloping'** and not **'backward-bending'**, and that increases in income tax create disincentives for the further supply of labour. (Refer back to Unit 13 at this stage for an explanation of the supply curve of labour.) An 'upward-sloping' supply curve of labour implies that increases in the marginal rates of income tax, being equivalent to cuts in wage rates, have a disincentive effect upon the supply of labour. Workers decide to supply less labour (choosing more leisure time instead) and they may also prefer the untaxed supply of labour in the informal **'black'** or **'underground' economy** to the more formal supply of 'taxed' labour in the 'overground' economy.

2 Supply-side economics and unemployment

'Supply-siders', and other more free-market orientated economists argue that the growth of voluntary unemployment explains much of the high level of unemployment occurring in the UK since the 1970s. Workers do not necessarily voluntarily leave their jobs and choose unemployment, but once unemployed (for whatever reason) they choose to remain unemployed for a much longer period than was previously the case. In part, this may be a **'discouraged worker'**

effect: repeated job rejections, in conditions of high unemployment, may discourage further attempts to find a job. **'Search theories'** have also been used to explain a growth in voluntary frictional unemployment. Suppose a worker earning £300 a week loses his job and that vacancies exist which pay £150 a week; other conditions of work being similar. The worker may choose to remain unemployed rather than to fill the vacancy because:
(i) the wage does not meet his aspirations; (ii) he is uncertain whether better-paid vacancies exist which he does not know about. Accordingly, unemployment is viewed as a **voluntary search period** during which an unemployed worker scans the job market for a vacancy that meets his aspirations. Voluntary unemployment ends either when the worker finds a vacancy which meets his aspirations or when he reduces his aspirations sufficiently, to accept the vacancy he knew about in the first instance.

Search theorists argue that such voluntary frictional unemployment has increased because, in the Keynesian era, the state created for the unemployed a **'safety net' of welfare benefits** such as unemployment pay. A higher real level of welfare benefits could then be used by the unemployed to finance a longer search period, thus delaying the decisions to reduce aspirations and fill a vacancy. Highly relevant here is the **replacement ratio**; **the ratio of disposable income when unemployed to disposable income in work**. An increase in the replacement ratio caused perhaps both by higher welfare benefits available to the unemployed and also, by fiscal drag and higher taxation affecting the low-paid, encourages workers with few skills to offer in the job market, to choose unemployment in preference to work. This is the **'unemployment trap'**, to which we referred in Unit 15.

Since **'supply-side' economists**, such as Professor Patrick Minford, have argued that much recent and current unemployment in the UK is 'voluntary frictional', it is not surprising that they recommend free-market orientated 'supply-side' policies as the appropriate remedy. Such policies include cuts both in marginal income tax rates and in welfare benefits, together with a tightening of rules to make benefits more difficult to claim. Supply-siders claim that tax cuts increase the incentive to work, while reducing the real value of benefits decreases the incentive to choose unemployment. Neo-Keynesians reply by arguing that tax and benefits cuts involve an unacceptable and socially divisive increase in inequality. They also believe that only a small part of current unemployment is of the 'voluntary frictional' kind, so therefore, free-market orientated supply-side policies will not have much affect on the rump of **involuntary structural unemployment** resulting from the deindustrialization process and from the effects of an over-valued exchange rate and decades of under-investment both by the private sector and by the state in social capital or infrastructure.

3 The Laffer curve

The assumption by supply-siders of an upward-sloping supply curve of labour leads on to the supply-side argument that high rates of income tax and the overall burden of income tax upon taxpayers create disincentives which eventually, as taxation increases, diminish national income and cause total tax revenue to decline. This can be illustrated by a **'Laffer curve'**, which we have drawn in Figure 23.1.

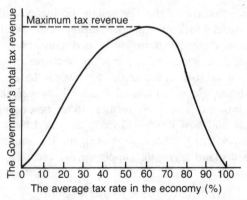

Fig. 23.1 A Laffer curve

The Laffer curve shows the government's total tax revenue as the average tax rate increases from 0 to 100 per cent. Tax revenue is zero when the tax rate is 0 per cent; and it is assumed also to be zero at an average tax rate of 100 per cent (there being no incentive to produce output other than for subsistence if any extra output is completely taxed away). In between these limiting rates, of 0 and 100 per cent, the Laffer curve shows tax revenue first rising and then falling as the average rate of taxation is increased. Tax revenue reaches its maximum at the highest point on the Laffer curve, after which any further increase in the average tax rate becomes counter-productive as total tax revenue falls.

Supply-siders have argued that the increase in the burden of taxation, that took place in the Keynesian era in the UK and USA, to finance the growing government sector, raised the average tax rate towards or beyond the critical point on the Laffer curve at which tax revenue is maximized. If this was the case, then the policy of tax cuts recommended by the supply-siders, would have the paradoxical effect of actually raising tax revenues. A growing national output, stimulated by lower tax rates, would yield higher total revenues despite the reduced tax rates, and the effect would be reinforced by a decline in tax avoidance and evasion as these activities became less worthwhile at less penal rates of taxation.

4 The choice between consumption and saving

As we have already noted, the central idea of supply-side economics is that fiscal policy works by changing relative prices or incentives. So far we have drawn attention to the **labour/leisure choice**, developing the policy implication of the Laffer curve that income tax cuts can stimulate the supply of labour; with the government actually benefiting from higher total tax revenues, despite lower tax rates, at a higher resulting level of national output. However, it is too simplistic to explain supply-side economics solely in terms of the theory that 'across the board' personal income tax reductions are self-financing; and that the prime aim of 'supply-sidism' is to secure more revenues for the government and to improve its budgetary position. Rather, the essence of 'supply-sidism' is the overcoming of the economy's inability to grow without a rapid rise in inflation, together with a reversal of the declining competitive position of industry.

Supply-siders argue that a second choice, facing individual economic agents, is as important as the labour/leisure choice. This is the **choice between consumption and saving**. The cost, to an individual, of spending a £ of income on consumption is the future income stream given up by not saving and investing the £. The present value of the income stream is in part determined by marginal tax rates. The higher the marginal tax rate on investment income, the lower is the value of the income stream that savings will yield. Thus, high rates of taxation levied on investment income, make current consumption of income cheap in terms of the investment income foregone. As a result, savings and investment decline. Supply-siders argue that the increased public spending and deficit financing of the Keynesian era stimulated aggregate demand; but that the Keynesians completely ignored the adverse effects we have just described of the higher levels of taxation that accompanied the Keynesian expansionism. As a result, expansionary Keynesian fiscal policies, designed to boost output and employment, led only to rising inflation, as the aggregate supply of output failed to respond to the demand stimulation. By contrast, the tax cuts advocated by supply-siders are not designed to stimulate aggregate demand. Instead they are intended to produce price incentives which encourage households to save rather than to consume; and businesses to invest so that the growth of the economy can proceed without the additional demand which results from higher incomes hitting the wall of stagnant national output and dissipating into inflation.

5 The Keynesian income/expenditure model revisited

Perhaps the most serious weakness of the Keynesian income/expenditure model, examined in Units 19 and 20, is the model's lack of a proper 'supply-side'. Within the model, the 45° line illustrated on a 'Keynesian cross' diagram, such as Figure 19.4, represents the Keynesian aggregate supply function. Following any increase or decrease of aggregate expenditure, the aggregate supply of output adjusts upwards or downwards to equal the level of aggregate expenditure at a new equilibrium level of national income. However, the model tells us little about a **key question of interest**: how much of the adjustment to the new equilibrium level of income will be a change in real output and how much will be represented by a change in the price level? Because of this inadequacy within the basic Keynesian model, another macro economic model, known as the **aggregate demand/aggregate supply model (or AD/AS model)**, has come into prominence in recent years.

6 The aggregate demand/aggregate supply model

The main differences relating to the nature of aggregate supply which separate Keynesians and supply-siders (together with most monetarists and other members of the 'radical right'), can be explained using the AD/AS model illustrated in Figure 23.2. In this figure we show **aggregate demand for**, and **aggregate supply of, real output as functions of the price level**. For the most part, there is little disagreement between Keynesians and supply-siders about the nature and shape of the aggregate demand curve; **it is the aggregate supply curve that is the centre of dispute and interest**. The AD curve shows demand for **real output** (in contrast to the **AMD** or **aggregate**

expenditure curve of the 'Keynesian cross' diagram which shows demand for **nominal output**). The AD curve is drawn downward-sloping, showing that the aggregate demand exercised in the economy for goods and services increases as the price level falls. There are two main explanations for this. The first is a **real balance effect** or **wealth effect**. Assuming a given **nomimal** stock of money in the economy, a decrease in the price level increases people's stocks of **real money balances**, i.e. the same amount of money will buy more. Thus people feel wealthier and demand more goods. Secondly, increased real money balances cause the rate of interest to fall, further stimulating consumption and investment spending.

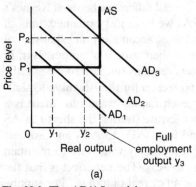
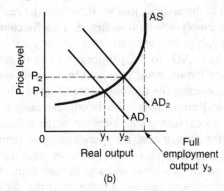

Fig. 23.2 The AD/AS model
(a) with an 'inverted L-shaped' schedule
(b) with an upward-sloping AS schedule

7 Keynesian aggregate supply

As we have noted, Keynesians and supply-siders disagree fundamentally over the specification of the **aggregate supply schedule**, which shows **how much real output firms are willing to supply at various price levels**. Figure 23.2(a) shows an **'inverted L-shaped' Keynesian aggregate supply function**. Following an expansion of aggregate demand, which shifts the aggregate demand function from AD_1 to AD_2, real output increases from y_1 to y_2, but there is no increase in prices. But once full employment is reached, at the level of real output y_3, any further increase in aggregate demand (e.g. to AD_3) causes prices and not output to rise. Figure 23.2(a) thus illustrates the 'traditional' and rather simple Keynesian view that an expansion of demand will **reflate** real output rather than **inflate** prices, providing the economy is below the full employment level of income.

8 Keynes's aggregate supply function

It is now generally agreed that the 'inverted L-shaped' aggregate supply function is not the one that Keynes himself had in mind in the 'General Theory'. We can distinguish between **Keynes's own aggregate supply function** and the **'Keynesian' function** we have just described, i.e. the aggregate supply function implicitly adopted by many followers of Keynes (the 'Keynesians'), but not by Keynes himself.

In contrast to the 'inverted L-shaped' AS curve, Keynes's AS function, depicted in Figure 23.2(b), is upward-sloping until the full employment level of income is reached. Following an expansion of demand from AD_1 to AD_2, the price level must rise to create the conditions in which firms are willing to supply more output. The difference between the two functions is explained by **different assumptions about the marginal productivity of labour**. With the 'inverted L-shaped' AS curve, it is assumed that the marginal product of labour is constant as output increases, until full employment is reached. But Keynes accepted the standard neo-classical assumption that firms face a declining marginal productivity of labour as they increase the supply of output in the short run. In this situation, the real wage rate paid by the firms must fall (to match the declining marginal product of labour), in order to persuade profit-maximizing firms to demand more labour and to increase the supply of output. Given a constant money wage rate (which is assumed for all **short-run** AS curves), a rise in price level reduces the real wage rate and produces the conditions in which firms are willing to employ more labour and supply more output. Hence, the upward-sloping AS function, showing that a rise in the price level is necessary to persuade firms to supply more output.

9 The supply-siders' aggregate supply function

It is important to emphasize that both the **Keynesian 'inverted L-shaped' AS function** and **Keynes's own upward-sloping AS function** are **short-run** functions, derived from assumptions about the short run marginal productivity of labour and a constant money wage rate. In particular, we must emphasize that **there will be a different short-run AS function for each and every money wage rate**. The supply-siders' short-run AS function, which is illustrated by the curves AS_1 and AS_2 drawn in Figure 23.3, is broadly similar to Keynes's upward-sloping AS curve. But, unlike Keynes's upward-sloping curve, the supply-siders' short-run AS curve lacks a vertical section. It remains upward-sloping at all price levels since supply-siders (along with most monetarists and Neo-classical economists) assume that firms continue, in the short run, to employ more labour and supply more output, as (at a constant money wage rate) the price level rises and the real cost of employing labour falls.

It is at this point in the analysis that we introduce the really **crucial difference between Keynes's AS function and the supply-side (and monetarist) AS function**. As we have just explained, in both Keynes's and the supply-siders' analysis, a rise in the price level must accompany an expansion of aggregate demand from AD_1 to AD_2 to induce firms to increase their supply of output. But, in Keynes's analysis, the money wage rate paid by firms to workers remains unchanged despite the increased price level eroding the real wage rate. There is thus no reason for the AS curve to shift. For supply-siders, and monetarists, this is not the case. For each money wage rate there is a different short-run AS curve, with an increase in the money wage rate shifting the short-run AS curve leftwards. If the government increases aggregate demand from AD_1 to AD_2 and workers then respond to the resulting higher price level by pushing up the money wage rate to maintain their real wages, then the AS curve shifts to the left from AS_1 to AS_2. The net effect is that the 'new' AD and AS schedules once again intersect at the initial level of real output y_n. For supply-siders, monetarists and New Classical economists, y_n is the **'natural' level of output** towards which market forces and a flexible price mechanism eventually adjust (it represents the **long-run equilibrium level of output or production potential** associated with the **'natural' levels of employment** and **unemployment** of labour which we investigated in Unit 22). The vertical line drawn in Figure 23.3, between the intersections of each pair of short-run AD and AS curves at this 'natural' or equilibrium level of output, is the **supply-siders' long-run AS schedule**. It carries the supply-side message, shared by most anti-Keynesians on the 'radical right', that the short-run expansionary effect on output and employment, resulting from the government increasing aggregate demand, is negated in the long run by the way the supply side of the economy responds.

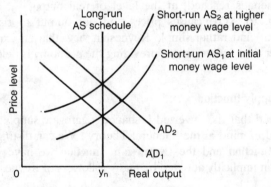

Fig. 23.3 The 'supply-siders' (monetarist/neo-classical) version of the AD/AS model

10 The growing influence of supply-side economics

Today many economists, who would not regard themselves as supply-siders, claim that their analysis has always incorporated supply-side effects. However, true believers in supply-sidism would dispute this claim. Be that as it may, few economists or politicians of whatever persuasion or 'ism', now call for large budget deficits as the way to achieve full employment; while almost all voice agreement with the idea that the tax structure should be used to create incentives for work, saving and investment. Arguably, by the 1990s, supply-sidism has become a more significant part of the now-dominant neo-classical revival than monetarism (since for many, monetarism has been discredited by the apparent breakdown in its central postulated relationship between the rate of growth of the money supply and inflation).

23.4 Links with other topics

As we have emphasized throughout this Unit, supply-side economics developed in the 1970s and 1980s as part of the wider neo-classical revival to replace the previous hegemony of Keynesian economics. The basic Keynesian macro-economic model, that the AD/AS model of the supply-siders replaced, is covered in Units 19 and 20. Monetarists and supply-siders, both being a part of the wider neo-classical revival and resurgence of free-market economics, share many similar views. Some of the major conflicts and controversies separating Keynesians and monetarists, which relate closely to the content of this Unit, are explored in Unit 24. Also of relevance are Unit 12 (on industrial policy) and Unit 13 (on trade unions and wages) in which the supply curve of labour is explained, which provides the micro-economic underpinning of much supply-side theory.

23.5 Question practice
Essay Questions

Question 1 Although many economists agree that the most important problems facing the UK economy lie on the 'supply-side' of the economy, there is much less agreement about the policies appropriate to deal with these problems. What are the 'supply-side' problems facing the economy and why is there disagreement about the appropriate policies? *(AEB: June, 1989)*

Understanding the Question Start your answer by explaining how supply-side economists believe that the stagflation of the 1970s resulted from Keynesian demand-management policies and the accompanying growth of the government sector and neglect of the supply side of the economy. Explain how supply-siders argue that Keynesian fiscal policy and 'interventionism' destroyed flexibility, incentives and competitiveness, and burdened the private sector with the high taxes necessary to finance the over-enlarged government sector. List and briefly describe particular supply-side problems, e.g. inflexible labour markets, wage rigidity, the poor investment record of British industry, a poorly trained labour force, etc.

You could, tackle the second part of the question by taking issue with the question, i.e. by arguing that the supply-siders have won the battle and that there is a wide measure of agreement on the appropriateness of free-market orientated supply-side policies to overcome the problems you have described Alternatively, you might argue that neo-Keynesians, while agreeing on the importance of supply-side problems, reject the supply-side programme of the 'radical right', believing instead in the need for **'interventionist' supply-side policies**, such as those we discussed in Unit 12. These would include nationalization (rather than denationalization) and a general extension of government planning in the economy. However, for free-market supply-siders, these are precisely the alleged 'failed policies' of the Keynesian era which contributed, along with demand management, to the emergence of the supply-side problems facing the economy.

Answer plan
1 Relate stagflation, and the breakdown of the Phillips relationship, to the ineffectiveness of demand management and the inability of the supply of output to increase to meet an expansion of demand.
2 List and briefly explain particular supply-side problems.
3 Explain how supply-siders recommend policies to create incentives, reduce government interventionism and expand the role of markets.
4 Go on to explain how neo-Keynesians, while accepting the importance of supply-side problems, reject the free-market approach and argue for a much more interventionist supply-side policy.

Question 2 'Micro-economic policies to increase aggregate supply, such as those directed towards training, enterprise and productivity, are more effective than expansionary macroeconomic policies in reducing unemployment.' Discuss. *(Oxford: June, 1988)*

Understanding the Question Much of the guidance notes given for Question 1 are also relevant for this question. However, the question does require either that you take issue with the view posed (arguing carefully whether you agree or disagree) or sit on the fence and adopt an 'it-all-depends' position.

Answer plan
1 Explain how, in Keynesian theory, expansionary macro-economic policies reduce demand-deficient unemployment.
2 Describe why supply-siders believe such policies are ineffective; contributing to stagflation, etc.
3 Argue that other types of policies will be appropriate for dealing with other causes of unemployment, frictional, structural, 'classical', etc.
4 Describe and assess the effectiveness of 'free market' micro-economic policies to increase aggregate supply.
5 Describe and assess the effectiveness of Keynesian, or interventionist, supply-side policies.
6 Argue a conclusion.

Multiple Choice Questions

Question 3 According to supply-side economists, all the following policies are appropriate for increasing aggregate supply **except**:
(a) rapidly increasing the money supply
(b) increasing government spending on retraining schemes
(c) reducing the monopoly power of trade unions
(d) encouraging the emergence of regional differences in wage rates.

Understanding the Question Alternatives (b), (c) and (d) are examples of particular micro-economic policies of the type often recommended by supply-side economists. While supply-siders dislike government spending, they do accept the need for properly-targeted spending, (for example, on the training of labour); though doubtless, they would prefer the private sector to undertake its own training. Alternative (a) is the correct answer; supply-siders, along with monetarists, believe in the need for a tight control over the growth of the money supply to secure control over inflation.

Question 4 In the aggregate demand/aggregate supply macro-economic model, a vertical AS curve:
(a) is, according to supply-side economists, the short-run AS curve but not the long-run AS curve
(b) is the Keynesian AS curve
(c) is the long-run Phillips curve
(d) locates the 'natural' or equilibrium level of real output.

Understanding the Question The vertical AS curve is the supply-siders' **long-run** AS curve, so alternative (a) is incorrect. The Keynesian AS curve is not vertical, so (b) is also wrong. Alternative (d) is the correct answer. Beware confusing the long-run Phillips curve (explained in Unit 22) with the supply-siders' long-run AS curve. Both are vertical curves, but the long-run Phillips curve locates the 'natural' level unemployment in the **labour market** whereas the long-run AS curve performs a similar function for the 'natural' level of output in the **goods market**. Both are closely related in supply-side and monetarist analysis.

Data Response Questions

Question 6   The United Kingdom Labour Market: Equilibrium or Disequilibrium?

The labour market in this country is one of the most studied but probably least understood of all markets. There are a wide range of views about the nature of the labour market. On the one side there are the 'equilibrium theorists', who argue that the labour market is not dissimilar to competitive markets, like that for cabbages or foreign exchange. At least they say it has more in common with such markets than is commonly supposed. Thus the price in each market, be it cabbages or labour, is determined by the equality of supply and demand. Equilibrium theorists argue that real wages adjust quickly to changes in supply and demand.

An important part of the equilibrium approach is the explanation it suggests for the pattern of rising real wages and unemployment. The explanation advanced is couched in terms of upward (leftward) shifts in labour supply, these reductions in the supply of labour being the result of increases in the value of social security benefits and of increasing pressure on the labour markets by trade union activity. In an equilibrium model, measured unemployment is then explained by the rational supply decisions by workers, although it is also recognised that there will be frictional unemployment even in a competitive labour market. Such frictional unemployment is, of course, an almost inevitable feature of a flexible, changing economy, and as such is not evidence of problems in the labour market. In the main, the argument put forward by the equilibrium theorists is a supply-side explanation of changes in measured unemployment. Put another way, they argue that the natural or equilibrium rate of unemployment increased substantially during the 1980s, largely due to these supply side effects.

The other or opposite view of the labour market is that it is more or less permanently in disequilibrium, with the supply of labour not being brought into equality with the demand, by smooth quickly adjusting real wages. According to this alternative, real wages are rigid, especially downwards. Hence a fall in the demand for labour, for example, will be reflected in an increase in unemployment, which is largely involuntary, and which will tend to persist. 'Disequilibrium theorists' generally advocate demand reflation as a means of reducing unemployment.

Source: *adapted from Lloyds Bank Review, number 165, July 1987*

(a) How would equilibrium theorists explain the pattern of relative wage rates?   (5)
(b) Why is frictional unemployment **not** regarded as 'evidence of problems in the labour market'? (second half of second paragraph)   (4)
(c) Explain the differences between the equilibrium and disequilibrium theorists' views of the causes of unemployment.   (7)
(d) Discuss the policies to reduce unemployment which are likely to be advocated by
    (i) equilibrium theorists (ii) disequilibrium theorists.   (9)

(*AEB: June, 1990*)

Understanding the Question The 'equilibrium theorists' mentioned in the passage are supply-siders, together with other rather similarly-minded members of the neo-classical revival, such as monetarists and New Classical economists. The 'disequilibrium theorists' are Keynesians. Disequilibrium theorists locate an important cause of unemployment on the demand-side of the economy (in terms of deficient aggregate demand) arguing that real wages and interest rates do not operate, in the manner postulated by the equilibrium theorists, to eliminate deficient demand. By contrast, the equilibrium theorists deny the possibility of deficient aggregate demand, except as a temporary phenomenon that a flexible price mechanism quickly eliminates. Disequilibrium theorists therefore, recommend the use of Keynesian-style reflationary policies to reduce unemployment; whereas equilibrium theorists reject these, believing instead in the need for the supply-side policies we have discussed in this Unit.

When answering part (b), it would be useful to divide frictional unemployment into two elements. Its traditional 'between-jobs' or transitional component is not usually regarded as a problem since a modern competitive economy, adapting to changing demand and technology, must always contain people moving between jobs and learning new skills. However, supply-siders now identify a 'voluntary frictional' unemployment explained in terms of search theory. The higher the replacement ratio (the ratio of disposable income out of work when unemployed to disposable income in work) the more rational it is for lowly-skilled workers with poor pay prospects to choose to live off state benefits, particularly if these can be supplemented 'unofficially' by untaxed income from employment in the 'black' economy.

23.6 Further reading

Lipsey, R. G., *An Introduction to Positive Economics*, 7th edition (Weidenfeld & Nicolson, 1989)
Chapter 33: The Aggregate Demand, Aggregate Supply Model.

Begg, D., Fischer, S., and Dornbusch, R., *Economics*, 3rd edition (McGraw Hill, 1991)
Chapter 26: Aggregate Supply, the Price Level, and the Speed of Adjustment.

24 Keynesianism and Monetarism

24.1 Points of perspective

In the preceding units, frequent mention has been made of Keynesian and monetarist views and of points of controversy and disagreement which separate economists of the two schools. In this unit we firstly gather together and summarize some of the themes of the earlier units, before extending the discussion to other aspects of the controversy such as the role of incomes policy and the international nature of inflation. Besides emphasizing that **Keynesianism** and **monetarism** are broad labels which encompass a wide variety of different viewpoints, we shall also note the existence of another school of thought, the self-styled **'radical-left'** or **neo-Marxian** school which rejects both Keynesianism and monetarism.

24.2 Underlying concepts

Monetarism takes its name from the belief held by all monetarists that inflation is explained by the **quantity theory of money**; according to strict monetarism **all** inflation is casued ultimately by a prior expansion of the money supply. In fact, monetarism means rather more than this, extending to encompass a large part of the pre-Keynesian or 'classical' view of how the economy works. As we have explained in Unit 23, monetarism has formed an important part of the **neo-classical revival** (or **'radical-right' revival**) which has also spawned other free-market orientated 'schools of thought', interrelated with monetarism, including the **New Classical** and **'supply-side'** schools.

1 Keynesianism

Keynesianism is a label attached to the theories and policies of those economists who claim to have inherited the mantle of the great English economist, **J. M. Keynes**. In *The General Theory of Employment, Interest and Money* published in 1936, Keynes created a theory of the working of the **whole economy**, and from this foundation modern macro-economics developed. Keynes argued that no automatic tendency exists for unregulated market forces to bring about full employment and that **persistent mass unemployment** could be caused by **deficient demand**. Before his death in 1946, Keynes adapted his theory of **deflation** and deficient demand to the problem of **inflation** caused by **excessive demand**. However, although he did not live to see it, the 'true' **Keynesian era** dawned in the years after 1945 when, in the United Kingdom in particular, Keynesianism became the new economic and political orthodoxy. Essentially, Keynesianism became associated with an **increased level of government intervention** in the economy, especially through **budget deficits** and **fiscal policy**, to 'fine-tune' or manage aggregate demand to a level consistent with achieving relative **full employment** and **economic growth** without excessive costs in terms of **inflation** or **Balance of Payments** crises.

2 Monetarism

Monetarism takes its name from the belief held by all monetarists that inflation is explained by the **quantity theory of money**; according to strict monetarism **all** inflation is caused by a prior expansion of the money supply. In fact, monetarism means rather more than this, extending to encompass a large part of the pre-Keynesian or 'classical' view of how the economy works.

Indeed, **'the New Classical Macro-economics'** is probably a better descriptive label than monetarism of the true roots of the views held by many members of the monetarist school.

3 Some fundamental issues of dispute

Later in the unit we shall examine some of the issues of dispute between Keynesians and monetarists on particular aspects of government policy. First, however, we shall look at some rather more fundamental differences in the views held by the two schools on the nature of the economy:

(i) The separation of 'real' and 'monetary' forces Many monetarists appear to accept the old 'classical' view (known as **the Classical Dichotomy**) that **real** and **monetary** forces in the economy are separate. Via the quantity theory of money, an increase in the money supply causes the price level to rise, but it leaves unaffected the **equilibrium** values of relative prices and levels of output and employment. This view, which is completely rejected by Keynesians, carries the implication that a policy of monetary expansionism will in the **long run** increase prices but not output and employment, though in the **short run** (a period of up to five or ten years according to Milton Friedman) some monetarists agree that monetary changes can primarily affect output.

(ii) The stability of market forces Monetarists see a market economy as a calm and orderly place in which the market mechanism, working through **incentives** transmitted by **price signals** in **competitive markets**, achieves a better or more optimal outcome than can be attained through government interventionism. In essence, risk-taking businessmen who will gain or lose through the correctness of their decisions in the market-place 'know better' what to produce than civil servants and planners cocooned by risk-free salaries and secured pensions. And providing that markets are sufficiently competitive, what is produced is ultimately determined by the wishes of consumers, who also know better than governments what is good for them. According to this philosophy the correct economic function of government is to act as 'nightwatchman' by maintaining law and order, to provide public goods where the market fails, and generally to ensure a suitable environment in which 'wealth-creating' private enterprise can function in competitive markets subject to minimum regulation.

This view of the correct economic role of government leads monetarists generally to **reject discretionary intervention** in the economy as a means of achieving goals such as reduced unemployment. At best, such intervention will be ineffective, at worst it will be destabilizing and damaging. To ensure that such intervention does not take place, governments should adopt, if necessary by law, **fixed** or **automatic policy rules**. Many monetarists recommend the adoption of a **fiscal rule** to balance the budget or reduce the PSBR to a fixed percentage of GDP; a **monetary rule** to expand the money supply in line with the growth of real GDP; and an **exchange rate rule** either to keep to a fixed exchange rate or to allow the exchange rate to float freely. (The debate between Keynesians and monetarists on the respective merits and demerits of discretionary policy and automatic rules is sometimes conducted in terms reminiscent of a motor manual. Thus Milton Friedman argues the advantage of a 'fixed throttle' increase in the money supply, rejecting the 'fine-tuning' of demand advocated by the Keynesians.)

In contrast, Keynesians adopt a rather different view of the functioning of an unregulated market economy. In particular, they stress:

(a) the **imperfect** nature of generally **uncompetitive markets**, the growth of **monopoly power** and **producer sovereignty**, and the importance of **uncertainty about the future** and **lack of correct market information** as potentially destabilizing forces; **and**

(b) the possible breakdown of **money linkages** between markets. In market economies money is used as a means of payment for market transactions, but people receiving money incomes from the sale of labour in the **labour market** may not necessarily spend their income on the purchase of goods and services in the **goods market**. Instead they may decide to hold idle money balances. Thus Say's Law that 'supply creates its own demand' breaks down and **deficient demand** causes **involuntary unemployment** of labour and other resources.

Thus monetarists emphasize the optimal aspects of a **competitive** economy in a state of **general** (and **fully employed**) equilibrium, and the role in attaining such an equilibrium of **private economic agents** reacting to **price signals** in conditions of near-perfect market information. In competitive markets the market mechanism working through **flexible** prices will move the economy towards a full employment equilibrium. In contrast, the Keynesians emphasize the **inflexible** nature of prices and particularly wages. They also see the economy in terms of **disequilibrium** rather than equilibrium. The economy is subject to the uncertainty of **random 'shocks'** or **autonomous changes** which, by inducing **destabilizing multiplier effects**, hold no guarantee of a smooth and orderly movement to a full employment equilibrium. By **managing the level of demand** the government can 'know better' than unregulated market forces. It can anticipate and counter the destabilizing forces existent in the market economy, achieving a better outcome than is likely in an economy subject to market forces alone.

In summary, therefore, monetarists lay great stress on the essentially **stabilizing** properties of market forces, seeing discretionary government intervention as **destabilizing** and **inefficient**. Conversely, Keynesians justify discretionary interventionism on the grounds that it **stabilizes** an inherently **unstable** market economy.

24.3   Essential knowledge

1 Keynesian objectives and instruments

In order to explain the principal points of difference between Keynesian and monetarist **policies**, we shall adopt an **objectives and instruments approach**. First we must identify the objectives, goals or targets which governments or their policy-makers wish to achieve. Once we have specified the **objectives**, the next stage is to **assign** a particular **policy instrument** to a particular objective.

In the earlier part of the Keynesian era, and especially in the 1950s and early 1960s, the Keynesian policy-makers in the United Kingdom relied on **one principal policy instrument** – the use of **discretionary fiscal policy**. Fiscal policy was used to achieve **three** policy objectives: **full employment**, **a satisfactory balance of payments** (and the **protection of a fixed exchange rate**), **and control of inflation**. In order to create full employment, tax cuts and increases in public spending resulting in a budget deficit were used to **expand demand**. However, an increased level of demand also raised imports and pulled up the price level. Eventually, either a balance of payments crisis or an unacceptable rise in the inflation rate, or both, would cause the policy-makers to initiate a reversal of policy in which fiscal policy would be used to **deflate** demand in order to protect the exchange rate or to reduce inflation. Thus Keynesianism became associated with **'stop-go'** management of the economy.

It is worth noting that in this era discretionary fiscal policy was used as the principal tool of demand management, partly because the Keynesians believed it to be more effective than discretionary **monetary policy**, but also because monetary policy was in the main assigned to **another objective**, that of **National Debt management**. Nevertheless, the role of monetary policy was not absolutely clear; it was also used as a **supplementary tool** of demand management to 'back up' fiscal policy, and as a means of protecting the exchange rate through high interest rates in the recurrent balance of payments crises of the era. In a credit squeeze, demand would be deflated through the use of monetary policy instruments such as open-market operations and the raising of interest rates.

During this first period of Keynesian management of the British economy, successive British governments were committed to preserving a fixed exchange rate. The **exchange rate** was thus a **target** rather than an **instrument** of the policy. But in the latter part of the Keynesian era in the later 1960s and the early 1970s, many Keynesians came to the conclusion that if 'stop-go' was to be avoided a **separate policy instrument** must be assigned to each of the **three principal objectives** of policy. Accordingly, the Keynesian **assignment rule** became:

INSTRUMENT		OBJECTIVE
Fiscal policy	:	Full Employment and Growth
Exchange Rate policy	:	Balance of Payments
Incomes policy	:	Control of Inflation
Monetary policy	:	National Debt Management

2 Keynesians and the exchange rate

The Keynesians believed that their ability to achieve sustained full employment and economic growth by means of expansionary demand management policies was severely **constrained** by the tendency of the balance of payments to go into serious deficit whenever full employment was approached. Increasingly in the early 1960s Keynesians argued in favour of abandoning the commitment to maintain a fixed exchange rate. **Devaluation** should be used as a policy instrument to 'look after' the balance of payments, leaving fiscal policy free to pursue the objective of full employment. (You should refer to Units 26 and 27 for a detailed explanation of the effects of a change in the exchange rate on the balance of payments.) The ideas of **'export-led growth'** and of the existence of a **'virtuous circle'** became fashionable amongst Keynesians in the 1960s. They argued that a devaluation (or downward float) of the exchange rate improves the competitive position of exports and worsens that of imports. The improved balance of payments position then stimulates growth which in turn stimulates productivity. The competitive position of exports then further improves as a result of falling average costs of production. The process continues, with exports stimulating growth, stimulating competitiveness and so on. Conversely, it was believed that an

overvalued exchange rate could explain Britain's predicament in the 1960s, trapped in a **vicious circle** of uncompetitive exports, slow growth, and a worsening balance of payments position.

Nevertheless, neither the 1967 devaluation of the £ nor its floating in 1972 succeeded in achieving for Britain the 'miracle' of export-led growth. Against this background, economists of the Keynesian persuasion increasingly turned their attention to **incomes policies**, and even to **import controls**, in the search for additional policy instruments with which to manage the economy successfully.

3 Keynesians and incomes policy

As it became increasingly clear that, on its own, discretionary fiscal policy or demand management was unable to secure both full employment and price stability, Keynesians, or Post-Keynesians, of the cost-push school turned their attention to **incomes policy** as the appropriate instrument to reduce inflation. However, many economists dispute the idea that an incomes policy should be regarded as a well-defined policy instrument. They argue that 'incomes policy' has become a label for a wide variety of **statutory** and **voluntary, short-term** and **long-term** policies for the **freezing, restraint** or **'planned growth'** of **wages**, **incomes**, and even **prices**. Incomes policies can vary from emergency ad hoc measures, usually of short duration in response to a panic or crisis, to the long-term forward planning of the growth of incomes, based on some social consensus.

Other economists take the view that the **control of inflation** is not necessarily the main objective of an incomes policy. Many Marxists argue that its main function is to **squeeze wages** so as to alter the distribution of income in favour of profits. A popular view is that incomes policies should be used to pursue a **'social fairness' policy** in which job evaluation replaces market forces as the determinant of wages. One result of this proliferation of interpretations as to what is meant by incomes policy is that it is exceedingly difficult to evaluate the effectiveness of incomes policies in controlling inflation. This is because it is almost impossible to compare a **'policy-on' period** with a period of **'policy-off'** as no one can agree on what exactly constitutes an incomes policy.

Nevertheless, the incomes policies introduced by successive British governments in the 1960s and 1970s went through four identifiable stages in the cycle of their rather short lives:

(1) Incomes policies have almost always been introduced as unthought-out and temporary measures by governments elected to office on an anti-incomes policy platform. Indeed, in the first months in office the government may well have been busy dismantling an earlier policy inherited from its predecessor. The first stage of an incomes policy has usually been a **wage freeze** introduced in response to a crisis–either of inflation or in the balance of payments. **Free collective bargaining** may be suspended for the duration of the wage freeze.

(2) Traditionally, governments have used the wage freeze as a breathing space for thinking out the detailed strategy of the second or **'planned growth of incomes'** stage. In this critical stage of an incomes policy, the government allows market forces to work but imposes constraints on their operation, particularly in the labour market. A **statutory** incomes policy imposes legally binding limits on free collective bargaining, and sometimes on prices as well. In contrast, a **voluntary** incomes policy will rely on exhortation, an appeal to the national interest and national unity, or to some form of **social contract** between government, employers and unions.

Restraint on the wage-bargaining process may take the form of a **maximum limit** for wage rises. Usually the government chooses a wage ceiling on the basis of the estimated rate of growth of productivity. For example, if productivity grows at 3 per cent, a limit on wage rises of 7 per cent should be consistent with 4 per cent inflation. In practice, however, an **upper limit** on wage rises becomes interpreted as the **norm**, or even as a **lower limit** which every self-respecting union negotiator must attempt to exceed.

(3) The second stage of an incomes policy has usually lasted as long as it is accepted as **socially fair** by the people upon whom it is imposed. In the third stage, the incomes policy begins to **disintegrate** when this consensus breaks down. Workers begin to resent and fight against the incomes policy when they see other groups in society successfully evading the policy. **Wage-drift** provides one form of evasion. In a period of incomes policy, workers may try to negotiate locally at the plant level rather than through national collective bargaining. It is usually much more difficult for the government to 'police' thousands of local agreements than the much smaller number of national collective agreements. Thus **total earnings** drift away from **basic wage rates** which are still usually negotiated nationally, but only certain groups of workers will benefit from the process. Other methods of evasion include **job re-gradings** and the tendency for higher-paid workers–particularly managers–to take a larger part of their real income in the form of **fringe benefits** or **perks**. The feeling of social unfairness will also intensify if certain types of income, such as profits and the income of the self-employed, are outside the bounds of the incomes policy, or if there is no restraint on prices.

In the third stage of incomes policy, workers begin to claim, and the government begins to allow, **special case treatment**, whereby certain groups of workers bypass or exceed the limits on pay rises. Some groups, usually the higher paid, claim **special case** status on the grounds of a higher than average rise in productivity, whereas others, usually the lower paid, argue that they merit special treatment on the basis of 'social fairness'.

(4) Incomes policies in the UK have **finally collapsed** under one of two sets of circumstances. Either the government, having lost its resolve, has allowed the policy to fade away in a spate of 'special cases', or the election of a new government has defeated the policy at the ballot-box. However, before too long an incoming government has usually found it necessary to reintroduce an incomes policy despite its avowed intentions. Even the monetarist Conservative Government elected in 1979 operated an **informal incomes policy** applied to wages in the public sector where the government is the employer! This incomes policy was a logical consequence of the **cash limits** and **external financing limits** imposed respectively upon government departments (and local government) and nationalized industries. Wage increases exceeding these limits would not be compatible with the government's achieving its PSBR and money supply targets.

Immediately following the final collapse of an incomes policy, there is usually a **'catching up' period** in which workers frantically attempt either to make up what they see as lost ground, or to restore differentials. Indeed, the sudden rise in the inflation rate which occurs in the catching-up period creates precisely the conditions in which a 'new' incomes policy is introduced to reduce the rate of inflation. Thus, because of the catching-up period between incomes policies, it is very difficult to assess just how effective incomes policies have been in reducing inflation.

4 Monetarists and incomes policies

Most monetarists completely oppose the use of an incomes policy except as an **informal policy** to control pay increases in the public sector, where the state is the employer. As we have explained, monetarists accept the neo-classical tradition of the allocative efficiency of market forces and retain a suspicion of the economic power of the state. Incomes policies are undesirable because they **interfere** with and **distort** the working of the market mechanism, and **extend the economic role of the state.** Nevertheless, some economists take up a more **eclectic** or **pragmatic** position between the extremes adopted by cost-push Keynesians and monetarists. The **eclectics** argue that an incomes policy may **sometimes** have a useful role in reducing inflationary expectations, without at the same time greatly distorting market forces.

5 Monetarist instruments and objectives

While the Keynesians have consistently searched for an ever-wider range of policy instruments with which to conduct the management of the economy, the monetarists have argued that the correct role of government is to minimize its intervention in the economy. While monetarists usually believe that **discretionary** monetary policy has a more powerful influence on the level of money national income than fiscal policy, it is wrong to draw the conclusion that monetarists advocate its use in the management of the level of demand. Not only would a discretionary monetary policy be **unpredictable** in its effects, the main effect of monetary expansion would be a **rising price level** rather than a growth of real output. Monetarists usually reject the use of **discretionary** economic management policies of any kind—fiscal policy, monetary policy, incomes policy and exchange rate policies. Instead, they argue that the economic function of government is to create the conditions in which market forces, working through price signals and private incentives, can properly operate. Nevertheless, it is still useful to analyze monetarist economic policy in terms of instruments and objectives, even though the monetarists prefer the announcement of **firm policy rules** to a discretionary intervention in the working of the economy:

(i) The **ultimate objective** of monetarist policy is to create conditions in which market forces and private enterprise can ensure full employment and economic growth.

(ii) **Control of inflation** is seen as a necessary condition or **intermediate** objective which must be achieved before market forces can work properly.

(iii) Monetarists believe that inflation is caused by an excessive rate of growth of the money supply. Therefore **control of the money supply** is a necessary intermediate (or immediate) objective of policy. Nevertheless, control of the money supply may be difficult to achieve. Some monetarists believe that it should be regarded as a general **indicator** of whether or not the policy is 'on course', and used in conjunction with other indicators or intermediate targets such as the **exchange rate** and the **rate of growth of Money GDP.**

(iv) Monetary policy cannot be separated from the **fiscal stance** adopted by the government. At the root of monetarism is the belief that the **levels of public spending and the PSBR** must be used as a policy instrument to achieve control over the rate of growth of the money supply. A tight fiscal stance and the reduction of both public spending and the PSBR as a proportion of GDP will also reduce undesirable 'crowding out' in the economy by freeing a greater volume of resources for use and employment in the private sector. Some monetarists recommend a **'balanced budget' fiscal policy rule.**

(v) Monetarists place considerable emphasis on **supply-side** or **micro-economic** policies which have the general objective of making markets more competitive. **Competition policy** and **industrial relations policy** (perhaps a euphemism for anti-trade union policy) are examples, together with cuts in income tax rates to promote supply-side incentives.

6 Monetarists and the exchange rate

Practical monetarism thus involves the adoption of **two automatic policy rules**:

(i) A **fiscal rule** to balance the budget or to reduce public spending and the PSBR as proportions of GDP;
and

(ii) A **monetary rule** to allow the money supply to grow at some predetermined rate, for example based on the rate of growth of real GDP.

There is much less agreement amongst monetarists on the form of a **third rule** to be adopted for the **exchange rate**. Monetarists generally fall into one of two camps, advocating either a **fixed** or a **freely floating** exchange rate. Those monetarists who have studied the inflationary process in a regime of fixed exchange rates such as existed before 1972 are sometimes called **international monetarists** or **global monetarists**. In such a system, the **world inflation rate** is determined by the rate of growth of the **world money supply**. For a country like the UK, the **domestic inflation rate** must converge with the world inflation rate to maintain the fixed exchange rate. The domestic money supply responds endogenously to 'accommodate', or finance, the rate of inflation 'imported' from the rest of the world. Thus, instead of changes in the domestic money supply causing inflation, with fixed exchange rates, the **'imported' rate of inflation changes the domestic money supply**. This is the reverse of the 'traditional' theory of monetarism, developed originally by Milton Friedman as appropriate either for a closed economy or for a system of floating exchange rates. Nevertheless, in a fixed exchange rate system, the rate of **world inflation** is still caused by **world monetary growth**.

At the beginning of the 'monetarist experiment' in the early 1980s, many monetarists seemed to prefer a completely free or cleanly floating exchange rate because this is consistent with their view that market forces and not the government should determine as far as possible the level of activity within the economy. As in the case of other forms of government intervention, many monetarists believe that an attempt by government to **manage the exchange rate** will create distortions and inefficiences and is in any case in the long run unable to defy market forces. We develop this theme in Unit 27. Additionally, a floating exchange has the advantage, in theory at least, of **isolating the economy from international inflationary pressure**. As has been just explained, with a fixed exchange rate, a country may **'import' inflation from the rest of the world**. Many monetarists, and also many Keynesians, argue that this is what happened in the 1960s when the USA expanded its domestic economy and built up a huge balance of payments deficit against the rest of the world. Because the dollar was the cornerstone of the **Bretton Woods system of fixed exchange rates** (to be explained in Units 26 and 27), the Americans managed to persuade other countries to maintain their fixed exchange rates against the dollar and to accept dollars in payment for US imports from the rest of the world. The resulting outflow of dollars from America into the reseves of the rest of the world greatly swelled international demand and, in the monetarist interpretation, added to the excessive rate of growth of the world money supply. If, instead, other exchange rates had freely floated against the dollar, the rest of the world would not have imported the dollars created by the American authorities. The American balance of payments deficit would simply have resulted in an excess supply of dollars on foreign exchange markets which would then have caused the exchange rate of the dollar to fall until the US deficit had been eliminated.

Nevertheless, the experience of floating exchange rates in the 1970s and 1980s has convinced many monetarists–and Keynesians as well–that a **floating exchange rate contributes to the inflationary process**. They argue that a **completely fixed** exchange rate provides a source of **discipline** for workers and business enterprises within the domestic economy. If, for example, workers bargain for wage increases of 10% when the average rate of growth of productivity is only 4%, then the domestic price level is almost sure to rise. But in a regime of freely floating exchange rates, international competitiveness need not be adversely affected. The exchange rate may simply fall to maintain the initial **relative price** of British goods compared with foreign goods. But the inflation process does not stop here. Workers may respond to the rising **money price** of imports by demanding even higher money wages in an attempt to increase the real wage. This causes a further rise in prices, followed by a fall in the exchange rate and further wage increases in a vicious inflationary spiral accompanied by a plummeting exchange rate.

The floating of the exchange rate may also remove a source of discipline from the behaviour of governments. Indeed, the acceleration in the rate of inflation experienced simultaneously by many countries in the 1970s has been explained in terms of the breakdown of the Bretton Woods system of fixed exchange rates in 1971 and 1972. Governments apparently felt free to reflate demand, hoping that a floating exchange rate would 'look after' the balance of payments. They also hoped that in a regime of floating exchange rates there would no longer be a need periodically to deflate demand in order to support the exchange rate. As a result simultaneous reflation by many countries in the early 1970s caused a world-wide increase in demand which world output was incapable of meeting, and inflation resulted.

Thus many economists, both monetarist and Keynesian, have swung round to the opinion that a fixed exchange rate is needed to impose the necessary **discipline** upon the behaviour of workers and firms in the setting of wages and prices, and upon government in avoiding the temptation to reflate demand 'irresponsibly'. Some monetarists even go as far as to recommend a return to a **gold standard system** of fixed exchange rates similar to the system that operated in the 19th century. Indeed, without going this far, the UK government has come to regard fixed interest rates with renewed favour as evidenced by the decision in October 1990 to join the exchange rate mechanism of the **European Monetary System (EMS)**.

7 'New School' and 'Old School' Keynesians

We have already mentioned that Keynesians of the cost-push school favour the use of an incomes policy as a means of controlling inflation. One group of Neo-Keynesians, or Post-Keynesians, whose members subscribe to the cost-push theory of inflation is the **Cambridge Economic Policy Group (CEPG)**. The members of the CEPG are also known as the **'New School' Keynesians**, a title which distinguishes them from the more traditional **'Old School'** supporters of demand management and discretionary fiscal policy. In common with monetarists, New School Keynesians are doubtful of the virtues of **short-term discretionary management** of the economy. Instead, they prefer a more **medium-term policy**, aimed at improving the **structure or supply side** of the economy. Nevertheless, in contrast to monetarists, the New School shares with the older school of Keynesians a belief in the need to increase rather than to reduce government intervention in the market economy. Members of the CEPG argued in the 1970s that a close link exists between the **budget deficit** and the **balance of payments**; in short, that a larger budget deficit has an adverse effect on the balance of payments. In consequence, the government's **fiscal stance** should be used to achieve a desired balance of payments target. This would mean that fiscal policy is unavailable for use as a policy instrument to secure the domestic target of full employment. The New School has at times recommended the use of **import controls**, not so much as a means of protecting the balance of payments, but as a policy instrument to achieve full employment by increasing the volume of domestically produced output.

To complete the picture, both incomes policy and the exchange rate have been recommended by various members of the New School as appropriate policy instruments to control inflation. However, different members of the New School hold different views which have been subject to frequent change and adjustment. In the early 1980s, New School views had a significant influence on the **Alternative Economic Strategy** adopted as **Labour Party economic policy**. As with the Old School of Keynesians, the New School attaches a relatively small importance to monetary policy in its assignment of policy instruments to policy objectives.

8 Keynesians, monetarists and the nature of aggregate supply

An important area of dispute between Keynesians and monetarists centres on assumptions made by each school about the nature of the **aggregate supply of real output** in the economy. 'Extreme' Keynesians believe that an expansion of aggregate demand, along an 'inverted L-shaped' aggregate supply curve, will reflate output (without inflation) until full employment is reached, when any further demand stimulation will cause prices to rise. For more 'moderate' Keynesians (and probably for Keynes himself), the AS curve is upward-sloping. In these circumstances, an increase in aggregate demand will stimulate both real output and prices until full employment is reached. However, for many monetarists, supply-side economists and other members of the neo-classical/'radical right' revival, the long-run AS curve is vertical, located at the 'natural' or equilibrium level of output in the economy. It carries the message that any demand stimulation will, in the long run, cause prices to rise rather than output. (For a more detailed discussion of these issues, refer back to Unit 23 on supply-side economics.)

9 A criticism of Keynesian and monetarist economics

With the decline of traditional or Old School Keynesianism, both monetarism and the New Keynesian School have had an influence upon the conduct of economic policy in the UK. The influence of the monetarist school has of course been considerable and often dominating. Nevertheless we should not conclude this unit without mentioning, albeit briefly, the arguments of another school of thought which attacks and rejects both Keynesianism and monetarism. This is the **'radical-left'** or **Neo-Marxian school**, which experienced something of a revival at the academic level in some British universities in the 1970s and 1980s, but which has had little or no influence upon the conduct of UK policy. Marxists analyze the problems of the British economy in terms of the historical development of **capitalism** as an **economic system**, and of the particular stage of development in which the British economy finds itself.

According to the Marxist view, Keynes made respectable the extension of the economic role of the state in a non-socialist economy. Government intervention could make the capitalist economy function better, without changing the fundamental nature of capitalism as an economic system. For a time Keynesian economic management did indeed contain and reduce the inconsistencies and contradictions which Marxists identify within the capitalist system, but it did not eliminate them. Marxists argue that this is demonstrated by the role of the state in capitalist economies such as the UK. On the one hand, the state provides necessary services which allow private capital to be more profitable. These services include the **management of demand**, the provision of **external economies**, and the maintenance of **social order**. But on the other hand, most of the economic functions of the modern state are not directly productive and the growth of the state imposes an increasing burden of taxation upon private capital. Marxists argue that in the short run the state has been able to reduce this burden and to achieve full employment, but only at the expense of pursuing inflationary policies. The modern state now finds itself in an impasse, with capitalism in a state of crisis. A further extension on Keynesian lines of the role of the state to restore full employment will either add to inflationary pressure or, by increasing the burden of taxation, it will erode the vital requirement for capitalist accumulation–the rate of profit.

Yet if the monetarists' alternative is adopted and the state 'rolled back' to become a mere 'nightwatchman' over the economy, the necessary functions of the state for private capital will not be performed. Thus Keynesian economic management will produce runaway inflation and declining profitability, whereas monetarism will result in mass unemployment and social conflict. According to Marxists, neither Keynesian nor monetarist economic management can deal with the true causes of the crisis, which lie within the nature of capitalism itself. The controversy between Keynesians and monetarists is irrelevant; only a change in the system, to **socialism**, will eliminate the crisis in capitalism. Needless to say, most 'orthodox' Keynesians and monetarists dispute the Marxian analysis, though some would accept that it usefully adds to the discussion about the current problems facing the economy. However, there is a widespread dismissal by Keynesians and monetarists of the Marxist view that the problems would somehow be eliminated or reduced if the capitalist system was replaced with socialism, and recent changes in Eastern Europe and the USSR have hardly added to the authority of Marxian economics or the Marxist interpretation of history.

24.4 Links with other topics

In this unit, which concludes our main section on macro-economic theory and policy, we have attempted to draw together many of the themes introduced in earlier units from Unit 14 to Unit 23. The essentials of the Keynesian national income-expenditure model are covered in Units 18 to 22. Units 14 to 17 cover areas of monetary and fiscal dispute between Keynesians and monetarists, including the topical issue of the importance of the PSBR and its effects upon the economy. Unit 22 concentrates on the dispute about the causes of unemployment and inflation, while Unit 23 surveys the main elements of 'supply-side' economics which, along with monetarism, forms an important part of the neo-classical revival.

We have made some mention in this unit of the impact that the balance of payments and the exchange rate have on the task of domestic economic management. This theme is developed in more depth in Unit 26 on the balance of payments and Unit 27 on the exchange rate.

24.5 Question practice

Essay Questions

Question 1 Distinguish between monetary and fiscal policy. Discuss the role of fiscal policy in the management of the economy by a 'monetarist' government.   (*AEB: June, 1989*)

Understanding the Question Many of the candidates who answered this question in 1989 wrote as follows: 'monetary policy is control of the money supply; fiscal policy is Keynesian demand management. Since monetarists reject Keynesian demand management, a 'monetarist' government does not have a fiscal policy.'

While there is an element of truth in this approach, it is only an element and the answer is much too narrow. You should define monetary policy more broadly as 'the part of the government's overall economic policy that attempts to achieve its objectives using monetary instruments such as controls on bank lending and the rate of interest'. Likewise, fiscal policy can be defined as 'the part of the government's overall economic policy that attempts to achieve its objectives using the fiscal instruments of taxation and public spending'. It is then useful to distinguish between the 'macro' and 'micro' elements of fiscal policy. At the macro level, a 'monetarist' government might use fiscal policy to reduce the overall size of the public sector to avoid 'crowding out'; and to create the fiscal conditions (via PSBR control) thought necessary for the success of a 'monetarist' monetary policy aimed at controlling monetary growth.

Under monetarism, it is useful to think of fiscal policy (at the macro level) being determined by the needs of monetary policy; while macro policy in general is subordinated to some extent below micro policy in a 'monetarist' government's overall economic strategy. Micro fiscal policy is essentially the 'supply-side' fiscal policy we described in Unit 23, centering on the role of tax cuts to create incentives to which private economic agents may respond.

Answer plan

1 Define both fiscal policy and monetary policy in the broad terms we have indicated.
2 Explain how a 'monetarist' government is likely to reject the use of fiscal policy as an instrument of short-term demand management, adopting instead a much more medium-term strategy.
3 Describe the more macro elements of 'monetarist fiscal policy, e.g. reducing public spending, balancing the budget, etc.
4 Describe the more micro elements and relate them to 'supply-side' economics, e.g. tax cuts to create incentives.

Question 2 Are monetarism and supply-side economics inextricably linked? (*Cambridge: June, 1988*)

Understanding the Question As the influence of Keynesianism diminished during the 1980s, a number of related terms and '-isms' became associated with the ascendency of monetarism. These included: **the neo-classical revival**; **New Classical economics**; the growth of the 'radical right' or the 'New Right'; Thatcherism (in the UK) and **Reaganomics** (in the USA); and, **'supply-side' economics**. All these terms are linked, relating to the re-emergence of an economic ideology centering on the virtues of free-market forces, competition and private enterprise or capitalism; and a distrust (even hatred) of state intervention in the economy and socialism. Most monetarists probably subscribe to the set of free-market beliefs associated with these various terms. Nevertheless, as we have explained in the Unit, (in strictly narrow terms) an economist is a monetarist if he believes that the quantity theory of money holds and that inflation is caused by a prior increase in the money supply. On this basis, for example, it is perfectly possible for a Marxist to be a monetarist, though in the author's experience, left-wing monetarists are almost non-existent! Often, however, monetarism is interpreted in the wider meaning (that we have also explained in the Unit) and this is where monetarism and 'supply-side' economics perhaps become inextricably linked. Both terms are associated (along with the other terms and 'isms' we listed) with the **'free-market revival'** and the decline of Keynesianism as an influence at both the government and academic levels.

Answer plan

1 Distinguish between the 'narrow' and 'wider' meaning of monetarism.
2 Define 'supply-side' economics (see Unit 23).
3 Explain that monetarism, narrowly defined, need not be inextricably linked with supply-side economics.
4 Explain how in its broader and more popular meaning, monetarism and 'supply-side' economics do tend to become inextricably linked as part of the wider 'free-market' revival.

Multiple Choice Questions

(a)	(b)	(c)	(d)
1, 2, 3 all correct	1, 2 only correct	2, 3 only correct	1 only correct

Question 3 Which of the following statements might represent the views of a monetarist economist?
1 Inflation is primarily caused by trade union behaviour.
2 An increase in government spending is likely to reduce spending by the private sector.
3 In the long term governments cannot reduce unemployment below the natural rate.

Understanding the Question The first statement is wrong since monetarists believe that **governments** cause inflation by expanding the money supply and by attempting to reduce unemployment below its natural rate. However, according to monetarists, trade unions may cause unemployment by refusing to accept a real wage at which employers will voluntarily employ all the labour force at the 'natural' rate of employment. Unemployment can temporarily be reduced below the natural rate of unemployment, but only at the expense of an accelerating inflation that will eventually make the level of employment unsustainable. Thus statement three is a correct summary of an important monetarist view. Statement two is also correct; monetarists believe that expenditure by the state often 'crowds out' private spending. Since 2 and 3 are correct, the answer is therefore **(c)**.

Question 4 The main areas of dispute between monetarist and Keynesian economists include:

1 whether statutory incomes policies should be used to control inflation;
2 whether changes in the money supply cause changes in the price level;
3 whether government policy should attempt to make the economy more competitive.

Understanding the Question The answer to this question is **(b)** since only the first two statements are correct. Monetarists reject the use of statutory incomes policies, while many Keynesians recommend that an incomes policy be used as the principal instrument to control inflation. The second statement relates to a major area of controversy between monetarists and Keynesians; a popular Keynesian view is that the money supply **responds** to rather than **causes** changes in the price level. In contrast, there is no general dispute between Keynesians and monetarists on the virtues of competition policy, though monetarists probably place a greater emphasis upon it.

Data Response Questions

Question 5

The rehabilitation of market forces in the early 1980s was seen at first as an aberration from the post-war concensus, and one that was likely to be short-lived. But I have little doubt that, as a longer perspective develops, history will judge that intervention and planning were the aberration, and that the market economy is the normal, healthy way of life.

Needless to say, belief in the system of free markets does not imply that markets are infallible, any more than examples of irrational market behaviour in any way undermine belief in the market system. What matters is that free markets bring greater benefits and fewer (and more readily corrected) costs than statism.

This is a truth increasingly recognized throughout the world: the lesson that the way to economic success is through the market-place.

(Source: N. Lawson, *The State of the Market*, IEA Occasional Paper 80, 1988.)

(a) What did Mr Lawson mean in referring to the 'post-war consensus'?   (6)
(b) Critically appraise the statement that 'free markets bring greater benefits and fewer (and more readily corrected) costs than statism'.   (14)
(c) What examples might Mr Lawson have had in mind in support of his case in favour of market forces?   (5)

(*London S Level, June, 1990*)

Understanding the Question At the economic level, the **'post-war consensus'** referred to the wide measure of agreement amongst economists (during the three decades after 1945) on the virtues of Keynesianism and the mixed economy. At the political level, this was the **'Butskellite consensus'**, named after two centerist politicians, one Conservative (Rab Butler) and the other Labour (Hugh Gaitskell), who were influential in ensuring that every British government, from 1950 until the election of Mrs Margaret Thatcher's Conservative administration in 1979, subscribed to the 'post-war consensus'. The mix of private and public ownership and market and non-market provision of goods and services were regarded as 'about right for Britain'. The election of a Labour government might extend the state sector at the margin, via some extra nationalization, while conversely a Conservative administration (prior to 1979) might tinker with denationalization; but there was general agreement on the virtues of Keynesian-inspired management of aggregate demand and of state provision of public and merit goods such as education and the National Health Service.

The second part of the question calls for a discussion of whether the benefits of free (and presumably competitive) markets, in terms of consumer sovereignty and the various types of efficiency we have explained at length earlier in this book, exceed the disadvantages resulting from the many examples of market failure we have also explained. Under **'statism'**, market failure is regarded as so serious that state intervention completely replaces the market. Nigel Lawson probably had in mind a much different role for the state: essentially a **minimalist 'enabling' role** to create the competitive conditions in which markets can function efficiently. The examples Nigel Lawson might have had in mind (in 1988), in support of his case in favour of market forces, would include any benefits he believed had resulted from the programmes of privatizaton and deregulation pursued in the 1980s. Since 1988 many of the economic changes taking place in Eastern Europe might also be cited; though the move towards the marketization of formerly Communist, and 'statist' economies, has also exposed some of the deficiencies of exclusive reliance on the virtues of the market.

24.6 Further reading

Morris, D., editor, *The Economic System in the UK*, 3rd edition (Oxford University Press, 1985).
Chapter 8: Objectives and Instruments.

Lipsey, B. G., and Harbury, C., *First Principles of Economics*, (Weidenfeld & Nicolson, 1988)
Chapter 45: Macroeconomic Controversies

25 Trade

25.1 Points of perspective

The underlying basis for trade is the same whether trade takes place between individuals or business enterprises, on a regional basis **within** a country or **internationally** between countries. Although in this unit we shall concentrate on international trade, the basis for all voluntarily undertaken exchange and trade is the belief that both parties can gain. Trade begins when an individual productive enterprise produces an output that is surplus to its own needs, which it is able to exchange for the surplus of some other individual or productive enterprise, increasing the **welfare** of both. Before the development of money, the exchange was achieved through barter. Nowadays, a commonly accepted currency serves as the medium of exchange for internal trade within a country, but **payments difficulties** prevent the full development of international trade. Countries may lack a means of payment acceptable to other countries, and risks and uncertainties about **exchange rates** may reduce trade. Deliberately imposed restrictions on trade, such as **tariffs**, and other forms of **import control** may create further **barriers to trade**.

World trade is dominated by the advanced industrial nations, whose exports and imports usually exceed 20 per cent of GDP. Because of the size of its huge domestic market the USA is somewhat of an exception, with the value of US exports and imports equalling only about 8 per cent of GDP. The largest proportion of the trade of industrialized countries (the **'North'**) is with each other, rather than with the less developed countries (LDCs or the **'South'**). A considerable growth in 'North/South' trade may be necessary if the development gap between the countries of the world is to be reduced.

25.2 Underlying concepts

1 The case for specialization and trade

The general case for specialization and trade centres on the proposition that countries or regions can attain levels of production, consumption and economic welfare which are beyond the **production possibility frontier** open to them in a world without trade. Assuming full employment of all factors of production, a country can only increase the production of one good or service by diverting resources away from the production of other goods. Whenever resources are scarce, the **opportunity cost** of increasing the output of one industry is the alternative output foregone in other industries in the economy. If, however, a country concentrates scarce resources and factors of production into producing the goods in which it is most efficient, total world production can increase. Gains from specialization and trade are possible if countries can agree to exchange that part of the output which they produce that is surplus to their needs. Having stated the general case for trade, we shall now examine some more specific arguments in favour of specialization and trade.

2 The benefits of competition

In Unit 6 we explained how market forces operating in a perfectly competitive market economy can, subject to rather strong assumptions, achieve a state of **economic efficiency**, defined as a combination of **productive** and **allocative efficiency**. Within an isolated and relatively small economy, markets may be too small to be competitive and monopoly may predominate. Exposure to international competition is likely to make markets more competitive and hence more efficient.

3 The benefits of economies of scale and division of labour

The benefits of division of labour were first recognized in the 18th century by the great classical economist Adam Smith. Smith discussed the division of labour in the context of workers specializing in **different productive tasks** within a factory which itself specialized in producing a particular type of product. He then went on to extend the analysis to specialization between regions and countries. Thus, it should be stressed that there are many different levels at which the benefits of the division of labour can be attained: division of labour within a plant; division between plants within a firm; division between firms within an industry; division between industries within a country; and finally division of labour between countries.

Adam Smith suggested three reasons why division of labour increased production and efficiency:
 (i) workers become better at a particular task–**'practice makes perfect'**;
 (ii) time, which would be lost when workers move between tasks, is saved;

(iii) more and better capital can be employed in production.

The latter advantage cited by Smith is particularly important, since it is closely related to the benefits of economies of scale. If a country specializes in producing the goods in which it is already most efficient, a large scale of production may allow it to benefit from increasing returns to scale and economies of scale. In other words, its industries become even more efficient, when, for example, long production runs allow firms to introduce more advanced forms of machinery and improved technology. In the absence of international trade, the limited extent of the domestic market may prevent a country from benefiting from economies of scale. Thus, by **extending the market**, international trade and specialization allows the full benefits of the division of labour and economies of scale to be achieved (though we should also note that the possibility of **diseconomies of scale** and other disadvantages of the division of labour form the basis of a case against trade).

5 Increasing the range of choice

The **international immobility** of some factors of production and the **unique allocation of natural resources** in each country mean that the production possibilities open to each country are different. In the extreme, the production of some goods or services may be exclusive to a particular country. A simple example will show in this situation how wider choice can result from trade. If there are just two nations (A and B) and one can only produce bread and the other jam, then if each country's production exceeds its needs, both countries can gain by trading their surplus rather than letting it rot. Thus the welfare of each nation is increased as they both have bread **and** jam, rather than bread **or** jam.

25.3   Essential information

1 The principle of comparative advantage

Even when there are no economies of scale or increasing returns to scale, the theory of comparative advantage indicates that gains can still be realized from international trade. This is easiest to show when each country in our two-country model has an **absolute advantage** in producing either bread or jam, but is able to produce the other commodity if it wishes.

(i) Absolute advantage We shall assume:

(a) Factors of production are perfectly mobile **within** each country and they can be instantly switched between industries. However, factors are **immobile** between countries, though final goods and services can be traded.

(b) There are **constant returns to scale** and **constant average costs of production** in both industries in both countries.

(c) Both commodities, bread and jam, are in demand in both countries.

(d) The **limited** resources and factors of production in each country are fully employed.

Suppose now that each country has equal resources and devotes half of its limited resources to bread production and half to jam. The production totals are:

	Bread (units)	Jam (units)
Country A	10	5
Country B	5	10
'World' total	15	15

The relative or **comparative cost** of bread production is lower in country A than in country B, but the position is reversed in the production of jam. Country A has an **absolute advantage** in bread production, whereas the absolute advantage in jam production lies with country B. If each country specializes in the production of the commodity in which it is most efficient and possesses the absolute advantage, we get:

	Bread (units)	Jam (units)
Country A	20	0
Country B	0	20
'World' total	20	20

The gains from specialization and trade equal 5 units of bread and 5 units of jam, provided that there are no transport costs.

(ii) Comparative advantage It is less obvious that specialization and trade are also worthwhile even when a country can produce **all** goods more efficiently at a lower comparative cost than other countries. This phenomenon is explained by the principle of **comparative advantage**, or a comparison of the **relative efficiency** of production in different countries rather than their absolute efficiency.

Suppose that country A becomes more efficient in both bread and jam production. If each country devotes half its resources to each industry, the production totals are:

	Bread (units)	Jam (units)
Country A	30	15
Country B	5	10
'World' total	35	25

Country A possesses an absolute advantage in both industries, but whereas A is six times as efficient in bread production, it is only 50 per cent more efficient in jam production. Nevertheless, if country B produces an extra unit of jam, it need give up only half a unit of bread. In contrast, country A must give up two units of bread in order to increase production of jam by one unit. We say that a country's comparative advantage lies in the good which it can produce **relatively cheaply**, at a **lower opportunity cost** than its trading partner. Country A (which has the absolute advantage in both commodities) possesses a comparative advantage in bread production, whereas country B (with an absolute disadvantage in both) has the comparative advantage in jam production.

If each country specializes **completely** in the activity in which it possesses a comparative advantage, the production totals are:

	Bread (units)	Jam (units)
Country A	60	0
Country B	0	20
'World' total	60	20

You will notice that compared with the situation without specialization and trade in which each country devoted half its resources to each industry, there is a gain of 25 units of bread, but a loss of 5 units of jam. Thus in the case where one country is more efficient in both activities we cannot say, without some knowledge of demand and the value placed on consumption of bread and jam by the inhabitants of the two countries, whether a **welfare gain** will result from **complete** specialization. We can be more sure of a welfare gain if **at least as much of one good** and **more of the other** results from specialization and trade. We can obtain this result by devising a situation in which country A, the country with the absolute advantage in both goods, decides not to specialize completely, but to devote some of its resources to jam production. For example, if country A produces 5 units of jam with one-sixth of its resources and 50 units of bread with the other five-sixths, then the production totals are:

	Bread (units)	Jam (units)
Country A	50	5
Country B	0	20
'World' total	50	25

Compared with the situation without specialization and trade, there is a gain of 15 units of bread.

2 The terms of trade

The rate of exchange of bread for jam, or the **terms of trade**, will determine the benefits of trade for these trading partners. The **limits to the exchange** are set by each country's **opportunity cost ratio**. In the example where country A has an absolute advantage in the production of both goods, country A will be prepared to give up no more than 2 units of bread for 1 unit of jam, whilst country B will require at least ½ a unit of bread for 1 unit of jam if trade is to be worthwhile. Thus the terms of trade must lie between ½ unit of bread and 2 units of bread for 1 unit of jam. The exact rate of exchange, or the relative price of the two commodities, will be determined by the strength of demand.

In the real world where millions of goods and services are traded, a nation's average terms of trade are measured with **index numbers**. The average prices of exports and imports are calculated using **weighted indices** and the export index is divided by the import index to give the terms of trade index. A rise in the index shows an **improvement** in a nation's terms of trade, indicating that a given quantity of exports now pays for more imports than previously. We shall examine the causes and effects of changes in the terms of trade in greater detail in Units 26 and 27. It is worth noting, however, that a rise in the exchange rate of the £, and a domestic inflation rate higher than that of our trading partners, can both 'improve' the terms of trade, but that the effects of the 'improvement' are not necessarily beneficial in other respects.

3 The case against trade

The case **for** specialization and trade is based on the proposition that all countries taken together will gain in terms of increased production, efficiency and welfare, providing that the terms of trade lie within the opportunity cost ratios. However, there is no guarantee that the gains are distributed equally amongst the trading countries. Although restraints on free trade will probably reduce world welfare, individual countries may feel that it is in their self-interest to restrict the freedom of trade. Not all the arguments put forward to justify restrictions on trade are strictly economic; social and political factors are also involved.

(i) Economic arguments:

(a) The protection of 'infant industries' This argument is quite strong when there is scope for industries to benefit from **economies of scale.** A newly established industry, in for example a developing country, may be unable to compete with other countries in which established rivals are already benefiting from economies of scale. Protection may be justified during the early growth of an 'infant industry'.

(b) To avoid the dangers of overspecialization The benefits which result from specializing in accordance with the principle of comparative advantage will not be obtained if the **disadvantages of the division of labour** outweigh the advantages. **Diseconomies of scale** may be experienced. Agricultural overspecialization can result in **monoculture**, in which the growing of a single cash crop for export may lead to soil erosion, vulnerability to pests, and falling agricultural yields in the future. Overspecialization can also cause a country to be particularly vulnerable to sudden changes in demand or in the cost and availability of imported raw materials or energy, or to new inventions and changes in technology which eliminate its comparative advantage. The greater the **uncertainty about the future**, the weaker the case for complete specialization, If a country is self-sufficient in all important respects, it is effectively **neutralized** against the danger of importing recession and unemployment from the rest of the world if international demand collapses.

(c) To cushion home employment The model of comparative advantage assumes that factors of production are both fully employed and perfectly mobile within countries. If large-scale unemployment exists, there is a case for using factors **inefficiently** rather than not to employ them at all. Countries may also regard as unacceptable the costs of **structural** unemployment resulting from complete freedom of trade. Structural unemployment occurs when old industries decline in response to changes in either demand or comparative cost and advantage. There is a case for **selective** and **temporary** import controls to ease the problems of adjustment to the new conditions, whilst still accepting that in the long run trade should be encouraged and that a country should adapt to produce the goods in which it possesses a comparative advantage. Indeed the **New Cambridge School** have argued that import controls will boost the economy to such an extent that, although the **structure** of imports will change, the **volume** of imports will not actually fall once growth has taken place. This is the **paradox of import controls**, a counter to the free-trade view that 'what keeps imports out, keeps exports in.'

(d) To prevent dumping Exports are sometimes sold at a price below their cost of production and below the market price in the country of origin. Dumping may be motivated by the need to obtain foreign currency or a foothold in a foreign market, or by the hope of achieving productive economies of scale.

(e) To avoid 'unfair' competition It is sometimes claimed that low-wage countries in the developing world exploit local labour in order to produce cheap goods and that such activity is unfair. However, the developing countries are simply specializing in producing goods in which a plentiful supply of labour gives them a comparative advantage. It is essentially a value judgement whether this is 'fair' or 'unfair'.

(f) To raise revenue Tariffs are sometimes justified as a means of raising revenue for the government, but in modern economies this is a comparatively unimportant source of government revenue.

(ii) Political and social arguments:

(a) Economic sanctions Economic sanctions have been used for centuries to buttress political decisions. An **embargo** on trade may weaken a political enemy and it may also encourage co-operation between politically sympathetic countries. Embargoes and other import controls are often imposed on trade in armaments and military goods.

(b) Restrictions are also commonly placed on the trade in harmful goods (demerit goods) such as narcotic drugs.

(c) Restrictions may be imposed for **strategic reasons**, to ensure that a country is relatively self-sufficient in time of war.

4 Arguments against protectionism and restrictions on trade

We have already covered the principal arguments involved, in our explanation of the case for trade. We have shown that, subject to some rather strong assumptions about the full employment of resources and the nature of demand, welfare losses will result if countries fail to specialize in accordance with the principle of comparative advantage. Countries may use import controls and other restrictions on trade to gain a **short-term** advantage at the expense of other countries (the **'beggar my neighbour'** principle). However, **retaliation** by other countries is likely to cause a **long-term** welfare loss which is experienced by all countries, since protection props up inefficient and monopoly producers and redistributes income in favour of the protected.

5 Methods of protection

The decision to protect is made deliberately by a government. The method chosen may affect demand, supply or price. The demand for goods can be influenced by **tariffs, subsidies** and **exchange controls.** Supply can be manipulated by **embargoes, quotas, administrative restrictions and voluntary agreement.**

(i) Tariffs Tariffs, which may be **specific** or *ad valorem*, are taxes placed on imported, but not on domestic, goods. The ability of a tariff to reduce imports depends upon its size and upon the **elasticity of demand** for the imported good. If the country which imposes the tariff produces **close substitutes**, demand for imports is likely to be price elastic, In these circumstances, a tariff will reduce imports by **switching** demand towards the domestically produced substitutes. Conversely, if demand for imports is price inelastic, the main effect of the tariff will be on import prices rather than on the quantity of imports. (Refer back at this stage to the analysis in Unit 15 on the various effects which follow an increase in expenditure taxes. A tariff is simply an example of an expenditure tax.)

(ii) Subsidies These are provided in many, often clandestine, forms to avoid GATT restrictions on subsidies and dumping. The provision of export credit, VAT remission and regional aid may reduce total costs for exporters and thereby distort trade by affecting market prices. The support given by government agencies, such as the Export Credits Guarantee Department and the British Overseas Trade Board, to British exporters is envied by her European rivals! At the same time, subsidies to domestic producers enable them to compete more easily with imported goods.

(iii) Exchange Control Some nations control the amount of currency which can be used for buying imports. Usually foreign currency earnings (from exports) are deposited with the central bank, which authorizes the withdrawals for the buying of imports. In this way, selective control of imports can be achieved. In Britain up to 1979 when exchange control was abolished, transfers of cash and overseas investment were limited to protect the Balance of Payments.

(iv) Embargoes As we have already mentioned, some goods are completely banned from entry into a country. This encourages smuggling and the development of black markets.

(v) Quotas The import of a certain quantity of goods may be allowed, usually via licensing arrangements, for example footwear into the UK. Although acting on supply rather than demand, a quota has the same effects as a tariff in that it raises prices and domestic output whilst cutting the volume of imports.

(vi) Administrative Restrictions, documents and procedures are used by many nations as a covert method of protection. A Japanese trading practice considered by other countries to be unfair has been the withholding of information on product specifications from foreigners but warning domestic producers of changes well in advance. Similarly, Britain has refused to admit poultry from countries which use vaccination rather than slaughter as the means of controlling foul pest.

(vii)Voluntary Agreements One government may try to persuade another to pressurize its exporters into limiting supplies to certain markets, for example Japanese government restraint over Japanese car exports to the UK in 1981.

6 The General Agreement on Tariffs and Trade (GATT)

Towards the end of the Second World War, the American and British governments decided to establish new international institutions which would have the general aim of preventing a breakdown of world trade similar to the collapse which had contributed to the inter-war depression. The intention was to create an **International Trade Organization** (ITO) to liberalize trade, and an **International Monetary Fund** (see Units 27 and 28) to supervise the post-war system of payments and exchange rates. Because the charter to establish the ITO was never ratified, GATT, which was originally a temporary substitute for the ITO, survived as the most important international forum for expanding world trade and seeking the **multilateral** reduction of tariffs and other barriers to trade.

The General Agreement which came into operation in 1948 was based on four principles:

(i) **Non-discrimination** The **'most favoured nation' clause** binds countries to extend reductions in tariffs to the imports of all GATT members.

(ii) **Protection through tariffs** Where protection is justified, it should only be through tariffs and not through import quotas and other quantity controls.

(iii) **Consultation between members**

(iv) **Tariff reduction through negotiation** GATT should provide the framework through which successive **rounds** of tariff reduction are negotiated.

The history of GATT can be divided into two. During the 1950s and the 1960s the economic climate was such that countries were willing to negotiate tariff reductions, culminating in the 'Kennedy Round' of 1967. In more recent years, the main achievement of GATT has been in preventing members from reintroducing protectionist measures rather than in achieving any further notable liberalization of trade. The main advantages of tariff cuts have accrued to the advanced nations. In order to extend the tariff reductions of GATT to developing countries and to help primary producers, the United Nations established the **United Nations Conference on Trade and Development** (UNCTAD). This started in 1964 and meets every four years. However, because the problems of the developing countries are so diverse, co-operative trade developments have been limited.

7 Regional economic groupings

(i) **Free Trade Areas and Customs Unions** GATT allows the continuation of any system of tariffs in operation when GATT was signed. It also allows the creation of either a **Free Trade Area** (FTA) or a **Customs Union** (CU), both of which aim to liberalize trade between members, without extending most favoured nation treatment to non-members. Members of a FTA, such as the **Latin American Free Trade Area** (LAFTA), are free to choose their trading policy with outsiders. Britain was a founder member of the **European Free Trade Area** (EFTA), but left in 1973 to join the **European Community** (EC). The EC is a Customs Union, in which a **common external tariff** restricts members' freedom of action. A Customs Union usually involves a much closer economic integration between members, who adopt **common policies** additional to the common external tariff.

With the creation of a **Single European Market** after 1992, the EC will develop into a proper **common market**, before perhaps becoming a full **Economic and Monetary Union** and evolving into a **Political Union**. Common economic policies have been established which either considerably replace the freedom of separate policy action in member countries (the CAP and the Common Fishery Policy) or supplement the policies of individual members (Regional and Competition Policy). Most members of the EC are also members of the exchange rate mechanism of the **European Monetary System** (Unit 27), which has been interpreted as a step towards full **Monetary Union**.

The effect on a country of its joining a Customs Union will depend on the **size of the common external tariff**. on whether the tariff is applied to all traded goods, and on the **pattern** of the country's trade. If a growing proportion of the country's trade is with the members of the CU, then there may be a strong case for joining, particularly if the common external tariff is high. However, FTAs are more consistent with the philosophy of GATT than are Customs Unions. The latter are more likely to encourage trade between members by diverting trade from non-members. The distortive effects of the common external tariff on trade with the rest of the world can depend on the extent to which the CU is 'inward'- or 'outward'-looking. Customs Unions can be **trade-diverting** or **trade-reducing** rather than **trade-creating**. They do not take comparative advantage to its logical conclusion, favouring instead internal producers against lower-cost external producers. The members of the EC claim to be outward-looking, citing for example the Lomé Convention of 1975 (subsequently renewed) which enables sixty less developed countries to export duty free to the EC, and without reciprocity.

(ii) **Suppliers organizations** Occasionally, producing countries co-operate in order to exploit the world market, for example by forming an international **cartel**. Primary producing countries justify the formation of agreements such as that of the **Organization of Petroleum Exporting Countries** (OPEC) in order to countervail the market power of industrial countries. For most of the 20th century, the terms of trade have moved against primary producers and in favour of industrial countries.

Indeed, the adverse effects of the terms of trade on developing countries, together with profit remittances to developed countries, may have far exceeded the benefits of any **aid**. By creating a monopoly in the supply of a primary product, countries hope to reverse the movement in the terms of trade. International producers' cartels are most effective when governments can control supply, when there is unity of purpose and action amongst members, and when the demand of the industrialized countries is greatest.

8 British trade

Major changes have taken place in the structure of Britain's exports and imports over the last thirty years. As Table 25.1 illustrates, in 1955 over one-third of the United Kingdom's trade was with developing countries, while less than a third was with other European countries. This reflected what was still partly a 'traditional' pattern of trade in which the UK exported manufactured goods, largely to Commonwealth countries and other developing countries, in return for imports of food and raw materials. This pattern is now completely out of date, the current pattern of British trade being dominated by the exchange of both exports and imports with **other industrial countries**, particularly those in the EC.

Table 25.1: The geographical pattern of Britain's trade

Visible trade by area	1955		1985		1989	
	Imports %	Exports %	Imports %	Exports %	Imports %	Exports %
EC	12.6	15.0	46.0	46.3	52.6	50.3
Other West Europe	13.1	13.9	17.1	12.0	12.7	8.7
North America	19.5	12.0	13.8	17.0	12.6	15.3
Other developed	14.2	21.1	7.5	4.8	7.7	5.8
Total developed countries	59.4	62.0	84.3	80.0	85.6	80.1
Centrally planned economies	2.7	1.7	2.2	2.0	1.9	1.9
Oil-exporting countries	9.2	5.1	3.3	7.6	1.9	6.2
Other developing countries	28.7	31.2	10.0	10.1	10.6	11.8

The United Kingdom is by no means unusual in its pattern of trade. The largest part of the international trade of all industrialized countries is with other industrial countries. However, what Table 25.1 does not show is a major structural change which has turned the UK from being a net exporter to becoming a net importer of manufactured goods. This change is illustrated in Tables 25.2 and 25.3. From the beginning of the Industrial Revolution until about 1983, the UK benefited from a balance of trade surplus in manufactured goods. But in recent years, the **balance of trade in manufactured goods** has moved severely into deficit, reflecting both the declining competitiveness of British manufacturing in international markets and the absolute decline of manufacturing output which occurred in the years of deindustrialization in the early 1980s. The deficit in manufacturing goods cannot be blamed completely on the poor performance of more traditional industries such as shipbuilding and automobiles; the UK has a rather serious deficit in the trade of high-tech 'sunrise' industries in the field of information technology. Although by 1987 manufacturing output in the UK had recovered to the level achieved before the onset of severe deindustrialization, the balance of trade in manufactured goods has continued to deteriorate, causing a re-emergence of the UK's 'traditional' current deficit problem, despite North Sea oil's continuing contribution to the payments position. Table 25.3 shows how severe the deficit in the visible balance of trade would be without the contribution of North Sea oil, which most commentators believe reached its peak in 1985.

Table 25.2: The commodity pattern of Britain's trade

Visible trade by commodity	1955		1985		1989	
	Imports %	Exports %	Imports %	Exports %	Imports %	Exports %
Food, beverages, tobacco	36.2	6.5	10.9	6.3	9.5	7.0
Fuel	10.4	4.6	12.4	21.3	5.2	6.6
Industrial materials and semi-manufacturers	47.9	35.3	31.4	28.4	30.2	28.7
Finished manufacturers	5.2	49.1	43.7	41.3	50.0	47.6
Others	0.3	4.5	1.6	2.7	5.1	10.1

Table 25.3: Visible balance of trade

	£m 1975	£m 1985	£m 1989
Food, beverages, tobacco	−2701	−3592	− 4875
Fuel	−3057	+8163	− 71
Industrial materials and semi-manufacturers	− 915	−2549	− 9540
Finished manufacturers	+3241	−3102	−15 907
Others	+ 99	−1031	+ 3250
Total	−3333	−2111	−27 143

Trade in oil has, in fact, had several effects on the geographical pattern and commodity composition of Britain's exports and imports. Besides contributing directly to exports via sales of oil to the rest of the world, North Sea oil production has resulted in a considerable saving of oil imports. Less directly, via its effect on the Balance of Payments and an over-valued exchange rate, North Sea oil production undoubtedly contributed to the uncompetitiveness of British manufacturing industry, particularly in the early 1980s. (This is the so-called 'Dutch disease' effect, which we explain in Unit 26, though high interest rates, resulting from a tight monetary policy, have probably been mainly to blame for an overvalued exchange rate.) Finally, a further development has been the growth in importance, since about 1970, of the oil-exporting countries, particularly in the Middle East, as a market for UK manufacturing exports.

25.4 Links with other topics

Although trade gives an international dimension to economics, the theory of trade is essentially based on the concepts of scarcity, production possibilities and opportunity cost, division of labour and economies of scale which we first introduced in Units 1 to 6. We now examine some of the complications, distortions and barriers to trade which result from the fact that countries may lack an acceptable means of payment for trade (Unit 26 on the Balance of Payments), while in Unit 27 we see how exchange rates can cause further distortions and uncertainties.

25.5 Question practice

Essay Questions

Question 1 In recent years there have been increased calls in many countries for the reintroduction of import controls.
(a) What forms may import controls take?   (10)
(b) Discuss the economic arguments for and against a return to trade protectionism.   (15)

(AEB: June, 1990)

Understanding the Question For the first part of the question, list and briefly describe the main forms of import controls; dividing them into physical restrictions, such as embargos and quotas on the one hand and on the other, tariffs and export subsidies which distort the relative prices of imports and exports. You might also mention how administrative procedures and bureaucracy can deter imports; and explain less direct forms of import control such as foreign exchange controls and the promotion of an undervalued exchange rate.

   Structure the second part of your answer around the 'free trade versus import control' arguments, making sure you introduce comparative advantage into your discussion. Import controls may be a 'second best' solution to counter the protectionism already introduced by other countries; you might argue that the 'first best' alternative would be to persuade all countries to abandon import controls.

Answer plan

1 Classify import controls into physical restrictions and policy measures that affect the relative price of imports.
2 List and briefly describe at least four types of import control.
3 Explain that protectionism already affects the pattern of world trade, arguably giving an unfair competitive advantage to those countries enjoying protection.
4 There is therefore, a case for those countries currently at a disadvantage to introduce retaliatory import controls.
5 Briefly explain some of the standard arguments in favour of protectionism: infant industry arguments; ensuring the orderly decline of 'sunset' industries; anti-dumping, etc.
6 Explain, using the principles of comparative advantage, how nevertheless, if all countries introduce protectionism, there will be an output and efficiency loss compared to a situation without protectionism.

Question 2

(a) Explain the difference between a 'free trade area', a 'customs union' and a 'common market'.   (10)
(b) To what extent does the European Community match the above theoretical models?   (10)

(Cambridge AS: June, 1989)

Understanding the Question Free trade areas (FTAs), customs unions and common markets are all examples of trading blocs in which free trade is promoted internally; while the whole bloc is protected against external competition to a greater or lesser degree. As we have explained in the Unit, each member of an FTA is free to choose its own tariff levels against non-members, whereas a customs union binds all its members to accept a common external tariff. To discourage imports from countries outside the FTA gaining low-tariff access to the markets of all the members (by entering the FTA via the member country with the lowest external tariff), FTAs normally have a **'country of original' rule**. For example, the rule might specify that 80 per cent of the content of any traded good must originate within a member country to qualify for tariff-free internal trade. A variation of the 'country of origin' rule is also used in customs unions such as the European Community. Japanese or American companies such as Nissan or General Motors, locating a factory in the UK, are required to manufacture a large proportion of their finished products from local components and raw materials in order to gain tariff-free access to the wider EC market.

The EC is in the process of achieving the transformation, to be completed in 1992, from customs union to full common market. Besides the abolition of all internal tariffs and other import controls, a full common market requires the abolition of restrictions on the movement of capital and labour between member countries, and the adoption of similar policies in member countries towards competition and trading restrictive practices.

Answer plan

1 Define precisely the three forms of trading bloc, emphasizing the differences that separate them.
2 Explain that the EC was established as a customs union, with aspirations of becoming a full common market, and possibly eventually an economic (and even a political?) union.
4 1992 marks the transition of the EC into a full common market. Explain its implications and any aspects in which you think the transition may be incomplete.

Questions 3 and 4 These refer to the following information:
In a simple model of international trade there are two countries, A and B, and two commodities, guns and butter. When each country divides its resources equally between the two products they produce as follows:

	Guns (units)	Butter (units)
Country A	600	400
Country B	800	200

Question 3 Assuming constant returns to scale, if each country specializes in producing the commodity in which it has a comparative advantage, total output will increase by:

(a) 200 units of guns
(b) 400 units of guns and 200 units of butter
(c) 200 units of guns and 200 units of butter
(d) 200 units of guns and 400 units of butter

Question 4 Which of the following would improve the terms of trade of country A?

(a) An increase in the world price of butter
(b) An increase in the world price of guns
(c) An increase in the volume of butter exports
(d) The imposition of a tariff on the exports of country B

Understanding the Questions This is a simple model of absolute advantage in which country A has an absolute advantage in the production of guns and B has an absolute advantage in butter. It is obviously the case that each country has a comparative advantage in the commodity in which it has an absolute advantage. Total 'world production' is 1400 units of guns and 600 units of butter without specialization, whereas output increases to 1600 guns and 800 units of butter when each country specializes in the activity in which it has a comparative advantage. The correct answer to Question 3 is therefore **(c)**.

The terms of trade move in a country's favour if its export prices rise relative to the price of imports. Since country A exports butter, the commodity in which it has a comparative advantage, the answer to Question 4 is **(a)**.

Data Response Questions

Question 5 Study Figure 1 and Figure 2 on pages 220 and 221, then answer the questions below.

(a) Describe and account for the pattern of world trade flows in 1982 shown in Figure 1.

(b) Briefly compare the growth of the international trade of industrialized countries with that of developing countries over the years 1972 to 1982.

(c) Discuss, with reference to the data, the trading problems of devloping countries in the nineteen-eighties.   (*AEB: November, 1986*)

Understanding the Question The most important single feature of Figure 1 is the importance of intra-trade between the advanced industrial areas. Other significant features of the pattern of world trade include: (i) the trade surplus of the oil-exporting developing countries, both with the industrial countries and with the non oil-producing developing world; (ii) the overall trade deficit of the non oil-producing developing countries with all other types of country; (iii) the relative unimportance in world trade of trade between the Communist or Eastern Trading Area and the rest of the world; and (iv) the relative lack of intra-trade between developing countries.

Having identified the main features of the pattern of trade – and having resisted the temptation merely to 'write out the data' – you must now account for the changes you have noted. As well as explaining the pattern in terms of comparative advantage and the effects of trading blocks, you might also introduce **dependency**, **technology gap**, and **product cycle theories**. A **dependency theory** explains the present pattern of trade in developing countries in terms of the fact that Third World countries possess

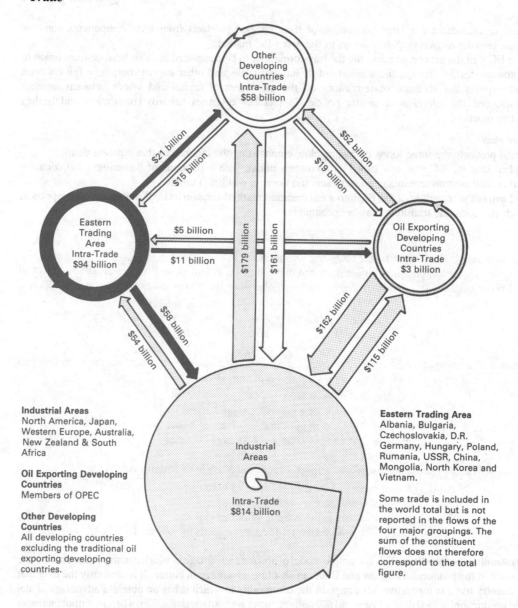

Figure 1: World trade flows

Source: *GATT International Trade* and *Barclays Bank Review*

little capital because the system of world trade and payments has been organized by the developed industrial countries to their own advantage. **Technology gap** theories explain the pattern of trade in terms of the nature of technical progress. Advanced industrial countries are usually the leaders and this gives them an advantage, reinforced by economies of scale, allowing long production runs, which the monopoly position of the innovating country creates. However, when the technology 'matures' and becomes available to other countries, comparative advantage may shift to the developing world. Indeed, Third World countries may take the lead in developing later generations of the new technology, and the original leaders may suffer the disadvantage of factories fitted with what has become out-of-date equipment. Often foreign subsiduaries of multi-national firms produce a good and export it back to the original pioneering country which has gone on to develop further products and technologies.

Like the technology gap theory, the **product cycle** theory explains the pattern of world production, specialization and trade in manufactured goods in terms of the nature of technical progress. Early in its **life cycle** and immediately following successful innovation, a product is likely to be strongly differentiated from competing products. At this stage of the product's life cycle, manufacture is usually located in the country of origin of the innovative company, where research and development facilities arte concentrated. However, at a later stage the company loses its monopoly over existing technology when the product becomes more standardized with agreed international specifications and when mass production combines economies of scale with the application of routine, relatively unskilled labour. The advanced economies lose their comparative advantage and production shifts to the newly industrializing countries of the developing world.

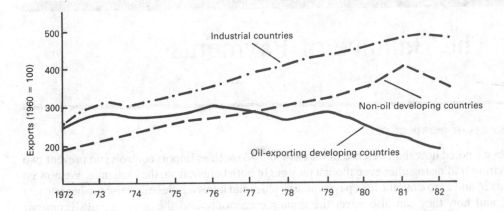

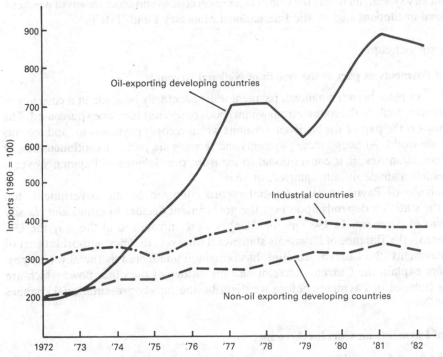

Figure 2: Growth in volume of world trade

Source: *Barclays Bank Review*, May 1984

25.6   **Further reading**

Begg. D., Fischer, S., and Dornbusch, R., *Economics*, 3rd edition (McGraw Hill, 1991).
Chapter 32: International Trade and Commercial Policy
Lipsey, R. G., *An Introduction to Positive Economics*, 7th edition (Weidenfeld & Nicolson, 1989).
Chapter 21: The Gains from Trade
Chapter 22: Barriers to Trade

26 The Balance of Payments

26.1 Points of perspective

In Unit 25 we noted how the existence of **barriers to trade** such as import controls can prevent two countries from trading together even though they might both benefit from the exchange. We now go on in Units 26 and 27 to examine how **payment difficulties and uncertainties** can cause further barriers to trade, and how they can also affect the domestic economy and the government's economic management thereof. This unit concentrates on a country's **balance of payments**, while Unit 27 looks at the interrelated question of the **exchange rate**. We also introduce important aspects of the **international monetary system**, including the role of **reserve currencies** and other means of payment, and of **international institutions** such as the **International Monetary Fund** (IMF).

26.2 Underlying concepts

1 The Balance of Payments as part of the system of National Accounts

Whenever trade takes place between nations, payment must eventually be made in a currency or means of payment acceptable to the country from whom goods or services have been purchased. The **Balance of Payments** is the part of the **National Accounts** which records payments to, and receipts from, the rest of the world. Although these payments and receipts are part of a **continuous flow** of currencies between countries, it is conventional to measure the Balance of Payments over a time-period of either a single month, quarter, or year.

Since the Balance of Payments is an official record collected by the government, the presentation of the statistics depends upon how the government decides to group and classify the different items of payment. In 1987 major changes were introduced in the way the UK Government presents the Balance of Payments statistics. However, the most important part of the Balance of Payments, the **Current Account**, has remained unaffected by the new changes. We shall therefore explain the Current Account and the nature of the other flows which are measured in the Balance of Payments before we describe the purely presentational changes introduced in 1987.

2 The Balance of Payments on Current Account

This measures the flow of expenditure on **goods** and **services** and broadly indicates the income gained and lost from **trade**. The Current Balance is the most important part of the Balance of Payments because it reflects the international competitiveness of the UK economy and the extent to which the UK is living within its means. If receipts from exports exceed payments for imports, there is of course a Current Account **surplus**. The Current Balance is obtained by simply adding the **Balance of Visible Trade** to the **Balance of Invisible Trade**.

(i) The Balance of Visible Trade Although visible trade is the most important single item in the Balance of Payments, it is perhaps the most simple to define. The Visible Balance measures the value in pounds sterling of **goods** exported, minus the value of goods imported. The Visible Trade Balance is often known simply as the **Balance of Trade**, a rather misleading term since it implies (falsely) that all trade, including invisibles (or services) are included, when in fact the Balance of Trade measures only trade in goods or visibles.

(ii) The Balance of Invisible Trade In general terms this measures the sterling value of **services** exported minus the value of services imported. However, the Invisible Balance includes a number of rather disparate items. For example, invisible **exports** include:

(a) a large part of the earnings of the City of London, insurance and brokerage services, etc.;

(b) the overseas earnings of British shipping and aviation services;

(c) expenditure by overseas governments on embassies and military bases in the UK;

(d) spending by foreign tourists;

(e) gifts of money from overseas residents to British residents;

(f) dividends or profits remitted to British residents owning capital assets overseas – the difference between such profit inflows and outflows is sometimes known as **net property income from abroad**.

Conversely any payments from British residents to overseas residents for shipping services, tourism, the upkeep of embassies, etc., are **invisible imports**. In recent years Britain's **net contribution to the EEC budget** has developed into an important invisible import. Some forms of **aid to developing countries** are also classified in the invisible account.

3 The changing nature of the UK Current Account

For most of the 20th century the British Balance of Payments on Current Account displayed a **deficit** on the balance of visible trade and a **surplus** on the invisible balance, both of which could be explained by the **principle of comparative advantage**. The emergence of other competing industrial countries reduced or eliminated Britain's comparative advantage in many manufacturing industries but, until very recently at least, she still retained her advantage in services. Whether the overall Balance on Current Account was in surplus or deficit in any single year depended on whether the invisible surplus was sufficient to offset the visible deficit.

From the 1970s onwards significant changes have occurred in the composition of the Current Account:

(i) The contribution of North Sea oil revenue moved the visible balance into surplus (for a while), both through import-saving and oil exports. From about 1976 onwards and reaching a peak in the mid-1980s, North Sea oil revenues transformed the Current Account from deficit into surplus.

(ii) However, this disguised the continuing deterioration of the balance of non-oil visible trade, reflecting the growing propensity to import in the UK and the uncompetitiveness of British manufacturers. Indeed, it is useful nowadays to divide the visible balance into the separate catagories of the **oil balance** and the **non-oil balance** of visible trade and also into the **balance of trade in manufactured goods** and **non-manufactures**. The balance of trade in manufactured goods remained in surplus from the 18th century through to the early 1980s, reflecting the importance of the United Kingdom as a manufacturing economy. In 1982, however, Britain's imports of manufactured goods began to exceed her exports of manufactures, moving the balance of trade in manufactured goods into deficit for the first time since before the Industrial Revolution. In part this reflects the fact that the revenues of North Sea oil have been largely used to finance improved short-term standards of living through the import of consumer goods and foodstuffs, rather than investment. It also reflects the **deindustrialization** process, or structural decline of a significant part of UK manufacturing industry which occurred in the early 1980s. Although since 1983 there has been a slow recovery of manufacturing output, the balance of trade in manufactured goods has continued to display a growing deficit.

(iii) The importance of invisible trade and services in the Current Account has continued to grow in recent years. Invisible exports accounted for 38.5 per cent of total credits in 1970, rising to 51.9 per cent in 1984 and 54.0 per cent in 1989. The contribution of invisible exports to Britain's total trade earnings is thus now greater than that of trade in goods. Invisible imports have also grown in relative importance, from 34.3 per cent of total imports in 1970 to 47.2 per cent in 1989. In part, the growth of invisibles, in both absolute and relative importance, reflects the changing pattern of world trade, in which the richest countries of the world increasingly trade services with each other. The spectacular growth of invisible exports reflects also a surge in dividend income, under net property income from abroad. Following the abolition of exchange controls in 1979, UK residents and companies invested large capital funds overseas. These investments are now profitable, remitting sufficient income to offset the falling contribution of North Sea oil to the visible trade account. However, in the early 1990s, the UK's invisible surplus has dwindled, causing the fear that it may disappear completely. Growing international competition in the provision of services (e.g. tourism, financial services), together with the outward interest payments required to service the capital flows that finance the Current Account deficit, have reduced the invisible surplus.

4 Capital flows Before 1987 the United Kingdom government divided the Balance of Payments into three sections:

(i) The Current Account;

(ii) Investment and Other Capital Flows (sometimes known as the Capital Account);

(iii) Official Financing.

In the presentational changes of the accounts introduced in 1987, **Investment and Other Capital Flows** and **Official Financing** have disappeared from the official accounts. They have been merged together into a new **Transactions in External Assets and Liabilities** section which, together with the Current Account, form the new official Balance of Payments tables.

However, before we can understand the new system of presenting the Balance of Payments, we must first explain the meaning of capital flows and official financing.

An **outward capital flow** takes place when a country's residents purchase assets in another country. Conversely, an **inward capital flow** describes a movement of capital funds into the country as residents of other countries purchase domestic assets. **Net capital flows** are, of course, the difference between outward and inward investment. A positive net capital flow over a period of years means that the country's residents – including its companies – are acquiring overseas assets which are greater in total than those of the country's own assets which are being acquired by the rest of the world. Following the abolition of exchange controls in 1979, the UK has been a very large net exporter of long-term capital. In a sense, UK residents have 'spent' North Sea oil revenues earned in the Current Account, on acquiring overseas assets which are likely to continue to pay dividends – received as invisible exports in the Current Account – long after North Sea oil has run dry. The UK is now the second largest owner of external capital assets after Japan. By contrast, the USA has become a net debtor nation in the sense that other countries now own more assets in America than the US owns in the rest of the world.

In order to understand further the importance of capital flows in the Balance of Payments, it is useful to distinguish between **long-term** and **short-term** capital flows.

(i) Long-term capital flows We can explain long-term capital flows by invoking the principle of comparative advantage, which explained the nature of visible trade. A long-term capital flow occurs when residents of one country buy up or invest in the productive resources **within** another country. They will do so if they believe that their financial assets can be more productively and profitably employed in the other country.

A net outflow of long-term capital means that there is more investment by British residents in real assets in other countries than there is foreign investment in Britain. Such an outflow includes both **real** or **direct investment**, when for example a British company buys or creates a foreign subsidiary, and **portfolio investment**, when British residents purchase the shares of overseas companies or the securities of foreign governments.

(ii) Short-term capital flows Since changes in comparative advantage usually take place relatively slowly, the long-term capital flows tend to be stable and predictable. Movements in the Balance of Payments resulting from the changing pattern of either trade or of long-term capital flows are said to be **spontaneous** or **autonomous**. In contrast short term capital flows are neither stable nor predictable, and they frequently occur in response to a change in the autonomous part of the Balance of Payments. A growing proportion of the short-term flows is extremely volatile **'hot money'** which, by flowing into – and just as quickly out of – countries, can destabilize the Balance of Payments, the exchange rate, and indeed the international monetary system as a whole. Hot money is the name given to the pool of 'footloose' hard currencies owned by governments, banks, businesses and private individuals, usually outside the exchange controls of the currency's country of origin. A major cause of the growth of hot money flows lies in the emergence of the **Eurodollar market** after 1957.

The pool of Eurodollars grew dramatically in the 1960s and 1970s when the USA persuaded other countries to accept payment for the US Balance of Payments deficit in dollars. Some of these dollars were received in payment for American imports, but others arose from capital investment overseas by American firms and the growth of overseas bank deposits owned by American residents. The early growth of the Eurodollar market was prompted by the imposition of restrictions by the American monetary authorities upon the domestic banking system. In the absence of exchange controls, it became more profitable for American residents to keep their dollars in overseas bank accounts, often in the subsidiaries of US banks, rather than in deposits held within the USA.

From these origins in the late 1950s and 1960s the Eurodollar market has grown, hugely supplemented by the injection of **'petrodollars'** after the oil crises in the 1970s when the OPEC countries accumulated large balance of payments surpluses matched by deficits in the oil-consuming industrial countries. The oil-producing countries placed a significant proportion of their oil revenues on deposit in the European banking system, thus adding to the pool of footloose hot money. Indeed the market is perhaps better called the **Eurocurrency market**. Although the dollar is still the most important currency deposited, other currencies such as sterling and the Deutschmark are also involved.

The European banks, including those in London, have developed a thriving business in the short-term borrowing and lending of international currencies, outside the exchange controls which may exist in their countries of origin. These Eurocurrency flows are extremely destabilizing because the sheer size of the hot money pool means that the financial markets and balance of payments of a single country can be overwhelmed by a sudden inward or outward flow which may often occur for essentially speculative reasons. A hot money flow into a country may be triggered by high rates of interest, by the belief that the exchange rate is undervalued, or by an event such as a Middle East war, when currencies are shifted into countries that are regarded as 'safe havens' for funds. The movement of funds into a country on a large scale itself puts upward pressure on the exchange rate since it creates a demand for the local currency on foreign exchanges, when for example government securities are purchased by the overseas owners of hot money. Conversely, a sudden outflow can cause a rapid deterioration in the balance of payments and downward pressure on the exchange rate.

5 Accommodating flows

Like all balance-sheets, the Balance of Payments must balance, at least in a strictly accounting sense. This means that all the items in the Balance of Payments must **sum to zero**. In principle, therefore, if the **autonomous** Current Account and capital flows are in surplus or deficit, the surplus or deficit must be financed by an equal **accommodating flow**, to make the balance-sheet sum to zero.

Traditionally, changes in **official reserves** and **official borrowing**, for example from foreign central banks or from the International Monetary Fund, were regarded as the principal accommodating flows. The current and capital flows added together formed the **Balance of Payments for Official Financing**, which was financed or accommodated by changes in reserves and in official borrowing in the third part of the Balance of Payments: the **Official Financing** section. For example, if the autonomous or spontaneous current and capital flows showed a deficit of −£2000m, this would be financed by a loss of reserves, or by official borrowing of + £2000m. (For accounting reasons, the loss of reserves would be represented by a plus sign!) In this way the Balance of Payments is balanced.

6 The 1987 changes in presentation of the Balance of Payments

We have just explained how, in principle, the Balance of Payments deficit or surplus, obtained by adding together the Current Account and capital flows, is financed or accommodated by changes in official reserves or by official borrowing. This reflects the fact that the Current Account and capital flows have traditionally been regarded as **spontaneous** or **autonomous**, i.e. based on the decisions of private economic agents to trade, while the Official Financing section of the Balance of Payments was purely **accommodating**. However, it is now realized that this separation of autonomous and accommodating flows is rather artificial. In recent years a Current Account deficit or surplus has been financed not so much by official financing involving a change in reserves, as by private sector capital flows. Indeed, such capital flows which finance or accommodate the Current Account have been actively encouraged and used by the authorities as an alternative to official financing. While it is usually difficult for the authorities to influence quickly the largely autonomous long-term capital flows (except through the imposition or removal of exchange controls and tax advantages), this is not true of short-term or 'hot money' flows. In the case of a Current Account deficit, the authorities may raise interest rates in order to engineer a hot money inflow, thereby avoiding the need to draw on official reserves to finance the deficit. Conversely, when North Sea oil revenues moved the Current Account into surplus, the authorities preferred to encourage a capital outflow rather than finance the surplus through an accumulation of reserves.

In large part, this reflects the change of the exchange rate regime from **fixed exchange rates** to **floating exchange rates**. As we explain further in Unit 27, when the exchange rate is fixed,

Table 26.1: The New Presentation of the Balance of Payments

		1989 £m
	Current Account	
	Visibles	−23 112
	Invisibles	+4045
A	Current Balance	−19 067
	UK external assets and liabilities	
	Transactions in assets	−84 419
	Transactions in liabilities	+88 462
B	Net Transactions	+4043
C	Balancing item	+15 024
	A + B + C	≡ 0

the authorities must actively use official reserves to finance a Balance of Payments deficit or surplus, in order to prevent the exchange rate moving from its fixed parity. When exchange rates were floated in the 1970s, this requirement largely disappeared, and the authorities preferred to allow private sector capital flows rather than changes in reserves to finance the Current Account. The entry into the exchange rate mechanism of the EMS, which took place in 1990, marks a return to a relatively fixed exchange rate. This implies that changes in official reserves must take place once again to support the exchange rate.

Table 26.1 shows the new presentation of the Balance of Payments which was introduced when the 1986 statistics were first published in 1987.

As we have already noted, there have been no changes in the presentation of the Current Account. However, the distinction between capital flows and official financing has now been dropped, reflecting the fact that in recent years private sector capital flows, rather than changes in reserves, financed any Current Account imbalance. The new **'transactions' section** of the Balance of Payments therefore comprises all private and public sector movements of capital funds. **'Transactions in assets'** measure the outward flow of funds, including investment flows, while **'transactions in liabilities'** represent the inward flow – the rest of the world's assets held in the UK being the United Kingdom's liabilities.

We have already explained that these changes reflect the decreased importance of official financing in the 1980s. Yet, by 1987 when the new presentation was introduced, the exchange rate was being managed by 'shadowing' the DM in preparation for full entry into the EMS. Thus, at a time when the exchange rate was becoming more like a fixed exchange rate, a new presentation of the Balance of Payments was introduced; more appropriate to a freely-floating system than a fixed system.

7 The Balancing Item

The official estimates of the Balance of Payments will seldom be accurate, because of the imperfect nature of data collection. For this reason, a **'Balancing Item'** – analogous to the residual error in the National Accounts – must be added or subtracted as the last item in the Balance of Payments in order to make the balance-sheet sum to zero. In the years following the first publication of the Balance of Payments, statistics for a particular year are constantly revised. A very large Balancing Item – as illustrated in Table 26.1 – means that not much faith should be attached to any interpretation of the first publication. It is usual for the figures for both the Current Account and capital flows to change and for the Balancing Item to become smaller as it is gradually 'allocated' to one or other of the 'real' items in the Balance of Payments. In this way, an apparent Current Account surplus on first publication may become a deficit when the figures are revised, or vice versa.

26.3   Essential knowledge

1 Balance of Payments equilibrium and disequilibrium

Although in an accounting sense the balance of payments always balances, this can obscure the fact that a country's payments may not be in a state of equilibrium. **Balance of Payments equilibrium** (or **external equilibrium**) is usually taken to mean that the **desired spontaneous** or **autonomous trade and capital flows** into and out of the country are equal over a number of years. A state of equilibrium in the balance of payments is perfectly compatible with the existence of **short-term** surpluses and deficits. But a **fundamental disequilibrium** in the balance of payments will exist if there is a persistent tendency for the autonomous flows out of the country to be greater or less than the corresponding inflows. When for example a persistent deficit occurs in the autonomous items in the balance of payments, it must be accommodated by a loss of reserves, by official borrowing or by 'unofficial' borrowing via a hot money inflow in the transactions section of the Balance of Payments.

2 The problem of a Balance of Payments deficit

While a short-run deficit or surplus on the Current Account of the Balance of Payments seldom poses a problem, the same is not true when a persistent imbalance indicates a fundamental disequilibrium. It is easy to see why a persistent deficit in the autonomous items in the Balance of Payments is a problem, since the resulting loss of reserves and need for borrowing cannot be maintained indefinitely. However, the extent of the problem depends on a number of factors, including the **size of the deficit, its cause** and the **exchange rate regime**.

Obviously, the larger the deficit the greater the problem is likely to be, but it also depends upon which items are in deficit. For example, an overall deficit caused by a long-term capital outflow may produce the long-term benefit of an eventual profits inflow in the invisibles section of the Current Account. In contrast, if the cause of the deficit lies in the Current Account the problem may be more serious. Although a trade deficit allows the country's residents to enjoy a higher standard of living than would be possible from the consumption of the country's output alone, it may also reflect the uncompetitiveness of the country's goods and services.

In the next unit we shall examine in some detail the effect of different exchange rate regimes upon the balance of payments. In this unit we can merely note that a payments deficit is usually considered more of a problem under **fixed exchange rates** than when the exchange rate is **freely floating**. In a floating regime the market mechanism may eliminate the cause of export uncompetitiveness and restore an equilibrium in the balance of payments. In contrast, when the exchange rate is fixed the government usually has to take action through **deflation, import controls, devaluation** of the exchange rate, or a combination of all three.

In the 1960s and 1970s it was widely believed that the British balance of payments posed a problem in the sense that in a fixed exchange rate regime the exchange rate was 'unavailable' as a policy instrument to cure the persistent payments deficit that Britain experienced at that time. This meant that the **internal** policy objectives of full employment and growth had to be sacrificed to the **external** objective of protecting the balance of payments and supporting the exchange rate, which imposed a serious **constraint** on the sustained achievement of the domestic policy objectives. Floating the exchange rate was regarded as an 'escape route' from this constraint; a floating exchange rate would 'look after' the Balance of Payments, allowing economic policy to be devoted to the internal objectives.

However, the experience of floating exchange rates after 1972–albeit **dirty** or **managed** floating rather than **clean** or **freely floating** exchange rates–has led to considerable disenchantment with this view. Countries have still intervened to protect the balance of payments and to support the exchange rate. In particular there has been a growing awareness of the effects of a falling exchange rate on the domestic inflation rate and the pursuit of internal policy objectives. It is now generally accepted that even with a floating exchange rate the Balance of Payments cannot be completely isolated from the pursuit of internal economic policy. These issues are discussed further in Units 25 and 27.

3 The problem of a Balance of Payments surplus

While it is generally accepted that a persistent Balance of Payments deficit is a problem, it is much less obvious that a surplus can also pose problems. Indeed, because a surplus is often regarded as a symbol of national economic success, many people argue that the bigger the surplus, the more successful the country must be. Nevertheless there are a number of reasons why a persistently large surplus is undesirable, even though a small surplus may be a more justifiable objective of policy:

(i) One country's surplus is another country's deficit It is impossible for all countries simultaneously to run surpluses. If countries refuse to reduce their persistently large surpluses, then deficit countries will find it difficult, and even impossible, to reduce their deficits. The danger then arises that deficit countries will resort to import controls and all countries may suffer from a consequent reduction or collapse in world trade. In recent years the danger posed to the development of world trade by excessive surpluses and deficits has been well illustrated by the problem of recycling the surpluses of the oil-producing countries, though these surpluses have now almost disappeared.

(ii) The 'Dutch disease' effect The growth of Britain's own oil trade surplus in the 1970s and 1980s illustrates another way in which a surplus can create a problem. In 1980 and 1981 the Current Account surplus, reinforced by hot money inflows, caused the exchange rate to rise to a level which decreased the competitiveness of non-oil visible exports in world markets, and increased the competitiveness of imports in the UK economy. This accelerated the **de-industrialization** of the British economy and caused much of the benefit of North Sea oil revenues to be 'lost' in financing imports and the upkeep of the growing number of unemployed. The effect of the balance of payments surplus upon the exchange rate and the domestic economy is called the **'Dutch disease'** after the experience of the Netherlands following the discovery and development of natural gas in the 1950s and 1960s.

(iii) In Keynesian terms, a balance of payments surplus represents an **injection of demand** into the economy, causing **demand-pull inflation** if output cannot be raised to meet demand.

(iv) The money supply and a balance of payments surplus In an open economy the domestic money supply is affected by the balance of payments; a surplus tends to increase and a deficit to decrease the money supply unless the exchange rate is freely floating. When the balance of payments is in surplus, the country's currency is in short supply on foreign exchange markets. If the authorities wish to prevent the exchange rate from rising in response to the excess demand, they must buy the foreign currencies being offered in the market, giving their own currency in exchange. The nation's foreign currency reserves expand, but only at the expense of an increase in the money supply. The process of selling the country's own currency and buying reserves in order to prevent the exchange rate from rising is an example of **exchange equalization**.

The extent to which a balance of payments surplus (or deficit) leads to an increase (or decrease) in the money supply depends upon the exchange rate policy being pursued. A 'clean' or pure float can eliminate the external imbalance with little or no change in either the reserves or the money supply, but if the exchange rate is fixed or managed quite large changes in both can result. The impact of the balance of payments upon the domestic money supply clearly poses a problem for **monetarist economic policy**, with its emphasis on the need to control the rate of growth of the money supply.

Indeed, when the Balance of Payments is in deficit, **Domestic Credit Expansion (DCE)** is a better measure of liquidity in the domestic economy than money supply measures such as M3 and M4. Broadly, DCE is the money supply plus (or minus) the Balance of Payments deficit (or surplus). Thus, when the current account is in deficit, DCE exceeds the money supply which falls as the authorities use reserves to 'buy back' pounds in order to support the exchange rate.

4 Policies to cure a fundamental disequilibrium in the Balance of Payments

We shall now discuss in more detail the various policy measures of **deflation**, the imposition of **import controls**, and **devaluation** (or a **managed** or **'dirty' downward float**), which can be used to correct a persistent balance of payments deficit. (In Unit 27 we shall discuss how a payments disequilibrium is **automatically** corrected without the need for government intervention under **freely floating** and **rigidly fixed (gold standard)** exchange rates.)

(i) **Deflation** Both **fiscal policy** and **monetary policy** can be used to deflate the level of demand in an economy in order to correct a payments deficit. Deflation is primarily an **expenditure-reducing policy** which cures a deficit by reducing the demand for imports. The increase in unused capacity produced by the deflation may also encourage firms to seek extra export orders, though many economists argue that a sound and expanding home market is necessary for a successful export drive since exports are usually less profitable than domestic sales. A deflation can also have a subsidiary **expenditure-switching effect** upon the Balance of Payments. Successful deflation results in the domestic inflation rate falling relative to that in other countries, thereby increasing the **price competitiveness** and demand for British exports, while reducing the demand for imports.

However, a deflationary policy usually involves severe costs, since in modern economies **output** and **employment** fall rather than the **price level**. For this reason, governments may use the **expenditure-switching policies** of import controls and devaluation as alternatives to expenditure-reducing deflation.

(ii) **Import controls** Import controls have a direct **expenditure-switching** effect upon the balance of payments. **Quotas** and **embargoes** reduce or prevent expenditure on imports, while **tariffs** or **import duties** discourage expenditure by increasing the relative price of imports. However, import controls do not deal with the underlying cause of imbalance – usually the uncompetitiveness of a country's industries – and they may provoke retaliation with an undesirable decrease in world trade and specialization. In any case, import controls may be 'unavailable' because of membership of a trading body such as GATT which discourages their use.

(iii) **Devaluation** The 'unavailability' of import controls as an effective instrument to correct a payments deficit has meant that the real policy choice has usually been between **deflation** and **devaluation**. Devaluation of a fixed exchange rate, or a managed or 'dirty' downward float, is essentially an **expenditure-switching** policy. By increasing the price of imports relative to the price of exports, a successful devaluation switches demand away from imports and towards domestically produced goods. Similarly, foreign demand for the country's exports increases in response to the fall in price.

However, the effectiveness of a devaluation (and of any expenditure-switching policy) depends in large part upon the **price elasticities of demand for exports and imports**. It is easy to see that when the demands for exports and imports are both highly elastic, a devaluation will improve the Balance of Payments. Overseas residents will spend more on British exports following a fall in their relative price, while British residents will spend less on imports. But it is rather more difficult to see what will happen if the demands are less elastic. Providing, however, that the **sum of the export and import elasticities is greater than unity**, it can be shown that a devaluation or downward movement of the exchange rate will reduce a payments deficit (and that a **re-valuation** will reduce a **surplus**). This is known as the **Marshall-Lerner condition** or criterion for a successful devaluation or revaluation.

5 Expenditure-reducing versus expenditure-switching policies

While the Marshall-Lerner condition is a **necessary condition** for a successful expenditure-switching devaluation, it is not a **sufficient condition**. A devaluation could fail if there were insufficient spare capacity within the domestic economy. Spare capacity is needed in order to **increase supply** so as to meet the switching of overseas and domestic demand away from foreign goods and towards the home-produced output. Thus it is far better ro regard an **expenditure-reducing deflation** and an **expenditure-switching devaluation** as *complementary* rather than as *substitute* policies in curing a payments deficit. Deflation alone may be unnecessarily costly in lost output and employment, yet may still be necessary to create the spare capacity and 'prepare the way' for a later successful devaluation.

6 The J-curve effect

Even if an expenditure-reducing deflation creates the spare capacity, a country's industries may still be unable **immediately** to increase supply following a devaluation. It may also be that the Marshall-Lerner condition is not met in the immediate period, since the demand for exports and imports is likely to be much more inelastic in the short run than in the long run. Thus the balance of payments may actually deteriorate before it improves. This is known as the **J-curve effect**. The deterioration in the balance of payments may reduce confidence in the eventual success of the policy, leading to capital outflows which destabilize both the balance of payments and the exchange rate. The existence of the J-curve effect, which can perhaps be minimized by an expenditure-reducing deflation prior to the devaluation, reduces the attractiveness of exchange rate adjustment as a policy to cure a payments deficit. And even when the benefits of the devaluation are realized, they may be relatively short-lived. The advantages of price competitiveness produced by the devaluation may be lost as a result of increased import prices raising the country's inflation rate.

7 The absorption approach to the Balance of Payments

Whereas the Marshall-Lerner condition illustrates the **elasticities approach** to the balance of payments, the need to deflate domestic demand in order to prepare for a later successful devaluation reflects the **absorption approach**. This examines the balance of payments in an essentially Keynesian way in terms of aggregate demand **absorbing**, or failing to absorb, a country's output. In Unit 19 we wrote the equilibrium condition for National Income as

$$Y = C + I + G + X - M$$

Rewriting the equation, we get:

$$X - M = Y - (C + I + G)$$

Thus the balance of payments $(X - M)$) will be in deficit if the economy consumes or **absorbs** more goods and services than it produces: if $(C + I + G)$ is greater than Y.

To put it another way, the balance of payments equals national output less national absorption. If unemployed resources exist, an expenditure-switching devaluation can reduce a payments deficit without having to reduce absorption, but if full employment exists, Y cannot increase. The balance of payments can only improve if the economy is deflated and domestic absorption reduced.

26.4 Links with other topics

The Balance of Payments is one part of the **National Income Accounts** which have been considered in Unit 18. The major **macro-economic issues and policies** considered in Units 15–17 and 19–24 all influence, and are often influenced by, the payments position. Similarly world trade (Unit 26) and international exchange rates, which we consider in Unit 27, have a significant impact upon a nation's balance of payments position and performance.

26.5 Question practice

Essay Questions

Question 1 During the 1980s, the United Kingdom's balance of trade in manufactured goods moved from surplus into deficit. Explain why and discuss whether it matters.   (*AEB: November, 1989*)

Understanding the Question This question links the Current Account of the Balance of Payments to the **deindustrialization** process discussed in Unit 12. For the first part of the 1980s, the deterioration in the balance of trade in manufactured goods was countered by North Sea oil's contribution to the Current Account, and by the strong state of invisible trade, particularly the earnings of financial services. This led the Conservative Government to argue that there is nothing intrinsicly superior about manufacturing compared to the service industries; and that the manufacturing trade deficit does not matter if the resulting hole in the current account is made good by the increased contribution of services, in which the UK might have a comparative advantage. The Conservative Government's opponents replied by arguing that a strong and varied manufacturing sector is vital for the economy's long term prospects; and that without manufacturing, there is little for service industries 'to service'.

By the late 1980s, the overall Current Account was in large deficit. The deficit in trade in manufactured goods continued to widen, while North Sea oil's contribution to the Current Account had lessened and the invisible trade surplus also dwindled. The Conservative Government continued to argue that the deficit did not matter.

The Government has argued that the deficit (unlike that of the 1970s, which had been caused by an excess of government spending drawing in imports) was purely a private sector matter that would eventually be self-correcting and that, therefore, it was not a problem for the Government. This is true so long as the 'rest of the world' is prepared to finance the Current Account deficit with private sector capital inflows – though it can be argued that the high interest rates required to encourage these inward 'hot money' movements themselves have a damaging effect on the economy and particularly on manufacturing industry.

Answer plan

1 Describe the changes in the balance of trade in manufactured goods that occurred during the 1980s.
2 Relate the changes to the overall state of the Current Account.
3 Suggest reasons why the changes occurred: e.g. changing comparative advantage; the effect of decades of loss of competitiveness; the 'mistakes' of government policy in the early 1980s leading to an excessively high exchange rate and interest rates; the effects of excessive consumer demand in the late 1980s, etc.
4 Outline the reasons why the decline may not matter.
5 Outline the reasons why the decline may matter.
6 Give your own personal view and conclusion.

Question 2 Why might a government wish to eliminate a surplus on its current account balance of payments? What measures could it use to achieve this end?   (*London: June, 1987*)

Understanding the Question Generally, the impact of the surplus is to increase demand for the country's output. In Keynesian terms this is represented by an injection of demand into the economy with consequent multiplier effects. If the economy is below full employment, a desirable increase in output may occur, but if the economy is fully employed or if there are production bottlenecks, the main effect may be inflationary. Monetarists emphasize the impact on the domestic money supply of the currency inflow associated with the surplus, also stressing the inflationary consequences.

We have described in the unit some of the other reasons why a large surplus may not be desirable – namely the effect on deficit countries and the 'Dutch disease' syndrome. Generally, however, there is less international pressure to reduce a surplus than a deficit, and a country may only take action if the undesirable effects on its own economy are obvious.

The policies to cure a surplus are the reverse of those to remedy a deficit, namely **reflation**, **revaluation** (or allowing the exchange rate to float upward) and the **removal of import controls**. You might also mention that if the surplus is on the Current Account, the **removal of exchange controls** might encourage a capital outflow which will counter the trading surplus. **Lower interest rates** might have the same effect.

Answer plan

1 Explain the meaning of a balance of payments surplus and its possible origins.
2 Outline why a government may wish to remove or reduce such a surplus. It is worth pointing out that a surplus is a success symbol and that most governments are reluctant to remove them.
3 Explain the main measures and how they will operate on the payments position. Reflation is mainly **expenditure-increasing** while other policy measures are **expenditure-switching**.

Multiple Choice Questions

Question 3   Selected UK Balance of Payments Figures 1986

	£m
Visible Balance	−8254
Invisible Balance	+7154
Net Transactions	−5758
Balancing Item	+6858

It is possible to conclude from these figures that in 1986 there was:
(a) a favourable balance of trade;
(b) a Current Account deficit;
(c) balance of payments equilibrium;
(d) a fall in Official Reserves.

Understanding the Question The data relates to the new method of presenting the Balance of Payments statistics introduced in 1987. The balance of trade refers to the visible balance, which was obviously in deficit or unfavourable. The correct answer is (b); the Current Account, which is the addition of the visible and invisible balances, showing a deficit of −£1,100m. Balance of Payments equilibrium refers to the Current Account; a deficit of −£1,100m seems to indicate disequilibrium. Finally, we cannot tell from the data whether the Official Reserves have risen or fallen.

Data Response Question
Question 4

'The prospect of a major Balance of Payments crisis remains the single most important danger for the UK economy in 1988. The re-emergence of the external constraint will be increasingly important in framing monetary policy through the year.

The manufacturing deficit looks set to worsen further due to two critical factors. The first is the UK's competitiveness. The restrained growth in unit labour costs in 1987 owed a great deal to rapid productivity growth on the back of sharply expanding production. In 1988 production will grow less rapidly, productivity gains will be slow, and unit labour costs could expand sharply.

Meanwhile, the exchange rate will not be allowed to come to the rescue on present policies.

The second factor is the strength of the domestic demand in the UK relative to its main trading partners. The OECD forecast real domestic demand growth of 3¾ per cent in the UK, 2½ per cent in the EC as a whole and only 1 per cent in the US. Under these circumstances the trend for the UK trade deficit has only one direction to go.'

(Adapted from: *The Times*, 15 February 1988)

(a) What is meant by 'UK competitiveness' (second paragraph)? (3)
(b) Analyse the reasoning behind the statement that 'The prospect of a major Balance of Payments crisis remains the single most important danger for the UK economy in 1988' (first paragraph). (6)
(c) How may the 'strength of domestic demand in the UK relative to its trading partners' cause Balance of Payments problems (fourth paragraph)? (5)
(d) Examine one short term and one long term measure likely to reduce the UK's Balance of Payments deficit. (6)

(*London: June, 1990*)

Understanding the Question

(a) Competitiveness can refer to prices of UK-produced goods, compared to the prices of similar goods produced in other countries, and it may also refer to the relative production costs, especially labour costs, of different countries.
(b) A rapidly deteriorating Balance of Payments deficit on current account could trigger a massive outflow on capital account. The resulting large-scale selling of sterling on foreign exchange markets, would cause an extremely rapid fall in the exchange rate. This might then fuel domestic inflation or result in high domestic interest rates if the authorities take action to support the exchange rate.
(c) A high level of domestic demand contributes directly to a deteriorating current account by drawing imports into the economy (via the marginal propensity to import). Less directly, it will cause a high rate of domestic inflation, reducing the competitiveness of UK industries.
(d) Raising interest rates is a short-term measure. A long-term measure could be any 'supply-side' policy to improve the underlying competitiveness of the UK economy.

26.6 Further reading

Burningham, D., editor, *Economics*, 3rd edition (Hodder & Stoughton, 1987).
Chapter 18: The Balance of Payments and its Adjustment.

Hardwick, P., *et al.*, *An Introduction to Modern Economics*, 3rd edition (Longman, 1990).
Chapter 28: The balance of Payments and Exchange Rates.

27 Exchange Rates

27.1 Points of perspective

In Unit 26 we emphasized how the method of restoration of equilibrium in the **Balance of Payments** depends in large measure upon the type of exchange rate that exists. In this unit we examine in greater detail the mechanisms through which **freely floating** and **completely fixed** exchange rates operate, before investigating various types of **managed exchange rates** that have existed in the world economy since 1945. We shall introduce the role of the **International Monetary Fund** (IMF) in providing the institutional framework within which modern exchange rates operate, and we shall comment on the **international payments difficulties** and the **problems of world liquidity** which exist today.

27.2 Underlying concepts

1 The simple theory of a freely floating exchange rate

Exchange rates and the existence of a **foreign exchange market** are necessary because different countries use different currencies to pay for **internal** trade. An exchange rate is simply the **external price** of a currency expressed in terms of gold, another currency such as the US dollar, or a weighted average of a sample of important trading currencies. For the sake of simplicity, we shall for the most part follow the convention of expressing the exchange rate of the pound sterling in terms of the dollar, but we shall also note when other expressions of the exchange rate are more appropriate.

In a regime of **freely** (or **cleanly**) floating exchange rates, the currency of a country is regarded as a simple commodity to be traded on foreign exchange markets, its price or exchange rate being determined by the forces of supply and demand. For the time being we shall assume that a currency is demanded on foreign exchanges only for the payment of trade (we are ignoring the complications caused by **capital flows** and **speculation**), that a country needs another country's currency to purchase imports from that country, and that all countries will immediately sell on the foreign exchange market any holdings of foreign currencies that are surplus to their requirements.

As in any market, the **demand** and **supply** curves for a currency (in this case the pound sterling) show the amounts of the currency which traders wish to buy and sell at various possible prices or exchange rates. Since we are assuming that people wish to hold foreign currency only for the purpose of financing trade, the slopes of the demand and supply curves for a currency will depend on the levels of exports and imports that are desired at each exchange rate. The lower the exchange rate of the pound, the more competitive are British exports when priced in foreign currencies and the greater the volume of exports. Thus the lower the exchange rate, the greater the demand for pounds on foreign exchange markets, since foreigners need more pounds to buy a greater volume of British exports at their current sterling price. The result is the downward-sloping demand curve for pounds illustrated in Figure 27.1.

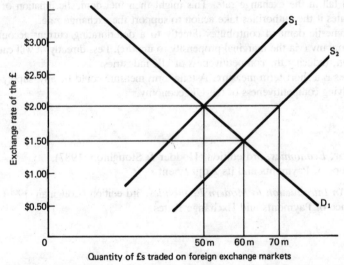

Fig 27.1 Exchange rate adjustment in a system of freely floating exchange rates

While exports generate a demand for pounds on foreign exchange markets, imports generate the supply of sterling needed to purchase the foreign currencies required to pay for the goods and services demanded. A fall in the exchange rate will reduce the competitiveness of imports when priced in sterling. Provided that the demand for imports is elastic, the quantity of pounds being supplied to pay for imports decreases as the exchange rate falls—and increases as the exchange rate rises—resulting in the upward-sloping supply curve of sterling in Figure 27.1.

Figure 27.1 illustrates an initial exchange rate of £1 = $2.00, the demand curve for sterling being D_1 and the supply curve of sterling S_1. Clearly this is an **equilibrium exchange rate** at which the demand for and the supply of sterling are equal. Since the value of exports (paid for in pounds) equals the value of imports (paid for in foreign currencies), the **balance of payments** is also in equilibrium! This point is well worth stressing: **exchange rate equilibrium** implies **balance of payments equilibrium** and vice versa. Indeed, the two concepts are merely different sides of the same coin, the one an equilibrium stated in terms of an equilibrium price (the exchange rate), and the other an equilibrium of quantities (currency flows). If the balance of payments is in equilibrium there will be no pressure for a change in the exchange rate.

Suppose now that for some reason, such as an increase in the quality competitiveness of foreign goods, the desire to buy imports increases at all existing prices expressed in sterling. More foreign exchange is demanded in order to purchase imports and the supply curve of sterling in Figure 27.1

shifts rightwards to S_2. $2.00 is no longer an equilibrium exchange rate, since foreigners now accumulate sterling holdings of £70m., whereas they only require £50m. to pay for their own purchases of British exports at this exchange rate. The market mechanism now operates to restore simultaneously equilibrium in the balance of payments and an equilibrium exchange rate. The sale by foreigners of the **excess supply** of pounds depresses or **depreciates** the exchange rate, thereby increasing the price competitiveness of British exports and reducing that of imports. The process continues until the new equilibrium exchange rate of $1.50 is reached. Conversely if the initial equilibrium is disturbed by an event such as the production of North Sea oil which moves the balance of payments into surplus, the exchange rate will rise or appreciate until the **excess demand** for sterling is eliminated and a new equilibrium is achieved.

2 The Marshall-Lerner condition and exchange rate stability

It is important to stress that the result illustrated in Figure 27.1 depends critically upon our assumption that the demand for imports is elastic. If demand is inelastic, more pounds will be needed as the exchange rate falls in order to pay for imports. The fall in the quantity of imports at lower exchange rates is insufficient to offset the effects of the higher sterling price of each unit of imports. In these circumstances a **downward-sloping (perverse** or **backward-bending)** supply curve for sterling results. The equilibrium exchange rate is still determined where the demand and supply curves intersect, but the equilibrium may not always be stable. The **stability condition** is provided by the **Marshall-Lerner criterion** which we introduced and explained in Unit 26. Provided that the sum of the elasticities of foreigners' demand for British exports and British demand for imports is greater than unity, there will be a tendency to move towards a stable equilibrium exchange rate. Even if the demand for imports is inelastic, provided that the **sum** of the export and import elasticities is greater than one and that supply is sufficiently elastic, then a floating exchange rate system will correct a disequilibrium in the balance of payments.

3 The simple theory of a completely fixed exchange rate

For much of the 19th century and part of the present century, the exchange rates of the world's most important trading countries were fixed in terms of gold. The system was known as a **gold standard system of fixed exchange rates**. There were two crucial aspects of the gold standard system. In the first place each country guaranteed to exchange its currency on demand for a certain physical quantity of gold at the **price** or **parity** at which it declared its currency on the gold standard. Thus if two or more currencies were on the gold standard, the exchange rate of one in terms of another was effectively fixed via the parities at which each currency could be exchanged for gold. The **full gold standard** in operation in Britain until the First World War meant that the country's note issue was **representative money** both inside and outside the country. The country's own citizens as well as foreigners could demand that the currency be exchanged for gold. Ownership of paper currency represented ownership of gold. However, in the **partial gold standard** or **gold bullion standard** adopted by the UK from 1925 until 1931, the country's citizens could only purchase gold from the Bank of England in bars of a considerable size. Internally, because of the shortage of it gold had been effectively **demonetized**.

The second essential feature of the gold standard system as a **mechanism for correcting Balance of Payments disequilibrium** was that a country on the gold standard agreed to the inflow and outflow of gold in payment for trade. Assuming that one country on the gold standard experienced a balance of payments deficit and another country simultaneously experienced a surplus, the following sequence of events was expected to take place:

(i) Gold would be shipped out of the deficit country and into the surplus country.
(ii) The money stock in the deficit country would automatically contract, directly in the case of gold coins and paper currency backed by gold; indirectly in the case of fractionally backed bank deposits. Conversely, there would be an automatic expansion of the money stock in the surplus country.
(iii) This would be followed by an automatic deflation of the price level (via the **quantity theory of money**) in the deficit country and an automatic inflation in the surplus country.
(iv) The falling **internal** price level of the deficit country would increase the competitiveness of its exports, while the rising price level within the surplus country would reduce its export competitiveness.
(v) The process would then continue until the restoration of equilibrium in the balance of payments of both countries.

4 The weaknesses of the gold standard mechanism

The 19th century gold standard displayed a number of weaknesses which make it extremely unlikely that it will ever be adopted again in pure form, though a minority of monetarist economists have called for its revival. The principal weaknesses in the gold standard were:

(i) the gold standard adjustment mechanism worked only very slowly. Internal price levels within countries did not respond quickly to gold inflows and outflows in the manner suggested by the simple quantity theory of money. Although a gold inflow might have an inflationary effect in a surplus country, prices and wages were usually 'sticky downwards' in a deficit country. Instead of **prices** falling in the deficit country, the main **deflationary effect** was **lost output** and **increased unemployment** which could persist for many years as a result of too high an exchange rate against gold. If the country's currency was overvalued against gold, only deflation would cure the payments disequilibrium.

(ii) Although the length of the adjustment period partly explains why deficit countries tended to run out of gold, an increasing shortage of monetary gold also contributed to the weakness of the gold standard system, despite the adoption of a **partial gold standard**, which allowed a greater proportion of a country's monetary gold to be available as an international means of payment. However, world trade expanded despite the world shortage of monetary gold largely because sterling took on the key role of a reserve currency, thereby supplementing gold and becoming an important source of world liquidity. The gold standard became a **gold exchange standard** in which key currencies on the gold standard, notably sterling, occupied a growing proportion of world reserves.

However, the reserve currency role of sterling involved a **contradiction** which eventually led to the downfall of the gold standard system in the 1930s, just as the contradictory role of the dollar later contributed to the collapse of the Bretton Woods system of fixed exchange rates in the 1970s. In order to become a reserve currency, and thereby provide the liquidity to finance the continuing growth of world trade, a key currency must be **transmitted** into the reserves of other countries. Only a large **Balance of Payments deficit** over a long period of time can provide the required **transmission mechanism**. In effect the other countries with whom a deficit country trades agree to accept payment in that country's currency without the country being required to reduce its deficit. The other countries then hold the 'excess supply' of the currency in their reserves for use as a means of payment. To be acceptable as a reserve currency, countries must be confident of the exchange value of the currency, yet the balance of payments deficit required as a transmission mechanism eventually destroys this very state of confidence. In the case of sterling in 1931 (and latterly of the dollar which was also on the gold standard), the currency eventually became vulnerable to speculative runs when external holdings of the currency, held both privately and officially in other countries' reserves, far exceeded the British (and American) gold reserves.

Thus the **liquidity-confidence problem** which forced the pound off the gold standard in 1931 led to the collapse of the gold standard system of fixed exchange rates as, one by one, most other leading trading countries followed suit. For the rest of the 1930s exchange rates either floated freely or were artificially depressed as countries attempted to escape from the Great Depression by gaining a competitive advantage at the expense of the rest of the world. This era established a bad reputation for floating exchange rates just as the experience of the 1920s had diminished the reputation of the gold standard. It is not surprising, therefore, that by the end of the Second World War, when the new **Keynesian orthodoxy** was advocating the **extension of economic management within countries**, its logic should be extended to the **management of exchange rates** and of the system of world payments **between** countries.

27.3   Essential information

1 Exchange rates and Balance of Payments adjustment

Before we investigate the advantages and disadvantages of freely floating and fixed exchange rates, we shall present a simple summary of the critical difference between the Balance of Payments adjustment mechanism under the two exchange regimes. Under a system of floating exchange rates, the **external price** of the currency (the exchange rate) moves up or down to correct a payments imbalance, without requiring an adjustment in domestic output or the **internal price level**. In contrast, under a system of fixed exchange rates it is the internal price level (together with the levels of domestic output and employment) which adjusts to cure the imbalance, the external price of the currency remaining unchanged.

2 The advantages of floating exchange rates

(i) An important advantage of a **freely floating** (or **flexible**) exchange rate stems from the nature of the adjustment mechanism just described. According to the simple theory of a freely floating exchange rate, the exchange rate should never be over- or undervalued for very long. In the event of a 'too-high' exchange rate causing export uncompetitiveness and a payments deficit, market forces should quickly adjust towards an equilibrium exchange rate which also achieves equilibrium in the Balance of Payments–provided of course that the Marshall-Lerner condition holds.

(ii) Correctly valued exchange rates are necessary if the world's resources are to be efficiently allocated between competing uses. If efficient resource allocation and use are to be achieved in a constantly changing world, market prices must be free to reflect the shifts in **demand** and **comparative advantage** that result from such events as resource discoveries and changes in technology and labour costs. A freely floating exchange rate may automatically adjust to gradual changes in demand and comparative advantage, whereas in a fixed exchange rate system a currency may become gradually over- or undervalued when demand or comparative advantage move either against or in favour of a country's industries.

(iii) It has been argued (rather naively as we shall later see) that when the exchange rate is freely floating, the state of the balance of payments ceases to be both a **'policy problem'** and a **constraint** upon the pursuit of domestic economic objectives. Governments can leave market forces to 'look after' the balance of payments while they concentrate on achieving full employment and growth. If the pursuit of domestic objectives causes the inflation rate to rise out of line with other countries, then, according to the **purchasing power parity theory**, the exchange rate will simply fall to compensate exactly for the higher inflation rate. In this way the competitiveness of the country's exports is always maintained. In a fixed exchange rate system, the country would **'import'** **unemployment** from the rest of the world as a result of its deteriorating competitiveness and because of the need to deflate the domestic economy in order to correct the payments deficit.

(iv) Equally, a 'responsible' country with a lower than average inflation rate benefits from a floating exchange rate which insulates it from **'importing' inflation** from the rest of the world. There are two ways of explaining this. If the rest of the world is inflating at a faster rate, a fixed exchange rate causes a country to 'import' inflation through the rising prices of goods it purchases abroad. Alternatively under fixed exchange rates, excess demand in countries with persistent balance of payments deficits causes inflationary pressure to be 'exported' to surplus countries. The deficit countries escape the full inflationary consequences of the excess demand generated by their economies.

(v) When the exchange rate is floating, a country's monetary policy (as well as its fiscal policy) can be completely independent of external influences. This is because the country has no need to keep official reserves to finance a payments deficit or to support the exchange rate. If for example the deficit increases, the exchange rate simply corrects the disequilibrium without any loss of reserves. The country's domestic money supply is unaffected by a change in the official reserves, and interest rate policy is not determined by the need to protect the exchange rate.

(vi) Because a country has no need to hold large official reserves of foreign currencies, resources which would otherwise be tied up in the reserves can be used more productively elsewhere.

3 The disadvantages of floating exchange rates

(i) It is often argued that floating exchange rates **increase business uncertainty** and lead to less specialization, trade, and investment than would otherwise take place. However, uncertainty is probably not the most serious problem that results from a floating exchange rate. Indeed, **hedging**, which usually involves the purchase or sale of currency three months in advance in the **'forward'** market, can considerably reduce the business uncertainties caused by floating exchange rates. It is also the case that fixed and managed exchange rates can on occasion be just as uncertain as floating rates, particularly when a currency is obviously overvalued, and a devaluation is expected.

(ii) It is also asserted that a floating exchange rate promotes an increase in **currency speculation** with all its **destabilizing** effects. There are a number of interesting aspects to this question. While it is undoubtedly true that there has been a growth in currency speculation in the modern era of 'dirty' floating, it may be less related to floating than to the growth of the pool of footloose 'hot-money'–itself a response to the role of the dollar in the Bretton Woods system of managed exchange rates. Secondly, there is far more scope for speculators to 'win' at the expense of governments in a managed exchange rate system than in a freely floating system. In the former case, a speculator engages in the 'one-way option' of selling currency to the central bank defending the currency, hoping to force a devaluation and to realize a capital gain when the currency is bought back at a lower price. If the pressure fails, the speculator will only make a small loss since he can buy back the currency at or near the original price. In a freely floating system, however, a speculator wishing to sell must find another wishing to buy–and in the consequent trading the speculator who guesses correctly gains at the expense of the one who guesses wrongly. The successful speculators are those who correctly sell when the exchange rate is too high and buy when it is too low. Their activity speeds the process of adjustment to an exchange rate equilibrium, stabilizing rather than destabilizing, and smoothing out rather than reinforcing temporary fluctuations.

However, during the regime of 'dirty floating' in the 1970s and 1980s, massive, essentially speculative, short-term capital flows or hot money movements have had seriously destabilizing effects upon the exchange rates, balance of payments and indeed the structure of the domestic economy of a number of countries. At the beginning of the 1980s, hot money flowed into the UK, forcing the exchange rate up to an uncompetitive level at a time when the British inflation rate was above that of her major trading partners. The overvalued exchange rate was a major cause of de-industrialization and unemployment.

By contrast, in 1985 the exchange rate fell to nearly $1.00 as hot money flowed out of sterling into the US currency causing the American economy to experience the problems of overvaluation. However, by the late 1980s and early 1990s, the pound was once again overvalued with a major cause being UK monetary policy. Since the early 1980s, UK monetary policy has relied almost exclusively on the use of interest rates to influence the demand for credit and bank lending. High interest rates, aimed at dampening domestic credit, have attracted capital flows into sterling, forcing up the exchange rate. Many commentators believe that an overvalued exchange rate, now 'locked in' to the rate at which the pound joined the exchange rate mechanism of the EMS in 1990, may once again contribute to renewed de-industrialization and the growth of unemployment.

(iii) We have already noted how fixed exchange rates have been blamed for the 'export' of inflation from one country to another. However, other economists believe that floating exchange rates are to blame for inflation and that fixed exchange rates in fact possess a **deflationary bias** which reduces inflation. If a country allows its inflation rate to exceed that of its trading competitors, its balance of payments will move into severe deficit. A growing export uncompetitiveness and import penetration will 'discipline' the domestic causes of cost-push inflation through an increase in the level of unemployment and the number of bankruptcies. At the same time the loss of reserves will put pressure on the deficit country to deflate its domestic economy in order to cure the imbalance, but the system is asymmetrical since no equivalent pressure is put upon the surplus country to cure its surplus.

In a floating exchange rate system no such discipline exists to make a country reduce its inflation rate. (Indeed we argued earlier that the lack of such a discipline is regarded by some as one of the virtues of floating exchange rates, allowing a country to pursue domestic objectives unconstrained by the need to support the balance of payments or the exchange rate.) In fact, however, a policy of pursuing domestic objectives irrespective of their effects on the exchange rate contains two serious dangers. In the first place, through the effects of a falling exchange rate upon import prices and hence upon domestic inflation, such a policy may unleash a **vicious circle** or **cumulative spiral** of ever faster **inflation** and **exchange rate depreciation** which eventually destabilizes large parts of the domestic economy and prevents growth and full employment from being attained. Secondly, a simultaneous expansion of demand in a large number of countries untrammelled by the consequences upon the exchange rate can add to excess demand and fuel inflation on a world-wide scale. In an individual country such inflation may be explained in cost-push terms since it appears to originate in increased import prices, but the true causes probably lie deeper in an international increase in money demand which far exceeds the short-run ability of industries, and particularly primary producers, to increase world supply.

4 The advantages and disadvantages of fixed exchange rates

The advantages and disadvantages of fixed exchange rates are closely but oppositely related to the disadvantages and advantages of floating exchange rates which we have already covered in some detail. In summary, we can state that the main advantages usually cited for fixed exchange rates are (i) certainty and (ii) the 'discipline' imposed on a country's domestic economic management and upon the behaviour of workers and firms. In contrast, the main disadvantages are (i) in some circumstances uncertainty may actually be increased, (ii) a currency may be over- or undervalued, in which case (iii) severe costs in terms of unemployment and lost output may be imposed on deficit countries, and (iv) in a rigid gold standard system there may not be an adequate adjustment mechanism successfully to cure a payments imbalance.

5 The experience of managed exchange rates

(i) **The Bretton Woods System** In earlier units we noted how in the 1940s **Keynesian economic policies** were first adopted **within** many countries to pursue growth and full employment through demand management and government interventionism. It is not surprising, therefore, that it was also the decade in which interventionism was extended to the international economy through the creation at the **Bretton Woods Conference** in 1944 of the system of **managed exchange rates** that came into full operation in 1947. Indeed Keynes himself was a principal architect of the new system, and of the **International Monetary Fund** (IMF) set up to supervise the post-war exchange rates. (The other functions of the IMF are explained in more detail in one of the questions at the end of this unit.)

By the 1940s it had become generally agreed that the **Great Depression** experienced by most countries in the 1930s had been deepened, if not caused, by a collapse of world trade. The collapse of trade was itself related to the failures of, firstly, the gold standard and, after 1931, of floating exchange rates to cure payments imbalances and to provide adequate world liquidity.

The United States and United Kingdom therefore decided to create a post-war system of managed exchange rates which they hoped would possess the **advantages of both fixed and floating exchange rates** with the disadvantages of neither system. They hoped that the Bretton Woods system would be both **more flexible** than the gold standard and **more stable** than the floating exchange rates of the 1930s.

The gold standard had failed for two main reasons: the shortage of gold and the lack of an adequate adjustment mechanism to correct a 'wrongly' valued currency. In the new system the dollar became the principal international reserve asset supplementing gold, being transmitted into other countries' reserves through the mechanism of the US payments deficit. The dollar also became the **pivot** or **fulcrum currency** in the new system. (Nevertheless, because the dollar remained on the gold standard, the 'new' system was still essentially a **gold exchange standard** in which other exchange rates were fixed, via the dollar, against gold.) The **adjustment mechanism** in the Bretton Woods system worked through the creation of a **zone of flexibility** around an **adjustable peg** exchange rate. **Market forces** were free to determine the day-to-day exchange rate of a currency within a **ceiling** and **floor** 1% each side of an agreed par value or 'peg'. A temporary balance of payments surplus would cause the exchange rate to rise towards the ceiling, whereas a deficit would depress the rate towards the floor.

Each country agreed to intervene in the foreign exchange market to keep the exchange rate within the zone of flexibility. This was achieved through a process of exchange rate management or **exchange equalization**. If the exchange rate was tending to rise through the ceiling, the country's central bank artificially increased the supply of its own currency by selling it on the foreign exchange market and buying reserves. Conversely, it would sell reserves and buy its own currency when the exchange rate was falling through the floor. A persistent tendency for the exchange rate to leave the zone of flexibility would indicate a fundamental disequilibrium in the balance of payments and a 'wrongly' valued exchange rate. In these circumstances the IMF rules allowed a country to adjust the par value of its exchange rate: to **revalue** in the case of a surplus and to **devalue** in the case of a deficit.

In this way it was hoped that countries could benefit from **'managed flexibility'**, but as time went by the system increasingly displayed signs of **'managed inflexibility'**. It suffered from many of the disadvantages of the gold standard and fixed exchange rates that we have already described. The IMF interpreted its rules in such a way that devaluation became effectively ruled out, except as a last resort, for countries suffering from persistent payments deficits. Such countries were expected to deflate, but this could be unsuccessful without a simultaneous pressure on surplus countries to reflate.

A number of factors eventually contributed to the final collapse of the Bretton Woods system in 1971/72. In the first place, it is exceedingly difficult to maintain relatively fixed exchange rates if the inflation rate in deficit countries is markedly higher than in surplus countries. It is no accident that the system worked best in the 1950s when inflation rates in the developed world were remarkably similar. In contrast the greatest strains on the system began to occur in the 1960s when divergent inflation rates began seriously to alter the relative export competitiveness of the world's major trading countries. As a result, pressures began to mount in many countries, including the UK, to use the exchange rate as a **discretionary policy instrument** to be specifically assigned to balance of payments management, leaving the country supposedly free to pursue its own internal objectives.

The final weakness in the Bretton Woods system concerned the contradictory role of the dollar as a reserve currency. We have already explained how, in the context of the reserve role of sterling in an earlier era, a reserve currency is transmitted into the ownership of other countries via the mechanism of a payments deficit in the country of origin, and how eventually this weakens or **softens** the currency, making it less desirable or acceptable as a reserve asset and means of international payment. For the dollar, this stage had been reached by the late 1960s when dollars held outside the USA far exceeded American gold reserves. Being the pivot currency of the Bretton Woods system, it was impossible to devalue the dollar so as to restore American trading competitiveness against other countries and to stem the speculative runs which were taking place against the dollar. The dollar could only be devalued against gold, and when in 1971 a series of dollar crises culminated in the dollar being taken off the gold standard and allowed to float, the Bretton Woods system collapsed at a stroke.

(ii) Dirty Floating Since the breakdown of the Bretton Woods system of managed exchange rates in 1971/72, countries have frequently intervened in the foreign exchange market by buying or selling their own currency in order to influence its exchange rate. At one extreme this can simply be regarded as a **smoothing operation** in a regime of otherwise clean or freely floating exchange rates, but when the intervention is designed to secure an **'unofficial' exchange rate target** it is better described as **dirty floating**. After an attempt in the **Smithsonian Agreement** of 1971 to patch up the Bretton Woods system of fixed exchange rates, the modern era of dirty floating was initiated in 1972 by the British decision to float the pound so that domestic economic objectives could be achieved without the need to defend the exchange rate. Most other currencies then quickly followed suit.

The British experience of dirty floating in the 1970s exhibited two interesting phases. In the initial stage up to about 1977, market forces aided by massive hot money movements out of sterling tended to depress the exchange rate. Since the British inflation rate was higher than that of most of her competitors, this was in line with the predictions of the **purchasing power parity theory**. However, the British government considered the fall in the exchange rate to be excessive and tried to intervene (unsuccessfully in the sterling crises of 1975 and 1976) to prevent the exchange rate falling beneath an unofficial exchange rate target (or **floor**) which the government had chosen. Both sterling crises culminated in the abandonment of the authorities' unofficial target, and the pound fell to a 'low' of about $1.55 in 1976.

In the late 1970s the authorities had to intervene in the market to try to prevent the exchange rate from rising. Hot money now moved into sterling because of North Sea oil revenues and the continued weakness of the dollar. Again the intervention was largely unsuccessful. A 'trade-off' appeared between the successful control of the domestic money supply and the exchange rate target. The authorities gave up the attempt to control the exchange rate because the sale of sterling involved was increasing the domestic money supply at an unacceptable rate. Thus the pound floated upward, becoming severely overvalued at a rate of over $2.40 early in 1981. This phase of recent history illustrates the consequences of domestic fiscal and monetary policy upon the exchange rate. A tight fiscal and monetary stance pushes up interest rates, attracts hot money, and therefore pushes up the exchange rate.

By the late 1970s the UK authorities were facing the dilemma of choosing between a **'low pound' target** (below $2.00) and a **'high pound' target** (above $2.00). A high exchange rate might reduce domestic inflation (a) through cheaper import prices and (b) through 'disciplining' domestic causes of cost-push inflation. However, this could also be a disadvantage if the 'discipline' led to an unacceptable loss of output and employment and to an acceleration of the deindustrialization process. In contrast, a 'low pound' target would increase the competitiveness of British industry, but it might fail to discipline inflation. Indeed it might lead to a vicious downward spiral of cumulative inflation and exchange rate depreciation.

As it happened, market forces and capital movements caused a rapid fall in the exchange rate in 1981. The British Government then appeared to settle for an exchange rate target of about $1.80 to $1.90–or approximately 90% of the pound's 1975 value as measured by the **effective exchange rate**, which is a **trade-weighted index** measuring the pound's value against a basket of leading currencies. In 1981 the Government operated its domestic policies so as to sustain the exchange rate within this range, but in 1982 and 1983 it allowed the exchange rate to fall towards a new 'low pound' target around or below $1.40. The fall in the exchange rate as shown by the effective exchange rate is rather less, providing perhaps a rather better indication of the real change in the pound's external value. The dollar exchange rate has become increasingly less useful, being distorted by American interest rates, political factors and speculation.

In the early 1980s, the Government frequently announced that the exchange rate should be left to market forces and that governments should not intervene to influence the exchange rate. However, by 1987, the Government's attitude had apparently changed; it had become 'unofficial' policy to intervene in the foreign exchange markets to maintain the pound's exchange rate against other European currencies, in preparation for entry to the system of fixed exchange rates represented by the **European Monetary System (EMS)**. The £ eventually joined the exchange rate mechanism of the EMS in 1990, at a 'high' rather than a 'low' parity. Before entry, industrialists, trade unionists and other lobbyists on behalf of manufacturing industry had argued that the £ be allowed to fall in order to join at a competitive rate. By contrast, monetarists and City lobbyists had advocated entry at a higher exchange rate, arguing that a 'high' £ is necessary in the fight against inflation. Entry at a 'high' DM 2.95 rate therefore represents a victory for the City and financial interests over the needs of manufacturing industry.

27.4 Links with other topics

Exchange rates have a great effect on trade and the balance of payments (Units 25 and 26). They also influence macro-economic policy, affecting the level of demand (Units 19 and 20) and inflation (Unit 22). We also saw in Unit 24 how Keynesians advocate a managed exchange rate while monetarists favour either a freely floating or a rigidly fixed regime.

27.5 Question practice

Essay Questions

Question 1
(a) What are the advantages and disadvantages of a stable exchange rate?   (12)
(b) How might a stable exchange rate be achieved?   (13)

(*AEB: June, 1990*)

Understanding the Question To a large extent, the advantages and disadvantages of a stable exchange rate are those of a fixed exchange rate (to which we have referred in the Unit). Advantages include the creation of a more stable business environment for a country's industries and exporters and (if the exchange rate is deliberately held fixed by the government) the disciplining of domestic sources of inflationary pressure. Amongst the possible disadvantages are a lack of competitiveness and an unnecessarily depressed economy, resulting from stability at an overvalued rate; and a certain loss of freedom to pursue domestic economic policies.

However, stability can also be associated with floating exchange rates, given orderly economic management and control of inflation within each country. A stable domestic economy can promote a stable exchange rate, as well as vice versa!

When answering the second part of the question, you must go further than simply stating that a stable exchange rate can be achieved by fixing it, or by joining a system such as the EMS. A developed answer requires a discussion of exchange equalization and a mention of how interest rates and possibly exchange controls might be used to promote exchange rate stability.

Answer plan
1 Explain the meaning of a stable exchange rate.
2 List and briefly discuss the advantages.
3 List and briefly discuss the disadvantages.
4 Explain how by purchasing or selling the country's currency on foreign exchange markets, exchange equalization can promote stability.
5 Explain how interest rates can be raised or lowered to encourage or discourage capital movements. Exchange controls can also be altered.

Question 2 Evaluate the role of the International Monetary Fund in the last two decades.

(*O & CSEB: June, 1980*)

Understanding the Question The IMF should be evaluated in terms of its success or failure in promoting a growing and freer system of world trade and payments. To achieve this general objective, the original Articles of Agreement of the International Monetary Fund specified that the IMF should:

1 promote international monetary co-operation;
2 promote stable exchange rates, maintain orderly exchange arrangements and avoid competitive exchange depreciation;
3 encourage full convertibility between currencies and an ending of exchange controls:
4 lend its resources to countries to enable them to correct payments imbalances without resorting to harmful restrictions on trade;
5 shorten periods of disequilibrium in the balance of payments of member countries.

Essentially the IMF has adopted **three roles**:

(i) **An advisory role** acting as a consultant and giving expert advice to members.

(ii) **'Policing' the Bretton Woods system of exchange rates** We have already described the system of exchange rates introduced at Bretton Woods in 1944 which was operational from 1947 to 1971. In summary, the system worked well until about 1960, but came under an increasing strain in the 1960s when inflation rates began to diverge and the dollar weakened. The system collapsed in 1971/72, since when the IMF has rather ineffectively attempted to produce orderly conditions in a world of dirty floating. In particular the IMF has discouraged countries from artificially depressing the exchange rate in an attempt to gain a competitive advantage at the expense of the rest of the world.

(iii) **A banking role** The Bretton Woods Agreement aimed to promote the orderly development of world trade by providing an adequate supply of **international liquidity** to tide deficit countries over **temporary** payments difficulties. We have already seen how the dollar provided the main source of **primary liquidity**, and how it eventually contributed to the downfall of managed exchange rates. Specially created **IMF reserves** were to provide a source of **secondary liquidity** to supplement the reserves held by individual countries. When the IMF was initially established, each member paid a **quota** (75% in its own currency and 25% in gold) into the IMF 'pool' of currency reserves which were to be available for member countries to draw upon in the event of a payments deficit. A deficit country could then draw upon the IMF currency 'basket' to supplement its own reserves when financing a temporary payments imbalance. The first part of a country's drawing entitlement is automatic, but beyond a certain limit the IMF can impose conditions upon any further loan. At regular intervals, the size of quotas and the Fund's overall reserves have increased.

Other methods of expanding the IMF's lending ability have included (a) the creation of **stand-by credits** in the mid-1950s; (b) **currency swaps**, and the **General Agreement to Borrow** in 1962, under which ten leading industrial countries (the **Group of Ten**) agreed to support each other's currencies through a supplementary IMF pool; and (c) the **Special Drawing Rights** (SDRs) scheme initially operated in 1970.

The creation of SDRs illustrates a most important aspect of the IMF's banking function. The Bretton Woods Agreement was essentially a compromise between the radical **Keynes plan** advocated by Britain and the more conservative **White plan** suggested by the USA. Keynes had envisaged a **world 'super bank'** issuing its own **world trading currency** (to be called **bancor**) which would effectively replace gold and national currencies in financing world trade. If the Keynes plan had been adopted, the IMF might have been able to expand the supply of world liquidity to meet demand without having to use national currencies such as the dollar. Because world trade grew much faster than the supply of IMF reserves, the burden of financing world trade was thrust upon the dollar, with the consequences we have already described.

Before the creation of SDRs, the IMF's lending ability was restricted by the size of the basket of currencies deposited by members. The Fund could only lend what it possessed, and many of the currencies it held were not very useful for the purpose of paying for trade. With the creation of SDRs or **'paper gold'**, the IMF could for the first time expand its lending ability without facing the constraints imposed by the size and composition of its currency basket. SDRs are essentially **book-keeping units of account** allocated by the IMF to each member. The allocation of SDRs can be expanded to keep pace with the growth of world trade. However, the usefulness of SDRs depends upon their acceptability. The creation of SDRs has not really solved the problem of world liquidity, since many countries lack trust in both the IMF and in SDRs. They regard SDRs as artificial man-made assets, far inferior to gold, an asset which has proved its value over thousands of years.

Thus opinions on the IMF are divided. One school of thought wishes to continue to expand both its regulatory or 'policing' powers and its role as a major source of world liquidity, while the opposing school regards the IMF as an unnecessary institution in a world in which the necessary discipline upon individual countries should still be imposed by gold.

Answer plan

1 Describe the functions of the IMF.
2 Explain how the early years of the 1970s mark a critical division between (i) the Bretton Woods system of exchange rates and 'dirty' floating and (ii) the development of the IMF's banking function before and after the creation of SDRs.
3 Evaluate the IMF's role in policing exchange rates.
4 Evaluate the banking role. Some economists argue that countries should possess a much greater automatic right to borrow from the IMF. They argue that the IMF wrongly insists on 'free market' domestic policies as a condition for lending. Other economists take the opposite view, arguing that as a banker the IMF has a duty to impose stiff conditions in order to ensure 'responsible' behaviour.
5 Discuss the criticism that the IMF is a 'rich man's club', assisting developed countries with their payments problems, while being insufficiently attentive to the needs of developing countries. In recent years the IMF has attempted to meet this criticism by expanding the facilities available to developing countries.
6 Lastly, explain that since the oil crises of the 1970s the liquidity problem facing the IMF may be less a problem of **shortage** of world liquidity than of its **distribution**, including the problem of **recycling oil revenues**, and the imbalance between 'North and South'.

Question 3 Examine the potential gains and losses from the United Kingdom's full participation in the European Monetary System.   (*Oxford: June, 1988*)

Understanding the Question The **European Monetary System** (EMS) which began operations in 1979 was initially a **'joint float'** of mainly EC currencies against the currencies of the rest of the world, though it was intended eventually to create a **European Monetary Fund**. Indeed, some people believe that the EMS is the first step along a path to a **full monetary union** within the EC, including the adoption of a common currency.

The currencies of the member countries of the EMS are fixed against each other, but with rather wider zones of flexibility than under the old Bretton Woods system, and exchange rates are also fixed against a **European currency unit** (ECU). Within the EMS, currencies can move within the relatively wide zones of flexibility, and, in theory at least, EMS rules require action by both surplus and deficit nations to keep the currencies within the permitted bands.

Initially, the United Kingdom decided to remain outside the exchange rate mechanism of system, but this decision contradicts the spirit if not the rules of Common Market membership. The EMS was established because it is difficult, if not impossible, to implement the **common economic policies** of the EC in a world of erratically floating exchange rates. The costs or benefits of joining the EMS, as a full member, are thus closely associated with the costs and benefits of Community membership.

A major benefit of EMS membership might be the ability to draw on the help of other members to deter destabilizing hot money movements into and out of the country. Britain might also benefit if a successfully established EMS eventually creates a new source of world liquidity which is able to take pressure off the reserve role of the dollar. Joining the EMS as a full member could also mean that the UK would achieve other benefits of a fixed-rate system. These might include a more stable business and exporting environment, and a source of external discipline against domestic cost-push inflationary pressures.

However, Britain might also be expected to suffer the disadvantages of any system of relatively fixed exchange rates. The EMS has tended to become a 'Deutschmark area' in which the German mark is the key currency. A strong DM might pull up the fixed values of the other currencies, leading to their overvaluation against the rest of the world. Although the zones of flexibility are designed to prevent this, great pressure could still be placed on the exchange rates of the other currencies, particularly if countries continue to experience highly divergent inflation rates. In Britain's case, the domestic costs of lost output and increased unemployment resulting from the deflationary policies necessary to reduce the inflation rate may be deemed too high; indeed many commentators felt that the severe deflationary policies of the early 1980s were 'preparing the way' for entry into the EMS.

Lastly, the **reserve role of sterling** might create severe problems, as the volume of sterling owned overseas and the attractiveness of London as a centre for hot money operations have caused much greater fluctuations in the exchange rate of the pound than in most other European exchange rates. This might place even greater pressure on the UK to deflate its economy in order to keep the sterling exchange rate steady against the EMS currencies.

Answer plan

1 Describe the main elements in the EMS.
2 Assess the advantages of membership to the UK:
 (i) the advantages of fixed exchange rates;
 (ii) European co-operation and the implementation of common economic policies;
 (iii) advantages resulting from a new source of world liquidity.
3 Assess the disadvantages:
 (i) the disadvantages of fixed exchange rates;
 (ii) the DM pulling up and overvaluing the other exchange rates;
 (iii) the domestic deflationary costs might be too high.
 (iv) a source of discipline against domestic cost-push inflationary pressures.

Multiple Choice Questions

Question 4 Other things being equal, which of the following is (are) likely to lead to a fall in the exchange rate of the pound sterling?
1 A fall in UK interest rates.
2 The Bank of England selling sterling for foreign currencies.
3 An increase in the UK inflation rate.

(a)	(b)	(c)	(d)
1,2,3 all correct	1, 2 only correct	2, 3 only correct	1 only correct

Understanding the Question The answer is **(a)** since all three are correct. A fall in British interest rates relative to those in other countries would lead to a capital outflow, deteriorating the balance of payments and causing the exchange rate to fall. Likewise a deliberate policy by the Bank of England of selling sterling on the foreign exchange market will increase the supply of sterling relative to demand, thereby depressing its price. An increase in the inflation rate relative to that in other countries will worsen the Current Account of the Balance of Payments, causing the exchange rate to fall via the Purchasing Power Parity theory.

Question 5 (Use the table in Question 4) Revaluation must have the effect of:
1 Improving the terms of trade.
2 Improving the Balance of Payments.
3 Increasing the country's official reserves.

Understanding the Question Revaluation inevitably improves the terms of trade since export prices expressed in the country's own currency rise relative to import prices. However, if the Marshall-Lerner condition is met, the balance of payments will deteriorate, though there may be a temporary improvement immediately after the revaluation – a **'reverse J-curve effect'**. If the Balance of Payments deteriorates following a revaluation, official reserves will tend to fall. Therefore the correct answer is **(d)**.

Data Response Questions

Question 6

'In Britain there is an obvious connection between a strong pound and the reduction in inflation. But a strong pound has its costs. Net exports are less than they would otherwise be, and the high interest rates required to keep sterling strong dampen domestic activity. These considerations suggest some fiscal stimulus – lower taxes or higher public spending – to offset high interest rates and a strong pound.'

(Source: S. Brittan, 'No magic rule for setting budget deficits', *The Financial Times*, 28 November 1985.)

(a) Carefully explain the 'obvious connection between a strong pound and the reduction in inflation'. (6)
(b) Examine in more detail the 'costs' of a strong pound. (7)
(c) Explain why high interest rates were 'required to keep sterling strong'. (3)
(d) Why does the author suggest a fiscal stimulus to offset high interest rates and a strong pound? (4)

(London: June, 1988)

Understanding the Question A strong pound reduces UK inflation in two main ways. Firstly, there is a direct reduction in import costs, and secondly (less directly), cost-push inflationary pressure, generated domestically by workers and firms through their wage bargaining and price-setting behaviour, is externally disciplined. However, the high interest rates, that might be needed to sustain a strong pound, can have both an inflationary and a deflationary impact. High interest rates contribute to inflation by increasing business costs and the RPI but are deflationary, to the extent that they take demand out of the economy. Indeed, such high interest rates contribute to the 'costs' of a strong pound: the loss of competitiveness, depressed demand, slower growth and increase in unemployment that result from overvaluation. And if sustaining a high exchange rate becomes the prime objective of economic policy, the government loses a lot of freedom to use policy, particularly monetary policy, to pursue other objectives. It is in this context that Samuel Brittan suggest the fiscal stimulus of tax cuts. Given that monetary policy is 'tied up' supporting the strong pound, fiscal policy could provide an extra policy instrument, via tax cuts, to offset the effect of high interest rates in raising business costs and depressing the level of demand in the economy.

27.6   Further reading

Begg, D., *et al.*, *Economics*, 3rd edition (McGraw Hill, 1991).
Chapter 33: The International Monetary System and International Finance

Griffiths, A. & Wall, S., *Applied Economics*, 4th edition (Longman, 1991)
Chapter 22: Sterling Exchange Rate

Index

Note: This index is not comprehensive. Many passing references have been omitted. It is intended only as a guide to the book